Cooperative Strategies in International Business

Cooperative Strategies in International Business

Farok J. Contractor
Graduate School of Management
Rutgers University

Peter Lorange
The Wharton School
University of Pennsylvania

Lexington Books
D.C. Heath and Company/Lexington, Massachusetts/Toronto

Library of Congress Cataloging-in-Publication Data

Cooperative strategies in international business.

    Papers presented in Oct. 1986 at a colloquium sponsored by the Graduate School of Management, Rutgers University and the Wharton School of the University of Pennsylvania.

    1. International business enterprises—Congresses. 2. Joint ventures—Congresses. I. Contractor, Farok J. II. Lorange, Peter. III. Rutgers University. Graduate School of Management. IV. Wharton School.

HD2755.5.C645   1988   338.8′8   86-46160

ISBN 0-669-14927-6 (alk. paper)

Published simultaneously in Canada
Printed in the United States of America
Casebound International Standard Book Number: 0-669-14927-6
Library of Congress Catalog Card Number: 86-46160

The paper used in this publication meets the minimum requirements of American National Standard for Information Sciences—Permanence of Paper for Printed Library Materials, ANSI Z39.48-1984. ∞™

88 89 90 91 92 8 7 6 5 4 3 2 1

To our children,
Anne Sophie, Cyrus, Erach, Per, and Sahm

Contents

Figures

Tables

Preface

The idea for a conference on the cooperative forms of international business was spawned during a lunch conversation in April 1985 between the two coeditors of this volume. We realized that the interest in joint ventures, coalitions, R&D partnerships, licensing, technology agreements, and other types of interfirm cooperation appeared to be growing. But, while these were receiving increasing scholarly scrutiny, the work done was scattered geographically in universities across the world, as well as fragmented conceptually in terms of the aspects of the phenomenon covered by each researcher.

The conference would, we hoped, not only draw scholars together but, by giving a ten-month lead time, commission new thoughts on the subject. In a few cases, we were able to induce authors who had not ventured into this topic before to come up with fresh insights. They succeeded. The colloquium, held in New Brunswick, New Jersey, in October 1986, represented researchers from twenty-seven universities in six nations and was quite possibly the first of its kind devoted specifically to cooperation in international business. Corporate representation was consciously limited to one well-known international joint venture, that between AT&T and Philips. Its chief executive, Mr. Al Stark, gave a detailed glimpse into the negotiation, formation, market and technological rationales, operating problems, and culture in his joint venture company. We were charmed and informed by his remarks as well as by his insightful participation in several sessions.

The cosponsorship of this effort by two schools, the Graduate School of Management at Rutgers University and the Wharton School of The University of Pennsylvania, was in itself a joint venture experiment in microcosm, from which we drew some interesting lessons about institutional and personal relationships. For the most part, this experiment was a happy success and very much a positive-sum game in the best tradition of cooperative relationships.

Acknowledgments

The papers on which the chapters in this book are based were presented in October 1986 at a colloquium organized by the Graduate School of Management at Rutgers University and the Wharton School of The University of Pennsylvania.

Partial support for the conference by the German Marshall Fund of the United States, the Office of International Programs, Rutgers University, and the Center for International Management Studies at the Wharton School is gratefully acknowledged.

We owe Cheryl Wagner special thanks for handling the surprisingly huge volume of correspondence that accompanies an effort of this sort. To Terry Reagan and Linda Brennan, we offer our appreciation for their organizational support at the meeting.

Professor William Dymsza offered to partially support the conference out of funds he had raised for his own research. While these were, in the end, not needed, we would like to record our appreciation for Professor Dymsza's characteristic generosity and his career-long support of international business scholarship.

Introduction and a Summary of the Issues

Until relatively recently, the study of international business management was substantially devoted to the problems of the multinational enterprise as a self-contained and internally controlled administrative system. The standard operating paradigm was a globally optimizing parent supervising a constellation of controlled or fully owned foreign affiliates. In this model, the firm's managers are principally occupied with issues such as internal efficiency, control, and optimization of a single administrative system—albeit one that straddles several nations and markets. The scholarly literature, textbooks, and business school curricula continue to reflect this preoccupation, especially in the United States.

Alternative Modes of International Business Operations

There is growing recognition, however, of the alternative modes of international business operations involving negotiated arrangements between two or more firms. In this model, companies cooperate by sharing control, technology, management, financial resources, and markets. While joint ventures remain the most visible and common mode of interfirm cooperation, there are several other institutional and legal forms, such as contractually defined joint programs or consortia, technology transfer or licensing agreements, and management service and franchising agreements, to name only the major types.

Numerically, these negotiated arrangements outnumber fully owned foreign subsidiaries by a factor of at least four to one for U.S.-based companies, as reported in the chapter by Contractor and Lorange. For European- and Japanese-based companies, the ratio is possibly higher because they are said to have a higher propensity than U.S. companies to engage in international joint ventures and contractual arrangements. We should quickly add that, while there are a great many cooperative ventures by number, they collectively account for about a third of the value of U.S. investments abroad. In terms of overall economic impact—measured by indices such as assets, sales, or employees—fully owned foreign affiliates continue to be the dominant and preferred vehicles for international strategy.

As to whether joint ventures and licensing are increasing their relative share of international business activity remains a problematic issue. In the early and mid 1980s there has certainly been a surge of interest, reflected in many announcements in the business press of corporate links being forged. The accounts of joint ventures being formed (in publications such as *Mergers and Acquisitions* or *Predicasts*, for example) have increased substantially. Companies are more willing today to factor the possibility of cooperation into their strategic planning, and more willing to selectively share their technology with other firms. But at the national or aggregate level, the data are unavailable or fragmentary and, therefore, inconclusive. One of the objectives of our conference on cooperative ventures was to spur further research on this topic.

In studying the international strategies of companies, one observes two contrary trends. One is the convergence of buyer preferences and technical standards in some industries. These contribute to the "internalization" advantages of conducting global operations under a single administrative entity. Centralized and full control over affiliates, unencumbered by the possibly variable objectives of partners, is important in such firms so that they can extract the efficiencies of global optimization. But investing and operating alone via fully owned subsidiaries, though optimal, may not be attainable. The most common example is the joint venture forced on a company because of government mandate, nationalism, or protectionism in that country. This is the traditional rationale for joint ventures in Japan, socialist countries, and several developing nations. Second, even if operating alone is an attainable strategy, it may be inferior to a strategy of cooperating or linking up with another firm. This was one of the significant themes of the conference. Under what conditions might a company *prefer* cooperation over a "going-it-alone" strategy? Many of the joint ventures, consortia, and technology-sharing agreements in the eighties were undertaken by preference over a fully owned subsidiary option. Each firm had the choice of independent action. There was no government mandate requiring a linkup. Yet, the firms chose cooperation over competition. This is the countertrend in international corporate strategy.

Changes in the International Business Environment

In recent years, the economic climate has fostered cooperation in several industries more strongly than in the past. The salient historical fact in the postwar period is the reduction in the United States's relative share of industrial output, from half the world total to well below a fifth. European and Japanese firms have regained the relative competitive position that they enjoyed in the first half of the century. In a crowded field, especially in maturing industries, cooperation has been proven often superior to outright competition.

Technological factors are important in explaining the propensity to cooperate. This is discussed in empirical studies in part III of the book. In industries characterized by rapid technical change and technological intensity, such as semiconductors and computers, only the very largest firms (and perhaps not even they) feel that they can independently carry the risks of accelerating research and development costs. At the same time, shrinking product cycles leave less time over which to amortize and recoup these costs. Thus firms, especially those that are *not* the largest in their industry, may cooperate in order to reduce the risk, in a manner akin to insurance pools. On the other hand, technological intensity may give such an advantage to the largest firms in an industry, through internalization advantages combined with a large market and production scale, that they may decide that independent action is a superior strategy to cooperation. How to translate these firm-level observations into empirical studies that compare industries remains a problem in the empirical papers in part III.

Fragmentation and multiple spin-offs in a technology can provide further impetus to cooperative ventures. For instance, a firm may feel that the only way it can keep in touch with many competing, emerging technologies is to be a member of various research coalitions at the same time—in short, diversifying its R&D portfolio by external memberships in several research ventures, while concentrating internally on one or two promising developments. The fragmentation may come from a multiplicity of market applications of a single technology. The firm may consider itself incapable of developing *all* the applications singlehandedly. For instance, optical disks lend themselves to storage of encyclopedias, music, mail-order advertising, movies, library catalogues, television programs, business and personal communications, and so on. Marketing in each application is very different and requires expertise that no one company can provide. Extensive licensing and joint ventures may result in a situation like the above example.

The declining U.S. share of world patents and the growing share of foreigners filing U.S. patents is symptomatic of a more fragmented strategy landscape. There are more players in the game in several industries. Some hold technology cards; others hold market cards—that is to say, they offer partners access to markets they control by being there first or because of nationalist, cultural, or political reasons.

Corporate policies in many firms have adapted to reflect the changing environment for international business in some industries. There is still the preference, especially in U.S.-based firms, for the go-it-alone strategy. But today, there is less inflexibility on the question. There is less neglect of incremental opportunities to selectively engage in a joint venture for a specific product or market, or to license technologies not at the core of the company's business. There appears to be more sophistication on the part of executives to delink the issue of control from the question of ownership. Many realize that there are ways of exercising control over joint venture affiliates, even minority ones, by means other than by formal agreements and equity percentages. Even in so-called arms-length licensing, the mutual vulnerability (and, hence, control) of the two firms is enhanced by spinning other activities around the technology transfer core. These may include supply of materials, ingredients, countertrade, or buyback of finished product, technology upgrades, joint business in third nations, and so on. The relationship is then multidimensional and long-term, as opposed to being a one-time transfer of capability between licensor and licensee.

The Contents of This Book

The book is organized into six parts. The first part, *Conceptual Frameworks,* has five normative chapters which describe various types of cooperative relationships and try to classify them. One of the key questions in strategy is "Why should firms cooperate?" That is to say, under what conditions might the choice of cooperating with another firm be superior to the alternative of independent action? One normative chapter deals with alternative types of cooperative arrangements under different technological systems.

The second part, *Trends in Cooperative Activities and Ownership Patterns,* contains three surveys of international companies. One shows an increasing trend in joint venture activity. The other two do not perceive any trend and propose that there may be long-term cycles over the decades.

Industry-level studies are grouped in part III, *Structure and Performance of Cooperative Ventures.* They use factors such as R&D intensity, firm size relative to industry, the relative sizes of the partners, concentration, diversification, experience level, and the existence of patents and intangibles to explain the structure of relationships, their success, and their mortality or failure over time.

The chapters in part IV, *Managing Cooperative Relationships,* treat the issue of cooperation from the perspective of a manager; several take a case study approach. The focus is on management behavior; on the character of the interpersonal relationships between executives in the parent organizations; on the rate and value of organizational learning about how to run cooperative businesses; and on the attributes of a successful joint venture manager.

Since many of the licensing, joint venture, and other cooperative relationships exist in the more regulated economies of the socialist and Third World nations, *A Focus on Developing Countries* is the title and theme of part V. One chapter examines the growing use of cooperative modes in LDCs as alternatives to the traditional investment pattern of fully owned affiliates. A second chapter examines several cases of successful and not-so-successful joint ventures in the developing world. The third chapter looks at countertrade and buyback arrangements as a form of interfirm cooperation.

Japanese firms are said to have a higher propensity to enter into cooperative arrangements. A special focus on *Cooperating with the Japanese* comprises part VI of the book. Two chapters treat human resource management and cultural aspects.

The other two examine patterns and structures of joint ventures between U.S. and Japanese firms. One chapter proposes, for upstream cooperative ventures (namely, those formed at the research, development, and commercialization stages of a project) that entrepreneurial U.S. firms may have an easier time finding, and be more successful with, larger Japanese firms as partners, than with U.S. partners.

It is hoped that these chapters will highlight and spur further research into this important, but relatively neglected, aspect of international business. Research interest in this topic is strong. Curiously, the international business curriculums in many schools of management in the United States still devote virtually no space to cooperative strategies. Standard textbooks barely devote a dozen pages to joint ventures and a couple of pages to licensing, management contracts, and joint R&D— a surprising lacuna, considering the frequency of these cooperative modes. Being scholarly in its content, this book is not aimed at students, but it can help remedy this lacuna, since it is aimed at our fellow academics, as well as at policy makers and strategists in international companies. The well-rounded manager today needs to master the arts of both competition and cooperation. Learning how to negotiate, to share technology, markets, and resources, and to handle multiple objectives of partners are skills the international manager needs as much as those of internal administration and control. This book is dedicated to fostering these skills.

Part I
Conceptual Frameworks

1

Why Should Firms Cooperate? The Strategy and Economics Basis for Cooperative Ventures

Farok J. Contractor
Peter Lorange

Nature is not always red in fang and claw. Cooperation and competition provide alternative or simultaneous paths to success. In business, as in nature, managers must learn the arts of competing and cooperating as equally valid aspects of corporate strategy. Cooperative aspects of international strategy have been relatively neglected until recently. In the past few years, however, there appears to have been a proliferation of international joint ventures, licensing, coproduction agreements, joint research programs, exploration consortia, and other cooperative relationships between two or more potentially competitive firms (Boston Consulting Group, 1985). The role of these relationships in international strategy is the focus of this chapter.

The traditional preference of international executives has largely been to enter a market or line of business alone. This seems to have been particularly true for the larger multinationals, especially those based in the United States. Among smaller international companies and those based in Japan, Europe, and developing nations, there seems to have been a higher propensity to form cooperative relationships (United Nations, 1978; Stopford and Haberich, 1976). Traditionally, cooperative arrangements were often seen as second-best to the strategic option of going it alone in the larger firms. Licensing, joint ventures, coproduction, and management service agreements have been viewed as options reluctantly undertaken, often under external mandates such as government investment laws or to cross protectionist entry barriers in developing and regulated economies. In several socialist and developing nations, this consideration remains important; association with local partners is more frequently necessary for market access and government permissions of various kinds.

What makes the recent spate of cooperative associations different is that they are typically being formed between firms in industrial free-market economies where

A small portion of this chapter is based upon concepts from Farok J. Contractor, "International Business: An Alternate View," *International Marketing Review*, Spring 1986, pp. 74–85.

there are few external regulatory pressures mandating a linkup. Instead of the traditional pattern of a large "foreign" firm trying to access a market by associating itself with a "local" partner, many of the recent partnerships involve joint activities in many stages of the value-added chain, such as production, sourcing, and R&D. These associations often involve firms of comparable rather than unequal size, both may be international in scope, and each may make similar rather than complementary contributions. Further, the territorial scope of some of these new cooperative ventures is global, rather than restricted to a single-country market as in the traditional pattern of joint ventures and contractual agreements. These new forms of cooperative ventures will be the focus of our discussion in this chapter.

The Incidence of Cooperative Arrangements in International Business

How important are cooperative arrangements such as joint ventures and licensing, compared with fully owned foreign subsidiaries? For U.S.-based companies, arrangements involving overseas partners, licensees, or local shareholders outnumber fully owned subsidiaries by a ratio of 4 to 1. Compared with the approximately 10,000 fully owned foreign affiliates, there are 14 to 15,000 affiliates in which the U.S. parent's share is less than 100 percent. Of the latter, in about 12,000 affiliates, the U.S. parent has a 10 to 50 percent equity position (minority affiliates roughly equal majority and fully owned affiliates put together).[1] In addition, there are some 30,000 overseas licensees in which U.S. firms or their affiliates have negligible or no equity stake (U.S. Department of Commerce, 1981).

The fact remains that many of the cooperative ventures, particularly those in which the U.S. company has a minority stake, are very small affairs. Hence, the preceding picture can be misleading. By indexes such as assets or number of employees, the fully owned foreign subsidiaries of U.S.-based multinationals continue to account for over two-thirds of the *value* of U.S. foreign investment, even if these subsidiaries are vastly outnumbered by the cooperative arrangements. Companies based in Europe and Japan are said to have a higher propensity than U.S. firms to enter joint ventures and licensing agreements. But the data remain fragmentary and incomplete, making it hard to verify these overall patterns of cooperative activities.

An Alternative Paradigm for Multinational Operations

Cooperative arrangements are numerous enough to suggest that our stereotype of the multinational corporation may need to be changed. Traditionally, it has been seen as a monolithic entity, controlling or owning its inputs and outputs, and expanding alone into foreign markets, based on its technological, managerial, and marketing dominance (see Caves, 1971). It could be seen as a transnational chain of control, "internalized" within the firm (Buckley and Casson, 1976). In this view, the corporation reserves for itself the gains from global vertical and/or horizontal integration.

Today, we are in a more negotiated, circumscribed, competitive world, at least as far as several industries are concerned. In many situations, the international firm is better seen as a coalition of interlocked, quasi–arms-length relationships. Its strategic degrees of freedom are at once increased by the globalization of markets (Levitt, 1983) and decreased by the need to negotiate cooperative arrangements with other firms and governments. In linking up with another firm, one or both partners may enjoy options otherwise unavailable to them, such as better access to markets, pooling or swapping of technologies, enjoying larger economies of scale, and benefitting from economies of scope. These benefits are detailed later. As a corollary, each partner is less free to make its own optimizing decisions on issues such as product development, transfer prices, territorial scope, and retention of earnings versus dividend payout.

The rest of this chapter falls into three broad areas. First, we shall discuss various types of cooperative arrangements, with particular emphasis on reviewing the broader strategic implications of the choice of various types of cooperative efforts. Next, we discuss in some detail various rationales for cooperation, identifying seven broad benefits from various types of cooperative efforts. Finally, we suggest a more formalized cost/benefit analysis for deciding to enter into a cooperative arrangement versus choosing the option to go it alone in a fully owned subsidiary.

The fundamental approach of this chapter is to focus on the predecision phase, the time before a commitment has been made to go for a joint venture or to expand strategically in a wholly owned mode. The emphasis is, thus, on planning, analysis, and design before one enters into such an arrangement.

Types of Cooperative Arrangements

Between the two extremes of spot transactions undertaken by two firms, on the one end, and their complete merger, on the other hand, lie several types of cooperative arrangements. These arrangements differ in the formula used to compensate each partner (the legal form of the agreement) as well as in the strategic impact on the global operations of each partner. Table 1–1 ranks these arrangements in order of increasing interorganizational dependence which is generally, but not necessarily, correlated with strategic impact (Pfeffer and Nowak, 1976). This ranking is at present only in the form of a hypothesis, since no empirical work exists comparing the various types of cooperative agreements on the extent of interorganizational dependence they create.

Table 1-1
Types of Cooperative Arrangements

	Typical Compensation Method	Extent of Interorganizational Dependence
Technical training/start-up assistance agreements	L	Negligible
Production/assembly/buyback agreements	m	↓
Patent licensing	r	Low
Franchising	r;m	
Know-how licensing	L;r	
Management/marketing service agreement	L;*r*	
Nonequity cooperative agreements in		Moderate
Exploration	$\pi_i = f(C_V, R_V)$	
Research partnership	$\pi_i = f(C_V, R_j)$	↓
Development/coproduction	$\pi_i = f(C_i, R_j)$	
Equity joint venture	α	High

α = fraction of shares/dividends.
r = royalty as a percentage of turnover.
L = lump-sum fee.
m = markup on components sold or finished output brought back.
π_i = profit of firm *i* in nonequity joint venture.
C_V, R_V = costs and revenues of the venture.
C_i, R_i = costs and revenues of the firm *i*.
R_j = revenues of the dominant partner.

For instance, technical training and start-up assistance agreements are usually of short duration. The company supplying the technology and training is typically compensated with a lump-sum amount and will thereafter have minimal links with the start-up company, unless, of course, there is an additional licensing agreement. Similarly, patent licensing involves a one-time transfer of the patent right. Compensation, however, is often in the form of a running royalty, expressed as a fraction of sales value. In component supply, contract assembly, buyback, and franchising agreements, the principal form of compensation for both partners is the markup on the goods supplied, although there could be a royalty arrangement as well, as typically is the case in franchising. The interdependence between the partners is thus somewhat greater because of delivery, quality control, and transfer-pricing issues associated with the supply of materials, as well as due to the global brand recognition in franchising.

Know-how licensing and management service agreements assume a closer degree of continuing assistance and organizational links. Studies show that most licensing involves the transfer of know-how which is unpatented but proprietary information (Contractor, 1983). It is not simply a matter of transferring a patent right or providing start-up training. It involves extended links between the two firms and ongoing interaction on technical or administrative issues. Payment in these cases will typically be in the form of a lump-sum fee plus running royalties.

The term *joint venture* often implies the creation of a separate corporation, whose stock is shared by two or more partners, each expecting a proportional share of dividends as compensation. But, many cooperative programs between firms involve joint activities without the creation of a new corporate entity. Instead, carefully defined rules and formulas govern the allocation of tasks, costs, and revenues. Table 1–1 gives three examples. Exploration consortia often involve the sharing of the venture's costs, C_V, and revenue from a successful find, R_V, by formula. By comparison, the costs of a research partnership may be allocated by an agreed-upon formula, but the revenue of each partner depends on what the company independently does with the technology created. In coproduction agreements, such as the Boeing 767 project involving Boeing and Japan Aircraft Development Corporation (itself a consortium of Mitsubishi, Kawasaki, and Fuji), each partner is responsible for manufacturing a particular section of the aircraft. Each partner's costs, C_i, are therefore a function of its own efficiency in producing its part. However, revenue, R_i, is a function of the successful sales of the 767 by the dominant partner, Boeing (Moxon and Geringer, 1984). Each of these examples involves different risk/return trade-offs for the parties. Table 1–1 lists the major types of cooperative arrangements, indicating how costs and revenues are typically shared, depending on the compensation method. Significantly also, the table indicates how interorganizational dependence increases as one proceeds from simple one-shot cooperative agreements to ongoing formal joint ventures.

The Broader Strategic Effects of Forming a Cooperative Venture

So far, we have considered costs and revenues directly associated with the cooperative venture itself. But the legal form that governs the allocation of tasks, compensation, and costs plus the broader strategy consequences are not necessarily that easy to interrelate. Seen in isolation, a cooperative venture may only be a simple start-up, technical training agreement, or standard patent license. But if the effect of this cooperative move is to create a long-term customer for a part or active ingredient, the strategic impact goes beyond the arrangement itself. Examples of this kind are frequently found, for instance, in the pharmaceutical industry's licensing practices or in automotive assembly agreements, where the nominal royalty accruing to the headquarters of the technology-licensing group typically will be vastly exceeded by the profit margin earned by the division that supplies the active ingredient for the drug or the automotive parts (Contractor, 1985).

On the other hand, there could be negative strategic impacts external to the venture itself. The worry of creating a future competitor is often overblown, but must be considered when entering into any cooperative venture or transferring technology or know-how to another firm. Let us consider two contrasting examples. A chemical company is helping to set up a PVC plastic plant with a Korean firm. The technology is mature, if not widely known in its most efficient production form. The PVC industry is globally decentralized, and delivery to customers from local sources is a more common pattern than imports. Hence, in this case, there may be little reason to fear that the company receiving the assistance will become a global competitor or otherwise impinge upon the strategy of the firm supplying the technology, except in the one country agreed upon. In this case, the geographic issue is clear.

However, the opposite case of the junior partner turning over time into a global competitor is also well documented. Reich (1984) and Abegglen (1982) relate many examples involving Japanese firms, including the celebrated stories of Western Electric licensing transistor technology to Sony for $25,000 and RCA assisting Japanese companies to make color-television receivers. How significant in cooperative agreements is this problem of being taken over by one's partner will depend on many factors such as the duration of the arrangement, the ability of each partner to go it alone on the partnership's expiration, and their resolve to independently keep up with technical and/or market-related changes in the industry. In this context, it may also be critical to assess the degree to which the relationship leaves the partners mutually interdependent and, thus, potentially vulnerable later on. This question must be assessed differently depending on whether the industry is characterized by global production-interaction efficiences or by adaptation to the unique country-level circumstances.

In industries "configured" to be country-based (Porter, 1986), are cooperative ventures less dangerous in terms of creating global competition? Yes, but only if the partner is a "local" firm unlikely to make its own direct investments in other countries. Otherwise, even if the industry is territorially fragmented or "multi-domestic," an improved technology can be easily spread by a partner that is already global in scope. Competition from a former joint venture partner or licensee is likely to be felt sooner and in greater intensity in geographically concentrated and global-scope industries.

In general, there are no comprehensive data on this question. Warnings have primarily been voiced vis-à-vis Japanese companies (for example, Reich, 1984; Hamel, Doz, and Prahalad, 1986). Overall, the opinion of the Office of Technology Assessment or of authors such as Contractor (1985) is that U.S. technology transferred to overseas licensees or joint venture partners does not induce a pervasive competitive threat, barring a few notable cases. The technology-receiving oganization is often local in orientation or remains one step behind; the rate of technical change may be rapid enough to diminish the danger from one transfer; or the terms of the agreement itself may limit the other partner via patents or other restrictive clauses. The potential threat can thus often be dealt with through careful creation of a "black-box position" for oneself, emphasizing legal and patent protection; maintaining some control over the venture through staffing; maintaining one's strong independent research momentum; and linking the partner up through a complete system of relationships. It is necessary to see all of these activities together when creating black-box protection (Lorange, 1986).

Overall, the benefits of international cooperative ventures will have to exceed the direct and indirect costs, such as creating competitors. Neither fashion nor phobia accounts for the fact that the number of cooperative arrangements vastly exceeds the number of fully owned subsidiaries as modes of international business organization. There must be de facto strategic rationales or benefits to these arrangements.

Rationales for Cooperation

In addressing the conditions necessary for entering into a cooperative relationship, we shall take the viewpoint of any one partner and examine the contribution it makes to a given venture's strategy. It is critical to keep the strategy of one partner in mind. How central is the particular business domain of a joint venture for the partner? What opportunity losses must the partner reckon with as offsetting the benefits from a joint venture, such as limitations on future strategic flexibility and alternative use of management's capacity? We shall examine the overall benefit/cost balance of cooperative relationships in a subsequent section of this chapter. For the moment, let us primarily discuss the benefits—the reasons for *forming* cooperative ventures.

In the broadest terms, joint ventures, licensing, and other types of cooperative arrangements can achieve at least seven more or less overlapping objectives. These are: (1) risk reduction, (2) economies of scale and/or rationalization, (3) technology exchanges, (4) co-opting or blocking competition, (5) overcoming government-mandated trade or investment barriers, (6) facilitating initial international expansion of inexperienced firms, and (7) vertical quasi-integration advantages of linking the complementary contributions of the partners in a "value chain." We have listed the major potential benefits that might be associated with each of these rationales in table 1–2. Each of these issues will be discussed in more detail in the following paragraphs.

When considering benefits from cooperative ventures in the broadest sense, they typically create value through either a *vertical* or *horizontal* arrangement. In considering the vertical value-addition process that takes place through a joint venture, it is useful to draw on the value chain approach suggested by Porter (1985, 1986). The *combined* efforts of all partners must add up to a value chain that can produce a more competitive end result. It is important that the partners have complementary strengths, that they together cover all relevant know-how dimensions needed, and that the strategies of the partners are compatible and not in conflict.

Table 1–2
Strategic Contributions of Joint Ventures

• *Risk Reduction*

Product portfolio diversification
Dispersion and/or reduction of fixed cost
Lower total capital investment
Faster entry and payback

• *Economies of Scale and/or Rationalization*

Lower average cost from larger volume
Lower cost by using comparative advantage of each partner

• *Complementary Technologies and Patents*

Technological synergy
Exchange of patents and territories

• *Co-opting or Blocking Competition*

Defensive joint ventures to reduce competition
Offensive joint ventures to increase costs and/or lower market share for a third company

• *Overcoming Government-mandated Investment or Trade Barrier*

Receiving permit to operate as a "local" entity because of local partner
Satisfying local content requirements

• *Initial International Expansion*

Benefit from local partner's know-how

• *Vertical Quasi Integration*

Access to materials
Access to technology
Access to labor
Access to capital
Regulatory permits
Access to distribution channels
Benefits from brand recognition
Establishing links with major buyers
Drawing on existing fixed marketing establishment

This table is adapted with permission from Farok J. Contractor, "An Alternative View of International Business," *International Marketing Review*, Spring 1986.

Instead of the partners making *complementary* contributions, an alternative model of cooperation is one in which the partners provide *similar* inputs to the venture. The rationales for the latter can be to limit excess capacity, to achieve risk reduction through joint efforts, and to save on costs, as we shall see shortly. Both models exist in international cooperative ventures, but their relative incidence and stability are not definitely known.

Let us now consider in more detail the seven areas for potentially generating benefits outlined in table 1–2.

Risk Reduction

Cooperative ventures can reduce a partner's risk by (1) spreading the risk of a large project over more than one firm, (2) enabling diversification in a product portfolio sense, (3) enabling faster entry and payback, and (4) cost subadditivity (the cost to the partnership is less than the cost of investment undertaken by each firm alone).

Developing, for instance, a new car or airplane is a multibillion dollar undertaking. First, to state the obvious, a joint new undertaking such as the Boeing 767 Project spreads the risk of failure (and the potential gains) over more than one party. This applies also to exploration consortia. But there are other subtler considerations, as can be illustrated by the General Motors–Toyota venture. To the extent that GM did not have to sink $2.5 billion into developing a new small car in the United States, it could invest the capital over a range of larger models (*Business Week*, March 1984). Given the public's fluctuating taste for smaller versus larger automobiles—something Detroit has been largely unsuccessful in predicting over the past two business cycles and oil shocks—a diversification of the product portfolio might insulate auto producers from such variability in demand, at least up to a point. Further, a joint venture can lower the total investment cost of a particular project, or the assets at risk, by combining expertise and slack facilities in the parent firms—the cost subadditivity factor. A good example is utility power pools that enable each regional electric company to make a lower investment than it would operating alone (Herriott, 1986). Finally, the experience of all the partners—their mutual sharing or abdication of markets in favor of the joint venture corporation—make for faster entry with a better design and a quicker payback. Faster entry and certification are also strong factors in pharmaceutical-industry licensing. The industry's complaint is that because certification takes a long time, the monopoly advantage of a patent is eroded and there is not enough time to recoup R&D costs. Clinical testing performed by a licensee often speeds up the certification process.

The risk-sharing function of coalitions may be especially important in research-intensive industries such as computers, where each successive generation of technology tends to cost much more to develop, while at the same time product life cycles might shrink, leaving less time to amortize the development costs. This observation appears to be contradicted by Friedman, Berg, and Duncan (1979), who showed a negative correlation between R&D intensity and the propensity to form joint ventures—as if to suggest that the more valuable a firm's proprietary technology, the more likely it is to go-it-alone. The apparent contradiction is possibly resolved when we consider that (1) Friedman, Berg, and Duncan's data are now a decade old, when the context for developing international strategies was markedly different and (2) industry-level studies typically are difficult to translate to the firm level. A leader such as IBM may well be able to carry on by itself, while the followers such as Siemens, Fujitsu, and Amdahl may have to form joint ventures to share development costs and risks.

Another dimension of risk reduction has to do with containing some of the political risk by linking up with a local partner. Such a partner may have sufficient political clout to steer the joint venture clear of local government action or interference. It may also be that the joint venture has come about as a result of the host government's industrial policy. In such a case, added political-risk reduction can be achieved; the government endorses the joint venture as being beneficial to its economic policy agenda. Government policies favoring joint ventures over fully owned investments are by no means peculiar to less-developed countries (LDCs). Japan has, in fact, been a role model for many developing nations (Contractor, 1983). European policies in this regard are outlined in Gullander (1976) and Mariti and Smiley (1983).

Economies of Scale and Production Rationalization

"I think world trade in built-up vehicles will be largely replaced by trade in vehicle components. . . . The distinction between imports and domestics could very well become meaningless" (Donald Peterson, president of Ford, in the *International Herald Tribune*, September 19, 1981). Underlying this remark are two distinct but related concepts. Production rationalization means that certain components or subassemblies are no longer made in two locations with unequal costs. Production of this item is transferred to the lower-cost location which enjoys the highest comparative advantage, thus lowering sourcing cost. But, there is an added advantage. Because volume in the more advantageous location is now higher, *further* reduction in average unit cost is possible due to economies of larger scale. General Motors, for instance, has an extensive global interchange between its affiliates and joint venture partners such as Isuzu and Suzuki (in which it has had an admittedly passive equity stake, so far). Japan serves as a source for transaxles—transmission plus axle subassemblies—for assembly in markets such as Canada, Europe, South Africa, and Australia. Brazil serves as a source of small engines for Ford's U.S. and European markets. Other examples are abundant.

In many situations, too, particularly in more mature businesses, there may be excess capacity and need for industrial restructuring. A joint venture approach may be a practical vehicle for achieving this. Thus, production can be rationalized and output levels reduced within the joint venture context, thereby avoiding a "winner-loser" situation and a protracted stalemate. High exit barriers can thereby be overcome.

Another example is a licensing/franchising operation for the servicing of marine engines and boats in ports all over the world. Ships are drawn to the internationally recognized brand name for the service facility so that they can enjoy identically high standards of service anywhere. Moreover, there are important economies of scale in centralized engine rebuilding, parts inventories, and training—savings passed on to the franchise holder and from there to the customer.

Potential synergistic effects of joint ventures can possibly also be inferred from the findings of McConnell and Nantell (1985), who show that the value of the shares of over two hundred firms listed on the New York and American stock exchanges was increased for those companies that had undertaken joint ventures.

Exchanges of Complementary Technologies and Patents

Joint ventures, production partnerships, and licensing agreements may be formed in order to pool the complementary technologies of the partners. Several alliances in the pharmaceutical and biotechnology fields, for instance, are built on this rationale. Each partner contributes a missing piece. By pooling know-how and patents, a superior product is expected. In general, it is important to consider joint ventures as vehicles to bring together complementary skills and talents which cover different aspects of state-of-the-art know-how needed in high technology industries. Such creations of "electric atmospheres" can bring out significant innovations not likely to be achieved in any one parent organization's "monoculture" context.

Moreover, *faster entry* into a market may be possible if the testing and certification done by one partner are accepted by the authorities in the other partner's territories. Or, one partner may cede the rights to a partially developed process to another firm which refines it further, with the fruits of the development to be shared in a joint venture. This is a typical pattern among smaller and larger firms (Doz, 1986). In this regard, it is useful to remember that a patent is not merely a right to a process or design; it is also a right to a *territory*. Often, the marketing or territorial right is the dominant strategic issue. By pooling or swapping patents, companies also pool or swap territories. Contractor (1985) describes such cross-licensing arrangements. Research partnerships can have a similar intent.

A closely related issue has to do with the pressures faced by a company that has invested heavily in developing a new technological breakthrough. But on its own, it may not have sufficient production or global marketing resources to secure a rapid, global dissemination of the new technology, making it hard to achieve an acceptable payback for its investment. A joint venture approach can be an important vehicle in achieving such dissemination and realistically securing the necessary payback. This may be especially true for smaller firms lacking the internal financial and managerial resources to make their own investments or expand rapidly.

Paradoxically, this may also be true in giant diversified firms. Let us take General Electric (GE) as an example: it has scores of foreign affiliates, as well as several hundred licensing or production contracts plus minority joint ventures. For a company with the number of products GE has, the potential country/product combination of activities must add up to over ten thousand. Not even a giant firm can invest in all of these. Direct investment in fully owned subsidiaries is reserved for the most interesting combinations, while many of the rest are handled by cooperative ventures. Stopford and Wells (1972) confirm in their study that the propensity to form joint ventures is higher when the entry entails product diversification. Berg, Duncan, and Friedman (1982) indicate that large average firm size and rapid growth in an industry correlate positively with joint venture formation.

Co-opting or Blocking Competition

Potential (or existing) competition can be co-opted by forming a joint venture with the competitor or by entering into a network of cross-licensing agreements (Telesio, 1977). The majority of these are defensive strategic moves. Besides other considerations mentioned earlier, blunting the Japanese auto penetration into the U.S. market is likely to have been one rationale for the GM–Toyota venture.

On the other hand, a joint venture may also be made in a more offensive vein. Caterpillar Tractor is said to have linked up with Mitsubishi in Japan in order to put pressure on the profits and market share that their common competitor Komatsu enjoyed in its important home market, Japan. Japan is said to generate 80 percent of Komatsu's global cash flow (Hout, Porter, and Rudden, 1982). Thus, even though the joint venture may not have great importance in itself for Caterpillar, it may act as a thorn in Komatsu's side and, thus, reduce its competitiveness outside Japan. Vickers (1985) suggests that many R&D partnerships are intended to quickly file patents to stake out the ground against competitors.

Of course, joint ventures are, quite properly, scrutinized by governments for their potential anticompetitive and welfare-limiting effects—but less stringently today, it seems, than a decade ago (Wassink and Carbaugh, 1986).

Overcoming Government-mandated Investment and/or Trade Barriers

Here we come to one of the oldest and still common rationales for joint ventures—in many instances, host government policy makes the joint venture form the most convenient way to enter a market. An abundance of examples can be found, particularly in developing countries. Over the past few years, for instance, joint ventures with China have received much attention. We also have frequent examples of joint venture agreements being complemented by barter or countertrade arrangements. General Motors' venture with LZTK in Yugoslavia is an example of this. The joint venture, in fact, produces castings which GM buys for its German assembly lines; in return, GM is able to sell more cars in Yugoslavia by way of countertrade (Barkas and Gale, 1981). These more or less protectionist policies are not exclusive to LDCs or planned economies. Mariti and Smiley (1983) describe how NATO prefers weapons systems developed by multinational consortia, whereby the purchasing countries can participate in parts manufacturing through a cooperative network. Japan is known for its more or less exclusionary policies, and this has been a major contributing factor to the hundreds of U.S. firms using the joint venture route as the most practical way to sell products in the Japanese market (Abegglen, 1982).

Facilitating Initial International Expansion

For medium- or small-sized companies lacking international experience, initial overseas expansion is often likely to be a joint venture. This may be especially true when the firm is from a socialist or developing country (Lall, 1981). In a cross-sectional study, Dunning and Cantwell (1983) show that the lower the GDP per capita of the host nation originating a multinational firm, the more likely it is to use joint ventures in its initial international expansion. In a typical scenario, such a firm has production capability, but lacks knowledge of foreign markets for which it depends on its partner. Embraer of Brazil, a highly successful aircraft manufacturer, was helped initially by its joint venture with Piper. It makes small commercial jets as well as fighters. Initially aiming for the Brazilian market, Embraer is now a strong exporter, landing orders even in the demanding U.S. market. It gives a good example of a joint venture partner that over time has been turning into a global competitor on its own.

In general, it is an expensive, difficult, and time-consuming business to build up a global organization and a significant international competitive presence. Joint ventures offer significant *time savings* in this respect. Even though one might consider building up one's market position independently, this may simply take too long to be viable. Even though acquisitions abroad might be another alternative for international expansion, it can often be hard to find good acquisition candidates at realistic price levels—many of the "good deals" may be gone. All of these considerations add to the attractiveness of the joint venture approach.

Vertical Quasi Integration

Several cooperative ventures involve each partner making essentially *similar* contributions, as described already. However, joint ventures, coproduction, research partnerships, and management or marketing service agreements can also be a form of vertical quasi integration, with each partner contributing one or more *different* elements in the production and distribution chains. The inputs of the partners are, in this case, *complementary*, not similar.

There is usually a strategic optimum, lying *in between* the extremes of complete vertical integration within one organization on the one hand and completely contractual relationships or out-sourcing on the other hand. Sometimes, a cooperative relationship with another firm is the best way to reach this optimal middle ground. Such ventures can be described as a mode of interfirm cooperation lying between the extremes of complete vertical integration (in one company) of the chain from raw materials to the consumer, to the opposite case where stages of production and distribution are owned by separate companies which contract with each other in conventional market mechanisms (Thorelli, 1986). Empirically, the latter case is observed only rarely. Examples may be found in pockets of the music and publishing industries. One even encounters firms with no assets other than an office that undertake production and sales by contracting out each stage to separate organizations, while they simply "manage" the entire chain (Miles and Snow, 1986). But such one-time contracts mean that none of the parties accept any obligation for future behavior. Strategic direction-setting in any long-term sense may become next to impossible.

A firm may therefore integrate vertically (own more than one stage of the chain), because it may more easily permit longer-run strategic decisions. There is a large literature on vertical integration (Richardson, 1972; and, for the international firm, Buckley and Casson, 1976). Briefly stated, its advantages are these: (1) avoidance of interfirm contracting, transactions, and negotiations costs (Williamson, 1975), (2) reduction in cost or achieving economies of scale from combining common administrative, production, transport, or information processing activities in two or more stages of production or distribution, (3) internalizing technological or administrative abilities and secrets within a single firm, (4) gaining a better understanding of strategy within the industry as a whole (enabling the integrated firm to outperform its more fragmented competitors), and (5) the ability to implement technological changes more quickly and over more stages of the value chain.

On the other hand, there are drawbacks to integration as well. These drawbacks can be overcome to a certain extent by linking up with another firm, where integrating entirely within one firm may be difficult. First, there is the matter of capital investment cost which may become too high for just one company to bear, especially when operating in a risky environment. We see that many joint ventures in uncertain investment fields such as semiconductor R&D or oil exploration are predicated simply on spreading the investment cost and risk.

Second, the vertically integrated firm tends to increase its fixed costs and, thus, its break-even point, thereby potentially increasing its vulnerability to cyclical fluctuation. In the aerospace industry, for instance, the cost of developing new airplanes is very high for even the largest participants, such as Boeing (Moxon and Geringer, 1984). The Boeing 767 is being built in a contracted coproduction cooperative venture with Japan Commercial Aircraft and Aeritalia. Not only are the development risks shared, but fixed costs of Boeing are lowered by contracting major portions of the aircraft to the other partners. There are other strategic advantages as well, such as helping the sales of the aircraft in Japan and Italy.

Third, forward integrating to internalize more elements of marketing channels requires market access, links with major buyers, and brand recognition which can be a critical impediment in international expansion. The history of Japanese firms expanding into the U.S. market shows that in the early stages, they would link up with established U.S. companies. This typically gave them a "beachhead" and a longer learning period before developing channels of their own. Lastly, Porter (1980) indicates some other strategic disadvantages of full integration, such as reduced flexibility to environmental or technological change, dulled incentives for an individual operating unit to remain competitive if internal transfer prices do not reflect their external values, and being deprived of the marketing or technical insights available from outsiders.

A middle position between the two extremes of full integration and purely contractual relationships is often optimal for many companies. Joint ventures, coproduction, management service agreements, and so on provide a means whereby each partner can contribute its distinctive competencies. Many of the specific obligations of each partner may be defined in auxiliary agreements. Because they share in the equity of the venture or share the profits by a formula, the firms typically perceive that they have an overlapping if not identical strategy. The relationship is neither purely contractual nor entirely integrative. We may describe it as a mode of quasi integration, as Blois (1972) puts it.

There are many typical examples. Take, for instance, the case of a hotel venture located in the Mideast. One partner, an international hotel chain based in the United States, supplies expertise to construct and start the hotel in terms of operating procedures, standards, and building codes. Thereafter, the other partner, a hotel company based in India, staffs and runs the operation under a profit-sharing management service contract, using local and expatriate Indian personnel who are hired at relatively modest salaries. The U.S. partner now provides worldwide brand recognition and a global reservation system.

Let us consider other examples of the contribution made by one of the partners. To carry out the production functions, an important bargaining chip in the so-called planned economies may simply be the permission to produce that one of the partners already has received from the government. In many nations, permission is necessary, even for local firms, before they can begin to produce; in several industrial sectors, foreigners may be excluded altogether. This is a similar but distinct issue from trade barriers, which involve an inability to sell.

In the latter case, what one partner seeks from the other is production destined for *other* markets. Take the case of Marine Resources in Seattle, a joint venture between Bellingham Cold Storage and Sovrybflot. It was perhaps the only joint venture in the United States with Soviet equity participation (Pereyra, 1981). The joint venture was predicated on the United States extending its offshore economic zone to 200 miles in 1976. The Russians being excluded, Americans now catch the fish. But the species available include many plebeian varieties such as pollock and whiting which have to be caught and processed quickly, in huge quantities, to make even a modest profit in international markets. U.S. fleets had neither the huge processing capacity of the Soviet motherships nor the expertise for international trade in such species. The factory ships are based in the Soviet Far East and have considerable excess capacity. At an early stage in the development of fisheries in the U.S. Northwest (with inexperience, slim profit margins, and a seasonal catch), investment in a factory ship was out of the question. Marine Resources contracted with American fishermen for supply of such species, with delivery to be made directly to affiliated Soviet factory ships in midocean; the processed catch was to be sold directly to other countries such as Japan and Korea. The joint venture had staff in Seattle, on-board representatives on the Soviet processing ships, and personnel in Nakhodka, Soviet Union.

Another variation on this theme of government production permission as a strategic contribution made by a partner can be exemplified by Kennecott's seabed mining consortium. To extract nodules from a depth of 3 miles is a speculative and costly venture; Killing (1983) reports that a full-scale test alone costs $150–200 million. Moreover, a large number of technical disciplines are needed, requiring expertise from several companies. For this reason, and in order to spread the risk of exploration, Kennecott formed a joint venture with companies from four industrial nations. But another crucial reason was political: to get the support of several governments at a time when negotiations on the law of the sea in the United Nations may have gone adversely against the mining companies. A similar consideration exists in the Airbus joint venture, except that, in this case, it is not a matter of production permission, but a question of improving the ability to sell the airplane to the national carriers of countries included in the joint venture.

Potential strategic advantages under the distribution-type joint venture category include rapid access to an existing marketing establishment, links with key buyers, knowledge of the local market and culture, and benefits from a recognizable brand name—in total, better market access. Let us now illustrate this with the following example. Tata is a large conglomerate based in India with extensive international contacts. India has potentially a fifth of the world's leather raw material base, but much is wasted. It seemed natural to invest in a leather-finishing operation to add value to the product in India before exporting it. Having tentatively decided to get into the high-quality end of the business, Tata faced the problem of not knowing anything about the international fashion leather market, notwithstanding its expertise in other industries. Instead of merely selling the leather as a commodity to independent European importers, a marketing joint venture was to be set up with TFR in France, a significant leather finisher and marketer in Europe. This would provide inputs to the factory in India regarding the exact color, texture, and other requirements of large European buyers. By making the leather to order instead of selling it to agents as a commodity, the operation earns higher margins. The French partner would make available an existing marketing establishment, links to key buyers, its name and reputation, and knowledge of the ever-shifting sands of fashion.

Being a natural substance, leather has inherent variability. Add to that the myriad of treatment methods, colors, and finishes, and one ends up with thousands of manufacturing combinations. To produce to a standard fit for the fashion market is, therefore, as much an art as a production science. In total, a successful operation requires close integration of the factory personnel with the marketing and manufacturing staff in Europe.

Let us give a few other brief examples to illustrate the span of variety in the forms of these distribution-type joint ventures. One New York–based partner in the restaurant business contributes marketing expertise in the case of a New York Chinese restaurant. The Sichuan Province of the People's Republic of China was to provide the Chinese chefs with local investors providing financing. The TRW–Fujitsu venture for the U.S. market was based on the idea of combining Fujitsu's hardware with TRW's existing distribution network. Fujitsu had no experience in selling in the United States, nor did it have much interest in making the potentially enormous expenditure of establishing its own sales organization from scratch. It wished to conserve resources for achieving greater strength in production.

Conversely, in the Fuji–Xerox venture in Japan, Fuji provided Xerox an entry into the Japanese market as well as links with key buyers (*Electronic Business*, March 1984). The latter is an important consideration in Japan because of the strong business conglomeration within Japan's commercial industry sectors (Burton and Saelens, 1982). Personal contacts and referrals within the group are necessary for sales success.

Two Basic Patterns for Joint Venture Formation

We have discussed seven strategic rationales for forming cooperative relationships. In the broadest terms, they involve risk reduction, cost reduction, and an ability to enter markets or enhance revenues in a manner not possible for each firm alone.

A distinction was drawn between ventures in which the partners make similar inputs ("horizontal" ventures) versus ventures in which the contributions of the partners are complementary, with quasi-vertical integration providing *synergy*. Examples of partners making roughly similar contributions are found in the natural resources sector, oil and mineral exploration, real estate development, R&D ventures, and perhaps in large aerospace projects as well, where the dominant considerations appear to be an *accretion* of resources for the large investment involved and a spreading of risk over more participants.

An Overall Benefit/Cost Framework for Analyzing Cooperative Relationships

Thus far, we have mainly examined the strategic benefits side of cooperative ventures, based on the question: what are the conditions necessary for their formation? In weighing costs against benefits, one approach might be to compare the cooperative venture with the fully owned foreign subsidiary option. For the rest of this chapter, let us assume that the firm has the option of making its own investment independently. The question we shall address is how managers should *compare* the "internalization" or "go-it-alone" option with the cooperative venture option. In brief, we shall compare the "100 percent–owned foreign subsidiary" with joint ventures, licensing, and other cooperative forms. Each option involves different organizational and ownership modes, but with the same ultimate market objective.

We begin with a general axiomatic statement. A cooperative mode will have certain incremental benefits as well as certain incremental costs over a fully owned operation. A cooperative venture (CV) may have the effect of increasing the project's revenues and/or decreasing costs over what could have been earned by a fully owned subsidiary; on the other hand, certain drawbacks endemic to cooperative relationships might decrease revenues and/or increase costs over the level of a fully owned operation.

Let us express this statement in axiomatic terms. A cooperative venture is preferred over a fully owned operation if:

| Incremental benefit of a cooperative form *over* a fully owned subsidiary | − | Incremental cost of a cooperative form *over* a fully owned subsidiary | > | Share of other partners' profit |

In brief, a firm would prefer a cooperative association over the go-it-alone option when the net incremental benefit of a cooperative mode is not only greater than zero, but in fact is greater than the profit share of the other partner/s—or if risk is reduced by the act of cooperating. Algebraically,

$$(R_1 + R_2) + (C_1 + C_2) - (R_3 + R_4) - (C_3 + C_4) > (1 - \alpha)\pi_{CV}$$

and/or if risks are reduced significantly.

The terms are defined as follows: *A cooperative venture, compared with an alternative form such as a fully owned subsidiary, will create:*

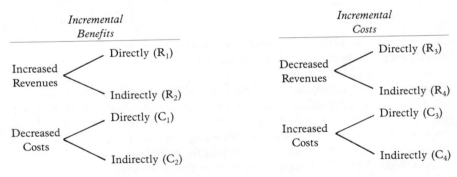

(Note that by *incremental* is meant the extra revenue or cost of a cooperative form over the fully owned option.)

π_{CV} is the expected profit of the cooperative venture. α is the equity share (or contractually defined share) in the venture of the firm doing this analysis. $(1 - \alpha)$ is the other partner's share. Tables 1–3 to 1–6 give further detail on each of the terms, R_1 to R_4 and C_1 to C_4.

Thus, the incremental net benefit of a cooperative venture over a go-it-alone alternative has to not only be positive, but moreover, be large enough to cover the other partner's share of the profits, leaving some further incremental gain for the company considering the alternatives. This statement shows why cooperative ventures are not easy to form or to sustain over time.

By *direct* is meant the revenue and cost increments directly impinging on the project itself. By *indirect* is meant the effect of undertaking the cooperative venture on the rest of the global enterprise (on other divisions of the company), on affiliates in other countries, and on overall strategy. The direct and the indirect revenues and costs do not always have the same directional effect, nor might they occur in the same location or time. A licensing agreement or a joint venture, for instance, may in itself be directly profitable, but it can be indirectly harmful if it creates a future competitor, perhaps in another part of the world. The benefits of cooperative ventures are summarized in tables 1–3 and 1–4.

Incremental Benefits of Cooperative Ventures

Higher Revenues from Cooperation. It should be noted that this analytical framework applies to all types of cooperative arrangements, whether they be licensing, joint ventures, or other agreements. Among the reasons why project revenues can be improved are the other partner's market knowledge, technology, market access, ties to important buyers and government, faster entry and, thus, more favorable cash flows. Indirectly, the company could benefit by having, for instance, technical or new-product ideas from the venture diffused to other parts of the company, a process studied by Lyles in chapter 17 of this book. Another indirect benefit is the possibility of having other divisions of the company handle (for a markup) products from the partner organization.

Lower Costs of Cooperative Ventures. Among the reasons why project costs may be lower under a cooperative form might be larger economies of scale and rationalization gains; government incentives available to joint ventures and licensing (but not to fully owned subsidiaries); lower capital investment and overheads due

Table 1–3
Increased Revenue from the Cooperative Venture Alternative over the Fully Owned Subsidiary

Direct (R_1)	Indirect (R_2)
Other partner's knowledge of market	More complete product line to help overall sales
Other partner's intangible assets such as technology, patents, and trademarks	Technical or new-product ideas learned from other partner and diffused to other parts of the company
Other partner's ties to government and/or important buyers	Markups on components or product trade with partner
One fewer competitor; hence, potentially larger market share	
Faster entry; improved cash flows	
Access to market otherwise foreclosed	

Table 1-4
Decreased Costs from the Cooperative Venture Alternative Compared to the Fully Owned Subsidiary

Direct (C_1)	Indirect (C_2)
Economies of scale from larger market share	Productivity and technical improvements diffused to other parts of company
Rationalization based on each partner nation's comparative advantage	
Government incentives and subsidies given to CVs only	
Lower capital cost and overhead due to using slack or underutilized equipment or design capabilities in each partner	
Less duplication of headquarters personnel	
Access through partner to cheaper raw materials and/or component inputs	
More productive technology or administrative methods contributed by one partner	

to utilizing slack capacity in the partner firms; and, finally, cheaper raw materials/component inputs and more productive methods acquired through the partner. Indirectly, other parts of the company might gain cost advantages from productivity gains and other efficiency improvements learned from the partner. This was probably an important consideration for GM when it linked up with Toyota.

Detrimental Aspects of Cooperative Ventures

Lower Revenues. Aspects of cooperative ventures leading to lower revenues and/or higher costs are summarized in tables 1–5 and 1–6. As opposed to the situation with fully owned investments, the firm may be constrained by its association and suffer a relative decline in revenues because it does not have the freedom to unilaterally

Table 1-5
Decreased Revenue from the Cooperative Alternative Compared to the Fully Owned Option

Direct (R_3)	Indirect (R_4)
CV association does not allow firm to expand into certain lines of business in the future.	Partner's desire to export decreases sales made by other affiliates in international markets.
Partner reaps the benefit of future business expansion that is not proportional to its future contribution.	Partner becomes more formidable competitor in the future.
Lower price is set at behest of partner.	

Table 1-6
Increased Costs from the Cooperative Venture Mode Compared to the Fully Owned Option

Direct (C_3)	Indirect (C_4)
Cost of transferring technology and expertise to partner	Increase in headquarters administrative, legal, and other overheads
Increased coordination and governance costs	Opportunity costs of executives and/or technicians assigned to CV
Pressures from partner to buy from designated sources or sell through its distribution channel	
Global optimization of MNC partner may not be possible for: Sourcing Financial flows Tax Transfer pricing Rationalization of production	

expand lines of business or because prices set in collaboration with the partner may be lower than one would like them to be. Indirectly, global revenues of one of the partners may decline because the other partner's desire to have the venture export might cut into potential sales of the firm in other territories. In general, revenue declines could occur in the future if the partner turned into a global competitor.

Higher Costs. Costs of a cooperative venture may exceed those of a fully owned, internalized operation due to the extra elements of having to negotiate and transfer technology and administer an enterprise jointly with another firm. (See table 1-6.) This is, in brief, the "transaction costs" argument. For a multinational firm, costs rise when global optimization may no longer be possible when it comes to sourcing, finance, tax, transfer pricing, and/or distribution due to the divergent objectives of the partners. Indirectly, cooperative ventures could entail somewhat higher headquarters costs as well as legal and technical overheads, compared with fully owned affiliates.

Risk-reduction Effects of Cooperative Ventures

Apart from the higher or lower costs and revenues of a cooperative venture compared with a fully owned subsidiary alternative, there are often important risk-reduction aspects.

Table 1-7 recapitulates these important risk-reduction effects of cooperative ventures in terms of lower investment, faster entry (and, thus, better payback), and potentially lower political risk. High tech venture companies, for instance, may have stakes in several ventures with different potential competitors and be engaged

Table 1–7
Risk Reduction

Lower capital investment at stake:
  Partial investment
  Excess capacity utilization
  Economies of scale
  Economies of rationalization and quasi integration

Faster entry and/or certification

Use CV as a guinea pig

For large risky projects:
  Limit risk per venture
  Diversify risk over several firms

Lower political risk

Lower asset exposure for medium- and small-sized firms

in ventures involving several technologies at various stages of development—a loose network of sometimes interlocking companies. The strategy may be to maintain a stake in and potential payoff from several (sometimes speculative) projects, with limited risk per venture, while diversifying risk exposure over several projects. A cooperative venture may in some instances be viewed as a "guinea-pig," perhaps to be brushed aside or taken over fully should it come up with a truly interesting discovery or market success. For medium- and small-sized firms, cooperative ventures are often the only realistic way to reduce risk to tolerable levels.

This framework can be used to analyze any cooperative venture (be it an equity joint venture, licensing agreement, or research partnership) and to compare it with the alternative of internal development. To recapitulate, the framework suggests making project calculations for both a fully owned and a cooperative option and then comparing the two. The cooperative mode is preferred if its net incremental profit over the fully owned alternative exceeds the profit share of the other partner, that is, if $(R_1 + R_2) + (C_1 + C_2) - (R_3 + R_4) - (C_3 + C_4) > (1-\alpha) \pi_{CV}$ In some cases, actual cash flow calculations have been made for the comparison (Contractor, 1985). At the least, the framework provides a useful strategic planning exercise, which helps in planning negotiation terms with prospective partners.

Conclusion: Cooperative Ventures as an Alternative Form of International Business Operation

In this chapter, we have examined the strategic-management and industrial-organization rationales for forming cooperative ventures. We have not explored the cultural or behavioral problems of running them, nor have we examined in much detail the causes of their failure or success. There is a large literature on those topics, exemplified by Sullivan and Peterson (1982) and Killing (1983). The thrust of that literature, perhaps unwittingly, seems to overemphasize the problems of running international joint ventures. There is, however, no hard evidence that their failure rate exceeds the normal corporate failure rate for comparable single-owner ventures. We have, however, claimed in this chapter that careful analysis prior to the decision of whether to go for a cooperative venture may be a most critical factor impacting future success of the cooperative venture (if such a venture is the decision outcome). The very fact that the partners have spent sufficient time to become truly clear about what they are entering into should be a major positive factor in this context.

The fact remains, nevertheless, that the strategic rationales prevailing when a cooperative venture was formed may shift over time. As a hypothesis for testing, let us propose that even though subsequent problems may develop (such as cultural difficulties, slower decision making, arguments over the rate and division of profits, disputes over sourcing, tensions in connection with the assignment of personnel, and disagreements on future expansion), these are still all less onerous problems when compared with an erosion of the fundamental strategic rationales proposed in this chapter. This erosion may come from external or environmental sources, such as when the technology contributed by one partner is obsolescent because of changes in the industry. Or the erosion may be internal, such as when one partner *learns* from the other, and the other partner then has nothing new to contribute. Ongoing viability of the venture depends on the *continuing* mutual dependence of the partners.

This chapter has specifically focused on the strategic and economic rationales for forming cooperative ventures. We have, by choice, not discussed "softer" issues which also should be assessed before reaching a decision on whether to form a cooperative venture. Such issues might include the anticipated ease of working with the other partner; possible language difficulties, cultural differences, style incompatibilities, and differences in values and norms; the anticipated "political" climate within the context of the partners' organization; and the presence of a sufficiently strong "mentor" who will push the cooperative venture. We acknowledge the importance of incorporating these types of assessments into the decision on whether to go for a cooperative venture. However, we feel that the relative importance of these softer issues might be relatively lessened if a careful planning process has been undertaken, so that both partners understand the fundamental strategic and economic rationales involved.

It is possible that cooperative ventures will grow in importance as a mode of international business operations. However, we cannot be sure; in terms of strategic management of multinational operations, we have a trend and a countertrend. On the one hand, through regional economic integration plus convergence of standards and buyer preferences, in some industries there is the possibility of producing for a world market, with relatively minor variations in each nation. Centralized control and full ownership of affiliates is important for the implementation of an efficient and strategic direction in such corporations. On the other hand, this chapter has pointed to examples in several industries where efficiency, risk-reduction, and other strategic rationales make the cooperative mode of organization superior to an internalization or go-it-alone strategy. Moreover, the traditional impetus for joint ventures, licensing, and other contractual forms remains in many countries. Economic nationalism, protectionism, transport costs, differing local cultures and standards, as well as the presence of entrenched domestic firms encourage a linkup with a local company as a means of serving the particular needs of a geographic market and/or for getting political permission to produce and tap natural resources. These traditional types of cooperative ventures remains ubiquitous.

Negotiated arrangements between international firms such as joint ventures and technology licensing agreements already vastly exceed controlled foreign affiliates by number, if not value. One model of the multinational corporation sees it as a closed, internalized administrative system that straddles national boundaries. An alternative paradigm proposed in this chapter is to view the international firm as a member of various open and shifting coalitions, each with a specific strategic purpose.

Notes

1. In the latest benchmark survey (U.S. Department of Commerce, 1985), the figures appear quite different. But this is an artifact of the data-collection method used.

An appendix to this chapter, "The Case of the Six Thousand Missing Affiliates," illustrates the data problem and provides further detail to the preceding figures.

Bibliography

Abbeglen, J. 1982. "U.S.–Japanese Technological Exchange in Perspective, 1946–1981." In C. Uehara (ed.), *Technological Exchange: The US–Japanese Experience.* New York: University Press.

Barkas, J.M., and Gale, J.C. 1981. "Joint Venture Strategies: Yugosalvia—A Case Study." *Columbia Journal of World Business,* Spring: 30–39.

Berg, S., Duncan, J., and Friedman, P. 1982. *Joint Venture Strategies and Corporate Innovation.* Cambridge, Mass.: Oelgeschlager, Gunn and Hain.

Blois, K.J. 1972. "Vertical Quasi-Integration." *Journal of Industrial Economics,* July: 253–72.

Boston Consulting Group. 1985. *Strategic Alliances.* Working Paper 276, Boston, Mass.

Buckley, P.J., and Casson, M. 1976. *The Future of the Multinational Enterprise.* New York: Holmes & Meier.

Burton, F.N., and Saelens, F.H. 1982. "Partner Choice and Linkage Characteristics of International Joint Ventures in Japan: An Exploratory Analysis of the Inorganic Chemicals Sector." *Management International Review,* 22(2): 20–29.

Business Week. 1984. "The All American Small Car is Fading." March 12: 88–95.

Caves, R.E. 1971. "International Corporations: "The Industrial Economics of Foreign Investment." *Economica,* February: 1–27.

Contractor, F.J. 1985. *Licensing in International Strategy: A Guide for Planning and Negotiations.* Westport, Conn.: Greenwood.

Contractor, F.J. 1983. "Technology Importation Policies in Developing Countries: Some Implications of Recent Theoretical and Empirical Evidence." *Journal of Developing Areas,* July: 499–520.

Contractor, F.J. 1983. "Technology Licensing Practices in U.S. Companies: Corporate and Public Policy Implications of an Empirical Study." *Columbia Journal of World Business,* Fall.

Cyert, R.M., and March, J.G. 1963. *A Behavioral Theory of the Firm.* Englewood Cliffs, N.J.: Prentice-Hall.

Doz, Y. 1986. *Technology Partnerships between Larger and Smaller Firms.* Draft paper. INSEAD, Fontainebleau, France, August.

Dunning, J., and Cantwell, J. 1983. *Joint Ventures and Non-Equity Foreign Involvement by British Firms with Particular Reference to Developing Countries: An Exploratory Study.* Working paper. University of Reading Economics Department.

Electronic Business. 1984. "The Winning Formula for U.S.–Japan Joint-Ventures." March: 182–85.

Friedman, P., Berg, S., and Duncan, J. 1979. "External vs. Internal Knowledge Acquisition: Joint Venture Activity and R&D Intensity." *Journal of Economics and Business,* 31(2): 103–10.

Gullander, S. 1976. "Joint Venture and Cooperative Strategy." *Columbia Journal of World Business,* Winter: 104–14.

Hamel, G., Doz, Y., and Prahalad, C. 1986. *Strategic Partnerships: Success or Surrender?* Paper presented at the Rutgers/Wharton Colloquium on Cooperative Strategies in International Business, New Brunswick, N.J., October.

Harrigan, K. 1983. *Strategies for Vertical Integration.* Lexington, Mass.: Lexington Books.

Herriott, S.R. 1986. *The Economic Foundations of Cooperative Strategy: Implications for Organization and Management.* Working paper. University of Texas at Austin.

Hout, T., Porter, M.E., and Rudden, E. 1982. "How Global Companies Win Out." *Harvard Business Review,* September–October: 98–108.

International Herald Tribune. 1981. *World Car* (Supplement), September 19.

Killing, J.P. 1983. *Strategies for Joint Venture Success.* New York: Praeger.

Lall, S. 1981. *Developing Countries in the International Economy.* London: Macmillan.

Levitt, T. 1983. "The Globalization of Markets." *Harvard Business Review,* May–June: 92–102.

Lorange, P. 1984. *Cooperative Strategies: Planning and Control Considerations.* Working paper. Wharton School, University of Pennsylvania, Philadelphia, October.

Lorange, P. 1986. *Cooperative Ventures in Multinational Settings: A Framework.* Working paper. Wharton School, University of Pennsylvania, Philadelphia, May.

Mariti, P., and Smiley, R.H. 1983. "Cooperative Agreements and the Organization of Industry." *Journal of Industrial Economics,* June: 437–51.

McConnell, J., and Nantell, J.R. 1985. "Common Stock Returns and Corporate Combinations: The Case of Joint Ventures." *Journal of Finance,* 40: 519–36.

Miles, R.F., and Snow, C.C. 1986. "Network Organizations: New Concepts for New Forms." *California Management Review,* 28(3).

Moxon, R.W., and Geringer, J.M. 1984. *Multinational Ventures in the Commercial Aircraft Industry.* Working paper (mimeo). University of Washington, Seattle.

Pereyra, W.T. 1981. "Some Preliminary Results of a U.S.-Soviet Joint Fishing Venture." *Journal of Contemporary Business,* 10(1): 7.

Pfeffer, J., and Nowak, P. 1976. "Joint Ventures and Interorganizational Interdependence." *Administrative Science Quarterly,* 21 (September): 398–418.

Porter, M.E. 1985. *Competitive Advantage: Creating and Sustaining Superior Performance.* New York: Free Press.

Porter, M.E. 1980. *Competitive Strategy: Techniques for Analyzing Industries and Competitors.* New York: Free Press.

Porter, M.E. 1986. "The Changing Patterns of International Competition." *California Management Review,* 28(2).

Reich, R.B. 1984. "Japan Inc., U.S.A." *The New Republic,* November 26: 19–23.

Richardson, G.B. 1972. "The Organization of Industry." *The Economic Journal,* September: 883–96.

Sinclair, S.W. 1983. *The World Car: The Future of the Automobile Industry.* New York: Facts on File.

Stopford, J.M., and Haberich, K. 1976. "Ownership and Control of Foreign Operations." *Journals of General Management,* Summer.

Stopford, J.M., and Wells, L. 1972. *Managing the Multinational Enterprise.* New York: Basic Books.

Sullivan, J., and Peterson, R.B. 1982. "Factors Associated with Trust in Japanese–American Joint Ventures." *Management International Review,* 22(2): 30–40.

Telesio, P. 1977. *Foreign Licensing Policy in Multinational Enterprises.* D.B.A. dissertation. Harvard University.

Thorelli, H.B. 1986. "Networks: Between Markets and Hierarchies." *Strategic Management Journal,* 7(1).

United Nations Economic and Social Council. 1978. *Transnational Corporations in World Development: A Re-Examination.* New York: United Nations.

U.S. Department of Commerce. 1981. *U.S. Direct Investment Abroad, 1977.* Washington, D.C.: U.S. Government Printing Office.

U.S. Department of Commerce. 1985. *U.S. Direct Investment Abroad, 1982: The Benchmark Survey.* Washington, D.C.: U.S. Government Printing Office.

Vickers, J. 1985. "Pre-Emptive Patenting, Joint Ventures and the Persistence of Oligopoly." *International Journal of Industrial Organization,* 3: 261–73.

Wassink, D., and Carbaugh, R. 1986. "International Joint Ventures and the U.S. Auto Industry." *The International Trade Journal,* 1(1): 47–64.

Williamson, O.E. 1975. *Markets and Hierarchies: An Analysis and Antitrust Implications.* London: Free Press.

Appendix:
The Case of the Six Thousand Missing Affiliates

Every five years, the U.S. Department of Commerce publishes an extensive survey on U.S. direct investment abroad.

Between the 1977 and 1982 surveys, the total number of foreign affiliates of U.S.-based firms was shown to have declined from 23,698 to 18,339. An affiliate is defined as a foreign corporation in which the U.S. company has 10 percent or more of voting securities. The surveys distinguish between minority affiliates (10 to 50 percent shareholding) and majority affiliates (one in which the U.S. firm has more than 50 percent of shares). Unfortunately, they do not inform us whether there is, in fact, a distinct foreign corporate entity functioning as a "partner" to the U.S. firm or whether the balance of the shares are merely held by passive "portfolio"-type local investors. Nevertheless, examining the data provides several insights, especially comparing the 1977 and 1982 figures. Eliminating bank parents and affiliates (which are but a minor subset), we have table 1A–1.

Table 1A–1
Nonbank Affiliates of Nonbank U.S. Parents

	Total	Majority	Minority
1977	23,641	11,909	11,732
1982	17,213	14,475	2,738

Source: U.S. Department of Commerce, *U.S. Direct Investment Abroad, 1977,* (1981) and *U.S. Direct Investment Abroad, 1982: The Benchmark Survey* (1985). Washington, D.C.: U.S. Government Printing Office.

The "loss" of over six thousand affiliates is substantially, if not almost entirely, explained by the more stringent criterion adopted in 1982 to cut off the tail of the distribution. In 1982, filing data with the Department of Commerce was reportedly mandatory for all U.S. firms with foreign affiliates that had total assets, sales, or net income of at least $3 million. For the 1977 survey, the comparable cutoff was only $500,000, roughly a quarter of the 1982 figure in real terms. This is the principal explanation for the fall in the number of affiliates and parents. (However, there are other minor factors which we may note, such as the marginal retrenchment of U.S. investment abroad between 1977 and 1982 in some countries and sectors such as energy and mining; the existence of a global recession in 1982; and the somewhat stronger dollar.)

Thus, the disappearance of over six thousand affiliates is more apparent than real. It is mainly caused by the new data-collection criterion. For example, the reported drop in employment by nonbank foreign affiliates is small, from 7.1 million in 1977 to 6.6 million in 1982. Total assets of nonbank affiliates actually increased from $490 million in 1977 to $751 million in 1982, which hardly suggests a drop in the value of foreign investment.

Several significant conclusions and hypotheses emerge:

1. The distribution of U.S. foreign investment, by size of both parents and affiliates, has a very long tail, consisting of rather small operations.

2. There are far more small U.S. firms investing abroad than is commonly realized (judging by the emphasis on large multinational strategy in the literature and even in this book). Their numbers are large, even though their share in total assets or employment is small.

3. Smaller U.S. firms are particularly prone to go in for minority foreign ventures, judging by the sharper "decline" in the "minority" category in table 1A-1, resulting from the higher cutoff criterion in 1982.

4. Although there is no unequivocal proof, the preceding lends credence to the hypothesis that the propensity to form joint ventures and cooperative relationships is negatively correlated with the size of the U.S. parent and foreign affiliate. (Again, this is in terms of number of relationships, not their size or economic impact.)

2

A Theory of Cooperation in International Business

Peter J. Buckley
Mark Casson

The Concept of Cooperation

To what extent are cooperative ventures really cooperative? What exactly is meant by *cooperation* in this context? In international business, the term *cooperative venture* is often used merely to signify some alternative to 100 percent equity ownership of a foreign affiliate: it may indicate a joint venture, an industrial collaboration agreement, licensing, franchising, subcontracting, or even a management contract or countertrade agreement. It is quite possible, of course, to regard such arrangements as cooperative by definition, but this fudges the substantive issue of just how cooperative these arrangements really are.

If not all cooperative ventures are truly cooperative, then what distinguishes the cooperative ones from the rest? To answer this question, it is necessary to provide a rigorous definition of cooperation. This chapter attempts to distill, from the common-sense notion of cooperation, those aspects of the greatest economic relevance. It is not intended, however, to preempt the use of the word *cooperation* for one specific concept. There is a spectrum of concepts—concepts variously known as cooperation, collaboration, copartnership, and so on—and a diversity of fields of application—employee-ownership of firms, intergovernment collaboration in economic policy, and so on; several different concepts will be needed to do full justice to the complex issues raised by cooperative behavior in the broadest meaning of that term.

Because the manifestations of cooperative behavior are so wide-ranging, it is desirable, within the scope of a single chapter, to restrict attention to a single case. The 50:50 equity joint venture (JV) has been chosen. It is argued that while genuine cooperation is a feature of some JVs, adversarial elements can be present too

A preliminary version of this chapter was presented to the joint seminar of the Swedish School of Business Administration, Helsinki, The Finnish School of Economics, and the University of Helsinki (kindly arranged by H.C. Blomqvist, T. Bergelund, and I. Menzler-Hokkanen) and to the staff workshop at the University of Reading. Steve Nicholas provided considerable encouragement, mixed with healthy skepticism. We are grateful to Farok Contractor, Peter Lorange, Peter Gray, Kathryn Harrigan, Ingo Walter, and others for their constructive comments.

and, in some cases, can dominate. The factors that govern the degree of cooperation are delineated. The organizational structure of the venture and the extent and nature of the other ventures in which the participants are involved turn out to be crucial. It is potentially misleading to analyze a joint venture in isolation from other ventures, for the extent of cooperation in any one venture is strongly influenced by the overall configuration of the ventures in which the parties are involved.

Coordination

The definition of *cooperation* advocated here is "coordination effected through mutual forbearance." This identifies cooperation as a special type of coordination. *Coordination* is defined as effecting a Pareto-improvement in the allocation of resources, such that someone is made better off, and no one worse off, than they would otherwise be. Coordination is an appropriate basis upon which to build a concept of cooperation, for it articulates the idea that cooperation is of mutual benefit to the parties directly involved (Casson, 1982).

Coordination sounds as if it must always be a good thing, but the following points should be noted about the way that the concept is applied in practice.

The Externality Problem. Coordination is defined with respect to all parties who are in any way affected by a venture, and not just those who join in voluntarily. Those who join presumably expect to benefit, but others who do not join may lose as a result. Sometimes the losers have legal rights which can be used to block the venture, or they can organize themselves into a club to compensate the beneficiaries for not going ahead. But when there are many nonprivileged losers who have difficulty organizing themselves, it is quite possible that a venture may go ahead even though the losers, as a group, suffer more than the beneficiaries gain.

Coordination under Duress. Coordination is defined with respect to an alternative position—namely, what would otherwise happen—so that what is assumed about this alternative position is crucial in determining whether coordination occurs. A voluntary participant may decide to join a venture simply because it is in such an adverse position that the alternative to joining would be absolute disaster.

In some cases, the adversity may be deliberately contrived by others—in particular, by other participants anxious to increase their bargaining power. Even where the adversity has not been contrived, other participants may still seek to take advantage of the unattractive nature of the alternatives available to the party concerned. A related point is that where adversity stems from a recent setback, the party may expect coordination to return it to a position as good as its original one, and it may regard as exploitative any terms that fail to do this.

Empty Threats and Disappointments. It is a party's perception of the outcome of a venture, and of the alternative position, that governs its decision concerning whether to join. These perceptions are subjective, in the sense that they depend upon the information available to the participant, and can vary, within the same situation, between one person and another. Expectations can be erroneous, so that a venture that effects coordination ex ante may turn out not to do so ex post. Astute individuals or managements may be able to influence the expectations of others to their own advantage. One participant may threaten another participant that if it does not join on onerous terms, the first participant will act to make the other participant's alternative position considerably worse than it would otherwise be. It is quite possible, therefore, for a participant to join a venture under a threat that subsequently turns out to have been empty and, either for this reason or for some other, to later regret having joined at all.

Autonomy of Preferences. In conventional applications of the concept of coordination, it is assumed that a party's objectives are unchanged by involvement in a coordinating venture. This assumption is relaxed when introducing the concept of commitment later on. Many economists consider it methodologically unsound to introduce endogeneity of preferences in this way, but in the present context, there are good reasons for doing so. Not everyone is likely to be convinced of its necessity, however.

Interfirm Coordination

Coordination applies first and foremost to people rather than to firms. In certain cases, however, a firm can be regarded as a person, as when it consists of a single individual who acts as owner, manager, and worker. In large firms, of course, these various functions are specialized with different individuals. The firm then becomes an institutional framework for coordinating the efforts of different people working together. This exemplifies *intrafirm* coordination. The focus of this chapter, however, is on *interfirm* coordination, in which one firm coordinates with another. It is analytically useful to separate the intrafirm and interfirm aspects of coordination by assuming that interfirm coordination takes place between single-person firms of the kind just described. Subject to this qualification, interfirm coordination may be defined as an increase in the profits of some firms that is achieved without a reduction in the profits of others.

It is also important to distinguish interfirm coordination from extrafirm coordination, which is coordination effected between firms on the one hand and households on the other. Extrafirm coordination is exemplified by trade in final product markets and factor markets. Because of externalities of the kind just described, certain types of interfirm coordination can damage extrafirm coordination to the point where coordination within the economy as a whole is reduced. It is well known, for example, that when firms collude to raise the price within an industry to a monopolist level, the additional profit accruing to the firms is less than the loss of consumer welfare caused by the higher prices and the associated curtailment of demand. Because the consumers are usually more numerous than the firms, it is difficult for them to organize effective opposition to this. Thus, when interfirm coordination is motivated by collusion, even though the firms gain, the economy as a whole may be a loser.

Forbearance

All the parties involved in a venture have an inalienable de facto right to pursue their own interests at the expense of others. It is one of the hallmarks of institutional economics—and transaction cost economics in particular—that it recognizes the widespread implications of this. It can manifest itself in two main ways: aggression and neutrality. An aggressive party perpetrates some act that damages another party's interests, while a neutral party behaves more passively: it simply refrains from some act that would benefit someone else. In either case, the party is deemed to cheat; if it refrains from cheating, it is said to *forbear*. Often, both options are available: the party can either *commit* a damaging act or merely *omit* to perform a beneficial one. Under such conditions, neutrality is regarded as *weak cheating* and aggression as *strong cheating*.

Forbearance and cheating can take place between parties that have no formal connection with each other. They also occur in the establishment of a venture. To fix ideas, this chapter focuses on the problem of sustaining a venture once operations have commenced. It is assumed that at this stage each participant has accepted certain specific obligations. Typically, a minimal set of obligations will have been codified in a formal agreement, while a fuller set of obligations has been made informally. Failure to honor minimal obligations represents strong cheating, honoring only minimal obligations represents weak cheating, while honoring the full obligations represents forbearance. In the special case where the obligations relate to the supply of effort, strong cheating involves disruption, weak cheating involves supplying a minimal amount of effort, and forbearance involves providing maximum effort.

The Incentive to Forbear

When only the immediate consequences of an action are considered, it often seems best to cheat. But when the indirect effects are considered, forbearance may seem more desirable. This means, intuitively, that forbearance appeals most to those agents who take a long-term view of the situation.

A short-term view is likely to prevail when the agent expects the venture to fail because of cheating by others. The risk of prejudicing the venture through its *own* cheating is correspondingly low, and there may be considerable advantages in being the first to cheat because the richest pickings are available at this stage.

Knock-on effects arise principally because of the responses of others. Their perceived importance depends upon the *vulnerability* of the party. A party is vulnerable if some course of action that might be chosen by another party would significantly reduce its welfare. Vulnerability encourages a party to think through how its own actions affect the incentives facing others. The more vulnerable the party is, the more important it is to avoid stimulating an adverse response from other agents. Each party can, to some extent, induce long-term thinking in other parties by threats that emphasize their vulnerability to its own actions. Partly because of this, the likely pattern of response by others, in many cases, is to match forbearance with forbearance, but to punish cheating. Confronted with this pattern of response, the optimal strategy in most cases is to do the same. Specifically, it is to forbear at the outset and to continue forbearing as long as others do. The situation in which all parties forbear on a reciprocal basis is termed *mutual forbearance*. According to the earlier definition, coordination effected through this mechanism is the essence of cooperation.

If other parties cheat, the victim has a choice of punishment strategies. These strategies differ in both the nature of the evidence required and the severity of the punishment inflicted.

Recourse to the Law. This method has very limited scope because many forms of cheating are perfectly legal. This is particularly true where weak cheating is concerned. Even where the law has been breached, the principle that the defendant is guilty until proven innocent, coupled with controls over what evidence is admissible in court, makes it costly, in many legal systems, for the victim to translate circumstantial information about cheating into convincing evidence.

Do-It-Yourself Punishment. This strategy is often much cheaper. The victim can rely upon its own assessment of the situation. It does not need to convince others of its case. There are two main problems with this strategy. First, the victim may have far more limited sanctions than the law and, indeed, in some cases (such as punishing theft), the victim may have lost, as a direct consequence of the crime, the very resources needed to inflict the punishment. Second, there may be a credibility problem. If the potential victim threatens to withhold promised bonuses, the threat will have little force if it is not trusted to pay them when they are deserved anyway. If it threatens to perform some seriously damaging action instead, it is possible that the victim may damage its own interests too—as when it threatens to undermine the entire venture—and this may create the belief that it will not actually do it. Despite these difficulties, do-it-yourself punishment is widely used. A common strategy is tit-for-tat, which matches acts of cheating with similar acts in kind. It has an appropriate incentive structure, is simple to implement, is not too costly, and is easily intelligible to other parties (Axelrod, 1981, 1984).

Residual Risk Sharing. In some cases, punishment is semiautomatic, as when each participant requires each of the others to hold a share in the residual risks of the venture. If anyone cheats, the venture as a whole suffers, and the value of their equity stake diminishes as a result. This device is particularly appropriate in ventures calling for teamwork, when it is difficult to pinpoint the individuals who are cheating. This means that incentives must be based, not on the inputs (because they are difficult to observe), but upon the joint output instead. This principle works well for small teams, but not for large ones, where the link between individual performance and the share of the team rewards is relatively weak. It is also dependent on there being less likelihood of cheating in the sharing out of residual rewards than in the supply of inputs—which is a reasonable assumption in many cases.

Although these three methods are substitutes in dealing with any one type of cheating, most ventures provide opportunities for various types of cheating. In this respect, the methods complement one another quite nicely. Formal agreements between participants are often drafted by professional lawyers to make them easy to enforce through the courts. The formalities typically refer to readily observable aspects of behavior on which convincing evidence is easy to collect. The law provides an appropriate punishment mechanism in this case. But the formal aspect of a venture cannot usually guarantee much more than its survival. True success can only come if informal understandings between the parties are honored as well (Williamson, 1985). In this context, legal processes are seriously deficient. A system of shared equity ownership provides a suitable incentive framework, but almost invariably needs to be supplemented by do-it-yourself rewards and punishments too.

Reputation Effects

We have noted that do-it-yourself arrangements often suffer from a credibility problem. One way of resolving this problem is for the potential victim to gain a reputation for always carrying out threatened reprisals. Reputations can have other benefits too. A party with a reputation for never being first to abandon forbearance gives partners a greater incentive to forbear themselves, for it increases the likelihood that if they too forbear, then the venture as a whole will reach a successful conclusion. A reputation for forbearance also facilitates the formation of ventures in the first place; it makes it easier for the reputable party to find partners because prospective partners anticipate fewer problems in enforcing the arrangements (Blois, 1972; Richardson, 1972).

A reputation is an investment. It requires a party to forgo certain short-term gains in order to save on future transactions costs. The most valuable reputation appears to be a reputation for reciprocating forbearance: never being the first to abandon it, but always taking reprisals against others who do. The factors most conducive to investment in reputation are as follows:

1. *The prospect of many future ventures in which the party expects to have an opportunity to be involved.* The number of ventures will be larger, the greater the party's range of contacts, the longer its remaining life expectancy, and the higher its expectation of the frequency with which new economic opportunities occur.

2. *The conspicuous demonstration of forbearance in a public domain.* A high-profile venture, with a large number of observers, and a dense network of contacts spreading information about it, facilitates reputation building. Conspicuous forbearance is favored by a cultural environment that is open rather than secretive. A dense network of contacts is most likely within a stable social group, in which few parties enter or leave.

3. *A propensity for observers to predict the future behavior of a party by extrapolating its past pattern of behavior.* This governs the extent to which a party can signal future intentions through current behavior. If peoples' attitudes are governed by prejudice based on superficial appearance rather than upon actual behavior, acquiring a reputation that is at variance with prejudice may prove very difficult.

Cooperation, Commitment, and Trust

To what extent can it be said that one contractual arrangement is more cooperative than another? To answer this question, it is necessary to distinguish between cooperation as an input to a venture and cooperation as an output from it. An arrangement that gives all parties a strong incentive to cheat requires a great deal of mutual forbearance if it is to be successful. Loosely speaking, it requires a large input of cooperation. In one respect, this is a weakness rather than a strength of the arrangement, since it means that in practice the arrangement is quite likely to fail. This is important when considering joint ventures later, for it does seem that joint ventures that begin by being hailed extravagantly as a symbol of cooperation have a high propensity to fail.

Cooperation may be regarded as an output when an arrangement leads to greater trust between the parties, which reduces the transaction costs of subsequent ventures in which they are involved. Focusing on cooperation as an output gives a perspective that is closest to the common sense view that cooperative ventures are a "good thing."

There is a connection, however, between input and output. This is because an arrangement that calls for a considerable input of cooperation and then turns out successfully enhances the reputations of the parties. First and foremost, it enhances their reputations with each other, but, if there are spectators to the arrangement, then it enhances their reputations with them too.

The connection between input and output suggests that some arrangements may be more efficient than others in transforming an input of cooperation into an output. More precisely, cooperation is efficient when a given amount of mutual forbearance generates the largest possible amount of mutual trust. Efficiency is achieved by devising the arrangement of the venture so as to speed up the acquisition of reputation. One reason why reputation building may be slow is that cheating is often a covert practice—it is more viable if it goes undetected—and so it may be a long time before parties can be certain whether or not an agent has cheated. The importance of this factor varies from one venture to another, depending upon how easy it is for agents to make their own contributions and monitor and supervise their partners at the same time.

Reputation Building

To speed up reputation building, it may be advantageous to create, within the arrangement itself, additional opportunities for agents to forbear reciprocally. Thus, a venture may provide for a sequence of decisions to be taken by different parties, in each of which the individual agent faces a degree of conflict between its own interests and those of others. Each agent (except the first-mover) has an opportunity to respond to the earlier moves of others. The essence of this reputation-building mechanism is that, first, the decisions are open and overt, rather than secretive and covert, and second, there is some connection between the overt decisions made by agents and their covert ones. In other words, the mechanism rests on the view that what the agent does when observed is a reflection of the way it behaves when not observed. Because of bounded rationality and the persistence of habits, it is difficult for most agents to adjust their behavior fully according to the conditions of observation. A sophisticated arrangement can set traps to catch agents off guard; provided agents do not face similar sequences of decisions too often, all but the cleverest and most alert are likely to unintentionally reveal something about the pattern of their unobserved behavior as a result.

This device has certain dangers, however, not least of which is that it increases the amount of discretion accorded to each party. For it is the essence of the deferred decisions that agents have discretion over how they use the information at their disposal. If they were instructed to follow a decision rule prescribed at the outset, then their only discretionary decision would be whether to cheat on the rule. The situation would revert to one that encouraged covert rather than overt behavior. To avoid creating excessive risks for the other parties, however, it is necessary to carefully control the amount of discretion by focusing the earliest decisions in the sequence upon issues that do not really matter. As the venture proceeds and trust grows, so the degree of real discretion can be increased. To start with, therefore, the situation may resemble a game in which only token gains and losses are made, and only as time passes does the game become fully integrated into the real world.

There are certain types of venture that naturally create game-playing situations. In long-term ventures in a volatile environment, for example, there is a very sound logic for deferring certain decisions until after the venture has begun—namely, that new information may subsequently become available that is relevant to how later parts of the venture are carried out. It may well be appropriate to delegate these decisions to the individuals who are most likely to have this information at hand. It then becomes possible to fine-tune the degree of discretion to the amount of trust already present. Thus, it is quite common to observe that when a number of parties work together for the first time, a tight discipline is imposed to begin with, which is then progressively relaxed as the parties begin to trust each other more.

Commitment

Up to this point, it has been assumed that cooperation is encouraged by appealing to the agents' enlightened self-interest—their incentive to cooperate is strengthened by reducing the cost of building up a reputation for reciprocity. It is also possible, however, to encourage cooperation by changing an agent's preferences so that the successful completion of the venture receives a higher priority than it did before. One way of doing this is to encourage the agent to perceive cooperation not as a means but as an end in itself. Cooperation then ceases to be based on strategic considerations—considerations that recommend cooperation as an appropriate means—and becomes based on commitment to cooperation in its own right.

It is worth noting, in this connection, that many everyday situations call for forbearance to be shown to people whom it is unlikely that one will ever meet again, and where there is, as a result, little incentive to forbear so far as self-interest alone is concerned. A typical situation arises in connection with unanticipated congestion in the use of a facility. When there is insufficient time to negotiate agreements between the users, and when there is either no system of priorities or the system in force is an inappropriate one, coordination may depend upon spontaneous forbearance. Examples include moving out of other people's way when shopping and giving way to traffic entering from byroads. The reason many people forbear in these situations, it seems, is that they derive welfare directly from their constructive role in the encounter.

It is likely that participation in certain types of venture can affect parties in a similar way. Indeed, participation in a venture may leave an individual far more oriented toward spontaneous cooperation than it was before. The main reason for this is the role of information sharing in a venture. It is characteristic of many ventures that agents are asked to agree to share certain types of information with their partners. This is principally because the agents who possess certain types of information (or are in the best position to obtain it) are not necessarily those with the best judgment on how to use it. Another reason is that information provided by an agent may act as an early warning that, due to environmental changes, it (and perhaps others too) has a strong incentive to cheat, which can be reduced, in everyone's interests, by a limited renegotiation of their agreement.

In asking people to share information, however, it is likely that the response will divulge some of their more general beliefs and their moral values too. Thus, the sharing of information provides those who stand to gain most from the successful completion of the venture with an opportunity to disseminate—whether deliberately or quite subconsciously—a set of values conducive to cooperation. In this case, a venture can promote cooperation simply by providing a forum for the preaching of the cooperative ethic.

The degree of commitment to a venture is likely to be conditional upon certain characteristics of the venture. The commitment of the partners is likely to be higher, for example, the more socially meritorious or strategically important the output is deemed to be. Commitment will also tend to be higher if the distribution of rewards from the venture, when it is successfully completed, is deemed equitable by all parties. Envy of the share of gains appropriated by another partner cannot only diminish motivation, but can encourage cheating—which may be "justified" as a means of generating a more equitable outcome. It is one of the characteristics of the JVs analyzed in the next section that, superficially at least, the distribution of rewards seems fair because it is based on a 50:50 principle. As subsequent discussion indicates, however, such equity may be illusory, and once any such illusion is recognized, the degree of commitment may fall dramatically.

The psychology of commitment, if understood correctly, can be used by one party to manipulate another. But securing commitment through manipulation is a dangerous strategy for, once it is exposed, some form of reprisal or revenge is likely. The commitment previously channelled into the venture by the victim of manipulation may be transferred and channelled into punishing the manipulator instead.

From the standpoint of economic theory, these propositions are equivalent to a postulate that an agent's preferences depend not only upon material consumption (or profit), but also upon the characteristics of the ventures in which it is involved. These characteristics relate both to the nature of the venture itself and to the extent of mutual commitment shown by the parties concerned. This postulate provides the basis for further developments of the theory of cooperation, which lie beyond the scope of the present chapter.

The Economic Theory of Joint Ventures

Analysis of the cooperative content of cooperative ventures must be based upon a rigorous theory of nonequity arrangements. Because nonequity arrangements can take so many different forms, it is useful to focus upon one particular type. The 50:50 equity joint venture (JV) seems appropriate because it is very much symbolic of the cooperative ethos. The main focus is on arrangements involving two private firms, for, although arrangements involving state-owned firms and government agencies are very important in practice (particularly in developing countries), they raise issues lying beyond the scope of this chapter. To the extent, however, that the state sector is primarily profit-motivated, the following analysis will still apply.

It is assumed that each partner in the JV already owns other facilities. It is also assumed that the JV is preplanned, and that the equity stakes are not readily tradeable in divisible units. This means, in particular, that the joint ownership of the venture cannot be explained by a "mutual fund" effect—in other words, it is not the chance outcome of independent portfolio diversification decisions undertaken by the two firms.

Working under these assumptions, theory must address the following three key issues.

Why does each partner wish to own part of the JV rather than simply trade with it on an arm's-length basis? The answer is that there must be some net benefit from internalizing a market in one or more intermediate good and/or service flowing between the JV and the parties' other operations. A *symmetrically motivated* JV is defined as one in which each firm has the same motive for internalizing. This is the simplest form of JV to study, and it is the basis for the detailed discussion presented later. (See also Buckley and Casson, 1985, chapters 2–4.)

Why does each firm own half of the JV rather than all of another facility? The force of this question rests on an implicit judgment that joint ownership poses managerial problems of accountability that outright ownership avoids. To the extent that this is true, there must be some compensating advantage in not splitting up the jointly owned facility into two (or possibly more) separate facilities. In other words, there must be an element of economic indivisibility in the facility. The way this indivisibility manifests itself will depend upon how the JV is linked into the firms' other operations.

1. If the JV generates a homogeneous output which is shared between the partners, or uses a homogeneous input which is sourced jointly by them, then the indivisibility is essentially an economy of scale.

2. If the JV generates two distinct outputs, one of which is used by one partner and the other by the other, then the indivisibility is essentially an economy of scope.

3. If the JV combines two different inputs, each of which is contributed by just one of the parties, then the indivisibility manifests itself simply as a technical complementarity between the inputs (a combination of a diminishing marginal rate of technical substitution and nondecreasing returns to scale).

Given that, in the light of the first two issues, each partner wishes to internalize the same indivisible facility, why do the partners not merge themselves, along with the JV, into a single corporate entity? The answer must be that there is some net disadvantage to such a merger. It may be managerial diseconomies arising from the scale and diversity of the resultant enterprise, legal obstacles stemming from antitrust policy or restrictions on foreign acquisitions, difficulties of financing because of stock market skepticism, and so on.

It is clear, therefore, that JV operation is to be explained in terms of a combination of three factors, namely internalization economies, indivisibilities, and obstacles to merger.

As noted in the introduction, there are many contractual alternatives to JV operation, but for policy purposes, particular interest centers on the question of when a JV will be preferred to outright ownership of a foreign subsidiary. Given that location factors, such as resource endowments, result in two interdependent facilities being located in different countries, the first of the three factors mentioned—internalization economies—militates in favor of outright ownership. It is the extent to which it is constrained by the other two factors—indivisibilities and obstacles to merger—that governs the strength of preference for a JV. The larger are indivisibilities, the greater the obstacles to merger; the smaller are internalization economies (relative to the other two factors), the more likely it is that the JV will be chosen (Casson, 1987, chapter 5). The interplay between these factors in governing the choice of contractual arrangements is illustrated by the following examples.

The Configuration of a JV Operation

The configuration of a JV operation is determined by whether it stands upstream or downstream with respect to each partner's other operations, and by the nature of the intermediate products that flow between them. A JV arrangement is said to be *symmetrically positioned* if each partner stands in exactly the same (upstream or downstream) relation to the JV operation as does the other. Figure 2–1 illustrates symmetric forward integration, and figure 2–2 shows symmetric backward integration. Sometimes an operation may be integrated both backward and forward into the same partner's operations. Figure 2–3 illustrates a symmetric buyback arrangement in which each partner effectively subcontracts the processing of a product to the same jointly owned facility.

Some writers seem to suggest that JVs are inherently symmetric—presumably because of the 50:50 symmetry in the pattern of ownership—but this is far from

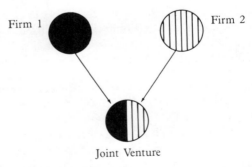

Firm 1

Firm 2

Joint Venture

Figure 2–1. Forward Integration into a Joint Venture

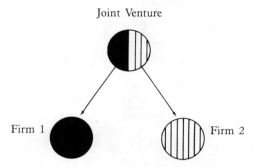

Figure 2-2. Backward Integration into a Joint Venture

actually being the case. JVs may, for a start, be asymmetrically positioned with respect to the partners' operations. Figure 2–4 illustrates a multistage arrangement in which one partner integrates forward into the JV and the other integrates backward; such an arrangement is quite common in JVs formed to transfer proprietary technology to a foreign environment.

Even if a JV is symmetrically positioned, it does not follow that it is symmetrically configured, for the intermediate products flowing to and from the respective partners may be different. It is only when both the positioning is symmetric and the products are identical that the configuration is fully symmetric in the sense we defined.

The fact that the configuration is symmetric does not guarantee that the motivation for internalization is symmetric too. If each partner, for example, resells the JV output within a different market structure, then the motivation for internalization may differ in spite of the fact that the configuration is symmetric.

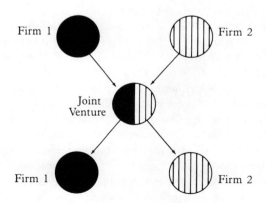

Figure 2-3. Buyback Arrangement

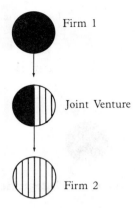

Firm 1

Joint Venture

Firm 2

Figure 2–4. Multistage Arrangement

The symmetry properties illustrated in figures 2–1 through 2–3 refer only to the immediate connections between the JV and the rest of the partners' operations. Each partner's operations may be differently configured from the others. This means that while the activities directly connected with the JV are symmetrically configured, the operations when considered as a whole may be asymmetric. Thus, the symmetry concept just used was essentially one of local symmetry, and not of global symmetry. While global symmetry implies local symmetry, the converse does not apply.

The distinction between local and global symmetry has an important bearing on the question of the distribution of economic power between the parties. It is important to appreciate that local symmetry does not guarantee that there is a balance of economic power between the parties to the JV. It is quite possible, for example, that one of the partners may own facilities that are potential substitutes for the jointly owned facility, while the other partner does not. This becomes important if the other partner could not easily gain access to an alternative facility should the first partner place some difficulty in its way. It may be, for example, that the first partner holds a monopoly of alternative facilities. This means that in bargaining over the use of the jointly owned facility, the first partner is likely to have the upper hand. It can use power either to secure priorities for itself through nonprice rationing or to insist on trading with the JV at more favorable prices. The fact that the JV is 50:50 owned implies only that residual income is divided equally between the partners; it does not guarantee that total income is divided equally. And, as we have argued, a locally symmetric configuration does not guarantee that total income will be divided equally. It is the symmetry of substitution possibilities that is crucial in this respect. Symmetry of substitution is likely to occur only with global symmetry, and this is a much less common type of configuration. One important consequence of this is considered in section 18 below.

*JV Operations Motivated by Lack of Confidence in
Long-Term Arm's-Length Contracts*

The next four sections illustrate how different motives for internalization manifest themselves in various contexts. Readers familiar with the most recent literature on internalization theory may prefer to proceed directly to section 16, where the main line of argument is resumed.

This section presents three simple examples in which both the configuration of the JV and the motivations for it are symmetric. The examples are designed to illustrate a progression from internalization involving no day-to-day operational integration between the JV and the partners' operations to internalization involving very close operational integration indeed.

Hedging against Intermediate Product Price Movements in the Absence of a Long-term Futures Market. Consider the construction industry, in which main contractors have to quote fixed prices for long-term projects, some of which require a large input of cement, which is liable to vary in price over the life of the project. For obvious reasons, the cement cannot be stored, and there is no organized futures market either. Cement has to be purchased locally for each project, and because the sites are geographically dispersed, there is no one supplier that can economically supply all the projects. Nevertheless, prices of cement at different sites tend to vary in line with each other, so that ownership of a cement-making facility at any one location will still help to hedge against price fluctuations in the many different sources of supply that are used. There are two major contractors of equal size who specialize in cement-intensive projects. Because of economies of scale in cement production, however, a cement plant of efficient scale generates much more cement than either contractor uses. There is one plant whose output price varies most closely with the average price of cement paid by the contractors, and so they each acquire a half of the equity in this plant. This is the most efficient mechanism available for diversifying their risks relating to the price of cement. It involves no operational integration whatsoever between the cement facility and the site activities.

Avoiding recurrent Negotiation under Bilateral Monopoly over the Price of a Differentiated Intermediate Product. Suppose there are two firms that are the only users of an intermediate product produced with economies of scale. It is difficult for either firm to switch away from the product, since it has no close substitutes. Upstream, therefore, there is natural monopoly, while downstream there is duopsony. Before any party incurs nonrecoverable setup costs through investment in specific capacity, it would be advantageous to negotiate once and for all long-term supply contracts for the product. Because of the difficulty of enforcing such contracts, however, the duopsonists may prefer to jointly acquire the upstream facility. This insures both of them against a strategic price rise initiated by an independent natural monopolist. The fact that both share in the residual risks also helps to discourage them from adversarial behavior toward each other. A modest degree of operational integration is likely in this case.

Operational Integration between Upstream and Downstream Activities in the Absence of Efficient Short-term Forward Markets. Extending the construction industry example, suppose that the two firms have long-term projects in hand at adjacent sites and require various types of form work to be supplied to mold the concrete foundations. The form work is customized and each piece has to be in place precisely on time. Both firms are skeptical about devising enforceable incentives for prompt supply by a subcontractor, as arms' length forward contracts are difficult to enforce in law. Because of the small scale of local demand relative to the capacity of an efficient-size team of workers, the two contractors may decide to secure quality of service through backward integration into a JV. Unlike the previous arrangements, this involves close day-to-day management of an intermediate product flow between the owners and the JV.

Quality Uncertainty

Quality uncertainty can manifest itself in many different contexts. Four examples are given next to demonstrate the ubiquity of this phenomenon.

Insuring against Defective Quality in Components. This example relates to forward integration involving two distinct flows of materials. Consider two components which are assembled to make a product. The quality of the components is difficult to assess by inspection, while other methods of assessment, such as testing to destruction, are expensive—not least in terms of wasted product. Reliable performance of the final product is crucial to the customer; failure of the final product is often difficult to diagnose and attribute to one particular component. Because of legal impediments, it is impossible to comprehensively integrate the assembly with the production of both components, and an independent assembler would lack confidence in subcontracted component supplies. If two independent component producers form a joint venture, however, then each can enjoy a measure of confidence in the other, since each knows that the other bears half the penalty incurred by the venture if it supplies a defective product to it. This is the JV analogue of the "buyer uncertainty" argument emphasized in the internalization literature.

Adapting a Product to an Overseas Market. This example involves the combination of two distinct but complementary types of know-how in the operation of an indivisible facility. The first type of know-how is technological and is typically embodied in the design of a sophisticated product developed in an industrialized country. The other is knowledge of an overseas market possessed by an indigenous foreign firm. The complementarity concerns their use in adapting the design and marketing strategy of the product to overseas conditions. The indivisible facility is the plant used to manufacture it overseas. Together, these elements make up the classic example of the use of a JV to commence overseas production of a maturing product.

Management Training and the Transfer of Technology. In some cases, a JV may be chosen as a vehicle for training (Kojima, 1978). Employees of a technologically advanced firm are seconded to a JV to train other employees who will remain with the venture when it is later spun off to the currently technologically backward partner. Training involves two inputs, rather than just the one that is usually assumed. It requires not only the knowledge and teaching ability of the tutor, but also the tutee's time, attention, and willingness to learn. The tutee may be uncertain of the quality of the tutor's knowledge and ability, and may demand that the tutor bears all the commercial risks associated with the early stages of the venture. The tutor, on the other hand, may be uncertain of the effort supplied by the tutee, which could jeopardize the performance of the venture if it were poor, and so the tutor may require the tutee to bear some of the risks as well. These conflicting requirements are partially reconciled by a JV that requires both to bear some of the risks and thereby gives each an incentive to maintain a high quality of input. Those incentives can be further strengthened, in some cases, by a buyback arrangement—or production-sharing arrangement as it is sometimes called—which encourages each party to use the output that the newly trained labor has produced and thereby gives an additional incentive to each party to get the training right.

Buyback Arrangements in Collaborative R&D. Buyback arrangements, which combine backward and forward integration, are particularly common in collaborative research. In the research context, both the inputs to and the outputs from the JV are services derived from heterogeneous intangible assets (that is, they are flows of knowledge).

Consider two firms, each with a particular area of corporate expertise, who license their patents and personnel to a joint research project (the indivisible facility). The planned output—new knowledge—is a proprietary public good, which is licensed back to the two firms. Each firm may be suspicious of the quality of the input supplied by the other firm, but the fact that the other firm not only holds an equity stake in the project but also plans to use the product of the research for its own purposes serves to reassure the first firm that the quality will be good (though there still remains a risk that personnel and ideas of the very best quality will be held back). Likewise, the fact that the firm itself has partially contributed to the production of the new knowledge is a reassuring factor when it comes to implementing this knowledge in downstream production.

Collusion

The role of indivisibility facilities in the previous discussion can, in fact, be taken over by any arrangement that either reduces the costs of two plants by coordinating their input procurement or enhances the value of their outputs by coordinating their marketing. The former is relevant to backward integration by firms into a JV, while the latter pertains to forward integration instead. The forward integration case, to be discussed shortly, shows the JV to be an alternative to a cartel.

Consider two firms that have identified an opportunity for colluding in their sales policy. They may have independently discovered a new technology, territory, or mineral deposit and wish to avoid competition between them in its exploitation. They may, on the other hand, be established duopolists operating behind an entry barrier, who would benefit from fixing prices or quotas to maximize their joint profits from the industry. (The nature of the entry barrier is irrelevant to the argument. It may be based on technological advantage, brand names, statutory privilege, or exclusive access to inputs, and so on.)

The main problem with a sales cartel is the mutual incentive to cheat by undercutting the agreed price—for example, by selling heavily discounted items through unofficial outlets. This poses an acute monitoring problem for each party. Channelling sales through a JV reduces the incentive to cheat, since the gains from cheating are partially outweighed by the reduction in profits earned from the JV. Economies in monitoring costs may also be achieved if both parties specialize this function with the JV.

Hostages: Internalizing the Implementation of Counterthreats

In an atmosphere of mutual distrust, an imbalance in the vulnerability of two parties to a breakdown of the venture can further undermine confidence in it. This suggests the possibility that instead of collaborating on a single venture, they should collaborate on two ventures instead. The function of the second venture is to counteract the imbalance in the first venture by giving the least vulnerable party in the first venture the greatest vulnerability in the second venture. Suppose, for example, that the two firms wished to collude in a product market where one firm has a much larger marker share, coupled with much higher fixed costs, than the other. This is the firm that is most vulnerable to cheating by the other. To redress the balance, it may be advantageous for the two firms to agree on some other venture—say, collaborative research—to run in parallel with a collusive JV to give the weaker firm an effective sanction against the stronger one. In such a case, the primary motive for the second JV concerns nothing intrinsic to the venture itself, but simply its ability to support the other venture.

It should be clear from the preceding examples that there are an enormous number of different forms that a JV operation can take. Each of the three main factors—the internalization motive, the indivisibility, and the obstacle to merger—can take several different forms. The internalization motive may differ between the firms. Add to this the considerable diversity of global configurations, and it can be seen that the permutations to which these aspects lend themselves make any simple typology of JV operations out of the question. While the economic principles governing the logic of JV operation are intrinsically quite straightforward, the way that environmental influences select the dominant factors in any one case is extremely complex.

Building Reputation and Commitment

It was established in the first part of the chapter that almost all coordinating activity calls for some degree of mutual forbearance and that, therefore, most ventures—even simple trade or team activities—involve an element of cooperation. It was also established that extensive reliance on mutual forbearance was not necessarily a good thing. The essence of cooperative efficiency, it was suggested, is that as a result of a venture, a small amount of mutual forbearance is transformed into a large amount of trust. Cooperatively efficient ventures will tend to accord all parties an opportunity to reciprocate forbearance within a sequence of decisions, observable to the others, calling for increasing levels of loyalty. Ventures of this kind are likely to be followed by a succession of other ventures involving the same parties—perhaps in the same grouping or perhaps in other groupings involving other parties with whom the original participants have established a reputation. (Propositions of this kind are certainly testable, even if the propositions regarding "quantities" of forbearance and trust, from which they derived, are not.)

Some ventures lend themselves naturally to an internal organizational structure that encourages participation. These ventures call for widespread decentralization of decision making, afford decisions of varying degrees of responsibility, and call for the sharing of information. They provide ample opportunity for overt behavior and only limited opportunity for covert behavior. These considerations suggest that certain motives for JV operation are far more conducive to cooperation than are others. It is, in fact, the combination of the motive and the main activity performed by the JV that seems to be crucial in this respect.

In the production sector, JVs that involve very little operational integration with the partners' other activities provide little opportunity for the partners to meet and interact on a regular basis. The greater the degree of operational integration, the greater is the regularity with which forbearance may have to be exercised when short-term holdups occur in production, and the greater are the opportunities for sharing information in the planning of production. Quality uncertainty provides a motive for both parties to open up their wholly owned operations to their JV partner once a certain degree of trust has been established, and so provides a natural route through which cooperation could progress to a point where it embraces production, product development, and basic research.

Joint R&D is naturally cooperative because it is based upon the sharing of information and, for reasons already noted, the sharing of information often leads to the emergence of shared values too. This may, perhaps, partly explain why collaborative R&D seems to enjoy a special mystique all of its own.

Of the various functional areas in which JV operations can occur, sales and procurement are the least promising so far as true cooperation is concerned. A dominant motive for JV operations in this area is collusion. Collusion affords large incentives to cheat and therefore requires a major input of cooperation. The maintenance of a high price in a static market environment—so characteristic of many collusive arrangements—does not, however, create much need for meetings at which open forbearance and reciprocity can be displayed. Collusion emphasizes the covert rather than overt dimensions of behavior. It therefore generates little output of trust. The most promising area for cooperation in marketing arises when a proprietary product is transferred to a new country, for then both the source firm and the recipient firm need to share information. Since the demand is uncertain, but has considerable growth potential, the market environment is dynamic rather than static, and so, unlike the case of collusion, it provides opportunities for deferring key decisions and delegating in a way that allows both parties to demonstrate forbearance.

The International Dimension

So far, nothing has been said specifically about the international aspects of JV operation. To a certain extent, this is deliberate, since there are no reasons to believe that the familiar factors of international cost differentials, tariffs, transport costs, and variations in the size of regional markets are any different for JVs than they are for other international operations. It can, however, be argued that the political risks of expropriation, the blocking of profit repatriation, and so on, are lower in the case of a JV than in the case of a wholly owned operation, though empirical support for this view is very limited, to say the least. Tax-minimizing transfer pricing, though not impossible with JVs, is more difficult to administer because of the need to negotiate the prices with the partner and to find a subterfuge for paying any compensation involved.

So far as the general concept of cooperation is concerned, the international dimension is much less important than the intercultural dimension. In purely conventional analysis of transaction costs, the focus is on the legal enforcement of contracts, and so the role of the nation state is clearly paramount, in respect to both its legislation and its judicial procedures. The mechanism of cooperation, however, is trust rather than legal sanction, and trust depends much more on the unifying influence of the social group than on the coercive power of the state. Trust will normally be much stronger between members of the same extended family, ethnic group, or religious group, even though it transcends national boundaries, than between members of different groups within the same country.

This means that in comparing the behavior of large firms legally domiciled in different countries, differences in behavior are just as likely to reflect cultural differences in the attitudes of senior management as the influence of the fiscal and regulatory environment of the home country. Cultural attitudes are certainly likely to dominate in respect of the disposition to cooperate with other firms. In this context, it may be less important to know whether a corporation is British or Italian, say, than to know whether its senior management is predominantly Quaker or Jewish, Protestant or Catholic, Anglo-Saxon or Latin, and so on. National and cultural characteristics are correlated, but not perfectly so. In some instances, such as Japanese firms, it has proved extremely problematic to disentangle them.

In the light of these remarks, it is clear that JV operations involving firms with different cultural backgrounds are of particular long-term significance. Once established, they provide a mechanism for cultural exchange, particularly as regards attitudes to cooperation. The success of this mechanism will depend upon how receptive each firm is to ideas emanating from an alien culture. Where the firm is receptive, participation in international JVs may have lasting effects on its behavior, not only in international operations, but in many other areas too.

Networks of Interlocking JVs

The recent proliferation of international JVs means that many firms are now involved in several JVs. Two JVs are said to interlock when the same firm is a partner in both. It is not always recognized as clearly as it should be that a set of interlocking JVs is an extremely effective way for a firm to develop monopoly power at minimal capital cost. By taking a part-interest in a number of parallel ventures, producing the same product with a different partner in each case, the firm can not only establish a strong market position against buyers of the product, but it can also create a strong bargaining position against each partner as well.

Once an individual partner is committed to a venture, it is vulnerable if the monopolist threatens to switch production to one of its other JVs instead. The partner has no similar option because the remaining facilities are all partly controlled by the monopolist. The vulnerable firm may be obliged to renegotiate terms under duress. Although the monopolist may stand to lose by withdrawing production from one JV, it will be able to recover most of these losses from enhanced profits arising from the JVs to which production is switched.

A situation of this kind is illustrated in figure 2–5. Firm 2 has the ability to switch production between the two downstream plants, but neither firm 1 nor firm 3 has this option because the only other plant is partly controlled by firm 2. Although each JV is symmetrically configured in a local sense, the overall situation is globally asymmetric. Superficially, it may seem that firm 2 is a "good cooperator" because it is involved in more JVs than either of the other firms, but in reality its claim to cooperate may simply be a subterfuge. Firm 2 can, in fact, not only exercise monopoly power against the buyers of downstream output, but also play off its partners against each other. In this case, it is conflict (not cooperation) and deception (not trust) that is the driving force in firm 2's choice of JV operation.

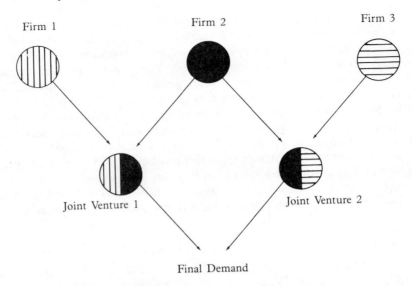

Figure 2-5. The Dominant Partner in Networks

Conclusion

Joint ventures are, first and foremost, a device for mitigating the worst consequences of mistrust. In the language of internalization theory, they represent a compromise contractual arrangement that minimizes transaction costs under certain environmental constraints. But some types of joint venture also provide a suitable context in which the parties can demonstrate mutual forbearance and thereby build up trust. This may open up possibilities for coordination that could not otherwise be entertained. The prospect of this encourages partners to take an unusually open-ended view of JV partnerships and gives JVs their political and cultural mystique.

An important role of JVs, from the limited perspective of internalization economics, is to minimize the impact of quality uncertainty on collaborative research and training. From the more open-ended perspective of long-term cooperation, however, JVs designed to cope with quality uncertainty are also well adapted to help partners to reciprocate and also to learn the values that inspire the other partner to unreserved commitment to a venture. Without doubt, JVs of this type offer a way forward to genuine cooperation in international economic relations in the future.

The analysis also suggests, however, that a degree of cynicism may be warranted in respect of the claims advanced for JVs of certain kinds. A JV may be merely a subterfuge, luring partners into making commitments that leave them exposed to the risk of renegotiation under duress. It may be a device for enhancing collusion—a practice that may be warranted if it is necessary to recover the costs of technological or product innovation, but not otherwise. It may represent a pragmatic response to regulatory distortion—as when a misguided national competition policy outlaws a merger between the partners that would afford considerable efficiency gains; the JV, in this case, is better than nothing at all, but is only second best to a policy of removing the distortion itself.

One of the most topical applications of the theory of the JV is to industrial cooperation and production-sharing arrangements involving Japanese firms. To what extent, for example, can quality uncertainty in the training process support the argument that the Japanese JV is an appropriate vehicle for tutoring partners in developing countries? Are Japanese JV networks in Southeast Asia merely agglomerations of independent JV operations, or are they part of a wider strategy to play off one partner against another in an effort to maintain low prices for Japanese imports and thereby assure the competitiveness of Japanese reexports?

Other questions may be asked, for example, of Western corporations that seem anxious to cooperate with the Japanese. Are they really interested in long-term collaboration in the development of leading-edge technologies, or is it their hope that token research collaboration with the Japanese can open the door to short-term cartellike restrictions on international trade? Do Western collaborators really hope to learn something of a cooperative ethic (and perhaps even a new system of values) from the Japanese, or are they merely interested in cooperation as a mask to disguise the replacement of competition by collusion?

There do not seem to be any easy answers to these questions. More empirical evidence is required. It is hoped that the analysis presented in this chapter affords a framework within which such evidence can be interpreted. So far, it is only possible to clarify the questions, but eventually it should be possible to answer them.

References

Axelrod, R. 1981. "The Evolution of Cooperation among Egoists." *American Political Science Review*, 75: 306–18.

Axelrod, R. 1984. *The Evolution of Cooperation*. New York: Basic Books.

Blois, K.J. 1972. "Vertical Quasi-Integration." *Journal of Industrial Economics*, 20: 253–72.

Buckley, P.J. and Casson, M.C. 1985. *Economic Theory of the Multinational Enterprise: Selected Papers*. London: Macmillan.

Casson, M.C. 1982. *The Entrepreneur: An Economic Theory*. Oxford, England: Blackwell.

Casson, M.C. 1987. *The Firm and the Market*. Cambridge, Mass: MIT Press.

Kojima, K. 1978. *Direct Foreign Investment*. London: Croom Helm.

Richardson, G.B. 1972. The Organisation of Industry. *Economic Journal*, 82: 883–96.

Williamson, O.E. 1985. *The Economic Institutions of Capitalism: Firms, Markets, Relational Contracting*. New York: Free Press.

3

Understanding Alliances: The Role of Task and Organizational Complexity

J. Peter Killing

omplexity is a key consideration in the design of corporate alliances. Managers of alliances created to undertake complex tasks using complex organizational processes require different skills and a much greater level of commitment than managers of simply organized alliances undertaking relatively simple tasks. It is important that both managers and researchers understand the nature and magnitude of these differences and the fundamental role that both task and organizational complexity play in the design of alliances.

This chapter provides definitions of task and organizational complexity and these definitions are used to plot a number of alliances on a complexity grid. Complex alliances are compared with simpler ones, and implications are drawn for managers trying to reduce the organizational complexity of alliances created to carry out tasks of moderate and high complexity. Among other things, this chapter argues that:

1. Alliances that undertake complex tasks do not always need to be organizationally complex. Task complexity does impact on organizational complexity, but so do a number of other factors.

2. Firms wishing to create an alliance to undertake a complex task should first enter a simpler alliance with their chosen partner, in order that a degree of mutual trust may be established, prior to the formation of the more complex alliance.

3. Relatively weak firms should be wary of entering alliances with strong firms, if those alliances are intended to take on complex tasks.

The ideas in this chapter are based on interviews with managers involved in fifteen alliances (approximately half of which were in the automobile industry) and an

This chapter was written with the assistance of Michael Wray and benefitted from the comments of Professors José de la Torré (UCLA), Jim Ellert (IMEDE), Nick Fry and Rod White (University of Western Ontario), and Paul Beamish (Wilfrid Laurier University). Funding was provided by both IMEDE and the University of Western Ontario.

extensive review of secondary data pertaining to alliances in the automobile industry. A list of the alliances discussed in the interview sessions is contained in table 3–1. However, the examples used in this chapter do not all derive from the study.

Three types of alliance were examined. These were traditional joint ventures, nonequity alliances, and minority equity alliances. Traditional joint ventures are created when two or more partners join forces to create a newly incorporated company in which each has an equity position and representation on the board of directors. Nonequity alliances are agreements between partners to cooperate in some way (to jointly carry out a research project, for instance), but they do not involve the creation of a new firm, nor does either partner purchase equity in the other. Minority equity alliances are similar to nonequity alliances in that joint activities are undertaken, but one parent does take an equity position in the other. The Austin Rover–Honda alliance, for example, is a nonequity alliance in which the two firms are working together to develop and produce, but not market, a number of different automobiles. The activities undertaken by the Ford–Mazda alliance are similar, but, because Ford owns 25 percent of Mazda, this is categorized as a minority equity alliance rather than a nonequity alliance.

Table 3–1
Alliance Sample

Company Visited	Alliances Discussed
A.P.M. Ltd.	A.P.M.–Smorgon (NE)
AT&T-Philips	APT (E)
Ford of Europe	Ford–Fiat (E–NC)
Ford, U.S.A.	Ford–Mazda (ME)
G.E.C.	Six research alliances, all parts of the Esprit program (NE)
General Motors	G.M.–Toyota (E)
Saab-Aircraft	Saab–Fairchild (E–T)
Saab-Automobile	Saab–Fiat (NE)
Porsche	Porsche–Audi (NE)
Volvo	Peugeot–Renault–Volvo (E) Joint Research Committee (NE)

Notes: APM Ltd. is an Australian company. All of the rest are European or American

(NE) = a nonequity alliance.

(E) = an equity alliance.

(E–NC) = a nonconsummated (never begun) equity alliance.

(ME) = a minority equity alliance.

(E–T) = a terminated equity alliance.

Other alliances are mentioned in the chapter that are not part of this sample.

Alliance Complexity

Although they used different words to do so, virtually all of the twenty or so managers interviewed in this study suggested that the key to successful alliance building is to create an alliance that is simple enough to be manageable. Complexity, they argued, leads to failure. When pressed as to what they meant by complexity, the managers highlighted two aspects: the complexity of the task the alliance was undertaking and the complexity of its organizational arrangements, as shown in figure 3–1.

Task Complexity

Three factors appear to importantly affect the complexity of the task that an alliance sets out to accomplish. These are the scope of activities the alliance undertakes, the environmental uncertainty surrounding these activities, and the adequacy of the skills within the alliance.

As indicated in figure 3–2, the scope of an alliance's activities will depend on its objectives, the number of business functions it encompasses, its duration, and the number of products it deals with and markets it serves. Some alliances, such as the 1979 Saab–Lancia alliance to jointly create a new car design, are very narrow in scope. This two-year alliance required engineers from the partners to work together to make basic calculations for the new model, to build prototypes, and to develop and test components. It involved no production and no marketing, and its objective was to reduce costs, rather than directly earn profits. In sharp contrast, Saab's 1980 alliance with Fairchild Industries was created to develop, produce,

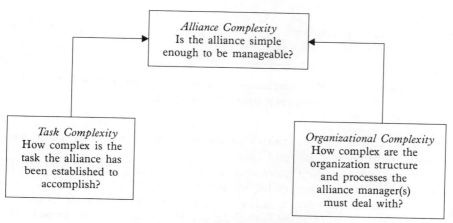

Figure 3-1. Alliance Complexity

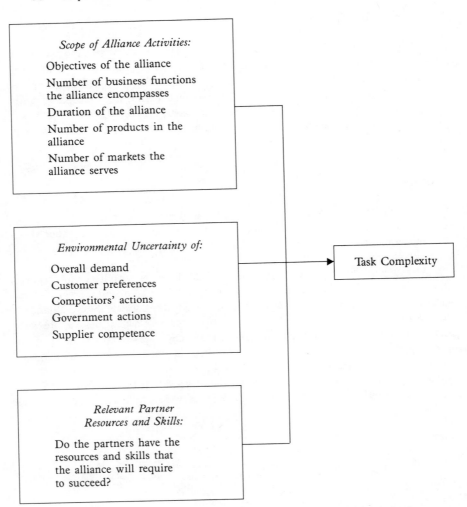

Figure 3–2. Task Complexity, Alliance Scope, Environmental Uncertainty, and Partner Skills

and market on a world scale a thirty-five–seat commuter aircraft. This venture was to earn profits and had no fixed duration.

The second important factor affecting task complexity is the degree of environmental uncertainty surrounding the activities of the alliance. The Saab–Lancia alliance involved a low degree of environmental uncertainty. Because its output was provided to its parents, the alliance did not have to contend with the potential unpredictability of customers or competitors. In fact, it was even possible to specify the tasks to be carried out by each partner and the alliance budget, before the alliance was formally created. The degree of environmental uncertainty in the Saab–Fairchild joint venture was much higher. The purpose of this alliance was to earn a profit in a very competitive market. The attitudes and actions of competitors, customers, and government agencies were important and often difficult to predict. Such uncertainty makes the management of an alliance much more difficult.

Finally, the resources, competence, and familiarity of the partners with the tasks at hand must be considered. What is a complex task for one pair of firms may be much simpler for another pair, because they already have a good knowledge, perhaps, of the products and markets involved. The greater the competences and resources of the partners in relevant areas, the less complex, to them, will be the task that they are undertaking. A summary of the major factors affecting task complexity is presented in table 3–2.

Organizational Complexity

Organizational complexity arises in alliances when personnel from the partner companies interact to make and implement decisions that affect both firms. As indicated in figure 3–3, the more frequent and less routine in nature are the interactions, the greater will be the organizational complexity.

Table 3–2
Factors Affecting Task Complexity

	Less Complex	*More Complex*
Alliance scope		
Alliance objective	Reduce costs for partner companies	Earn profits
Number of business functions included in alliance	Few	Many
Number of products included	Few	Many
Number of markets to be served	Few	Many
Intended duration of venture	Short	Open-ended
Environmental uncertainty	Low	High
Relevant partner resources and skills	High	Low

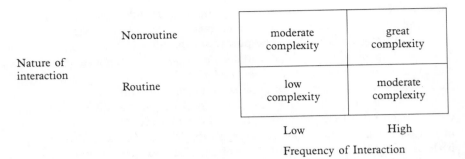

Figure 3–3. **Organizational Complexity**

Causes of Difficulty

The rationale underlying figure 3–3 is that interactions between personnel from the partner firms are likely to be a source of difficulty because (1) initially, at least, they will not know one another very well, (2) they may hold differing opinions, attitudes, and beliefs, and (3) they may have different objectives for the alliance.

Don't Know Each Other. It can be difficult for managers who do not know each other well to work together effectively. If a marketing manager from one partner provides a market estimate to a production manager from the second partner, for example, the production manager may have difficulty deciding how to interpret the estimate. How reliable a forecaster is the marketer? Is the marketer an optimist or a pessimist? Is he likely to come in with a new forecast in two weeks time? A general manager who has to assess both the estimates of a marketing manager and a production manager's view of the constraints he faces is in an even more difficult position. Until such managers come to know each other, interactions between them can be difficult.

Differing Opinions, Attitudes, and Beliefs. It is quite likely that personnel from the partner companies will have differing opinions, attitudes, and beliefs. These differences will stem naturally from the corporate cultures of the firms involved, and they may be accentuated further if the firms are of different nationalities. One group of European managers, for example, was frustrated by the short-term financial outlook of their U.S. partner plus the fact that the Americans placed no value on continuity, changing managers every two years or so, with the result that just as the Europeans were getting to know someone, they had to begin again. Language can also be a problem; more than one alliance partner has chosen an interface manager on the basis of language skills rather than on the basis of whether that person was the best for the job. Possibly even worse off are the firms that appoint interface managers who cannot speak the partner's language.

Differing Objectives. It is no revelation to suggest that the partners in an alliance often have differing objectives. The more joint decision making is called for in such an alliance, the more these differences in activities will be highlighted. Thus, a joint venture, for example, in which the general manager has to refer many decisions to a board, which will contain executives from both partners, will probably be very difficult to manage well. The situation will be even more difficult if the partners have equal influence in the decision-making process.

Factors Affecting Organizational Complexity

Four factors that affect the organizational complexity of an alliance are listed in figure 3–4 and described briefly. All of these factors are likely to impact on both the nature and the frequency of interaction between personnel from the partner companies.

Number of Partners. The more partners there are in an alliance, the greater is the potential for organizational complexity. This complexity will make itself felt at the board of directors level. The board will consist of members from each partner, all of whom will be expecting, to a greater or lesser extent, to be involved in the decision-making process. An alliance with more than three partners may be quite unmanageable unless each partner has a well-defined role and sphere of influence from the outset, which may include one or more partners agreeing to play a relatively passive role.

Role of Each Partner. The more partners see themselves as having an equal role in managing an alliance, the more organizationally complex the alliance will be. When decision making is shared, there is a need for more (and probably less routine) communication between the partners than would otherwise be the case. For the reasons listed earlier, decision making between partners is likely to be time-consuming and difficult.

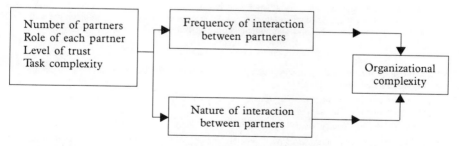

Figure 3–4. Factors Affecting Organizational Complexity

Previous research by Killing categorized joint ventures according to the role played by each partner.[1] Descriptions of dominant-parent, split-control, shared-management, and independent joint ventures are given in table 3–3, as are similar categorizations for nonequity and minority equity alliances.[2] The role played by the partners in an alliance will tend to reflect the quantity and similarity of skills and resources that each brings to the alliance. Generally, the more similar the skills and more equal the contribution, the more likely is a shared–decision-making alliance.[3] This relationship is illustrated in figure 3–5.

Table 3–3
Alliance Types and Decision-making Roles

Traditional Joint Ventures

Two or more partners join forces to create a new incorporated company in which each has an equity position and representation on the board of directors.

Independent ventures: Joint ventures in which the venture general manager is given a great deal of autonomy to manage as he sees fit.

Dominant parent ventures: Joint ventures in which one parent plays a dominant managerial role.

Split-control ventures: Joint ventures in which each parent plays a separate and distinct role, say, marketing on one hand and technology transfer on the other.

Shared-management ventures: Joint ventures in which both parents play an active managerial role so all significant decisions are shared.

Nonequity Alliances

Nonequity alliances are agreements between partners to cooperate in some way, but they do not involve the creation of a new firm, nor does either partner purchase equity in the other.

Trading alliance: An agreement between firms that are actual or potential competitors to buy and/or sell technical information, goods, or services. See text for examples.

Coordinated-activity alliance: An agreement between firms to coordinate activities and perhaps share information to the benefit of all partners. Research alliances in which the total task is divided between the partners, each of whom works separately on the problem, are often of this type.

Shared-activity alliance: An agreement between firms to work directly together to achieve a common objective. An example is the joint research laboratory employing fifty engineers which was established by Bull, ICL, and Siemens in 1984.

Multiple-activity alliance: A nonequity alliance that has many component parts. The Honda–Austin Rover alliance, for example, involves production under license of two cars, the joint design and development of two other cars, and component supply agreements.

Minority Equity Alliances

Minority equity alliances are similar to nonequity alliances except that one parent has taken a minority equity position in the other.

Passive minority equity alliance: One in which the equity acquisition has been made, but no joint programs have been undertaken.

Single-activity minority equity alliance: One in which one joint activity has been undertaken.

Multiple-activity minority equity alliance: One such as Ford–Mazda, in which a number of joint activities have been undertaken subsequent to Ford's purchase of 25 percent of Mazda.

		Dissimilar	Similar
Equality of partner contributions	Equal	split control	shared decision making
	Unequal	dominant partner or split control	one partner probably dominates

Dissimilar   Similar

Similarity of partner skills

Figure 3-5. Skills, Contributions, and Decision-making Roles

Level of Trust. If the partners in an alliance have previously worked together and established a degree of trust or at least a level of "mutual forbearance,"[4] organizational complexity is likely to be less than it otherwise would be.[5] In some alliances, there is a lot of dysfunctional interaction between the partners because they do not particularly trust one another. Neither is willing to let the other play a dominant role in any area, even though it may have little skill or knowledge of its own to add to the managerial process. The greater degree of trust between the partners, the less "unnecessary" interaction there will be between them.

Task Complexity. The simpler the task that an alliance has been created to carry out, the simpler can be its organizational arrangements. Perhaps the simplest of all alliances is the trading alliance in which firms that are otherwise competitors agree to buy or sell goods and/or services to one another. Peugeot's continuing sale of diesel engines to Ford of Europe is a good example. Typically, nonroutine decisions have to be made by both firms at the outset, addressing, on the one hand, "Do we want to sell to a competitor?" and, on the other, "Do we want a competitor's engine in our car?" However, once these nonroutine issues are settled and terms are set, the interface between the firms is typically handled by functional managers (of shipping, purchasing, and so on) doing their normal jobs.

Alliances undertaking tasks that require the combining of skills and resources provided by both parents need more complex organizational arrangements. If a joint venture is being formed, personnel are likely to be provided by each parent, and these people will have links both to the joint venture's general manager and to their original company. If a nonequity alliance is being formed, interfaces will be created between the partners using committees and boards at a number of hierarchical levels. Each of these integrative devices adds to the complexity of the alliance.

Combining Task and Organizational Complexity

The alliances surveyed in this chapter (plus a few others documented in case studies) were plotted according to their task and organizational complexity. A sampling of the results is shown in figure 3-6. As expected, the relationship between the two types of complexity was not linear—factors other than task complexity do impact on organizational complexity. The Peugeot–Renault–Volvo venture, for example, was off the diagonal largely because of the number of partners involved (three) and the Showa–Packard alliance was located as shown because it was dominated by one partner. There were not, however, any organizationally simple alliances formed to carry out very complex tasks, nor were there any very organizationally complex alliances created to carry out very simple tasks. Thus, there is an "alliance envelope" in which alliances are likely to take place.

The critical issue facing managers is how to create an alliance with no unnecessary organizational complexity, bearing in mind that it has to be capable of accomplishing the task for which it was created. The arguments presented in this chapter suggest that reducing the number of partners, increasing the degree of trust between them, and separating their roles in the alliance are all important. Figure 3-7 indicates how these variables (with the exception of the number of partners, which is treated as fixed for this illustration) interact. The exhibit should be read as saying that an alliance of task complexity x (which is a split-control alliance with a low degree of trust between the partners) will have organizational

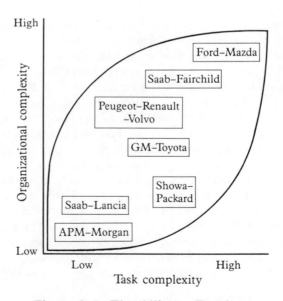

Figure 3-6. The Alliance Envelope

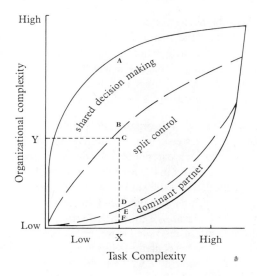

High

Organizational complexity

Y

Low

A

shared decision making

B

C

split control

D
E
F

dominant partner

Low   X   High

Task Complexity

Note: Within each alliance type, low-trust alliances are at the top, high-trust alliances at the bottom. Thus:

Point A is a low-trust, shared–decision-making alliance.
Point B is a high-trust, shared–decision-making alliance.
Point C is a low-trust, split-control alliance.
Point D is a high-trust, split-control alliance.
Point E is a low-trust, dominant-partner alliance.
Point F is a high-trust, dominant-partner alliance.

Figure 3–7. Alliance Types

complexity y. If the level of trust increases, the organizational complexity will decrease, but only so far.

The dominant-partner band in figure 3–7 is narrower than the split-control or shared–decision-making bands, reflecting the fact that the degree of trust between the partners in a dominant-partner alliance is likely to be less important than in the other two types. This is because there will be less interaction between the partners in a dominant-partner alliance. Of course, the passive partner has to have sufficient trust to allow the dominant partner to continue to dominate (if, indeed, the passive partner has any choice in the matter once the alliance is formed). But, on a week-to-week basis, the partners in such an alliance will typically have little contact. The managerial implications of figure 3–7 for managers in alliances of low, moderate, and high task complexity are outlined in the following sections.

Low Task Complexity. Alliances undertaking simple tasks do not usually face a high degree of uncertainty. Whether companies are trading components or jointly developing a new car design which will be separately exploited by the partners, the economics of the alliance are generally quite clear for each firm at the outset. Because the economics and the major activities of the alliance can be specified in advance, there is need for little other than a nominal degree of trust between the partners. In fact, as figure 3–7 suggests, whether there is a high or low degree of trust between the partners in such an alliance will make little difference— organizational complexity in either case will be low.

Moderate Task Complexity. The organizational complexity of alliances formed to carry out moderately complex tasks can vary from quite low to rather high, depending upon the role played by each partner and the degree of trust between partners. Dominant-partner alliances result in the least organizational complexity, but are not always appropriate, particularly if the skills of both partners are critical to the success of the alliance. If the split-control or shared–decision-making models are used, trust will be very important, because if the partners trust one another, joint decision making and consultation will be restricted to topics and situations in which they are truly important. In fact, if firms are contemplating an alliance to undertake a moderately or highly complex task, they could be well advised to try something simpler first, so a degree of trust can be established prior to the major undertaking.

High Task Complexity. Unless one partner is dominant, these alliances are organizationally complex. They typically comprise a major business undertaking, such as the Saab–Fairchild alliance described earlier, or there are a significant number of component parts to the alliance, as is the case in the Ford–Mazda and Austin Rover–Honda alliances. Because of the complexity of these alliances, their total payoff and the ultimate distribution of the payoff between the partners is much less clear at the outset of the alliance than is the case in simpler alliances. Thus, reassessments, renegotiations, and reorganizations are quite likely. There will be a need for a high degree of mutual forbearance. The danger to a weak company that has entered such an alliance with a strong company is that it may be putting itself at risk in this continuing series of renegotiations. Each new bargaining session may reveal new weaknesses or reemphasize existing ones to the point that the weaker company may find itself in an increasingly poor position in the alliance.[6]

As mentioned earlier, potential partners may be well advised not to jump directly into an alliance of high task complexity. Both the Ford–Mazda and Austin Rover–Honda alliances were built carefully, one piece at a time. Ford and Fiat, on the other hand, tried to create a full-blown complex alliance in 1985 and it did not work. Saab and Fairchild did create a complex alliance in 1980, but, in 1985, Fairchild pulled out, taking a write-off of hundreds of millions of dollars in the process. A complex alliance is a difficult place to begin a relationship.

Conclusions

The purpose of this chapter has been to create a framework for analyzing alliances. It suggests that if managers and researchers explicitly consider both the task and organizational complexity of alliances they are working with, they may gain new insights into their performance problems or opportunities. A high level of complexity in alliances is not a given; complexity is a factor that can and should be managed.

Notes

1. J.P. Killing, "How to Make a Global Joint Venture Work," *Harvard Business Review*, volume 60 (3), 120–27, 1982.

2. The notion of a "split-control" alliance, although not using this terminology, was presented in J.A. Cantwell and J.H. Dunning, "The New Forms of International Involvement of British Firms in the Third World," Proceedings of the European International Business Association, 1984.

3. For a discussion of the relationship between ownership and control, see J.P. Killing, *Strategies for Joint Venture Success* (New York: Praeger, 1983); and J.L. Schaan "Parent Control and Joint Venture Success: The Case of Mexico," unpublished doctoral dissertation, University of Western Ontario, 1983.

4. *Mutual forbearance* is a term taken from chapter 2 in this book by P.J. Buckley and M. Casson, "A Theory of Cooperation in International Business," which captures the notion that alliance partners would "deliberately pass up short-term advantages" which they could take at the expense of their partners, in the interests of keeping the alliance alive.

5. The role of trust in alliances is described in more detail by Paul Beamish, "Joint Venture Performance in Developing Countries," unpublished doctoral dissertation, University of Western Ontario, 1984.

6. A similar argument is documented in G. Hamel, Y. Doz, and C.K. Prahalad, "Strategic Partnership: Success or Surrender," prepared for the Rutgers-Wharton Conference on Cooperative Strategies in International Business, held in New Brunswick, N.J., in October 1986.

4
Some Taxonomies of International Cooperative Arrangements

Franklin R. Root

I nternational cooperative arrangements between firms of different nationalities are of many kinds serving many purposes. Discussions about interfirm cooperation in international business, therefore, are apt to founder on misunderstanding stemming from a failure to specify the exact form of cooperation in question. For the same reason, generalizations about cooperative arrangements are often so abstract as to lack empirical meaning or so contingent as to defy empirical testing.

As a modest effort to improve this situation, this chapter offers some taxonomies that classify international cooperative arrangements into types or categories that possess distinctive features of interest to international managers as well as to international business scholars.

Nationality and Cooperation Dimensions of International Cooperative Arrangements

I define an *international cooperative arrangement* as any form of long-term cooperation between two or more independent firms headquartered in two or more countries that undertakes or supports a business activity for mutual economic gain. *Long-term* does not refer to any specific period of time, but, rather, to a duration that exceeds the duration needed to complete arm's-length, open-market transactions. The firms in question may be private or state enterprises. This definition of international cooperative arrangements is expressed in table 4–1.

Moving from left to right, the matrix indicates three arrangements with respect to *interfirm* cooperation.

Open-market transactions begin and end with the exchange of an economic good between two firms. They are temporary, ad hoc connections between a buyer firm and a seller firm that involve minimal, if any, cooperation.

Interfirm cooperative arrangements designate any form of long-term cooperation between two or more firms. For instance, if a firm purchases inputs under a long-term supply contract with a second firm, sells its product to (or through) middlemen under a distributor agreement, or enters a manufacturing joint venture with another firm, then it is engaged in an interfirm cooperative arrangement.

Table 4–1
Two Dimensions of International Cooperative Arrangements:
Nationality and Cooperation

	Cooperation		
Nationality	*Open-market Transactions (Trade)*	*Interfirm Cooperative Arrangements*	*Intrafirm Cooperative Arrangements*
Uninational	No or minimal short-term cooperation	Domestic	Going it alone
Binational	No or minimal short-term cooperation	International cooperation	Going it alone
Multinational	No or minimal short-term cooperation	International cooperation	Going it alone

Intrafirm cooperative arrangements confine long-term cooperation to elements of the same business enterprise. That is to say, the firm "goes it alone" by dealing with other firms only through open-market transactions.[1]

Moving downward, the matrix indicates three levels of nationality. *Uninational* means that the firms in question belong to the same nationality or country. Therefore, any interfirm cooperative agreements are *domestic* in nature and excluded from my definition. *Binational* indicates two firms (or a parent company and its controlled affiliate) belonging to two different countries. *Multinational* indicates three or more firms (or a parent company and its controlled affiliates) belonging to three or more different countries.

The individual cells in table 4–1 are labelled to indicate the result of intersections between the nationality and cooperation dimensions. Only the binational interfirm and multinational interfirm categories contain international cooperative arrangements as defined in this chapter.

Contractual Agreements and Equity Joint Ventures along the Value-added Chain

Figure 4–1 structures international cooperative arrangements by their link in the value-added chain and by ownership. The vertical side of the figure lists the principal links in the value-added chain of a representative firm. International cooperative arrangements may cover a single link in the chain or two or more links. Because each of the two or more participants has its own value-added chain and because each may contribute complementary resources, a cooperative arrangement often covers two or more links. When, for example, a foreign firm enters an equity joint

Value-added Chain	Ownership	
	Contractual Agreements	*Equity Joint Ventures*
R&D	1	2
Raw materials/ component manufacture	3	4
Assembly	5	6
Marketing	7	8
Distribution/ customer service	9	10

Figure 4–1. International Cooperative Arrangements Classified by Link in the Value-added Chain and by Ownership

venture with a local firm, the former commonly contributes technology (R&D) while the latter contributes marketing, distribution, and customer service resources, and both partners may contribute resources for production.

Moving from left to right, the ownership dimension classifies international cooperative arrangements into *contractual agreements* and *equity joint ventures*. Under contractual agreements (such as licensing, franchising, technical assistance, and coproduction), the participants commit resources to a business activity, but they do *not* share the ownership or profits of a venture. In contrast, participants in equity joint ventures share the ownership of an enterprise, receiving compensation in the form of profits or dividends. The significance of this distinction is twofold: (1) owners have a legal right to manage the enterprise and (2) owners assume the market and nonmarket (environmental) risks of the enterprise.

A firm may enter into a cooperative agreement or joint venture to *obtain* resources that pertain to any link or set of links in its value-added chain. (The firm, of course, must pay for these resources with money or with its own resources.) We can use figure 4–1 to position an international cooperative arrangement by ownership and by the location on the value-added chain of the resources *obtained* through the arrangement by one of the participants.[2] To illustrate, we use cell numbers to designate the positions of some international cooperative arrangements. An international supply agreement occupies cell 3; it is a contractual agreement through which the firm obtains raw materials or components. Under a foreign distributorship agreement, the firm obtains marketing and distribution services (cells 7 and 9). In the same way, a representative licensing agreement occupies cells 3, 5, 7, and 9 of the licensor firm; a turnkey contract, cells 1, 3, and 5 of the customer firm; a contract-manufacturing agreement, cells 3 and 5 of the firm contracting production out; a coproduction agreement, cell 5 for a Western firm cooperating with, say, a Polish firm; and an equity joint venture, cells 8 and 10 for the foreign firm obtaining marketing and distribution skills from a local partner firm.

The form of international cooperative arrangement that offers the highest degree of interfirm cooperation is the equity joint venture which I shall refer to simply as "joint venture."

Mission and Geographic Scope of International Cooperative Agreements

Table 4–2 classifies international cooperative arrangements by mission and by geographic scope. A firm may participate in an international cooperative arrangement to obtain (1) technology that can lead to new products or to lower production costs for old products, (2) components or assembly of products at lower costs, and/or (3) entry into a country market or into regional/global markets.

One of these objectives will be the *dominant mission* of the arrangement as perceived by that firm. This dominant mission may not be the only mission, but any other missions become *subordinate missions.*[3] Other partner firms in the same arrangement may have different perceptions of the mix of dominant and subordinate missions. But the perceptions of *all* partners must be complementary and remain so if the arrangement is to avoid fundamental conflicts between them.

Table 4–2
International Cooperative Agreements Classified by Dominant Mission and Geographic Scope

	Geographic Scope		
Mission	*Home Country*	*Foreign Country*	*Regional/ Global*
Technology sourcing	X		X
Components/ assembly sourcing	XX		X
Market entry		XX	X

Agreement on the *mission mix* that harmonizes the interests of the individual partners should be regarded by managers as the key requirement for the success of international cooperative arrangements.

As perceived by a given partner, the dominant mission of an international cooperative arrangement is to provide technology, components/assembly, or market entry with reference to its own (domestic) country, a designated foreign country, a multicountry region, or the entire globe. The location of the given partner's *operations* that are supported by a cooperative arrangement providing technology or components/assembly, or the location of the *target-market* of an arrangement providing market entry defines the *geographic scope* of the venture. It follows that the geographic scope of a cooperative venture may not be the same for all participants.

The most frequent combinations of mission and geographic scope from the perspective of a U.S. partner-firm are indicated in table 4–2 with an *XX*. The most frequent *mission* is probably market entry and the most frequent *geographic scope* is a single foreign country that contains the target market. Distributor/agent contracts, licensing, franchising, technical agreements, service contracts, and joint ventures with local partners are specific forms of this combination.

Probably the next most frequent mission and geographic scope of international cooperative agreements for U.S. firms is sourcing components/assembly abroad for the home country (United States). Particularly in the past decade, U.S. firms facing growing foreign competition in their home markets have responded by sourcing components and assembly in foreign countries either through their own subsidiaries or through cooperative arrangements with foreign firms.

Somewhat less frequent combinations of mission and scope are indicated with an *X*. In recent years, U.S. firms in some industries, such as steel, have begun to source technology (particularly production technology) to improve their operations in the United States.

As more U.S. multinational firms have moved toward a global strategic focus, they have increasingly participated in arrangements with foreign firms (many of whom are also multinational) to obtain technology, inputs, or entry for production and marketing with a *regional* or *global* scope. Because these global arrangements involve prominent firms, they have attracted much attention from both academic scholars and the public at large. Variously dubbed strategic or corporate alliances, strategic or international coalitions, and global strategic partnerships, their widespread appearance is so recent that one can only speculate on their future role in international competition. The remaining cells have been left blank in table 4–2 to indicate their comparative rarity. U.S. firms seldom enter international cooperative arrangements to provide market entry to the United States, for it is unlikely—although not impossible—that a foreign firm would possess marketing access unavailable to a local firm. Other unlikely combinations are for a U.S. firm to use international cooperative arrangements whose dominant mission is to source technology or inputs in a foreign country to support production *only* in that country.

Fiduciary Risk and Environmental Risk Exposure of International Cooperative Arrangements

Table 4–3 distinguishes international cooperative arrangements by their exposures to *fiduciary* and *environmental risks*. The fiduciary risk of a given participant in an international cooperative arrangement is the probability that the other participant or participants will fail to carry out their responsibilities under the arrangement. In addition to performance failure, I interpret fiduciary risk also to include disclosure risk: the risk that the other participants will use the proprietary knowledge of the given participant for their individual gain outside the arrangement to the detriment of the given member.

Environmental risk exposure is the *size* of a given participant's assets (both financial and real) that would be directly affected by changes in the political, economic, competitive, and other aspects of the cooperative arrangement's environment. I interpret environmental risk as *downside* risk so that risk exposure becomes the maximum possible loss of assets from adverse changes in the environment.

Fiduciary risk is comparatively low for an open-market transaction because it is limited to that transaction. Fiduciary risk can be minimized for both seller and buyer by making payment for a good simultaneous with its receipt. This is commonly done in international trade by maintaining the exporter's control (ownership) of a good until the importer either makes payment (documents against payment) or commits in writing to make payment at a determinable time in the future (documents against acceptance). Also, it is possible to obtain insurance against the risk of nonpayment by the buyer. Of course, fiduciary risk can never be fully eliminated in market transactions because there is always the possibility of deception, fraud, and bankruptcy.

Table 4–3
Fiduciary Risk and Environmental Risk Exposure of International Cooperative Arrangements

Fiduciary Risk	Environmental Risk Exposure		
	Low	*Middle*	*High*
Low	Open-market transactions		Intrafirm cooperative arrangement
Middle		50:50 or majority joint ventures	
High	Cooperative agreements, minority joint ventures		

Environmental risk exposure is also comparatively low for open-market transactions because the assets of a participant are limited to a single transaction and, more importantly, the exposure is short-term only. Hence, it is much easier to make reliable assessments of environmental risk for spot market transactions than for long-term cooperative arrangements. Furthermore, the risk of nonpayment arising from adverse environmental changes (notably, exchange inconvertibility) is commonly insurable by government agencies, such as the Export-Import Bank in the United States.

The fiduciary risk of *intra*firm cooperative arrangements is comparatively low because the participants are all members of the same firm subject to the authority of their superiors and a reward system that encourages behavior that advances the interests of the firm.[4] But environmental risk exposure is comparatively high because all the assets associated with a venture are owned by the same firm.

In contrast, fiduciary risk is comparatively high for international cooperative agreements and minority joint ventures because a participant can exert only a limited influence over the behavior of the other participants. Any agreement is conditional upon the continuing belief of each participant that the benefits exceed the costs of the agreement. On the other hand, environmental risk exposure is comparatively low because each participant is contributing only a share of the venture's assets. For the same reasons, joint ventures have a comparatively high fiduciary risk and a comparatively low environmental risk for the minority partner. Insofar as the minority partner can increase control through bargaining power (a subject discussed later), then it can reduce the fiduciary risk.

Majority and 50:50 joint ventures are classified as having fiduciary and environmental risks at a middle range lying between comparatively high and low risks.

For international cooperative arrangements, then, there is a trade-off between fiduciary risk and environmental risk exposure. After a firm's managers have used their relative bargaining power to the full, they can acquire more control over a venture only by increasing ownership and their firm's exposure to environmental risk.

Relative Bargaining Power, Ownership, and Control

A key issue in international cooperative arrangements is management control. Who is to run the arrangement? The importance of control to a given partner depends mainly on the strategic role (mission) of the cooperative arrangement for that partner. In general, we can say that the greater the significance of an arrangement for the growth and profitability of a partner (that is, its strategic importance), the more that partner wants to control it. Other things being equal, therefore, a firm wants more control over a cooperative arrangement that is providing inputs for the firm's operations in several countries or providing end products for a global market than it wants over an arrangement providing inputs and products for a single country (unless that country is a very large one, notably the United States).

Basically, a firm gains more control over an international cooperative arrangement through *ownership* or through *bargaining power*. To get more control through ownership, a firm must either transform an international cooperative agreement (such as licensing) into an equity joint venture or—if the arrangement is already an equity joint venture—increase its equity share. By investing in the arrangement, a firm assumes the opportunity cost of the investment (the next best alternative use of the capital funds) and also a higher exposure to environmental risk.

A firm can gain greater control over a contractual agreement by enhancing its bargaining power with the other participants. To do so, a firm must make the arrangement more dependent on the availability of the firm's proprietary resources (such as technology or market entry) that would be costly or impossible for other partners to replace. Hence, a firm may need to contribute more "strategic" resources to the cooperative arrangement (such as the latest technology) and thereby assume a greater fiduciary risk.

The dependence of managerial control on the intersection of bargaining power and ownership is shown in table 4-4. (Table 4-4 excludes nonequity international contractual agreements in which control depends only on bargaining power.) *Weak control* indicates that the firm has no certain influence over the strategic direction of the joint venture. *Shared control* indicates that agreement between the firm and its partners is necessary for any decisions on the strategic direction of the joint venture. *Strong control* indicates that the firm can overrule other partners on the strategic direction of the joint venture. Let us look first at the bargaining power dimension. When a firm's relative bargaining power is weak, then it will have only weak control—even with a 50:50 joint venture—and only shared control with a majority joint venture. At the other extreme, when its relative bargaining power is superior, then it can have shared control even when it is a minority partner.

Table 4–4
Relative Bargaining Power, Ownership, and Control in International Joint Ventures

Relative Bargaining Power of Partner A	Ownership of Partner A		
	Minority joint venture (less than 50%)	*50:50 joint venture (50%)*	*Majority joint venture (more than 50%)*
Inferior	Very weak control	Weak control	Shared control
Equal	Weak control	Shared control	Strong control
Superior	Shared control	Strong control	Very strong control

When a firm's relative bargaining power is equal to that of its partner, then it will need a majority joint venture to have strong control.

With respect to the ownership dimension, a majority joint venture gives a firm strong control unless its bargaining power is inferior when it is compelled to share control. At the other extreme, a minority joint venture gives a firm only weak control unless the firm's superior bargaining power forces its partner(s) to share control.

A Dynamic Taxonomy: Shifting Net Benefits

The preceding taxonomies do not *directly* consider changes over time in international cooperative arrangements although they imply that changes in value-added activities, mission, geographic scope, fiduciary and environmental risks, bargaining power, and ownership will affect arrangements. I offer, therefore, a final taxonomy on the continuing viability of international cooperative arrangements.

A firm enters an international cooperative arrangement when it concludes that (1) its incremental benefits of participation exceed its incremental costs and (2) these incremental net benefits exceed those of open-market transactions or of intrafirm cooperative arrangements that would accomplish the same mission. But these initial net benefits may not remain positive for some or all of the partner firms. Net benefits may become negative for a firm because of changes in its economic, political, technological, or competitive environments or because of changes in its own strategy and capabilities.

An example of an arrangement in which the net benefits of one participant became negative is the joint production agreement between General Electric and Rolls Royce, Ltd. Under the 1984 agreement, the two firms were to manufacture two families of engines, a medium-size Rolls Royce engine and a large-size General Electric engine. The agreement collapsed when Rolls Royce beat out General Electric for a $850 million contract with British Airways for *high-powered* engines. This strategy shift by Rolls Royce into large-size engines made that company a direct competitor of General Electric, which now considered the agreement detrimental rather than beneficial to its interests.

The consequences of shifts in the net benefits of partner firms for the viability of an international cooperative arrangement are shown in figure 4–2. For simplicity, we assume that there are two partners to the arrangement, *A* and *B*. When the net benefits of both partners remain positive, then the arrangement continues. In contrast, the arrangement is dissolved when the net benefits of *either* partner or of *both* partners become negative. When the net benefits fall to zero for either or both partners, the viability of the arrangement is indeterminate within this taxonomy: a partner is indifferent to participation or withdrawal because its benefits are exactly matched by its costs.[5]

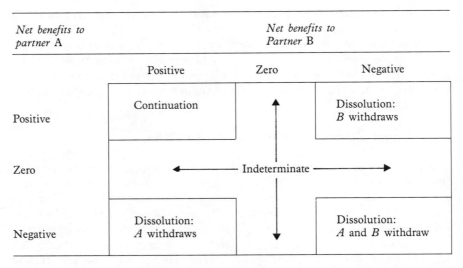

Figure 4–2. Continuation and Dissolution of International Cooperative Arrangements: Shifting Net Benefits

Classifying International Cooperative Arrangements According to the Taxonomies

In closing, table 4–5 shows the use of the foregoing taxonomies by classifying three actual international cooperative arrangements which, it so happens, are all equity joint ventures involving U.S. firms.[6]

The NII–NKK joint venture was started in 1984 when the U.S. firm, National Intergroup, Inc., sold 50 percent of National Steel to the Japanese firm, Nippon Kokon, the number 2 producer in Japan. NII obtains from NKK technology in both new products (corrosion-resistant galvanized sheet steel) and in production (improvements that will raise productivity, enhance quality, and cut costs). This technology will enable National Steel to compete more effectively in the U.S. market. The partners share control through equal representation on National's board although U.S. managers run the company on a day-by-day basis.

AT&T of the United States and Philips of The Netherlands started a 50:50 joint venture, called AT&T & Philips Telecommunications, V.V., in 1983 to market digital telephone switching equipment to countries throughout the world. AT&T, the manufacturer of the equipment, obtains through the joint venture access to Philips's worldwide distribution network. Although AT&T has three votes and Philips only two votes on the board, managers of the joint venture are drawn from both parent companies and control is shared by them.

American Motors Corporation and a Chinese state enterprise established in 1983 the Beijing Jeep Corporation, Ltd. to manufacture four-wheel drive vehicles

Table 4–5
Some International Cooperative Arrangements Involving U.S. Firms Classified by the Taxonomies

Taxonomies	International Cooperative Arrangements		
	NII/NKK	AT&T & Philips	A.M.C./China
Nationality[a]	BN	BN	BN
Location on value-added chain[b]	R&D	MK+D/S	MK+D/S
Ownership[c]	50:50	50:50	o > 50
Dominant mission[d]	T	ME	ME
Geographic scope[e]	HC	R/G	FC
Fiduciary risk[f]	M	M	H
Environmental risk exposure[f]	M	M	L
Relative bargaining power[g]	E	E	E
Control[h]	SH	SH	W

Note: The arrangements are classified from the perspective of the U.S. partner firm.
[a]BN = binational; MN = multinational.
[b]R&D = resources obtained by the U.S. partner; CM = component manufacture; A = assembly; MK = marketing; D/S = distributor/customer service.
[c]Ownership percentage share of U.S. partner: contractual agreement—0; minority joint venture—0 > 50; 50:50 joint venture—50:50; or majority joint venture—50 > 100.
[d]T = technology sourcing; CA = components/assembly/sourcing; ME = market entry.
[e]HC = home country; F = foreign country; R/G = regional/global.
[f]L = low; M = middle; H = high.
[g]I = inferior; E = equal; S = superior.
[h]W = weak; SH = shared; ST = strong.

in China. A.M.C. owned 31 percent of the joint venture. As of mid-1986, the venture has assembled eight hundred Cherokees from kits imported from A.M.C.'s operations in the United States. All of these vehicles have been sold in China. A.M.C. has faced delays in dollar payments and only the threat of a pullout has remedied this situation for the present. It would appear that A.M.C.'s perception of the dominant mission and geographic scope of the joint venture—market entry into China—conflicts with that held by the Chinese government: the manufacture of jeeps for sale in export markets. A.M.C. has only weak control over the joint venture.

Notes

1. The concept of "firm" used here is an economic organization under a single top management and direction. Hence, a parent company with controlled affiliates constitutes a single firm. When those affiliates are located in the same country as the parent, the firm is

designated "domestic." When affiliates are located in second or third countries, then the firm is designated "binational" or "multinational." There is no ownership percentage that unambiguously distinguishes controlled from noncontrolled affiliates. In this chapter, I assume that ownership of more than 50 percent creates a controlled affiliate and that relations between the parent and a controlled affiliate are *intrafirm* relations.

2. We can, of course, position a cooperative arrangement along the value-added chain by resources *provided* by a firm. Both perspectives are important. To decide on participation in an arrangement, managers must assess both which resources they will obtain from the arrangement and which resources they will provide to it.

3. International cooperative arrangements that provide only inputs of technology, components, or assembly used in a firm's product(s) represent an alternative to *backward* integration of the firm. International cooperative arrangements that provide only market entry represent an alternative to the *forward* integration of the firm through controlled foreign marketing affiliates. These two forms of cooperative arrangement may be called "quasi-vertical integration." International cooperative arrangements that provide both the production and marketing of a firm's product(s) in a foreign location represent an alternative to geographic diversification or *horizontal* integration through controlled foreign production/marketing affiliates. This arrangement may be called "quasi-horizontal integration."

4. Fiduciary risk is not fully absent even in a single firm, and it is probably higher for international firms with subsidiaries in several foreign countries than it is for domestic firms.

5. This indeterminacy is resolved by assumptions with respect to a partner's alternative opportunities to accomplish the same mission: other cooperative arrangements, open-market transactions, or intrafirm transfers. When one of these alternative opportunities offers positive benefits, then the partner will withdraw from the existing cooperative arrangement. Conversely, it will remain in the arrangement when alternative opportunities offer only negative benefits. Indeterminacy persists only when all opportunities to accomplish the firm's mission offer zero benefits.

6. I do not classify these arrangements by net benefits because all remain viable. However, the net-benefits taxonomy may be used *prospectively* by posing the question for each participant firm: in which direction are its net benefits moving? Answers to this question indicate whether the viability of the arrangement is becoming stronger or weaker.

5

A Technology-Transfer Methodology for Developing Joint Production Strategies in Varying Technological Systems

Kofi Afriyie

P olitical and economic considerations have led many less-developed countries (LDCs) to frown upon and sometimes reject outright the wholly owned subsidiary as a vehicle of foreign direct investment. Consequently, many host nations, including some industrialized countries (ICs), require some form of joint participation by host and foreign partners in the equity and managerial control of enterprises in various sectors of national economies.

A major outcome of this changing mode of foreign investment is that multinational investors are not only learning to form production coalitions in host countries, they also now face the reality of sharing technology with host partners through a variety of licensing agreements (Contractor, 1985). Hence, a key element in the foreign investment decision centers on developing a set of criteria that decision makers can use to choose among competing modes of technology transfer.

Reflecting the importance of technology-related issues in foreign direct investment, a substantial number of studies on international technology transfers have appeared in the literature.[1] However, despite the rich collection of studies on technology transfers, key issues examined in this chapter remain unresolved regarding the nature of technology itself, on the one hand, and the transfer process, on the other.

First, there appears to be no consensus on what constitutes a technology or a technological system in an industry or related industrial group. As a result, many empirical works on technology transfers are not comparable. Hence, generalizations that may enhance our understanding of technology-transfer processes are difficult to make.

Second, despite the lack of comparable data and information, policy prescriptions for suppliers and recipients of technologies tend to point to lessons of technology acquisitions and transfers in industries among selected countries.[2] Such prescriptions

I am grateful to the following for their helpful comments: Paul Beamish, Farok Contractor, Peter Lorange, Charles Oman, and Jean-Louis Schaan.

implicitly assume that generalizations about the transfer process are possible. However, it is impossible to draw general conclusions on technology transfer activities given the lack of convergence in data and methodology. Hence, our understanding of how the transfer process affects choice of strategies and innovation in varying technological environments may be severely limited.

This chapter addresses these issues and begins by asking: can we be more precise in our definition of *technology* and what constitutes a technological system? If we can, it may be possible to identify more precisely the requirements and mechanisms for developing effective technology-transfer strategies. The ultimate goal of this chapter, therefore, is to present a framework that outlines decision paths for selecting technology-transfer strategies and the modes of such transfers.

The approach used in this chapter is to identify some of the common strands of knowledge accumulated from past studies on technology transfer and present a typology of the transfer process within a technological system. It is an attempt to raise the level of technological analysis beyond the anecdotal by proposing a framework that sets the conceptual boundaries of technological systems. The framework should allow replication and comparability of studies and thereby enhance our ability to make generalizations about the transfer process. The basic assumption in this chapter is that the principal agents of transfers of technology are commercial and economic enterprises that are engaged in the transformation of resources to produce and sell goods and services in more than one national market.

Studies on International Technology Transfers

The pioneering work of Eckaus (1955) revealed the potential problems that exist in transferring production techniques among countries with different factor proportions. Later studies focused on the efficiency effects of capital-labor substitutions in LDCs using aggregate production functions (Arrow, Chenery, Minhas, and Solow, 1961). The shortcomings of the aggregate production function approach led to a shift toward a micro view of examining factor intensities, technology acquisition, and transfers in manufacturing enterprises in LDCs (Mason, 1971, 1973; Morawetz, 1974; Forsyth and Solomon, 1977; Rhee and Westphal, 1977). Several studies concluded that a wide range of technological choices permit increases in productivities (Mason, 1973; Pack, 1976; Morley and Smith, 1977). These studies have used various measures of capital and labor intensities in determining levels of technology acquisition and transfers by foreign firms in different host countries. However, since there appear to be no universal or optimal levels of factor intensity in generating productivity, the usefulness of these capital-labor measures as guides to corporate or public policy is rather limited.

With the findings that the transfer of technology can lead to substantial costs to the donor (Teece, 1977; Contractor, 1981; Mansfield, 1981) and to the recipient (Dahlman and Westphal, 1982), research focus has shifted to a search for optimal entry strategies of foreign-based firms in host markets. Contractor (1985) has proposed that the licensing option to market entry may not only be profitable, but, in many cases, a superior strategic mode of entry relative to other forms of foreign investment.

The current predominant view relating market-entry strategy to levels of technology transfer is that those firms that invest in products and processes utilizing standard and stable or mature technologies are those most likely to enter into joint ventures in host markets (Grosse, 1980; Contractor, 1981; Mason, 1978), whereas those with a leading edge in technology tend to avoid joint ownership participation in host markets. However, recent empirical work suggests that an increasing number of competitors comprising U.S., Japanese, and European technologically intensive firms are engaged in cooperative ventures involving technology acquisition, sharing, and transfers.[3]

The variety of approaches, information, and shifts in focus in the study of technology-transfer processes point to a need to define the conceptual boundaries of technological systems (as distinct from technological capabilities). In this regard, I present a methodology that would, first, enhance comparability of studies and, ultimately, provide guidelines for policy analysis. I begin this task by examining the nature of the technological problem.

Definitional Problems and Confusions

In order to understand the nature of the transfer process, we need to first understand what constitutes technology. Technology has been defined in a variety of ways. Some writers define it as a society's stock of knowledge that is applied in productive activities. Hence, technological change will necessitate a change in that stock of knowledge (Yotopoulos and Nugent, 1976, p. 145). To others, technology is yet another factor of production that belongs to the domain of such traditional factors as labor and capital (Lindert and Kindleberger, 1982, pp. 65–68). Technology is sometimes seen as a relationship between science and technique with human interaction forming the link between the two (Ellul, 1964). A definition of technology, in the anthropological sense, is "a cultural system concerned with the relationship between humans and their natural environment" (Terpstra and David, 1985, p. 148).

This definitional problem is further compounded by the traditional tendency to characterize technological activities in dichotomous terms such as *appropriate* versus *inappropriate, labor-intensive* versus *capital-intensive, process* versus *product, bundled* versus *unbundled, embodied* versus *disembodied,* and *small-scale* versus *large-scale.*

A close examination of these definitions and characterizations of technology reveals differences that go beyond mere semantics (Frame, 1983, pp. 5–7). A basic contention of this chapter is that the lack of general agreement in defining technology ultimately affects policy choices in ways that may not lead to desirable outcomes.

Rather than discard the preceding definitions, it is possible to identify the elements that are inherently common to the foregoing definitions of technology with the object of providing an eclectic point of departure for developing a methodology to guide technology-transfer policies.

The methodological framework proposed in this chapter is developed in two stages. The first stage presents a spectrum of technological capabilities. The second stage presents a typology of technological environments based on the degree of interaction among elements of the technological capabilities identified in the first stage. This two-stage approach is designed to provide decisionmakers a framework for choosing joint venture partners and technological elements that are prime targets for transfers in cooperative agreements.

Technological Systems: A Spectrum of Capabilities

A fundamental proposition of this chapter is that, for foreign-based firms, the basis for identifying technology-transfer needs begins with an examination of the technological system of a host industry. This proposition is based on the rationale that the ultimate constraining factor for an investing firm is the host country's technological environment. Thus, even if the initial legal hurdles of entry through a joint venture are overcome by a foreign-based firm, the technological capabilities available in the core or allied industries will ultimately affect the profitability of operations and the survival of the firm.

Relying on current technological concepts, I argue that, for a firm to evaluate a technological system, it must begin by examining the spectrum of capabilities in an industry or allied industrial groups.

Despite the lack of unanimity in defining technology, the literature is replete with what constitutes elements of technology.[4] Using the range of activities and definitions of technology, we can develop a spectrum of technological capabilities (figure 5–1). Three generic components or subsystems emerge from the literature on technology: (1) the basic knowledge subsystem, (2) the technical support system ("software"), and (3) the capital-embodied technology ("hardware"), denoted K, S, and H, respectively, in the figure. Each of these subsystems would comprise sets of elements involving activities and specific as well as general functional capabilities. These elements are depicted as K_i, S_i, and H_i ($i = 1, 2 \ldots n$) as in figure 5–1.

Examining figure 5–1 in relation to current studies on technology transfers and policy analysis, there appears to be a focus of attention biased toward research and development (R&D) activities of firms (K_3) and hardware, particularly finished products (H_1) and machinery and equipment (H_3). The roles of other elements of the knowledge infrastructure—such as the stock of theoretical and conceptual knowledge (K_1), techniques (S_1), and design capabilities (S_2)—appear to receive little or no attention in the literature on technology transfer. It is evident from figure 5–1

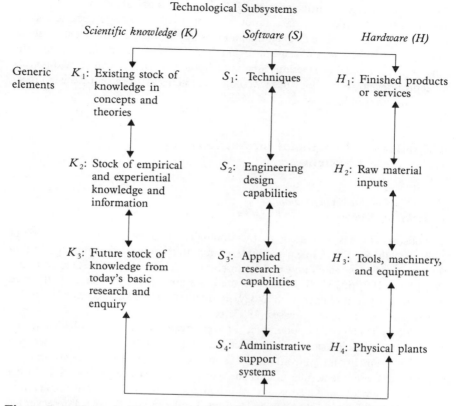

Figure 5-1. Generic Elements and Components of a Technological System

that traditional characterization of technologies as dichotomous dimensions fails to recognize the complexities of technological systems.

Pavitt (1985) has argued that technological knowledge is highly differentiated and specific to firms and the products they produce. In this chapter, whereas I acknowledge the existence of differentiated knowledge in each industry, I also suggest that in every technological environment, there are general capabilities that are transferrable among industries and firms and that these transferrable capabilities are key to the technology-transfer process.

Rather than posit a static technological system, I suggest that the spectrum of capabilities that exist in an industry is constantly being affected by existing contextual variables in the socioeconomic, political, and cultural environment. Thus, the level of activity that exists in, say, K_3 (the accumulation of knowledge through basic research and development) will depend on educational facilities, available scientific skills, and the priorities attached to R&D by firms and central authorities through the latter's incentive schemes. Thus, a technological system, comprising the three basic subsystems or components and their respective generic sets of elements, provides a range of potential and shifting interactions among subsystems and elements. In the second stage of the methodological framework, I examine the concept of functional interactions among technological subsystems. Based on this concept, I develop a typology of technological systems as a basis for decision making in the transfer process.

A Typology of Functional Interactions in a Technological System

The Nature of Interactions among Technological Subsystems

The observation has been made that technological progress and innovation do not automatically occur as a linear sequential function from basic research, continuing through applied research and ending in commercial development (Dahlman and Westphal, 1982, p. 131). Likewise, Frame has argued that the often hypothesized causal link between science, technology, productivity, and economic growth, in that order, does not hold in all cases (1983, p. 8).

Rather, as Heertje has observed, modern inventions and technological developments are conscious and persistent efforts undertaken by firms to enhance product improvement and innovation (1973, pp. 69–71). Such efforts suggest that the existence of close interactions among some or all of the basic components and their respective elements in a technological system may be an indication of the viability and level of maturity of that system. Indeed, Dahlman and Westphal observe that frequent interchange of technological information occurs among suppliers and producers, and that R&D activity is found in the capital goods ("hardware") sectors as well as in the supporting intermediate inputs ("software") sectors (1982, p. 132).

If the preceding observations are correct, we can conclude that a technological system is highly interactive if its subsystems or components comprise activities that share *common functional capabilities* and *goals*. It then follows, from Heertje (1973) and Dahlman and Westphal (1982), that the greater the interaction among components of a technological system, the greater the viability of that system in terms of its ability to promote the development of productive sectors of an economy. Next, I present a series of hypothesized levels of functional interactions within technological systems and suggest potential technology-transfer requirements.

From previous analysis, we can identify a continuum of levels of interactions among technological subsystems on the basis of functional capabilities in each subsystem. At one extreme, we can envisage a technological system with no functional interaction among the subsystems, K, S, and H. In this case, activities in the knowledge, software, and hardware subsystems do not share any common functional capabilities.

An example of such a technological system might be one in which the development of basic research in, say, organic chemistry has no commercial or other transactional links to the production of fertilizers. The production of the final product, fertilizers, may be possible only when skills, inputs, and technical know-how are imported from other technological systems. Under some circumstances, *reverse engineering* may allow a manufacturer to produce a finished product (hardware, H_1) without necessarily understanding the fundamental principles and physical laws underlying the proper working of the product.[5]

At the other end of the spectrum, we can envisage an extremely high level of functional interaction among the knowledge, software, and hardware subsystems. In this case, the hardware component comprises activities that are completely and functionally dependent on the software base, and collectively S and H depend on the available stock of knowledge within the system.

An example will be the existence of basic research in the computer and mathematical sciences which also leads to commercial application with strong transactional links to the production of programming languages and other computer software capabilities. The latter in turn leads to the development of compatible computer hardware.

In practice, however, we are likely to observe varying degrees of interactions among the subsystems within the extremes just described. A typology of a possible range of interactions among subsystems is presented in figure 5–2. Type I levels of interaction in a technological system are those that involve at least two technological components whose activities share common functional capabilities with strong transactional links, whereas type II levels involve the development of activities concentrated solely in specific subsystems with little or no transactional or commercial links to each other. Such a subsystem development bias is illustrated in R_5, R_6, and R_7, in figure 5–2.

The typology presented in figure 5–2 can be used as a basis for classifying industries, sectors of the economy, or countries according to the degree of functional interactions among technological subsystems as just described. Such a scheme can then be used to detect possible technological strengths and weaknesses and, hence, potential technology- transfer needs. Identification of such needs might in turn form the basis for a firm to formulate technology-transfer policy that is consistent with the firm's overall strategy.

Scope of Technology Agreements: Partners, Modes, and Costs of Transfers

A specific application of the typology presented in figure 5–2 centers on the development of criteria for choosing venture partners and determining the scope of technology-transfer agreements within type I and type II technological environments (figure 5–2). For a wholly owned foreign firm, the transfer of technology to a host firm or agency is possible on an arm's-length basis. In the absence of an explicit agreement, however, it is unlikely that a wholly owned foreign firm will transfer

Hypothesized Functional Interaction (R_j)	*Set Notation and Venn Diagram*	*Potential Demand for Technology Transfers*

Type I Technological System: The Case of Subsystem Interaction

Interaction of elements of all subsystems.	$R_1 = K \cap S \cap H$	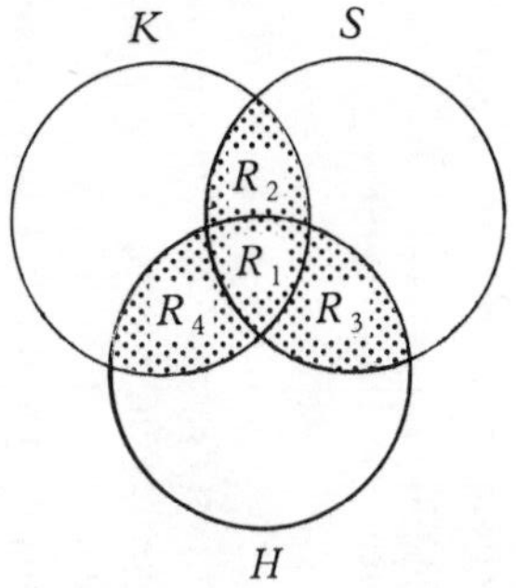 • Low potential demand for transfers of elements in the system.
Interaction of elements of software and knowledge subsystems. No interaction with hardware.	$R_2 = K \cap S \cap H'$	• Potential hardware transfers.
Interaction of elements of software and hardware subsystems. No interaction with the knowledge base.	$R_3 = S \cap H \cap K'$	• Potential knowledge transfers.
Interaction of knowledge and hardware subsystems. No interaction with the software base.	$R_4 = K \cap H \cap S'$	• Potential software transfers.

Type II Technological System: The Case of Subsystem Noninteraction

Knowledge accumulation bias: stock of knowledge with no interaction with other subsystems.	$R_5 = K \cap S' \cap H'$ $= K \cap (S \cap H)'$	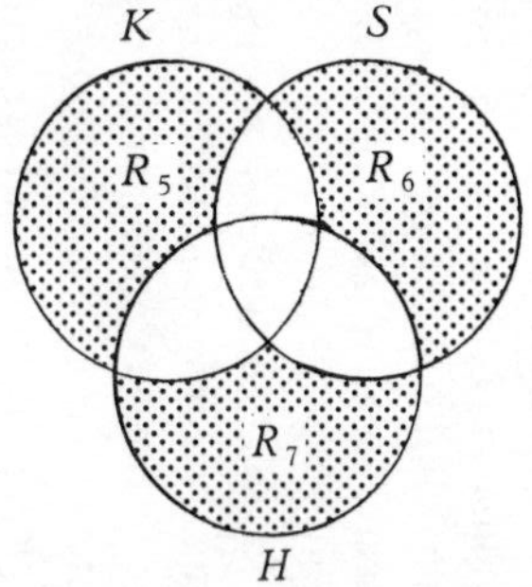 • Potential software and hardware transfers that can functionally utilize existing knowledge base.
Software development bias: software elements with no interaction with other subsystems.	$R_6 = S \cap K' \cap K'$ $= S \cap (K \cap H)'$	• Potential hardware and knowledge transfers that can functionally utilize existing software system.
Hardware development bias: hardware elements with no interaction with other subsystems.	$R_7 = H \cap K' \cap S'$ $= H \cap (K \cap S)'$	• Potential transfers of knowledge and software that can functionally utilize existing hardware system.

Figure 5-2. A Typology of Levels of Functional Interactions in a Technological System and Potential Transfer Needs

technology to any entity in the host country beyond the sale of hardware (H_1 through H_4 in figure 5–2).

Increasingly, however, as a result of host-country regulations, a foreign firm has to choose its host partner(s) as part of a limited range of available entry strategies. Under such circumstances, the foreign firm has the option of explicitly negotiating a technology-transfer agreement with the host counterpart or simply avoiding any technology-related agreements. The critical assertion here is that, even in the absence of explicit licensing agreements, de facto technology transfers can still occur through imitations and other means to alter the competitive positions of the partners.[6]

Thus, the choice of cooperative venture partners can hardly be separated from a firm's policy on technology transfer. Critical questions that foreign investing partners must address include the following: How can knowledge of the host technological environment assist the foreign firm in choosing its host partners? Would the choice of joint venture partners help the firm in formulating its future technology policy and determining the scope of transfer agreements? I address these questions by using the preceding typology (figure 5–2) to determine the link between the choice of venture partners and technology-transfer policy.

We can draw some *prima facie* policy conclusions from the typology. First, it would seem that the higher the degree of interaction among technological subsystems (type I environment), the less likely the need for a *unidirectional* technology transfer, namely, a transfer originating from a foreign firm to a host recipient partner. Conversely, the smaller the degree of subsystem interaction (type II environment), the greater the likelihood of unidirectional technology transfer from the foreign partner to the host counterpart. If these observations are correct, transfer costs to the supplier and recipient of technology are likely to be higher in type II environments relative to those in type I, notwithstanding any import controls that may be imposed on the parties to a technology transfer by the host country. Transfer costs are discussed later in this chapter.

From the foregoing analysis, it appears that a foreign firm can choose partners based on the potential demand for technology transfers by both supplier and recipient as identified in figure 5–2. In type I environments, cooperative agreements are likely to involve very specific and narrowly defined elements of the K, S, and H subsystems (figure 5–1). These might include licensing agreements such as those involving aspects of basic and applied R&D, patents for specific processes, as well as supplier agreements for raw material inputs and specialized equipment. Host partners are more likely to possess technologies that are comparable in terms of function to those possessed by the foreign partner. Examples of these types of cooperative agreements include those concluded by firms such as National Intergroup, Inc., and Nippon Kokon in the steel industry and among JVC, Thorn-EMI, and Thomson in the VCR market. These firms also compete with each other in the global market. Under such circumstances, the potential transfer needs of the host firm are likely to be motivated by considerations of production efficiency leading to low-cost operations, quality, and the desire to enhance the firm's long-term competitive advantage.

The factors that are likely to influence the foreign partner's choice of host partners are summarized in table 5–1.

Because of the greater likelihood of missing links within type II technological environments (figure 5–2), cooperative agreements are more likely to be broad in scope relative to agreements in type I environments (table 5–1). For example, a foreign firm might construct a turnkey plant producing an entire line of chemical

Table 5–1
Strategic Factors Affecting Cooperative Agreements by Type of Technological Environment

Type of Dominant Cooperative Agreement	*Factors Influencing Choice of JV Partners*
Type I Environment	
1. "Hardware" agreements: Product technology Supply of specialized hardware inputs (H_1 through H_4)	Limited product adaptation for host and/or export market Production of standardized products Low manufacturing and labor costs in host country
2. "Software" agreements: Blueprints Patents, brand names, and trademarks Techniques and design capabilities Process technology Relevant managerial know-how	Appropriation of rents through licensing of know-how and other capabilities in S_1 through S_4 which are either not easily duplicable or becoming obsolete to supplier Collaboration with host partner on basic research for long-term product development
3. "Knowledge" agreements: Stock of basic research knowledge now "public good" to supplier	Low R&D costs in host country
Type II Environment	
4. Combined software and hardware agreements: Potential elements as in type I	Available "knowledge" base in host country, hence potential demand for "software" and "hardware" capabilities to utilize stock of knowledge
5. Combined hardware and knowledge agreements: Potential elements as in type I	Short-term gains for supplier of hardware Low R&D and labor costs in host country Available software capabilities in host country, hence potential demand for hardware inputs
6. Combined knowledge and software agreements: Potential elements as in type I	Low labor costs in host country Some host interest in basic knowledge as innovation becomes key national goal Available host hardware capabilities, hence potentially low manufacturing costs Likely host demand for software capabilities Some host interest in basic knowledge as innovation becomes a key national goal

products (H_4 in figure 5–1) and also provide the host partner with the concomitant applied research and quality-control functions (S_3 and S_1 in figure 5–1).

Alternative Transfer Modes

The identification of strategic factors that potentially affect the choice of cooperative venture partners and the scope of agreements does not necessarily determine the *mode* by which a supplier firm might transfer technology to a host recipient partner. Undoubtedly, the choice of a particular mode of technology transfer will depend on the nature of the technological environment (figures 5–1 and 5–2) and agreements reached by the parties involved (as described in table 5–1) as well as the firm's overall strategy, among other factors. I identify four alternative modes of transferring technology:

The Complementarity Mode. Each partner contributes technical inputs in which that partner has a distinct production advantage. The Pratt and Whitney Company has collaborated with Rolls Royce in this mode within the commercial aircraft industry.

The Substitution Mode. One partner's technology is used entirely or almost to the exclusion of the other partner's technology. The latter's contribution might be to provide market access to the former or to contribute managerial skills to the venture. The General Motors–Toyota venture in California comes close to the substitution mode.

The Fusion Mode. Welding together of each partner's technology leads to the production of a "third" technology that is distinct from the original inputs of each partner. Examples of such a transfer mode include cooperative ventures involving AT&T and Philips in the telecommunications industry, and a consortium of Japanese companies and Boeing in the aircraft industry.

Arm's-Length Supplier Agreement. This occurs essentially through trade in one or more elements of technology, usually in the hardware category, between a foreign supplier firm and a host recipient. Although there is no data available to determine the magnitude of such transactions, this may be the most widely used mode of transferring technology in the global market today.

In a type I technological environment where a high degree of interaction exists among subsystems K, S, and H, all four modes of transfer can be used at varying degrees of effectiveness. On the other hand, in type II technological environments where the development of the K, S, and H subsystems occur in isolation with little or no transactional links with each other, the modes of transfer are likely to be limited to *complementarity* of inputs and *arms's-length transactions*. Since, by definition, a type II system would lack critical production links among the three subsystems, the substitution and fusion modes are largely irrelevant in the transfer process within a type II environment.

Technology-transfer–Cost Trade-offs

In choosing to enter a host market through a cooperative venture, it is assumed that firms would perform an implicit or explicit cost-benefit analysis of their investment. Contractor and Lorange (1985) have proposed a comprehensive cost-benefit framework for analyzing cooperative ventures. The cost variables they propose that are relevant to the technology-transfer portion of the overall cooperative venture are (1) the indirect costs associated with losing competitive advantage in the future as a result of licensing technology to a venture partner today and (2) the direct cost of transferring technology to the host partner.[7] In light of the methodological framework presented earlier in this chapter, we might add to those costs (3) the opportunity cost of choosing one or a combination of some of the four modes of complementarity, substitution, fusion and arm's-length transaction in transferring technology to a partner.

It is possible for firms to reduce some or all of these costs. How can firms realize this potential cost reduction? First, if we reexamine the spectrum of generic elements and technological capabilities presented in figure 5–1, it is apparent that the cost of acquiring and transferring each technological capability will differ from element to element. For example, some of the components of the knowledge base such as the existing stock of conceptual and theoretical knowledge (K_1 in figure 5–1), may well exist as public goods in the host and/or foreign environment such that the cost of acquiring and transferring them would be insignificant relative to other components in the technological spectrum.

A second way for firms to attempt to minimize technology-transfer costs is to gain access, through venture partners, to skilled labor, knowledge, and software institutions such as quasi-government R&D organizations and autonomous state-funded multidisciplinary research institutes. Kaynak (1985) has noted that some of these institutions are effective bodies for developing technological capabilities in LDCs.[8] It is not always likely that a wholly owned foreign firm would easily gain access to these public institutions in the event that the firm needed to obtain some element of host technological capability, because search costs are likely to be high without adequate local knowledge. In contrast, a cooperative venture involving foreign and host partners stands a better chance of gaining access to host technological capabilities and consequently reducing search costs for those capabilities.

Third, some of the recommended cooperative agreements outlined in table 5–1 have the dual effect of (1) minimizing transfer and development costs through cost sharing and utilization of existing production facilities of the host partner and (2) enhancing new-product development that utilizes host-country capabilities and/or materials; hence, products are more likely to be "environmentally appropriate" to the host market than those produced and imported entirely from abroad.

Conclusion: Research and Policy Implications

The methodological framework proposed in this chapter introduces a systematic approach that may be employed in policy analysis of technology transfers. However, there is room for refining some of the proposed variables in this chapter. For example, the degree of interaction among technological subsystems can be explored in a variety of ways. One way would be to estimate the volume of transactions that occurs among subsystems using measures such as purchases from one technological subsystem by another within, say, the intermediate goods market.[9] This calls for expertise that many recipient or donor firms may not possess. Nevertheless, the lack of expertise does provide venture partners the opportunity to search for innovative tools for evaluating technology-transfer activities.

Furthermore, the role that product demand in a host or export market plays in determining the type and mode of transferring technology must be investigated. How does market demand compare with a firm's strategic interests in determining the type, level, and mode of technology to be transferred? Notwithstanding these research and policy challenges, this chapter suggests that a systematic framework is necessary to identify the interactions, overlaps, and confusions that characterize research and policy analysis involving technology transfer processes.

Although the analysis has focused on the foreign supplier of technology in a cooperative venture, the framework proposed in this chapter can equally be used by a host partner and public policy makers in evaluating technologies acquired from a foreign partner or any entity outside the host technological environment. Naturally, the cost-benefit calculations in this case would differ from those made by a foreign partner.

Without the tool of a systematic framework for analyzing technology-transfer processes, it is possible that cooperative partners may miss valuable market opportunities, while host-country policies may not take into consideration the full range of existing technological capabilities within and outside the host environment. Ultimately, a better understanding of the transfer process is possible when research methodologies are designed to take into consideration the complexities of the technological environment.

Notes

1. For a rich collection of recent works, see Samli (1985) and Rosenberg and Frischtak (1985).

2. See, for example, reported cases of successful technology transfers in Dahlman and Westphal (1982).

3. Contractor (1985) reports several cases of such technologically intensive cooperative ventures in the global market.

4. Terms that describe constituents of technology include *embodied* and *disembodied* technology (Mason, 1978), *software* and *hardware* (Weiss and Jequier, 1984), and *composite* technology (Kaynak, 1985).

5. See Dahlman and Westphal (1982).

6. Abbleglen (1982) and Reich (1985) report cases where Japanese licensees have become competitors of their former U.S. licensors of technology.

7. Contractor and Lorange, (1985, pp. 45–47).

8. Kaynak (1985) reports the successful outcomes of selected licensing agreements from low- and medium-income countries such as India, Republic of Korea, the Philippines, Thailand, and Turkey.

9. Several attempts have been made to measure the fit of technology with other organizational variables. See, for example, Alexander and Randolph (1985) in the case of measuring technology fit with structure as a predictor of performance. Comparable methodologies can be used to measure functional interactions among technological subsystems.

Bibliography

Abbleglen, J. 1982. "U.S.–Japanese Technological Exchange in Perspective, 1946–1981." In C. Uehara (ed.), *Technological Exchange: The U.S.–Japanese Experience.* New York: University Press.

Alexander, J.W., and Randolph, W.A. 1985. "The Fit between Technology and Structure as a Predictor of Performance in Nursing Subunits." *Academy of Management Journal*, 28(4): 844–59.

Arrow, K., Chenery, H., Minhas, B., and Solow, R. 1961. "Capital Labor Substitution and Economic Efficiency." *Review of Economics and Statistics*, 43(1): 225–50.

Contractor, F.J. 1981. *International Technology Licensing: Compensation, Costs, and Negotiations.* Lexington, Mass.: Lexington Books.

Contractor, F.J. 1985. *Licensing in International Strategy: A Guide for Planning and Negotiations.* Westport, Conn.: Quorum.

Dahlman, C., and Westphal, L. 1982. "Technological Effort in Industrial Development: An Interpretative Survey of Recent Research." In F. Stewart and J. James (eds.), *The Economies of New Technology in Developing Countries.* London and Colo.: Frances Pinter and Westview.

Eckaus, R.S. 1955. "The Factor Proportions Problem in Underdeveloped Areas." *American Economic Review*, 45: 539–65.

Ellul, J. 1964. *The Technological Society.* New York: Alfred A. Knopf.

Forsyth, D.J.C., and Solomon, R.F. 1977. "Choice of Technology and Nationality of Ownership in Manufacturing in a Developing Country." *Oxford Economic Papers*, 29(2): 258–82.

Frame, J.D. 1983. *International Business and Global Technology.* Lexington, Mass.: Lexington Books.

Grosse, Robert E. 1980. *Foreign Investment Codes and the Location of Direct Investment.* New York: Praeger.

Heertje, A. 1973. *Economics and Technical Change.* London: Weidenfeld and Nicolson.

Kaynak, E. 1985. "Transfer of Technology from Developed to Developing Countries: Some Insights from Turkey." In A.C. Samli (ed.), *Technology Transfer: Geographic, Economic, Cultural, and Technical Dimensions.* Westport, Conn.: Quorum.

Lindert, P.H., and Kindleberger, C.P. 1982. *International Economics,* 7th ed. Homewood, Ill.: Richard D. Irwin.

Mansfield, E. 1981. *International Technology Transfer: Rates, Benefits, Costs, and Public Policy.* Unpublished paper. Philadelphia: University of Pennsylvania.

Mason, R.H. 1971. *The Transfer of Technology and the Factor Proportions Problem: The Philippines and Mexico.* Research report no. 10. New York: United Nations Institute for Training and Research.

Mason, R.H. 1973. "Some Observations on the Choice of Technology by Multinational Firms in Developing Countries." *Review of Economics and Statistics,* 55(3).

Mason, R.H. 1978. "Technology Acquisition in the Pacific Basin: Direct Foreign Investment versus Unpackaged Technology." In R.H. Mason (ed.), *International Business in the Pacific.* Lexington, Mass.: Lexington Books.

Morawetz, D. 1974. "Employment Implications of Industrialization in Developing Countries: A Survey." *Economic Journal,* 84: 491–542.

Morley, S.A., and Smith, G.W. 1977. "Limited Search and the Technology Choices of Multinational Firms in Brazil." *Quarterly Journal of Economics,* 91(2): 263–88.

Pack, H. 1976. "The Substitution of Labour for Capital in Kenyan Manufacturing." *Economic Journal,* 86 (March): 45–58.

Pavitt, K. 1985. "Technology Transfer among the Industrially Advanced Countries: An Overview." In N. Rosenberg and C. Frischtak (eds.), *International Technology Transfer: Concepts, Measures, and Comparisons.* New York: Praeger.

Reich, R.B. 1984. "Collusion Course." *The New Republic,* February 27: 18–21.

Rhee, Y.W., and Westphal, L.E. 1977. "A Micro, Economic Investigation of Choice of Technology." *Journal of Development Economics,* 4: 205–38.

Rosenberg, N., and Frischtak, C. (eds.). 1985. *International Technology Transfer: Concepts, Measures, and Comparisons.* New York: Praeger.

Samli, A.C. (ed.). 1985. *Technology Transfer: Geographic, Economic, Cultural, and Technical Dimensions.* Westport, Conn.: Quorum.

Teece, D.J. 1977. "Technology Transfer by Multinational Firms: The Resources Cost of Transferring Technological Know-how." *Economic Journal,* 87: 242–61.

Telesio, P. 1979. *Technology Licensing and Multinational Enterprises.* New York: Praeger.

Terpstra, V., and David, K. 1985. *The Cultural Environment of International Business.* Cincinnati, Ohio: South-Western.

Todaro, M. 1981. *Economic Development in the Third World.* New York and London: Longman.

Weiss, C., Jr., and Jequier, N. 1984. *Technology, Finance, and Development: An Analysis of the World Bank as a Technological Institution.* Lexington, Mass.: Lexington Books.

Yotopoulos, P.A., and Nugent, J. 1976. *Economics of Development: Empirical Investigation.* New York: Harper & Row.

Part II
Trends in Cooperative Activities and Ownership Patterns

6

Trends in International Collaborative Agreements

Michael Hergert
Deigan Morris

The use of collaborative agreements has become an important phenomenon in international business. During the past ten years, cooperative agreements have grown from almost zero to the point where new ventures are announced on nearly a daily basis. Academic research is just starting to come to grips with this significant change in international commerce. This chapter summarizes the findings of an ongoing research program into international collaborative agreements.

The increasing use of collaborative agreements has begun to attract the attention of researchers into business strategy. However, careful analysis of this phenomenon has been hampered by the lack of systematic data collection on the motivations for, incidence of, and implications of collaborative agreements. This is particularly true for agreements between international partners. To address this need, the INSEAD Business School in Fontainebleau, France, began collecting data in the mid-1970s on the occurrence of international collaborative agreements.

The data base was compiled from public announcements of collaborative agreements reported in the *Economist* and *Financial Times* over the period 1975–86. As of mid-1986, there were 839 agreements in the data base. Information was collected on the type of collaborative agreement, current status, strategic rationale, participants, ownership structure, announced purpose, and industry setting. The conclusions drawn from this sample must be tempered with a qualification on the source of the data. Although both the *Economist* and *Financial Times* are international in scope, the data may tend to have a European orientation and may reflect weaker coverage of deals originating in regions outside of Europe (such as between the United States and Japan). Furthermore, only major ventures are likely to receive publicity in the international media. While announcements of collaborative agreements appear constantly in the business press, many small deals will go unreported. Finally, the source of information for many of the articles is likely to be press releases by participating firms. These releases may not be totally unbiased descriptions of the structure and strategy of the agreements. Firms may wish to mislead their competitors about the true aims of their activities and may purposely misrepresent themselves to the business press.

The fact that every day sees the announcement of fresh agreements should not be construed as a sign of enthusiasm on the part of participating companies. The converse is in fact true. Any other viable alternative would be seized upon. Evidence for this interpretation comes from reports in the financial press of agreements that run into difficulties or are abandoned, the testimony of executives with first-hand experience, and an appreciation of the technological, economic, and managerial obstacles to successful collaboration.

For the purposes of this chapter, a collaborative agreement was defined to be a linkage between companies to jointly pursue a common goal. These agreements are very different from traditional relationships between companies, and it is these differences that make collaborative agreements so difficult to manage. A collaborative agreement may be viewed as an intermediate position along a spectrum of inter-firm dealings encompassing arms-length transactions at one end and full mergers at the other. Collaborative agreements are characterized by the following four attributes:

1. The main purpose of a collaborative agreement is to share risks and rewards among the participants. As a general rule, companies are only willing to share risks and rewards on the condition that they also share in the decision making. Therefore, the first attribute of a collaborative agreement is that responsibility for managing the project is shared by the participants. This is in contrast to some large projects (for example, construction) in which project leadership is vested in one company designated as the prime contractor.

2. Another attribute of collaborative agreements is that they only cover part of the activities of the participants. The participants therefore maintain their individual identities and have activities that are not included in the agreement. The significance of this characteristic is that it is difficult to insure a proper separation between projects that are part of the agreement and those that are not. Consequently, there is the danger of know-how leaking from one type of project to another. A merger is a special case where collaboration is total, individual identities are lost, and there is no distinction between projects. Thus, a merger is marriage and not a collaborative agreement.

3. The next attribute of collaborative agreement is that partners provide inputs (funding, skills, personnel) to the project on a continuing basis. There is thus a continual transfer of resources from the partners to the project and a continuing dialogue between the partners about what resources are needed, how they are to be used, who is to supply them, and how the costs will be shared.

4. The final attribute of collaborative agreements is that the total project cannot be broken down into independent subprojects with well-defined performance characteristics and interfaces. Consequently, progress in one subproject influences the problems to be tackled by and the progress of others. The quality and frequency of communications between project teams therefore has a significant impact on outcomes.

An Explosion in Activity

The use of international cooperative agreements surged during the first half of the eighties. As shown in figure 6–1, the number of collaborative agreement announcements between the three major trading blocs has increased steadily from 1979 to 1985.

This explosion in cooperative behavior represents a significant change in the nature of international commerce. The growth in international collaboration is particularly evident between U.S. and European firms, although all three trading blocs show substantial increases. A variety of authors have speculated as to why this strategy is becoming so popular. (See, for example, Harrigan, 1985, or Hall, 1984). Some of the recurring themes behind collaboration are:

Capital requirements beyond the scope of a single firm,

Excess capacity resulting from a change in technology or industry economics,

New production methods which make modular design and manufacturing possible, thus allowing partners to divide responsibility for subassemblies,

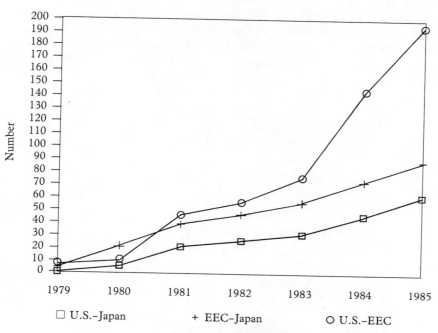

Figure 6–1. Cooperative Agreements, 1979–85

Large scale economies, which extend beyond the market of a single firm,

The emergence of global products, such as the world car,

The desire to share substantial risks embodied in single projects,

A desire to enter new geographic markets outside the domestic operations of one or more of the participants.

Strategic advantages as well as economic necessity have combined to make collaboration a dominant pattern in the international marketplace.

Patterns of International Collaboration

An analysis of the nature of collaborative agreements between international partners reveals several patterns. First, it is interesting to note what types of firms are most likely to collaborate. An examination of the list of collaboration participants in the INSEAD data base reveals that agreements are most likely to arise between large corporations that are already multinational in nature. The home markets for collaboration partners are concentrated in a relatively few economic zones. Figure 6-2 provides an illustration of who is collaborating with whom.

It appears from figure 6-2 that a majority of the collaborative agreements are struck between partners within the European Community or between U.S. and European firms. The Japanese are less active in cooperative ventures than their U.S. and European counterparts. The dramatic rise in the use of collaborative agreements

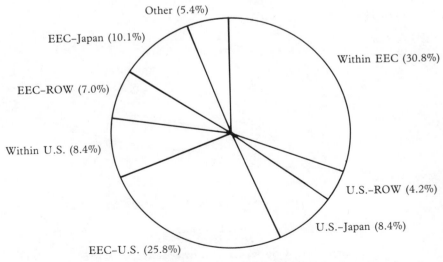

Figure 6-2. Worldwide Collaboration Partners

had led to fear and speculation that U.S. firms are "selling their birthright" to the Japanese (Reich and Mankin, 1986). The distribution of cooperative agreements seems to refute this argument. There are far more collaborations formed between Americans and Europeans than between Americans and Japanese. It is also evident from figure 6–2 that most of the international cooperative agreements are made between firms from the three major trading blocs. It is particularly striking to note the participation rate of European firms in international collaboration. Approximately 74 percent of all collaborative agreements involve at least one partner from Europe.

Figure 6–3 sheds more light on the patterns of European collaboration. It appears that the French are the most active of the Europeans in participating in collaborative agreements. As the French show a relatively small percentage of their agreements with firms outside the three major trading blocs, it appears that they tend to favor agreements with industrialized partners, particularly in the United States. Italian firms show a similar pattern of collaboration.

The Germans are noteworthy for their relative lack of participation in cooperative ventures. Given Germany's size and industrial output, the number of agreements is rather small. However, the Germans could argue that they are the "best citizens" of the European Community in that 57 percent of their cooperative agreements are with partners within the EEC. Along this dimension, the British

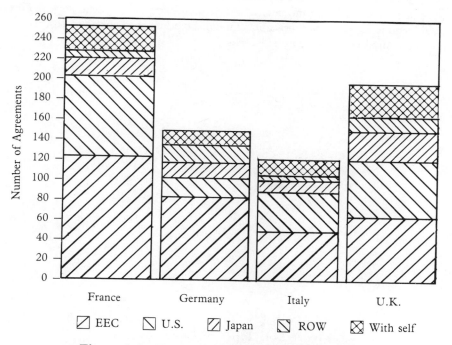

Figure 6–3. European Collaboration Partners

are the least likely to collaborate with European partners. Only 34 percent of Britain's agreements are inside the EEC. This may reflect, among other things, the relatively strong ties between Britain and the Commonwealth nations. Interestingly, there is no obvious tendency for British and U.S. firms to cooperate. The French and Italians are both more likely to choose a U.S. partner. The British, on the other hand, show the highest proportion of deals with Japanese firms.

The vast majority of collaborative agreements are between 2 partners. Approximately 81 percent of the agreements in the INSEAD data base are between 2 firms. Roughly 9 percent of the deals were between 3 partners, and 5 percent were between 4 firms. There are occasional references to agreements between 20 or more corporations, but these are quite unusual. It is also interesting to note the types of partners who are most likely to collaborate. The cooperative agreements in the INSEAD data base were categorized according to Michael Porter's framework for industry analysis (Porter, 1980). Surprisingly, relatively few agreements are made between participants in the vertical stream of production activity. As shown in figure 6-4, only 14.7 percent of the collaborative agreements were between a buyer and supplier. Most of the agreements occur between two rivals. Over 71 percent of the deals are struck between two competitors in the same market. Only about 14 percent of the collaborative agreements are between two firms to make an entry into a new market. The implication is that collaborative agreements seem to be an intramarket rather than intermarket phenomenon. This would tend to support the motivations for collaboration, such as risk or cost reduction by competitors, as described earlier.

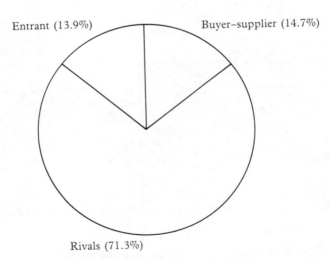

Entrant (13.9%)　　　　　　Buyer–supplier (14.7%)

Rivals (71.3%)

Figure 6–4. Types of Collaboration

The Industrial Settings of Collaboration

Although collaborative agreements are being used with increasing frequency, they are concentrated in relatively few industries. Figure 6–5 is an illustration of which industrial sectors are the most active participants in cooperative agreements. Five major industrial sectors account for 87 percent of all collaborative agreements.

The relative concentration of collaborative agreements in the few industrial sectors shown in figure 6–5 is not surprising, given the incentives for collaboration mentioned earlier. All of these sectors are typified by high entry costs, globalization, scale economies, rapidly changing technologies, and/or substantial operating risks. For example, the development costs of a large-scale digital switching system are probably in excess of $1 billion. This led British Telecom, General Electric, Plessey, and Standard Telephones and Cable to embark on a joint development project for a digital exchange (System X) in the mid-seventies. Not only are the capital requirements for entry into this market enormous, but there are substantial risks that the product will be difficult or impossible to sell after development, due to technological obsolescence and difficulties in securing contracts from foreign government buyers. This project is a good example of how difficulties in managing the collaborative effort can eventually undermine the entire program, as the System X collaboration was eventually abandoned in favor of the appointment of a prime contractor. Similar motivations for collaboration can be applied to the costs and risks associated with a new world car or commercial airliner.

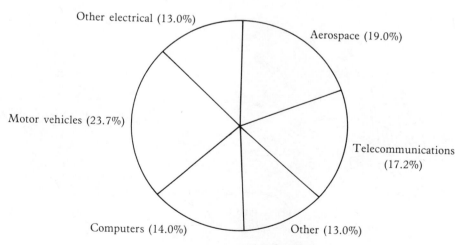

Figure 6–5. Collaboration by Industry

Other electrical (13.0%)

Aerospace (19.0%)

Motor vehicles (23.7%)

Telecommunications (17.2%)

Computers (14.0%)

Other (13.0%)

The industrial setting for collaboration varies markedly between trading blocs, as shown in figure 6–6. The aerospace industry is a good example of the differences between industry sectors according to trading blocs. The aerospace industry has the leading share of collaborations between U.S. and European firms, with approximately 26 percent of all agreements. However, it is unusual for the Japanese to collaborate in aerospace ventures with either the Americans or Europeans. Aerospace accounts for only 12 percent of Japanese–American agreements and 9 percent of Japanese–European agreements. This probably reflects the historically weak competitive position of the Japanese in aerospace, although Japanese firms

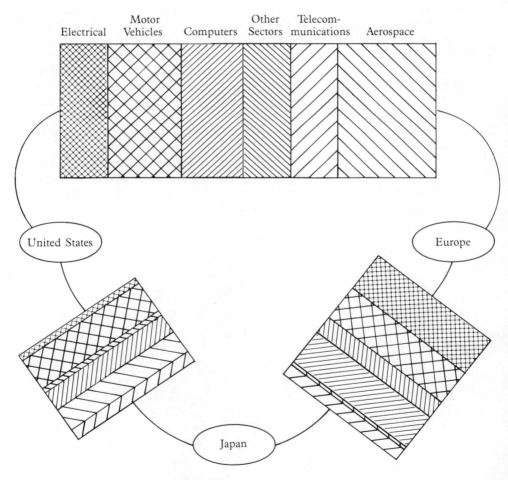

Figure 6–6. Collaborative Agreements by Sector between Trading Blocs

are beginning to become more active in this area. The computer industry is another example where the Japanese have formed relatively few cooperative ventures. On the other hand, the Japanese are quite active in noncomputer electrical goods and motor vehicles.

U.S. firms show a fairly balanced rate of participation across the six sectors shown in figure 6–6. They are most active in aerospace and telecommunications, and least in noncomputer electrical products. The Europeans participate in computers and aerospace, but are less active in telecommunications.

Purposes of Collaboration

The factors just mentioned are the driving forces behind cooperative agreements. The INSEAD data base also provides information about the strategic rationale behind collaboration as well as the type of collaborative venture formed. Figure 6–7 illustrates the distribution of announced objectives for each agreement. It is interesting to note that the largest number of cooperative ventures are formed to engage in joint product development (approximately 38 percent). If the agreements in which eventual production and/or marketing are included, this figure rises to 64 percent. It appears that cooperative behavior begins to occur very early in the product-development cycle. Part of the tendency to collaborate on early stages of product development may be explained by the difficulties in managing the partnership as the project gets closer to its eventual market. Speaking at the European

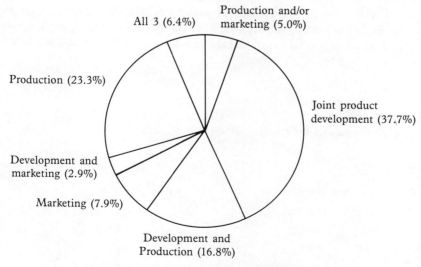

Figure 6–7. Purpose of Collaboration

Management Forum in Davos, an executive from Philips noted that cooperation is simpler on precompetitive development, as the rewards from eventual sales are distant. However, as the project nears the marketing phase, the incentive to cheat on a partner or to benefit at each other's expense may become strong. The implication is that collaboration becomes more difficult to create and sustain as markets evolve. Early establishment of a cooperative relationship between partners during the product-development cycle may help to encourage goal congruence as the product comes to market and cash flows begin to appear.

The motives for collaboration vary by international trading bloc. Table 6–1 is a cross-tabulation of types of agreements across international partners. It appears that collaborative ventures within the EEC are even more likely to be joint development projects than would be predicted from figure 6–7. The same is true for collaborations between American firms; very few ventures are started between American partners to engage in joint marketing. Conversely, the Japanese are not very active in collaborating on joint development projects with either the Europeans or Americans. They are more likely to form agreements for the purpose of marketing or production. The incidence of production collaborations between European and Japanese firms is particularly high.

Although the growth in collaborative agreements is a relatively recent phenomenon, some partnerships have already been aborted. Most of the collaborations (roughly 90 percent) in the INSEAD data base are still in operation. Approximately 5 percent of the ventures have been discontinued.

Collaboration between international partners has become an important aspect of international commerce. A growing number of companies have initiated joint projects, perhaps without fully realizing the many obstacles they are likely to confront. Collaborative agreements offer the potential to share risks and rewards beyond the capabilities of individual firms. However, it will only be the companies with skill and sensitivity toward resolving the managerial challenges that are likely to realize success from collaboration.

Table 6–1
Type of Collaboration by Economic Bloc

	Development	Marketing	Production	Development and Production	Development and Marketing	Production and Marketing	Development, Production, and Marketing
EEC	82	10	35	47	3	5	13
U.S.	32	2	12	2	3	2	3
Japan	8	2	4	0	0	0	0
EEC–U.S.	67	14	36	25	5	9	13
EEC–Japan	20	8	22	8	3	5	3
U.S.–Japan	8	10	15	11	4	9	2

Bibliography

Hall, R.D. 1984. *The International Joint Venture.* New York: Praeger.
Harrigan, K. 1985. *Strategies for Joint Ventures.* Lexington Mass.: Lexington Books.
Porter, M. 1980. *Competitive Strategy.* New York: Free Press.
Reich, R., and Mankin, E. 1986. "Joint Ventures with Japan Give Away Our Future."
    Harvard Business Review, 64 (2): 78–86.

7

Joint Venture Cycles: The Evolution of Ownership Strategies of U.S. MNEs, 1945-75

Benjamin Gomes-Casseres

Today's business periodicals are full of reports of new joint ventures between international companies. Consultants claim that "no company can stay competitive in the world today single-handedly" (Kenichi Ohmae in *Business Week*, 1984). Even top U.S. antitrust officials now believe that joint ventures "will play a vital role in promoting the growth and international competitiveness of the American economy" (McGrath, 1984). To many observers, it seems as if the era of the wholly owned subsidiary in international business is passing. Such a trend can have important implications for how multinational enterprises (MNEs) are managed and for public policies in both host and home countries.

Although anecdotal evidence suggests that the use of joint ventures by MNEs has been rising, we unfortunately have little comprehensive data on this question from 1976 to 1986. Some studies found that the use of joint ventures has increased (Hladik, 1985), while others claim that there has been little change since the 1970s (Ghemawat, Porter, and Rawlinson, 1986; Kobrin, chapter 8 in this book). On the basis of this fragmentary information, it is hard to predict future trends. But a careful look at the extensive data available up to 1975 provides important clues to how MNEs' ownership strategies evolved over time; this knowledge can inform our speculation about future trends.

This chapter argues that the evolution of multinational ownership strategies depends on trends in the underlying factors that drive ownership decisions. Elsewhere (Gomes-Casseres, 1985, 1987), I developed and tested a cross-sectional model of when and why MNEs form joint ventures with local partners. Here, I examine how this behavior changed over time. In particular, the factors that were found to be important in cross-sectional tests will be used to explain striking cycles of joint venture formation in the 1945-75 period.

I received valuable comments on this chapter from Louis T. Wells, Jr., Donald R. Lessard, Kim B. Clark, Robert O. Schlaifer, Bruce Kogut, and participants at the October 1986 Rutgers/Wharton Joint Research Colloquium on Cooperative Strategies in International Business. The Harvard Business School's Division of Research provided financial support, and the Multinational Enterprise Project at Harvard and the Strategic Planning Institute in Cambridge, Mass., gave me access to their data. The views expressed here are mine.

The analysis in this chapter is based on data on over five thousand foreign manufacturing subsidiaries of 180 large U.S. MNEs (all *Fortune 500* companies) that was collected by Harvard's Multinational Enterprise Project. Only joint ventures with local partners were considered; a subsidiary was classified as a joint venture if the MNE owned between 5 percent and 95 percent of its equity. Industry characteristics of four-digit SIC groups were derived from the PIMS data base; host-country characteristics were derived from the World Bank. General results from analyses of these data were consistent with clinical data collected from five MNEs in 1985 (Gomes-Casseres, 1985).

Historical Trends in Joint Venture Use

Postwar Trends

Since the early 1960s, researchers have claimed that the use of joint ventures by U.S. MNEs had been increasing (Friedmann and Kalmanoff, 1961; Stopford and Wells, 1972; Hladik, 1985). This indeed was the long-term trend in the data used here. With significant fluctuations, the yearly share of joint ventures in new manufacturing subsidiaries grew from about 10 percent in the first decade of this century to over 50 percent in the early 1960s (figure 7–1).

But just as striking as this rising trend was a sharp *decline* in joint venture use during most of the 1960s. The yearly share of joint ventures in new subsidiaries fell continuously from 55 percent in 1961 to 31 percent in 1968. This trend has not been reported in the extensive literature on international joint ventures.

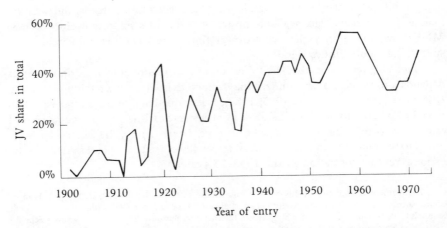

Figure 7–1. Three-Year Moving Averages of Share of Joint Ventures in New Manufacturing Subsidiaries, 1900–75

A closer look at the postwar period reveals other surprising patterns. There appears to have been two-and-a-half cycles in MNEs' use of joint ventures at entry. From 1946 to 1951, the yearly share of joint ventures in new entries rose from 15 percent to over 50 percent; after that, it fell to 28 percent in 1955. Then came another rise to the 55 percent peak in 1961, followed by the decline to 31 percent. A third increase began in 1969, with the share of joint ventures reaching 41 percent in 1975. The three-year moving averages plotted on the solid line in figure 7–2 clearly show these trends.

These joint venture entry patterns appear to be closely correlated to trends in ownership changes after entry. Joint ventures established at the peaks of the cycles were more likely to be changed into wholly owned subsidiaries than others. This is evident from the varying gap between the dotted and solid lines in figure 7–2. On average over the 1945–75 period, 21 percent of joint ventures were eventually reorganized into wholly owned subsidiaries. But 27 percent of joint ventures formed in the two peaks of the cycles (1950–52 and 1960–62) underwent this change, compared to 16 percent of the joint ventures formed during the troughs (1954–56 and 1967–69).

Explaining Patterns of Joint Venture Use

These patterns suggest that ownership choices at entry and changes made after entry were motivated by the same underlying behavioral processes. Indeed, my cross-sectional tests using 1975 data (Gomes-Casseres, 1985 and forthcoming) and Franko's (1973) suggest that both entry choices and ownership changes after

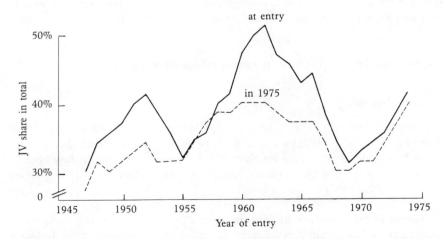

Figure 7–2. Three-Year Moving Averages of Shares of Joint Ventures in Manufacturing Subsidiaries at Entry and in 1975 for Subsidiaries Entering in 1946–75

entry depend on the costs and benefits of different ownership structures. Other studies have also highlighted the firm, industry, and host-country characteristics that affect these costs and benefits (Tomlinson, 1970; Stopford and Wells, 1972; Fagre and Wells, 1982).

Briefly, in the absence of host-government restrictions on foreign ownership, joint ventures were used by the MNEs when they needed contributions from local partners that were costly to acquire contractually. This occurred, for example, when the MNE had little previous experience in the subsidiary's country or industry. On the other hand, joint ventures were not attractive when it was costly to arrange contracts that reduced potential conflicts of interest between the local partner and the MNE. This often occurred when the subsidiary was vertically integrated with the MNE's operations elsewhere or when the MNE followed other globally integrated strategies (Gomes-Casseres, 1987).

When host governments restricted foreign ownership, MNEs might be forced to accept joint venture structures, but they often negotiated exceptions to the restrictive regulations. A host government's power to enforce ownership restrictions then depended on what it had to offer the MNE and vice versa. For example, MNEs would often accept joint ventures in return for a protected market.

Do these and other factors that are useful in explaining cross-sectional patterns also account for the historical changes in joint venture use just described? As I will show, they played a role in the evolution of ownership strategies of MNEs in the sample, but none of these factors can account fully for the cycles observed in the data. Rather, the cycles may have been generated by systematic and closely related changes in global competition and corporate strategies. These findings suggest that the increasing use of cooperative strategies being reported today may be only one stage in a process that could well reverse itself in the future.

Factors behind Changes in Ownership Strategies

Country Factors

Conditions in the host country help determine whether an MNE needs the help of local partners to compete successfully. Previous studies have shown that the need for such contributions diminish with an MNE's familiarity with the host country and with the level of income of host-country consumers (Davidson, 1980; Gomes-Casseres, 1985, 1987).[1]

Geographic Distribution of Investment. These country factors probably accounted for the long-term upward trend in joint venture use since the early 1900s. Early in the century, the MNEs invested mostly in Canada and Europe. In the 1910s and 1930s, investments in Latin America began to increase, but the flow to Europe was still strong. During World War II, the share of investments to Latin

America rose sharply, while that to Europe fell. After the war, the MNEs generally invested in a more diverse group of countries than before. Over time, therefore, these firms ventured into less and less familiar territories, making joint ventures more attractive.

But geographic shifts in MNEs' investments do not seem to account for the postwar cycles noted earlier. The share of investment going to Europe increased gradually after the war, while that to Latin America fell (figure 7–3). These trends suggest that the use of joint ventures should have decreased gradually over the period, as European countries were more familiar to the MNEs and had higher per capita incomes than Latin American nations. Consequently, these shifts cannot explain the rise in joint venture use in the late 1940s, the late 1950s, and the early 1970s.

That the geographic mix of investments did not account for the cycles in joint venture formation is also evident from figure 7–4. Joint venture use at entry rose both in Europe and in Latin America in the late 1950s, and declined in the late 1960s. The data for Canada, Australia, and South Africa also show the decline in joint venture use in the 1960s. Joint venture use in most regions also rose sharply in the 1970s. If changes in the geographic mix of investments were behind the aggregate patterns in figure 7–2, then one would not expect to find these patterns repeated in each major region of the world.

Host-government Policies. One country factor that partly accounted for the evolution of MNE ownership strategies in the 1960s and 1970s was the impact of host-government ownership restrictions. As has been shown elsewhere, such restrictions influenced MNEs' ownership choices even though the firms could often bargain successfully for exceptions to the regulations (Fagre and Wells, 1982; Lecraw, 1984; Gomes-Casseres, 1985).

During most of the period, new subsidiaries in "restrictive" countries were more likely to be joint ventures than those in "open" countries.[2] (See figure 7–5.) The enforcement of restrictive policies also seems to have become stricter over time, as the spread between joint venture entry levels in the two groups of countries increased from the 1950s to the 1960s. Restrictive countries thus seemed to "get their way" more often in the 1960s than before. Another reason for this trend may have been that many of the countries classified as restrictive only instituted their regulations in the late 1950s.

Consistent with this argument, the decline in joint venture use in the 1960s may have resulted partly from the deterrence effect of the restrictive policies (Gomes-Casseres, 1985). The more insistent stance of restrictive governments in the 1960s led to a declining share of investment going to these countries (figure 7–6), so that the overall use of joint ventures by firms in the sample decreased. For reasons to be examined shortly, the share of investment to restrictive countries began to grow again in the 1970s, encouraging a new rise in the use of joint ventures.

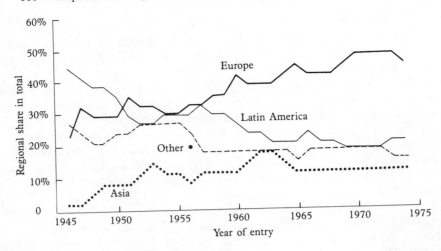

•Other = Canada, Australia, South Africa.

Figure 7–3. Three-Year Moving Averages of Shares of Major Regions in New Manufacturing Subsidiaries, 1946–75

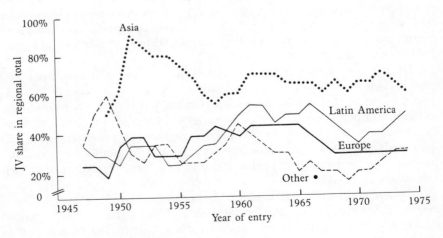

•Other = Canada, Australia, South Africa.

Figure 7–4. Three-Year Moving Averages of Shares of Joint Ventures in New Manufacturing Subsidiaries, by Major Regions, 1946–75

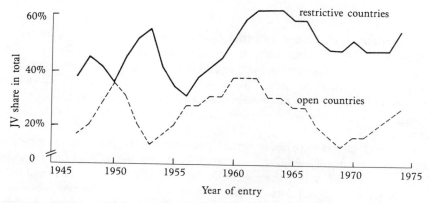

Figure 7–5. Three-Year Moving Averages of Shares of Joint Ventures in New Manufacturing Subsidiaries in Open and Restrictive Countries, 1946–75

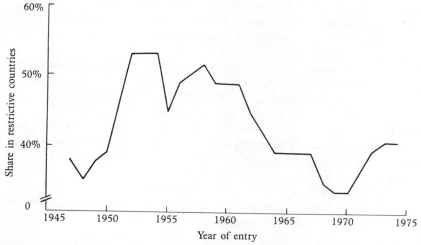

Figure 7–6. Three-Year Moving Averages of Share of New Manufacturing Subsidiaries That Were in Restrictive Countries, 1946–75

But host-government policies again offer only a partial explanation of the cyclical patterns in ownership strategies. The rise and fall in joint venture use, with a peak around 1961, occurred in data for *both* restrictive and open countries (figure 7–5). In fact, this pattern is even more striking in the latter than in the former. The rise in the 1970s is also most striking in the data for open countries. Clearly, other factors must have been at work there.

Industry Factors

Cross-sectional tests have shown that industry factors too can affect ownership strategies. For example, subsidiaries in marketing-intensive industries were less likely to be joint ventures than others, because global marketing strategies often conflicted with interests of local partners. Similarly, the R&D intensity of subsidiaries' industries and the extent to which subsidiaries depended on local inputs of natural resources could also affect ownership choices (Stopford & Wells, 1972; Gomes-Casseres, 1987).

But such factors were not important in explaining the evolution of ownership strategies over time. Overall, the industry mix of new subsidiaries in the sample changed little, and, where there were shifts, these did not seem responsible for changes in the aggregate patterns of joint venture use. The share of new subsidiaries in pharmaceuticals, for example, declined gradually from about 19 percent of total entries in the late 1940s to 5 percent in the early 1970s. But, since joint ventures were seldom used in this industry, this suggests a constantly increasing share of joint ventures in new entries, not the cyclicity apparent in the data. Other sectors showed no clear trends. The share of new subsidiaries making electrical and electronic components fluctuated more or less randomly between 5 percent and 10 percent, and that of new subsidiaries in the automotive sector varied widely between 2 percent and 11 percent.

There were fewer shifts in the distribution of investment across broader categories.[3] The shares of subsidiaries making intermediate goods, capital goods, and durable and nondurable consumer goods remained roughly constant during the postwar period (figure 7–7). The use of joint ventures in each of these categories, however, did vary over time (figure 7–8). The patterns in all but intermediate goods correspond closely to the aggregate trends in figure 7–2. Shifts in the mix of investment among these categories therefore could not have caused the aggregate patterns.

Because the cyclical pattern in joint venture use is so pervasive across both industries and countries, it is natural to think that it may have been due to something in the nature of the MNEs themselves, in the mix of firms going abroad, or in the global environment. These possibilities are considered next.

Firm Factors

Several characteristics of the firms investing abroad seemed to have influenced patterns in joint venture formation. In particular, previous studies found that if an MNE had a lot of experience in a new subsidiary's industry, it was less likely to enter into a joint venture than otherwise (Gomes-Casseres, 1985, 1987). Conversely, the MNE was more likely to form a joint venture if it was small relative to its competitors (Stopford and Wells, 1972; Gomes-Casseres, 1985). There were important changes over time in each of these factors.

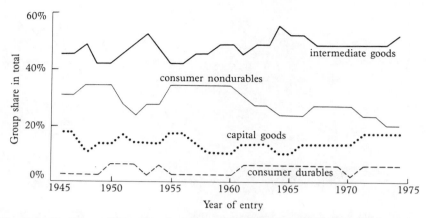

Figure 7-7. Three-Year Moving Averages of Shares of Industry Groups in New Manufacturing Subsidiaries, 1946-75

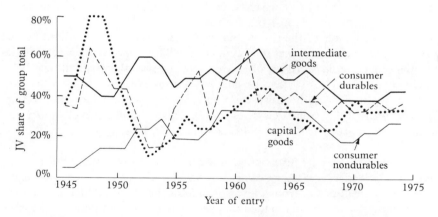

Figure 7-8. Three-Year Moving Averages of Shares of Joint Ventures in New Manufacturing Subsidiaries, by Industry Group, 1946-75

Industry Experience. As could be expected, the industry experience of U.S. MNEs in the sample grew as they expanded abroad; later investments were more likely than earlier ones to be in industries in which each firm was already active abroad (figure 7-9). This implies that the MNEs' preference for joint ventures should have decreased over time, perhaps leading to the decline in joint venture

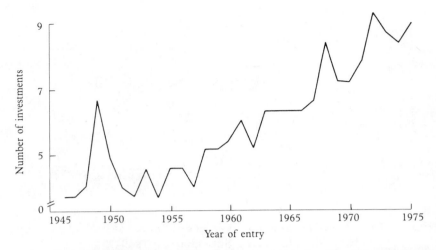

Figure 7-9. Average Number of Foreign Investments That Each Parent Firm Had in the Industries of New Subsidiaries, 1946-75

formation in the 1960s. But what led to the increasing use of joint ventures in the late 1940s, the late 1950s, and the early 1970s?

One explanation for the rise in joint ventures in some periods might be that the MNEs were diversifying as they went abroad. The number of new subsidiaries that were outside each MNE's main product line increased sharply in the late 1940s and then again gradually after the late 1950s (Gomes-Casseres, 1985, p. 431). Previous studies showed that this factor sometimes encouraged joint ventures (Stopford and Wells, 1972; Gomes-Casseres, 1987). This trend might explain increases in joint venture use in the late 1940s and the late 1950s.

Size of Firms. The size distribution of the parent firms of new subsidiaries also seemed to have affected aggregate ownership patterns. The proportion of subsidiaries of relatively small parent firms rose at the end of the 1940s and fell in the early 1950s, perhaps contributing to the first peak in joint venture formation shown in figure 7-2.[4] But after that, the patterns in the size distribution of MNEs do not correspond to those in joint venture activity (figure 7-10).

In addition, the ownership strategies of the relatively small and large firms in the sample showed similar trends. Both followed the apparently cyclical patterns discussed earlier (Gomes-Casseres, 1985, p. 429). Thus, like the other firm factors I have described, this variable may have contributed to the aggregate trends in some periods, but it cannot explain them fully.

The aggregate patterns in joint venture use could, of course, have resulted from the combined effects of the country, industry, and firm factors already discussed. The trends in some of these factors may have encouraged joint ventures in certain periods,

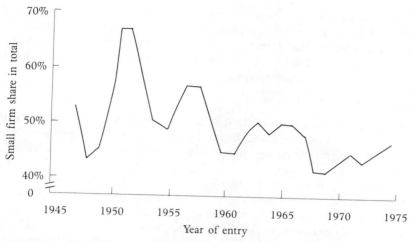

Figure 7-10. Three-Year Moving Averages of Share of New Manufacturing Subsidiaries Accounted for by Relatively Small Firms, 1946–75

while trends in other factors discouraged them in other periods. But for systematic cyclical patterns to result from this combination, some other process must have orchestrated the various opposing forces. If the trends in these variables were unrelated to each other, their combined effect would not show a systematic pattern—the rate of joint venture formation would have varied more or less randomly. The next section suggests what processes may have coordinated the various factors into a systematic joint venture formation cycle.

A Joint Venture Formation Cycle?

The interplay of two broad processes might help explain the regular patterns observed in the historical data on joint venture formation. The first is the changing nature of global competition. Ownership policies are part of an MNE's overall corporate strategy, which in turn is influenced by its competitive environment. As such, these policies may change as the pace and nature of global competition changes. Because MNEs often match each other's competitive moves, such changes can result in aggregate shifts in corporate strategies.

The second process contributing to a joint venture formation cycle may be the changing organizational capabilities of firms, such as their technical and marketing skills, their knowledge of foreign environments, and the scope of their operations. These capabilities evolve as firms learn to compete in new industries and become familiar with new environments, and as opportunities for global integration grow. As a result, the emphasis of corporate strategies may shift from *expanding* the firm's capabilities to *exploiting* existing capabilities. While joint ventures have been found to be attractive in the former strategies, they can be costly in the latter (Gomes-Casseres, 1985).

Phases of the Cycle: A Conceptual Model

These two processes are closely related, and their combination could result in a cycle of joint venture formation. To see this, picture a world at rest, so to speak, where firms compete in an oligopoly, but where none has a persistent advantage over another. Then introduce an exogenous factor that upsets this balance, such as an innovation or new market that opens up new areas for competition.

The firms will now scramble to gain new advantages over their competitors. Due to the follow-the-leader nature of oligopolistic competition, there will be pressure on follower firms to match the moves of leaders (Knickerbocker, 1973). While the strongest firms may be able to exploit the new opportunity by themselves, many other firms will need to form joint ventures that can provide them with technologies, markets, raw materials, or other sources of competitive advantage. Joint ventures will thus be used to expand these firms' capabilities. Because there are inevitably more followers than leaders in this game, the aggregate rate of joint venture formation will increase.

But these joint ventures also make it more difficult for each firm to rationalize its newly expanded operations and coordinate its many ventures into a cohesive force. The local interests of joint venture partners often conflict with those of MNEs pursuing globally integrated strategies, because many policy decisions of a joint venture will have global costs and benefits that are important to the MNE but that are not felt by the local partner. Thus, while opportunities for global integration by the MNE grow as the firm expands, they cannot yet be exploited fully. Also, as the MNE expands abroad, it acquires additional experience and resources, thus diminishing the potential benefits it can receive from joint ventures. Joint ventures at this stage will also cut into the profits that the MNE can appropriate from its newly acquired capabilities.

As a result, there comes a point when the opportunity costs of not exploiting fully the capabilities that the firms have built begin to exceed the benefits of further expansion of these capabilities. The basis of competition then shifts to integration and coordination rather than expansion. Again, firms in the oligopoly will be pressed to follow each other's leads in this direction. Because joint ventures are not attractive in this new type of strategy, the rate of joint venture formation will decrease; in addition, the firms will seek to buy out their partners in existing joint ventures.

That is the conceptual model. Does it fit the reality of the period 1946–75? Only incomplete evidence exists to evaluate this, because such concepts as the "nature of global competition" and the relative benefits of "expanding" or "exploiting" a firm's capability are difficult to quantify.

Evidence for the Cycles

During the period 1946–75, there were apparently two and a half cycles of joint venture formation. The first ran from 1946 to 1955, with a peak in 1951; the second, from 1956 to 1968, with a peak in 1961. A third cycle seemed to begin in 1969. Among these, the second cycle seems to fit the model best, but the patterns in the other periods may be partly explained by the model.

The First Cycle. Immediately after the end of World War II, there was much uncertainty about the future state of the European and Japanese economies. U.S. MNEs that had already established operations in these areas began to reconstruct war-torn plants, but expansion of these operations and the entry of new MNEs did not begin until the late 1940s and early 1950s, when the Marshall Plan fueled the beginning of a rapid recovery.

In the years around 1950, many relatively small U.S. MNEs expanded abroad and many MNEs invested in industries outside their main product lines (figure 7–10 and surrounding text). These factors encouraged the greater use of joint ventures in these years. This pattern also may have been part of the Marshall Plan's efforts, when "all sorts of channels were used to transmit not only goods but also technology to European industry, even though it was clear that industry would eventually represent a threat to U.S. exporters" (Vernon, 1972, pp. 87–88).

But there seems to have been a limit to this early expansion and diversification of U.S. MNEs in the post–World War II period. Within a few years, local European and Japanese firms became stronger competitors and the U.S. firms went back to investing in subsidiaries in their main product lines. Faced with greater local competition, the proportion of smaller MNEs in total entries also declined (figure 7–10). As a result, the use of joint ventures declined to a low point in 1955.

The Second Cycle. By the second half of the 1950s, however, consumer demand had also begun to recover in Europe and Japan, and many less-developed countries had embarked on import-substitution strategies. These changes provided the incentive for an unprecedented expansion in U.S. direct investment abroad. Not only did the number of manufacturing subsidiaries of U.S. MNEs increase in this period, but it did so at an accelerating pace.

The annual percentage increase in the number of subsidiaries of MNEs in the sample rose from about 4 percent in the late 1940s to 12 percent in the early 1960s (figure 7–11). After the peak in the rate of foreign expansion in the early 1960s, the pace of new entries declined gradually, with many fluctuations; by the early 1970s, it had again reached the level of the early 1950s.

The acceleration of foreign expansion by U.S. MNEs from about 1953 to 1960 went hand in hand with their increased use of joint ventures at entry. During this period, it seems, U.S. MNEs competed fiercely against each other to establish operations in new markets. As a result, many formed joint ventures with strong local

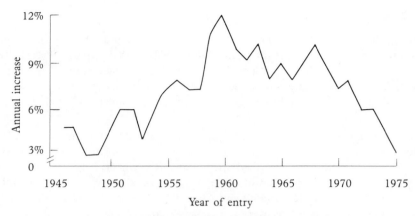

Figure 7-11. Annual Percentage Increase in the Number of Manufacturing Subsidiaries of U.S. MNEs, 1946-75

firms as a way of rapidly expanding their competitive advantages vis-à-vis other firms in the oligopoly. (In these years, few European and Japanese firms were part of this oligopoly; that phenomenon appeared in the 1970s, as will be noted later.) The rate of joint venture formation thus rose in all the major regions to which U.S. MNEs went (figure 7-4).

Then, in the 1960s, U.S. MNEs began to consolidate and rationalize the extensive foreign operations that they had built up. In Europe, the formation of the EEC encouraged cross-border integration. Vernon suggested that, while the formation of the EEC may have provided some incentive to investments by U.S. MNEs, "the more important effect was probably on the functions of the plants established by U.S. enterprises in the EEC, which might otherwise have been less specialized and less extensively linked across the borders of Europe" (Vernon, 1972, p. 89). In other areas, too, exports of subsidiaries of U.S. MNEs grew during the 1960s. Especially in the less-developed countries, this increase in exports seemed to have been partly due to the MNEs' access to world markets.

This increase in the global integration of MNEs' subsidiaries in the 1960s is consistent with the model I have presented. After the rapid expansion that provided the MNEs with footholds in many new markets came a period of consolidation, when the firms turned to ways of exploiting the global scale economies of their newly expanded networks. Under these conditions, joint ventures became costly due to the conflicts that could arise between the global interests of the MNE and the local interests of the partners.

Further evidence that the 1960s was a period of consolidation and integration of the MNEs' foreign operations comes from studies of the firms' organizational structures. Stopford and Wells (1972) traced the various stages in U.S. MNEs' organizations and reported that many of the subsidiaries set up in Europe in the late 1950s at first were relatively autonomous operations. Later, they became more closely controlled by headquarters. Franko found that these organizational changes were closely related to the MNEs' "tolerance" for joint ventures (1973).

The motivation for this pattern of organizational evolution is similar to that behind the joint venture formation cycle presented here: "The transitory nature of autonomy is clear. The first phase of expansion, involving autonomous subsidiaries, is likely to give way rapidly to a new phase when controls and organization are introduced." In the first phase, "the need for learning exceeds the desire for control." (Stopford and Wells, 1972, p. 21.) By the end of 1966, all 170 firms in Stopford and Wells's study had developed international divisions to coordinate their international activities. In fact, many were already in the process of abandoning these divisions in favor of structures that provided even better coordination among all the firm's activities, foreign and domestic—the so-called global structures (ibid., pp. 21, 25).

It seems, therefore, that the 1960s was indeed a period of consolidation and integration of the operations of U.S. MNEs. This process allowed the firms to exploit fully the extensive network of subsidiaries that they had built up during the preceding years. In the 1960s, the firms tended to form fewer new joint ventures, as those that they already had were fulfilling their function of teaching the MNEs about new environments and new technologies. Instead, the firms invested in new wholly owned ventures and they began to buy out their partners in the joint ventures. Most of the evidence that Franko (1973) found for the "instability" of joint ventures was from this period.

A Third Cycle? Toward the end of the 1960s, this process seemed to have advanced far enough that the firms could begin to look again for new expansion opportunities. By this time, the competitive environment had begun to change again. Newly industrializing countries in Asia and Latin America had begun to grow rapidly, and even before the oil-price hike in 1973, the oil-exporting countries in Africa and the Middle East had developed attractive markets.

In addition, Japanese and European MNEs had grown to the point where they presented a threat to U.S. firms in many of these third-country markets. Also, they were usually more willing than U.S. MNEs to accept joint ventures imposed by restrictive host-country governments. And more governments began to impose such conditions on foreign investors.

This is the period in which some U.S. MNEs that had earlier resisted joint ventures slowly began to change their ownership strategies. General Motors is a case in point. It had no joint ventures before 1970, but acquired several in the first half of the decade. Its managers explained that this was due to a variety of factors, among which was increased competition from European producers, pressure from host governments, entries into new and unfamiliar countries, and the gradual recognition that Japanese small cars and trucks fit the needs of consumers in some countries better than U.S. models did (Gomes-Casseres, 1985, pp. 569–73).

Conclusion: Whither Global Competition?

The changing environment of the 1970s thus provided new incentives for joint venture formation, and a new cycle seemed to have begun. Unfortunately, no data are available for the period after 1975 comparable to those used in this chapter. Fragmentary evidence cited earlier suggests that the rate of joint venture formation has remained high, and no indication of a downturn has yet been unearthed.

But recent studies also stress the dilemmas that MNEs currently face when attempting to respond to both local and global pressures at the same time (Doz, Bartlett, and Prahalad, 1981). And there are suggestions that the advantages of global integration and coordination are increasing, while the barriers to globalization are coming down (Porter, 1986; Flaherty, 1986).

It is thus conceivable that the net benefits of joint ventures in expanding the MNEs' capabilities will once again be exceeded by the net benefits of wholly owned structures in exploiting global economies of scale. While in the initial stages of globalization, joint ventures may help a firm achieve such scale, they are not necessarily the best way to exploit it in later stages. (Of course, this process may in the future occur only in specific industries or regions instead of across the board, as seemed to have happened in 1946–75.)

Indeed, some recent research suggests that global strategies have been evolving in three stages (Hamel and Prahalad, 1985). In the first stage, MNEs build a global presence. In the second, they begin to coordinate operations in order to retaliate against each other's moves. In the third, they rationalize global operations to gain world-scale volume and reputation.

These stages correspond closely to the cycle of joint venture formation I have discussed. In the first stage, joint ventures may be useful to help a firm expand abroad. In the second, the drawbacks of joint ownership begin to appear as the local partners hinder the MNE's global coordination. In the final phase, a firm with wholly owned subsidiaries can compete better than one with joint ventures.

Thus, in industries where global competition is evolving in these directions, we might see a decrease in the use of joint ventures. In other words, while cooperative strategies today seem to be the wave of the future, the wave may well crest. The analysis here at any rate suggests that, in joint venture formation as in so much else, what goes up, must come down.

Notes

1. The preferences of consumers in high-income countries were similar to those of consumers in the MNEs' home market (the United States), so that the MNEs were not likely to need marketing inputs from local partners.

2. Restrictive countries were defined as those where the government had policies discouraging 100 percent foreign ownership (based on surveys by the U.S. Department of

Commerce). They were: France, Mexico, Japan, Spain, Australia, Brazil, Venezuela, the Philippines, Colombia, New Zealand, India, Iran, South Korea, Pakistan, Peru, Malaysia, Nigeria, Indonesia, Ecuador, and Sri Lanka. All other countries were classified as "open."

3. This analysis used the industry definitions in the PIMS data base.

4. Relatively small parent firms were defined as those with assets smaller than the average for sample firms in the same industries. Note that even these "small" firms were *Fortune 500* companies.

References

Business Week. 1984. "Are Foreign Partners Good for U.S. Companies." May 28.

Davidson, W.H. 1980. *Experience Effects in International Investment and Technology Transfer.* Ann Arbor: University of Michigan Press.

Doz, Y.L., Bartlett, C.A., and Prahalad, C.K. 1981. "Global Competitive Pressures and Host Country Demands: Managing Tensions in MNCs." *California Management Review*, Spring: 63–74.

Fagre, N., and Wells, L.T. 1982. "Bargaining Power of Multinationals and Host Governments." *Journal of International Business Studies*, Fall: 9–23.

Flaherty, M. 1986. "Coordinating International Manufacturing and Technology." In M.E. Porter (ed.), *Competition in Global Industries*. Boston: Harvard Business School Press.

Franko, L.G. 1973. *Joint Venture Survival in Multinational Corporations*. New York: Praeger.

Friedmann, W.G., and Kalmanoff, G. (eds.). 1961. *Joint International Business Ventures.* New York: Columbia University Press.

Ghemawat, P., Porter, M.E., and Rawlinson, R.A. 1986. "Patterns of International Coalition Activity." In M.E. Porter (ed.), *Competition in Global Industries*. Boston: Harvard Business School Press.

Gomes-Casseres, B. 1985. *Multinational Ownership Strategies.* Unpublished doctoral dissertation. Harvard University, Graduate School of Business Administration, Boston.

———. forthcoming. "Joint Venture Instability: Is It a Problem?" *Columbia Journal of World Business.*

———. 1987. *Ownership Structures of Foreign Subsidiaries: Theory and Evidence.* Working paper. Harvard Business School, Boston.

Hamel, G., and Prahalad, C.K. 1985. "Do You Really Have a Global Strategy?" *Harvard Business Review*, July–August: 139–48.

Hladik, K.J. 1985. *International Joint Ventures: An Economic Analysis of U.S.-Foreign Business Partnerships.* Lexington, Mass.: Lexington Books.

Knickerbocker, F.T. 1973. *Oligopolistic Reaction and Multinational Enterprise.* Boston: Harvard Business School Press.

Lecraw, D.J. 1984. "Bargaining Power, Ownership, and Profitability of Transnational Corporations in Developing Countries." *Journal of International Business Studies*, Spring–Summer.

McGrath, J.P. 1984. *Remarks of the Assistant Attorney General to the 18th Annual New England Antitrust Conference*, Harvard Law School, Cambridge, Mass., November 2.

Porter, M.E. 1986. "Competition in Global Industries: A Conceptual Framework." In Michael E. Porter (ed.), *Competition in Global Industries*. Boston: Harvard Business School Press.

Stopford, J.M., and Wells, L.T., Jr. 1972. *Managing the Multinational Enterprise: Organization of the Firm and Ownership of the Subsidiaries.* New York: Basic Books.

Tomlinson, J.W.C. 1970. *The Joint Venture Process in International Business: India and Pakistan.* Cambridge, MIT Press.

Vernon, R. 1972. *Sovereignty at Bay.* New York: Basic Books.

8

Trends in Ownership of U.S. Manufacturing Subsidiaries in Developing Countries: An Interindustry Analysis

Stephen J. Kobrin

Joint ventures have been a major concern in the international business literature and, as this book and the conference from which it is drawn indicate, attention has increased in recent years. Systematic empirical data on international joint ventures have been difficult to obtain, however, especially since the Harvard Business School's Multinational Enterprise data base was last updated in 1975. As a result, many of the recent comprehensive studies of ownership patterns and determinants either rely on data by now a decade or more old (for example, Fagre and Wells, 1982; Gomes-Casseres, 1985), draw on a sample that is restricted by industry and geographic area (Lecraw, 1984), or limit the population to joint ventures rather than all subsidiaries (Hladik 1985).

This chapter reports a 1986 survey of large, international, U.S.-based manufacturing firms that provides comprehensive data on ownership of subsidiaries in developing countries. It analyzes trends and preferences at the industry level and concludes that there has not been a noticeable increase in the proportion of joint ventures in developing countries.[1]

Ownership preferences have been analyzed theoretically from two major perspectives: strategy and internalization (competition and transaction cost in Kogut's, 1986, terms). Examples of the former include Stopford and Wells (1972) and, of the latter, Rugman (1981) and Hennart (1986). While the two approaches differ in assumptions and levels of analysis (firm versus transaction) and they illuminate different aspects of the problem, imperfect markets are central to each and they tend to converge at the broad level of explanation. All else being equal, managers prefer a wholly owned subsidiary when unambiguous control renders the exploitation of assets more efficient and effective.

With apologies to John Dunning, I take an eclectic approach to explanation, drawing on both streams of the literature as appropriate. As I do not deal with country- or partner-specific factors that increase the benefits of shared ownership, the focus of this chapter is on industry characteristics that influence preferences for unambiguous control: it is an examination of ownership rather than joint ventures.

I begin by reviewing ownership patterns over time and then examine interindustry differences. Next, I analyze differences in preferences in terms of underlying industry characteristics. I then explore intraindustry variation and host-country policies. To close, I draw some conclusions about trends over time.

The Study

The study is restricted to relatively large and international U.S. manufacturing firms. (Although smaller firms are of interest, their very large numbers would have made it impossible to obtain a representative sample.[2]) Using the Conference Board's *Key Company Directory* (1983), 203 firms were identified that are equivalent in size to the Fortune 500 largest industrial firms and have at least 20 percent of their sales generated abroad. Firms in extractive sectors (petroleum or mining), conglomerates that could not be classified by industry, and those in sectors that are export based (such as aircraft) were eliminated, leaving 162 firms. The population is roughly equivalent to the Harvard Multinational Enterprise Project's 187 companies with two exceptions: extractive firms and conglomerates are not included and the minimum foreign ownership is 20 percent rather than 5 percent.

Public sources (*Moody's Industrial Manual*, 1984; *Who Owns Whom?* 1984/85; Stopford, Dunning, and Haberlich, 1980) were used to identify manufacturing subsidiaries in non-European developing countries and to determine parent ownership and the products produced.

The next step was a mail survey of the 139 firms that had manufacturing subsidiaries in developing countries. Each was sent an exhibit summarizing the public-source data and asked to identify those subsidiaries actually manufacturing product, to make necessary additions or deletions, and to supply information on ownership and products produced. Eleven firms that no longer manufacture in developing countries were removed from the population, leaving 128. Seventy-five (58.6 percent) responded, providing usable data on 563 subsidiaries in 49 countries. Industrial sector and percentage of sales generated abroad were compared for respondents and the population; chi-squared tests reveal a nonsignificant probability that the two distributions are not identical.

Trends Over Time

There have been remarkable changes in the developing countries during the past twenty-five years. This period was marked by the end of formal colonialization, development, and nation building in much of the Third World, the emergence of group consciousness in the developing countries as manifest in the United Nations declarations on permanent sovereignty over natural resources and OPEC, the development of considerable managerial and technological capabilities in some countries, and the appearance of a number of newly industrializing countries which are beginning to compete in world markets.

The rather high level of North–South tension prevalent in the 1970s affected relations between investors and host countries. One manifestation was the emergence of specific restrictions on foreign ownership of business investment. The Andean Pact's Decision 24 called for phased divestment in many sectors. Restrictive legislation was passed in a number of important countries, including Mexico (1971), India (1973), Indonesia (1974), and Nigeria (1977). (See Kobrin, 1984).

The ownership restrictions were applied first to the extractive sectors and, by the mid-1970s, traditional foreign-owned equity concessions were replaced by either joint ventures or contractual arrangements in many natural-resource ventures. In petroleum, the change was revolutionary. Virtually every important oil-producing country expropriated at least some of its industry by 1976 (Kobrin, 1985).

After the wave of extractive nationalizations, equity ownership—especially wholly owned subsidiaries—appeared to be a very tenuous vehicle for international business involvement in developing countries. Some observers assumed that it was only a matter of time until manufacturing investment would be affected significantly. For example, Contractor (1984) argued that there has been significant growth in joint ventures due to the erosion of multinational corporation (MNC) bargaining power and changed attitudes of American managers.

The data from the present analysis do not support a conclusion that there has been a move away from wholly owned subsidiaries by U.S. manufacturing multinationals in the developing countries. The vast majority of the subsidiaries (62 percent) of the firms surveyed are still wholly owned (90 percent or more); 15 percent are majority joint ventures; 5 percent, equal shares; and 18 percent, minority joint ventures.

While differences in samples render intertemporal analyses problematic, some rough comparisons can be made. Stopford and Wells (1972) use the Harvard data base and report the 1966 distribution of ownership of manufacturing subsidiaries in developing countries (less Ceylon, India, Pakistan, and Mexico, which restrict ownership). They found 61 percent wholly owned, 16 percent majority, and 23 percent minority ownership. Removing the four countries from my data, the comparable figures are: 66 percent, 15 percent, and 19 percent, respectively.

Two differences in the populations (previously noted) should result in a lower mean level of ownership in the Harvard data. First, they include manufacturing affiliates of extractive firms, which even in the midsixties faced more pressure to share ownership than firms in the manufacturing sector.[3] Second, subsidiaries with 5–19 percent foreign ownership are included in the Harvard study, but not in mine.

A more comprehensive comparison with the 1975 Harvard data (Curhan, Davidson, and Suri, 1977) for all developing countries is presented in table 8–1. As can be seen, 55 percent of the Harvard firms were wholly owned in 1975 as compared to 62 percent in my data in 1985. The relative differences in distribution across majority, co-owned, and minority ventures are comparatively minor.

Table 8–1
Ownership by Region
(percentage of subsidiaries)

	Minority	50:50	Majority	Wholly Owned	Total
1985 data					
Latin America	19.0	3.1	8.2	69.7	100.0
Northern Africa	30.8	11.5	38.5	19.2	100.0
Africa	18.2	4.6	27.3	50.0	100.0
Asia	15.2	8.5	22.6	53.7	100.0
Total	18.4	5.1	14.5	62.0	100.0
1975 Harvard data					
Latin America	16.6	7.7	16.0	59.6	100.0
Northern Africa	37.9	11.6	22.1	28.4	100.0
Africa	17.6	3.3	24.2	54.9	100.0
Asia	20.9	10.4	20.9	47.8	100.0
Total	18.7	8.3	17.8	55.3	100.0

The interregional differences are of interest and are statistically significant. Seventy percent of the subsidiaries in Latin America were wholly owned in 1985, as compared with only 54 percent in Asia, 50 percent in Africa, and 19 percent in the Mideast. (The absolute numbers of subsidiaries in the last two regions are small.) The interregional distribution of ownership revealed in the 1975 Harvard data is comparable, increasing confidence in the validity of at least gross cross-temporal comparisons. The reasons for the regional differences are complex and include differences in host-country preferences (as will be discussed), the industry distribution across regions, and the average age of subsidiaries.

Nominally, the percentage of wholly owned subsidiaries in 1985 is marginally higher than that reported by comparable respondents in 1966 and 1975. Taking the differences that bias the Harvard data downward into account, it appears prudent to conclude that there has not been a significant increase in the proportion of joint ventures in manufacturing subsidiaries of U.S. manufacturing firms in the developing countries in the past two decades.[4]

The revolution in ownership that took place in the extractive sectors in the 1970s does not appear to have spread to manufacturing. As Oman notes, "compared to the extractive industries, it [the fragmentary evidence] suggests that the traditional form of FDI [foreign direct investment] is by no means becoming obsolete or being systematically superseded by the new forms" (1984, p. 47).[5]

Gomes-Casseres's (1985) data is consistent with these findings. He finds cycles in joint venture formation, with the yearly share of joint ventures as a proportion of new subsidiaries rising through the early 1960s, then declining sharply over that decade, and then rising modestly from 1969 to 1975 (the last year the Harvard data is available) to a peak lower than that of 1961. An observer taking a cross section in 1975 would find that the proportion of joint ventures among subsidiaries entering in the mid-1970s was roughly similar to that for entries in the early 1960s. It appears that these conclusions hold for developing as well as developed countries (1985, p. 422).

It should be noted that focusing on stocks may well understate trends. While there have been a number of attempts to develop data on joint ventures over the past decade, they do not include data on all subsidiaries abroad. Hladik (1985), for example, gathered data on manufacturing joint ventures from 1974 to 1982 from public sources. While she found an increase in joint venture formation over that period, in both the high- and middle–low-income countries, it is impossible to calculate whether there has been an increase in the proportion of joint ventures (relative to all new entries) without more comprehensive data. A comparison of the 1975 and 1985 cross sections does not suggest a visible increase in the proportion of manufacturing subsidiaries that are joint ventures.

There are a number of possible explanations for the difference in ownership patterns in the extractive and manufacturing sectors. As I argue elsewhere (Kobrin, 1980, 1985), although host-country ownership is of the essence in the extractive sectors, it is often only a means to other ends in manufacturing. In a developing country, where oil or mining dominates both the domestic economy and trade, national political and economic control may well be inconsistent with foreign ownership. As the events of the 1970s demonstrate, petroleum producers believe that stategic control over natural resources requires dominant ownership. (See Kobrin, 1986.)

In manufacturing, ownership is often a means to an end: technology transfer, development of local managerial skills, increasing local content, or illuminating transfer-pricing practices. As local administrative, managerial, and technical skills have improved, Third World countries have developed the capability to substitute behavioral control through regulation for direct control through ownership. The ends can be achieved through more efficient means (Kobrin, 1985).

As a result, host countries may accept 100 percent foreign ownership in exchange for meeting other performance requirements. In two recent cases in Mexico, for example, Ford and IBM were allowed exceptions to the Mexican law limiting foreign ownership to 49 percent in exchange for technology transfer, increased investment, and an increased commitment to exports (*Business Week,* January 1984; *New York Times,* July 25, 1985). In these cases, a modicum of state control was achieved without national ownership.

The continued dominance of wholly owned subsidiaries may also reflect the deteriorating economic conditions in many developing countries in the early 1980s. Balance of payments problems (especially external debt) increase the desirability of inflows of foreign direct investment and constrains a host country's freedom of action as international organizations and commercial banks tend not to look fondly on ownership restrictions and other performance requirements. Furthermore, widespread economic problems may have led to disenchantment with state ownership and some shift to market solutions as manifest in the privatizations taking place in both developed and developing countries.

Developments in the manufacturing industries—particularly increased technological intensity and global integration—have also had an important impact on ownership patterns. Both the case study and quantitative literature on bargaining power conclude that there is no evidence of the systematic shift in bargaining power from MNCs to host countries observed in the extractive industries in the manufacturing sector (Gereffi and Newfarmer, 1985; Kobrin, 1986). Trends in technology and integration have strengthened the desire for unambiguous control in many industries. I now turn to an analysis of interindustry differences in ownership preferences and of the implications for trends in ownership patterns.

Interindustry Differences

Parent firms and subsidiaries are divided into thirteen industrial sectors based on "Forbes Annual Report on American Industry" (1986). Table 8–2 reports ownership patterns by subsidiary industry. Instruments, electronics, and computers are virtually wholly owned, as less than 15 percent of subsidiaries are joint ventures in each case. At the other end of the scale, over 72 percent of subsidiaries in the paper products industry are joint ventures. Drugs and pharmaceuticals (78 percent wholly owned), processed foods (72 percent), and construction materials (71 percent) are all well above the average (62 percent wholly owned), while apparel (50 percent), automobiles (51 percent), and chemicals (53 percent) are well below.

Table 8–2
Ownership by Subsidiary Industry
(percentage of subsidiaries)

Sector	Minority	50:50	Majority	Wholly Owned	Total
Apparel	16.7	16.7	16.7	50.0	100.0
Auto	33.3	2.2	13.3	51.1	100.0
Chemicals	18.2	7.8	20.8	53.3	100.0
Computer	14.3	0.0	0.0	85.7	100.0
Construction materials	0.0	14.3	14.3	71.4	100.0
Drugs and pharmaceuticals	3.5	0.0	19.0	77.6	100.0
Electronics	11.1	2.8	0.0	86.1	100.0
Electrical equipment	14.3	7.1	14.3	64.3	100.0
Food	11.8	1.8	14.6	71.8	100.0
Household products	11.3	9.7	12.9	66.3	100.0
Industrial machinery	29.4	0.0	5.9	64.7	100.0
Instruments	11.1	0.0	0.0	88.9	100.0
Paper products	37.9	13.8	20.7	27.6	100.0
Total	18.4	5.1	14.5	62.0	100.0

Chi-square	98.45
Degrees of Freedom	39
Probability	000.00

The data for the automobile industry is misleading, as the sector is heterogeneously comprised of parts producers, assembly plants, and large-scale automotive production ventures. If the nine subsidiaries that produce automobiles in relatively large markets (1982 GDP of at least $40 billion) are considered separately, different conclusions are drawn. Eight are wholly owned, the sole exception being a subsidiary in South Korea. (Franko, 1985, comes to similar conclusions, arguing that virtually all of the subsidiaries engaged in full-scale automobile manufacturing are wholly owned. He specifically mentions the Korean venture as an exception.

Although joint ventures are almost equally divided between majority (52 percent) and minority (48 percent) ownership for the sample as a whole, there are some interesting interindustry differences. Sixty-eight percent of automotive joint ventures are minority shares as are 83 percent of those in industrial machinery. On the other hand, 85 percent of pharmaceutical ventures, 67 percent of those in household products, 61 percent in chemicals, and 60 percent in electrical equipment are majority-owned. While I shall return to the subject, it is interesting to note that the two industries that exhibit a marked preference for minority holdings are characterized by the absence of assets that generate a return to unambiguous control. (Recall that the automotive subsidiaries where ownership is shared are parts suppliers, component plants, and small assembly operations.)

The Propensity for Joint Ventures

While strategic and transaction-cost approaches to explanation are quite different theoretically, they generally converge when it comes to the factors explaining preference for sole ownership. Stopford and Wells (1972) found that four strategies are associated with a strong preference for wholly owned subsidiaries: use of marketing techniques to differentiate products, rationalization of production, control of raw materials, and innovation in the development of new products. While the third is less applicable to the manufacturing sector, marketing intensity, technological intensity, and global integration have formed the core of virtually all explanations for variation in ownership preferences ever since.

Theories of the MNC or foreign direct investment taking an internalization approach (Buckley and Casson, 1976; Dunning, 1980; Teece, 1981; Rugman, 1981) argue that foreign investors possess certain advantages or firm-specific assets (technology or capital) which market imperfections allow the firm to contain and make proprietary. The combination of firm-specific advantages and market imperfections results in a MNC preference for ordering economic transactions through its own internal administrative hierarchies (vertical or horizontal integration) rather than the external market (Teece, 1981) and provides it the economic power to do so. Thus, as assets such as proprietary technology and the ability to market differentiated products are more efficiently exploited through unambiguous control, there will be a preference for sole ownership.

As global integration of production increases the probabilities that the objectives of the MNC and a local partner will conflict (Doz and Prahalad, 1984; Porter, 1986), it makes joint ventures more costly and increases the returns to unambiguous control. Thus, the greater the extent of the global integration of production, the lower should be the propensity to create joint ventures.

Previous empirical tests have confirmed the relationship between a preference for unambiguous control and technological and advertising intensity and global integration. Fagre and Wells (1982) and Lecraw (1984) found that indicators of all three explanations correlated significantly and positively with increased MNC ownership.

The results of this analysis provide additional confirmation of the relationship between these factors and preferences for unambiguous control. As there are only thirteen industry groups, statistical analysis is not appropriate. However, the implications of the cross tabulations presented in table 8–3 are quite clear. Each cross tab compares industry ownership (dichotomized as numbers of firms above and below the sample mean) and a single explanatory variable.

High levels of technological intensity and advertising expenditures are clearly associated with a preference for wholly owned subsidiaries. In each case, the cell where a low proportion of wholly owned subsidiaries and a high score on the relevant explanatory variable intersect is empty. All four industries that are R&D-intensive are more than 62 percent wholly owned. The same holds true for the three industries (household products, processed foods, and pharmaceuticals) that are advertising-intensive.[6]

Global integration is measured by an unweighted average of the percentage of parent exports sold to affiliates and the percentage of affiliate sales to other affiliates (Bureau of Economic Analysis, 1985). Four of the five industries that are highly integrated (computers, electronics, instruments, and pharmaceuticals) tend

Table 8–3
Cross Tabulations
(number of industries)

Variable	< 62% Wholly Owned	> 62% Wholly Owned
R&D		
Low	4	5
High	0	4
Advertising		
Low	4	6
High	0	3
Global integration		
Low	3	5
High	1	4

to be wholly owned. The exception is automobiles, which is relatively integrated globally, but below average in terms of the propensity for sole ownership. As I have noted, however, the industry is heterogeneous and, if one considers only large-scale automotive production, sole ownership is the rule.

This analysis of joint venture preferences is obviously limited and partial. Aggregating at the industry level requires focusing on costs of joint ventures and ignoring the potential benefits. The analysis is static, using ownership as of 1985 without adjusting for the date of entry of the subsidiary. Last, cross-country differences are ignored.

That being said, the results confirm theory and are in accord with other empirical studies. What is of most interest is how little has changed since the Stopford and Wells study, which was based on 1966 data. Despite the marked changes in the strategy and structure of multinational firms—primarily the evolution of global competition—and the social, economic, and political transformation that has taken place in the Third World, the factors shaping ownership preferences of U.S. manufacturing firms appear to be relatively constant. The rate and nature of change in those factors have significant impacts on trends in ownership. I return to this topic after a discussion of intraindustry variation and host-country preferences.

Intraindustry Differences

Aggregation at the industry level obscures considerable firm-by-firm variation in the propensity for joint ventures in developing countries. Although differences in the number of subsidiaries per firm and the distribution across countries make comparison difficult, there is considerable variation in the proportion of joint ventures within some industries.

In general, there is much less intraindustry variation at the ends of the spectrum than in the middle. While it is admittedly arbitrary, I analyze intraindustry variation in ownership propensity in terms of the proportion of firms in an industry whose percentage of wholly owned subsidiaries is more than twenty percentage points above or below the industry mean. In three industries where wholly owned subsidiaries dominate—computers, instruments, and pharmaceuticals—few firms are outside the range noted (25 percent, 20 percent, and 0 percent, respectively). While 88 percent of electronics subsidiaries are wholly owned, three firms have no joint ventures and three very small firms share ownership in half to one third of their subsidiaries.

At the other end of the spectrum, paper products, automobiles, and chemicals—which are all well below the sample mean—report relatively few firms outside of the range (33 percent, 18 percent, and 29 percent, respectively). There is considerable variation in industries nearer the grand mean: food products (50 percent of the firms out of the range), household products (40 percent), industrial machinery (40 percent), and electrical equipment (66 percent).

Thus, in industries where joint ventures are relatively rare, where unambiguous control over an asset is very desirable, firm-by-firm variation in ownership patterns is quite limited. The same holds in industries where joint ventures are more prevalent, where one presumes the returns to unambiguous control are low. In the middle ground, where returns to unambiguous control over assets are in a state of flux and probably declining, there is much more intraindustry variation in ownership propensity.

While to some extent this reflects differences in geographic distribution and, thus, country preferences and bargaining power (see Kobrin, 1986), it also reflects differences in strategy and managerial preferences. The differences in strategy may result from variation in underlying factors that affect preferences such as technological intensity or global integration. However, they also reflect differences in managerial preferences resulting from firm history and individual experience and background. This would appear to be a fertile ground for further research.

Host-Country Policies

Although this analysis has focused on the relationship between MNC characteristics and ownership preferences, it is clear that host-country preferences and policies are important determinants of the propensity for joint ventures. In the 1982 *Benchmark Survey,* U.S. Foreign Investors report that local ownership regulations exist in a majority of developing countries (Bureau of Economic Analysis, 1985, p. 139). Beamish (1985) found that government pressure was the dominant reason for entering a joint venture in developing countries (57 percent of respondents). Reviewing performance requirements, a recent United Nations Centre on Transnational Corporations report (1985) concluded that increased local ownership continued to be a major objective in developing countries.

The U.N. Centre on Transnational Corporations (UNCTC) divides developing countries into three groups with respect to ownership policies: no restrictions, restrictions applied only at entry (including phased divestment policies), and those that attempt to force at least partial divestment of existing foreign subsidiaries (UNCTC, 1985, p. 45). Table 8–4 contains a cross tabulation of ownership and host-country policy, using the country-subsidiary as the unit of analysis ($n = 565$).

As can be seen, there are significant differences between the "all investment" category and the other two. In the seven countries attempting to restructure existing investment (India, Indonesia, Malaysia, Pakistan, Ghana, Kenya, and Nigeria), only one-third of the subsidiaries are wholly owned and one-quarter are minority joint ventures. While the difference between the first two categories is less marked (71 percent wholly owned in countries without restrictions compared to 64 percent in those requiring local ownership at entry), there are interesting differences in the frequency of minority joint ventures. Only 11 percent of the subsidiaries in countries without restrictions are minority joint ventures, as comapred with 28 percent

Table 8–4
Ownership by Host-country Policy
(percentage of subsidiaries)

Host-country	Minority	50:50	Majority	Wholly Owned
None	6.9	4.4	18.1	70.6
New investment	22.4	5.2	8.2	64.2
All investment	25.3	6.7	34.7	33.3
Total	18.4	5.1	14.5	62.0

Chi-square	60.611
Degrees of Freedom	6
Probability	000.0

in countries applying restrictions at entry. (It should be obvious that cross-sectional analysis underestimates the effectiveness of policy in the second category as the date of entry is ignored.)

Analysis of the 160 subsidiaries in the unrestricted countries is also of interest. While this group is certainly not a representative cross section—it does not include Brazil, Mexico, Venezuela, or the larger Asian markets—it does provide a vehicle for analysis of ownership preferences in the absence of host-country pressure. Seven industries have ten or more subsidiaries in this group of countries. While the mean proportion of wholly owned subsidiaries is higher than in the sample at large (71 percent versus 62 percent), the distribution by industry is generally unchanged from the results in all countries. Electronics, pharmaceuticals, household products, and processed foods report a proportion of wholly owned subsidiaries well above the mean, while automobiles, chemicals, and paper products are below the average.

The paper industry and chemicals are of particular interest. Only 29 percent of paper subsidiaries are wholly owned in cases where no restrictions apply, compared to 28 percent for all countries. Figures total 58 percent versus 53 percent for chemicals. This suggests that it is the underlying substantive factors rather than regulation that are most important in determining the propensity for joint ventures. While ownership restrictions—particularly when applied to all existing investment—are effective, and surveys indicate that government pressure is an important motivation for shared ownership in developing countries, firms do not automatically revert to wholly owned subsidiaries where the choice is theirs. The decision appears to be a function of the costs of a joint venture, which have been discussed in this chapter, and the benefits, which have not.

Conclusion

What can be said about the future? Will U.S. manufacturing multinationals make increased use of joint ventures and other "new forms" of investment or will they retain their current preference for sole ownership? The question is complex and depends on trends in host countries as well as MNCs; only a partial answer can be attempted here.

If ownership preferences are a function of assets that make unambiguous control through internalization more efficient, changes in preferences could take place as a result of (1) a change in the nature of the asset (such as maturation of technology) or (2) changes in the environment that lower the costs of market (or quasi-market) transactions. I will focus only on the former.

Technology, marketing, and global integration are at the core of most explanations of ownership preferences. Changes in any of these factors that reduce the returns to unambiguous control should reduce the propensity to prefer wholly owned subsidiaries; to the extent that technology matures, for example, one would expect preferences for sole ownership to decline.

While the evidence is fragmentary and anecdotal, it does not lead one to expect an increase in shared ownership. On the contrary, the technological intensity and degree of global integration of many industries appear to be increasing, which should result in continued, or even increased, pressure for sole ownership.

Dunning and Pearce (1985) provide a comparison of R&D expenditures as a percentage of sales for large MNCs in seventeen industries for 1977 and 1982. All but one of the industries show an increase, with the average being 22 percent. While it is possible that technological developments can actually reduce the MNC's leverage (See Grieco, 1982), in the main, increasing technological intensity should result in a continued preference for wholly owned subsidiaries.

The evidence for global integration is more anecdotal, but I suspect that most observers would agree that many important industries have become even more integrated over the past decade. As I have noted, integration results in a conflict between the global objectives of a MNC and the local objectives of the host-country partner (public or private) that results in costly friction. Integrated MNCs prefer unambiguous control and should have the bargaining power to maintain it.

The trends, or lack of them, in ownership preferences can be partially explained by increases in the intensity of technology and degree of global integration. Furthermore, there is no reason to expect that there will be marked changes in ownership preferences on the part of U.S. manufacturing MNCs in the foreseeable future. While changes at the level of managerial preference are certainly possible—MNCs could well trade ownership for other advantages or accept other means for maintaining control—there is no basis for forecasting systematic change.

Notes

1. A previous paper used ownership to test the applicability of the bargaining hypothesis to the manufacturing sector in developing countries at the country-subsidiary level of analysis. See Kobrin (1986).

2. Relatively few large firms account for most of sales and assets. For example, in 1975, 180 U.S. manufacturing multinationals accounted for 71 percent of sales of U.S. direct investors abroad (Curhan, Davidson, and Suri, 1977).

3. Worldwide, they report 70 percent of nonextractive subsidiaries are wholly owned, compared with 44 percent of manufacturing subsidiaries of petroleum firms and 35 percent of those of mining firms. See Stopford and Wells (1972, p. 134).

4. That does not mean that the overall percentage of joint ventures has not increased. Given that European and Japanese investors have a greater propensity to share ownership and that their relative share of direct investment has increased over time, one would expect—ceteris paribus—the proportion of joint ventures to have increased.

5. Oman (1984) defines traditional FDI as including both wholly owned and majority joint ventures and new forms as minority joint ventures and nonequity or contractual arrangements.

6. R&D expenditures as a percentage of sales are taken from Bureau of Economic Analysis (1985). Advertising expenditures as a percentage of sales are from Bureau of Economic Analysis (1984).

References

Beamish, P. 1985. "The Characteristics of Joint Ventures in Developed and Developing Countries." *Columbia Journal of World Business* (Fall): 13–20.

Buckley, P., and Casson, M. 1976. *The Future of the Multinational Enterprise.* New York: Holmes and Meier.

Bureau of Economic Analysis. 1984. *The Determinants of the Input-Output Structure of the U.S. Economy, 1977.* Washington, D.C.: U.S. Department of Commerce.

Bureau of Economic Analysis. 1985. *U.S. Direct Investment Abroad: 1982 Benchmark Survey.* Washington, D.C.: U.S. Department of Commerce.

Business Week. 1984. "Ford's Better Idea South of the Border." (January): 43.

Conference Board. 1983. *The Key Company Directory.* New York.

Contractor, F. 1984. "Strategies for Structuring Joint Ventures: A Negotiations Planning Paradigm." *Columbia Journal of World Business* (Summer): 30–39.

Curhan, J., Davidson, W., and Suri, R. 1977. *Tracing the Multinationals: A Source Book on U.S. Based Enterprise.* Cambridge, Mass.: Ballinger.

Doz, Y.L., and Prahalad, C. 1984. "Patterns of Strategic Control within Multinational Corporations." *Journal of International Business Studies* (Fall): 55–72.

Dunning, J. 1980. "Explaining Changing Patterns of International Production: In Support of the Eclectic Theory." *Oxford Bulletin of Economics and Statistics,* 41 (November): 269–95.

Dunning, J., and Pearce, R. 1985. *The World's Largest Industrial Enterprises: 1962–1983.* New York: St. Martin's.

Fagre, N., and Wells, L., Jr. 1982. "Bargaining Power of Multinationals and Host Governments." *Journal of International Business Studies* (Fall): 9–24.

Forbes. 1986. "Forbes Annual Report on American Industry." (January 13): 4.

Franko, L. 1985. *New Forms of Investment in the Developing Countries: Practices of U.S. Companies in the Automobile, Auto Parts, Food Processing, Pharmaceutical, and Computer Industries.* Unpublished manuscript.

Gereffi, G., and Newfarmer, R. 1985. "International Oligopoly and Uneven Development: Some Lessons From Industrial Case Studies." In R. Newfarmer (ed.), *Profits, Progress, and Poverty.* Notre Dame: University of Notre Dame Press, 385–436.

Gomes-Casseres, B. 1985. *Multinational Ownership Strategies.* B.D.A. thesis, Harvard Business School.

Grieco, J. 1982. "Between Dependency and Autonomy: India's Experience with the International Computer Industry." *International Organization,* 36 (Summer): 609–32.

Hennart, J.F. 1986. *A Transaction Costs Theory of Equity Joint Ventures.* Unpublished manuscript.

Hladik, K. 1985. *International Joint Ventures: An Economic Analysis of U.S. Foreign Business Partnerships.* Lexington, Mass.: Lexington Books.

International Directory of Corporate Affiliations: Who Owns Whom? 1984/85. National Register Publishing Company.

Kobrin, S. 1980. "Forced Divestment of Foreign Firms in Developing Countries." *International Organization,* 34: 65–88.

Kobrin, S. 1984. "Expropriation as an Attempt to Control Foreign Firms in LDCs: Trends from 1960–1979." *International Studies Quarterly,* 28: 329–48.

Kobrin, S. 1985. "Diffusion as an Explanation of Oil Nationalization." *Journal of Conflict Resolution,* 29: 3–32.

Kobrin, S. 1986. *Testing the Bargaining Hypothesis in the Manufacturing Sector in Developing Countries.* Unpublished manuscript.

Kogut, B. 1986. *Joint Ventures: A Review and Preliminary Investigation.* Unpublished manuscript.

Lecraw, D.J. 1984. "Bargaining Power, Ownership, and Profitability of Transnational Corporations in Developing Countries." *Journal of International Business Studies* (Spring/Summer): 27–43.

Moody's Industrial Manual. 1984. New York: Moody's Investors Services.

New York Times. 1985. "IBM Concessions to Mexico." July 25.

Oman, C. 1984. *New Forms of International Investment in Developing Countries.* Paris: Organization for Economic Cooperation and Development.

Porter, M. 1986. "Competition in Global Industries: A Conceptual Framework." In M. Porter (ed.), *Competition in Global Industries.* Boston: Harvard Business School Press.

Rugman, A. 1981. *Inside the Multinationals.* New York: Columbia University Press.

Stopford, J., Dunning, J., and Haberlich, K. 1980. *World Directory of Multinational Enterprises,* vols. 1 and 2. New York: Facts on File.

Stopford, J., and Wells, L., Jr. 1972. *Managing the Multinational Enterprise: Organization of the Firm and Ownership of Subsidiaries.* New York: Basic Books.

Teece, D. 1981. "The Multinational Enterprise: Market Failure and Market Power Considerations." *Sloan Management Review* (Spring): 3–17.

United Nations Centre on Transnational Corporations. 1985. *Transnational Corporations in World Development: Third Survey.* London: Graham and Trotman.

Part III
Structure and Performance of Cooperative Ventures

9

Entrepreneurship over the Product Life Cycle: Joint Venture Strategies in the Netherlands

Sanford V. Berg
Jacob M. Hoekman

J oint ventures can be an important component of corporate strategy over the product life cycle. They can be used as a vehicle for taking innovative steps in market niches, for responding to changes in broader economic circumstances, and for reallocating resources out of declining markets. Joint venture activity by the two hundred largest Dutch manufacturing, transport, and trade companies illustrates how firms respond to rapidly changing economic environments over the product cycle. The pattern of joint venture (JV) activity provides support for viewing JVs as entrepreneurial from the parents' perspective. In short, entrepreneurship breaks through repetitive processes, allowing more rapid adjustment to changing technological and commercial opportunities.

Because of the diverse roles played by cooperative ventures, no single theory can explain the phenomenon. However, certain commonalities tend to be present. First, each parent can be viewed as bringing particular contributions to the new entity. Second, the decision to create a joint venture, rather than utilize an alternative organizational form (such as merger or license arrangement), represents a project-specific linking of firm-specific components. For example, one parent may bring a strong technological component, while the other contributes distribution channels. This combining of strengths leads to potential disputes over the initial valuation of contributions and the sharing of the profits. Valuations that are project-specific (and dependent upon continuing links with parents) are highly problematic. To avoid initial misrepresentation by either parent and to insure incentives for continued support, joint ownership provides a splitting of the returns.

The first half of this chapter presents a model that emphasizes situation-specific aspects of JVs. The approach is useful in characterizing the entrepreneurial motivations underlying cooperative activity. The second half describes patterns of JV activity in the Netherlands. In many cases, technology-intensive cooperative ventures

The support of the Center for International Economics and Business Studies at the University of Florida and the research assistance of Subhasis Das are gratefully acknowledged.

allow the Dutch to keep pace with rapidly changing environments. Yet, stable industries, such as cement and steel, can also gain from JV activity. No single explanation of JV patterns emerges from this discussion—although the reduction of transactions costs may be one reason for industry-specific use of this organizational form.

Joint Contributions and the Division of Returns

Economics has often borrowed from biology, comparing competition to a natural selection process, describing diffusion of production technologies in terms of imitation, and relating innovation to hybridization. Such metaphors can provide fresh insights into the function of joint ventures in the marketplace. The concept of market niche is particularly appropriate, drawing as it does from ecology. A niche is the specific role that a certain kind of animal or plant fills in the ecosystem, preserving the balance of the system. Similarly, a JV, like any new entrant, moves the system toward equilibrium or balance.

Like the case of an ecosystem, external shocks and random variations can disturb an industry equilibrium. Firms continually search for ways to obtain profit and avoid losses; changes in the marketplace force firms to adjust their product and production strategies. For example, demand growth or technological opportunities present firms with choices regarding the best organizational form for rapid response.

Two firms can pool their corporation-specific resources in response to market opportunities via mergers, licensing arrangements, sell-offs, or JVs. If a joint venture organizational form is chosen, the cooperating units are not likely to have a tranquil process wherein contributions are identified and the proceeds are shared. (See chapter 20 in this book.) Similarly, their ecological counterparts sometimes experience disruptions when temporary niches arise. To better understand the role of joint ventures in a corporte environment, we propose a conceptual framework for analyzing the contributions to and returns from a joint venture.

The Product Cycle and Joint Ventures

The niche concept seems to fit best in the product cycle theory of industrial organization. This theory suggests that a product basically moves through four stages: introduction, expansion, maturity, and decline. By definition, the introduction stage is dominated by an innovating monopolist. In the expansion stage, sales take off, but the product is still in the process of maturing technically. The maturity stage is reached once the product has a reasonably secure market and stable technology. The decline stage (which can be held off for a long time) is usually announced by the rise of a superior product or less expensive substitute.

Despite large organizations being characterized by inflexibility, they are continually seeking to acquire footholds in markets by introducing new products. Expansion requires the scaling up of production runs and investments in new capacity.

During the maturity phase, vertical integration may prove to be a viable strategy—taking advantage of stable production processes and steady sales. In the decline phase, the product line may be dropped or sold off to a less growth-oriented firm. Throughout the process, joint ventures represent vehicles for combining resources with other firms, thus shortening the time needed to adapt to the onset of the next phase.

Historical evidence suggests a speeding up of the product cycle. Technology-intensive industries, such as consumer electronics, offer rewards to those enterprises that can create the new product, fill the new niche most rapidly, and handle the later phases with appropriate policies. Organized entrepreneurship, which is meant to duplicate the functions of a pioneering company, can take place with the assistance of wholly owned subsidiaries or joint ventures. Some JVs may prosper in a strongly turbulent environment, where an individual firm approaches the limits of its current capabilities. As an organizational form, the JV covers a wide range of functions and can operate in the unstable peripheral areas of the big corporation. Thus, the JV is uniquely suited to combine the strengths of separate entities.

A distinction can be made among four main strategies: penetration, expansion, consolidation, and pullback. A penetration strategy refers to the creation of a new market or an attempt to establish a significant position in a nonfamiliar, already existing market (diversification). Expansion efforts are made to maintain positions in rapidly growing markets, whereas a consolidation strategy is generally designed to protect profitability and market share when the product has become mature. Finally, a pullback strategy focuses on the withdrawal from declining markets or the withdrawal from markets where the competitive position of the corporation is too weak to survive. We will consider the role of the JV with respect to these strategies.

JVs are well suited for penetration and timely expansion. The main characteristic of penetration strategies is that they create competition as firms move into a relatively unexplored market. A second penetration strategy involves launching a substitute product in an unfamiliar market. It is easy to see the usefulness of a JV for an existing corporation that sells different products from its partners but has distribution networks in that region of the national or international market. Expansion strategies also characterize much JV activity, as the new entity is used to extend the parents' spheres of corporate influence.

Consolidation and pullback can also be facilitated by JVs. In the consolidation strategy, JVs are used to achieve vertical and horizontal intergration. Vertical integration through a JV may serve several purposes besides cost reduction. JVs could be used to set up entry barriers by integrating backward with a raw-materials producer. Alternatively, JVs could reduce competition among existing market participants by dividing up markets and equalizing cost structures, thus limiting competitive price cuts. However, horizontal integration could also increase competition by strengthening weaker firms. Cooperative ventures may also serve to prevent destructive competition and to realize economies of scale. JVs become part of a pullback strategy when it is used to reorganize supply in deteriorating markets.

The joint venture format can easily accommodate the peculiarities of the different stages of the growth cycle. Alternative organizational forms are not always suitable. For example, the merger is generally irreversible. Similarly, horizontal cartels or vertical trade agreements can be unstable or forbidden by law. And a wholly owned subsidiary cannot benefit from (temporary) cooperation with another entity. Although the joint venture fills the gaps between the other corporate forms, the form has been characterized as "unavoidable" and a "necessary evil" due to the managerial problems it presents. It is usable in places and at times where other cooperative forms are either not applicable or less efficient.

Some would argue that strategy and the nature of the environment impose the particular interorganizational form. For instance, when a firm wants to diversify by taking over a promising small company that is likely to resist such a move, a joint venture could be undertaken. Cooperation may only be an intermediate step to the attainment of complete takeover or it might be self-limiting in nature—allowing each parent to share in the other's strength.

Timing of Product Introduction

Scherer (1967) developed a useful analytical framework for examining incentives for corporate cooperation. Figure 9–1 depicts the present value of costs and benefits from introducing a product at particular points in time. Here, we explore the date of product introduction, where time is shown on the horizontal axis. V_1 is a project benefit function and is negatively sloped; the curve represents the present value of revenues minus production costs at different points in time. It does not include R&D or other set-up costs associated with the project. The potential date of product introduction is shown on horizontal axis.

1. Earlier introduction allows more periods of product monopoly.
2. Earlier introduction has potential for permanent enhancement of the innovator's market share, sometimes called a "first-mover advantage."

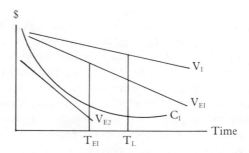

Figure 9–1. Benefits, Costs, and Timing of Product Introduction

3. Delayed introduction increases the probability that a rival will preempt the market, reducing sales for the firm that delays.

The project cost, C_1, falls as the firm delays the introduction date:

1. Costs fall when time compression of development is reduced, since errors are avoided when the process is more sequential.

2. Costs decrease since information from one step may save money in a subsequent one if acquired in time.

3. Costs increase when time is compressed, due to diminishing returns to additional scientists and engineers (given the state of scientific and technical knowledge).

4. Costs increase when time is compressed since parallel (duplicative) approaches may be required to hedge against uncertainty regarding the technical feasibility of alternative solutions.

In figure 9–1, for benefit curve V_1 and cost curve C_1, the optimal time of introduction is T_1, where the slope of the benefit function equals the slope of the cost function (where marginal cost equals marginal revenue). Earlier introduction would reduce the net profitability of the project, as would later introduction.

An increase of market rivalry causes the benefit function to shift downward and take on a steeper slope since the increased likelihood of competitive imitation further diminishes the potential benefits of late introduction. Two possible effects of competition are shown in the figure. An increase in the number of equal-sized rivals can shift the benefit function downward to V_{E1}, but benefits remain above the R&D cost function. In this case, increased rivalry creates a competitive stimulus, which increases the firm's R&D effect and compresses the introduction date to T_{E1}. Expected profits would be lower if the firm delayed introduction until T_1. However, excessive rivalry—including rapid imitation—could shift the benefit function to V_{E2}. Under such circumstances, the project would not be undertaken by the firm.

This analytical framework can be applied to the decision to cooperate on a project (Berg, Duncan, and Friedman, 1982). Differences in risk aversion and opportunity sets lead to situations in which JVs can be mutually advantageous. Consider the response of a large firm when confronted with the prospect of a joint venture. For illustrative purposes, suppose the small firm approaches the large firm with some new R&D-intensive product which is developed beyond the level achieved by the large firm. If a cooperative venture is formed, the benefit curve of the large firm may be the relevant one (reflecting distribution channels or goodwill), while the lower cost of the smaller firm is available to the new ventures. Whether this speeds up or delays introduction depends on the slopes of the benefit and cost curves of the two firms. Introduction of the product may be delayed, especially since the benefit function of the large firm becomes less steep due to the co-option of a potential rival. However, that effect may make the project feasible, as when V_{E2} shifts to V_{E1} in figure 9-1.

For a more complete characterization of a JV, consider figure 9-2. The small firm's innovation cost function over time, C_S, is below the large firm's cost function C_L for completion of comparable projects. Figure 9-2 presents three possible results in the market. Panel (a) presents a figure of a large firm and a small firm in the process of developing similar projects. This graph assumes neither is aware of the other's corporate strategies. (Both firms are unaware of the other's interest in the project, and neither knows the development costs of the other.) For either firm, the project is feasible alone. The slope and position of the V functions reflect corporate perceptions of technological and commercial opportunities. V_L lies above V_S since the large firm is presumed to have stronger distribution channels for the product.

Figure 9-2(b) depicts the reaction of the large firm to the information that the smaller one is a potential rival. V_L' has shifted in, reflecting competitive pressures. If a cooperative venture is formed, assume for now that the original benefit curve of the large one is the relevant one (reflecting marketing strengths), while the lower developmental costs of the smaller firm are available to the new venture. Whether this speeds up or delays introduction of the innovation depends on the slopes of the various curves. In the (b) example, introduction is actually delayed compared with independent projects, but duplication of effort is eliminated, yielding real resource savings.

Figure 9-2(c) illustrates another venture that delays introduction. Here, the large firm would not have even initiated the project since V_L is everywhere below C_L. Thus, dramatic savings in R&D costs are not achieved in this example, although the net benefits to industry from this innovation *have increased*. Note that the assumptions that $C_S = C_{JV}$ and $V_L = V_{JV}$ are very strong, since they imply costless access to each parent's strengths and no synergies. Modifying the assumption does not affect the basic point, however. For example, see Ordover and Willig (1985) for another characterization of the time trade-offs.

A key problem that arises is the sharing the gains of such cooperation. The relevant opportunity cost for each firm is the profits of going it alone. Cooperation is advantageous if the expected stand-alone profit for either of the cooperating firms is less than the share of the expected profits each gets by cooperating. If there were only one allocation that satisfied these constraints, then there would be no room for dispute. However, this situation is seldom, if ever, the case. Consider figure 9-2(b). Once the large firm is aware of the small firm's effort, the net profit from its project is distance YX. The net profit for the small firm going it alone is UV (assuming it was already aware of the large firm's program—and was relatively unaffected by the change from T_L to T_L'). For simplicity, we let $T_S = T_L'$, so each would introduce the product at the same date. The implied net profit from a joint venture would be ZV, which is greater than $YX + UV$.

The key question is how to evaluate the contributions and how to divide the gains for the JV. Should the benefit shares be proportional to stand-alone profits

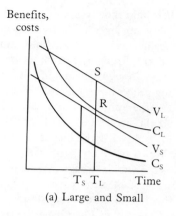

(a) Large and Small

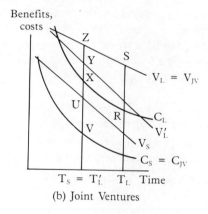

(b) Joint Ventures

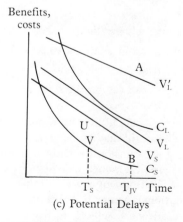

(c) Potential Delays

Figure 9–2. The Timing of Product Introduction with JVs

or to stand-alone costs? Or should they be split down the middle after stand-alone profits are allocated? If the gains are due to diversification, how are they to be allocated? We know from game theory that any allocation in the core is feasible. A further complication is that a firm's perception of its contribution may be different from that of its partner. Also, problems of indivisibilities exist with many inputs in the manufacturing process. For example, if we consider managerial skill of the personnel involved in the joint venture, it is possible that one partner will feel that it has contributed the key executives; hence, it should be compensated for that loss. This position could easily be disputed by the other partner, leading to a stalemate about sharing of profits.

Consider other sources of potential disagreement. What if the large firm doubts whether V_S is feasible and the small firm questions C_L, so the stand-alone profits are called into question? Furthermore, each may doubt the exact value of what the other is contributing (low C_S and high V_L). Given the transactions costs associated with precisely establishing such values, the 50:50 division reflects an economizing decision rule. As Murrell has shown, "share rents can solve transactional problems when fixed rents have high transactions costs and internal organization cannot be used because of monitoring problems" (1983, p. 283). The characteristics of JVs relevant to transactions cost analysis include:

1. Jointly determined inputs. (The value of the JV depends on how each partner continues to support the venture.)
2. Joint outputs. (The JV obtains net revenues and also provides information to each parent regarding further commercial and technological opportunities.)
3. Complex specification of production processes (so contracts are always incomplete).
4. Long payoff periods on investment (where the returns require stable ongoing relationships).
5. Costly monitoring of internal operations (making external supervision difficult).
6. Variability and nonmeasurability of relative contributions (noted previously).
7. Informational asymmetries (noted previously).
8. Project specificity. (Sunk costs can be significant, requiring joint commitments.)

JVs can reduce the organizational failures that would arise under alternative contractual arrangements. There still may be bargaining over the values of the contributions, but ultimately the division depends on both parents benefitting.

To summarize the theoretical model, note how project specificity is central to the gains to cooperation. As more potential partnerships arise, the value of the respective contributions (and options) narrow the bargaining range. The establishment of agreed-upon market values leads to sell-offs or licensing arrangements. However, with transactions costs and associated disagreement regarding contributions and opportunity costs, an entrepreneurial joint venture becomes more likely. Of course, for a JV to work, there has to be basic agreement regarding the fundamental benefits from cooperation.

Empirical Examination of Dutch Domestic JVs

With a conceptual framework now established, we turn to patterns of joint venture activity. Because of the openness of the economy, the Netherlands presents many opportunities for cooperative activities. Here, we consider domestic JVs, many of which involve foreign partners.

Patterns of Domestic JV Activity

Hoekman (1984) identified a sample of 520 Dutch JVs as of 1981. Information was collected on the two hundred largest Dutch manufacturing, transport, and trade companies (based on turnover figures published by *Het Financieele Dagblad*). Detailed data were obtained from the financial press, annual reports, and, in particular, "Dochterondernemingen en deelnemingen in het Nederlandse bedrijfsleven," Deventa 1981. Data used in the analysis include industrial classification, parental links (vertical, horizontal, or diagonal), and national/international orientation. Five basic categories are identified in table 9–1, with hybrids also shown. The child can have parents from several groups. A ∩ B, for example, reflects the population of Dutch JVs in which companies from category *A* and category *B* participate. Note that the Netherlands has roughly 10,000 participations and wholly (or partially) owned subsidiaries. Thus, pure joint ventures correspond to 5 percent of the entire population of subsidiaries and participations.

Table 9–1 indicates that only 4 percent of the Dutch JV population were joint subsidiaries among Dutch companies with a turnover that did not exceed 200 million guilders. On the other hand, the two hundred biggest Dutch corporations, excluding the financial sector, participate in more than 60 percent of the joint ventures. Similar patterns also emerge when analyzing comparable Swedish, U.S., and German data. Although the size of Dutch corporations is related to the number of joint venture participations, there are many more factors other than turnover that influence the number of JV participations by a firm, including the nature of the industry and differences in the strategies adopted by these firms. Given the governance problems associated with multiple parents plus the significant increase in transactions costs when going from two to three parents, 70 percent of the JVs had only two partners. (See table 9–2.)

Industries of Parent Firms

The relationship between the nature of an industry and the number of joint ventures by corporations within this industry can be analyzed from two points of view:

Table 9–1
The Composition of the Dutch Joint Venture Population

Category	Number of Joint Ventures	Percentage of the Population
A	104	20
B	38	7
C	21	4
D	12	2
E	37	7
A ∩ B	42	8
A ∩ C	62	12
A ∩ D	25	5
A ∩ E	53	10
B ∩ E	20	4
C ∩ D	20	4
Rest	86	17
Total	520	100

Source: Hoekman (1984).

A = joint subsidiaries in which only Dutch companies participate. The parents do not operate in the sector of financial services, but have a worldwide turnover of 200 million guilders or more.

B = joint ventures established by Dutch companies operating in the sector of financial services.

C = joint ventures with parents among the other private companies of Dutch origin.

D = joint subsidiaries in which Dutch government institutions participate.

E = joint ventures undertaken by two or more foreign groups in the Dutch market.

Table 9–2
Partners per Dutch Joint Venture

Number of Partners per Joint Venture	Number of Joint Ventures	Percentage of the Population
2	363	70
3	88	17
4	27	5
5	17	3
6	9	2
7	5	1
8	11	2
Total	520	100

Source: Hoekman (1984).

1. The intrinsic characteristics of the respective sector: technological opportunities, capital intensity, product range, and the nature of the production process or

2. Its external position: the stage the respective industry occupies in a manufacturing process and, consequently, its dependence on other segments.

It is interesting to contrast Dutch and German JV activity. Table 9–3 shows the JV participations of 92 of the largest German corporations classified by the primary industry of the parent firm. The exceedingly high number of JV participations in some industries reflects unique features of German industrial structure. However, the same basic patterns arise for the 200 and 100 largest Dutch corporations (shown in tables 9–4 and 9–5, respectively). The tables reveal that joint ventures are mostly undertaken by groups operating in petroleum extraction and processing, primary

Table 9–3
The Ninety-two Biggest German Corporations Grouped According to Their Main Activity

Industry	Number of Corporations	Common Domestic Turnover, 1978 (million deutsche marks)	Number of Joint Venture Participations [a]	Average Number of Joint Ventures per Corporation
Electricity production	2	15,921	92	46.0
Coal extraction	2	5,447	37	18.5
Chemicals	9	64,721	106	11.8
Petroleum refining	9	76,234	232	25.3
Rubber and miscellaneous products	1	1,915	2	2.0
Metal production	8	61,975	435	54.4
Mechanical	3	13,199	76	25.3
Engineering machinery	5	19,506	23	4.6
Motor cars	7	72,013	5	0.7
Electro technical industry	8	62,644	40	5.0
Food	3	12,426	7	2.3
Tobacco	3	11,845	2	0.7
Building/ construction	5	14,435	5	1.0
Wholesaling	11	36,155	45	4.1
Retailing	11	44,269	8	0.7
Transportation	2	7,445	8	4.0
Other services	2	7,683	0	0.0
Unclassifiable	1	2,850	10	10.0
Total	92	530,683	1,133	12.4

Source: Hoekman (1984).
Note: In the top 100 German corporations, there are eight mutual joint ventures. These are, consequently, left out of the table.
[a]This regards only joint ventures established in Germany, among the 92 involved companies.

Table 9-4
The Two Hundred Biggest Dutch Companies Classified According to Their Main Activity

Industry	Number of Corporations	Common Domestic Share in the Production of the Turnover[a]	Percentage of Total Turnover	Number of Joint Venture Participations in the Netherlands[b]	Percentage of Total[c]	Average Number of Joint Ventures per Corporation
Chemicals	20	26,457	13.4	53	10.2	2
Oil extraction/ petroleum refining	7	36,160	16.3	59	11.4	8.4
Metal production	3	5,754	2.9	23	4.4	7.7
Mechanical engineering	11	4,836	2.4	34	6.6	3.1
Shipbuilding	3	2,162	1.1	14	2.7	4.6
Other transportation equipment	4	3,807	1.9	2	0.3	0.5
Electrotechnical industry	9	11,603	5.9	14	2.7	1.5
Food	43	34,147	17.2	42	6.1	1.0
Building and construction	20	11,922	6.0	106	20.4	5.3
Printing and publishing	9	4,311	2.2	10	1.9	1.1
Paper and cardboard	4	3,262	1.6	6	1.2	1.5
Textiles	3	944	0.4	11	2.1	3.7
Lumber and wood products	1	453	0.2	–	0	–
Glass/clay/cement/ asphalt products	4	1,256	0.6	23	4.4	5.7
Retailing	7	15,456	7.8	13	2.5	1.9
Wholesaling	21	22,003	11.1	48	9.2	2.3
Car retailing	15	6,786	3.4	–	0	–
Transportation and storage	9	6,526	3.3	61	11.8	6.8
Tourism	1	248	0.1	–	0	–
Total	200	198,115	100	519	100	2.6

Source: Hoekman (1984).

[a]In millions of guilders (1980).

[b]Contrary to the German figures, this column does not regard only the mutual joint ventures of the companies on the list, but also their other participations in joint subsidiaries established in the Netherlands.

[c]The share of the industry as a percentage of the total number of joint venture participations of the two hundred corporations.

Table 9-5
The One Hundred Biggest Dutch Companies Classified According to Their Main Activity

Industry	Number of Corporations	Common Domestic Turnover, in 1980 (million guilders)	Number of Mutual Joint Venture Participations in the Netherlands		Average Number of Joint Ventures per Corporation	
			a	b	a	b
Chemicals	10	22,496	14	24	1.4	2.4
Oil extraction/ petroleum refining	7	36,180	8	35	1.1	4.4
Metal production	2	5,458	9	15	4.5	7.5
Mechanical engineering	3	2,783	8	12	2.7	4.0
Shipbuilding	1	1,633	4	10	4.0	10.0
Other transportation equipment	4	3,807	–	1	–	0.2
Electrotechnical industry	4	10,436	2	4	0.5	1.0
Food	26	27,712	15	25	0.6	1.0
Building and construction	10	8,701	36	60	3.6	6.0
Printing and publishing	4	3,414	1	3	0.2	0.7
Paper and Cardboard	2	2,720	1	3	0.5	1.5
Textiles	1	463	–	1	0.0	1.0
Glass/clay/cement/ asphalt products	1	450	14	17	14.0	17.0
Retailing	6	11,395[a]	5	9	0.8	1.3
Wholesaling	10	14,433[a]	16	29	1.6	2.9
Car retailing	5	2,820[a]	–	–	0.0	0.0
Transportation and storage	3	4,667	7	16	2.3	5.3
Lumber and wood products	1	453	–	–	0.0	0.0
Total	100	160,021	140	264	1.4	2.6

Source: Hoekman (1984).

Notes: This table is meant to make the Dutch data comparable to the German data presented in table 9-3.

The mutual joint ventures are subdivided into (a) complete mutual joint venture and (b) complete mutual joint ventures taken together with all the joint subsidiaries in which two or more Dutch top one hundred corporations own together the majority of the shares.

[a] As with the German figures, the turnovers of the wholesale and retail sectors are multiplied by 0.75 in order to account for their relatively small added value.

metals and metal production, chemicals, and mechanical engineering. This pattern reappears in French and U.S. data.

The Dutch and German figures differ in the building and construction sector, transportation, and electrotechnical industry. The high joint venture activity in the Dutch building and construction industry is influenced by the presence of several important, worldwide operating groups in the domain of hydraulic engineering. Furthermore, the transport industry in the Netherlands has a strong international position, reflecting the favorable geography of the country, whereas the Dutch electrotechnical industry is a rather modestly developed sector (except for Philips). This fact may account for the small number of Dutch joint ventures in the electrotechnical industry. In both countries, wholesaling has some kind of intermediate position with respect to the number of joint venture participations. It is impossible to say anything about the building material industry, coal extraction, and electricity production, because in one of the countries, the top one hundred firms are not represented in these sectors.

Linkages between parent firms are shown in figure 9–3 for Germany and figure 9–4 for the Netherlands. The figures show that the number of joint venture linkages among the top 88 firms in Germany is 17.5 times greater than those among the top 100 companies in the Netherlands. This situation is due to several reasons. First, the turnover of Germany's top 88 is 3.5 times larger than that of the Dutch top 100. The larger size promotes JV activity. Also, the number of joint ventures with 4 or more partners is 11 times larger in Germany than in the Netherlands. This is significant because a 3-partner joint venture gives only 3 cases of JV participations (interfirm relations), whereas a 10- partner joint venture generates 45 mutual linkages.

Figure 9–3, the German case, shows that the interfirm linkages within the same industry appear mainly in petroleum refining and metal production. Interfirm linkages among industries are also highly developed between metal production on the one side and firms from other industries: electricity production (453), coal extraction (147), petroleum refining (326), mechanical engineering (188), and engine building (265). There are also very strong affinities between the electricity producers and the chemical industry, petroleum refining, and also mechanical engineering. Note that some of these project JVs may be relatively short-lived. The key point is that mutual benefits are expected—reflecting cost savings or revenue enhancements (which could involve larger markets or market power).

The Dutch case, contained in figure 9–4, shows that the most outstanding linkages are those between building and construction and the building materials sector, between transportation and petroleum refining, between metal production and building materials, as well as that between wholesaling and food. Interfirm linkages within industries (horizontal participations) are to be found in petroleum refining, building, and food.

These descriptive statistics lead us to conclude that the closer the sectors are to the final consumer, the greater the tendency to reduce JV activity. When differentiated

No.		1	2	3	4	5	6	7	8	9	10	11	12	13	14	15	Total
1	Electricity production	49	54	91	133	453	88	75	–	7	–	–	–	7	33	3	993
2	Coal extraction	54	5	41	33	147	32	25	–	2	–	–	–	3	18	–	360
3	Chemicals	91	41	39	65	207	67	38	–	5	–	1	–	7	27	–	588
4	Petroleum refining	133	33	65	108	326	60	56	–	7	–	–	–	7	28	–	813
5	Metal production	453	147	207	326	679	188	266	–	32	–	–	5	37	81	3	2,425
6	Mechanical engineering	88	32	67	60	188	15	32	–	6	–	–	2	4	28	2	524
7	Engine building	75	25	38	56	266	32	–	2	13	–	–	–	5	16	–	528
8	Car industry	–	–	–	–	–	–	2	1	–	–	–	–	–	–	–	3
9	Electrotechnical industry	7	2	5	7	32	6	13	–	22	–	–	5	–	1	–	99
10	Paper industry	–	–	–	–	–	–	–	–	–	–	–	–	–	–	–	–
11	Foods	–	–	1	–	–	–	–	–	–	–	1	–	–	–	–	2
12	Building and construction	–	–	–	–	5	2	–	–	5	–	–	2	–	–	–	14
13	Wholesaling	7	3	7	7	37	4	5	–	–	–	–	–	4	2	–	76
14	Retailing	33	18	27	28	81	28	16	–	1	–	–	–	2	2	–	236
15	Transportation	3	–	–	–	3	2	–	–	–	–	–	–	–	–	–	8
	Number of corporations per industry	3	2	11	6	9	8	7	5	8	1	6	4	10	10	2	6,665 87

Note: Twelve corporations out of the German top 100 are left out of account, namely the already mentioned eight mutual joint ventures in the top 100, two corporations that are not specifically operating in a certain industry, and two corporations in the field of other services.

Figure 9–3. Interindustrial Linkages Originating in the Mutual Joint Venture Activities of the Eighty-eight Biggest Corporations in West Germany, 1975

No.		1	2	3	4	5	6	7	8	9	10	11	12	13	14	15	16	Total
1	Building materials	—	—	—	—	13	—	—	—	—	—	—	11	—	—	—	—	24
2	Textiles	—	—	—	—	—	1	—	—	—	—	—	—	—	—	—	—	1
3	Chemicals	—	—	6	4	3	1	—	1	3	—	3	3	—	—	—	—	24
4	Petroleum refining	—	—	4	39	1	4	—	4	1	—	—	—	3	—	24	—	80
5	Metal production	13	—	3	1	—	1	—	—	—	—	—	2	1	—	—	—	21
6	Mechanical engineering	—	1	1	4	1	—	—	4	2	—	—	1	3	—	—	—	17
7	Publishing/printing	—	—	—	—	—	—	—	—	—	1	—	—	—	1	—	—	2
8	Transportation[a]	—	—	1	4	—	4	—	—	2	—	—	—	6	—	2	—	19
9	Electrotechnical	—	—	3	1	—	2	—	2	—	—	—	—	—	—	—	—	8
10	Paper/wood processing	—	—	—	—	—	—	1	—	—	2	—	—	—	—	—	—	3
11	Foods	—	—	3	—	—	—	—	—	—	—	13	—	8	—	—	—	24
12	Building/construction	11	—	3	—	2	1	—	—	—	—	—	40	6	—	3	—	66
13	Wholesaling	—	—	—	3	1	3	—	6	—	—	8	6	3	1	13	—	44
14	Retailing	—	—	—	—	—	—	1	—	—	—	—	—	1	3	—	—	5
15	Transportation and storage	—	—	—	24	—	—	—	2	—	—	—	3	13	—	5	—	47
16	Car retailing	—	—	—	—	—	—	—	—	—	—	—	—	—	—	—	—	0
	Number of corporations per industry	2	1	7	7	2	5	3	5	4	4	22	10	13	5	6	4	385 100

Figure 9–4. Interindustrial Linkages Originating in the Mutual Joint Venture Activities of the One Hundred Biggest Dutch Companies in Terms of Worldwide Turnover

aAll except one are joint ventures of the former shipbuilding group RSV. The car industry has only one joint venture, namely a joint subsidiary between DAF-Trucks and Philips (electrotechnical sector).

products are involved, firms prefer to go it alone. The JV activity that does occur is in the form of backward integration. Also, the horizontal interfirm linkages tend to arise in the relatively mature raw materials processing sectors. Such ventures presumably reflect the consolidation stage of declining industries. For instance, German steel firms, Dutch building and construction firms, and the integrated oil companies are active participants in JV activity.

Corporate Strategy and Industry of the Child

Two characteristics of JVs are important in the context of our model of organized entrepreneurship over the product cycle. First, the analyst must determine the *strategy* of corporations: whether or not the firm focuses on diversification or verticalization. Second, the analyst needs to identify the status of a corporation: whether it is an independent group or a subsidiary of one or more foreign groups. The 175 biggest Dutch corporations, considering the Dutch share in the production of their turnover, were ranked in groups of 25 and analyzed as far as these characteristics are concerned. When determining whether a corporation follows a policy based on diversification or vertical integrating, the corporation in question was required to have 10 percent or more of its turnover in activities not belonging to its core business. The results of the data collection effort are shown in table 9–6, which leads us to conclude that diversifying and vertically integration corporations are very active in JV participations. For example, the largest 25 firms were also the most active joint venturing firms: 48 percent of them had a significant share of turnover outside their core industry. These firms had 89 percent of the JV participations. Of the next 25 firms, only 20 percent were diversifying, but these firms did 75 percent of the JV activity within the group. The table also shows a clear relationship between diversification and turnover. Dutch foreign subsidiaries engaged in relatively little JV activity—perhaps their parents handled interorganizational projects. Other aspects of individual companies other than strategy and status are also important determinants of decisions to undertake JVs. Such factors include organizational structure of companies and their management philosophies. Unfortunately, a more detailed study would be required to uncover such factors at the firm or industry level.

Recognizing problems of differentiating between different types of JVs, we estimate that 39 percent of Dutch JVs were vertical between parent and child, 28 percent horizontal, and the rest diagonal. This result contrasts with comparable U.S. figures where the highest percentage is of horizontal JVs (45 percent) and diagonal JVs accounted for less than 10 percent. However, our analysis includes a broader range of industries, including banking and insurance.

Table 9–7 contains Dutch JV data grouped on the basis of the industry of the child. It shows that the most important domains with a high joint venture activity (eighteen or more) are chemicals, mechanical engineering, food and allied products, building and construction, wholesaling, transport and storage, (real estate)

Table 9-6
Strategy and Status of Dutch Corporations and Their Joint Venture Activity

Groups of 25 Corporations Ranked According to Their Average Turnover	Number of Joint Venture Participations per Group	Diversifying or Verticalizing		(Foreign) Subsidiaries		Rest	
		% of the 25	% of the JV	% of the 25	% of the JV	% of the 25	% of the JV
1st–25	209	48	89	36	5	16	6
2nd–25	105	20	75	32	4	48	21
3rd–25	74	24	73	32	6	44	21
4th–25	51	8	40	52	43[a]	40	17
5th–25	50	16	76	48	6	36	18
6th–25	25	12	64	40	8	48	28
7th–25	6	—	—	44	33	56	66

Source: Hoekman (1984).

Note: Participations of banks, insurance and investment companies or the Dutch government are left aside when defining the status of a corporation.

[a]This determination is based on the industry classification used in Annex I. Contrary to this classification, the transport and transhipment activities are treated as two separate industries. The same goes for pharmacy and the other chemical industries as well as for metal processing and mechanical engineering.

Table 9–7
The Dutch Top Two Hundred Joint Ventures Grouped According to Industry

Industry	Number of Joint Ventures	Percentage of Total
Chemicals	24	7
Petroleum extraction/refining	5	2
Metal production	3	1
Mechanical engineering	23	7
Shipbuilding	1	0.5
Other transportation equipment	1	0.5
Electrotechnical industry	4	1
Food	18	6
Building and construction	22	7
Printing and publishing	10	3
Paper and cardboard	3	1
Textiles	8	2
Building materials	29	9
Wood processing	—	—
Retailing	2	1
Wholesaling	33	10
Car retailing	—	—
Transport and storage	45	14
Tourism	9	3
Extraction (other)	1	0.5
Banking	9	3
Insurance	1	0.5
Other commercial services	21	7
Investments, in particular real estate	41	12
Unknown	6	2
Total	320	100

Source: Hoekman (1984)

investments, and engineering and consulting—more than 80 percent of the 320 examined joint subsidiaries are located in these industries. The Dutch JVs reveal another division: production (36 percent), marketing in the sense of distribution (11 percent), services (34 percent), and real estate investments (12 percent). The joint venture may be an investment activity of the parents or could be a support firm for the parents' activities. Forty percent of the JV participations of the one hundred biggest Dutch companies can be ascribed to the investment category. Table 9–8 shows the relative frequency of the different functions served by Dutch JVs during the period under study.

Evaluation of Domestic JVs

We would need to examine joint ventures at the individual corporation level in order to answer the following questions:

Table 9–8
The Strategy Functions of the Joint Venture Participations of the Dutch Top One Hundred Corporations

Functions	Frequency of Appearance	Percentage of Total
Assuring or creating distribution channels	58	11.3
Product development	9	1.8
Economies of scale through pooling of (financial) resources	57	11.1
Know-how pooling	84	16.4
Acquiring a higher productivity by merging into a joint venture	21	4.1
Rescuing a subsidiary by transforming it into a joint venture[a]	5	1
Aspiring at takeover	2	0.4
Assuring supplies	47	9.2
Market control	14	2.7
Disinvestment	7	1.4
Supporting other firms[b]	6	1.2
Export	21	4.1
Penetrating new markets/industries	113	22
Risk spreading	38	7.4
Market division	3	0.6
Risk sharing	27	5.3
Total	512	100

[a]This is, for instance, the case of Spinnerij Nederland (Spinning-mill Holland), a joint venture of various textile producers and the Dutch government.

[b]An example in this respect is the iron foundry De Globe. Since 1981, this previously independent company has become a joint subsidiary of Estel and LIOF (a local investment company of the Dutch government). They undertook this joint venture in order to prevent bankruptcy of De Globe (*Het Financieele Dagblad*, April 27, 1981).

1. What significance do JV networks acquire in their respective industries?
2. Is there any pattern to be found in the activities promoted by JVs?
3. What is the function of interorganizational linkages?

These issues are left to more detailed industry studies to be conducted by others. However, we note that cement and steel illustrate firm activity in stable industries. The more technology-intensive JVs better fit the time-cost trade-off model introduced in this chapter's section "Timing of Product Introduction." However, the scale-economy/market-power trade-offs warrant being highlighted for both mature and declining industries. For example, the building/cement/concrete industry has one of the few extensive joint venture networks in the Netherlands. The most extensive linkages are between Estel and ENCI: both corporations deliver raw material (blast furnace slag and limestone) for current production. The trigger for joint ventures in this industry is probably to be found in the homogeneity of the product, cement. Since price is the only competitive tool (because of the impossibility of product differentiation), cartellike activities are common in the cement industry. However, JVs and mergers seem to have partially replaced cartels. Other European countries including Germany and France have similar JVs in cement, though there is little evidence of such organizational forms in the U.S. industry. Britain has fewer JVs because cartels are officially allowed in the cement industry there.

Joint ventures in the concrete industry have another source. First is the pressure to integrate forward (into the building industry) or backward (into the cement industry) in order to assure sales and supplies, respectively. Second, economies of scale play a role here since the transport of concrete is relatively expensive. Consequently, the production of concrete is geographically decentralized. However, to make decentralization profitable, the firms have to achieve a sufficient plant size via cooperation.

Looking at the steel industry, it appears that JV activity is widespread in almost all the major industrial countries. However, different factors were responsible for the JV activity in the steel industry of different countries. For instance, in the United States, antitrust policy limits further merger activity—a restriction that might stimulate the undertaking of JVs. France, on the other hand, had created high tariff barriers in order to protect itself from the world market before it joined the EEC in 1958. By means of coordinating practices (via cartels) and the formation of joint subsidiaries (achieving economies of scale), the steel corporations were able to create market conditions that enabled them to preserve their independence. Finally, in West Germany, the four former joint regional steel sales agencies, the Watzstake-Ronbane, were a stimulus to adopt other forms of cooperation. A structurally different national steel industry involves the British Steel Co., which has been nationalized; however, even this company was involved in at least twenty JV subsidiaries, most vertical in nature.

This brief overview of the steel industry allows us to draw several conclusions. First, joint ventures fulfill a significant vertical integration function for firms in the mature steel group. Furthermore, JVs need not be designed to reduce competition: purposes include spreading risk (to insure the access to various iron ore sources), undertaking programs that are too extensive for individual companies to handle (mining, coastal projects), achieving economies of scale (transport), and/or insuring untroubled supply and distribution.

Specific industry studies can give us some valuable insights into the workings of JVs. Often, we observe competition between parent firms, who simultaneously cooperate in terms of specific JVs. Nevertheless, JV networks might reduce competition because:

1. The JV can create common interests if it represents a substantial part of the turnover of the parents. In such a situation, the parents are hostage to each other; they will be compelled to follow lines of conduct that impose at least mutual respect. This implies tacit agreements or market divisions.

2. The JV may also serve as a meeting point for the top executives. The executives take this opportunity to survey the opposition and search for areas of common interest.

Generally speaking, it seems unlikely that joint venture networks are set up in order to restrain competition. For instance, in the case of the European naphtha market (where joint venturing plays an important role), the European Commission had to conclude, starting from an examination of the quantities of traded naphtha and price trends, that there are no restrictive practices between firms or abuses of dominant positions calling for action under Articles 85 and 86 of the EEC Treaty (Seventh Report on Competition Policy, Brussels, 1978, p. 51). Subsequently, the commission announced a further investigation with respect to the way in which the companies that control those joint ventures compete with each other. Similarly, Rockwood (1983) concluded that JVs involved in leasing and exploring oil and gas prospects in offshore Texas, Louisiana, and California have had a positive impact on the level of economic performance. However, there are exceptions. For instance, a joint venture can also serve as a joint sales office and actually act like a cartel or be entered to create a shared monopoly position.

Thus, the appearance of JV networks can be considered endogenous to an industry, with the following factors playing important roles: the extent to which the interests of the involved companies coincide, the opportunities available for entering JVs, and the payoffs from cooperation in earlier JVs.

Conclusion

After noting the "worst-case" industries for the entrepreneurial model, it is very easy to characterize the engineering and chemical JVs as involving the sharing of technological and managerial skills. Berg, Duncan, and Friedman (1982) found the knowledge-acquisition motivation to be strong in the United States. External knowledge acquisition via JVs served as a substitute for internal R&D programs at the individual parent-firm level. The increased technological competition in the parent industries was reflected in higher R&D intensity for those manufacturing industries with relatively more JV activity.

The Dutch data go beyond manufacturing, so a broader set of motivations is likely, including risk reduction. However, innovation includes identifying new markets and new uses for old products—as well as introducing new technologies. Thus, the entrepreneurial model of innovation via JVs still applies to services, including wholesaling, banking, and transportation. Given the geography and history of the Netherlands, its comparative advantage lies in these areas. No one should be surprised if large firms regularly choose JVs to fill niches, penetrate, and expand where new opportunities arise. Nor are the gains to efficient consolidation and pullback unaffected by the possibility of joint projects.

The theoretical framework and descriptive data presented here underscore the interesting issues raised by joint venture activity. As an organizational form, JVs represent a relatively understudied category. Since JVs continue to be established and to thrive in some industries, we can conclude that they fulfill some unique roles in our economic ecosystem. In particular, a strong case can be made for their representing a form of cooperative entrepreneurship.

Bibliography

Berg, S.V., Duncan, J., and Friedman, P. 1982. *Joint Venture Strategies and Corporate Innovation.* Cambridge, Mass.: Oelgeschlager, Gunn & Hain.
Hoekman, J.M. 1984. *The Role of the Joint Venture in the Strategy of Corporations.* Universiteit van Amsterdam.
Jacquemin, A.P., and de Jong, H.W. 1977. *European Industrial Organization.* London: Macmillan.
de Jong, H.W. 1985. *Dynamische Markttheorie.* Leiden: Stenfert Kroese.
Murrell, P. 1983. "The Economics of Sharing: A Transactions Cost Analysis of Contractual Choice in Farming." *Bell Journal of Economics,* 14 (1): 283–93.
Ordover, J.A., and Willig, R.D. 1985. "Antitrust for High-Technology Industries: Assessing Research Joint Ventures and Mergers." *Journal of Law and Economics,* 28: 311–33.
Rockwood, A. 1983. "The Impact of Joint Ventures on the Market for OCS Oil and Gas Leases." *Journal of Industrial Economics,* 31: 453–68.
Scherer, F.M. 1967. "Research and Development Resource Allocation under Rivalry." *Quarterly Journal of Economics,* 81: 359–94.

10

A Study of the Life Cycle of Joint Ventures

Bruce Kogut

Joint ventures, like any form of organization, undergo a cycle of creation, institutionalization, and, with high probability, termination. The additional complexity of a joint venture is that its creation is the product of two or a few existing organizations which, by right of equity ownership, jointly—though not necessarily equally—may exercise control. Of course, if the partners had nonconflicting goals, the management dilemma of a joint venture would be no greater than the problems inherent in any subsidiary–corporate headquarters relationship. But joint ventures are often, though not exclusively, created due to competitive motives, either between the partners or relative to other firms. Herein lies the irony, namely, that the competitive conditions that motivate the creation of a joint venture may also be responsible for its termination.

The relationship between the motivations to create and to terminate implies the need to analyze issues of stability from the perspective of the life cycle of a joint venture. Recent work in organizational theory has shown, for example, that the early history of an organization molds the patterns of behavior into relatively inert institutional structures. Similarly, the motivations of the partners to cooperate mold the institutional structure of the joint venture and influence their future behavior.

This chapter seeks to develop a few theoretical perspectives on the creation and termination of joint ventures. The first section presents data on the mortality of joint ventures. The second describes three theories of joint ventures from the perspectives of transaction cost economics, strategic behavior, and organizational ecology. The subsequent section reviews the literature on joint venture stability and relates previous findings, where possible, to the three theoretical perspectives. In addition, a few representative hypotheses are statistically tested. In the fourth section, a case history of an international joint venture is analyzed from the perspectives of the three theories. The final section presents a set of conclusions.

I would like to acknowledge the helpful criticism on an earlier draft by Erin Anderson and John Kimberly, as well as the research assistance of Bernadette Fox. The research for this chapter has been funded under the auspices of the Reginald H. Jones Center of the Wharton School of the University of Pennsylvania through a grant from AT&T.

Descriptive Statistics of Joint Venture Mortality

Because there has been little cross-sectional research on mortality rates of joint ventures over time, this section reports mortality rates according to age, function, industry, and country. Information on joint ventures was taken from the publication *Mergers and Acquisitions*. A questionnaire was sent to one of the parent companies of 475 joint ventures. Despite a response rate of 55.5 percent, only 148 questionnaires were usable due to either refusal to give pertinent information, the decision not to invest following the published announcement, or a misclassification by the respondent of nonequity contracts as a joint venture. Only ventures located in the United States were used so as to eliminate the effects of government regulations in other parts of the world. A domestic venture is between only U.S. partners; an international venture includes at least one non-U.S. firm. By looking only at ventures located in the United States, differences in business and political conditions can be reduced as influences on stability.

As seen in table 10–1, instability rates peak in years 5 and 6 for the sample of all joint ventures, though this trend is more pronounced for international ventures. Rates of termination by acquisition (whether by the partners or by a third firm) appear slightly more stable than those by dissolution. Studies on business failure rates, in general, show dissolution rates to be roughly 10 percent a year for small start-ups (Reynolds, 1986). While the mortality rates are not much different than what we find for joint ventures, the difference is that these ventures are started and owned by existing firms with the requisite financial resources.

In table 10–2, mortality rates are lower for production, financial service, and development of new products. However, statistical tests that correct for age of the

Table 10–1
Hazard Rates for Joint Ventures by Acquisition and Dissolution as a Percentage of Those at Risk

	Age						
	1	*2*	*3*	*4*	*5*	*6*	*>6*
Domestic joint ventures terminated	5.6	13.5	5.1	12.7	10.4	8.3	25.9
Dissolved	4.2	7.5	1.7	3.6	10.4	5.6	14.8
Acquired	1.4	6.0	3.4	9.1	0	2.7	11.1
International joint ventures terminated	3.9	5.4	10.8	4.2	20.0	24.0	12.6
Dissolved	2.6	2.7	3.1	2.1	14.3	12.0	6.3
Acquired	1.3	2.7	7.7	2.1	5.7	12.0	6.3
Both international and domestic joint ventures terminated	4.7	9.3	8.1	8.7	14.7	14.8	20.9
Dissolved	3.4	5.0	2.4	2.9	12.0	8.2	11.6
Acquired	1.3	4.3	5.7	5.8	2.4	6.6	9.3

Table 10-2
Mortality Rates by Function

	Total		Alive		Dissolved		Acquired	
	Number	Percentage	Number	Percentage	Number	Percentage	Number	Percentage
Research	7	4	3	42.9	4	57.1	0	0
Development of existing products	28	1	15	53.6	5	17.9	8	28.6
Development of new products	50	3	30	60.0	12	24.0	8	16.0
Production	69	4	40	58.0	16	23.2	13	18.8
Marketing and service	72	4	37	51.4	19	26.4	16	22.2
Financial service	10		6	60.0	4	40.0	0	0
Natural resource development	24	1	12	50.0	8	33.3	4	16.7

Table 10-3
Mortality Rates by Industry

	Total		Alive		Dissolved		Acquired	
	Number	Percentage	Number	Percentage	Number	Percentage	Number	Percentage
Resources	19	12.8	10	52.6	7	36.8	2	10.5
Paper and allied products	4	2.7	3	75.0	1	25.0	0	0
Chemicals and allied products	27	18.2	16	59.3	6	22.2	5	18.5
Petroleum and coal products	4	2.7	1	25.0	2	50.0	1	25.0
Rubber and miscellaneous plastic products	3	2.0	2	66.7	0	0	1	33.3
Primary metal industries	7	4.7	3	42.9	0	0	4	57.1
Fabricated metal products	4	2.7	3	75.0	0	0	1	25.0
Machinery, except electrical	18	12.2	12	66.7	2	11.1	4	22.2
Electrical and electronic equipment	16	10.8	11	68.8	4	25.0	1	6.3
Transportation equipment	4	2.7	2	50.0	1	25.0	1	25.0
Instruments and related products	6	4.1	2	33.3	3	50.0	1	16.7
Other manufacturing industries	7	4.7	2	28.6	1	14.3	4	57.1
Communications	3	2.0	1	33.3	0	0	2	66.7
Utilities	3	2.0	1	33.3	2	66.7	0	0
Wholesale trade	2	1.4	2	10.0	0	0	0	0
Financial services	9	6.0	2	22.2	6	66.7	1	11.1
Real estate and construction	5	3.4	4	80.0	1	20.0	0	0
Other services	7	4.7	3	42.9	2	28.6	2	28.6
Total	148	99.9	80	54.1	38	25.7	30	20.2

Table 10-4
Mortality Rates by Country of Joint Venture Partner

	Total		Alive		Dissolved		Acquired	
	Number	Percentage	Number	Percentage	Number	Percentage	Number	Percentage
United States	70	47.3	33	47.1	22	31.4	15	21.4
Britain	9	6.1	4	44.4	2	22.2	3	33.3
Japan	23	15.5	15	65.2	2	08.7	6	26.1
Scandinavia	8	5.4	4	50.0	4	50.0	0	0
Switzerland	3	2.0	1	33.3	1	33.3	1	33.3
Germany	10	6.8	7	70.0	1	10.0	2	20.0
France	4	2.7	1	25.0	3	75.0	0	0
Netherlands	3	2.0	3	100.0	0	0	0	0
Belgium	5	3.4	3	60.0	1	20.0	1	20.0
Malaysia	1	.7	1	100.0	0	0	0	0
Canada	12	8.1	8	66.7	2	16.7	2	16.7
Total	148	100.0	80	54.1	38	25.7	30	20.2

venture show only that ventures including marketing and after-sales service have significantly higher mortality rates. (The nature of these tests is described in the next section.) Particularly interesting is the difference in how ventures terminate according to function. Development of new products shows a higher rate of dissolution than acquisition, which makes sense given the risk attached to development. But development of existing products shows a tendency to terminate by acquisition, presumably because the development risk is lower and partners may differ in their valuations placed on the product.

In table 10–3, mortality rates are given for ventures by industry as defined by SIC codes. Because of the lower number of cases in some industries, it is difficult to infer mortality trends. However, when the ventures are aggregated into services, manufacturing, and resources, the statistical tests show a significantly higher mortality rate for services.

Table 10–4 presents data by the second partner's country. Again, it is important to caution against inferences without controlling for age. The Japanese joint ventures tend to be younger, which explains why the statistical tests do not show a significantly higher probability of termination. Interestingly, the Japanese ventures show a high rate of termination by acquisition when compared to the total sample. Of these six acquisitions, five were by the Japanese partner. When grouping the ventures into international and domestic categories, the tests show a higher probability of termination for international ventures, when correcting for age effects.

Theoretical Explanations

The central thesis of this chapter is that the reasons for the termination of a joint venture frequently lie in the motives responsible for its creation. There are many possible explanations for the creation of joint ventures. Many of these explanations, however, are variants of three theoretical perspectives, namely, transaction costs, strategic behavior, and organizational behavior. Though all three of these are complementary, they differ also in important ways.

Transaction cost economics has been developed by a number of scholars working on the determinants of the firm's boundaries. The most influential statement of transaction-cost economics is associated with Williamson (1975, 1985). His argument is that institutional design reflects efforts to *minimize* the sum of production and transaction costs. Production costs are simply the costs usually associated with the transformation process, with factors including the costs of inputs, the degree of scale economies, and the efficiency of the productive technology. Transactions costs are less well specified, but represent the costs of monitoring efforts, of investing in ways to bond performance, and of cheating. Since it is difficult to observe these costs, Williamson proposes instead to focus on the conditions that are likely to lead to high transaction costs. He lists three: asset specificity (or the degree to which assets are dedicated to transacting with a particular economic partner), uncertainty (which represents the difficulty of predicting and observing cheating), and frequency (which influences whether there is sufficient volume to justify a fixed investment in establishing an organizational solution). All of these conditions are necessary; none is sufficient.

There have been few attempts to extend transaction costs to joint ventures, with the notable exception of Stuckey (1983), and Buckley and Casson (chapter 2). One approach is to analyze the unique organizational properties of a joint venture and the transaction hazards to which they are addressed. What sets a joint venture apart from other organizational forms is that the parties share ownership of the assets and derived revenues and, thus, share monitoring and control rights, which (even if not exercised) are still valuable. There are, thus, two issues: (1) joint investment in ownership and (2) control and monitoring rights. Joint investment addresses the issue of creating incentives to perform, for what better incentive is there than requiring both parties to put up the capital or capitalized assets? Joint investment is, thus, a form of *mutual hostage positions* which mitigate the incentives to shirk or to behave contrary to fiduciary responsibility. Along with ownership comes the right to monitor and control, though to what extent is frequently the subject of negotiation. Of course, complete ownership also provides these benefits, but due to obstacles to merger and to differentiated abilities among the partners, both parties are forced to venture outside (see Buckley and Casson, chapter 2).

Unlike transaction-cost theory, strategic-behavior explanations rest, not on predicting that a joint venture will be chosen if it represents the minimum-cost institution, but if it maximizes profits. As Contractor and Lorange point out in chapter 1, the motives for strategic behavior are plentiful, from defensive arrangements which hurt other competitors to collusive arrangements to enhance market power, perhaps at the expense of buyers. To many researchers, strategic-behavior and transaction-cost–economics are compatible approaches, for once two firms decide to collude, many of the issues of bilateral bargaining discussed by Williamson are also relevant to the design of the collusive agreement.

Though compatible, the two approaches differ in terms of predicting institutional choice. Consider the following example of a firm that sources components outside for internal assembling into a product sold as a final good. A firm implicitly calculates the degree of asset specificity, uncertainty, and frequency; it decides that the sum of the transaction and economic costs favors a buy decision. Unexpectedly, consumers suddenly insist on, and are willing to pay a premium for, greater quality of components. Asset specificity, frequency, and uncertainty have not changed their values.

Transaction-cost economics would predict no change in the buy decision; strategic behavior implies a move toward a make decision because the importance of quality has increased and the downstream assembler is under greater incentives to appropriate the rents. One way to handle this problem is to rig the analysis to look like a cost-minimizing issue. For example, it could be posited that the downstream firm compares the revenue stream under internal manufacture to that under outside purchase, calls this difference an opportunity cost, and then proceeds to minimize the sum of transaction, economic, and opportunity costs. But if this solution is to be permitted, then every situation can be reduced ad hoc to comply with transaction costs. For the point of view of what is of analytical interest, it is empirically and theoretically important to separate out reasons of appropriability of revenue streams derived from strategic positioning in a particular product market from reasons of minimizing costs. What is the point of a theory if there is no variance to be explained?

Another explanation for joint ventures is derived from organizational theory and stresses cooperative motivations. The basis of this perspective is that firms can be conceived as organizations embodying different skills. To the extent that these skills are embedded in complex organizational routines, the transfer of organizational skills through the market or through a license may be impeded. Moreover, since organizational knowledge is very likely to be what Polanyi (1967) calls "tacit," the transfer of organizational knowledge can only be carried out if the organization is itself replicated.

This perspective has a straightforward implication for joint ventures. If a firm desires to sell a portion of its technological competence, it may do so by a spot market, by a license agreement, by acquiring or being acquired by another party, or by a joint venture. Let us rule out acquisitions by assuming that the technology being transferred is only a small portion of the total value of the firm. A common mechanism by which to transfer technology but still control its use is the licensing agreement. But if the knowledge is organizationally bound, a license may be an inadequate mechanism by which to transfer tacit knowledge. In this case, a joint venture serves as a vehicle that better allows for the transfer and imitation of complex and tacit organizational routines.

As discussed in the later sections, the three theoretical perspectives on the motives for joint venture creation have direct implications for the causes of instability. Both transaction-cost and strategic-behavior explanations view joint ventures as derived from a competitive dynamic, vis-à-vis either the parties to the venture or other competitors. It stands to reason, therefore, that changes in the parameters influencing the competitive positioning of the partners may lead to destabilizing their cooperation. An organizational-knowledge argument, however, views termination as the completion—successful or not—of the attempt to transfer complex technological routines. In this case, termination is planned.

Perspectives on Joint Venture Stability

Most studies that have analyzed joint venture stability have concentrated on the competitive dynamics between the partners to the neglect of the competitive nature of the industry and of the completion of technology transfer. Partner competition is, however, consistent with transaction-cost and strategic-behavior theories of joint venture creation, for it stands to reason that changes in the values of the parameters found to influence joint venture creation should influence stability. To isolate the factors that influence joint venture stability requires analyzing the stability of the cooperative and competitive incentives among the partners. Changes in the environment, of strategies, and of bargaining power over the life of the venture can affect dramatically the longevity of cooperation.

The importance of partner conflict has been confirmed by several studies. Franko (1971) analyzed joint venture instability in terms of strategic change, as proxied by whether the U.S. partner reorganized its international activities. Stopford and Wells (1972) looked at conflicts between the desire of a U.S. multinational to control the joint venture as a subsidiary and the desire of the country partner to maximize local profits. Hladik (1985) found a similar pattern in her analysis of whether an overseas venture carried out exporting.

The most detailed studies of partner-conflict explanations for joint ventures have been carried out by Killing (1982, 1983) and two colleagues, Schaan (1985) and Beamish (1985). These studies are especially relevant to transaction-cost explanations, since their focus is principally on the governance properties of joint ventures. Killing argues that since dual control is inherently problematic, ventures dominated by one of the partners are more likely to be stable. Based on a sample of thirty-seven ventures, Killing finds support for his thesis, though statistical tests were not provided. In summarizing his Ph.D. thesis work, Beamish (1985) qualifies Killing's results by showing that ventures where the local partner is dominant or shares control reveal higher rates of instability in LDCs. Schaan (1985) was able to specify more clearly the link between dominant control and performance. Through a study of ten joint ventures in Mexico, he concluded that satisfactory performance is more likely to the degree to which parents fit control mechanisms to their criteria for success, presumably because otherwise there is likely to be confusion over how each partner can exercise power to achieve its objectives without infringing upon its partner's authority.

No matter what the initial agreement on control and ownership may have been at the start of a venture, environmental and strategic changes over time may shift the relative bargaining power among the partners. Harrigan (1985), in particular, has stressed motives of strategic behavior as an explanation of joint venture creation and stability. See also chapter 12. Among other factors, she proposes that partner asymmetries, the durability of the advantages each partner brings, and the existence of exit barriers tend to stabilize ventures. Empirical tests in chapter 12 show some support for the influence of asymmetry on stability.

These studies suggest several possible explanations for joint venture instability. Since many of these explanations are of managerial and scholastic curiosity, I have gathered a number of hypotheses from the aforementioned authors and tested them against a sample of 148 joint ventures. Based upon this data, a few hypotheses prevalent in the literature may be tested. Killing states clearly two hypotheses:

Hypothesis 1: Dominant joint ventures are more stable than shared-control joint ventures (Killing, 1982, 1983).

Hypotheses 2: Joint ventures formed between firms that differ significantly in size are less stable because many additional problems arise (Killing, 1983, p. 123).

While it is not possible with the available data to specify many of Harrigan's suggestions, the following statements can be tested:

Hypothesis 3: "Concentrated settings will be more attractive settings for joint ventures because firms operating within oligopolies can focus on mutually desirable goals with greater ease" (Harrigan, 1985, p. 124).

Hypothesis 4: Ventures with a partner having market access are more stable because access is a more durable advantage than technology (Harrigan, 1985, pp. 59, 83).

The hypotheses are tested by using a partial likelihood model. This model treats the influence of the explanatory variables (or covariates) as influencing linearly the log of the hazard function. The method works, not by comparing ventures that terminated to those that did not, but by the order of terminations and censorship (that is, ventures still existing when last observed). Effectively, estimates on the covariate coefficients are derived by a procedure that compares ventures that terminated early to those terminating later.

The specification of Killing's hypotheses are straightforward. Because, as noted earlier, ownership and control theoretically and, as Killing's data shows, in practice are correlated, stability should be higher for ventures when one partner has majority control. The ratio of the asset size of the larger partner to that of the smaller is a fair approximation for hypothesis 2. Hypothesis 3 uses an eight-firm concentration ratio at the four-digit SIC code level; unfortunately, such data are only available for manufacturing industries. (Tests using four-firm concentration ratios did not alter the results substantially.) Hypothesis 4 is specified by a dummy variable indicating whether the venture includes a marketing and distribution activity. Hypotheses 1 and 2 are related to transaction-cost–theory explanations; numbers 3 and 4 bear a greater relevance for strategic-behavior theories.

Table 10–5 provides a list of the variables, their sources, expected signs, and the results. A positive coefficient means that a variable acts to increase the likelihood of termination; a negative coefficient means a decrease in the likelihood of termination. As a control for industry conditions, a dummy variable is included; it takes a value of one if industry shipments at the four-digit SIC level are greater than the median, while it takes a value of zero otherwise.

The results do not support the hypotheses. Majority share is correctly signed but highly insignificant. (When replaced by a dummy variable for whether the

Table 10-5
Summary of Variables and Results

Hypothesis	Variable	Source	Expected Sign	Partial Likelihood Estimate
1	Majority share owner	Questionnaire	−	−.25 (−0.62)
	Shipment growth	Unpublished data from U.S. Dept. of Commerce	−	−.46 (−1.28)
2	Relative size	Moody's	+	−.0001 (−.85)
	Shipment growth	See above.	−	−.51 (−1.49)
3	Concentration	Bureau of Census 1977, 1982	−	.01 (1.69*)
	Shipment growth	See above.	−	−.51 (−1.59)
4	Marketing activity	Questionnaire	−	.56 (1.73*)
	Shipment growth	See above.	−	−.56 (−1.76*)

* = significant at .10 or better

venture had a partner who had dominant equity, the results remained the same.) Hypothesis 2 carries the reverse sign as predicted, but is also insignificant. The sign reversal is not surprising, for it could be argued logically that the greater the difference in asset sizes between the partners, the more likely it is that one firm will dominate; thus, by Killing's contention, the venture should be more stable. Hypothesis 3 is contradicted, as the higher the degree of concentration, the more likely it is that the venture will terminate; the relationship is significant at .10. This result also contradicts Kogut's (1986a) hypothesis that the higher the concentration rate, the higher the entry barriers and the more likely any venture's survival. The result may imply that in concentrated industries, the competitive incentives for the partners to defect increases. Hypothesis 4 is also contradicted. Ventures with marketing activities are more likely to terminate. The Shipment growth variable is correctly signed in all the estimations, but significant only in the fourth regression.

These results should be viewed as discounting any simple statement on the causes of joint venture instability. At the same time, some of these relationships may be confirmed when other important influences are considered. There is a danger, in other words, of specification error.

Some current work suggests, in fact, that joint venture stability is influenced jointly by competitive incentives among the partners and competitive changes in industry structure. In recent work, Kogut (1986a) found that the likelihood of termination is decreased when partners to the venture have other ongoing agreements. Mutual forbearance, to use Buckley and Casson's terminology, is enhanced when disrupting the venture may affect other transactions. This result supports the transaction-cost explanation of hostage positions stabilizing economic relationships. Moreover, it was found that whereas ventures located in growing industries are more likely to survive, those located in industries that are becoming more concentrated and to which both partners belong are more likely to terminate. This result is consistent with transaction-cost argument, but is particularly pertinent to strategic-behavior argument.

Whereas the statistical tests given in Kogut (1986a) confirm the influence of competitive dynamics between the partners and within the industry on joint venture stability, they do not examine terminations due to completion of the transfer of organizational knowledge. Nor do these tests provide rich insight into the origins of shifts in bargaining power among the partners. For this purpose, the following section examines a case history of a joint venture in terms of the reasons for its establishment and reasons for its demise.

A Life History of a Joint Venture

In 1983, the Honeywell Corporation and L.M. Ericsson signed a multifaceted agreement for the sale of a telecommunication switch and for joint development of technology. In January 1987, it was publicly announced that their joint research venture had been terminated and acquired by Ericsson. While the factors influencing the creation and termination of the venture are many, the following analysis concentrates on the motives and concerns of the two partners, the process of institutionalization, and the influences on stability.

In the early 1980s, the Honeywell Corporation was involved in the production of control equipment and systems and, to a lesser but still significant extent, in the manufacture and sale of information systems products and services. The control business had been the primary business of Honeywell since its founding. The information systems businesses, on the other hand, had been acquired from other firms (such as General Electric and RCA) during the 1960s and 1970s. Honeywell's aggressive acquisitions placed it in the second tier of the industry, with IBM occupying the premier position. However, its computer investments had come at a cost and had not earned the profitability of its other businesses.

In the late 1970s, Honeywell recognized the possibility to consolidate its control and information systems businesses by linking the two by a smart private branch exchange (PBX). The convergence of its two major product groups is the key to a major new strategy to offer "intelligent buildings" which integrate telecommunications, data processing, and system controls. Honeywell was searching for a stable and long-term source of supply of PBXs.

In the 1970s, L.M. Ericsson had captured the leading share of the non–United States public digital switching market and was a major provider of telecommunication services and products, including cable and cellular radio products. Despite its international strength, its U.S. position was weak and consisted mostly of the cable sales from L.M. Ericsson Inc. (Its U.S. joint venture, of which it owned 50 percent and Anaconda—which ARCO had acquired—owned the other 50 percent.) Ericsson was, therefore, looking for an entry into the U.S. private telecommunications market, which promised substantial growth following deregulation and recent product innovations. Ericsson hoped to build a large market for its MD-110 PBX. A sale to a major customer would provide critical market share to support the costs of entry and software development to adapt the MD-110 to the demands of the U.S. market.

Whereas an agreement for Ericsson to supply Honeywell with the MD-110 would meet the goals of both parties, there were critical areas of instability that would persistently endanger a simple supply contract. Honeywell, for its part, would be dedicating significant resources to interface with the MD-110 switch. What would happen if L.M. Ericsson developed a different line or divested the business? For Ericsson, Honeywell would be incorporating the PBX into its products and, thus, drawing away potential customers. More importantly, Honeywell's further development of the software and hardware to interface with its equipment would enhance its abilities to develop and manufacture its own PBX. How could Ericsson guarantee that it is not giving up technology to a competitor?

The critical decision was made to solve these problems before the agreement was signed. The cooperative framework was divided into four separate agreements. One agreement established the pricing for a long-term supply of the MD-110. Two other agreements provided for a sale of technology from Ericsson to Honeywell and a licensing provision by which Honeywell can choose itself to manufacture the PBX. Thus, the fears concerning loss of technology and future supplies were assuaged. The sale of technology is particularly interesting, for it implies that Ericsson recognized that it could not protect its technology. By selling the technology, the future cooperation is left unencumbered over the use and leakage of the proprietary knowledge. If the parties cannot agree on the pricing of the technology, then without adequate protection, cooperation on the long-term supply is itself destined to fail.

The fourth agreement established the Honeywell Ericsson Development Company (HEDC) as a 50:50 joint venture (in the legal form of a partnership) in order to develop software for the adaptation of the MD-110 to the U.S. market. The partnership not only shared the fixed costs and risks of developmental work, but also served the important function of bringing together the research efforts of both parties, thereby creating personal trust and team learning between Ericsson and Honeywell.

The use of multiple clauses to the agreement fits well with transaction-cost arguments. The licensing contract eliminated some of Honeywell's dependence on a single source for a critical component. The technology agreement resolved an issue that would otherwise be destabilizing. Finally, the joint venture served not only to share development costs, but to enhance the cooperation between the firms.

The joint venture was also critical to the successful transfer of knowledge between the firms. Both firms had started development efforts prior to the agreement. Much of this knowledge was being produced by engineering teams which had not yet codified the work in process. By bringing the engineering teams together and then circulating some of the people back to the partner organizations, the requisite know-how was transferred between the two firms.

Since the central task of HEDC was to develop software applications and transfer the products back to the partner firms, the institutional structure of the venture mirrored these objectives. The venture was controlled through three organizational entities: the board of directors consisting of 3 executives from each firm; the executive board consisting of 2 executives from each; and a project planning board consisting of 3 executives from each and including the project planning manager of the joint venture. Over time, the executive board was dropped as redundant. The board of directors met twice a year and was chaired by a Honeywell executive since the venture itself was headed by a former Ericsson manager. It had the primary task of overseeing progress and ascertaining whether the venture was progressing on what was called the "project road map." This road map was a careful statement incorporated into the agreement which laid out the research projects and objectives for the venture. The project planning board was the critical linchpin between the venture and the market planning groups in the partner organizations. A concern raised in the negotiations was whether the venture might stray from the partner strategies. The function of the project planning board was to keep the development activities of HEDC in line with the partners' marketing objectives.

Over the first year and a half of operations, HEDC grew to over 160 engineers and successfully tested the first major development project: the integration of voice and data signals. However, several problems inherent in the beginning of the venture began to emerge. First, since Ericsson and Honeywell already had established facilities in the United States, HEDC was split between Anaheim and Dallas, the former close to Ericsson's operations, the latter to Honeywell's. Because of the geographic isolation, separate projects were allocated to each location, though visits were frequent and coordination was closely maintained. Second, whereas both firms wanted integrated voice/data communication capabilities, the other projects were not always of equal importance to the partners. This difference was especially evident regarding a packet switch which was more valuable to Ericsson's efforts in promoting electronic mail.

In late 1985, Honeywell chose to reduce drastically its cost commitment to the venture and some fifty engineers were released to their parent organizations. As a result, HEDC consolidated its operations to its Anaheim location. Despite the dismissal, the projects remained largely on track. Still, in late 1986, Honeywell decided to pull out entirely, leaving HEDC to become a wholly owned part of Ericsson's U.S. operations. (Ericsson had acquired a 100 percent ownership of L.M. Ericsson Inc. the previous year.)

Though terminated, the venture could hardly be considered a failure. Both the supply and technology agreements remain in force, even though Ericsson and

Honeywell occasionally confront each other as competitors in the PBX market. Moreover, the venture succeeded in adapting the switch to the U.S. market and transferring the software know-how of both firms to each other. In this sense, termination reflected the completion of the limited objectives of the original agreement. Finally, through the acquisition of HEDC, Ericcson obtained an ongoing research facility critical to its plans for further product development and adaptation.

The Honeywell and Ericsson agreement illustrates three important issues. First, a joint venture is frequently only a part of a multiplicity of contracts between the partners. To understand the joint venture, it is necessary to analyze it from the perspective of the total relationship, if not from its position in the wider cooperative network of the partners.

Second, the history of the venture suggests that there was a possible shift of bargaining power in the course of the relationship. Initially, Ericsson was in possession of a switch that had already been proven outside the United States and of proven capabilities in leading developments in digital communication technologies. Honeywell offered the clout of a large-purchase contract and some software application know-how. But, over the course of time, Honeywell acquired growing familiarity in the development of the relevant technologies. On the other hand, the disappointment of Ericsson's other businesses in the United States increased the importance of Honeywell as a potential customer for other products and, possibly, as a partner in other areas. However, the incentives for Honeywell to contribute its marketing strengths to a venture with Ericsson diminished once the requisite technology had been transferred.

The shift in bargaining power raises a third issue concerning whether it was a missed opportunity for Ericsson to restrict the agreement. Like Honeywell (but to a far lesser extent), Ericsson also acquired firms in information systems, and it was to the information systems division that a considerable amount of investment was allocated for the purpose of entering the U.S. market. From the vantage point of hindsight, it is interesting to speculate on whether a broader coalition with Honeywell in return for the contribution of its technology would not have advanced Ericsson's information systems strategy. The timing for this coalition is past. Honeywell is currently joining its information systems businesses in a joint venture with other partners, and Ericsson has signed an agreement with DEC for development efforts located in Stockholm. On the other hand, the stability of the wider Honeywell–Ericsson agreement may reflect the decision to limit cooperation. In this sense, the endurance of their cooperation represents a successful response to both transaction-cost hazards and the requirements of technology transfer, as well as the avoidance of the turbulence involved in coordinating strategies in the information technologies market.

Conclusion

Both theory and empirical studies point to the importance of competitor incentives for the formation and termination of a joint venture. Ventures are a means to resolve competitive conflicts inherent in economic relationships or to affect the competitive positioning of firms relative to rivals, including buyers and suppliers. But ventures motivated on the basis of competition are vulnerable to changes in the bargaining power of the partners and in the competitive structure of the market. Whereas the design of the venture and overall partner relationship can mitigate competitive incentives, the sources of destabilizing pulls are often inherent in the original motivations to establish the venture.

This perspective casts a sobering light on the cooperative motivations for a joint venture. A joint venture is indeed a pooling of assets under the joint ownership and control of a few partner firms. But though cooperative in intent, joint ventures are troubled by the enduring influence of competitive rivalry on stability. To the extent that firms are committed to each other through other agreements, the design of the overall relationship between the partners can attenuate the incentives to terminate. But, it would be foolhardy to view a joint venture as anything but the institutional cooperation between firms within a larger competitive context.

Joint ventures play, however, another role outside of resolving or affecting competitive factors; namely, such ventures are vehicles by which knowledge is transferred and by which firms learn from each other. The Honeywell–Ericsson agreement is a fine example of cooperation for the objectives of sharing the costs of knowledge generation and of transferring complex knowledge. Imitation is frequently the goal of a joint venture, and when imitation is complete, the sign of success is termination. In this sense, it would be a mistake in the efforts to pinpoint the competitive sources for joint venture creation and termination to swing the pendulum too far and obscure the cooperative merits.

Bibliography

Beamish, P.M. 1985. "The Characteristics of Joint Ventures in Developed and Developing Countries." *Columbia Journal of World Business*, Fall: 13–20.
Berg, S., and Friedman, P., 1977. "Joint Ventures, Competition, and Technological Complementarities." *Southern Economic Journal*, 43 (3): 1330–37.
———. 1981a. "Impacts of Domestic Joint Ventures on Industrial Rates of Return." *Review of Economics and Statistics*, 63: 293–98.
———. 1981b. "Impacts of a Pooled Cross-Section Analysis, Domestic Joint Ventures on Industrial Rates of Return." *Review of Economics and Statistics*, 63.
Duncan, L. 1982. "Impacts of New Entry and Horizontal Joint Ventures on Industrial Rates of Return." *Review of Economics and Statistics*, 64: 120–25.
Franko, L.G. 1971. *Joint Venture Survival in Multinational Corporations.* New York: Praeger.
———. 1976. *The European Multinationals.* London: Harper & Row.
Hannan, M.T., and Freeman, J.H., 1976. "The Population Ecology of Organizations." *American Journal of Sociology*, 82: 929–64.
———. 1984. "Structural Inertia and Organizational Change." *American Sociological Review*, 49: 149–64.

Harrigan, K.R. 1985. *Strategies for Joint Ventures.* Lexington, Mass.: Lexington Books.

Hladik, K.J. 1985. *International Joint Ventures: An Economic Analysis of U.S. Foreign Business Partnerships.* Lexington, Mass.: Lexington Books.

Killing, J. 1982. "How to Make a Global Joint Venture Work." *Harvard Business Review,* 60 (3): 120–27.

———. 1983. *Strategies for Joint Venture Success.* New York: Praeger.

Kimberly, J.R. 1975. "Environmental Constraints and Organizational Structure: A Comparative Analysis of Rehabilitation Organizations." *Administrative Science Quarterly,* 20: 1–9.

Kimberly, J.R., and Miles, R.H., (eds.). 1981. *The Organizational Life Cycle.* San Francisco: Jossey-Bass.

Kogut, B. 1986a. *Cooperative and Competitive Influences on Joint Venture Stability under Competing Risks of Acquisition and Dissolution.* Working paper. Reginald H. Jones Center, The Wharton School, University of Pennsylvania, Philadelphia.

———. 1986b. "On Designing Contracts to Guarantee Enforceability: The Case of East–West Trade." *Journal of International Business Studies,* 17: 47–62.

———. 1987. "Joint Ventures: Theoretical and Empirical Perspectives." Mimeo.

McKelvey, B. 1983. *Organizational Systematics: Taxonomy, Evolution, Classification.* Berkeley, Calif.: University of California Press.

Nelson, R., and Winter, S., 1982. *An Evolutionary Theory of Economic Change.* Cambridge, Mass.: Harvard University Press.

Polanyi, M. 1967. *The Tacit Dimension.* New York: Doubleday.

Reynolds, P.D. 1986. "Organizations: Predicting Contributions and Survival." Mimeo.

Schaan, J.L. 1985. *Managing the Parent Control in Joint Ventures.* Presented at the Fifth Annual Strategic Management Society Conference, Barcelona, Spain.

Stinchcombe, A.L. 1965. "Social Structure and Organizations." In J.G. March (ed.), *Handbook of Organizations.* Chicago: Rand McNally.

Stopford, M., and Wells, L., 1972. *Managing the Multinational Enterprise.* New York: Basic Books.

Stuckey, A. 1983. *Vertical Integration and Joint Ventures in the Aluminum Industry.* Cambridge, Mass.: Harvard University Press.

Williamson, O.E. 1975. *Markets and Hierarchies: Analysis and Antitrust Implications.* New York: Free Press.

———. 1985. *The Economic Institutions of Capitalism.* New York: Free Press.

11
R&D and International Joint Ventures

Karen J. Hladik

I nternational joint ventures have become an important competitive force in many industries today. This chapter focuses on one aspect of the joint venture decision—the decision to pursue collaborative R&D. International R&D ventures have been formed in a number of industries including aircraft and aircraft engines, pharmaceuticals, telecommunication equipment, and computers. Many of these ventures have been highly successful. Airbus Industries, a partnership between French, German, British, and Spanish aircraft manufacturers, for example, has developed new commercial aircraft that have made it a viable competitor to Boeing in world markets.

Nevertheless, other ventures have encountered costly, often insurmountable problems in their collaborative R&D efforts. The purpose of this chapter is to examine both the benefits of joint venture R&D and the sources of some of their difficulties, as summarized in table 11–1. A sample of 334 U.S.–foreign joint ventures tests the effect that various of these factors have had on the likelihood that joint venture partners pursue collaborative research.

The chapter concludes by examining the ways that joint venture partners might avoid some of the potential difficulties with joint R&D. Strategies for circumventing these difficulties can involve similarities in size and technical assets between the partners, prior working relationships, and a clear delineation of what technologies will be made available to the joint venture and which will be held back.

Benefits of Joint Venture R&D

There are several reasons why joint venture R&D can be an attractive strategy for some firms. The benefits of joint R&D are based on the pooling of complementary resources provided by the different partners. While one partner may contribute certain critical resources, such as technological skills and assets, another partner may be helpful in providing financing, complementary technical know-how, or access to the large domestic or international markets for the product of the joint R&D effort.

Table 11-1
Factors Affecting the Joint R&D Decision

Potential Benefits

1. Spreading costs and risks of R&D
2. Access to technology and technical know-how
3. Access to markets
4. Competitive positioning

Potential Problems

1. Risks of sharing proprietary know-how
2. Desire for control
3. Agreement on design specifications
4. Minimum efficient scale in R&D
5. Government policies and regulations

The contributions of each partner are determined by both the assets at its disposal and its comparative advantage in different inputs. In some cases, the contributions are clear-cut. Each partner may possess one set of key resources and be deficient in others. In other joint ventures, there may be an overlap of skills and resources. The principle of comparative advantage may then guide the particular mix of contributions, as in the design of the Boeing 767. There, Boeing took responsibility for the wings, cockpit, and final assembly, while Aeritalia SAI undertook the rudder and fins, and a consortium of Japanese firms developed the main body of the aircraft. In still other types of R&D ventures, the lines of comparative advantage are less clear, with even greater similarity in the assets that each partner brings to the agreement. In many Europe-wide ventures, for example, each partner provides some financing, some technology, and some market share. Several of the most important benefits of joint venture R&D are discussed next.

Spreading the Costs and Risks of R&D

One of the most frequent motivations behind collaborative R&D agreements is the ability to spread the costs and risks of R&D between the joint venture partners. In many industries, the development of new products can be extremely expensive. In the aerospace industry, for example, the cost of developing a new aircraft engine is at least $1.5 billion. New telecommunication equipment such as computerized digital switches can cost up to $1 billion. Such projects are difficult, if not impossible, for one firm to finance alone. Joint venture research is one way in which a firm with limited financial resources can participate in new-product development and stay at the forefront of technology. Joint venture partners typically pool financial resources, and, in some cases, obtain additional funding from their governments. In the Eureka project (Europe's high technology cooperative R&D venture), governments can supply up to 50 percent of their companies' research budget.

Even if a firm is able to raise the necessary financing on its own, there are several risks involved that can also put R&D beyond the financial capabilities of many firms in the industry. The first risk is the obvious possibility that the expected R&D breakthrough does not occur, does not occur fast enough, or requires more financial or technical resources than originally expected.

The second type of risk has to do with assessing future consumer demand for the product. This is a problem with any new-product introduction, but in many high technology industries, for example, there may be a considerable lead time between the start of research efforts and the time the new product reaches the consumer. During this time, market factors can change, reducing or diverting consumer demand even before the product reaches the marketplace.

A further risk involves the actions of a firm's competitors. In order for an investment in R&D to pay off, a firm needs to achieve a certain market share. This share is dependent on the number and quality of rival products competing for the same market. When a firm begins research on a new product, just as it faces uncertainty over the success and timing of its own research activities, it faces even greater uncertainty over the outcome of its competitors' efforts. There is the risk that a competitor could develop a better product. The competition could also develop it faster—a problem in markets where consumers have an immediate or one-time need for the product or face high switching costs. Finally, even if customer demand remains as expected and competitors have similar timing in reaching the market, rival firms risk dividing the market in such a way that no one firm can achieve an economic return on its R&D investment.

The costs and risks of R&D can present a firm with two unattractive alternatives. It can pursue expensive R&D and face highly uncertain returns on its R&D investment. Otherwise, it can forgo aggressive R&D efforts and risk falling behind in the technical expertise necessary for the next generation of product development. By sharing R&D expenses, joint venture partners reduce their financial exposure to the uncertainties surrounding R&D investment. Similarly, by freeing up funds, joint R&D can allow firms to diversify their financial investment over several R&D efforts—spreading the risk inherent in any one project.

Access to Technology and Technical Know-how

Just as joint venture research can reduce a firm's financial exposure to the risks of R&D, it can also reduce the various risks themselves through the sharing of other, nonfinancial resources. One important attribute of a joint venture partner, in this respect, can be the technology it brings to the agreement. A firm may look to a partner to provide access to new technology or proprietary know-how or else to provide technical skills complementary to its own.

Chinese–foreign joint ventures are typical examples of R&D agreements where one partner, the foreign firm, provides the bulk of the technical expertise. The Chinese government has shown a distinct preference for partnerships that promise technology sharing and new-product development. The McDonnell Douglas aircraft-assembly venture, for example, includes a provision that Chinese scientists and technicians work with McDonnell Douglas on new aircraft design. For its part, the Chinese partner provides complementary resources to the venture—in this case, some access to the large Chinese market.

More commonly, there is a greater degree of overlap between the technical resources and contributions provided by each of the partners. One partner, however, may have a comparative advantage in technical ability and take the lead in joint R&D work. This has been the case, for example, in a number of joint ventures in the telecommunication industry. In the AT&T-Philips venture, AT&T provided most of the underlying technology and technical know-how used in developing the next generation of digital switching equipment. Philips, while also contributing technical skills to the joint development work, concentrated its resources on its comparative advantage in marketing and production.

Other joint venture partners have had more closely matched R&D capabilities and have structured their product development to integrate the two sets of technologies and technical skills accordingly. One example has been the Pratt & Whitney–Rolls Royce V2500 turbofan jet engine project. In this case, the notion of comparative advantage, which often determines which partner takes the lead in R&D activities, can be applied at the more micro level of deciding what partner does what part of the R&D. In the development of the V2500, Pratt & Whitney had the comparative advantage in the hot-section technology and Rolls Royce concentrated on the fan and compressor sections. This combination of know-how can allow the development of new products which far exceed the technical capabilities of any one firm.

Access to Markets

Another advantage of joint venture R&D over independent R&D efforts is the access that a joint venture can provide to large domestic and international markets. Given the fixed costs of innovation, the larger the market, the higher the joint venture's expected rate of return from R&D activities. A number of studies have shown, in fact, that R&D investment is positively influenced by the expected domestic and international sales of the product (Schmookler, 1966; Mansfield, Romeo, and Wagner, 1979).

Immediate access to a large market can be especially important in industries where product lifetimes are short. Expected sales are dependent on both market size and the length of time over which the product is sold in these markets. As the time factor grows shorter, market access can become critical to the viability of R&D investment.

Joint ventures with a local partner may also be the only way to enter into an important domestic market. Thus, for example, Beatrice Food formed a joint venture with CITIC, its Chinese partner, to develop and market a new fruit drink for the protected Chinese market. McDonnell Douglas's involvement in joint air-craft design with China's Shanghai Aircraft Industrial Corporation was motivated in part by the anticipation of future aircraft sales to that country.

Other country markets may be characterized by less formal barriers to entry. Still, foreign firms may find it difficult to penetrate these markets without local marketing expertise. A joint venture partner may provide the know-how or estab-lished local distribution channels through which to market the new product. Japanese linkups with U.S. pharmaceutical firms, for example, take advantage of both the Japanese and U.S. parents' home-country distribution networks to market new pharmaceutical products. Foreign partners have also been of critical value in markets where important customers have been state-owned enterprises or govern-ments which favor national suppliers.

Traditionally, U.S. firms have looked to foreign partners as a means of enter-ing the host-country market alone. While local markets are still a consideration, it has become increasingly important to insure access to international markets as well. The AT&T–Philips alliance, for example, benefits from both Philips's inter-national marketing network and its European identity which makes it a more accept-able supplier to nationalist EEC markets. AT&T–Philips has made major sales of telecommunication equipment to the Dutch telephone authority and won smaller orders in Britain, Colombia, and Saudi Arabia, where Philips had established marketing channels. This type of international presence not only creates a larger customer base for the joint venture's telecommunication products, but also diver-sifies the risk of being tied to the economic uncertainties associated with any one country or regional market.

Competitive Positioning

As mentioned earlier, one of the risks involved in costly R&D activities is the uncer-tainty surrounding future competition. Joint venture R&D with potential com-petitors can reduce this risk in two important ways. First, by creating an alliance between two or more firms in the industry, the joint venture reduces the number of competitors splitting the market. Second, if this cooperation takes place at the initial stages of product R&D, firms have the opportunity to develop common technical standards which form the basis for subsequent product design and develop-ment. This can insure a greater degree of compatibility between product lines within an industry. Hence, firms face a smaller risk of an all-or-nothing gamble—that either their technology becomes the industry standard or much of the accumulated technological expertise becomes worthless.

ESPRIT, the European Strategic Program for Research and Development in Information Technology, was established with these considerations in mind. Com-panies in the alliance share basic R&D information at the "precompetitive" R&D stage before actual product design takes place. This insures that products such as telecommunication equipment, computers, and other high technology products conform to common technical standards rather than being based on an array of incompatible technologies developed by different European firms.

Sources of Problems with Joint Venture R&D

The benefits of joint venture research are counterbalanced by a wide range of difficulties. The failure rate of joint ventures, in general, is high. The problems are heightened when the partners are of different nationalities and when collaboration occurs at the base of each firm's competitive advantage—new-product development.

This section describes some of the major problems of joint R&D. Some joint ventures have successfully resolved these difficulties. Others have led to failure, either failure to establish the partnership in the first place or failure in the eventual dissolving of the agreement.

Risks of Sharing Proprietary Know-how

The biggest concern in most R&D partnerships is the reluctance to share proprietary technical know-how outside of the parent firm, even with a joint venture partner. A firm may well possess the technical skills or resources that would make R&D a profitable activity for the joint venture. It may hesitate, however, before sharing this know-how with a subsidiary that is only partially under its control. The risk is heightened by the possibility that, if the joint venture dissolves, the firm providing valuable technical skills to its partner may well have been training its future competitor.

This issue has been raised concerning cooperation between U.S. producers of aircraft and aircraft engines and foreign partners. In particular, recent cooperation between U.S. aircraft manufacturers and Japanese firms, such as on McDonnell Douglas F-15 Eagle fighter and on the Boeing 767, has been questioned (U.S. General Accounting Office, 1982; Reich, 1986).

Desire for Control

Another difficulty involves control of the joint venture. This is particularly true if the joint venture is involved in the development of new products for world markets. In many high technology industries, strategic flexibility and the desire to remove bureaucratic interference have favored majority control over 50:50 partnerships.

At the strategic level, a firm attempting to coordinate its operations in a global market may seek to insure that the joint venture fits in with these other activities. Without majority control of the venture, this may cause problems. A partner may want to make certain, for example, that new-product development is complementary to its existing product line to encourage tie-in sales of these new products as well. The firm may also seek to avoid markets where it sells its own competitive products.

At the personal level, human nature can also be an important factor in the creation and success of joint venture efforts. Where ownership control of the joint venture is concerned, personal and corporate pride and nationalist feelings can block involvement in important new ventures where the firm does not have majority control.

The proposed Ford–Fiat partnership in Europe was an example of these difficulties. The joint venture would have split expensive development costs, provided each partner with access to valuable technology, extended market coverage by merging Ford's strength in Northern Europe with Fiat's marketing strength in the South, and consolidated competition in the fragmented European market. Nevertheless, there was a deadlock in negotiations over the issue of control. According to one source, conversations with Ford and Fiat executives indicated that: "while both sides agreed the merger would be a perfect marriage, each side considered itself too strong to give up control" (Cohen, 1985). Since both firms are major competitors in the global automobile industry, each considered control of the joint venture important to its coordination with other worldwide operations. On the human level, personal pride and nationalist sentiment may also have contributed to the breakoff of negotiations. According to one Italian government official, "The abandonment of control to Ford would have been a political bombshell" (ibid).

Agreement on Design Specifications

Joint ventures can stir up a number of difficult issues concerning control. One of the most frequent sources of conflict, however, has to do with the ability to influence product design. Problems related to design specifications often surface at the negotiation stage. Firms can enter discussions with their own ideas concerning the technology to be used to develop the product, the level of technical sophistication, and the expense involved. If a firm produces other products in the industry, it may want to insure that the joint venture is compatible with the rest of its product line or its own user needs. In the proposed GTE–Siemens joint venture in digital telephone exchange systems, one of the difficult points in negotiations involved the integration of two types of electronic switching technologies. GTE, for example, was committed to the GTD-5 switch used by its local phone companies. Abandoning the GTD-5 switch in favor of Siemans' technology would have involved substantial replacement costs, a transition GTE was unwilling to make (Hudson and Guyon, 1986).

The requirements for product design can be very specific. In another case, Dassault, the French aircraft manufacturer, withdrew from talks with four other European firms on the design and production of a new jet fighter. The talks broke down in 1985 after two years of negotiations. A key disagreement concerned the weight of the aircraft. France needed a lighter aircraft, no greater than 9.5 tons, designed for ground attack. Britain and West Germany, on the other hand, raised the weight specifications to 9.75 tons, more in line with their requirements for an air-to-air combat fighter. The heavier aircraft also contained different air-to-air missiles, radars, and ECM equipment than Dassault was willing to accept. According to an interview with Bruno Revellin-Falcoz, Dassault's directeur-général technique, "trying to add up and accommodate all the requirements could have ended up with a very bad compromise. The aircraft would have been heavier, more sophisticated and very expensive as a result" (*Interavia*, 1986).

Problems relating to the design of the joint venture product can continue even after the operational requirements are agreed upon. Asked whether there was any resistance to abandoning Philips's PRXD technology in the AT&T–Philips joint venture, AT&T–Philips President Al Stark indicated that there were some problems since "there are always people who are wedded to a technology because it's part of them, and that's understandable" (Williamson, 1985). He also indicated, however, some opportunities for utilizing this expertise on the interface between the two technologies.

Minimum Efficient Scale in R&D

Another potential difficulty in collaborative R&D is the issue of economies of scale. While R&D may be profitable for the joint venture, it may be even more profitable for the parent firm if it is centralized rather than carried out over several R&D sites.

This may be especially true if the firm's greatest technical assets are the know-how and skills of a few key technical personnel. In that case, the firm may be reluctant to divide its technical staff. The problem is generally heightened when the R&D sites are located in different countries or are otherwise geographically distant from each other.

Government Policies and Regulations

Legal barriers and delays can add to the complication and expense of establishing a joint venture. Legal considerations vary with the specific details of the joint venture and the country or countries involved. Some potential problems are summarized next.

One possible concern is antitrust. R&D agreements, however, may receive special treatment. Under EEC regulations, for example, collaborative research efforts have received special exemptions from general antitrust guidelines. The justification has been that rather than hindering competition, R&D ventures can allow European firms to develop new products which they would not otherwise have the resources to design on their own. There are many more restrictions, however, when the partnership extends beyond research into manufacturing and marketing. Also, there are differences among individual European countries, with the greatest problems in antitrust clearance appearing to be in Germany. Germany's Federal Cartel Office has prohibited a number of joint ventures which had received clearance under the EEC special exemption for R&D agreements.

Other legal considerations can affect the organizational structure of the joint venture and, hence, the costs of starting up and operating the partnership. European joint ventures, for example, face a situation where company law varies from country to country. For legal reasons, this may mean setting up individual subsidiaries in every country in Europe where the joint venture does business. Furthermore, despite the attractiveness of Europe-wide cooperative agreements, it is not yet possible to establish a joint venture with a legal, "European" identity. A joint venture must be incorporated in one country and, hence, risk being associated with that national identity. A joint venture that seeks to create a European rather than a national image faces extra complexities and costs in establishing its operations. For example, European Silicon Structures (a European joint venture to develop custom-made microchips) incorporated its operations in Luxembourg and set up subsidiaries in nine countries. It was estimated that this added about 20 percent to the joint venture's first-year costs (Hemp, 1986).

Another potential difficulty with foreign joint venture R&D is the extent of local patent regulations. Many LDCs provide inadequate protection in this area. China's patent law, for example, only went into effect in April 1985. Before that, invention was treated as a public good. Because of the risk of having to share the economic rewards from R&D, foreign investors may decide to pursue R&D closer to home where they have more experience and control over the dissemination of technical know-how.

Empirical Testing

The discussion up to now has highlighted some of the factors that can benefit or discourage joint venture R&D. A number of examples have shown how these factors have influenced joint R&D decisions in telecommunications, aerospace, automobiles, and other industries. While these examples were helpful in describing a range of considerations that have come up in actual R&D ventures, it is also useful to generalize further to aggregate trends in international joint venture activity. This section, therefore, summarizes the empirical results in Hladik (1985), which examines the strength of various influences on joint R&D over a broad sample of international joint ventures.

Data Base

The data base is part of an ongoing project by the author to compile information on newly formed joint ventures. The data base currently covers over 420 international joint ventures between U.S. and foreign firms, as referenced by the *F&S Index of Corporate Change*, a periodicals index published by Predicasts, Inc.

The data base catalogues a range of information on each of the joint ventures. Among the items included are data on the parent firms, ownership shares, the geographic range of the joint venture (particularly whether it exports outside the host country), and its functional activities including R&D. One of the most interesting topics, though not always the most readily available, is the resources being combined through the joint venture, particularly any financial or technical agreements between the partners. Further information on the methods used in compiling the data base is provided in chapter 4 of Hladik (1985).

The statistical work discussed here is based on a broad sample of international joint ventures formed between 1974 and 1982. The sample conforms to a number of criteria including that each joint venture be in one of the manufacturing industries (SIC codes 2000–3999), that it be located outside of the United States, and that the U.S. partner have been a 10 percent and 90 percent equity stake in the venture. Between 1974 and 1982, the number of U.S.–foreign joint ventures roughly doubled from the first half to the second half of the sample period. Over half of these joint ventures were in one of three manufacturing sectors: (1) chemicals and allied products, (2) nonelectrical machinery, and (3) electrical and electronic equipment.

Joint R&D was defined as any type of product or process development carried out by the joint venture partners. Over the sample, this included both basic R&D, such as the design of state-of-the-art products for world markets, and more adaptive types of development activities, such as modifying a product or process for a foreign market. While collaborative R&D was more the exception than the rule in this time period, the percentage of joint ventures with R&D operations almost tripled from the beginning to the later years of the sample. By 1982, 20 percent of the U.S.–foreign joint ventures formed in that year included some type of collaborative R&D. While the presence of joint R&D varied considerably across the thirteen manufacturing sectors, electrical and electronic equipment and instruments had the highest concentration of R&D joint ventures in the sample.

Hypotheses

The following hypotheses are based on the earlier discussion of some of the positive and negative factors that can affect joint R&D. The actual variables tested and their expected signs are summarized in table 11–2.

Costs and Risks. As mentioned earlier, one advantage of joint R&D is the ability to spread the costs and risks of R&D between the joint venture partners. This incentive is the greatest in those industries where the expense of R&D and the technical rivalry among competitors are particularly high. Industry R&D (*INDR&D*), the average R&D expenditure as a percentage of net sales in the joint venture's industry, is one measure of this type of environment. *INDR&D* is expected to have a positive influence on the likelihood of joint R&D.

Access to Technology. Access to technical resources may also influence collaborative R&D. The resources include the technical assets of both U.S. and foreign partners and

Table 11-2
Expected Effect of Variables on Joint R&D

Variable Name	Explanation	Expected Sign
INDR&D	Average R&D to sales ratio in industry	+
USTECH	U.S. firm's R&D as % of net sales	+ or −
FTECH	Dummy variable = 1 if foreign firm contributes know-how or resources	+
GDP/C	GDP per capita in host country	+
POP	Population of host country	+
INTL	Dummy variable = 1 if joint venture intends to export	+
FPARTNER	Dummy variable = 1 if foreign partner operates in international markets	+
MES	Minimum efficient scale in R&D operations in the industry	−
GOVT	Dummy variable = 1 for certain countries offering incentives for joint R&D	+

the general technical environment of the host country, such as the availability of scientists and technicians as well as access to information and communications facilities. The U.S. firm's technical resources (*USTECH*) are estimated by its R&D expenditure as a percentage of its net sales. The foreign firm's technology (*FTECH*) is represented by a dummy variable set equal to 1 if there is any indication that the foreign firm contributes technical know-how or resources to the joint venture, and 0 if otherwise. The GDP per capita (*GDP/C*) serves as a proxy for the availability of technical personnel and resources in the host country. All three variables should be positively related to a joint venture's involvement in R&D operations.

Access to Markets. Given the indivisible nature of innovation, the joint venture's ability to spread these costs over a large market should affect its expected rate of return on R&D and, hence, the decision to undertake joint R&D investment. Expected market size includes both domestic and foreign markets. Furthermore, it reflects the joint venture's ability to access these markets through local and foreign distribution channels. The population of the host country (*POP*) is used as a proxy for local market demand. Market demand also reflects income per capita (*GDP/C*), though this variable was factored out for separate treatment as discussed previously. The joint venture's presence in international markets (*INTL*) is represented by a dummy variable set equal to 1 if the joint venture intends to export and 0 otherwise. The foreign partner's international marketing experience or distribution network (*FPARTNER*) is represented by another dummy variable equal to 1 if the foreign partner operates in international markets outside its home country and 0 if there is no indication of foreign activity. *POP, INTL,* and *FPARTNER*, as indicators of expected market demand for the joint venture's products, should all have a positive effect on the likelihood of joint R&D.

Proprietary Know-how. A potential hurdle to joint R&D is the risk of sharing proprietary know-how with another firm. The U.S. firm's possession of technical resources (*USTECH*) was mentioned earlier as a possible incentive to joint R&D, assuming that the joint venture has access to this technology. The U.S. parent's reluctance to share this know-how, however, may reverse this effect. R&D intensity may indicate a firm that derives its competitive strength from innovative activity and, hence, one that might be highly protective about the proprietary assets and know-how it has acquired. If this is a predominant consideration, *USTECH* would have a negative rather than a positive influence on the joint venture's involvement in R&D. It is not possible to test this counterhypothesis on *FTECH*, however, since *FTECH* is a more narrowly defined variable controlling for technology already being transferred to the joint venture.

Minimum Efficient Scale. A further disincentive to joint R&D may be a high minimum efficient scale in R&D operations (*MES*). This variable measures the minimum efficient scale of R&D in the joint venture's industry. At higher levels, it may argue against the decentralization of R&D away from the U.S. parent firm's main R&D facilities; hence, likelihood of joint R&D in the sample would be lower.

Government Policy and Regulations. There are a variety of host-country laws and regulations that can either encourage or hinder joint venture R&D. In general, these are hard to quantify and compare in any rigorous manner between countries. The earlier discussion mentioned some potential problems. The testing here controls for the positive influence that government policies and regulations can have. The literature on joint R&D identifies some countries offering specific inducements to R&D between foreign firms and local partners: Brazil, France, India, and Japan (Behrman and Fischer, 1980). A dummy variable for host-government incentives (*GOVT*) was set equal to 1 for joint ventures in these countries and 0 otherwise. *GOVT* should have a positive effect on the likelihood of joint R&D.

Results

Since only the presence or absence of R&D was observable for each of the joint ventures in the sample, the empirical tests were constructed using a probit qualitative choice model. The probit model estimates the effects of the nine explanatory variables described concerning the likelihood of joint R&D. The maximum likelihood estimates for a sample of 334 U.S.–foreign joint ventures from 1974 to 1982 are shown in equation 11.1:

$$
\text{R\&D} = -2.810 + 0.158\text{INDR\&D} - 2.032\text{USTECH} + 1.162\text{FTECH}
$$
$$
(3.583) \qquad\qquad (-0.784) \qquad\qquad (4.829)
$$
$$
+ 0.058\text{GDP/C} + 0.001\text{POP} + 0.405\text{INTL} + 0.650\text{FPARTNER}
$$
$$
(2.225) \qquad\; (1.836) \qquad\;\; (1.799) \qquad\quad (2.802)
$$
$$
- 0.050\text{GOVT} - 0.002\text{MES}
$$
$$
(-0.227) \qquad (-1.473) \hspace{4cm} (11.1)
$$

The dependent variable, *R&D*, is a dummy variable set equal to 1 if the joint venture undertakes R&D and 0 otherwise for 49 R&D joint ventures and 285 non–R&D joint ventures.

The mean of the dependent variable is 0.15 and χ^2 (8) = 185.2.

(t-statistics are shown in parentheses. A two-tail t-test was used in the case of *USTECH* which had alternative sign predictions. Otherwise, a one-tail test was employed.)

Overall, the model satisfactorily identifies some of the important determinants of joint venture R&D activity. The likelihood ratio test is used to test the null hypothesis that the estimated coefficients are, as a whole, insignificantly different from zero. At χ^2 = 185.2, the null hypothesis can be rejected with the equation being statistically significant at better than a 99 percent level.

As a measure of the model's explanatory power, one can consider the number of observations in which the model correctly predicts the presence or absence of joint R&D—a statistical test called the correct classification criterion. For each joint venture observation, the equation gives the likelihood of R&D activity. Assuming that a probability of 50 percent or greater indicates a positive prediction and a probability of 50 percent or lower indicates a negative prediction, the model successfully predicts the presence or absence of joint R&D 88 percent of the time. Even at stricter cutoffs, such as a 75 percent probability for a positive prediction and a 25 percent probability for a negative prediction, the success rate is still greater than 75 percent. These results strongly support the viability of the model, though the danger of an upward bias due to the low frequency of joint R&D in the sample needs to be kept in mind (Amemiya, 1981).

Turning to the individual coefficient estimates, a number of variables exert a positive influence on the likelihood of joint R&D. The coefficients on *INDR&D, FTECH, GDP/C, POP, INTL,* and *FPARTNER* are all significantly different from zero at the 95 percent confidence level or better. These results are consistent with hypotheses concerning potential incentives for joint R&D—namely, the ability to share the costs and risks of R&D associated with the joint venture's industry, access to technical skills and resources, and access to larger domestic and international markets.

The effect of host-government policy, *GOVT,* does not have a positive effect as expected on joint R&D in this sample. The equation was reestimated to see what effect this would have on the coefficients and standard errors of the remaining variables. The coefficients and standard errors were barely affected, implying that the poor result for this variable may be due to weak data rather than statistical difficulties associated with multicollinearity.

Of the variables expected to have a negative effect on the likelihood of joint R&D, only *MES* is significant at the 90 percent confidence level. This implies that if economies of scale in R&D are high, the U.S. parent firm may very well find it more profitable to centralize R&D in one location, most typically at the parent firm's home-country facilities.

The coefficient on *USTECH* is negative though insignificant. The standard error on the coefficient prevents us from inferring too much from this first test. It is interesting, however, to see that the most R&D-intensive U.S. parent firms are not the most likely to support R&D in their foreign joint venture subsidiaries. In fact, the negative sign on the coefficient lends more support to the counterhypothesis. Namely, it appears that R&D-intensive U.S. parents might find it more profitable to conduct R&D in alternative sites to the joint venture, perhaps wishing to avoid the risks of sharing proprietary technical know-how.

As a further attempt to gain some insight into the relationship between *USTECH* and joint R&D, the model was reestimated controlling for the interaction between *USTECH* and *FTECH*. The hypothesis was that if both the U.S.. firm and the foreign partner were technically skilled, collaborative R&D would be more mutually attractive. In that case, it is possible that neither partner would contribute all of the technical skills and resources, and that both could benefit from the other partner's know-how. A new variable, *TECH2*, was formed as the product of *USTECH* and *FTECH* for values of *USTECH* greater than the sample mean. *TECH2*, therefore, controls for joint ventures between two technically endowed partners.

The results are presented in equation 11.2. (t-statistics appear in parentheses.) *TECH2* is positive as hypothesized and significant at the 90 percent confidence level. Interestingly, the independent effect of *USTECH*, controlling for those cases where both partners are technically endowed, is now more pronounced. The coefficient on *USTECH* is negative and significant at the 90 percent confidence level. This conforms with the previous hypothesis that an R&D-intensive U.S. parent might find it more profitable to conduct R&D itself rather than share technical development skills with a joint venture partner. Furthermore, it suggests that this reluctance might only be a deterrent when the flow of technology to the joint venture is one-sided.

$$R\&D = -2.781 + 0.167 INDR\&D - 6.546 USTECH + 0.970 FTECH$$
$$(3.647) \qquad (-1.423) \qquad (3.546)$$
$$+ 0.060 GDP/C + 0.001 POP + 0.405 INTL + 0.684 FPARTNER$$
$$(2.324) \qquad (1.924) \qquad (1.784) \qquad (2.918)$$
$$+ 0.009 GOVT - 0.001 MES + 7.573 TECH2$$
$$(0.037) \qquad (-1.454) \qquad (1.456) \qquad (11.2)$$

Mean of dependent variable = 0.15.
$\chi^2 (8) = 182.9$.

Conclusion

This chapter has discussed some of the benefits and drawbacks of joint R&D activities. It has further tested the broader applicability of these factors across a sample of U.S.–foreign joint ventures. Firms, however, may be able to influence the balance of benefits and problems through their choice of joint venture partner and through carefully defined goals and boundaries to joint activities. Unfortunately, data are particularly sparse on this point. This section discusses three strategies which merit further attention.

Similarity of Partners

Some evidence suggests that similarities in size, financial resources, and technical assets may be important considerations in evaluating potential joint venture partners. The empirical results presented earlier, for example, indicated that two technically endowed partners had a greater likelihood of pursuing joint R&D than two partners whose flow of technology was more one-sided. The benefits of similar partners, preferably large ones, were summarized by one executive whose company was involved in a large fiber optics joint venture. According to his experience, if the partners are comparable in sophistication and size, "they are likely to have similar values and control systems, similar tolerance for losses, and appetite for risk" (*Business Week*, 1984). These can be key considerations in high-cost, high-risk R&D ventures.

Similarities in size among partner firms have also been linked to issues of control. Here, case evidence is mixed. One possibility is that an even balance of power could improve the joint venture relationship. This view was expressed by American Motors Corporation's president and CEO in describing AMC's search for a suitable alliance: "I do believe that the same size of manufacturers has a better chance to work together than a very big one and a very small one. I think you have to have a certain balance of weight between the two. If not, it is not a relationship, it is a takeover" (Johnson, 1985). On the other hand, two evenly matched partners, each vying for control, could actually derail efforts to structure or operate a joint venture, as was the case in the Ford–Fiat joint venture negotiations discussed earlier.

Previous Working Relationships

Another possibility for minimizing the risks of joint venture activity is to seek a partner that is already well known to the firm. Joint ventures can evolve from a relationship as a customer or a supplier, from licensing or royalty agreements, or from various training arrangements. Through these initial ties, each firm acquires information concerning the potential partner's skills and deficiencies, reducing the uncertainties of whether a profitable match is possible. Certain considerations such as the corporate culture and the fit between key personalities can, in fact, be difficult to evaluate outside of a working environment. Prior working relationships also have the advantage of allowing mutual trust and goodwill to develop—an important factor in the negotiation and operation of R&D joint ventures that might involve the sharing of proprietary technical skills and resources.

Many recent U.S.–foreign joint ventures have developed out of a prior association between the partners. The AT&T–Philips joint venture, for example, was preceded by annual meetings between company executives to discuss patent cross licenses. Occasionally, there is a cultural bias for the gradual evolution of business relationships. In China, Chinese–foreign partnerships often develop from very tentative, modest "flirtations" such as technical seminars and training visits between Chinese and foreign firms.

Clear Delineation of Technology Contributed to a Joint Venture

As has been discussed, firms involved in joint R&D must often face the real and perceived risks of sharing proprietary know-how with others outside of the firm. Similarities in technical sophistication and prior working relationships between the parties may reduce some of these risks. A more direct approach has been to limit R&D cooperation to only one stage of the R&D process, thus reducing the exchange of proprietary data where possible. Two such limited R&D arrangements, interface and precompetitive R&D, are discussed next.

Interface cooperation typically involves independent R&D efforts by each of the partners. The flow of proprietary data is then confined to linking the different components at the final stages of product design. As a further precaution, the physical separation of technicians and scientists provides an additional check on the flow of proprietary information. This type of arrangement may be especially appropriate for joint ventures subject to antitrust scrutiny or other types of government restrictions on cross-national technology flows. This was the case in the Pratt & Whitney–Rolls Royce V2500 turbofan engine venture. The partners each developed one section of the engine, but joined forces to link the separate R&D efforts into a final product. The limits on cooperation, however, were indicated by Pratt & Whitney as follows: "We will have to know the interfaces, and there obviously will be some exchange of data involved in that. But we will not have to get into the details of the technology. There will be rigid restraints. The U.S. government will see to that" (Fink, 1983).

Interface cooperation has benefited in recent years from technical breakthroughs in communications capabilities. These include advances in voice and facsimile transmission and in video teleconferencing which can be used to transfer test data between different R&D locations. In the development of the Boeing 767, for example, voice and facsimile transmission became a critical resource and "technical solutions and decisions were communicated on a daily and almost colloquial basis" (Clutterbuck, 1981).

Precompetitive cooperation links resources at the opposite end of the R&D spectrum. Partners typically work together to create basic technologies and scientific know-how, yet then pursue independent efforts in designing products for the marketplace. By restricting the flow of technical know-how to the earlier phases of R&D, firms can maintain the proprietary skills and know-how associated with later stages of product design.

Precompetitive R&D has several additional advantages. One benefit is that it can help develop common technical standards. Thus, for example, high technology products made by different firms can still be used together, reducing the risk of fragmenting the market between several technologically incompatible products. Second, since each partner develops its own products to compete in the marketplace, antitrust may be less of an issue. Finally, control over product design and development can be attractive to firms coordinating activities over several markets, product lines, and interfirm linkages as well—the latter being of particular importance in many global industries today.

References

Amemiya, T. 1981. "Qualitative Response Models: A Survey." *Journal of Economic Literature*, 19: 1483–536.

Behrman, J.N., and Fischer, W.A. 1980. *Overseas R&D Activities of Transnational Companies*. Cambridge, Mass.: Oelgeschlager, Gunn & Hain.

Business Week. 1984. "Are Foreign Partners Good for U.S. Companies?" May 28: 60.

Clutterbuck, D. 1981. "The Jigsaw with Bits in Three Countries." *International Management*, August: 17.

Cohen, R. 1985. "Ford–Fiat: How Their Contest of Wills Prevented a 'Perfect Marriage' in Europe." *Wall Street Journal*, November 21: 34.

F&S Index of Corporate Change. 1974–1982. Cleveland, Ohio: Predicasts.

Fink, D.E. 1983. "Pratt, Rolls Launch New Turbofan." *Aviation Week & Space Technology*, November 7: 29.

Hemp, P. 1986. "Pan-European Ventures Face Difficulties." *Wall Street Journal*, April 1: 36.

Hladik, K.J. 1985. *International Joint Ventures: An Economic Analysis of U.S.-Foreign Business Partnerships*. Lexington, Mass.: Lexington Books.

Hudson, R.L., and Guyon, J. 1986. "GTE, Siemens Venture Could Become Power in Digital Phone Exchange Sales." *Wall Street Journal*, January 20: 6.

Interavia. 1986. "Dassault and Co-operation." March: 325.

Johnson, R. 1985. "AMC Eyes Japan for Joint Venture." *Automotive News*, July 29: 55.

Mansfield, E., Romeo, A., and Wagner, S. 1979. "Foreign Trade and U.S. Research and Development." *Review of Economics and Statistics*, 61: 49–57.

Reich, R. 1986. "A Faustian Bargain with the Japanese." *New York Times*, April 6: F2.

Schmookler, J. 1966. *Invention and Economic Growth*. Cambridge, Mass.: Harvard University Press.

U.S. General Accounting Office. 1982. "U.S. Military Coproduction Assist Japan in Developing its Civil Aircraft Industry: Report to the Chairman's Subcommittee on Trade, Committee on Ways and Means, House of Representatives, by the Controller General of the U.S." Vol. 50, no. 83004812.

Williamson, J. 1985. "AT&T–Philips' President Al Stark Talks about the Union of Two Industry Giants." *Telephony*, 209: 45.

12
Strategic Alliances and Partner Asymmetries

Kathryn Rudie Harrigan

Three recent flurry of articles about joint ventures (and other forms of strategic alliance) suggest that yet another "fad" has captured the interest of strategists and scholars of strategic management. Although the jury is still out with regard to the efficacy of cooperative strategies—because reported success rates for interfirm ventures are low (Harrigan, 1985; Levine and Byrne, 1986)—use of strategic alliances continues. Despite the many problems that firms have encountered in using joint ventures and other cooperative strategies (and because cooperation is likely to play an increasingly important role among firms' strategy options in the future), there is considerable interest among managers in discovering a recipe for successful venturing.

Do differences among sponsoring firms with respect to each other (and in relationships with their jointly sponsored ventures) influence the efficacy of their strategic alliances? Because managers must narrow the field in their quest to find the perfect venturing partner, a rigorous study of similarities and relationships between venture partners (and their effects on performance) may provide helpful insights about firms' successes in using joint ventures in their diversification strategies.

Literature Review and Hypotheses

Strategic alliances. Strategic alliances—joint ventures, cooperative agreements, and so forth—are partnerships among firms that work together to attain some strategic objective (Berg, Duncan, and Friedman, 1982; Killing, 1983; Pate, 1969). "Joint ventures" create a jointly owned entity, while nonequity forms of cooperation do not (Harrigan, 1985). For the purposes of my analysis, however, the unit of observation is *the venture* and all business activities where partners may cooperate

This chapter is based on materials contained in K.R. Harrigan, *Strategies for Joint Ventures* (1985), and K.R. Harrigan, *Managing for Joint Venture Success* (1986), both Lexington, Mass.: Lexington Books. Permission to use is gratefully acknowledged. Research support from the Strategy Research Center, Columbia University, and suggestions from its chairman, William H. Newman, are also gratefully acknowledged.

are referred to as "ventures"—regardless of their ownership form and status as a separate organizational entity.

Sponsor–Sponsor and Sponsor–Venture Relationships.

Diversification. Strategic alliances bring together partners that may be horizontally or vertically related to each other, but need not be related to each other at all. The ventures that they create may be horizontally or vertically related to either (or both) sponsoring firms, or they may constitute an unrelated diversification for sponsoring firms. Related diversification strategies have generally been found to perform better than unrelated diversification strategies (Bettis, 1981; Bettis and Hall, 1982; Montgomery, 1979; Montgomery and Singh, 1984; Rumelt, 1974), with some notable exceptions (Michel and Shaked, 1984; Rajagopalan and Harrigan, 1986). How does the relationship between sponsoring firm and venture influence its performance (if at all)? My null hypothesis concerning diversification is that horizontally and closely related ventures are expected to perform better than ventures that are vertically related (or unrelated to their sponsors) in terms of venture success, survival, and duration. Results suggest that the hypothesis cannot be rejected.

Partner Asymmetry. Harrigan (1985) argues that ventures are more likely to succeed when partners possess complementary missions, resource capabilities, managerial capabilities, and other attributes that create a strategic fit in which the bargaining power of the venture's sponsors is evenly matched. Partners' needs to be engaged in a particular strategic alliance are stabilizing to the relationship, while a wide variety of asymmetries are destabilizing to a venturing relationship. Thus, partners will stay together as long as they need each other and their venture remains successful, unless the terms invoked by the bargaining agreement's "divorce clause" are so egregious that they constitute an exit barrier that perpetuates a partnership long after its usefulness to at least one of the partners has expired (Caves and Porter, 1976; Harrigan, 1980; Porter, 1976). Over 12 percent of the ventures in operation in 1986 in my sample were not mutually judged successful by their sponsors.

How do partner asymmetries—in relative asset size, national origin, and venturing experience levels—influence venture performance (if at all)? My null hypothesis concerning partner asymmetry is that significant asymmetries among sponsoring firms are expected to be stabilizing to a venturing relationship (in terms of survival and duration) because partners each need what the other can supply, but they are expected to be harmful to venturing performance (in terms of success) because their heterogeneity exacerbates differences in how partners value their venture's activities. Results suggest that this hypothesis also cannot be rejected.

Variable Measurement and Rationale

Venture Performance

Venture performance is determined in this analysis by considering all three indicators—venture survival, duration, and sponsor-indicated assessments of success. Survival is indicated by coding whether the venture was operating in 1985, and 3.5 percent of all ventures were formed before 1975 and still operating as jointly owned ventures in 1986. Duration is measured by the number of years between when a venture was formed and was terminated (or 1986, if the venture is still operating). Success was determined by asking the venture's sponsors. If one of the sponsoring firms did not judge the venture to be a success, it was coded as not being a mutual success. Note that if exit barriers are high, successful strategic alliances are not necessarily indicated by long-lived ventures, and short-lived ventures can be judged as successes from both sponsors' perspectives if they have achieved their strategic purpose.

Success Rates. Of the ventures studied 45.3 percent were mutually assessed to be successful by their sponsors. The greatest relative successes were enjoyed by ventures in the metals fabrication, petrochemicals, pharmaceuticals, and programming (films) industries, as seen in table 12–1.

Ongoing Ventures. Venture survival may indicate successful performance, depending upon when the venture was created. Of the ventures studied 45.2 percent were ongoing at the end of 1985, and 59.3 percent of those ongoing ventures were mutually judged to be successful by their sponsors (26.8 percent of total). A full 66.7 percent of the ventures that were not ongoing at the end of 1985 were judged to be unsuccessful by one or more of their sponsors (36.6 percent of the total sample). A further breakdown by product type is given in table 12–1. The greatest proportions of ongoing ventures at the end of 1985 were found in the communications equipment, computers and peripherals, farm and industrial equipment, financial services, pharmaceuticals, and programming (films) industries.

Venture Duration. The average life span of a venture was 3.5 years (with a standard deviation of 5.8 years). Of the ventures studied 42 percent lasted more than 4 years, 86 percent of them lasted less than 10 years, and 2.6 percent of them lasted 20 years or more. Of the ventures that were mutually assessed to be successful by their sponsors, 50 percent lasted at least 4 years. The longest-lived ventures were found in the metals processing, mining, programming (films), and petrochemicals industries.

A total of 6.6 percent of the ventures studied lasted one year (or less) after formation. Of the ventures that were mutually assessed to be successful by their sponsors, 4.7 percent lasted one year or less. The shortest-lived ventures were

Table 12-1
Mean Values for Entire Sample

	Percentage Termed Success	Percentage Ongoing	Years Duration	Maximum Years
Automobiles	50.0	22.7	4.2	9
Communications equipment	38.1	65.5	3.0	9
Communications services	40.4	38.6	4.4	22
Computers and peripherals	37.9	58.6	3.5	12
Electronic components	32.4	16.9	2.9	6
Engines	43.2	45.9	3.6	6
Farm and industrial equipment	27.3	54.5	3.1	6
Financial services	41.9	54.7	4.9	16
Heavy machinery	33.3	23.8	7.3	20
Light machinery	11.1	0.0	6.0	8
Medical products	37.1	31.4	4.3	14
Metals fabrication	62.5	50.0	6.4	14
Metals processing	33.3	33.3	9.3	23
Mining	50.0	22.2	9.8	21
Office equipment	38.5	15.4	7.4	26
Petrochemicals	63.9	49.3	10.3	46
Pharmaceuticals	55.9	74.2	5.0	34
Precision controls	43.3	46.6	3.7	10
Programming (films)	87.5	75.0	8.0	16
Programming packaging	41.4	17.2	2.7	6
Software and data bases	40.0	44.0	3.7	11
Steel	39.4	45.5	6.1	26
Videotape recorder and videodisk players	38.1	42.9	4.9	12

found in the communications equipment, computer and peripherals, electronic components, farm and industrial equipment, and programming packaging industries, but this result may primarily be due to their recent formation.

Partner Asymmetries

Independent variables were constructed as follows: (1) *Horizontal partners* were estimated using a dummy variable indicating whether partners were horizontally related in a substantial portion of their products, markets, technologies, and competitive activities. (2) *Vertical partners* were estimated using a dummy variable indicating whether partners were vertically related (that is, had a buyer–seller relationship with each other) in a substantial portion of their business activities. (3) Asymmetries in partners' *horizontal linkages* with their venture were estimated using an index, a dummy variable indicating whether parent 1 was horizontally related to the venture multiplied by a dummy variable indicating whether parent 2 was horizontally related to the venture. (4) Asymmetries in partners' *vertical linkages* with their venture were estimated using an index, a dummy variable indicating whether parent 1 was vertically related to the venture multiplied by a dummy variable indicating whether parent 2 was vertically related to the venture. (5) Asymmetries in partners' *relatedness linkages* with their venture were estimated using an index, a dummy variable indicating whether the R&D, production, or marketing activities of parent 1 were related to those of its venture multiplied by a dummy variable indicating whether the R&D, production, or marketing activities of parent 2 were related to those of its venture. (6) Asymmetries in sponsoring firm *nationalities* were estimated using an index, a dummy variable indicating whether parent 1 was a U.S. firm multiplied by a dummy variable indicating whether parent 2 was a U.S. firm. (7) Partner *size* asymmetry was estimated using the absolute value of the difference between a scaling (from 0 to 99) indicating the asset size of partner 1 and a scaling (from 0 to 99) indicating the asset size of partner 2. (8) Partners' *venturing experience* asymmetry was estimated using the absolute value of the difference between parent 1's number of cooperative arrangements and parent 2's number of cooperative arrangements.

Table 12–2 and 12–3 show mean values by industry for the partner asymmetry variables. Analysis of the effects of industry traits on venture performance appear elsewhere (Harrigan, 1986, 1987), and results from these other studies suggest that the performance of joint ventures (and other forms of cooperation) is more heavily influenced by their industry's structural traits than by the partnership and diversification traits examined herein.

Methodology

Information concerning sponsoring firms' relationships with each other and with their ventures was obtained in three stages: (1) construction of background papers on each industry using archival data, (2) validation using field interviews and survey questionnaires (completed in advance of the delphi interviews), and (3) a three-round delphi-method questionnaire (Harrigan, 1985, 1986, 1987). The influence of sponsoring-firm asymmetries on venture performance was tested by studying 895 strategic alliances competing in twenty-three industries during the years 1974–1985. Ventures operating within the target industries were the units of analysis.[1]

Estimates of the independent and dependent variables just described were obtained and refined from interviews and questionnaires using an iterative, delphi-like procedure (Delbecq, Van de Ven, and Gustafson, 1975; Holmer, 1967; Van de Ven, 1976). Interviews, telephone conversations, follow-up letters, transcripts, and comments on preliminary drafts of each industry vignette provided revised estimates of these factors until estimates for the 895 ventures' competitive contexts were developed in a procedure described in Harrigan (1986, 1987).

Table 12–4 shows the distribution of sponsoring firms' nationalities, and table 12–5 shows the distribution of pairings of sponsoring firms by nationalities. Note that at least one of the sponsoring firms was based in the United States in 93.4

Table 12-2
Sponsoring Firm Differences across Industries for Strategic Alliances Affecting Commerce in the United States

	Sponsors Horizontally Related to Each Other	Sponsors Vertically Related to Each Other	Both Sponsors Horizontally Related to Venture	Both Sponsors Vertically Related to Venture	Both Sponsors Related to Venture's Activities	Both Sponsors Unrelated to Venture's Activities
Automobiles	100.0%	0.0%	100.0%	0.0%	100.0%	0.0%
Communications equipment	14.6	30.9	5.5	9.1	18.2	14.6
Communications services	21.1	22.8	19.3	24.6	26.3	1.8
Computers and peripherals	55.2	31.0	55.2	6.9	72.4	1.7
Electronic components	63.4	19.7	56.3	19.7	88.7	0.0
Engines	83.8	8.1	81.1	2.7	83.8	0.0
Farm and industrial equipment	81.8	9.1	81.8	0.0	90.9	0.0
Financial services	32.6	12.8	34.9	20.9	69.8	0.0
Heavy machinery	61.9	23.8	28.6	0.0	52.4	9.5
Light machinery	66.7	0.0	66.7	0.0	66.7	0.0
Medical products	34.3	8.6	34.3	0.0	34.3	11.4
Metals fabrication	62.5	0.0	37.5	0.0	62.5	25.0
Metals processing	33.3	22.2	22.2	0.0	55.6	33.3
Mining	44.4	11.1	50.0	0.0	55.6	22.2
Office equipment	30.8	7.7	34.6	0.0	42.3	19.2
Petrochemicals	25.7	41.2	13.2	21.3	56.6	6.6
Pharmaceuticals	48.4	43.0	45.2	1.1	91.4	2.2
Precision controls	46.7	33.3	46.7	0.0	73.3	26.7
Programming (films)	42.9	42.9	42.9	0.0	42.9	0.0
Programming packaging	24.1	44.8	0.0	62.1	0.0	3.5
Software and data bases	20.0	40.0	12.0	28.0	20.0	4.0
Steel	63.6	15.2	57.6	6.1	84.9	3.0
Videotape recorders and videodisk players	33.3	33.3	14.3	47.6	14.3	19.1

Table 12–3
Substantial Differences in Partners' Asset Sizes, National Origins, and Venturing Experience Levels by Industry

	Partners are of significantly different asset sizes.	Partners are both based in the United States.	Partners have significantly different venturing experience levels.
Automobiles	13.6%	0.0%	18.2%
Communications equipment	16.4	65.5	34.6
Communications services	5.3	91.2	17.5
Computers and peripherals	27.6	34.5	36.2
Electronic components	23.9	67.6	22.5
Engines	13.5	43.2	13.5
Farm and industrial equipment	0.0	18.2	9.1
Financial services	7.0	62.8	4.6
Heavy machinery	14.3	33.3	0.0
Light machinery	0.0	100.0	0.0
Medical products	8.6	62.7	14.3
Metals fabrication	0.0	37.5	0.0
Metals processing	11.1	33.3	0.0
Mining	11.1	72.2	0.0
Office equipment	7.7	53.6	23.1
Petrochemicals	24.3	70.6	11.0
Pharmaceuticals	29.0	43.0	9.7
Precision controls	23.3	20.0	40.0
Programming (films)	0.0	71.4	42.9
Programming packaging	20.7	96.6	6.9
Software and data bases	16.0	88.0	32.0
Steel	3.0	30.0	0.0
Videotape recorders and videodisk players	4.8	47.6	23.8

Table 12–4
Distribution of Sponsoring Firms' Nationalities for Strategic Alliances Affecting Commerce in the United States

Belgium	0.7%	Korea	0.4%
Brazil	0.1	Netherlands	2.5
Canada	1.3	Puerto Rico	0.1
Denmark	0.4	Saudi Arabia	1.0
Finland	0.1	Spain	0.1
France	4.2	Sweden	1.8
Germany	5.8	Switzerland	2.0
Honduras	0.1	United Kingdom	6.3
Italy	2.9	United States	93.4
Japan	17.0		

Note: n = 895. Two sponsors were coded for each venture. Probability that a particular nationality would be represented in a strategic alliance was calculated by summing nationalities for each sponsor and subtracting number of ventures where sponsors' nationalities were identical.

Table 12–5
Distribution of Sponsor Pairings by Nationality for Strategic Alliances Affecting Commerce in the United States

Belgian	with German	0.1%	French	with Japanese	0.2%
Belgian	with Italian	0.1	French	with Swedish	0.1
Belgian	with U.S.	0.5	French	with U.S.	3.0
Brazilian	with U.S.	0.1	German	with German	0.5
British	with British	0.3	German	with Italian	0.3
British	with German	0.2	German	with Japanese	0.3
British	with Italian	0.1	German	with Swiss	0.1
British	with Japanese	0.7	German	with U.S.	3.7
British	with Puerto Rican	0.1	Honduran	with U.S.	0.1
British	with Saudi	0.1	Italian	with Italian	0.1
British	with U.S.	4.6	Italian	with Japanese	0.2
Canadian	with Canadian	0.1	Italian	with Swedish	0.1
Canadian	with U.S.	0.8	Italian	with U.S.	1.8
Danish	with French	0.1	Japanese	with Japanese	0.7
Danish	with U.S.	0.3	Japanese	with Saudi	0.1
Dutch	with Dutch	0.2	Japanese	with Spanish	0.1
Dutch	with German	0.2	Japanese	with Swiss	0.1
Dutch	with U.S.	2.0	Japanese	with U.S.	14.4
Finnish	with U.S.	0.1	Korean	with U.S.	0.5
French	with British	0.1	Saudi	with U.S.	0.8
French	with French	0.3	Swedish	with U.S.	1.6
French	with German	0.2	Swiss	with Swiss	0.3
French	with Italian	0.1	Swiss	with U.S.	1.5
			U.S.	with U.S.	57.2

percent of the ventures studied. Both sponsoring firms were based in the United States in 57.2 percent of the ventures studied. All of the strategic alliances examined affected commerce within the United States regardless of the national origins of the venture's sponsors.

Results Concerning Diversification

Venture Performance and Related Diversification

Sponsors are related (in product, market, or technology) to their venture.
Table 12–6 depicts the relatedness of sponsoring firms to their ventures by industry. A total of 59.6 percent of the ventures studied were related diversifications for both of their sponsors, while 51.4 percent of these related ventures were mutually assessed to be successful by their sponsors (30.6 percent of the total sample). Significant differences between firms 1 and 2 in sponsor–venture relationships are reported in the section summary. The greatest proportions of ventures that were closely related to their sponsoring firms' activities were found in the automobile, computer and peripherals, electronic component, engine, farm and industrial equipment, financial services, pharmaceuticals, precision controls and robotics, and steel industries.

Table 12–6
Differences in Sponsoring Firms' Product-Market Relatedness
to Venture by Industry

	Unsuccessful		Successful	
	Mean	*Standard Deviation*	*Mean*	*Standard Deviation*
Automobiles	1.00	0.00	1.00	0.00
Communications equipment	0.18	0.39	0.19	0.40
Communications services	0.15	0.36	0.43	0.51
Computers and peripherals	0.64	0.49	0.86	0.35
Electronic components	0.85	0.36	0.96	0.21
Engines	0.71	0.46	1.00	0.00
Farm and industrial equipment	0.88	0.35	1.00	0.00
Financial services	0.64	0.48	0.78	0.42
Heavy machinery	0.43	0.51	0.71	0.49
Light machinery	0.67	0.58	*	*
Medical products	0.23	0.43	0.54	0.52
Metals fabrication	0.67	0.58	0.60	0.55
Metals processing	0.50	0.55	0.67	0.58
Mining	0.56	0.53	0.56	0.53
Office equipment	0.44	0.51	0.40	0.52
Petrochemicals	0.35	0.48	0.69	0.47
Pharmaceuticals	0.88	0.33	0.94	0.24
Precision controls	0.76	0.44	0.69	0.48
Programming (films)	*	*	0.43	0.53
Programming packaging	0.00	0.00	0.00	0.00
Software and data bases	0.20	0.41	0.20	0.42
Steel	0.90	0.31	0.77	0.44
Videotape recorders and videodisk players	0.08	0.28	0.25	0.46

*Cannot be calculated.

Relatively fewer related ventures have been formed since 1974 (64.1 percent of the ventures formed before 1975 as compared with 58.6 percent of the ventures formed after 1974). And pre-1975 related ventures were more likely to be mutually judged successful than those formed after 1974 (64.3 percent versus 48.5 percent, respectively). The related diversification variable adds little predictive power in regression models of venture survival, but it is positively signed and statistically significant in predicting venture duration and success. (R^2 equals .02 and .008, respectively.)

Summary. A larger percentage of strategic alliances are related to both of their sponsoring firms than are unrelated to them. Venture success rates are slightly less than proportional for the subsample that is related to both sponsoring firms. This result suggests that simply "sticking to one's knitting" alone—venturing in activities that are close to sponsoring firms' strategic cores—is not enough to insure venture success. A larger percentage of strategic alliances that are related to both sponsoring firms were formed before 1975 and they were proportionally successful. Ventures related to both sponsoring firms are more likely to be judged a success by both sponsoring firms and more likely to be longer in duration than ventures with asymmetrical patterns of sponsor–venture relatedness.

Venture Performance and Horizontal Diversification

Sponsors are horizontally related to their venture. Table 12–7 depicts the horizontal relatedness of sponsoring firms to their ventures by industry. A total of 36.1 percent of the ventures studied were horizontal diversifications for both of their sponsors. A full 51.7 percent of these horizontally related ventures were mutually assessed to be successful by their sponsors (18.7 percent of the total sample). Significant differences between firms 1 and 2 in sponsor–venture relationships are reported in the section summary.

Table 12–7
Differences in Sponsoring Firms' Horizontal Relatedness to Venture by Industry

	Unsuccessful		Successful	
	Mean	Standard Deviation	Mean	Standard Deviation
Automobiles	1.00	0.00	1.00	0.00
Communications equipment	0.09	0.29	0.00	0.00
Communications services	0.09	0.29	0.35	0.49
Computers and peripherals	0.47	0.51	0.68	0.48
Electronic components	0.52	0.50	0.65	0.49
Engines	0.67	0.48	1.00	0.00
Farm and industrial equipment	0.75	0.46	1.00	0.00
Financial services	0.28	0.45	0.44	0.50
Heavy machinery	0.29	0.47	0.29	0.49
Light machinery	0.67	0.58	*	*
Medical products	0.23	0.43	0.54	0.52
Metals fabrication	0.67	0.58	0.20	0.45
Metals processing	0.00	0.00	0.67	0.58
Mining	0.44	0.53	0.56	0.53
Office equipment	0.38	0.50	0.30	0.48
Petrochemicals	0.04	0.20	0.18	0.39
Pharmaceuticals	0.32	0.47	0.56	0.50
Precision controls	0.35	0.49	0.62	0.51
Programming (films)	*	*	0.43	0.53
Programming packaging	0.00	0.00	0.00	0.00
Software and data bases	0.20	0.41	0.00	0.00
Steel	0.70	0.47	0.38	0.51
Videotape recorders and videodisk players	0.08	0.28	0.25	0.46

*Cannot be calculated.

The greatest proportions of ventures that were horizontally related to their sponsors were found in the automobile, engine, and farm and industrial equipment industries.

Relatively more horizontally related ventures have been formed since 1974 (29.4 percent of the ventures formed before 1975 as compared to 37.5 percent of the ventures formed after 1974). But pre-1975 horizontally related ventures were more likely to be mutually judged successful than those formed after 1974 (68.9 percent versus 48.9 percent, respectively). The horizontal diversification variable adds little predictive power in regression models of venture survival and duration, but it is positvely signed and statistically significant in predicting venture success. (R^2 equals .01.)

Summary. Ventures that are horizontally related to both sponsoring firms are more likely than others to be judged a success by both sponsoring firms. A larger percentage of strategic alliances that are horizontally related to both sponsoring firms were formed after 1974 than before 1975, although venture success rates are more than proportional for both time periods.

Venture Performance and Vertical Diversification

Sponsors are vertically related to their venture. Table 12–8 depicts the vertical relatedness of sponsoring firms to their ventures by industry. Of the ventures studied, 13.9 percent were vertical diversifications for both of their sponsors; 46.8 percent of these vertically related ventures were mutually assessed to be successful by their sponsors (6.5 percent of the total sample). Significant differences between firms 1 and 2 in sponsor–venture relationships are reported in the section summary. The greatest proportions of ventures that were vertically related to sponsoring firms were found in the communications services, financial services, petrochemicals, programming packaging, software, and videotape recorder and videodisc player industries.

Relatively fewer vertically related ventures have been formed since 1974 (22.2 percent of the ventures formed before 1975 as compared with 12.1 percent of the ventures formed after 1974). And pre-1975 vertically related ventures were more likely to be mutually judged successful than those formed after 1974 (50 percent versus 45.6 percent, respectively). The vertical-diversification variable adds little predictive power in regression models of venture duration and success, but it is negatively signed and statistically significant in predicting venture survival. (R^2 equals .01.) This result may be due to the larger proportion of vertically related ventures that were formed (and subsequently terminated) early in the lives of U.S. industries to provide missing infrastructures. Similar patterns have been observed in the use of joint ventures in other newly industrializing economies (Leff, 1978).

Table 12–8
Differences in Sponsoring Firms' Vertical Relatedness to Venture by Industry

	Unsuccessful		Successful	
	Mean	Standard Deviation	Mean	Standard Deviation
Automobiles	0.00	0.00	0.00	0.00
Communications equipment	0.05	0.24	0.14	0.36
Communications services	0.23	0.43	0.26	0.45
Computers and peripherals	0.05	0.23	0.09	0.29
Electronic components	0.19	0.39	0.22	0.42
Engines	0.05	0.22	0.00	0.00
Farm and industrial equipment	0.00	0.00	0.00	0.00
Financial services	0.30	0.46	0.08	0.28
Heavy machinery	0.00	0.00	0.00	0.00
Light machinery	0.00	0.00	*	*
Medical products	0.00	0.00	0.00	0.00
Metals fabrication	0.00	0.00	0.00	0.00
Metals processing	0.00	0.00	0.00	0.00
Mining	0.00	0.00	0.00	0.00
Office equipment	0.00	0.00	0.00	0.00
Petrochemicals	0.12	0.33	0.26	0.44
Pharmaceuticals	0.00	0.00	0.02	0.14
Precision controls	0.00	0.00	0.00	0.00
Programming (films)	*	*	0.00	0.00
Programming packaging	0.53	0.51	0.75	0.45
Software and data bases	0.40	0.51	0.10	0.32
Steel	0.10	0.31	0.00	0.00
Videotape recorders and videodisk players	0.38	0.51	0.63	0.52

*Cannot be calculated.

Summary. Ventures that are vertically related to both sponsoring firms are less likely to be operating after 1985. Results suggest that the time when this particular form of diversification through cooperative strategy is appropriate has passed in many mature industries. A larger percentage of strategic alliances that are vertically related to both sponsoring firms were formed before 1975 than after 1974, although venture success rates are more than proportional for both time periods.

Venture Performance and Unrelated Diversification

Sponsors are unrelated to their venture. Table 12–9 depicts the unrelatedness of sponsoring firms to their ventures by industry. Only 6.3 percent of the ventures studied were unrelated diversifications for both of their sponsors, while 23 percent of these unrelated ventures were mutually assessed to be successful by their sponsors (1.5 percent of the total sample). Significant differences between firms 1 and 2 in sponsor–venture relationships are reported in the section summary. The

Table 12–9
**Differences in Sponsoring Firms' Unrelatedness
to Venture by Industry**

	Unsuccessful		Successful	
	Mean	Standard Deviation	Mean	Standard Deviation
Automobiles	0.00	0.00	0.00	0.00
Communications equipment	0.21	0.41	0.05	0.22
Communications services	0.00	0.00	0.04	0.21
Computers and peripherals	0.03	0.17	0.00	0.00
Electronic components	0.00	0.00	0.00	0.00
Engines	0.00	0.00	0.00	0.00
Farm and industrial equipment	0.00	0.00	0.00	0.00
Financial services	0.00	0.00	0.00	0.00
Heavy machinery	0.14	0.36	0.00	0.00
Light machinery	0.00	0.00	*	*
Medical products	0.18	0.39	0.00	0.00
Metals fabrication	0.00	0.00	0.40	0.55
Metals processing	0.50	0.55	0.00	0.00
Mining	0.33	0.50	0.11	0.33
Office equipment	0.31	0.48	0.00	0.00
Petrochemicals	0.10	0.31	0.05	0.21
Pharmaceuticals	0.00	0.00	0.04	0.19
Precision controls	0.35	0.49	0.15	0.38
Programming (films)	*	*	0.00	0.00
Programming packaging	0.06	0.24	0.00	0.00
Software and data bases	0.07	0.26	0.00	0.00
Steel	0.05	0.22	0.00	0.00
Videotape recorders and videodisk players	0.31	0.48	0.00	0.00

*Cannot be calculated.

greatest proportions of ventures that were unrelated to sponsoring firms were found in the communciations services and equipment, petrochemicals, and precision controls and robotics industries.

Relatively fewer unrelated ventures have been formed since 1974 (9.2 percent of the ventures formed before 1975 as compared with 5.7 percent of the ventures formed after 1974). But, post-1974 unrelated ventures were more likely to be mutually judged successful than those formed before 1975 (21.4 percent versus 23.8 percent, respectively). The unrelated-diversification variable adds little predictive power in regression models of venture duration and survival, but it is negatively signed and statistically significant in predicting venture success. (R^2 equals .01.)

Summary. Ventures unrelated to both sponsoring firms are less likely than others to be successful. A larger percentage of strategic alliances that are unrelated to both sponsoring firms were formed before 1975 than after 1974, although venture success rates are low for both subsamples.

Results Concerning Partner Asymmetries

Venture Performance and Partner Relationships

Sponsors are horizontally related to each other. Table 12–10 depicts the horizontal relationships of sponsoring firms to each other by industry. A total of 42.2 percent of the ventures studied were formed by sponsors that were horizontally related to each other, and 51.6 percent of those ventures between horizontally related partners were mutually judged to be successful (21.8 percent of the total). Sponsoring firms were most likely to be horizontally related to each other in the automobile, computer and peripherals, electronic component, engine, farm and industrial equipment, light and heavy machinery, metals fabrication, and steel industries.

Relatively more ventures between horizontally related sponsors have been formed since 1974 (38.6 percent of the ventures formed before 1975 as compared to

Table 12–10
**Sponsoring Firms' Horizontal Relationships
to Each Other by Industry**

	Unsuccessful		Successful	
	Mean	Standard Deviation	Mean	Standard Deviation
Automobiles	1.00	0.00	1.00	0.00
Communications equipment	0.18	0.39	0.10	0.51
Communications services	0.12	0.33	0.35	0.49
Computers and peripherals	0.47	0.51	0.68	0.48
Electronic components	0.56	0.50	0.78	0.42
Engines	0.71	0.46	1.00	0.00
Farm and industrial equipment	0.75	0.46	1.00	0.00
Financial services	0.30	0.46	0.36	0.49
Heavy machinery	0.57	0.51	0.71	0.49
Light machinery	0.67	0.58	*	*
Medical products	0.23	0.43	0.54	0.52
Metals fabrication	0.67	0.58	0.60	0.55
Metals processing	0.17	0.41	0.67	0.58
Mining	0.33	0.50	0.56	0.53
Office equipment	0.25	0.45	0.40	0.52
Petrochemicals	0.10	0.31	0.34	0.48
Pharmaceuticals	0.32	0.47	0.62	0.49
Precision controls	0.53	0.51	0.38	0.51
Programming (films)	*	*	0.57	0.53
Programming packaging	0.18	0.39	0.33	0.49
Software and data bases	0.33	0.49	0.00	0.00
Steel	0.80	0.41	0.38	0.51
Videotape recorders and videodisk players	0.23	0.44	0.50	0.53

*Cannot be calculated.

43 percent of the ventures formed after 1974). But pre-1975 ventures between horizontally related sponsors were more likely to be mutually judged successful than those formed after 1974 (66.1 percent versus 49.2 percent, respectively). The horizontal-partners variable adds little predictive power in regression models of venture duration and survival, but it is positively signed and statistically significant in predicting venture success. (R^2 equals .01.)

Sponsors are vertically related to each other. Table 12–11 depicts the vertical relationships of sponsoring firms to each other by industry. A total of 26.4 percent of the ventures studied were formed by sponsors that were vertically related to each other, and 49.8 percent of those ventures between vertically related partners were mutually judged to be successful (13.1 percent of the sample). Sponsoring firms were most likely to be vertically related to each other in the programming packaging, petrochemicals, pharmaceuticals, entertainment programming, and software industries.

**Table 12–11
Sponsoring Firms' Vertical Relationships
to Each Other by Industry**

	Unsuccessful		Successful	
	Mean	Standard Deviation	Mean	Standard Deviation
Automobiles	0.00	0.00	0.00	0.00
Communications equipment	0.24	0.43	0.43	0.51
Communications services	0.12	0.33	0.39	0.50
Computers and peripherals	0.39	0.49	0.18	0.39
Electronic components	0.21	0.41	0.17	0.39
Engines	0.14	0.36	0.00	0.00
Farm and industrial equipment	0.13	0.35	0.00	0.00
Financial services	0.10	0.30	0.17	0.38
Heavy machinery	0.21	0.43	0.29	0.49
Light machinery	0.00	0.00	*	*
Medical products	0.00	0.00	0.23	0.44
Metals fabrication	0.00	0.00	0.00	0.00
Metals processing	0.33	0.52	0.00	0.00
Mining	0.22	0.44	0.00	0.00
Office equipment	0.00	0.00	0.20	0.42
Petrochemicals	0.45	0.50	0.39	0.49
Pharmaceuticals	0.56	0.50	0.33	0.47
Precision controls	0.12	0.33	0.61	0.51
Programming (films)	*	*	0.29	0.49
Programming packaging	0.47	0.51	0.42	0.51
Software and data bases	0.33	0.49	0.50	0.53
Steel	0.05	0.22	0.31	0.48
Videotape recorders and videodisk players	0.31	0.48	0.38	0.52

*Cannot be calculated.

Relatively more ventures between vertically related sponsors have been formed since 1974 (24.8 percent of the ventures formed before 1975 as compared with 26.6 percent of the ventures formed after 1974). But pre-1975 ventures between vertically related sponsors were more likely to be mutually judged successful than those formed after 1974 (73.7 percent versus 45.2 percent, respectively). The vertical-partners variable adds little predictive power in regression models of venture duration and success, but it is positively signed and statistically significant in predicting venture survival. (R^2 equals .03.)

Summary. A larger percentage of strategic alliances were formed by partners that are horizontally related to each other than by those vertically related to each other, although venture success rates were about the same for either pattern of partner relatedness. A larger percentage of strategic alliances between pairs of horizontally related and vertically related partners were formed after 1974, but the success rate for both types of ventures was higher before 1975. Ventures between horizontally related partners were more likely than those between vertically related partners to be judged a success by both sponsoring firms. Ventures between vertically related partners were more likely to survive through 1985 (regardless of when they were formed).

Venture Performance and National Origins of Venture Sponsors

Partners are both U.S. firms. Table 12–12 depicts the proportions of partners that are based in the United States by industry. A total of 57.1 percent of the ventures studied were sponsored by firms that were both incorporated in the United States, and 41.1 percent of these U.S.-sponsored ventures were mutually assessed to be successful by their sponsors (23.4 percent of the total sample). U.S. sponsors were found most frequently in the communications equipment and services, electronic components, financial services, medical products, mining, programming packaging, petrochemicals, entertainment programming, and software industries. Non-U.S. sponsors were found most frequently in the automobile (primarily French, Italian, Japanese, and Swedish partners), communications equipment (primarily Canadian, Japanese, and Swedish partners), computer and peripherals (Japanese partners), engines, (British and German partners), heavy machinery (German partners), metals fabrication (Japanese partners), and processing (French partners), pharmaceuticals (German, Italian, Japanese, and Swiss partners), precision controls and robotics (German, Japanese, and Swedish partners), steel (Japanese partners), and videotape recorder and videodisk player industries (British, Dutch, and Japanese partners).

A full 95 percent of the unsuccessful automobile ventures had at least one non-U.S. sponsor, as did 68 percent of the successful automobile ventures. A total of 47 percent of the unsuccessful precision controls and robotics ventures and 46 percent of the unsuccessful videotape recorder and videodisk player ventures had

Table 12-12
Both Sponsoring Firms Based in the United States by Industry

	Unsuccessful		Successful	
	Mean	Standard Deviation	Mean	Standard Deviation
Automobiles	0.00	0.00	0.00	0.00
Communications equipment	0.76	0.43	0.48	0.51
Communications services	0.97	0.17	0.83	0.39
Computers and peripherals	0.39	0.49	0.27	0.46
Electronic components	0.73	0.45	0.57	0.51
Engines	0.67	0.48	0.13	0.34
Farm and industrial equipment	0.25	0.46	0.00	0.00
Financial services	0.78	0.42	0.42	0.50
Heavy machinery	0.21	0.43	0.57	0.53
Light machinery	1.00	0.00	*	*
Medical products	0.59	0.50	0.69	0.48
Metals fabrication	0.67	0.58	0.20	0.45
Metals processing	0.50	0.55	0.00	0.00
Mining	0.89	0.33	0.56	0.53
Office equipment	0.69	0.48	0.30	0.48
Petrochemicals	0.63	0.49	0.75	0.44
Pharmaceuticals	0.56	0.50	0.33	0.47
Precision controls	0.12	0.33	0.31	0.48
Programming (films)	*	*	0.71	0.49
Programming packaging	0.94	0.24	1.00	0.00
Software and data bases	0.80	0.41	1.00	0.00
Steel	0.30	0.47	0.54	0.36
Videotape recorders and videodisk players	0.31	0.48	0.55	0.45

*Cannot be calculated.

at least one non-U.S. sponsor, as did 35 percent of the successful precision controls and robotics ventures and 12 percent of the successful videotape recorder and videodisk player ventures.

Meanwhile, 56 percent of the successful engine ventures and 50 percent of the successful farm and industrial equipment ventures had non-U.S. sponsors, as did 19 percent of the unsuccessful engines ventures and 38 percent of the unsuccessful farm and industrial equipment ventures. Also, 45 percent of the successful computers and peripheral equipment ventures and 26 percent of the successful communications equipment ventures had at least one non-U.S. sponsor, as did 36 percent of the unsuccessful computers and peripheral equipment ventures and 11 percent of the unsuccessful communications equipment ventures.

Relatively more ventures between partners of differing national origins have been formed in the United States since 1974 (30.1 percent of the ventures formed before 1975 as compared with 45.5 percent of the ventures formed after 1974). Pre-1975 ventures where both sponsors were U.S. firms were more likely to be mutually judged successful than those formed after 1974 (58.9 percent versus 36.4

percent, respectively). The national-origins variable (as coded in this analysis) adds little predictive power in regression models of venture survival, but it is negatively signed and statistically significant in predicting venture success. (R^2 equals .01). It is positively signed and statistically significant in predicting venture duration. (R^2 equals .01.)

Summary. A larger percentage of strategic alliances between firms based in the U.S. were formed before 1975 than after 1974. More joint ventures (and other forms of cooperation) between firms of differing national origins are being formed now than in the past. This may be because competitive necessity forces managers to be less ethnocentric in their firms' searches for new products, customers, technologies, and resources than they once were (Harrigan, 1984). Although the Hofstede (1980) measure of cultural distance was not used in my analysis to test this hypothesis, comments from interviewed managers lead me to suspect that cultural homogeneity among sponsors is more important to venture success than symmetry in their national origins. For example, several observers noted that General Motors' values are more similar to those of its partner, Toyota, than to those of Ford Motor.

Venture Performance and Sponsors' Levels of Venturing Experience

Partners' experience levels vary. Table 12–13 depicts the proportions of partners with significantly different levels of venturing experience by industry. A total of 35 percent of the ventures studied were formed by sponsors with about the same level of venturing experience, and 8 percent were formed by sponsors with an experience level difference of more than ten ventures. Moreover, 39.5 percent of the ventures formed by sponsors with about the same level of venturing experience were mutually assessed to be successful (7.6 percent of the total sample), while 43.1 percent of the ventures formed by sponsors with an experience-level difference of more than ten ventures were mutually assessed to be successful (3.5 percent of total sample). Significant differences between firms 1 and 2 in sponsor–venture relationships are reported in the section summary. The greatest differences in sponsors' levels of venturing experience were found in the computer and peripheral, precision controls and robotics, and software industries. Partners were most evenly matched in their venturing experience levels in the engine, farm and industrial equipment, financial services, light and heavy machinery, and medical products industries.

Relatively fewer ventures between partners with the same level of venturing experience have been formed since 1974 (24.2 percent of the ventures formed before 1975 as compared with 18.2 percent of the ventures formed after 1974). Pre-1975 ventures between sponsors of similar venturing experience were more likely to be mutually judged successful than those formed after 1974 (43.2 percent versus 38.5 percent, respectively). Relatively more ventures between partners with vastly different levels of venturing experience have been formed since 1974 (2 percent of the

Table 12–13
Differences in Sponsoring Firms' Venturing Experience Levels by Industry

	Unsuccessful		Successful	
	Mean	Standard Deviation	Mean	Standard Deviation
Automobiles	1.3	0.8	5.6	5.4
Communications equipment	4.8	4.8	6.4	5.6
Communications services	4.2	4.7	3.7	3.7
Computers and peripherals	8.0	6.9	7.9	6.9
Electronic components	5.8	4.4	4.4	3.5
Engines	4.8	6.7	2.2	3.8
Farm and industrial equipment	1.8	1.6	3.3	4.2
Financial services	3.1	4.6	3.1	3.2
Heavy machinery	1.4	2.0	0.7	1.3
Light machinery	0.0	0.0	*	*
Medical products	2.1	3.1	4.0	3.8
Metals fabrication	3.3	2.5	0.8	0.8
Metals processing	2.5	2.5	0.7	0.6
Mining	2.0	2.1	2.8	1.8
Office equipment	4.1	5.2	3.5	3.6
Petrochemicals	3.3	2.9	2.9	2.9
Pharmaceuticals	2.9	2.7	4.0	3.1
Precision controls	5.6	7.0	7.8	5.3
Programming (films)	*	*	6.1	2.3
Programming packaging	4.1	4.1	3.3	1.7
Software and data bases	4.8	6.4	7.7	7.4
Steel	2.0	1.6	1.7	0.9
Videotape recorders and videodisk players	6.2	5.7	3.6	2.1

*Cannot be calculated.

ventures formed before 1975 as compared with 9.3 percent of the ventures formed after 1974). The finding that pre-1975 ventures between sponsors of vastly different venturing experience were less likely to be mutually judged successful than those formed after 1974 (33.3 percent versus 43.5 percent, respectively) suggests that experienced partners are now more willing to help their less-experienced counterparts learn to use strategic alliances effectively. The venturing-experience variable adds little predictive power in regression models of venture success, but it is negatively signed and statistically significant in predicting venture duration. (R^2 equals .02.) It is positively signed and statistically significant in predicting venture survival. (R^2 equals .01.)

Summary. Most of the ventures formed in recent years were between partners with dissimilar venturing experience levels. The impact of such dissimilarity on venture success is negative (although *not* statistically significant). A larger percentage of strategic alliances formed by partners with similar experience levels were formed before 1975 than after 1974, although venture success rates are more than proportional for both time periods.

Venture Performance and Sponsors' Relative Asset Sizes

Partner's asset sizes vary. Table 12–14 depicts the proportions of partners with significantly different asset sizes. Differences in sponsoring firms' asset sizes were scaled (through arithmetic transformation) from 0 to 99. A total of 24.6 percent of the ventures studied were formed by partners of similar asset size. Only 2 percent of the ventures studied were formed by partners with asset-size differences that were coded at the very high end of the scale, while 52.7 percent of the ventures formed between partners of similar asset sizes were mutually judged to be successful by their sponsors (13 percent of the total sample). The greatest differences in sponsors' asset sizes were found in the electronic component, computer and peripherals, pharmaceuticals, and precision controls and robotics industries.

Relatively fewer ventures between partners of the same asset size have been formed since 1974 (30.1 percent of the ventures formed before 1975 as compared with 23.5 percent of the ventures formed after 1974). Pre-1975 ventures between sponsors of similar asset size are more likely to be mutually judged successful than those formed after 1974 (67.4 percent versus 48.9 percent, respectively). Relatively

Table 12–14
Differences in Sponsoring Firms' Asset Sizes by Industry

	Unsuccessful		Successful	
	Mean	Standard Deviation	Mean	Standard Deviation
Automobiles	15.9	10.4	20.9	19.1
Communications equipment	21.8	15.9	24.0	13.0
Communications services	19.7	12.7	10.0	8.5
Computers and peripherals	29.0	13.5	22.0	17.3
Electronic components	23.9	16.0	21.7	17.4
Engines	23.8	18.6	11.6	8.9
Farm and industrial equipment	13.8	6.9	21.7	5.8
Financial services	14.9	11.7	16.9	13.4
Heavy machinery	20.4	14.5	22.1	16.3
Light machinery	8.3	2.9	*	*
Medical products	21.4	16.3	19.6	10.3
Metals fabrication	16.7	10.4	8.0	6.7
Metals processing	23.3	19.9	8.3	5.8
Mining	18.3	14.0	10.6	7.3
Office equipment	23.8	13.2	9.5	8.0
Petrochemicals	27.2	19.6	20.5	17.3
Pharmaceuticals	31.2	17.6	25.1	15.9
Precision controls	14.4	11.7	39.2	23.3
Programming (films)	*	*	7.9	7.0
Programming packaging	26.8	18.3	7.1	5.0
Software and data bases	20.3	16.7	22.0	14.6
Steel	13.5	10.8	15.0	10.0
Videotape recorders and videodisk players	16.9	12.0	11.9	8.8

*Cannot be calculated.

more ventures between partners of vastly different asset size have been formed since 1974 (1 percent of the ventures formed before 1975 as compared with 2 percent of the ventures formed after 1974). The asset-size variable adds weak predictive power in regression models of venture survival, duration, or success (because coefficient values in all cases are close to zero and R^2 equals .02, .01, and .01, respectively).

Summary. More ventures are being formed now by partners of different asset sizes than in the past. A larger percentage of strategic alliances formed by sponsoring firms of similar asset sizes were formed before 1975 than after 1974, although venture success rates are more than proportional for both time periods.

Conclusion

Results suggest that ventures are more successful where partners are related (in products, markets, and/or technologies) to their ventures or horizontally related to them than when they are vertically related or unrelated to their ventures. Results suggest that ventures last longer between partners of similar cultures, asset sizes, and venturing experience levels. Also, results suggest that ventures last longer when their activities are related (in products, markets, and/or technologies) to both of its sponsors' activities.

Given the great disparity in means (and standard deviations) by industry shown in tables 12–1 through 12–14, it appears that partners' traits and sponsor–venture relationship traits do not offer much explanatory power in models of venture survival, duration, and success. These results are consistent with Harrigan's (1986, 1987) findings that partners' and sponsor–venture relationship traits are less important in determining which cooperative strategy to embrace than industry traits are. They suggest that venturing firms should worry *less* about their partners' traits and *more* about the competitive needs that their ventures are intended to address when their managers use strategic alliances.

Note

1. The sample industries included automobiles (3.5 percent of sample), communications equipment (3.9 percent), communications services (7.2 percent), computers and peripherals (4.9 percent), electronic components (12.1 percent), engines (4.1 percent), farm and industrial equipment (1.0 percent), financial services (8.0 percent), heavy machinery (3.3 percent), light machinery (0.6 percent), medical products (4.9 percent), metals fabrication (0.8 percent), metals processing (1.2 percent), mining (2.9 percent), office equipment (4.5 percent), petrochemicals (14.2 percent), pharmaceuticals (4.9 percent), precision controls (3.3 percent), programming (films) (0.4 percent), programming packaging (4.9 percent), software and data bases (2.9 percent), steel (3.7 percent), and videotape recorders and videodisk players (2.5 percent).

References

Berg, S.V., Duncan, J.L., Jr., and Friedman, P. 1982. *Joint venture strategies and corporate innovation.* Cambridge, Mass.: Oelgeschlager, Gunn & Hain.

Bettis, R.A. 1981. "Performance differences in related and unrelated diversified firms." *Strategic Management Journal,* 2: 379–92.

Bettis, R.A., and Hall, W.K. 1982. "Diversification strategy, accounting determined risk, and accounting determined return." *Academy of Management Journal,* 25(2): 254–65.

Caves, R.E., and Porter, M.E. 1976. "Barriers to exit." In D.P. Qualls and R.T. Masson (eds.), *Essays in industrial organization in honor of Joe S. Bain.* Cambridge, Mass.: Ballinger, 39–69.

Delbecq, A.L., Van de Ven, A., and Gustafson, D.H. 1975. *Group techniques for program planning.* Glenview, Ill.: Scott Foresman.

Harrigan, K.R. 1980. *Strategies for declining businesses.* Lexington, Mass.: Lexington Books.

Harrigan, K.R. 1984. Innovation by overseas subsidiaries. *Journal of Business Strategy* (Summer): 47–55.

Harrigan, K.R. 1985. *Strategies for joint ventures.* Lexington, Mass.: Lexington Books.

Harrigan, K.R. 1986. *Strategic alliances: Form, autonomy, and performance.* Working paper. Columbia University, New York.

Harrigan, K.R. 1987. "Joint ventures: A mechanism for creating strategic change." In A. Pettigrew (ed.), *The management of strategic change.* London: Basil Blackwell (in press).

Hofstede, G. 1980. *Culture's consequences: International difference in work-related values.* Beverly Hills: Sage.

Holmer, O. 1967. *Analysis of the future: The delphi method.* Santa Barbara, Calif.: RAND Corporation.

Killing, J.P. 1983. *Strategies for joint venture success.* New York: Praeger.

Leff, N.H. 1978. "Industrial organization and entrepreneurship in the developing countries: The economic groups." *Economic Development and Cultural Change,* 26(4): 661–75.

Levine, J.B., and Byrne, J.A. 1986. "Odd couples." *Business Week* (July 21, 1986): 100–6.

Michel, A., and Shaked, I.M. 1984. "Does business diversification affect performance?" *Financial Management Journal,* 13 (Winter): 18–25.

Montgomery, C.A. 1979. *Diversification, market structure, and firm performance: An Extension of Rumelt's work.* Unpublished doctoral dissertation. West Lafayette, Ind.: Purdue University.

Montgomery, C.A. and Singh, H. 1984. "Diversification strategy and systemic risk." *Strategic Management Journal,* 5: 181–91.

Pate, J.L. 1969. "Joint venture activity, 1960–1968." *Economic Review.* Federal Reserve Bank of Cleveland, 16–23.

Porter, M.E. 1976. "Please note location of nearest exit: Exit barriers and strategic and organizational planning." *California Management Review,* 19(2): 21–33.

Rajagopalan, S., and Harrigan, K.R. 1986. *Diversification and market performance: In defense of the unrelated diversification strategy.* Presented at the 50th Academy of Management Meetings, Chicago, August 13–16.

Rumelt, R.P. 1974. *Strategy, structure, and economic performance.* Cambridge, Mass.: Harvard University Press.

Van de Ven, A.H. 1976. "On the nature, formation, and maintenance of relations among organizations." *Academy of Management Review,* 1: 24–36.

13

Network Analysis for Cooperative Interfirm Relationships

Gordon Walker

Interorganizational relationships have long been a subject of study for sociologists interested in exchange behavior, particularly in the context of an organizational community. The favored analytical construct for posing and testing hypotheses about these relationships is the network (Laumann, Galaskiewicz, and Marsden, 1978). This chapter explores how network approaches to understanding and predicting interorganizational behavior might be applied usefully to cooperative relationships between private-sector firms in an international context.

A common motivation of sociological research on interorganizational networks has been to uncover links between the pattern of organizational relationships and the social structure of the community, indicated by characteristics of organizational leaders (Laumann and Pappi, 1976). For this reason, the bounds of the community were quite restricted, usually defined by the geographic limits of a moderate-sized town or region; and the results indicated how economic decision making reflected in interorganizational behavior in the community was related to its social structure and to problems of coordinating exchange. The extensive investigations of interlocking directorates among corporations in a national economy (Pennings, 1984) represent an expanded version of this line of research, but focus more on regional differences and patterns of interorganizational or intersector control (Burt, 1980a; Mintz and Schwartz, 1981) than on characteristics of individual leaders.

The focus on shared membership patterns in a geographic community restricts the generalizability of this research tradition to interfirm cooperative relationships across national boundaries. Furthermore, the economic purpose and context of commercial interfirm cooperative relationships differentiates them from the types of relationship that sociologists have traditionally examined from a network perspective. The network metaphor, however, has become increasingly useful as a means of describing an emerging part of the global commercial context.

In what ways, then, can the research tradition on interorganizational networks contribute to a better understanding of global network behavior among for-profit enterprises? The present chapter addresses this question by proposing two tasks for network analysis: (1) identifying the extent of a firm's cooperative strategy and (2) evaluating the relative efficiency or strategic value of a cooperative relationship.

Because they use different theories and techniques, the applications of network analysis to the two problems just presented emphasize different aspects of the administration and content of cooperative relationships. In a competitive context, interfirm cooperation typically implies the existence of an administrative system that is at least in part specialized to the relationship and established to manage exchange within it. Composed of selection processes, incentive structures, and conflict-resolution practices, the system leads to the virtual absence of opportunist behavior in the relationship over a specific period of time.

The operational content of a cooperative relationship between for-profit firms, furthermore, can be narrowly focused on a single good or service, such as the single-source relationship between Fujitsu and ICL for the design and production of a specialized LSI CMOS chip, or broad in scope, as many joint ventures tend to be (Harrigan, 1985). Also, relationships can be vertical to the firm (in the sense of providing inputs to it or its contracting partner) or horizontal (in the sense of both partners jointly producing a product for a specific market).

Although their approaches to relational governance and content differ to some extent, the two network-application problems rely on the same basic assumption: that an adequate understanding of a particular cooperative relationship can be achieved only by analyzing the network of transactions in which the cooperative relationship is embedded. The importance of this assumption should become evident as the problems are dealt with in this chapter.

Identifying Cooperative Strategy

Harrigan (1985, p. 58) argues that firms may develop an expertise in forming joint ventures and implies that this capability may be part of the firm's corporate strategy. Her argument can be extended to cooperative relationships in general and resembles Nelson and Winter's (1982) theory of routines in organizations. However, in an interorganizational rather than intraorganizational context, the routines that dominate a relationship may not be the firm's but those of the organization with which it cooperates. Therefore, the number of a firm's relationships does not necessarily indicate that it has a cooperative strategy. The firm may simply be an attractive and willing partner that on its own cannot develop the type of relationship it currently enjoys or has enjoyed in the past.

Furthermore, a transaction initiated by a firm may reciprocate an earlier transaction with the same partner. Although reciprocity may be an important condition for the success of relatively simple cooperative relationships (Axelrod, 1984), its implications in complex institutional contexts are not straightforward (Gouldner, 1959). Therefore, it should not be seen as either a necessary component or sufficient indicator of cooperative strategy.

Identifying firms with cooperative strategies thus requires decomposing an organization's relationships into three parts—the strategic or "extensive" component, the passive or attractive component, and a reciprocity component. (See the log-linear model described in Holland and Leinhardt, 1981; Fienberg and Wasserman, 1981; Frank et al., 1985.) Estimating the component weights requires information on the relationships the firm's partners have with other firms and, therefore, an inventory and analysis of all the interfirm relationships in the network.

Differences in the administrative systems that are used to manage cooperative relationships obviously imply different opportunities for self-seeking behavior and, consequently, the development and application of different practices within the firms involved for managing cooperative relationships. In general, the more extensive the interaction for administrative purposes required of cooperating firms, the more extensive the routines applied to or developed to manage the relationship. The coordination and oversight procedures in an administrative system set up by a firm to manage a large multifunction joint venture with another firm, for example, are likely to be more extensive than the procedures a firm sets up to manage routine transactions with a large number of cooperating firms through a separate central coordinating unit (for example, SWIFT, which manages international funds transfers for member banks). Thus, including relationships based on different types of administrative mechanisms in the network complicates the interpretation of the results regarding their implications for cooperative strategy.

Furthermore, while a firm may be strategic in its cooperative relationships in one function, it may be attractive or passive in its relationships in another activity; likewise, it may have developed contracting expertise in vertical relationships but not in horizontal relationships. These distinctions imply that the more restricted the content of the relationships in the network that is analyzed, the stronger the inference that can be made about the character of the firm's cooperative strategy. For example, the results of analyzing a network of complex joint ventures involving a variety of value-chain activities would be more difficult to interpret than the results of analyzing a network of technology-development relationships alone.

However, a firm may reciprocate one type of cooperative relationship in the past, for example, a research and development partnership, with the same or another type of relationship in the present. To identify cooperative strategy and to understand and explain how cooperative relationships over time are constrained by competitive forces and the obligations of past cooperation, the network should be analyzed both for the specific period of cooperation and for the period of competition in which the cooperative relationships are embedded.

Defined in terms of the network, cooperative strategy is separable from the mix and matching of assets in interfirm dyads. It can be predicted by such organizational characteristics as size in revenues or personnel, extent and type of product-market diversification, and degree of vertical integration. Furthermore, in conjunction with these characteristics and with measures of dyadic fit, estimates of a firm's network attributes can be used to predict the success or failure of its ventures. Thus, cooperative strategy, as estimated through the network analysis previously suggested, may be an intermediate variable, independent of measures of asset complementarity, in models of effectiveness in interorganizational relations.

Evaluating Cooperative Relationships

Whether interfirm cooperation involves a supply contract for one or both firms or serves them as an avenue to enter new markets and technologies, the relationship's stability and success depend on its administrative efficiency relative to other institutional means for achieving the same goals. (See Kogut, 1986.) The two institutions whose administrative reqirements for sourcing or diversification strategies have traditionally been opposed are internal organization and the competitive market (Williamson, 1975, 1979; Teece, 1980, 1982), and the network in which a cooperative relationship is embedded may affect its comparative advantage over these alternatives.

Two definitions of a relationship's network position—centrality and niche membership—suggest in different ways how the network may add value to the relationship. These definitions suggest different approaches to the problems of identifying types of relationships, in terms of both content and administrative structure, and of choosing an appropriate method for analyzing the network.

Centrality

Centrality in a network is primarily a characteristic of individual firms, although the overall centrality of the network can be determined by aggregating the centrality measures of the firms that compose it. Centrality reflects the firm's position in structure of the network and may be an element in the firm's strategy. However, the structure of the network is generally beyond the control of the firm. Thus, centrality indicates a strategy based on the exploitation of current market forces rather than the development of cooperative strategy routines that extend the firm's reach in the network.

Vertical relationships, which are inherently directional between firms, give meaning to being central in the network; horizontal relationships do not. However, a central location in networks defined by different types of vertical flow will imply different benefits to the firm from its cooperative links to other firms. Market exchange does not constitute interfirm cooperation, as defined in this chapter, since no specialized administrative mechanism has been established to govern the transactions. Consequently, to qualify as cooperative arrangements, vertical flows of goods and services require idiosyncratic governance structures, as are found in many single-source relationships, for example. Because these types of supply relationship typically involve, by implication, specialized assets (see, for example, Williamson, 1983), detailing the network of relationships can be quite difficult and a dyadic approach is probably more productive (Williamson, 1981). On the other hand, flows of information and technology or skills between, as opposed to within, firms may require specialized governance mechanisms (see Teece, 1980) but not specialized assets. Consequently, centrality may be most meaningful in networks of firms whose members are linked for information or technology-transfer reasons.

Firms will engage in cooperative relationships for information and technology-transfer reasons with other firms that possess skills and resources to generate valuable information or technology or that are positioned in the network to access and transmit them. Note, however, that although technology transfer takes place between firms to govern property rights, information is passed between individuals. Therefore, technology-based networks are composed of organizations; but information networks are composed of people.

Cooperative relationships among firms for information purposes may therefore be implicit, since the specialized governance mechanisms are interpersonal and difficult to detect accurately. This is especially true for firms, such as professionalized organizations, that depend on information crucially to develop and market products and services and, therefore, whose human-resource policies focus on employees' positions in the network of information flow as critical resources.

The choice of firms that compose the network of cooperative relationships in which centrality adds value to the interfirm arrangements therefore depends partly on what assets are strategic for a focal firm. The importance of particular families of technologies for a firm's product-market competitiveness would lead to choosing as members of the network firms transferring those technologies. Whether the focal firm is central in that network becomes a matter for analysis.

Perhaps the most current operationalization of centrality is Freeman's betweenness measure (1977, 1979). The betweenness measure has been shown to be superior to other centrality indices in predicting the outcomes of small-group experiments (Freeman, 1979). In addition, it has a relatively straightforward interpretation based on network structure. The centrality of a firm is a function of the number of geodesics on which it lies, controlling for the number of paths possible, given the size of the network. Geodesics are the shortest paths between two network members. Thus, central-network members act as brokers of relationships between other members.

Centrality as betweenness may add value to an interfirm relationship and, therefore, make interfirm cooperation a preferred mode of organizing exchange for several reasons. First, centrality may indicate a niche of expertise and confer prestige. However, in networks of cooperative relationships as defined in this chapter, reputation should be less important because moral hazard has been minimized through specialized administrative mechanisms rather than through reliance on position in the network structure as an indicator of trustworthiness. Consequently, the prestige and expertise that a central firm acquires is valuable for dealing with firms outside the cooperative network. When the internal broker becomes an external broker (see Boorman and Levitt, 1982), it may charge a premium to outside firms that want to access information or technology through the network rather than through the competitive market.

Second, a central position may give the firm the ability to forecast technological and market changes sooner than its product market competitors. Whether it can translate this knowledge into an effective strategy depends on its current business and operating-level capabilities and on its commitments to its partners in the cooperative network, some of whom may compete in the markets that are changing. This problem may be especially acute in research and development consortia, such as MCC, in which central firms emerge because the group has grown too large for full-channel communications to be maintained.

Last, centralized firms may be well positioned when cooperative networks are decomposed into subnetworks because expansion has made the original administrative system inefficient (Blau, 1970). A network such as SWIFT, for example, will face pressure to reorganize as the increasing number of banks strains the system's capacity. The decomposition rules will necessarily take the positions of current centralized brokers into account. (See Zannetos, 1965.) As the locations for new administrative centers for the subnetworks, these brokers should develop new institutional competencies that may be generalizable to the administration of capabilities related to achieving a strategic advantage in competitive markets. The proposition that administrative skills appropriate for establishing and maintaining cooperative relationships can be transferred to the competitive arena is controversial, however, and difficult to test.

Niche Membership

The concept of niche, originating in community ecology research in population biology, has become current in studies of organizations primarily as a designator of the market or environmental segment to which firms have specialized their capabilities (Hannan and Freeman, 1977; Porter, 1980; Carroll, 1985). When the environment is construed as interorganizational relationships, however, it is no longer exogenous to the firms being studied; the firms in the network cannot be split into two groups, one responding to environmental change and the other producing it. The concept of niche applies then to a group of firms that have relationships with the same other firms in the network or to the relationships that link such a group to these firms.

The meaningfulness of network analysis focused on niche identification depends on the relative homogeneity or comparability of the relationships composing the network. Relative homogeneity is important because each type of relationship implies a specific set of constraints and opportunities for network members. For example, firms that share a niche in a network of vertical relationships have the same or similar suppliers which are managed through cooperative contracts rather than through competitive markets; in turn, firms in the niche may supply other niches in the network with the same or other goods and services. Thus, niches, like firms, may be more or less central in a network of vertical relationships. This is not so for niches in networks of horizontal relationships that involve the joint development of product markets and, therefore, imply symmetric contributions by firms that make centrality meaningless.

Niches in a network of cooperative relationships are components of its structure. The major analytical technique for modelling network structure is blockmodelling (White, Boorman, and Breiger, 1976; Arabie, Boorman, and Levitt, 1978). As Breiger (1976) points out, the two concepts that give the technique meaning are structural equivalence and pattern. Structural equivalence refers to commonality among network members in terms of their relationships with the rest of the network. If two firms have relationships with the same set of other firms in the network, this pair are structurally equivalent. Blockmodelling partitions the firms in the network into groups whose members are structurally equivalent. Each group or block of firms occupies a niche. Pattern is the structure of relationships among the blocks and is represented in a blockmodel, an array in which an entry of 1 in a cell indicates a relationship between two blocks and an entry of 0 indicates no relationship. Because pattern represents relationships among blocks, it is possible to identify niches that are strategically placed in the network.

A blockmodel of an interorganizational network may provide several types of information about the population of firms and about each firm individually. First, the structural equivalence of firms indicates that they draw on a common resource and information base in that they have relationships with roughly the same set of firms in the network. A fit between the distribution of organizational capabilities in the network and its structure indicates what kinds of relationships exist between blocks, since the capabilities of a firm determine to a large extent the types of relationships it can enter into effectively. The following analysis of upstream joint ventures among the nineteen dominant firms in the aluminum industry illustrates the types of information that blockmodelling can provide.

Stuckey (1983) proposes that two strategic groups, majors and diversifiers, compose the dominant group of firms in the aluminum industry and that upstream joint ventures among these firms for the supply of bauxite, alumina, and primary aluminum are formed for a variety of reasons. Primary among these are economies of scale, technology transfer from the majors to the diversifiers, and oligopolist collusion among the majors; the latter two reasons are directly related to network structure. First, a core and periphery pattern is suggested by the flow of technology from the majors to the diversifiers. Second, the prevalence of joint ventures among the majors which facilitates collusion and the absence of joint ventures among the diversifiers suggest that the majors are an "inbred" block, while the diversifiers are an "outbred" block. The pattern of interfirm relations proposed is thus a reflection of firm attributes. Table 13–1 shows this pattern as Stuckey presents it.

An analysis of the network shows something quite different. The procedure involved two algorithms, CONCOR (Breiger, Boorman, and Arabie, 1975) and CALCOPT (Walker, 1985), to determine the blocks of structurally equivalent firms

Table 13–1
**Structure of the Network of Upstream Joint
Ventures in the Global Aluminum Industry
as Suggested by Stuckey's Analysis**

Majors	Diversifiers
Alusuisse	Anaconda
PUK	Amax
Reynolds	CVRD
Kaiser	Elkem-Spiger-Verket
ALCAN	Gove Alumina
	Grangesburg
	Martin Marietta
	National Steel
	Noranda
	Phelps Dodge
	Revere
	Riotinto Zinc
	Shell

Blockmodel

	Majors	Diversifiers
Majors	1	1
Diversifiers	1	0

in the network. CONCOR split the firms into two blocks and these blocks into two blocks each and so on until a specified number of blocks were formed. Analyses were performed for two, four, and six blocks. At the two-block level, Stuckey's core and periphery pattern should emerge; and at the four- and six-block levels, subgroups within the majors and diversifiers should become apparent. CALCOPT takes as input the CONCOR ordering of the firms into blocks and reassigns the firms among the blocks according to changes in a target function (see Boorman and Levitt, 1983) based on the intra- and interblock densities of joint venture activity. In essence, increases in this target function represent clarification of the network structure as indicated by the density matrix from which the blockmodel is derived. The version of CALCOPT used in this chapter requires partitions of three or more blocks as input.

The results for the two-group model are shown in table 13–2. Note that although four of the majors are found in block I, two majors, Alusuisse and PUK, are found in block II. Block I is dominated by the large-scale multilateral joint ventures, and block II by bilateral ventures associated with its majors. The main finding here is that the core and periphery model of majors and diversifiers does not exist.

At the four-group level (see table 13–3) the majors and diversifiers share memberships in all blocks except block III, which is composed of PUK and

Table 13-2
Results of CONCOR Analysis of Global Aluminum Industry Joint Venture Network, Two-Block Model

Group I	Group II
Majors	*Majors*
Reynolds	Alusuisse
Kaiser	PUK
ALCAN	
ALCOA	
Diversifiers	*Diversifiers*
Anaconda	Amax
CVRD	Elkem-Spiger-Verket
Grangesburg	Gove Alumina
Martin Marietta	Noranda
National Steel	Phelps Dodge
Riotinto Zinc	Revere
Shell	

Density Matrix

	I	II
I	.314	.068
II	.068	.25

ALCAN, the majors with the greatest number of joint ventures. Both blocks I and II contain majors and diversifiers that are involved in ventures with block III; members of block I do not venture with each other to any degree, while members of block II do, due to the large-scale MRN and Alpart joint ventures. Block IV has the most contact with block III and no contact within itself. At this level of analysis, the core and periphery pattern appears; the core, however, is not the full set of majors, but PUK and ALCAN alone. The dominance of PUK and ALCAN in this model is striking and clearly shows that the roles of the majors in the network structure are different.

The six-block results presented in table 13-4 show the structure of the network in greater detail. First, PUK and ALCAN are in separate blocks, IV and V, respectively. ALCAN is the only member of block V, indicating its unique position in the network, and PUK is paired with Anaconda. ALCOA and Reynolds are together in block I, but Alusuisse and Kaiser are in different blocks, II and III, respectively. The majors are, thus, almost equally distributed across the blocks, indicating that they are not structurally equivalent, contrary to the structure suggested by Stuckey's assertions.

Table 13-3
Results of CALCOPT Analysis of Global Aluminum Industry Joint Venture Network, Four-Group Model

Block I	*Block II*	*Block III*	*Block IV*
Majors	*Majors*	*Majors*	*Majors*
Kaiser	Reynolds	PUK	none
Alusuisse	ALCOA	ALCAN	
Diversifiers	*Diversifiers*	*Diversifiers*	*Diversifiers*
Amax	Anaconda	none	Elkem-Spiger-Verket
Grangesburg	Shell		Gove Alumina
Martin Marietta			Phelps Dodge
National Steel			Revere
Noranda			
Riotinto Zinc			

Density Matrix

	I	II	III	IV
I	.05	.14	.67	.08
II	.14	.38	.63	.06
III	.67	.63	.5	.13
IV	.08	.06	.13	0

Furthermore, although the pattern of the six-block model is strongly outbred, the core and periphery pattern found in the four-block model is repeated with both block IV (the PUK group) and block V (ALCAN), as the core and the other blocks as the periphery. In the six-block model, moreover, the intersection of blocks IV and V indicates that the core blocks are strongly integrated; the periphery blocks, on the other hand, are loosely connected to each other. Firms in the same block do not participate in joint ventures with each other (with the exception of block II), are connected similarly to PUK and ALCAN, and have roughly similar relations with the other periphery blocks.

The key to this structure is the large multilateral joint venture established to achieve scale economies. ALCAN participates in four of these, PUK in three, Reynolds in two, and Kaiser, ALCOA, and Alusuisse in one. However, the large ventures themselves do not themselves constitute blocks (1) because ALCAN and PUK participate in more than one of these large ventures and (2) because of differences among the majors in the diversifiers they venture with bilaterally. ALCAN's multilateral joint ventures connect it to all other blocks, and PUK's multilaterals join it to all blocks except block II. Technology transfer between majors and diversifiers also occurs across blocks, as in the core and periphery model suggested by Stuckey's assertions. However, the blockmodelling results show that the majority of the majors, in spite of their technological expertise, lie outside the core because

Table 13-4

Results of CALCOPT Analysis of Global Aluminum Industry Joint Venture Network, Six-Block Analysis

Block I	*Block II*	*Block III*	*Block IV*	*Block V*	*Block VI*
Majors	*Majors*	*Majors*	*Majors*	*Majors*	*Majors*
Reynolds ALCOA	Alusuisse	Kaiser	PUK	ALCAN	none
Diversifiers	*Diversifiers*	*Diversifiers*	*Diversifiers*	*Diversifiers*	*Diversifiers*
Amax Gove Alumina Riotinto Zinc	CVRD Elkem-Spiger-Verket Phelps Dodge Shell	Grangesburg Martin Marietta National Steel	Anaconda	none	Noranda Revere

Density Matrix

	I	II	III	IV	V	VI
I	0	.16	.15	.5	.6	0
II	.16	.16	0	.2	.4	.2
III	.15	0	0	.38	1.0	0
IV	.5	.2	.38	0	1.0	.25
V	.6	.4	1.0	1.0	0	0
VI	0	.2	0	.25	0	0

they do not participate in the large ventures as extensively as PUK and ALCAN. The integration of the majors for the maintenance of oligopolist competition, therefore, occurs across blocks rather than within a single block composed of the majors alone; and the large joint ventures are the integrating mechanism.

An alternative to defining a network niche as a group of firms is to define it as a cluster of relationships between firms. Thus, the effectiveness of cooperative relationships may depend on their location in the network structure. In particular, relationships that are located in dense interblock regions, construed as niches, may be more successful than those in sparse regions. This proposition is based on the assumption that cooperative ties can involve the transfer or sharing of a variety of goods and services and typically require relatively complex administrative mechanisms tailored to them. For example, relationships involving joint technology-development activities should be governed differently than relationships involving joint manufacturing or marketing. The match between the governance mechanism and the types of goods and services exchanged should determine the effectiveness of the cooperative venture. Why, however, should efficient matches occur in dense regions of the network?

Granovetter (1985) has suggested that interfirm relationships are embedded in a social context that reinforces the accomplishment of the tasks for which the relationships are established. In the absence of this context, the effectiveness of the relationship declines. Dense regions of the network can be interpreted as aggregates of mutually supporting interfirm relationships. Walker and Townsend (1987) found that in high-density regions, whether within or between blocks, relationships tended to have a higher degree of fit between the way they were governed and the reasons motivating them. Extending their analysis to a population of private-sector firms would entail identifying networks with sufficient density and heterogeneity to allow for differentiated but equally supportive relational contexts in its dense regions. Sparse regions represent locations in the community ecology that are experimental, deviant, leading-edge, or failing. In any case, relationships in these areas should be less well governed than those in the regions that represent the mainstream.

Conclusion

This chapter has attempted to outline the contributions of various types of network analysis to research on cooperative relationships. In particular, the network was proposed as a contextual factor that contributed to the identification of cooperative strategy and to the evaluation of cooperative relationships in comparison with other institutional mechanisms (specifically, internal development and competitive market contracting) for achieving the same strategic goals.

The important problems confronted in the management of well-bounded, formally planned networks (as found, for example, in supplier tiering by powerful buyers and in consortia for technology development) were not discussed in this chapter. They were omitted primarily because methods for analyzing large-scale networks of cooperative relationships seemed less appropriate to them than team theory, game theory, and models of clique formation in small groups, particularly regarding the issue of coalition formation by network members.

Only three of the many network-analysis techniques and approaches currently in use (see Burt, 1980b for a partial review) were discussed and only one of these, blockmodelling, illustrated. The problems of testing the value of these methods are numerous. Defining the network boundary, identifying the basic units of the cooperative relationships that compose the network, identifying the relevant organizational attributes that are related to the firm's cooperative behavior, and understanding how the internal structure of the firm and the competitive structure of the industry contribute to and confound the importance of cooperative relationships are all significant tasks in this type of research. Isolating the network and its effect clearly depends on controlling these tasks effectively. Continuing to confront these problems, however, would contribute substantially to our understanding of how firms establish and maintain cooperative relationships.

Bibliography

Arabie, P., Boorman, S.A., and Levitt, P.R. 1978. "Constructing Blockmodels: How and Why." *Journal of Mathematical Psychology*, 17: 21–63.

Axelrod, R. 1984. *The Evolution of Cooperation.* New York: Basic Books.

Blau, P. 1970. "A Formal Theory of Differentiation in Organizations." *American Sociological Review,* 35: 201–18.

Boorman, S.A., and Levitt, P.R. 1982. "The Network Matching Principle: A Model of Efficient Resource Allocation by Informal Social Networks in Non-profit and Other Non-market Social Structures." *Economics Letters,* 10: 1–7.

Boorman, S.A., and Levitt, P.R. 1983. "Blockmodelling Complex Statutes: Mapping Techniques Based on Combinatorial Optimization for Analysing Economic Legislation and Its Stress Point over Time." *Economics Letters,* 13: 1–9.

Breiger, R.L., 1976. "Career Attributes and Network Structure: A Blockmodel Study of a Biomedical Research Specialty." *American Sociological Review,* 41: 117–35.

Breiger, R.L., Boorman, S.A., and Arabie, P. 1975. "An Algorithm for Clustering Relational Data, with Applications to Social Network Analysis and Comparison with Multidimensional Scaling." *Journal of Mathematical Psychology,* 12: 328–83.

Burt, R.S. 1980a. "Autonomy in a Social Topology." *American Journal of Sociology,* 85: 328–83.

Burt, R.S. 1980b. "Models of Network Structure." *Annual Review of Sociology,* 6: 79–141.

Carroll, G. 1985. "Concentration and Specialization: The Dynamics of Niche Width in Populations of Organizations." *American Journal of Sociology,* 90: 1262–83.

Fienberg, S., and Wasserman, S. 1981. "Categorical Data Analysis of Simple Sociometric Relations." In S. Leinhardt (ed.), *Sociological Methodology:* 156–92. San Francisco: Jossey-Bass.

Frank. O., Hallinan, M., and Nowicki, K. 1985. "Clustering of Dyad Distributions as a Tool of Network Modelling." *Journal of Mathematical Sociology,* 11: 47–64.

Freeman, L.C. 1977. "A Set of Measures of Centrality Based on Betweenness." *Sociometry,* 40: 35–41.

Freeman, L.C. 1979. "Centrality in Social Networks: Conceptual Clarification." *Social Networks,* 1: 215–39.

Gouldner, A.W. 1959. "Organizational Analysis." In R.K. Merton, L. Broom, and L.S. Cottrell, Jr. (eds.), *Sociology Today.* New York: Basic Books.

Granovetter, M. 1985. "Economic Action and Social Structure: A Theory of Embeddedness." *American Journal of Sociology.*

Hannan, M.T., and Freeman, J. 1977. "The Population Ecology of Organizations." *American Journal of Sociology,* 82: 929–64.

Harrigan, K.R. 1985. *Strategies for Joint Ventures.* Lexington, Mass.: Lexington Books.

Holland, P., and Leinhardt, S. 1981. "An Exponential Family of Probability Distributions for Directed Graphs." *Journal of the American Statistical Association,* 76: 33–50.

ICL Technical Journal. 1985. 4: 3.

Knoke, D., and Rogers, D.L. 1978. "A Blockmodel Analysis of Interorganizational Networks." *Social Science Research,* 64: 28–52.

Kogut, B. 1986. *Joint Ventures: A Review and Preliminary Investigation.* Working paper. Wharton School, University of Pennsylvania, Philadelphia.

Laumann, E.O., Galaskiewicz, J., and Marsden, P.V. 1978. "Community Structure as Interorganizational Linkages." *Annual Review of Sociology,* 4: 455–84.

Laumann, E.O., and Pappi, F. 1976. *Networks of Collective Action: A Perspective on Community Influence Systems.* New York: Academic Press.

Mintz, B., and Schwartz, M. 1981. "Interlocking Directorates and Interest Group Formation." *American Sociological Review,* 46: 851–69.

Nelson, R., and Winter, S. 1982. *An Evolutionary Model of Economic Change.* Cambridge, Mass.: Harvard.

Pennings, J. 1984. *Interlocking Directorates.* San Francisco: Jossey-Bass.

Porter, M. 1980. *Competitive Strategy.* New York: Free Press.

Stuckey, J. 1983. *Vertical Integration and Joint Ventures in the Aluminum Industry.* Cambridge, Mass.: Harvard University Press.

Teece, D. 1980. "Economies of Scope and the Scope of the Enterprise." *Journal of Economic Behavior and Organization,* 1: 233–47.

Teece, D. 1982. "Towards an Economic Theory of the Multiproduct Firm." *Journal of Economic Behavior and Organization,* 3: 39–63.

Walker, G. 1985. "Network Position and Cognition in a Computer Software Firm." *Administrative Science Quarterly,* 30: 103–30.

Walker, G., and Townsend, E. 1987. *Relational Congruence and Interorganizational Effectiveness: A Community Ecology Perspective.* Working paper. Department of Management, Wharton School, University of Pennsylvania, Philadelphia.

White, H., Boorman, S.A., and Breiger, R.L. 1976. "Social Structure from Multiple Networks. I: Blockmodels of Roles and Position." *American Journal of Sociology,* 81: 730–80.

Williamson, O.E. 1975. *Markets and Hierarchies.* New York: Free Press.

Williamson, O.E. 1979. "Transaction Costs Economics: The Governance of Contractual Relations." *Journal of Law and Economics,* 22: 3–61.

Williamson, O.E. 1981. "The Economics of Organization: The Transaction Cost Approach." *American Journal of Sociology,* 87: 548–77.

Williamson, O.E. 1983. "Credible Commitments: Using Hostages to Support Exchange." *American Economic Review,* 73: 519–40.

Zannetos, Z. 1965. "On the Theory of Divisional Structures: Some Aspects of Centralization and Decentralization of Control and Decision Making." *Management Science,* 12: 49–68.

14

Entering the United States by Joint Venture: Competitive Rivalry and Industry Structure

Bruce Kogut
Harbir Singh

T
o cooperate is a choice among alternatives. These alternatives include acquisition, internal development, joint ventures, licensing, and nonequity contracts. In a sense, any kind of economic transaction that is not motivated by coercion is a form of cooperation. It is not cooperation per se, but rather the design and characteristics of the cooperation that differentiate among institutional alternatives.

Recent explanations of the choice among ways to structure cooperation have focused prominently upon differences in costs assigned to each alternative.[1] These costs are often characterized as of two kinds. One consists of the costs of economic production, including R&D and distribution, as well as transportation and fiscal levies. The other consists of transaction costs, which are derived from the precautions required to monitor and bond parties to an agreement so that they will meet their fiduciary promises, as well as the loss attached to defections from the agreement that cannot be economically observed. This type of analysis, which is labeled *transaction-cost theory*, leads to the prediction that parties will choose the alternative that minimizes the sum of production and transaction costs.

The framing of cooperation as choice among alternatives that minimizes costs is especially pertinent to the penetration of firms into foreign markets because the initial market share cannot frequently justify the high fixed costs of relying upon internal development. These costs are derived not only from the building of plants, but in the distribution of experience regarding the host country and culture. For many companies, the costs of acquiring experience are most tangibly realized in the hiring and training of managers and workers and in the adaptation of products to the local market.

We thank Ommer Khaw, Eirene Chen, and Craig Stevens for their research help. This research has been funded by the Reginald H. Jones Center of the Wharton School, University of Pennsylvania, under a grant from AT&T.

However, costs are not the only criterion that might differentiate alternatives.[2] The competitive rivalry and structure of the market may also influence the choice among institutional alternatives, especially if the timing of the investment is of importance. For example, competitors may pursue strategies of international preemption in which acquisitions of national firms are promoted in order to speed the process of establishing a market presence. Or, in growing industries where R&D investment is important, foreign entrants may create joint ventures with larger firms in order to acquire technology from incumbents for use in their home markets or to gain marketing arms for their own innovations. Which institutional alternative is chosen, therefore, depends subtly on the structure of competition and the maturity of the market.

Little is empirically known regarding the relationship between strategic timing and the choice among institutional alternatives. This chapter provides a preliminary investigation into strategic motivations. The first section reviews the central findings of previous studies. The second section statistically investigates the significance of strategic contextual variables on entry choice. The next details the empirical investigation. The concluding section discusses future directions.

Summary of Previous Work

There have been surprisingly few statistical studies of the determinants of entry choice into a foreign country. Despite the paucity, there has been a reassuring consistency in the significance of particular variables. Because some studies compare acquisition versus wholly owned greenfield (a new start-up investment) while others compare joint ventures and acquisitions, the main results must be understood with some care. For the sake of exposition, only studies regarding greenfield, acquisition, and joint ventures are described.[3]

Experience. In a number of studies, previous investments in a country have been shown to encourage subsequent decisions to favor wholly owned investments. Davidson (1980) found evidence for a pattern of internationalization whereby firms move from exporting to partial equity investments to wholly owned operations. Dubin (1976) found that greater international experience favors wholly owned greenfield investments over acquisitions. Steuber et al. (1973) found that the percentage of equity share in a U.K. subsidiary by a foreign firm increased with the multinationality of the parent. However, neither Caves and Mehra (1986) nor Kogut and Singh (1986) found that previous investment in the United States influenced the choice of entry. (Caves and Mehra looked at acquisition versus greenfield, controlling for degree of ownership; Kogut and Singh looked at joint venture versus wholly owned greenfield/acquisition.) Wilson (1980) also did not find support for the theory that experience encourages greenfield over acquisition for a sample of entries made by U.S., British, German, and Japanese firms.

Size. Size of the investing firms and the target investment also have been found to be influential. In a sample of entry decisions by large multinational corporations, Dubin (1976) found that relatively smaller firms tended to acquire relatively more frequently than larger firms, though he did not control for other factors. In a multivariate test, Wilson (1980) confirmed Dubin's findings, which were also corroborated by Caves and Mehra (1986). In comparing joint ventures and acquisitions by non–U.S. firms entering the United States, Kogut and Singh (1986) found that the larger the investing firm, the more likely it was to enter by acquisition; the smaller the U.S. firm, the more likely the non–U.S. firm was to acquire than to utilize a joint venture.

Diversification. Studies have looked at the influence of both regional and product diversification on entry choice. Since acquisitions require a payment for exiting assets in excess of the valuation by the market, a firm will acquire only if there is a contribution to reducing risk that shareholders themselves cannot achieve or if it has existing resources that can put the acquired assets to better economic use. Dubin (1976) found, in fact, that firms with extensive multinational operations are less likely to enter by acquisition than by greenfield investments, presumably because they have already achieved regional diversification. However, Caves and Mehra (1986) did not confirm this result in their study on acquisition and greenfield entries into the United States and Kogut and Singh (1986) also found no influence on the acquisition versus joint venture decision.

Numerous studies have found that diversified firms, in general, reveal higher rates of acquisition, a pattern confirmed for international activity as well. Dubin (1976), Wilson (1980), and Caves and Mehra (1986) found that the greater the product diversity, the more likely a firm will acquire rather than enter by greenfield investment. Kogut and Singh (1986) did not find that product diversity influenced the joint venture versus acquisition choice in their sample. Stopford and Wells (1972) found, however, that firms tend to rely on local equity participation if the foreign subsidiary is diversified into other product lines than the parent. In their study of foreign investment in the United States, Stopford and Haberich (1978) found that joint ventures are used more commonly relative to wholly owned investments for diversified subsidiaries.

Product Differentiation. Stopford and Wells (1972) found the greater the product differentiation, the greater the likelihood of requiring local assistance in the form of a joint venture partner for the provision of local marketing know-how.

Strategic (or Intangible) Assets. Another explanation for entry choice is derived from the transaction costs of transferring certain assets between firms. Brand labels, technology, or the production or provision of quality are subject to degradation or undesired diffusion unless controlled through equity ownership.[4] Alternatively, control over strategic assets is required in order to affect the market position of the firm vis-à-vis rivals. Most empirical studies have indeed confirmed the relationship of strategic assets to increasing ownership levels. Stopford and Wells (1972) and Fagre and Wells (1982) both found that increasing R&D and marketing and advertising intensity of the U.S. parent led to a greater likelihood of wholly owned entry. Using the same but updated data base, Gatignon and Anderson (1986) confirmed the relationship of increasing equity ownership to the intensity of R&D, marketing, and advertising. Franko (1971) found that ventures were more likely to revert to wholly owned status when marketing and advertising were perceived as important to the parents; a similar result was not found by Franko for R&D.

Intrafirm Coordination. Franko (1971) and Stopford and Wells (1972) noted that joint ventures posed obstacles to the intrafirm coordination of the international activities of the U.S. firm investing overseas. Hladik (1985) indeed found that the greater the interdependence of the foreign subsidiary on the U.S. parent, the more likely was entry by a wholly owned operation.

Industry Structural Variables. Numerous studies of foreign direct investment have found a positive relationship between FDI and industry characteristics. Few studies have, however, researched the relationship between industry structure and choice of entry. Kogut and Singh (1986) found no relationship between industry marketing and advertising intensity and acquisition/joint venture choice, though some evidence for a positive relationship between industry R&D and joint venture was suggested. In their study, Caves and Mehra (1986) found no relationship between R&D, marketing intensity, and the acquisition/greenfield choice.

Country Factors. Despite strong evidence for country variation in the relative frequency of entry modes, few studies have investigated the underlying motivations. Franko (1976) found a higher use of joint ventures by European firms than by U.S. firms. Wilson (1980) also found significant country differences. In part, these patterns might reflect differences in the direction of investment flows, since many developing countries restrict equity shares. But even when controlling for host-country effects, country patterns emerge. The statistical investigations by Kogut and Singh (1986) of entry into the United States showed significant support of the theory that cultural distance leads to a greater use of joint ventures or wholly owned greenfield investment over acquisition, presumably because acquisitions require substantial costs involved in the integration of foreign management. Other reasons (such as illiquidity or differences in industry structures across countries) have been suggested, but not substantially studied.[5]

An Investigation of Strategic Motivations

The preceding summary shows an impressive degree of replication of results across studies. However, replication of these results has not led to agreement on interpretation.

In particular, the findings regarding the relationship of intangible assets to a preference for wholly owned entry and on concentration in consumer durable industries to acquisition is consistent with either a transaction-cost or strategic-behavior explanation for entry choice.

The importance of competitive rivalry on international investment behavior has well known support, despite the lack of empirical studies. The Hymer-Kindleberger/Caves theory of foreign direct investment and Vernon's theory of international product life cycle of trade and investment rests (implicitly in the case of the former and explicitly in the case of the latter) on the presumption that international investment is a response to oligopolist rivalry. The research by Knickerbocker (1973) showed that competitive rivalry in moderately concentrated industries led to a follow-the-leader pattern in the overseas investment behavior of U.S. multinational corporations. Graham (1978) found that European direct investment into the United States followed previous U.S. investment in Europe and that this pattern was more pronounced for industries of higher concentration, R&D expenditures, and product differentiation.

However, whereas the relationship of investment behavior to competitive rivalry is well documented, the implications for the choice of entry mode are less clear.[6] Though there is little theoretical guidance on the exact relationship of timing to institutional choice, some recent work suggests a number of structural variables, principally industry growth and market structure, that are likely to be of importance. Spence (1979) showed analytically that preemptive strategies are more viable in industries that are growing and not yet mature. Das Gupta and Stiglitz (1980) analyzed the influence of market structure and competition on R&D expenditures and the rate of innovation and found the greater the degree of monopoly or of competition in R&D, the greater the R&D expenditure level. These studies suggest that conditions of industry growth, technological intensity, and degree of rivalry are important influences on investment behavior.

A few analytical studies have considered the relationship of competitive rivalry to institutional choice. Eaton and Kierzkowski (1984), for example, argue analytically that a firm will transfer technology to another firm if demand is highly varied and if there are significant set-up costs to entering new market segments. Vickers (1985) analyzed the use of joint ventures as a way for incumbents to curtail preemptive behavior in R&D investments that might lead to lower industry profits. He found that joint ventures are encouraged if the nature of the technological innovation is likely to be incremental rather than radical. The results of Vickers and Eaton and Kierzkowski suggest that innovation, future market size, and the structure of rivalry influence institutional choice.

Empirical Investigation

The robustness of the conclusions of analytical models of competitive rivalry is highly sensitive to assumptions regarding the nature of the technology, the degree of competition, and the nature of demand. Though the theory is not sufficiently detailed to provide precise guidance for empirical studies, a number of structural variables are suggested as important for influencing the choice of institutions. For the purposes of a preliminary investigation, we focus upon four variables that analytical theories have argued to be significant: the ratios of R&D, and marketing/advertising expenditures, to industry sales; market concentration; and industry growth.

The influence of these variables on institutional choice is analyzed in the context of foreign entry into the United States. Previous studies have found that foreign firms enter the United States frequently for the acquisition of technology or for market access (Ajami and Ricks, 1981). For the purposes of a preliminary investigation, we focus on the choice between joint venture versus acquisition or greenfield investment. By a *joint venture*, we mean the pooling of assets into a distinct legal institution with ownership shared between two or a few parties which possess varying degrees of control over the use and fruits of the assets. *Acquisition* refers to the direct purchase of the assets of a company. By *wholly owned acquisition*, we mean that the foreign firm has bought 100 percent equity or majority equity with the remainder dispersed across many shareholders. Wholly owned greenfield entry is a *de novo* investment which is under the control of only the foreign firm. We do not consider entry by equity participation where the foreign firm buys a minority percentage in an existing firm. (Data are discussed shortly.)

Whether they enter by a joint venture or a wholly owned operation is likely to be sensitive to structural conditions. We hypothesize the following relationships between structural variables and the choice of entry by joint venture versus wholly owned acquisition or greenfield investment.

Size *(LGREL)*. Two important determinants of entry choice are the size of the entering firm and the target investment. The larger the entering firm, the more managerial and financial resources are available for an acquisition or greenfield investment. On the other hand, the larger the required investment, the more a joint venture is required. These considerations are reflected in the variable *LGREL*, which is the natural log of the ratio of the asset size of the foreign firm over the asset size of the acquired firm, joint venture partner, or the minimum efficient scale of investment.

Industry R&D Intensity *(R&D)*. Previous studies have found that the greater the R&D intensity, the more likely entry will be by a wholly owned activity (Stopford and Wells, 1972; Gatignon and Anderson, 1986). This relationship has largely been explained by the transactional hazards of selling technology through a market. However, most of these studies assumed that the entering firm possessed the technology. From a strategic standpoint, whether a joint venture or wholly owned entry is encouraged depends on the motivational assumption and the structure and maturity of the industry. In the case of the United States, foreign entry is often motivated by the desire to access U.S. technology in order to compete more effectively in other regional markets or to acquire the capability to adapt products to the U.S. market. When controlling for relative size of the foreign firm and requisite investment, it can be expected that the foreign firm will prefer a joint venture with an incumbent with proven technological resources rather than an investment insofar as the value of the technology to the foreign firm may not justify paying a premium over market price for ownership of all the U.S. partner's assets, especially when postacquisition costs of international coordination and integration are included. If these assumptions are correct in the aggregate, then it can be expected that the higher the ratio of R&D expenditures to sales (*R&D*) for an industry, the more likely the entry will be a joint venture.

Industry Marketing and Advertising Intensity (*MAD*). Stopford and Wells (1972) found that firms with high marketing expenses tend to prefer wholly owned activities. Caves and Mehra (1986) found a tendency toward acquisition over greenfield in consumer-durable industries where brand labelling is likely to be of strategic value. Unless competing through an international brand label, a firm is likely to enter by an acquisition of a firm with existing brand recognition rather than enter by a *de novo* investment. A joint venture is discouraged, however, since the U.S. partner, as the national firm, is unlikely to share control over its marketing expertise and brand labelling in a marketing-intensive industry. Moreover, since the foreign firm can be expected to be entering the United States for market penetration when the industry is marketing- and advertising-intensive, the long-term benefits of joint venturing relative to an acquisition or greenfield investment are weaker. Therefore, we can expect a negative relationship between MAD and entry by joint venture.

Industry Growth (*SHIPG*). A major structural feature stressed by theoretical work is the degree of industry growth. Again, which institutional alternative is promoted is dependent upon the competitive assumptions. Rivalry among foreign firms in a growing industry may lead to an international acquisition strategy as firms compete to establish a presence in different national markets. On the other hand, if foreign firms are competing against U.S. incumbents, joint ventures may speed entry by eliminating start-up and integration costs attached to greenfield investments and acquisitions, respectively. As a result, no prediction of the sign of the relationship between industry growth and entry choice is made. Shipment growth is measured as the percentage increase in price-deflated industry shipments, evaluated as the average of the shipments at the time of the venture and two years prior over the average of the shipments five or seven years prior, minus one.

Degree of Industry Concentration (*CONC*). Degree of industry concentration will also influence the competitive behavior of entrants. Industries that are concentrated are likely to be characterized by a high degree of interdependence. Greenfield entry is therefore to be competitively destabilizing and, thus, discouraged through the threat of retaliation. Acquisitions are less likely to threaten the industry consensus, but, given the implication that the number of important targets is small, the premium paid for control may arguably increase with concentration, thus discouraging an acquisition. (The empirical work on this supposition is, however, far from clear.) A joint venture, on the other hand, represents a cooperative entry with one of the incumbents and may be favored under conditions of interdependence. We predict, therefore, that concentration should be positively signed. Concentration is measured as the percentage of four-digit SIC industry sales of the top eight firms in 1982. To test these hypotheses, we regress the choice of entry by a wholly owned investment versus joint venture using a logit model on a sample of 108 manufacturing entries in the United States between 1981 and 1984.[7] The results are given in table 14–1. A positive sign means that the variable encourages entry by joint venture; a negative sign means that it encourages entry by acquisition or a wholly owned greenfield investment. The results of the first regression show some support for a strategic-behavior explanation. *R&D* is positively signed and significant at the .01 level. *SHIPG* is positively signed, but is shy of significance at the .1 level. *MAD* is signed as expected, but is insignificant. *LGREL* is correctly signed and significant at .01. *CONC* is positively signed, but insignificant.

These results show that joint ventures are encouraged under three conditions: when the target investment is large relative to the size of the investing firm, when the industry is intensive in R&D, and, with weak evidence, when the industry is growing. The finding regarding industry growth suggests that foreign firms tend

Table 14–1
Logit Estimates of Influences on Decision to Enter by Joint Venture

	Full Sample	High-growth Industries	Low-growth Industries
LGREL	−7.60	−6.71	−6.59
	(−2.69[a])	(−2.11[b])	(−2.26[b])
RND	.51	.65	.41
	(2.40[a])	(1.84[c])	(.84)
MAD	−.48	−.49	−1.23
	(−.85)	(−.78)	(−.43)
SHIPG	2.62	—	—
	(1.61)	—	—
CN882	.02	.06	.03
	(.83)	(.77)	(.86)
CONSTANT	3.10	.60	3.31
	(1.53)	(.23)	(1.37)
	n = 108	n = 55	n = 53

[a]$p < .01.$
[b]$p < .05.$
[c]$p < .1.$

to enter growth markets by teaming up with U.S. incumbents. The incentive for a U.S. partner to use a joint venture is likely to increase the more the joint venture may serve to stabilize competition in a growing industry.

The finding on *R&D* suggests that firms may not seek complete ownership if entry is for the purpose of accessing technology, possibly for application elsewhere in the world or possibly for adapting products to the U.S. market. Another interpretation is that the foreign firm is seeking a marketing joint venture partner in order to sell its product innovations manufactured in wholly owned operations. The latter interpretation preserves the transaction-costs arguments that activities intensive in technology increase the need for control and, thus, discourage joint ventures.

These considerations suggest an interaction between shipment growth and the other strategic variables. When an industry is growing, joint venture incentives increase if cooperation preserves stability in concentrated industries. Incentives for joint ventures for technological access are greater in growing and R&D-intensive industries. Incentives for joint ventures in mature and R&D-intensive industries, if such ventures occur at all, are more likely to reflect considerations of market access. In mature and marketing-intensive industries, acquisitions are promoted as a way to acquire brand labels. The importance of brand-label recognition increases, arguably, with the maturity of the industry. Since entry is likely to be less destabilizing in growing industries than in mature ones, no prediction is made for *CONC* in high-growth sectors.

To test the interactive effects of shipment growth on the structural variables, the sample was partitioned into high-growth and low-growth industries, with median shipment growth as the breakpoint. *LGREL* is maintained as a control variable. The results, given in regressions in table 14–1, show that the effect of only *R&D* differs depending on the growth of the industry. This finding suggests that foreign firms tend to joint venture for rapid technological access or product adaptation in growing and R&D-intensive industries. However, the incentives for cooperation lessen as the industry matures. None of the other estimations suggest significant interactions between industry age and the remaining structural variables. In short, the results suggest that timing is critical in growing and technologically intensive industries.

Conclusion

The preceding results show some support for the importance of strategic motivations on entry choice. Any interpretation is, of course, preliminary and is dependent upon the assumptions concerning rivalry among foreign firms and U.S. incumbents. For example, whether joint ventures in R&D-intensive industries are a means by which foreign firms seek technology to preempt rivals at home can only be confirmed by specifying directly the structure of the overseas markets. Clearly, to address empirically these issues is of greater complexity than can be resolved by the preceding tests.

Unquestionably, our results can be interpreted as supportive of a transaction-cost perspective. In this view, the tendency to create joint ventures in R&D-intensive and growing industries reflects the opportunity costs due to delays when entry is by greenfield investment. If greenfield and acquisition entries were to be separated (which we could not do, given the size of the sample), this hypothesis could be tested. But, it should be noted that, in any event, although it is possible to transform the problem into a transaction-cost framework, the value of the opportunity cost derived from delays in entry is strategically determined. The influence of timing on the choice of entry is an outcome of competitive rivalry and is only indirectly, via the notion of opportunity costs, amenable to transaction-cost explanations. (See chapter 10 by Kogut in this book.) The results of this chapter warrant a closer examination of the influence of competitive behavior in product markets on the choice among institutional alternatives.

Notes

1. The literature in this area is expansive and is split between writers concentrating on international transactions and those concentrating generally on the question of institutional choice. Seminal examples of the former are Buckley and Casson (1976), Rugman (1981), and Hennart (1982); of the latter, Williamson (1975, 1985).

2. A comparison of transaction-cost and strategic explanations is given by Kogut in chapter 10 of this book.

3. The following summary has benefited from Caves (1982, chapter 3).

4. For a statement of these kinds of risks, see Walker (1987).

5. See Caves (1982, p. 85) for a brief discussion of some of these studies.

6. Caves and Mehra (1986) provide some suggestive evidence that competitive rivalry influences the acquisition versus Greenfield investment choice.

7. The data is described in detail in Kogut and Singh (1986).

References

Ajami, R.A., and Ricks, D.A. 1981. "Motives of Non-American Firms Investing in the U.S." *Journal of International Business Studies*, 13 (Winter).

Buckley, P.J., and Casson, M. 1976. *The Future of the Multinational Enterprise*. New York: Holmes & Meier.

Caves, R.E. 1982. *Multinational Enterprise and Economic Analysis*. Cambridge, England: Cambridge University Press.

Caves, R.E., and Mehra, S. 1986. "Entry of Foreign Multinationals into U.S. Manufacturing Industries." In M. Porter (ed.), *Competition in Global Industries*. Cambridge, Mass.: Harvard University Press.

Das Gupta, P., and Stiglitz, J. 1980. "Uncertainty, Industrial Structure and the Speed of R&D." *Bell Journal of Economics*, 11: 1–28.

Davidson, W.H. 1980. "The Location of Foreign Direct Investment Activity: Country Characteristics and Experience Effects." *Journal of International Business Studies*, 12 (Fall): 9–22.

Dubin, M. 1976. *Foreign Acquisitions and the Spread of the Multinational Firm.* D.B.A. thesis. Graduate School of Business Administration, Harvard University, Boston.

Eaton, J., and Kierzkowski, H. 1984. "Oligopolistic Competition, Product Variety, Entry Deterrence and Technology Transfer." *Rand Journal of Economics*, 15 (1): 99–107.

Fagre, N., and Wells, L. 1982. "Bargaining Power of Multinationals and Host Government." *Journal of International Business Studies* (Fall): 9–23.

Franko, L.G. 1976. *The European Multinationals.* Stanford, Conn.: Greylock.

Franko, L.G. 1971. *Joint Venture Survival in Multinational Corporations.* New York: Praeger.

Gatignon, H., and Anderson, E. 1986. *The Multinational Corporation's Degree of Control over Foreign Subsidiaries: An Empirical Test of a Transaction Cost Explanation.* Working Paper no. 86–035. Marketing Department, The Wharton School, University of Pennsylvania, Philadelphia. 1986.

Graham, E.M. 1978. "Transatlantic Investment by Multinational Firms: A Rivalistic Phenomenon?" *Journal of Post-Keynesian Economics*, 1: 82–99.

Hennart, J.F. 1982. *A Theory of Multinational Enterprise.* Ann Arbor, Mich. University of Michigan Press.

Hladik, K.J. 1985. *International Joint Ventures: An Economic Analysis of U.S. Foreign Business Partnerships.* Lexington, Mass.: Lexington Books.

Knickerbocker, F.T. 1973. *Oligopolistic Reaction and Multinational Enterprise.* Boston: Division of Research,Graduate School of Business Administration, Harvard University, Boston.

Kogut, B., and Singh, H. 1986. *Entering the United States by Acquisition or Joint Venture: Country Patterns and Cultural Characteristics.* Reginald H. Jones Working Paper Series. The Wharton School, University of Pennsylvania, Philadelphia.

Rugman, A.M. 1981. *Inside the Multinationals.* New York: Columbia University Press.

Spence, A.M. 1979. "The Investment Strategy and Growth in a New Market." *Bell Journal of Economics*, 10 (1): 1–19.

Steuber, M.D. et al., 1973. *The Impact of Foreign Direct Investment on the United Kingdom.* London: Department of Trade and Industry.

Stopford, J., and Wells, L. 1972. *Managing the Multinational Enterprise, Organization of the Firm and Ownership of the Subsidiaries.* New York: Basic Books.

Vickers, J. 1985. "Preemptive Patenting, Joint Ventures, and the Persistence of Oligopoly." *International Journal of Industrial Organization*, 3: 261–73.

Walker, G. 1987. *Strategic Sourcing and Transaction Costs.* Mimeo. Wharton School, University of Pennsylvania, Philadelphia.

Williamson, O.E. 1985. *The Economic Institutions of Capitalism.* New York: Free Press.

Williamson, O.E. 1975. *Markets and Hierarchies Analysis and Antitrust Implications.* New York: Free Press.

Wilson, B. 1980. "The Propensity of Multinational Companies to Expand through Acquisitions." *Journal of International Business Studies*, 12 (Spring/Summer): 59–65.

Part IV
Managing Cooperative Relationships

15

International Cooperative Ventures in the Commercial Aircraft Industry: Gains, Sure, But What's My Share?

Richard W. Moxon
Thomas W. Roehl
J. Frederick Truitt

International cooperation is a fact of life in the commercial aircraft industry. Most new programs involve international teams, and all major competitors participate in one or more international cooperative ventures. The motivations for cooperation are clear. Risks and complementary resources are shared, access to national markets is assured, and the number of competitive products are reduced. The advantages of cooperation seem to have become more persuasive to competitors in the aircraft industry in recent years, as the investment needed for a family of aircraft or engines is formidable, market and competitive uncertainties are enormous, and governments are more willing to utilize their control of market access to gain an increased role in the industry. Economies of scale and experience favor globally integrated competitors, but government pressures limit the ability of firms to achieve this global ideal. International cooperation is one response to the pull of globalization against national constraints.

While the potential gains to competitors from international cooperation are clear, there are also costs. Cooperation implies the sharing of proprietary information, with possible adverse competitive consequences. Management control is diluted, and decision making may be cumbersome. And while there may be a net gain for all participants, there is no assurance of equal distribution of costs and benefits. In short, there exist questions of how the gains are to be shared and how the interests of each partner will be protected. This chapter looks at the elements of bargaining power that determine the distribution of gains, the way contracts are designed to protect vital interests, and how ventures change over time as cooperative relationships develop.

The authors gratefully acknowledge financial support for this project received from the Office of University Research of the U.S. Department of Transportation and from the Pacific Rim Project of the University of Washington.

The Ventures Studied

The four most significant nonmilitary international cooperative ventures were chosen for detailed analysis from about a dozen contemporary aircraft and engine ventures. The ventures are summarized in table 15–1.

Airframe Industry and Market

The commercial airframe industry is concentrated in a mere five producers. Only Boeing offers a full family of aircraft. Fokker and British Aerospace sales are concentrated in very narrow product lines, while McDonnell Douglas and Airbus fall in the middle. The major companies and their aircraft are listed in table 15–2.

Table 15–1
Major International Collaborations in the Commercial Aircraft Industry

Venture	Partners	Countries	Share	Products
Airbus Industrie	Aerospatiale Deutsche Airbus British Aerospace CASA	France West Germany U.K. Spain	37.9% 37.9 20.0 4.2	Medium-haul, twin-engine wide-body aircraft: A300, A310, and A320
Boeing-Japan	Boeing JADC[a] MHI[b] KHI[c] FHI[d]	U.S. Japan		JADC has about 15 percent of the airframe as a risk-sharing program participant on the 767 for production of fuselage panels, doors, and composite structures such as wing fairings. Participation on the 7J7 is expected to be 25 percent of total program.
CFM International	GE Snecma	U.S. France	50.0% 50.0	High-bypass turbofan engines in low-thrust (20–25,000-lb.) market segment
International Aero Engines	Pratt & Whitney Rolls Royce Japan Aero Engines[e] MTU[f] Fiat	U.S. U.K. Japan West Germany Italy	30.0 30.0 19.9 12.1 8.0	High-bypass turbofan engines in the 25,000-lb. thrust range

[a]The Japanese consortium is JADC (Japan Aircraft Development Corporation) in the development stage and JAC (Japan Aircraft Corporation) in the production stage.

[b]Mitsubishi Heavy Industries.

[c]Kawasaki Heavy Industries.

[d]Fuji Heavy Industries.

[e]JAE is a cooperative venture among Ishikawajima-Harima Heavy Industries (IHI) (60 percent), Mitsubishi Heavy Industries (MHI) (15 percent) and Kawasaki Heavy Industries (KHI) (25 percent).

[f]Motoren-und-Turbinen-Union.

Table 15–2
Large Commercial Aircraft Companies and Programs

Company	Country and Ownership	Aircraft	Capacity
Boeing	U.S. Private	737 757 767 747	103–150 186–220 211–330 452–550
McDonnell Douglas	U.S. Private	DC-9/MD-80 DC-10	90–180 250–330
British Aerospace	U.K. Government/private	BAe 146	93–120
Fokker	Netherlands Private	F-28/100	65–107
Airbus Industrie	Multinational Government/private	A300 A310 A320	220–375 210–265 149–179

Although most companies participate in both civil and military programs, the vagaries of the market and the high levels of risk associated with this industry have threatened the existence of each company in the last generation of airplanes. The search for scale and experience economies through increased unit sales has resulted in competition becoming increasingly global in character; global competition and high levels of investment in development of risky new aircraft for uncertain markets have tempted all companies in the industry to consider international collaboration on new projects.

Airbus Industrie

Airbus is the oldest and most ambitious of the cooperative ventures in aircraft, involving the "national champions" of four European countries in the development of a complete family of large commercial jet aircraft. The original A300 wide-body was followed by the A310 and the A320, currently in the development stage. Airbus now proposes to introduce at least two new models, giving it a range of planes to rival Boeing's. Airbus was originally a partnership of the U.K., French, and German aerospace companies. Partnership shares were renegotiated to accommodate Britain's withdrawal, its eventual return, and inclusion of the Spanish. Airbus management coordinates the engineering and manufacturing activities of the member companies, and it handles marketing and product support. The amount and type of work allocated to each member company are negotiated for each aircraft, and Airbus contracts with member companies to design and produce certain assemblies in return for a share of the revenues.

The formation of Airbus was in response to the realization that none of the individual European companies had the resources to challenge U.S. firms, and that cooperation was needed to preserve an independent European capability. International cooperation gave Airbus preferential access to several national airlines, and coordinated government funding provided a sound financial base. While the venture has been a technical success and has given the U.S. companies a tough competitor for aircraft orders, the venture continues to require capital infusions from its government supporters and is not a financial success.

Boeing and the Japanese Consortium

The Boeing–Japan relationship began in the early 1970s. The first postwar Japanese attempt to enter the commercial aircraft industry, the YS-11 turboprop, was a modest technical success, but a serious commercial failure. The YS-11 experience made Japanese companies and government, which had played an important role subsidizing development and production of the YS-11, very cautious about future commercial aircraft projects. Sobered by the financial failure of their first attempt, the Japanese companies were determined to reduce the risk of their next foray into aircraft by seeking out experienced foreign partners.

In the early 1970s, Boeing was open to the idea of including partners in plans for the next generation of aircraft. Boeing's harrowing experience in the then recent aircraft depression made it receptive to arrangements that would reduce the burden of developing new types of airliners to meet changing world market demand. Foreign firms were obvious candidates.

While the Japanese hoped to be included as partners, the deal struck with the Japanese consortium was for "risk-sharing subcontracting" on the manufacture of rear- and center-body sections, wing ribs, and composite structures (doors and wing fairings) for the 767. The contract called for the Japanese consortium to assume the risk of tooling for a production level of eight planes per month, with payment based on the assumption that five hundred planes would be produced during a given period. In that sense, the contract was "risk-sharing," since the Japanese companies would make a profit only if the expected level of demand materialized. The Japanese also assumed the foreign-exchange risk involved in the contract. Ownership remained with Boeing, as did the responsibility for overall design and marketing. Thus, the relationship was a subcontracting relationship, albeit a very substantial one with an unusual "risk-sharing" twist. Japanese companies provided assistance in the design stage, sending more than one hundred engineers to Boeing at one point. Boeing provided the Japanese consortium with the technology required to design and make individual parts, though the overall design of the plane itself remained Boeing's responsibility. Japanese government support was limited to the design phase, with 50 percent of the R&D amount being supported by government loans.

The 767 has been in production since 1983, but the expected level of sales has not materialized. While production was planned for eight aircraft per month, current production is approximately two per month, and both Boeing and the Japanese companies have idle capacity.

The Boeing cooperation with Japan has continued with a new Memorandum of Understanding (MOU), signed in March 1986, to build a 150-seat narrow-bodied plane, currently labeled the 7J7, to be powered by new technology, unducted fan (UDF) engines. As of mid-1987, some details of the project are still tentative, and the date of availability to airlines has been moved back one year to a goal of 1993. Neither side has made an irrevocable commitment at this point, but it is clear that if the project goes forward, there will be several differences between it and the earlier 767 project. Japanese participation will be increased in the amount of work, in their number of stages of the project, and in project decisions, though it appears that the overall design responsibility will remain with Boeing. At the peak of the design work, over five hundred Japanese engineers may be assigned to the project, half in Seattle. Japanese government support will continue to be given in the form of loans for somewhat more than half of the research and development costs.

Aircraft Engine Industry and Market

High development costs, overcapacity, and severe competition have reduced the number of commercial engine manufacturers to just three major international competitors—Pratt & Whitney (P&W), General Electric (GE), and Rolls Royce (Rolls)—and a dozen smaller national producers. In the commercial aircraft market, the three principal competitors produce high-bypass turbofan engines for three segments—high, medium, and low thrust. The exact boundaries of each segment are flexible over time and a particular engine model series can experience competitive pressure from below or above as engine thrusts are increased or deceased. But only two of the three competitors share most of the business in each of the three segments: GE and P&W in the high end, P&W and Rolls in the medium segment, and CFM International (a GE—Snecma joint venture) and P&W in the low end. A third producer in a segment almost always leads to production below economic scale, pressure on prices, and the threat of financial catastrophe for at least one of the engine manufacturers. Even two active producers in a small segment can mean overcapacity.

Pratt & Whitney dominated the commercial jet engine market during the 1960s. General Electric concentrated on military engines, and Rolls engines were used on aircraft having limited commercial success. However, in the early 1970s, General Electric staged a significant move into commercial production using the technology it had developed for military programs. Its CF6 series of high-thrust engines was followed by the CFM56 series of low-thrust engines, and, by 1978, GE had become a strong number two in the industry. Rolls suffered from its commitment to the commercially unsuccessful Lockheed L-1011 and today has the smallest share of the commercial market. Table 15–3 shows the engines produced by the three major competitors.

CFM International

CFM International, a joint subsidiary company owned in equal shares by GE and Snecma, was formed in 1974 after three years of discussions between GE, Snecma, and the French and U.S. governments. The venture manufactures and markets the CFM56 line of turbofan engines. GE is a large, diversified U.S. multinational

Table 15–3
Market Segments for High-bypass Commercial Turbofan Engines

Company	Engine	Thrust (000 lbs.)	Airframe Application
High-thrust			
GE	CF6-6...– 80	42–62	DC-10, A300, A310, B747, B767
P&W	4000	50–60	B747, B767, A300, A310, *MD-11*
P&W	JT9D-7...70A	46–56	B747, B767, A310, DC-10
Rolls	RB211-22B	42–56	L-1011, B747
Medium-thrust			
Rolls	RB211-535	37–40	B757
P&W[a]	2037	38	B757
Low-thrust			
IAE	V2500	25	*A320, MD-89*
CFM Intl	CFM-56	18–25	DC-8-70R, KC-135R, E-3, E-6, B737, *A320*
P&W	JT8D	14–21	B727, DC-9, B737, MD-80s

Note: Planes in *italics* (for example, *A320*) were not delivered as of the end of 1986.
[a]With MUT and Fiat.

company whose engine group is one of the big three international competitors. Snecma is one of the dozen small national military manufacturers and is 90 percent owned by the French government.

The beginnings of the CFM joint venture lie in the coproduction arrangements between GE and both MTU of Germany and Snecma on the heavy-thrust CF6 engine. The CF6 was launched in an attempt to satisfy the requirements of both the McDonnell Douglas DC-10 and the Lockheed L-1011, but Lockheed's choice of the Rolls Royce RB211 left GE with only one commercial customer for the CF6. The use of Snecma and MTU in the coproduction and final assembly of the CF6 engines was part of GE's successful attempt to secure acceptance of the CF6 as the lead engine on the Airbus 300.

After the initial success of the CF6, GE saw the potential for an engine in the low-thrust range of the market, using the core technology of the F101/110 engine developed for the B-1 bomber. Snecma was chosen as the partner in the CFM International joint venture to produce the CFM56 engine. Slowed by U.S. government concern about the transfer of militarily sensitive technology in the high-pressure core, CFM did not actually introduce the CFM56-2 into service until 1982. The CFM56 has now evolved into a family of engines, and GE and Snecma have agreed to continue their collaboration into the development of the new unducted fan engine. Even though Snecma will have only 35 percent of the new project, it will definitely be more than a subcontractor and will have a key role in UDF program financing, development, and production. The CFM56 venture supported GE's reentry into the commercial engine business and gave Snecma its first successful access to the commercial market.

CFM International is legally two joint subsidiary companies, one in France and one in the United States, with the same 50:50 ownership, same small staff, and same simple management structure. CFM International provides one program management, a single customer interface, and a single, integrated marketing and product-support program fully backed by each parent company. CFM International sells services to GE and Snecma and buys services and hardware (the component modules of the engines) from its parents. While GE and Snecma each specialize in the manufacture of certain sections of the engine, both GE and Snecma maintain their own assembly lines. CFM International takes title to the engines and sells them to the customer. Expenses of GE and Snecma are not merged and profits are not shared. Only the revenue to CFM International from the sale of engines is shared on the basis of the approximately 50:50 work split.

International Aero Engines

International Aero Engines (IAE) is the newest and most complex of the cooperative ventures. It was formed in 1983 to design and build a new jet engine designated the V2500 for the 25,000-pound–thrust market segment. It is comprised of seven partner firms from five countries. The shares of work performed by each partner differ slightly from the ownership shares. IAE is incorporated in Switzerland, a favorable site for legal and tax purposes. A separate entity has been created to coordinate development, production, and product support as well as to handle all marketing. The management team is headquartered in the United States and the engineering team in Britain. As in the Airbus and CFM International ventures, revenues rather than profits are shared. Managers assigned to the joint venture by the member companies are nominal employees of the venture, but remain on the payrolls of the individual firms.

International Aero Engines brought together two international teams that had been working on proposals for similar engines. One team was comprised of Rolls Royce and three Japanese companies, and the other combined U.S., German, and Italian companies. With a General Electric-Snecma engine already entering this market segment, the prospect was for three competing engines, encouraging consolidation and cooperation. Although the Rolls effort with the Japanese had already made significant progress, it became evident that a larger engine was needed, requiring a major redesign and added investment. Pratt & Whitney had just made a major investment in an engine that was not selling well, the PW2037, and was in the midst of development of a new engine series, the PW4000. These investment requirements in the face of market uncertainty convinced Rolls and P&W to join forces. It was also felt that using the special expertise of the different partners could speed development, an important consideration given the pressure from the GE-Snecma engine. It is too early to judge the commercial and managerial success of this venture.

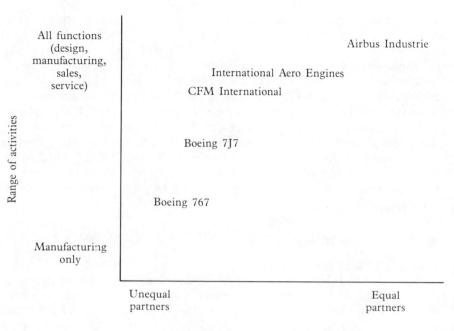

Partner sizes and competitive positions

Figure 15-1. Types of International Cooperative Ventures

To summarize, the main characteristics of the four ventures just described are presented in figure 15-1. The ventures vary along two important dimensions: the nature of the cooperation and the characteristics of the partners. Some ventures involve cooperation primarily in manufacturing, while others include substantial cooperation in engineering, marketing, and product support. Some involve cooperation among relatively equal partners, while others bring together the major players and smaller industry participants. The Boeing cooperation with Japan on the 767 represents one extreme of minimum cooperation between very unequal partners, the other extreme of equal partners being Airbus. CFM International, IAE, and the proposed Boeing–Japan cooperation on the 7J7 represent intermediate positions. While the issues involved in distributing the gains of cooperation are similar across all ventures, their relative significance seems to vary across these different types of ventures.

Analysis

While many issues are subject to negotiation in any international cooperative venture, three stand out as particularly important. These are:

1. The *strategic direction* of the venture: What product-market segment will be addressed by the venture, and what will be the timing of product introduction?

2. *Technology transfer and information sharing:* How much information will be transferred, and how can each partner's proprietary interests be protected while allowing the venture to operate successfully?

3. *Management control and decision making:* Who has authority for what decisions and what, if any, independence is given to the joint entity?

Potential partners operate in uncertain environments with imperfect information on future trends in the industry and on the motivations and behavior of other firms with which they are negotiating. Yet, in the analysis of international cooperative ventures, it is assumed that partners are rational in their negotiating behavior, given the information they can gather and process. They recognize the interests of the different parties to the negotiations and what each party stands to gain or lose. Each partner wishes to maximize its own long-term competitive position and assumes that others have similar goals. Thus, while short-term objectives in a particular venture are important, each party realizes that ventures can potentially result in longer-term benefits if successful.

Strategic Direction

In a new cooperative program, each partner will look for: (1) synergy between the new program and its existing programs, (2) the best adaptation to its perception of its future environment, and (3) compatibility with its own resources. The basis for cooperation between partners is the different portfolios of resources each partner brings to the venture. If the objectives of the partners are compatible, conflicts with regard to differing perceptions of the competitive environment, differing resource constraints, and divergent views on timing can—with good management and some luck—be overcome.

Airbus Industrie

Differing goals and resources of the Airbus partners have caused major conflicts regarding the strategic direction of the joint venture. Some of these disputes result from differing interests of individual companies, while others are engendered by government sponsors. The French, driven by the importance of maintaining a military capability independent of the United States, seem most committed to the preservation of a major air transport manufacturing industry and, hence, the establishment of a family of aircraft that can compete with the U.S. firms. They are prepared to invest heavily to achieve this goal, while the British and the Germans are more cautious, being concerned that new programs have attractive commercial prospects.

The French have therefore argued aggressively for more rapid introduction of new models than have their partners. The financial requirements of developing a full range of planes have strained all the partner companies, but some more so than others, partially due to differing attitudes and, hence, financing policies on the part of the sponsoring governments.

While fitting the venture's products to the existing portfolios of the partner enterprises has not been a problem for Airbus, other conflicts have existed regarding strategic direction. Each partner is concerned with the particular requirements of the airlines in its national market, and these differ widely. Lufthansa, for example, has consistently pushed Airbus to introduce a long-range aircraft and was not enthusiastic about the A320, for which it had no need.

Tensions in the Airbus consortium have always encouraged the Airbus partners to continue to explore possibilities outside of the venture. While the ideal of European cooperation has been an important goal, it has at times conflicted with the best commercial prospects. Both the British and the French have considered partnerships with the U.S. firms, and MBB, the parent of Deutsche Airbus, works outside the Airbus venture on the Fokker 100.

The fact that all the Airbus partners are either government-owned or dependent on their governments for financing means that the wider aerospace portfolios of the governments sometimes cause conflicts among the partners. Conflicts among the interests of airframe, engine, and components producers are common. The CFM-56 engine, for example, is used on the Boeing 737-300, a competitor for the Airbus A320. Rolls Royce in the early days of Airbus cancelled development of an engine to be used by Airbus in order to focus on an engine for a competitive Lockheed plane. The design of aircraft can also be affected by the interests of national producers of aircraft parts. In the early days of Airbus, the British wanted to design a plane making maximum use of European components, since they felt they had the strongest European parts industry. When they withdrew from the venture, the French and Germans deemphasized the use of European components and countered the natural tendency of even U.S. airlines to buy a U.S.-produced plane by increasing Airbus use of U.S. parts, thus increasing the marketability of their planes in the United States.

Boeing and the Japanese Consortium

At first glance, the strategic direction of Japan in the commercial aircraft industry might argue against a Boeing–Japanese partnership. The Japanese government through the Ministry of International Trade and Industry (MITI) has declared commercial aircraft production a targeted industry. Certainly, the companies participating in the consortium have the financial depth, engineering, and production strengths and history of manufacturing and export marketing success to be credible candidates for an independent reentry into the commercial aircraft industry. However, Japan's negative experience with the YS-11, reluctance to subsidize production, flaccid defense policies, small domestic market, and the existence of profitable and less risky alternative lines of business lead the Japanese consortium members to be very risk-averse in their ventures into the commercial aircraft industry. This risk aversion has strengthened Boeing's hand in negotiations and makes the strategic direction of Boeing and the Japanese compatible.

Boeing wants to maintain the capability to provide a full line of planes, thus making continuous use of its design experience. Unused, this key element of Boeing's competitive position can atrophy, but strategic alliances that increase the number of new planes designed have value to the company. While each new plane alone is risky, the payoff to Boeing is higher, as it can maintain the full product line. Peak levels of demand on finance, engineering, and production engineering skills have always forced Boeing to introduce at least some level of cooperation with its major assembly suppliers, and the Japanese provide a major source of these scarce resources. Japanese manufacturers have justly acquired a worldwide reputation for highest quality, competitive price, and prompt delivery. In extending its range of procurement and production to Japan, Boeing gains by diversifying its sources. This encourages its domestic suppliers to work to the efficient Japanese standard.

While there have been conflicts in the Boeing–Japan relationship, product design was Boeing's responsibility on the 767, and this responsibility maintained Boeing's vital interest in making sure that the new plane contributes most positively to Boeing's existing portfolio of products. Even on the 7J7 where Japan is a partner, Boeing retains the upper hand in this crucial area. However, it must consider very carefully—in light of Japan's 25 percent shared partnership—Japanese concerns. But, without an existing line of aircraft, Japanese companies can more easily defer to Boeing's wishes.

Timing is a potentially more contentious issue. If there is technology transfer, and the receiving firm expects to use that technology elsewhere in the firm, then earlier dates for go-ahead on production have high value. From Boeing's perspective, careful management of a portfolio of planes means that delay may be appropriate at times. The 7J7 project presents such timing conflicts. Faced with a fast-selling plane below the 150-seat range (the 737) and a narrow-body plane (the 757) that needs to become established in the market just above, Boeing wants to be sure its 150-seat entry adds sufficient value to its portfolio of planes to warrant displacement of its two existing planes. Japanese firms, with no significant participation in the 737 and 757, are more anxious to move ahead rapidly on the 7J7. This explains the Japanese irritation when Boeing postponed the 7J7 to adopt the UDF engine and fly-by-wire technologies, and when lack of orders forced a further one-year delay. Again, however, Boeing's overriding strategic interests, as well as the actions of competitors and developments in the market, reduce the influence of the Japanese on the timing decision.

In summary, we see that the strategic directions of Boeing and the Japanese consortium make for a relationship with potential gains for both. The apparent direct challenge of independent competition from the Japanese consortium is of little threat to Boeing. Problems of product design and timing are not inconsequential, but on balance are outweighed by the advantages in a complementary relationship of differing portfolios and compatible medium- to long-term goals.

CFM International

GE and Snecma brought complementary portfolios and objectives to their joint venture in the early 1970s, but timing of the introduction of the CFM56 was influenced by delay caused by the U.S. government. Both partners needed each other to penetrate the commercial engine market.

GE brought a long history of technical firsts in jet engine manufacturing, a concentration in military engine manufacturing, and a strong international focus and commitment to its collaboration with Snecma. GE needed access to markets, financing, engineering, and manufacturing capacity. Snecma's ability to contribute half of the $1 billion development cost of the CFM56 was very important to the completion of this engine, as GE's management had doubts about introducing a new engine in a soft market. Access to European markets was an even more important strategic consideration for GE. Snecma was also heavily concentrated in military engines, but had no commercial success. Snecma had accumulated experience working with GE on the CF6 engine, and no other competitor was likely to be interested in a joint venture for a new engine. Thus, there was little serious tension between GE and Snecma on the issue of strategic direction.

As in the Boeing–Japanese cooperation, the dominant partner has controlled decisions on product design and the timing of product introduction. With no existing portfolio of large commercial engines, Snecma had less stake in the decision of which type of engine to introduce, and it could acquiesce to GE's plans.

While the GE–Snecma relationship is long-standing and, by almost any standard, a successful one, neither GE nor Snecma has committed the majority of its resources to CFM International. Both partners are free to talk to other potential partners about joint ventures outside the market segment covered by the CFM56. In 1984, GE and Rolls signed a risk- and profit-sharing agreement (scrapped in November 1986) for joint participation in the development of derivatives of GE's high-thrust engine and Rolls's medium-thrust engine. Engines in the heavy- and medium-thrust segments face tough competition from Pratt & Whitney, and collaboration would have reduced the number of competitors in two market segments and improved prospects for all three competitors. Following GE's lead, Snecma announced in 1985 that it was considering another international collaboration with Rolls Royce to jointly develop an engine in the lowest end of the market.

International Aero Engines

Neither Pratt & Whitney nor Rolls Royce had an engine in the size category of the V2500 engine, so there was a common strategic need between both major partners.

All partners were agreed on the need for rapid development of the engine, given the competition from CFM International. The engine also fit the requirements of the Japanese, who were looking for an engine that would be suitable for its proposed aircraft project with Boeing. Nevertheless, as the program goes forward, it is clear that there are potential conflicts between the major partners in the venture concerning what is good for the venture and what is good for each partner.

The decisions of some airlines may involve choices among an aircraft using one of the partner's engines and another aircraft using the joint venture's engines. Although neither partner has a directly competing product, the needs of airlines can be satisfied by different engine and plane combinations, thus creating indirect competition. This conflict has been addressed at least partially by making the joint venture responsible for marketing, rather than leaving it in the hands of the partners.

To summarize, the strategic direction of a cooperative venture seems most contentious in partnerships that must contend with a partner's existing portfolio of products. Unequal partners or partners having few other activities directly related to the joint venture seem more likely to develop long-term compatible relationships, with the senior partner dominating the decisions on product introduction and timing. Thus, the Boeing–Japan, Airbus, and CFM International ventures seem to be broadening to a whole family of products, while IAE may be limited to one product line.

Technology Transfer and Information Sharing

Sharing resources is an important motivation in international ventures, but sharing may have important consequences on the partners' long-term competitive positions. Technology providers are wary that their contributions may be used to mount an independent competitive challenge at a later date. Nevertheless, they are mindful of the need to insure that sufficient technology is transferred to satisfy the technology recipient and to accomplish the performance expected in the current partnership. Furthermore, if the alternative to participation and sharing technology in a joint project is a significant delay or cancellation, the technology provider may see cooperation, even with the leakage that such cooperation might entail, as the only way to continue to maintain and develop its own technology and avoid atrophy from disuse. The recipient is concerned that the technology received is appropriately priced and that it makes a net improvement to the enterprise's capabilities.

Contracts for technology transfer and information sharing are designed to minimize or control opportunistic behavior and to insure a fair sharing of the gains from transfer. Because of the difficulties in writing and enforcing appropriate contracts, ventures are designed either to make it impossible to inappropriately acquire technology (as through modular product design) or to link the sharing of information to long-term commitments. An alternative approach would be for the technology provider to explicitly assume the most opportunist behavior from the technology recipient and price its technology accordingly. But, as we shall see in the next section such an approach could well preclude the trust and rapport building we believe is necessary for the effective operation of complex organizational relationships.

Airbus Industrie

In Airbus, the technology issue has revolved around the allocation of work, rather than the transfer of technology between firms. Work sharing has serious implications for the development or maintenance of enterprise and national capabilities. In the original Airbus partnership, the division of work was particularly contentious, with Britain and France vying for design leadership and assembly. The French prevailed in exchange for agreement to use a Rolls Royce engine. After Britain pulled out of Airbus, France clearly dominated, with Germany ceding design leadership and the most sophisticated manufacturing to the French.

In the current partnership, each national partner specializes—Britain in the wings, Germany in the fuselage, and France in the cockpit and assembly. This allows economies of production, but the non-French partners fear they are losing system-integrating and higher technology capabilities. Britain argued on the A320, for example, that it should have a larger share of the higher technology avionics and related work. Thus, work allocations remain a critical issue and encourage individual partners to seek other ventures on which complementary technological abilities can be maintained. Since successful experience in a given technology is likely to influence allocations on new programs within Airbus, such activities outside the venture are pursued by the individual firms in an effort to increase bargaining power within the consortium.

Boeing and the Japanese Consortium

Boeing's required transfer of production and design technology to the Japanese firms has been a sticking point in negotiations, since the value can only be certain after the transfer. While the price paid for subassemblies on the 767 (at Boeing's internal cost) was a way to finesse the problem, on the 7J7 there has had to be a value set in the MOU for Boeing's disproportionate noncapital contributions to that venture.

Defining the technology to be transferred is also a major problem for the venture. It is in the interest of the Japanese to define the pool of technology to be as wide and as deep as possible, arguing that the full benefits from any cooperation will accrue to the venture only when the maximum amount of technology is transferred. The breadth of technology is relatively easy to define and police, since areas can be defined as "off-limits" to the partner, and compliance can be easily monitored. For example, access to the technology of large autoclaves used by Boeing in composite materials was kept off limits to Fuji engineers, even though the Japanese made smaller composite parts for the 767.

Depth of technological access has proved more difficult to regulate, since the contract explicitly gives the Japanese access to information necessary to produce the parts they are assigned. From Boeing's perspective, at some point the information-sharing benefits are less than the costs of leaking technology, yet this limit is not easily identified in advance. Much of the ongoing difficulties of the 767 contract involved a perception by the Japanese that all information related to a part was to be transferred, while Boeing wanted to monitor the flow of technology and make decisions regarding further transfers consistent with the calculus just mentioned.

Boeing believed that design and marketing were key elements in maintaining its competitive position. In the 767 project, it was able to make a contract barring the Japanese consortium from participating in these key elements. Delay in signing the actual contract also permitted Boeing to accomplish much of the design work before the Japanese consortium could be brought in. Boeing chose the assemblies on which design and manufacturing work would be done by the Japanese, and it was adamantly opposed to the transfer of cockpit and wing technologies. Use of delay and off-limits strategies will be more difficult in the 7J7 contract, since the level of participation and the difference in technology level is now such that a contract without some elements of design and marketing would be unattractive to the Japanese. As the Japanese get closer to Boeing's technological capabilities in some areas, the most awkward contracting problems on technology sharing are likely to develop.

Boeing's relationships with the Japanese consortium involve several elements that make a long-term relationship likely. The initial 767 contract was for five hundred shipsets, and the consortium was required to make a commitment to production facilities for the overly optimistic monthly rate of eight shipsets. Much of this investment was specific to the Boeing relationship and, thus, costly for the firms if the contract relationship were short-term. Boeing also made a large commitment, primarily in staff and engineering time, to indoctrinating the Japanese in "the Boeing way." Again, this was a commitment to an ongoing relationship, even as its ostensible objective was to provide a monitoring system for the performance of Japanese production.

For the new 7J7, both sides can take advantage of the commitments made in the previous project. Techniques for monitoring performance under the contract have been set up by both partners, and information is now exchanged via computer for all stages of the design and production process. Personnel on both sides have had experience in resolving conflicts under the previous contract. Thus, a second contract, even if the parties have become more equal in status, may be easier to develop. Although the long-term relationship requirement can be implicit because of commitments that are difficult to reverse, Boeing has made the long-term commitment explicit on the 7J7. The Japanese are not permitted to engage in production of a competing plane, thus requiring a commitment to a single cooperative relationship in a given product class. Thus, several methods—including a kind of mutual hostage taking—are being used by both the Japanese consortium and Boeing in an imperfect attempt to limit opportunistic behavior on each side while strengthening the competitive position of both partners.

CFM International

The flow of technology has been an important issue from the beginning of the CFM venture. The technological advantage enjoyed by GE is largely the result of GE's work on three military engines with U.S. government–funded research. The U.S. government objected to the possible loss of the militarily sensitive high-pressure core that GE intended to use in the CFM56, and this objection delayed the production of the CFM56 until a solution could be found. The solution was the modularization of the CFM56. The militarily and politically sensitive core of the CFM56 is shipped as a sealed black box which prevents Snecma access to the high-pressure section of the engine. The modular solution was relatively easy to accomplish in this case. GE had already been moving in the direction of modularization of military engines in order to simplify the service and support problems under adverse servicing conditions. And, since GE had done most of the overall development on the CFM56 itself, it was in a position to carve up and modularize the engine without leaking key technologies from the core.

Even though there is widespread admiration for the modular-design solution to the technology-flow problem—plus agreement that this approach kept the sensitive technology from Snecma—there is also the widespread belief that the engine paid a performance penalty for this arrangement, that the "walled-off technology" approach irritated the French partners, and that this approach cannot be repeated on the unducted fan engine because, for example, the pod and thrust reverser are integral parts of the power plant.

GE's technological superiority is acknowledged by a project management fee paid by Snecma and by the fact that GE provides virtually all product support. Snecma entered the CFM International venture as the technologically deficient partner and remains technologically subordinate to GE today. But the technology-development dowry of $500 million Snecma brought with it from the French government provided capital necessary to sustain the CFM56 development through the uncertain period of cash-flow problems in the 1970s.

International Aero Engines

This venture seems to have been designed to minimize the amount of technology transferred. Work was assigned to the partners to take advantage of their unique capabilities (for example, Rolls Royce in fan blade technology, Pratt & Whitney in high-pressure turbine blade technology, MTU in the low-pressure turbine). Like the CFM56, the engine has a modular design that limits the need for each partner to understand the technology outside a single module. While this design is partly for ease of maintenance, it also satisfies both the concerns of the U.S. Department of Defense regarding transfer of the engine core technology and the competitive concerns of the major partners.

Minimizing technology transfer clearly conflicted with other objectives of the joint venture. Ownership percentages were allocated partially for purposes of defining management control, and they did not translate into an easy assigning of a corresponding percentage of work. Note that the total ownership percentage for the P&W-led half of the team is 50.1 percent, versus 49.9 percent for the Rolls–Japanese half. The work percentages, however, give the Rolls side over half the work. Limits on technology transfer could also cause difficulties in carrying out the testing and refining of the overall engine system. Finally, limiting technology transfer was clearly not the optimum arrangement for the minor partners. MTU, for example, has been reported to wish to move beyond the low-pressure turbine work that it has been assigned in several cooperative arrangements.

To summarize, the issue of information sharing is obviously contentious between industry leaders and aggressive junior partners, as illustrated in the Boeing–Japan partnership. That contract illustrates that both irreversible investments and explicit prohibitions are used to limit opportunistic behavior in such relationships. In ventures between more equal partners, information sharing is, on the one hand, more dangerous, but, on the other hand, easier to control. Sharing critical information could provide a rival with an edge in a battle of equals. But, if both partners contribute relatively equal amounts of technology to the venture, the protection of each partner's technology may be held hostage to appropriate behavior. This exchange of hostages is an alternative, although a more dangerous one, to the approach of building walls around key technologies taken by GE in the CFM International relationship.

Financial limitations have been built into all of the agreements examined here simply through the form that the ventures take. The four ventures examined here are revenue-sharing, not cost–and–profit-sharing arrangements. The partners share revenues according to an agreed formula which takes account of the amount of work to be done by each (and the estimated cost) as well as other contributions of each partner. This provides an incentive for cost control and minimizes the amount of production cost and financial information to be shared. Finally, we observe that the issues involving the distribution and flow of technology in joint ventures follow two distinct patterns. In ventures where one partner is clearly the technological leader, the issue is what kind of check valve mechanism governs the flow, while in ventures where neither partner has an overwhelming technological superiority, the issue is a bargaining problem over which partner will get the choicest piece of the project and subsequently enjoy the most exciting and useful technological growth in filling its part of the joint venture contract.

Management and Decision Making

Partners in a cooperative relationship link themselves together to achieve certain benefits, but retain a desire to control the direction of the venture as it develops. As conditions in the industry change, an individual partner's view of the role of the joint venture may change, leading this firm to argue for a change in the venture's strategy or operations. Individual firms wish to maintain flexibility and resist giving veto power to their partners. Contracts must recognize this reluctance to be bound by the priorities of others. Offsetting this, however, is the need to respond quickly and smoothly to changes in the environment. This may require some autonomy for the joint venture, or at least a rapid decision process by the parents. To the extent that the venture is a key element in a partner's broader strategy, the more insistent will it be to retain control. If this is true for two or more partners, it may be difficult to reach the optimum level of autonomy for the venture. The presence of a government as participant or backer will further complicate the autonomy issue because the government is likely to have national goals outside the specific project partnership that may conflict with the goals of private-firm partners.

Airbus Industrie

Much of the conflict within Airbus stems from differences in overall national goals, resources, and industrial portfolios of the governments involved. Although subject to strong influence of governments, Airbus has developed a fairly autonomous management structure and independent central staff for operational decisions and strategy formulation. Such independence has been needed to decide what is best for the enterprise as a whole and at least to provide an independent voice to offset the interests of its individual partner firms and government masters.

Boeing and the Japanese Consortium

Establishment of a flexible but controllable organization has been important to Boeing in both the contracts. As in other partnerships where one firm dominates, the 767 organization gave ultimate authority to Boeing. Boeing carefully tracks the flow of production through the system in all its projects, so it was natural to ask the Japanese to supply the same sort of information to Boeing. While useful for production scheduling, this "unobtrusive monitoring" enabled Boeing to carefully track the performance of the Japanese under the contract at a cost that was not burdensome. Disputes occurred, but the overall control of the system gave the dominant firm the right to threaten a unilateral decision—"do it the Boeing way"—if negotiations failed. Ironically, the right to dictate a decision often led to dispute resolution that involved a good deal of compromise.

An example of this give-and-take is the process of adjusting to lower levels of 767 production. Since the contract clearly stated that the Japanese firms had to accept the risk that the level of eight shipsets would not be met, Boeing was not obliged to compensate them when sales materialized at only 25 percent of the expected rate. But Boeing allocated additional work on other planes in order to offset to some degree the lower-than-expected level of work on the 767. Boeing's response preserved the integrity of the original contract and eliminated other minor disputes.

The actual share of the Japanese in the ventures with Boeing is a complex, potentially contentious, and gradually unfolding problem area. The relationship on the 767 was clearly an unequal one. But Japanese firms are now under pressure to show results in the form of increased participation on the 7J7. This pressure comes from the government but also from the private partners due to their desire for profits from participation.

The 7J7 shows signs of a true partnership, with Japanese firms having both a larger portion of the work—25 percent of the entire project rather than 15 percent of the airframe production—and more responsibility in all areas of the project. This deeper and wider relationship has forced the firms to try to form a more complex form of business relationship. No longer able to rely on "the Boeing way" as a means of dispute resolution, the two firms have had to develop a much more detailed set of plans for handling the upcoming venture. And, since Boeing is experimenting with a number of new management techniques to encourage communication among functional groups and meet very ambitious cost targets, managing the relationship with the Japanese is likely to be complex. After signing the MOU in March 1986, working groups spent more than a year developing concrete statements about various parts of the project and defining work shares (i.e., which firm would build what?). Given Boeing's discomfort with what will be its first deal of this type, it seemed to take special care in formulating the contract. This concern can in itself cause timing disagreements. If the nature of the market and the potential problems in the development and production of the aircraft become clearer over time, the longer Boeing waits, the more explicit the contract can be, and the more contingencies can be effectively covered in the contract.

The previous experience on the 767 will permit Boeing and the Japanese firms to assess more easily the capabilities and the strategies of the other partner and to anticipate contingencies. Still, when the nature of the contract changes as much as it seems to have done between the 767 and the 7J7, the new requirements of the more equal partnerships may make this previous experience less valuable than conventional wisdom suggests.

Government participation in the funding of the Japanese consortium complicates management issues by introducing an additional actor with different constraints and objectives into the decision-making process. The Japanese government does not have the wisdom or the power to direct solutions to consortium problems or to transform the consortium into a single, smoothly functioning entity. It does, however, have enough influence to complicate and delay the decision-making process of the consortium. The government brings in its influence on the Japanese consortium a different, economywide perspective, less appreciation for the specific risks of benefit/cost trade-offs for individual firms, and a lack of technical sophistication. The substantial risk aversion of individual firms is conditioned by their intimate knowledge of their own product and technology portfolios and concern about their abilities to deal with the problems of variable production rates under permanent employment constraints in this very cyclical industry. This knowledge and concern may not be fully appreciated by government bureaucrats.

Government's insistence on sharing work in a consortium format and its concern for spreading the technology spin-off benefits of a partnership with Boeing as widely as possible could complicate management of the Boeing–Japanese company relationships in the consortium by directing the allocation of work away from the most efficient—in Boeing's view—allocation arrangement. The move to partnership status for the Japanese on the 7J7 means that Boeing cannot as freely control either the total quantity of work allocated to the consortium or the allocation of work within the consortium, but must accede more readily to both the rivalries of the individual Japanese partners and the priorities of the Japanese government. In fact, a whole new culture of cooperation and accommodation needs to be inculcated in Boeing middle management in order to deal effectively with the design and production problems of the 7J7.

CFM International

While the CFM collaboration is structured as a 50:50 joint venture, it is clearly not a collaboration of equals. GE is the senior and dominant partner in the relationship, with much of this dominance based on GE's superior technology. GE is not only a much larger firm, it has a much vaster experience in military and civil engine production. GE's work share on the CFM56 includes the most technologically advanced parts of the engine. GE's clear leadership has prevented some of the problems of slow decision making experienced by other international joint ventures.

The structure of CFM International has the outward appearance of a classic 50:50 joint venture, but this outward orthodoxy conceals an unusual underlying arrangement. Although a separate entity, it is very thinly staffed and major decisions are made by GE personnel with input from Snecma. Ironically, this flexibility for rapid response was not relevent for CFM International's initial response problem in the 1970s, which required a slowed development process because of technology-sharing delays. However, the ability to respond quickly with the CFM56-3 and CFM56-5 is more important as Boeing and Airbus maneuver on the 737-300, A320, and 7J7.

The GE–Snecma relationship in CFM International is buoyed on both ends by the coproduction agreements on the CF6 and the prospect for a future relationship on the UDF. Even though CFM International covers only the 20,000–25,000-pound CFM56, the total GE–Snecma relationship spans two very different and noncompetitive engines in two distinct market segments. The advantage of working simultaneously on two engines is that both parties can go down the learning curve faster (including the learning of each others' operations) and smooth production. The latter consideration is especially important to Snecma because European employment practices make it more difficult to accommodate variable production rates. The limited nature of the CFM International relationship permits the partners to explore other collaborations, but also offers the chance to stay together for the next generation of engine development.

International Aero Engines

This venture has an independent management group to coordinate development, manufacturing, marketing, and product support. Development, manufacturing, and product support responsibilities are delegated to the individual companies. IAE retains control of marketing, however, to minimize conflicts of interest between the IAE product and those of the major partners. The joining of two major partners, Pratt & Whitney and Rolls Royce, means that there is no single clear leader of the program. The chief executive is from Pratt & Whitney, with his deputy from Rolls Royce. These two firms share the managerial positions at the vice presidential level, and in each functional area the vice president is from one of the firms while the assistant vice president is from the other. Management of the project is split in two, with engineering in Britain and program management in the United States, with attendant possibilities for overhead buildup and communications difficulties.

To summarize, the issue of control is most difficult in ventures among equals, where decisions must clearly be shared. Among unequals, the dominant partner is in control, but must bear in mind the interests of the minor partners and avoid tempting them to seek other options. In none of the cases examined here does the cooperative venture have a great deal of autonomy from its parents. Such autonomy would be desirable from the joint venture's view, but is impossible for a parent that is pursuing a broader strategy. The links of engineering, manufacturing, and marketing between the joint venture and a partner's independent programs make it impossible to operate the joint venture independently. Only if almost all of the commercial aircraft business of the various partners is put into the joint venture, thereby severing most links to a broader strategy, would autonomy seem to be possible. Airbus is the closest to this situation, but the wider portfolios of the governments limit the venture's independence even there.

Bibliography

Aerokurier. 1982. "Snecma/GE CFM56: Engine for a new airliner generation." September: 1010–1019.

Airbus Industrie. 1982. *Briefing*. Blagnac, France.

Andrews, J. 1985. "The big six: A survey of the world's aircraft industry." *The Economist,* June 1: 1 Survey to 24 Survey.

Aviation Week and Space Technology. 1983. "Pratt, Rolls launch new turbofan." November 7: 28–29.

Aviation Week and Space Technology. 1985a. "Snecma, GE consider joint development of unducted fan." February 25: 27–28.

Aviation Week and Space Technology. 1985b. "Snecma takes share of GE unducted fan, talks with Rolls on smaller engine." May 27: 20.

Bacchetta, M., and De la Torre, J. 1980. *Airbus Industrie.* Fontainebleau, France: European Institute of Business Administration (INSEAD).

Bluestone, B., Jordan, P., and Sullivan, M., 1981. *Aircraft industry dynamics.* Boston: Auburn House.

Demisch, W.H., and Demisch, C.C. 1984. "The jetliner business." New York: First Boston Research, October 5, mimeo.

Frankel, O. 1984. "Flying high: A case study of Japanese industrial policy." *Journal of Policy Analysis and Management* 3: 405–420.

Franko, L.G. 1971. *Joint venture survival in multinational corporations.* New York: Praeger.

General Electric Company. Undated. *A case of a successful joint venture: CFM International.*

Giget, M. 1978. *Le secteur aerospatial.* Paris: Groupe d'etudes des problèms Sociologiques, Economiques et Stratègiques liès aux Techniques Nouvelles (SEST).

Giget, M. 1981. *Evolution de la position relative des industries aeronautiques civiles de L'Europe et des Etats-Unis sur le marche mondial 1955-1985.* Paris: Group d'etudes des problèms Sociologiques, Economiques et Stratègiques liès aux Techniques Nouvelles (SEST).

Hagrup, K. 1980. *The aerospace industry of Western Europe.* Stockholm: Teknisk Hogskolan Stockholm, Institutionen for Trafikplanering.

Harrigan, K.R. 1985. *Strategies for joint ventures.* Lexington, Mass.: Lexington Books.

Hatakeyama. 1979. *YX keikaku no hassoku to wagakuni no kokuki kogyo (The inauguration of the YX project and the Japanese aerospace industry).* Koseiken series no. 130. Tokyo: Koku Seisaku Kenkyukai, December 25.

Masten, S.E. "The organization of production: Evidence from the aerospace industry." *Journal of Law and Economics* 27 (October): 403–418.

Ministry of International Trade and Industry, Tsushosangyosho: Sangyo Kozo Bangikai. 1980. *Hachijunendai no tsusan seisaku bijon.* Tokyo: Tsusanssho Chosakai, 91–92.

Mowery, D.C. 1986. *Multinational joint ventures in product development and manufacture: The case of commercial aircraft.* Pittsburgh: Carnegie-Mellon University.

Mowery, D.C. and Rosenberg, N. 1985a. "Commercial aircraft: Cooperation and competition between the U.S. and Japan." *California Management Review* 27 (Summer): 70–92.

Mowery, D.C., and Rosenberg, N. 1985b. *The Japanese commercial aircraft industry since 1945: Government policy, technical development, and industrial structure.* Occasional paper of the Northeast Asia-United States Forum on International Policy, Stanford University, Stanford, Calif.

Moxon, R.W., and Geringer, J.M. 1985. "Multinational ventures in the commercial aircraft industry." *Columbia Journal of World Business* 20 (Summer): 55–62.

Moxon, R.W., Roehl, T.W., and Truitt, J.F. 1985. *Emerging sources of foreign competition in the commercial aircraft manufacturing industry.* Washington, D.C.: U.S. Department of Transportation.

Newhouse, J. 1982. *The sporty game.* New York: Knopf.

Raiffa, H. 1982. *The art and science of negotiation.* Cambridge, Mass.: Harvard University Press.

Roehl, T.W., and Truitt, J.F. 1987. "Japanese industrial policy in aircraft manufacturing." *International Marketing Review* 4 (Summer): 21–32.

Rubin, P. 1981. *Japan air transport handbook.* Bokyo: Ikaros.

Stopford, J.M., and Wells, L.T., Jr. 1972. *Managing the multinational enterprise.* New York: Basic Books.

Teece, D.J. 1986. "Firm boundaries, technological innovation, and strategic management." In Thomas, L.G. (ed.), *Economics of strategic planning.* Lexington, Mass.: Lexington Books.

Tomlinson, J.W.C. 1970. *The joint venture process in international business: India and Pakistan.* Cambridge, Mass.: MIT Press.

U.S. Department of Commerce, Industry Analysis Division. 1984. *A competitive assessment of the U.S. civil aircraft industry.* Washington, D.C.

Williamson, O.E. 1979. "Transaction cost economics: The governance of contractual relations." *Journal of Law and Economics* 22 (October): 233–261.

16
Joint Venture General Managers in LDCs

Jean-Louis Schaan
Paul W. Beamish

T he number of joint ventures is growing worldwide at an increasing pace. For example, *Mergers and Corporate Policy* (1983) reported a 59 percent increase between 1981 and 1983 in the number of international joint ventures involving U.S. firms.

In the developing countries, the use of joint ventures is even more pronounced. As early as 1973, Vaupel and Curhan had noted that joint ventures, not wholly owned subsidiaries, were the predominate organization form used by multinational enterprises in LDCs.

With the prevalence of joint ventures in LDCs, the demand for joint venture general managers (JVGMs) has increased. Life as the head of a joint venture is characterized by a unique tension inherent in this particular organizational form. Double parenting exacerbates the difficulties and challenges that are a normal part of managing internationally, while creating new ones as well.

The JVGM's role differs from that of general manager in a wholly owned subsidiary. Their task is more complicated in a variety of ways: with essentially two bosses and two sets of expectations, they must simultaneously accommodate the interests of two partners. They often face a great deal of ambiguity in terms of defining both parents' criteria of success and must deal with issues of commitment and communication between the two parents. At the same time, they have less job security—if either parent or the board of directors disapproves of them, they may well have to move.

Among all these disadvantages, JVGMs do have several things to look forward to. They have two sets of resources and skills with which to work. They can often produce at better economies than competitors in the LDC by gaining quality and technical expertise from the MNE and knowledge of the local economy, politics, and customs from the local partner. A framework developed by Mintzberg (1980) provides a brief overview of the JVGM's role as compared to that of the general

The authors wish to acknowledge the financial support provided by the Plan for Excellence and the Center for International Business Studies, School of Business Administration, the University of Western Ontario, and the research assistance of Ms Itrath Qizilbash.

Table 16-1
The Role of the GM: Three Perspectives

I[a] *As They Apply to GM of WOS in a DC*	*II As They Apply to GM of WOS in an LDC*	*III As They Apply to GM of JV in an LDC*
Interpersonal Roles		
1. Figurehead role Represents the organization on ceremonial occasions.	As in column I. However, additional legal requirements in each country necessitate greater emphasis in this role.	As in column II, plus increased number of occasions due to ceremonial situations relating to two nationalities.
2. Liaison role Interacts with other managers and groups outside the organization unit.	Very prominent. Must also frequently interact with government officials. May have problems if GM is an expatriate and working/dealing with nationals outside organizational unit.	As in column II.
3. Leader role Establishes relationships with subordinates (motivating, supervising) and exercises formal authority within the organizational unit.	More complex than in column I. May find it difficult to motivate and supervise nationals due to different values, ethics, and so on.	More complexity than in column II. Must do this with expatriates and nationals who are likely from different countries. Hence, must understand how to motivate people from other countries.
Informational Roles		
1. Monitor role Receives and collects information from both inside and outside the organizational units.	Outside information searching may be harder for an expatriate in an LDC than in a DC. Dealing with subordinates who are nationals may be hard.	Monitoring is more easily done here as JVGM and managers may have access to information from two organizations.
2. Disseminator role Transmits information to members within the organizational unit.	Can talk to nationals, but general managers are usually expatriates; therefore, they may have communication breakdown.	General managers usually are nationals themselves. Hence, role is easier.
3. Spokesperson role Informs those outside the organizational unit.	Again, due to GM's being expatriate, the spokesperson role is often difficult.	Being national, it would be easier. However, there are more groups (partners) for information to be conveyed to.

Table 16–1 continued

I[a] *As They Apply to GM* *of WOS in a DC*	II *As They Apply to GM* *of WOS in an LDC*	III *As They Apply to GM* *of JV in an LDC*
Decision-Related Roles 1. *Innovator role* Initiates change.	Easier than JVGM due to need to convince only one superior. More complex than in column I since physical distance means GM cannot rely on others.	Very prominent role. Must convince both parents and the board of directors.
2. *Resource-allocation role* Decides where efforts and energies will be directed.	Similar to column I. Not too difficult since there would be one set of objectives to achieve rather than conflicting goals as in column III.	Very difficult due to two sets of resources and expectations.
3. *Negotiator role* Deals with situations involving negotiations on behalf of the organization.	Due to GM being expatriate, role may be difficult. As well, presence in an LDC environment may complicate negotiaions.	Perhaps the primary skill required of the JVGM.
4. *Disturbance-handler role* Takes charge when crises arise and the organization is threatened.	Handles individually. Gets support from direct superior if needed, but as above.	Has other influences (both parents and board of directors) which complicate the decision.

[a]This column is from Mintzberg (1980).

manager of a wholly owned subsidiary in a foreign country and a wholly owned subsidiary (WOS) in its home country. (See table 16–1.)

The role of JVGMs is to balance these opportunities and risks and make them work for them. Achievement of this difficult task can make for a successful venture.

The purpose of this chapter is to analyze the unique features of joint venture general management in LDCs. It begins with the identification and discussion of the major pressures that determine the JVGM's strategic and operating context. It then examines how JVGMs respond to those pressures. The chapter concludes with a discussion of the implications of the study's findings for JVGMs, managers in parent organizations, and researchers.

Methodology

This research is derived from two larger studies conducted by the authors (Schaan 1983; Beamish 1984) which involved in total nearly 75 joint ventures in LDCs. Schaan conducted 39 personal interviews in 4 countries—Canada, Mexico, the United States, and France. Beamish conducted 46 interviews in Canada, the United States, Great Britain, and two Caribbean nations. Questionnaires were used in some instances to supplement the interview observations.

Data for this chapter were obtained primarily from personal interviews with managers involved in 22 core joint ventures. In most cases, interviews involved managers at 3 levels: the JVGM, multinational parent (MNC) representative, and LDC parent representative. In total, 17 JVGMs were personally interviewed. The MNC parent held a majority position in 4 JVs; 6 JVs were 50:50; and the MNC parent held a minority position in 12 JVs.

Twelve JVs were managed at the time of study by a JVGM appointed by the MNC parent. Among them, 6 were nationals from the MNC's country, 4 were local nationals, and 2 were third-country nationals. The JVGMs of the other 10 JVs were appointed by the local parent and 4 of them were the local parent itself.

Of the 22 core joint ventures, 7 were successful, 9 were unsuccessful, and 6 had been turned around. Half operated in Mexico, with all but one of the balance located in the Caribbean.

The performance of the JVs by ownership category is presented in table 16–2. The data suggest that the JVs where the MNC holds a minority position have greater chances to succeed than where it holds a majority position.

Among the unsuccessful JVs, two-thirds were staffed with expatriates and one-third with local nationals, while the proportions are reversed for the successful JVs—two-thirds are managed by local JVGMs and one-third by expatriates. Hence, a local JVGM seems to have greater chances to run a successful operation than an expatriate.

The core ventures were carefully selected to be representative of common types of joint ventures in LDCs. All but one of the twenty-two ventures had been in operation for at least three years. Focus was placed on the manufacturing sector. Most of the ventures were in low-medium technology-intensive sectors such as food processing and production of nondurable consumer goods. All of the ventures were between a multinational enterprise from a developed country and a private local

Table 16–2
Ownership and Performance of Sample JVs

	MNE Majority	*50:50*	*MNE Minority*
Successful	25%	67%	75%
Unsuccessful	75	33	25

organization from the LDC. Half of the firms exported, with exports totaling up to 25 percent of sales.

The difficulty of securing cooperation from managers in LDCs plus the limited availability of joint ventures that met the specified requirements meant that a pure random sample could not be employed. For example, Beamish employed a stratified sample in that, where possible, both high and low performers in the same industry and same country were examined. Schaan, in turn, used a convenience sample.

The core ventures had sales between $1.0 and 543.0 million in U.S. dollars. Average market share for the core ventures was 42 percent, with a high standard deviation. The joint ventures had been in operation for an average of 11.5 years.

Only one of the core ventures had an effective monopoly position. In the other cases, either local manufacturing competition existed, or tariffs were low enough to allow competitive import.

The data analysis methods used included content analysis, frequency of response, and nonparametric statistical tests such as the Kolmogorov-Smirnov one-sample test.

What Makes It Difficult to Manage a Joint Venture in an LDC?

Meeting the Expectations of Two Parents

JVGMs tend to be evaluated on the basis of one dimension or a combination of dimensions (such as their ability to meet each parent's expectations, to achieve the joint venture's strategic objectives, or simply to maintain a good working relationship with managers from parent organizations). A challenge facing JVGMs is not only that the parent organizations may have different sets of expectations, but, more importantly, that those expectations are seldom clearly communicated and that they change over time.

In 70 percent of the joint ventures studied, JVGMs indicated that they had had in the past—or still had at the time of the interview—difficulties in understanding what the criteria of their parents were. In most cases, JVGMs were not handed a clear set of criteria by the two parents. Typically, they had to learn over time, through a trial and error process, what they had to do well to make each parent happy.

The ambiguity thus created by the parents was in most cases unintended. However, in about 10 percent of the joint ventures studied, at least one of the parents was reluctant to make its expectations clear, fearing that it would weaken its bargaining power in its dealings with its partner.

Managers in parent organizations use a complex function of expectations in forming a judgment regarding how successful a joint venture is. They use a combination of quantitative (financial and economic) and qualitative criteria, with each criterion carrying a specific weight in the function. Further, both the criteria and the weights change over time. As a result, JVGMs need to be perceptive enough to read the signals sent by managers from the parent companies, and adapt their personal and company's strategies to respond to changes in expectations.

Differences in the parents' expectations were found in the following areas:

in the dimensions used (growth versus ROI versus dividends, for example)

in the time orientation (short-term versus long-term)

in the level of achievement (aggressiveness of the criteria)

in the degree of specificity: growth versus growth in sales of 20 percent

Managing a joint venture so as to meet two (or more) sets of expectations is a difficult task in itself. However, it becomes an impossible one if the expectations are incompatible and there is no room or no willingness on the part of the parents to compromise. Joint ventures where this was the case did not survive very long.

It is difficult for a JVGM to meet simultaneously all criteria for one parent, let alone for two or more parents. Therefore, managing a joint venture involves a subtle balancing act between the parents' priorities, the joint venture's strategic and operating priorities, and the personal objectives, beliefs, and values of the managers representing the various stakeholders in the joint venture. This research shows that, in most cases, managers in the parent organizations have a satisficer's attitude toward a joint venture's performance. Such an attitude indicates that JVGMs have an opportunity to reach some sort of compromise which may be acceptable to the parents. Compromise is the rule rather than the exception in joint ventures. However, in the words of a Mexican manager, "to insure the long-term success of the joint venture, compromise must be perceived by all sides as being a mutual thing."

Finally, the observed differences in expectations regarding "good management practice" have been explained by Reynolds (1979) on the basis of the parents' attitudes toward the role of management in five areas: (1) the source and the scope of the manger's authority, (2) status, (3) personality versus position, (4) responsibility for decision making, and (5) responsibility for future events.

Insuring the Economic Viability of the Joint Venture

The joint venture characteristic of greatest interest to both managers and researchers is performance. Most of the existing research on joint ventures is normative, related in one way or another to performance. Yet, the amount of research in which the impact of these prescriptions is directly assessed against a measure of performance is limited, particularly for joint ventures in developing countries.

Use of only a foreign-partner managerial assessment represents an incomplete method of assessing joint venture performance. Since joint ventures are jointly owned, it is reasonable to examine whether both partners were satisfied with performance. Because one partner is a local firm and one is a foreign firm, we would expect differences in how performance might be assessed. In the country where the joint venture was located, the MNE partners were never strictly dependent on local earnings in determining their overall return. However, venture profits were often the only source of revenue for local partners, and, as Reynolds (1979) notes, the joint venture was much more often the major industrial interest of the local partner. The foreign partner, therefore, might still be earning a good overall return from the business (through raw material sales, royalties, and so on) when the venture itself was generating little, if any, profit. This did, in fact, occur in a number of cases.

In one case, the expatriate general manager claimed he could run it on a break-even basis in the local country and the parent company would still find it lucrative. In this case, the local partner was not satisfied with the performance of the venture.

Those joint ventures in which at least one partner was unsatisfied with performance were considered unsatisfactory performers. Overall, of the twenty-two core ventures, fourteen were classified as satisfactory performers using this system. The ventures can be further subdivided into satisfactory and unsatisfactory performers according to differences in partner assessment of performance. (See table 16–3.)

Joint managerial assessment was the sole performance measure used in the core ventures. Use of this measure is consistent with the way most JVGMs would assess performance. Nonetheless, one task of the JVGM is to continue reminding parent companies that there has to be *joint* satisfaction if the business is to remain viable.

Drawing from the Partners' Contributions

A mutual long-term need between joint venture partners is another significant variable associated with the success of joint ventures. In Beamish's study (1984), partner needs were categorized into five groups with three items in each group. These five groups encompassed: (1) needs for items readily capitalized, (2) human

Table 16–3
Joint Venture Performance: Mutual Response Measure

	Satisfactory		*Unsatisfactory*		
	Performance is satisfactory to both partners.	Performance had been unsatisfactory, but later turned around.	Performance is unsatisfactory from one partner's perspective.	Venture is currently performing poorly or has ceased operations.	Total
Total	8	6	4	4	22

resources needs, (3) market access needs, (4) government/political needs, and (5) knowledge needs. These needs were further broken down into long-term needs, short-term needs, and unimportant needs according to three different perspectives: the MNCs in high-performing ventures, those in low-performing ventures, and the local general managers. This is a useful reference guide for JVGMs. (Table 16–4 shows the correlation between the three perspectives and the three time frames.)

The managers of the MNCs in the high-performing ventures rated local management and local knowledge as key ingredients to long-term success. Here, local management includes general managers and functional managers. Knowledge of the local economy, politics, and culture make up the local-knowledge category.

The MNCs with low-performing ventures did not have any long-term needs for their partners. They felt that the local partner could not provide advantages and had formed the venture only for government/political reasons.

Table 16–4
Summary of Partner Contributions

	To MNCs in High-performing JVs	To MNCs in Low-performing JVs	To Local General Managers
Needs steadily or increasingly important over time	Local business knowledge General managers Knowledge of local economy, politics, and customs Functional managers		Better export opportunities
Needs decreasingly important over time	Local political advantages Avoid political intervention	Avoid political intervention Meet existing government ownership requirements	Raw material supply Technology or equipment
Unimportant needs	Inexpensive labor Raw material supply Technology or equipment	Inexpensive labor Raw material supply Technology or equipment Functional managers Access to local market Better export opportunities	Speed of entry Local political advantages Inexpensive labor Knowledge of local economy, politics, and customs

Source: Beamish, P.W., "Joint Venture Performance in Developing Countries." Unpublished doctoral dissertation. University of Western Ontario, 1984, p. 103.

Local general managers deemed better export opportunities a need of long-term importance. As JVGMs, they wanted to see their ventures successful in the long run. Better export opportunities allowed the joint venture to increase sales and profits.

In the short term, local general managers hoped to gain raw material supply and technology or equipment from the parents. This is as one would expect since they are only beginning operations and need the assistance from the parents.

Local general managers noted four items as unimportant contributions of their parents: speed of entry into a country, local political advantages, inexpensive labor, and knowledge of the local economy, politics, and customs. Given that two of the three of the foreign-supplied GMs had low-performing ventures, our view is that if these GMs had solicited feedback from the local partner, they might have been more successful.

In the high-performing venture, the JVGM was a national of the local country and ranked this knowledge need low. This is a legitimate claim because as a national, he already would have the necessary background knowledge in this area.

Foreign-supplied GMs would do well to use local contributions. The JVGMs that have a successful venture look for contributions from the local parent.

JVGMs must be aware of their MNE parent's views on the importance of the local partner's contributions. By enabling the JVGM to see if the parent is acting as one would in a successful or unsuccessful venture, the JVGM can insure that the MNC parent realizes the benefits to be gained from the local parent and can use these assets to become or maintain its successful posture.

This is key information for a JVGM. Knowing the importance of need and commitment, a JVGM can act in a way to achieve the needed amounts of both to improve the prospects for joint venture success. As intermediary, the JVGM can facilitate a trust relationship by involving the local partner in decisions affecting the joint venture even when there is no specific policy stated to involve the partner in a particular decision. By simply informing the partner of the activities of the joint venture, and involving the partner, the likelihood of success increases.

Managing in an Environment Constrained by the Parents' Control Practices

The analysis of the parent companies' control practices shows that JVGMs generally have less autonomy than they want to think they have. In particular, the JVs' boards of directors have been found to play a major role in the decision-making process, greater than in the joint ventures operating in developed countries. An explanation for this is that in LDCs, in addition to the level of uncertainty and the foreign parent's desire to be in control, there is a lack of managerial depth and the board of directors constitutes a mechanism for transferring the parents' expertise.

Control refers to the process through which a parent company assures that the way a joint venture is managed conforms to its own interests. From a JVGM's perspective, an understanding of the parents' control practices serves two purposes. First, it helps map the boundaries of authority within which one is expected to operate. Second, it helps identify opportunities for independence (areas of freedom from parent authority or involvement).

Parent companies have been found to exercise control through both positive and negative mechanisms. A parent uses positive control when it is in a position to influence activities or decisions in a way consistent with its own expectations and interests. It uses negative control when it is in a position to prevent decisions or activities it does not agree with from being implemented. (Refer to table 16–5 for details.) Negative mechanisms such as a veto right over major decisions are particularly useful to parents in a minority shareholder's position.

An analysis of the parent companies' control practices in joint ventures suggests that the autonomy of a JVGM is determined by how the following issues are actually implemented in a given case:

What JVGMs Can and Cannot Do. In all joint ventures, there were decisions and/or activities that were unequivocally under the responsibility of one parent, of both parents, or of the JVGM. Of course, for many decisions, the lines were not clearly defined. But for those decisions or activities that could be identified as being the prerogative of a given party to the joint venture, the allocation of authority was done in one of two ways.

First, for all the joint ventures studied, the allocation was the result of negotiations during the planning phase of the joint venture and was formally ratified in the joint venture agreement. Differences existed regarding which decisions should be made by whom depending on the area of expertise (such as technology or marketing) brought by a parent or on the control policies of the parent. (For example, two large U.S. multinationals had a policy to appoint the finance manager and to make all operating financial decisions.)

Second, the allocation could be the result of an implicit understanding and agreement of the parents regarding their respective territories of influence. This happened in cases where one parent would demonstrate greater expertise in a specific area than its partner or the JVGM.

What JVGMs Need to Get Approval for and to Whom JVGMs Report. As in most companies, JVGMs had to get approval for their strategic and operating plans, their budgets, appointments of joint venture top managers, and capital budgeting decisions. However, a distinctive characteristic of the joint ventures was that, although JVGMs want to see their reporting relationship to the board, in 40 percent of the Mexican joint ventures, the JVGM had to clear specific issues with one parent before being allowed to discuss them with the other parent. Further, it was expected that no surprises would be brought up during the board meetings.

What JVGMs Need to Achieve; What Targets Are Set by Parents. In a minority of cases (20 percent), JVGMs were given specific goals to achieve in terms of

Table 16–5
Positive and Negative Control Mechanisms

Positive	*Negative*
Ability to make specific decisions	
Ability to design:	Board
(1) Planning process	
(2) Appropriation requests	Executive committee
Policies and procedures	Approval required for:
Ability to set objectives for JVGM	(1) Specific decisions
	(2) Plans, budgets
Contracts: management	(3) Appropriation requests
technology transfer	(4) Nomination of JVGM
marketing	Screening/no objection of parent
supplier	before ideas are discussed with other
Participation in planning or budgeting	parent
process	
Parent organization structure	
Reporting structure	
Staffing	
Training programs	
Staff services	
Bonus JVGM tied to parent results	
Ability to decide on future promotion of JVGM (and other joint venture managers)	
Feedback: strategy/plan budgets, appropriation requests	
JVGM participation in parent's worldwide meetings	
Relations with JVGM: phone calls, meetings, visits	
Staffing parent with someone with experience with joint venture	
MNC level Mexico	
Information meetings with other parent	

Source: Schaan, J.-L., "Parent Control and Joint Venture Success: The Case of Mexico. Unpublished doctoral dissertation. Unviersity of Western Ontario, 1983, p. 249.

sales, profits, or market share. However, in a greater number of cases (60 percent), they were given very specific personal objectives such as conducting a market study or hiring and developing a new marketing manager.

Who Sets Policies, Procedures, and General Management Practices. In 70 percent of the Mexican joint ventures, the joint venture's policies and procedures were a replication of one parent's. Since in each of those cases, the JVGM had been appointed by the parent who had established the policies and procedures, the JVGM had a clear understanding of the joint venture's operating rules.

What Role Managers in Parent Companies Play. Two crucial elements in determining the JVGM's autonomy are the personal style of managers from the parent companies and the amount of trust between people. In some joint ventures, the JVGM received calls on a periodic basis from managers in a parent company who wanted to make sure there were no surprises, while in other joint ventures, JVGMs would be left alone (unless they would ask for help) until the next board meeting.

How Do JVGMs Respond to Those Challenges?

Parents' Versus Joint Venture's Agenda

As JVGMs learn how to live and manage under double parenting, they tend to develop an agenda of their own which differs in an important way from that of their parents. While managers from parent companies tend to decide on the joint venture's success based on how well the joint venture meets their own expectations, the JVGMs' judgment is based on the avoidance of bad relationships between the parties involved. In other words, managers in the parent companies tend to use indicators centered around the idea of achieving specific results, while JVGMs tend to use indicators centered around the idea of preventing bad relationships from developing. The following quotes capture the essence of the JVGMs' concern:

JVGM 1: If the joint venture is able to accomplish a desired result without too much "noise," it is a sign of future prosperous relationships.

JVGM 2: For the joint venture to be successful, I have to grow, to achieve the objectives set by the vice president for Latin America, to maintain the leadership position we have in Mexico, and to maintain a trust relationship between the Canadians and the Mexicans.

JVGM 3: A good indication of the success of the joint venture is that one parent has been able to run the joint venture without interference from the other parent.

In cases where the JVGM is a national of the host country, an important item on the agenda is the joint venture's contribution to the country's economic and social development. Nationalist concerns appear to play a more important role in LDCs than in developed countries and are noted in joint ventures staffed with national top managers, be they appointed by the local parent or the multinational parent.

Parents' versus Joint Venture's Interests

JVGMs tend to see their allegiance to the joint venture first and to the parents second. This applies to the vast majority of JVGMs interviewed, whether they come from one parent or not. When trying to resolve differences between the parents, they find that the joint venture's interests should be placed first and that the parents' interests should come second.

Essentially, JVGMs want to stay away from situations where one parent is perceived to win and the other to lose over a specific issue. JVGMs who try to satisfy one parent more than the other, or who are perceived as trying to do so, sooner or later are going to erode their credibiltiy and jeopardize their working relationship with the partner that feels discriminated against.

When managers refer to a joint venture's interests, they implicitly conceptualize a criterion of what is good or bad for the joint venture. This criterion may be operationalized in a number of ways, depending on the manager, the joint venture, the circumstances in which it is used, and so on. For instance, one manager may decide that anything that improves the competitive posture of the joint venture is in its best interest. Another manger may decide that when facing a choice, the alternative expected to yield the highest profit has to be selected (assuming the joint venture is considered as a profit center). Meanwhile, in one of the joint ventures assigned a common set of objectives by its parents, a manager may decide that anything consistent with these objectives is in the best interest of the joint venture.

When the joint venture has been assigned a set of agreed upon objectives or is considered as a profit center by its two parents, it is easy to decide what is in the best interests of the joint venture. However, it is important to recognize that the joint venture's interests are a reflection of the interests of the parents who define them; they are not independent. The separation between the joint venture's and a parent's interests occurs when the joint venture intends to carry out an activity that is consistent with its interests, as defined by its objectives, but that is contrary to a parent's interests. The typical example given by managers is when a MNC parent wants the joint venture to cut exports to foreign countries it can serve through a wholly owned plant that has a temporary overcapacity problem. In this case, what is in the best interest of the joint venture is no longer in the best interest of the parent—and conversely. Here, the joint venture's position is well understood—it was originally defined (or at least agreed upon) by the parent itself.

In cases where the joint venture does not have a specific set of objectives assigned, managers use the term *joint venture's interest* to refer to undefined, nonexplicit objectives that the joint venture would strive for, were it an independent company (for example, increase market share, maximize profits, or improve profitability). In this sense, the joint venture's interests are not necessarily a reflection of the parents' interests; they are simply a concept, an ideal, that managers feel is useful to settle a conflict between the two parents. They suggest that rather than seeing one partner win and the other lose over a specific issue, it might be better to see the joint venture win, even if in practice it is the same thing.

JVGMs' Time Orientation

The JVGMs' concern with preventing major clashes between and/or with the parents prompts them to be very prudent with the short-term impact of their decisions. As

Table 16–6
Time Orientation of the Parties Involved in Ten Mexican Joint Ventures as Reflected in Their Main Criteria of Success

JV	MNC Parent	Local Parent	JVGM
1	*Long-term:* Optimize long-term shareholder's value through consistent real growth in earnings	*Short-term:* Yearly growth rate Operating efficiency	*Short-term:* Sales and profit growth Profit margin on net sales
2	*Short-term:* Profitability Growth	*Long-term:* Growth Joint venture as a tool to diversify parent's portfolio in hotel business	*Short-term:* Growth Profitability Successful middleman
3	*Long-term:* Market share Growth Search for opportunities in Mexico and other Latin American nations	*Short-term:* Meet budgets *Long-term:* develop growth potential	*Short-term:* Meet budgets No "noise"
4	*Short-term:* Profits, growth, and quality of its brand	*Short-term:* Operating results *Long-term:* Profits Growth Future Prospects	*Short-term:* Avoid conflicts Achieve plan
5	*Short-term:* Return on net assets Dividends Business runs smoothly	*Short-term:* Profitability Contribution to Mexico Self-financing	*Short-term:* Be a successful diplomat *Long-term:* Growth
6	*Long-term:* Build long-term profit base Achieve strategic plan Identify future growth opportunities	*Short-term:* Contribution to parent through transfer prices	*Short-tesrm:* Monthly results Profits, ROI
7	*Short-term:* Achieve mission ROI Dividends	*Long-term:* Protection against erosion of money Fiscal benefits Mission (growth and exports)	*Short-term:* Maintain peace partners Achieve plan (one year)

Table 16–6 continued

JV	MNC Parent	Local Parent	JVGM
8	*Short-term:* Achieve mission ROI Dividends Operating results *Long-term:* Successful implementation of strategy	*Short-term:* Short-term growth in sales and profit	*Short-term:* Operating results *Long-term:* Maintain leadership in Mexico Maintain trust between partners
9	*Long-term:* Volume growth Market share Vehicle to look for opportunities into Mexico	*Short-term:* Profitability Supplies from joint venture Information on market *Long-term:* Future growth	*Short-term:* Meet budgets Profitability
10	*Short-term:*[a] Profits *Long-term:*[a] Reestablish parent's reputation in Mexico	*Short-term:* Dividends *Long-term:* Build asset base in hotels and land for development	*Short-term:* Growth Profitability Be a successful middleman

Source: Schaan, J.-L., "Parent Control and Joint Venture Success: The Case of Mexico." Unpublished doctoral dissertation. University of Western Ontario, 1983, p. 210.
[a]After 1978.

shown in table 16–6, JVGMs from the ten Mexican joint ventures were short-term–oriented, while there was no such clear pattern for managers from the parent companies.

Three major factors were found to reinforce the JVGMs' short-term orientation:

1. In all joint ventures, at least one parent had a short-term orientation.
2. All JVGMs had a bonus tied to their joint venture's yearly results.
3. JVGMs frequently report to the joint venture's board of directors and/or to the executive committee. For instance, 75 percent of the boards of the Mexican joint ventures studied met at least four times a year.

By holding JVGMs accountable through such close scrutiny, managers from parent companies inevitably trigger the JVGMs' short-term orientation. It does not mean that JVGMs are not concerned with the long-term health of the joint venture, but that when trade-offs have to be made, the short-term considerations carry the biggest weight in decision making.

Not all JVGMs are alike, though, and it was observed that JVGMs with limited-term contracts (two–three years) had, not surprisingly, a shorter time orientation than JVGMs with longer-term contracts.

The JVGM as Diplomat: Facilitating Commitment, Trust, and Communication

Commitment is one of the key variables associated with the success of joint ventures—something with which the JVGM must be concerned. There are four levels of commitment relevant to joint ventures: (1) commitment to international business, (2) commitment to joint venture success, (3) commitment to the particular joint venture, and (4) commitment to the particular venture partner. Table 16–7 provides a summary of the questionnaire responses, including those from the JVGMs.

In the high-performing joint ventures, commitment in all four areas was high. Two of the four questions in every category were characteristic at a .10 level of significance or better. This suggests that commitment is indeed associated with success.

In the aggregate, the JVGMs felt that there was commitment from the MNC. At least one question from each level was rated as characteristic at a .20 level of significance or lower. Also, JVGMs felt that the increase in number of nationals employed was an important factor in joint venture success. This relates directly to the importance of LDC contribution of knowledge of the local economy, politics, and customs as well as knowledge of local business practices. By having nationals employed as managers (and even as the JVGM), this knowledge is gained. This was also characteristic of the equity-holding general managers.

The JVGMs felt that the parents should have contingency plans available for assistance. This was true for the aggregate as well as the equity-holding and non-equity-holding managers. This shows that the JVGMs would like to have visible support from their parents in case the joint venture runs into difficulties.

In aggregate, the JVGMs felt that commitment to the particular joint venture (in terms of the joint venture interests being placed first) was important. This reduces the conflicts of two sets of objectives or directions from the parents. Unfortunately, this was not characteristic from the MNC parents' points of view. The JVGMs must work to convince the parents of the importance of the joint venture's interests being placed first.

Also, in this category, the willingness to visit and offer assistance by the parent was viewed as important by the JVGMs. This again shows the importance of parent assistance to the JVGM. Fortunately, this was also characteristic of the MNCs in high-performing ventures. This is a positive sign because those MNCs and JVGMs already have something vital in common—the willingness to visit and offer assistance.

For the nonequity JVGMs, the parents' willingness to commit resources was also very important. This is probably due to managerial confidence—if the joint venture needs something, it is comforting to know that the parents would give it to the joint venture if necessary.

Table 16-7

Commitment: Significance Levels of Questionnaire Responses

Abbreviated Statement from Questionnaire	Aggregate of 12 MNC Executives	MNC Executives in 7 High-Performing Ventures	MNC Executives in 5 Low-Performing Ventures	Aggregate of 6 General Managers	The 3 Equity-holding General Managers	The 3 Non-equity-holding General Managers
1. Foreign investment	.20	—	—	—	—	—
2. LDC foreign investment	—	—	—	—	—	—
3. Adapt products	.10	.05	—	—	—	—
4. Nationals employed	.01	.01	—	.01	.05	—
5. Willing to form JV	—	.10	—	—	—	—
6. Minority JV	(.20)	—	(.05)	—	—	—
7. Cost benefit of JV	.15	—	—	—	—	—
8. Forming contingency plans	.15	.05	—	.05	.10	.15
9. Making the venture work	—	—	—	.20	—	—
10. MNE willing to visit	.01	.01	.15	.11	.05	—
11. Commit resources	.15	—	—	—	—	.05
12. Developing skills	.10	.01	—	.01	.05	.05
13. Will change procedures	(.10)	—	—	—	—	—
14. Holding regular meetings	.05	.05	—	.20	.20	—
15. All discussions	.05	.10	—	—	—	—
16. Additional time	—	—	—	—	—	—

Source: Beamish, P.W. "Joint Venture Performance in Developing Countries." Unpublished doctoral dissertation. University of Western Ontario, 1984, p. 128.

Notes: Numeric values in parentheses that the statement is uncharacteristic of the respondents. Unbracketed values indicate the statement is characteristic.

Kolmogorov-Smirnov one-sample test used to derive significance levels.

Items 1, 2, 14, and 16 related to commitment to international business.

Items 3, 4, 5, and 6 relate to commitment to the joint venture structure.

Items 7, 8, 10, and 13, relate to commitment to the particular joint venture.

Items 9, 11, 12, and 15 relate to commitment to the particular partner.

The JVGMs also viewed commitment to the particular venture partner as important. The willingness of the parent to hold regular meetings was deemed characteristic of the MNCs in high-performing ventures. These meetings encompassed an information session for the MNCs as well as feedback from them. In successful ventures, there was this free flow of information. In Reynolds' (1979) study of joint ventures in India, he similarly noted:

> For the Indian, the choice of a partner is not so much the finding of an individual with whom he can feel compatible, since the individual partner-representative is likely to change every few years. It is more important to discover a company whose operating philosophy attracts individual managers who are likely to prove compatible.

The lack of parent commitment could also be seen in cases where there was no structure at headquarters to deal with the joint venture, or where there was structure, but a lack of allocated resources for the venture to operate efficiently. Successful control requires that a parent be committed to a joint venture and be prepared to allocate resources to exercise this control.

The JVGM must also facilitate trust and open communications in the joint venture and between the parents. In turn, trust and communication will increase the parents' commitment toward the joint venture. Managers in successful parent companies have been found to spend time and money to maintain and develop a trust relationship with the JVGM or with their partners in order to increase the accuracy of information obtained through informal channels and discussions with managers from the joint venture or the local partner. Formal reports are not sufficient information for determining what is really going on in the joint venture.

JVGMs are in a unique position to develop an understanding of the parents' idiosyncrasies with respect to verbal, nonverbal, and written communications. They often have to serve as an interpreter by explaining the meaning of what is communicated, clarifying misunderstandings, and teaching managers in the parents' organizations about their partners' codes and languages. The negative impact of poor communications on the partners' working relationship was also noted by Reynolds (1979) in his study of Indian–U.S. joint ventures.

Trust between the partners is a critical ingredient in the successful resolution of conflicts. This has been found to be particularly true for joint ventures in LDCs where the quality of interpersonal relationships is a better predictor of successful conflict resolution than legal and contractual considerations. As a result, JVGMs need to help the parents build a relationship where trust is an important component. Also, they must avoid situations that may jeopardize trust because, once lost, it is extremely hard to rebuild. This also applies to their own relationship with the parents.

The trust-communication-commitment characteristics are truly integrated. By developing and maintaining an open communication system with the joint venture and with the partner, the parent is able to (1) better understand the joint venture's problems and offer better solutions, (2) become aware of changes occurring in the joint venture business or in its partner's expectations, and (3) keep in touch with its partner, hence showing commitment to the joint venture and contributing to a trust relationship.

The JVGM is often the center of all the interaction between the two partners. By understanding the importance of open communication to a trusting relationship and how it achieves a higher level of commitment from the partners, the JVGM as diplomat can strive to open barriers that may be blocking this profitable cycle.

Implications

Implications for JVGMs

In order to cope with the political and interpersonal constraints of their job, JVGMs must show great sensitivity to the parent companies' differences in culture, management style, and expectations. Being under the scrutiny of two or more parents, they have to reconcile the achievement of their personal and career objectives with the parents' objectives and with the unique strategic and operating imperatives of running a company in an LDC.

Since a distinct advantage of a joint venture over a wholly owned subsidiary is its access to the skills and resources of two parents, JVGMs have an implicit opportunity to use this advantage to their benefit. However, a potential limitation is that the need for parent support is generally crucial in the early stages of a joint venture, at a time when the JVGM has not yet built networks with the parents.

Implications for Managers in Parent MNCs

Staffing. Managers in parent companies should be prepared to staff joint ventures in LDCs with local managers. This is all the more important when there is a tendency in an MNC parent to insist on providing management personnel to the joint venture. This is frequently the case in large MNCs which tend to duplicate their managerial systems and processes in their foreign subsidiaries or for companies having little or no experience in LDCs or with joint ventures. In those two sets of circumstances, they appoint expatriates in the belief that it reduces uncertainty, by facilitating communications between the joint venture and the parent and by appointing as joint venture managers individuals whose managerial style and practices are known. However, such practice does not recognize that the skills and knowledge required to successfully manage a joint venture in an LDC are very different from managing a wholly owned subsidiary in a developed country. For example, dealing with the local elites, businesspeople, politicians, and the local partner is a highly subtle exercise in diplomacy which may prove more important than the ability to run an operation effectively.

Developing a Working Relationship. In order to avoid surprises, to understand the operating context of the joint venture, to be able to ask the right questions, and to interpret the answers, managers in the parent companies need to manage their relationships with the JVGM on the one hand and with the partner(s) on the other hand. In joint ventures, as in marriages, a relationship is something built over time, not something that is there when one needs it.

A good example is provided by the experience of the vice president in a parent company involved in joint ventures around the world. The vice president made it a point to spend 50 percent of his time abroad with the local partners discussing business matters. For him, developing a personal relationship was a key for a healthy long-term business relationship.

Implications for Researchers

Most research on joint ventures has emphasized issues from the parents' perspectives and very little attention has been paid to the JVGM. This chapter presents some of the dimensions that define the JVGM's strategic and operating decision-making context. However, this area needs to be conceptually strengthened, particularly a comparison of the role of the JVGM with that of the general managers in wholly owned subsidiaries. Useful designs to research such topics could control for parent company effect by comparing a number of subsidiaries of one multinational firm, or they could focus on cross-national comparisons.

Conclusion

Ambiguity is inherent to the practice of management. An important element in the successful performance of general management activities is the ability to find one's way in a complex web of people, structures, and roles. This is also true for general managers of joint ventures operating in LDCs. Here, the complexity is heightened by the double parenting, the geographic as well as the cultural "distance," and the general infrastructure in which the joint venture operates. In that sense, a major challenge facing JVGMs in LDCs is that in addition to being good general managers, they also have to be good diplomats, able to operate constantly within two or more frames of reference and sets of values, and able to successfully manage the idiosyncrasies of their parents.

Bibliography

Beamish, P.W. 1984. *Joint venture performance in developing countries.* Unpublished doctoral dissertation. University of Western Ontario, London, Ontario, Canada.

Franko, L. 1976. *The european multinationals.* New York: Harper & Row.

Janger, A.R. 1980. *Organization of international joint ventures.* New York: Conference Board.

Killing, P. 1983. *Strategies for joint venture success.* New York: Praeger.

Lecraw, D. 1983. "Performance of transnational corporations in less-developed countries." *Journal of international business studies,* Spring/Summer.

Mintzberg, H. 1980. *The nature of managerial work.* Englewood Cliffs, N.J.: Prentice-Hall.

Reynolds, J.L. 1979. *Indian–American joint ventures: Business policy relationships.* Washington, D.C.: University Press of America.

Schaan, J.-L. 1983. *Parent control and joint venture success: The case of Mexico.* Unpublished doctoral dissertation. University of Western Ontario, London, Ontario, Canada.

Vaupel, J.W., and Curhan, J.P. 1973. *The world's multinational enterprises.* Cambridge, Mass.: Harvard University Press.

17

Learning among Joint Venture-Sophisticated Firms

Marjorie A. Lyles

More firms are utilizing joint ventures for the first time to increase their strategic capabilities and global competitiveness. Yet, the use of cooperative alliances among firms, in particular, joint ventures, is a controversial topic to both academics and practitioners (Pfeffer and Salancik, 1978; Pennings, 1981). Strategic and international management theorists have studied individual joint ventures to determine the reasons for formation, the factors for success, and the cultural implications (Franko, 1971; Killing, 1982; Stopford and Wells, 1972). Economic analysis has attempted to provide economic rationales for joint ventures and their impact on research and development (Berg, Duncan, and Friedman, 1982; Harrigan, 1985; Hladik, 1985; Pfeffer and Nowak, 1976). Prior studies have not led to a greater understanding of the joint venturing process from a corporate viewpoint nor how learning accumulates from past experience. Thus, for strategic management, two critical questions remaining are to what extent firms have learned from this process and whether joint venturing contributes to a firm's strategic capabilities.

This chapter documents the learning that has occurred in firms that have been successful at operating multiple joint ventures in an international context. It seeks to determine how these firms developed new programs and structures, innovated, and created new frames of reference in order to adapt and to learn. It builds upon the work of Chandler (1962), Cyert and March (1963), and Miles (1982), who have addressed the learning process in complex organizations as they coped with environmental stress. It attempts to fill the gaps in the research on joint ventures by exploring how joint venturing experiences have increased the competitive edge of the parenting firms. For our purposes, a joint venture (JV) is considered to be an independent entity formed by two or more parent firms.

The term *learning* refers to the development of insights, knowledge, and associations between past actions, the effectiveness of those actions, and future actions (Fiol and Lyles, 1985). Learning is the process in which growing insights and

Funds for this research were supplied by the Research Board and the Department of Business Administration at the University of Illinois, Urbana, and the Hewlett Fund.

successful restructuring of organizational problems reflect themselves in structural elements and outcomes (Chandler, 1962; Chakravarthy, 1982; Hedberg, 1981; Miller and Friesen, 1980). Hence, learning is both action outcomes and changes in the state of knowledge. When seen in a learning context, a host of issues about joint venturing activities may be better understood by both the researcher and the practitioner.

Longitudinal studies in the strategic management field are rare. Rarer yet are research studies that aim to understand the learning that takes place as firms attempt to survive and change under dynamic environmental conditions. While organizational learning has recently been identified as important in strategic management, it has received remarkably little attention by researchers. For these reasons, this chapter is exploratory in nature and will attempt to allow the important issues to emerge from the data (Glaser and Strauss, 1967).

The chapter addresses the issue of *whether* learning occurred in joint venture-experienced firms, *how* it occurred, and *what* was learned. It represents a subset of an ongoing research project on JV-sophisticated firms. Four firms (two U.S. and two European) were chosen to participate in the analysis based on their extensive JV experience. Table 17–1 gives a summary description of the firms. Table 17–2 gives their corporate characteristics. The chapter begins by identifying the conceptual framework used to assess the learning patterns. It then presents the results of interviews conducted with each firm on the firm's joint venturing experiences and what has been learned. Finally, implications are suggested.

The Learning Framework: Levels of Learning

Organizational adjustment is an essential element of a firm's ability to survive and to sustain competitiveness over time. Fiol and Lyles (1985) suggest that it is necessary

Table 17–1
Description of Firms

Company	Gross Sales	Major Lines of Business
C1	$7.2 billion	Chemical products, coatings, pharmaceuticals, consumer products, miscellaneous products
C2	$6.3 billion	Air conditioning, chemicals, plastics, industrial products, financial services, protective services, transportation equipment
C3	$3.5 billion	Industrial chemicals, petroleum equipment, defense equipment, performance chemicals, specialized machinery
C4	$2.0 billion	Brewing, soft drinks, wine

Table 17–2
Corporate Characteristics

Characteristics	C1	C2	C3	C4
Corporate structure	Worldwide products overseen by regional general managers	Worldwide products	Worldwide products interface with international department	Regional general managers
Culture	Entrepreneurial	Protective	Introspective	Introspective
Management approach	Decentralized	Centralized	Decentralized	Centralized
JV motivations	Diverse	Sell technology, get royalties	Sell technology, get market	Sell technology, get market
Current pace of JV formation	Steady	Slowed	Slowed	Steady
Definition of JV success	Profitability and operating ease	Profitability	Profitability and operating ease	Stability and performance
JV industries	Mature	Mature	Mature	Mature
Areas of JV	Main business area	Main business area	Main business area	Main business area

to separate mere adjustment decisions from deeper changes, such as in the belief structures, values, and norms. They argue that learning occurs at two levels—higher and lower. Lower–level learning may be apparent from observing the actions that are taken and the structural changes that are made. On the other hand, higher-level learning represents changing associations, frames of reference, and programs that beg a methodology that analyzes the more in-depth functioning of an organization. In order to study learning in JV-sophisticated firms, it is necessary to look not only at the way the JVs were implemented, but also to examine the attitudes and values of the management.

Figure 17–1 represents the framework for determining if learning occurred and what learning occurred as a result of these joint venturing activities. The figure shows the interrelatedness of lower-level and higher-level learning and the roles that unlearning and experimentation play in creating new learning. Each of these will be discussed next.

Lower-Level Learning. Lower-level learning is a result of repetition and routine and involves association building. Cyert and March (1963) identify standard operating procedures or success programs, goals, and decision rules as illustrative of learning based on routine. It occurs in contexts that are well understood and where management thinks it can control the situation (Duncan, 1974). Two types of lower-level learning will be discussed: success programs and management systems.

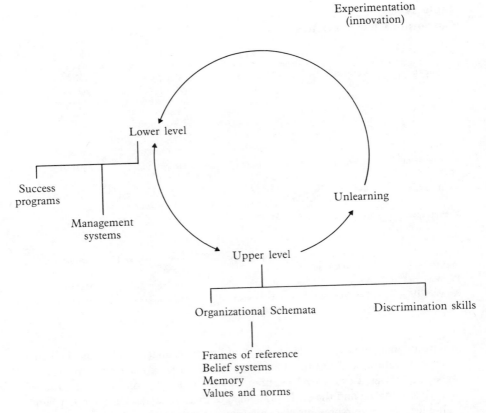

Figure 17-1. Learning Framework

Success Programs. Organizations that exist for any length of time develop standard methods for handling repetitive decisions which become standard operating procedures. These are successful methodologies which have worked in the past, and organizations resist changing them. They can be quickly utilized so there is no need to reassess the decision situation each time it arises (Cyert and March, 1963).

Management Systems. Galbraith (1973) suggests that firms will also develop management systems to handle their information-processing needs in repetitive, unchanging situations. The management systems include the policies, hierarchies, rewards, and administrative systems that reflect how the organization has learned to handle recurring situations. It is generally traumatic for the organization to restructure or to implement new management systems (Cyert and March, 1963).

Higher-Level Learning. The adjustment of overall missions, beliefs, and norms is higher-level learning. It has long-term effects and impacts the whole organization, not just the joint venture or a division. Over time, every organization faces the needs for renewal and for reanalysis of its mission and basic capabilities. Evidence suggests that higher-level learning often results in new frames of reference, new skills for problem formulation or agenda setting, new values, or unlearning of past success programs (Lyles and Mitroff, 1980; Miller and Friesen, 1980; Starbuck, 1983). Three types of higher-level learning will be discussed next: discrimination skills, unlearning, and innovation.

Discrimination Skills. An organization that can utilize different success programs and management systems for different situations has learned to discriminate. In other words, higher-level learning includes the ability to discriminate among different decision situations and to choose appropriate behaviors or actions for each situation.

Unlearning. Firms that can unlearn and reframe their past success programs to fit with changing environmental and situational conditions will have a greater likelihood of survival and adaptation (Hedberg, 1981; Starbuck, 1983). Unlearning is particularly important at the strategic level where each decision situation may be unique and where past success may not be an indication of future success. Miles (1982) argues that negative performance feedback precipitates the search for new methods for handling decisions and problems. Hence, unlearning is triggered by mistakes, failures, or poor performance.

Innovation or Experimentation. The ability to develop fresh approaches to situations or problems indicates a new dimension to higher-order learning. Experimentation may generate conceptual leaps in the development of associations and may result in the changing of the old success programs or norms. It represents a disassociation with the reinforcement of past behaviors and a reaction to the momentum that builds up (Starbuck, 1983). Innovation or experimentation may be closely tied to unlearning and is necessary for organizational renewal and the development of new capabilities.

This chapter describes the learning that is reported by the upper management of four JV sophisticated firms. It determines whether lower- and higher-level learning is reported and what patterns emerged. Next, the methodology will be discussed.

Methodology

Four firms were selected based on their long histories with joint venturing and their current involvement in multiple JVs. Each has at least thirty years of JV experience, at least twenty ongoing JVs, and experiences with a variety of JV configurations in numerous locations.

306 • *Cooperative Strategies in International Business*

A triangulation of data-collection methods was used to query each firm about its JV experiences, about specific JVs, and about the learning that occurred. In-depth interviews were conducted with corporate management, staff and line management, and the JV management. At least eight people were interviewed at each firm, with the maximum number being about forty. The interviews were conducted in the United States and in Europe and lasted an average of two hours. The companies and the individual managers were very cooperative and allowed the researcher to return for multiple interviews. In this manner, the researcher had the opportunity to raise additional questions, to clarify certain events, or to probe deeper regarding an event. To verify the verbal reports, two other kinds of data were necessary: publicly available information (such as annual reports and newspaper clippings) and company archival data (such as minutes from board meetings and memos).

The interviews were semistructured. All participants were asked to reconstruct their personal involvement in JVs, the historical evolutions of the firm's JV strategies, and the factors affecting future JV decisions. Questions regarding past joint ventures were straightforward; they included the reporting or management structures, the amount of involvement of the parent firm in the JV, and the successes and failures.

Data from the interviews were coded and were verified by the archival data, the person interviewed, or other informants. Alternative viewpoints about events were identified and served as probes for later interviews or they were verified by the other data.

This methodology is appropriate because information about a firm's learning is not available outside that firm, it requries an in-depth analysis, and learning is a lagged phenomenon. Although the sample size of four firms is small, an in-depth analysis of each firm was possible. The interviews built statements based on reconstructed logic, but the events could be verified by checking them in the formal reports or external documents. Statements of learning were perceptual and subject to individual biases and judgments; however, the use of multiple informants helped to minimize this bias.

Results

Each firm was analyzed to determine its JV approach based on the interviews, the detailed information about specific JVs, and the archival data. (See figure 17–2.) The firms varied between allowing the JV decentralized control versus centralized control from the parent. Three of the four firms licensed their technology to the JVs, but one firm licensed its technology but also received technologies from its partners. Three firms were willing to take minority positions, and all of the firms wanted their partners to have an active part in the management of the JVs. Each also said that they would prefer wholly owned subsidiaries to JVs. However, JVs

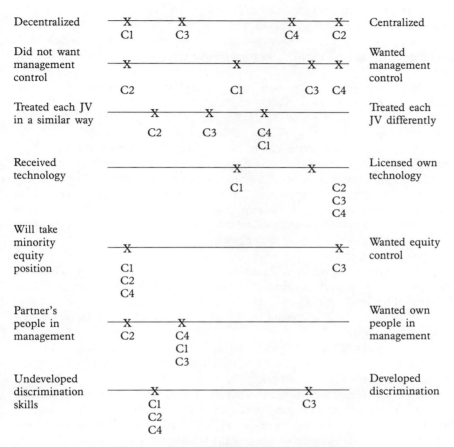

Figure 17–2. Profile of JV Approaches

were a necessary component of their global competitiveness. Next, the analysis of the learning framework is presented.

Success Programs/Management Systems

The two types of lower-level learning represent ways of doing things that were successful in the past. The research looked for decision rules or ways of handling JVs that are repeated and worked well and for structures, reporting systems, management methods, and so on, that were repeated across the JVs.

Two firms said there was a usual way of handling JVs and two firms said there was not. The two "yes" firms had different approaches to their success programs. Firm C1's approach was decentralized, allowing each JV to make important decisions about its operations, with guidance provided by the parent corporation. C1 provides the technology, but no management contracts. It maintains control of the JV through informal means such as socialization of the management and low turnover among the management. "Get good people and give them freedom" was the rule.

On the other hand, C2's usual way is to have 50 percent equity, not to participate in the management, and to maintain control over the technology. The management of C2 claim that this is changing. One person said, "There was a usual way, but it is changing. We were not ready to place our people in a JV. We wanted our 50 percent equity position. Now we are willing to place our technology into minority positions wherever new opportunities are coming."

Both firms that have a usual way to do things also said that in the future, there were not going to be any rules. The two other firms said they have no hard and fast rules in their approaches, except that they do require the use of their financial reporting systems. All four firms indicate that what they had learned over time is that flexibility is the best approach.

Discrimination Skills. One higher-level learning technique is the ability to discriminate between when a certain behavior or action is appropriate and when it is not. This is situational analysis. The researcher looked for certain decision rules for defining the attributes of the JVs that meant they would be treated one way versus another.

Three firms said they are flexible on the question of discrimination skills. One respondent said, "I would say that it's a case of being realistic. I think we are realistic in adjusting to the local situations."

Although the respondents indicate that the firms are becoming better at changing their management techniques based on the situation, the researcher found little evidence of this in three of the firms. The JV data and the interviews did not indicate any decision rules for segmenting the JVs into situations where one method would be used versus another. In C2, however, where there was a usual way for handling JVs, discrimination skills were required to determine when this usual way was appropriate.

Unlearning. Part of learning is unlearning and reframing past behaviors or success programs that are no longer appropriate. To determine if unlearning occurs, one must look for environmental jolts, mistakes, failures, critical incidents, and changes in the success programs or management systems. Table 17-3 summarizes the events mentioned by the respondents. Two categories, future conflicts and partner rapport, were identified within three firms as influencing their learning. Both of these concern maintaining a good partner relationship.

Future Conflicts. Partners should acknowledge at JV formation that there may be mixed motives and hidden agendas within both firms. One firm formed a JV

Table 17–3
Unlearning/Mistakes

Types	Firms			
	C1	*C2*	*C3*	*C4*
Building in Future Conflicts	X		X	X
Partner Rapport Issues	X	X		X
Technology Transfer Issues		X	X	
Cultural Issues				
Human Resource			X	
Futurist Issues	X	X		
Equity Issues				X
Partner Choice				X

to have its products manufactured and marketed in a particular country. As time passed, the parent company acquired the skills necessary to market the product itself—and it thought that its skills were better than the JV's. This created a conflict.

What the firms learned is to accept that the JV's reasons for being may change over time and to recognize that they want to acquire their partner's skills over a period of time. One person said, "The only general learning is that you have to be very, very careful that you think of all the potential conflicts of interest. It's more likely in your core business, core countries, than on the fringe." It appears that when the firms had comparatively less JV experience, they believed that a JV was forever and that there would be minimal conflicts.

Partner Rapport. Issues relating to maintaining partner rapport were frequently mentioned. These were verbalized as "lessons" such as "You should treat your partners with 49 percent as if they were yourself," "Have the firm's president meet with top partners when he is travelling," and "The ventures have got to satisfy the real desires of both parties to be successful." These were seen as important as the firms learned to deal with the ambiguity of the JVs' futures.

Partner Choice. This is important because of the potential for conflict. The firms would not choose a partner with the same international aspirations as theirs because they would then meet them head-on somewhere. Also, they have learned not to form a JV with people who want the JV as a way to save their own company, as a life buoy.

Technology Transfer. The two U.S. firms view technology transfer as an area in which they made mistakes. They said that it takes experience to recognize that once you license your mature or stable technology, you sell your business and create a new competitor.

Cultural Issues. Cultural differences have been discussed in the literature as a problem in JVs because of country differences and firm differences (Wright, 1979). None of the firms mentioned this as a reason for a mistake or failure, although it was mentioned as important for getting along with your partner.

Innovativeness. Innovativeness indicates an ability to move away from the learned responses of the success programs and to experiment with new approaches. Table 17–4 summarizes the responses.

It was expected that as firms gained JV experience, they would become more risk-taking as they grew comfortable with joint venturing. Three firms indicated that they were more risk-taking now than before. One respondent from the fourth firm said: "You take the decision that has the most pros and cons and the best risk profile. So in this respect, we look at JVs like any other alternative." This last firm is also the firm that had the most flexibile approach to JVs.

From analysis of the interviews, it became clear that two different kinds of risk were being discussed. The first, financial risk, indicates whether the firms would be willing to forgo financial returns. Managerial risk, the second, represents giving up control over the JV decision making or the technology. Taking a smaller equity position, licensing the technology, or participating in management were indications of this kind of risk.

This analysis shows that three firms would *not* forgo financial returns or sacrifice profitability. If they foresaw that the JV might be a financial risk, they would not be involved. One person said, "Early on, we didn't go into JVs because of profitability. I think today, we will not go into them unless they are going to be profitable. Early on, we went for market share."

On the other hand, two firms indicated that they would take managerial risks. One person said, "We are willing to take risks by starting with a small equity position and expecting to increase our share over time." Another person from the same firm said, "As a large company, you must be willing sometimes to take a minority

Table 17–4
Innovations: Taking Risks

	Firm C1	Firm C2	Firm C3	Firm C4
More risk taking				
Yes		X	X	X
No	X			
Taking financial risks				
Yes		X		
No	X		X	X
Taking managerial risks				
Yes	X		X	X
No		X		

interest with a smaller partner." With the right partner, it is possible to take risks on the amount of the equity position.

The JV-experienced firms reconfirm the importance of profitability since there is no reason to sacrifice profitability because you are in a JV. However, it is possible to take risks when you are referring to the management systems. Three firms are trying new ways of doing things. The new ways include developing lateral communication links, being more open to different kinds of partner firms, licensing a technology that had been closely protected, and forgoing some control in order to get the "name" utilized.

Transference of Learning. The respondents unanimously agreed that there was a transference of learning from multiple JV experiences, although some of it was indirect and informal. For example, the single-sector firm, C4, reported: "We were finding out, from experiences elsewhere in the world, that our partners are less interested in our business than we are. They had many other operations in other business areas. We slowly started to understand that we had to contribute much more to the management."

The transference takes place through the people and is influenced by the organizational structure. One respondent said: "The type of people you need in managerial/operational positions in a JV is different from the type of people you need in a wholly owned subsidiary because they need more diplomatic qualities." These same people develop networks that serve to disseminate their experiences.

The firms use their joint venture experiences as a credential which makes it easier for them to form new joint ventures. They are viewed as better partners and they have experienced people. One person said, "We now have a cadre of people well qualified to enter JV negotiations and well qualified to handle problems in JVs, and that is the result of experiences that began in the 1950s."

Table 17–5 summarizes the methods used for the transference of learning. It lists the topics that emerged from the interviews. The respondents recognize that top management, in its role of overseeing all the joint ventures, plays an active role in sharing the lessons learned. Communication and socialization of managers become important methods for the transference of these lessons and norms.

Learning Patterns

The learning within the four firms was demonstrated in several ways. These firms have a high frequency of joint ventures and place importance on them as a means for implementing their overall strategic direction. Joint ventures are recognized by each of the firms as a necessary condition for maintaining global competitiveness. Hence, these firms say that JVs help them to reach their goals. The evidence of continued JV usage and of meeting strategic goals provides insight into the experience gained and into the learning that occurred.

Table 17–5
Transference of Learning

	Firm C1	Firm C2	Firm C3	Firm C4
Methods of Transference				
Top management overseeing process	X	X	X	X
International operations			X	
Training and socialization			X	X
Direct management JV experience		X	X	X
Management networks	X	X		
Topics				
Geographic/cultural knowledge			X	X
Development of partner relations	X	X	X	X
Management systems		X		X
Interrelatedness of JVs		X	X	X
JV negotiation/management skills				X
Time orientation (long/short)	X			X

The organizational histories and statements by the management reveal how the firms learned. They are transmitted by the people, by the sharing of experiences, by the development of organizational stories, and by the development of management systems. The backgrounds of the individual managers reveal the extensive direct experience in the forming, managing, negotiating, and problem solving with the JV partners and management. The upper-level management of these firms provide the medium for the transference of the learning.

What the firms learned from their JV experiences is somehow both unique and general. It is unique in the sense that each firm has its own unique characteristics and histories, and it is general in the sense that there exists some pattern to the learning that is generalizable across the firms. Six learning patterns were gleaned from the interviews:

Routine success programs and management systems can be used successfully for joint venturing if the firm enacts its environment. Firms in joint ventures operate in the most complex of environments. They are dealing not only with environmental complexity in their home markets, but also with cultural complexity and the environmental stress of multiple markets. Strategic management researchers appear to argue that in environments of high uncertainty and complexity, firms should attempt to operate with flexibility and in a decentralized mode (Lawrence and Dyer, 1983; Meyer, 1982). In this analysis, we find that three of the firms are doing just that, namely, operating in a very flexible, decentralized manner.

Yet, the fourth firm presents an alternative to this approach. It has maintained the use of its usual way of handling JVs by enacting the environment. It has chosen to set up JVs only in environments that meet certain criteria and then to use its success programs. It is operating under the same environmental conditions as the other firms, but sets constraints on the elements that it considers as most important, namely, the partner firms, technology, and extent of management involvement.

Initial decisions about licensing, equity position, and management relations, although appropriate at the time they were made, frequently constrained choices and created conflicts later. Since the firms were among the first to use JVs, they began cautiously without prior knowledge or experience or the ability to learn from their peers' experiences. Consequently, each developed comfortable ways or success programs for handling the JV management. These reflect the cultures and norms of the parent firms which were accepting of new cultures and management approaches.

Nonetheless, the initial reasons for the JVs and the original management systems became obsolete over time (Harrigan, 1985). Lyles (1986) documents how the desire for involvement and the desire for control change over time. The initial contracts, legal statements, or agreements focused attention on the wrong set of issues. This came as a surprise to the parent firms' management. It also created conflicts in their relationships with their partner firms. The firms in this sample learned to accept such changes as part of the nature of joint venturing and to recognize the need for continuing conversations with their partner firms.

The importance of partner rapport increased over time. Many of the JVs that these four firms maintained were over ten years old. In fact, some were over twenty years old. Then firms experienced industry changes, market maturation, and their own growth and development. Initially, it did not seem that partner firms were closely investigated—they were chosen because they were known by the parent firms. Now, however, partner firms are chosen for good business reasons. With time, the firms in the study have learned how to assess markets, partners, and potential contributions of partner firms.

There is the knowledge that JV management is difficult and time-consuming and, as a JV matures, that it is harder to control (Prahalad and Doz, 1981). Therefore, it is very important to have a good partner and to maintain a good relationship with that partner. Social relations with a partner remain important because they help to build trust into the relationship.

Management attitudes have changed over time from viewing JVs as a choice to viewing them as a necessary evil. A widely held belief among researchers and practitioners is that if one wants to do business on a global scale, it is necessary to utilize JVs (Hout, Porter, and Rudden, 1982). The firms in this sample have learned that it is not easy to maintain a relationship over time and that a JV takes more time than a wholly owned subsidiary. Joint venturing is still uncomfortable; it is particularly difficult for the U.S. firms to loosen their grip on management controls (Lyles and Reger, 1987).

The complexity, uncertainty, and ambiguity of JVs is still uncomfortable for the firms, but more accurate knowledge of the future probability of certain events has come with experience. With the growth of their experience base, the firms have begun to identify certain events that may occur during a JV's life. For example, these firms have learned that partners may acquire their partners' skills, that partner firms may be merger targets and may change hands, and that technology can be a valuable asset in joint venturing. With this increased knowledge, these JV-experienced firms are better able to anticipate major issues and how to handle them.

The development of higher-level learning spreads to all levels of the organization. The organizational learning was incorporated into the respondents' statements and was evident in the belief systems, the norms, and the values espoused. Joint venturing was an accepted norm of doing business. All four firms sought to increase their global competitiveness by introducing and marketing their products, technologies, and name recognitions abroad. Joint venturing was one acceptable method for doing this.

Good partner rapport was an accepted value. It is extremely important because each firm has to have the reputation of being a good partner. The world is getting smaller, and the partner firms within an industry generally know each other. A firm has to have the reputation of being competent but also compassionate and trusted. Fairness in negotiations and recognition of their partners' own competence became essential norms for the managers dealing with JVs. These were learned attributes of the JV-experienced firms.

Strategic Implications

This chapter has addressed the learning that has occurred in JV-sophisticated firms. I have pointed out some of the learning patterns that emerged and the nature of the higher-level learning patterns. The firms have built upon their experiences and maintained flexibility in their approaches to JVs. This has resulted in multiple experiences, successes, experimentations, and failures that have led to the richness of their own corporate histories and schemata. It creates a depth to the organization that transcends highly decentralized organization structures. It reaffirms that the experiences, beliefs, and norms are transmitted through the people and management of the firms (Martin, 1982).

The JV experience of these firms may be viewed as a "window of opportunity" for increasing their global competitiveness. It creates a competitive advantage for them by establishing their presence worldwide, by giving them information about operating in various countries and about environmental events, and by helping them develop a skill base that has prior knowledge of the likelihood of certain events. This increases their strategic capabilities and provides them a competitive advantage (Jemison, 1986; Lenz, 1980). It provides them power and influence.

The firms recognize that the quality of their partner relationships may be just as important as the JV mission since they may affect the firm's corporate global strategy (Thorelli, 1986). This provides them a sense of caution and patience. It provides them a motivation to develop their reputations as trustworthy bedfellows, which allows them to influence others. It provides them a strategic advantage over firms with less experience.

The strength of this analysis lies in the in-depth nature of the investigation of each firm. However, it is only the first step in analyzing the importance of learning as a strategic capability. Future investigations need to address whether the learning patterns are useful to other firms and whether the learning process can be further analyzed.

Bibliography

Berg, S.V., Duncan, J., and Friedman, P. 1982. *Joint venture strategies and corporation innovations.* Cambridge, Mass.: Oelgeschlager, Gunn & Hain.

Chandler, A. 1962. *Strategy and structure.* Cambridge, Mass.: MIT Press.

Chakravarthy, B.S. 1982. "Adaptation: A promising metaphor for strategic management." *Academy of Management Review,* 7: 735–44.

Cyert, R.M., and March, J.G. 1963. *A behavioral theory of the firm.* Englewood Cliffs, N.J.: Prentice-Hall.

Dunbar, R.L. 1981. "Designs for organizational control." In P.C. Nystrom and W.H. Starbuck (eds.), *Handbook of organizational design,* vol. 2. Oxford, England: Oxford University Press.

Duncan, R.B. 1974. "Modifications in decision structure in adapting to the environment: Some implications for organizational learning." *Decision Sciences,* 705–25.

Fiol, C.M., and Lyles, M.A. 1985. "Organizational learning." *Academy of Management Review,* 10 (4): 803–13.

Franko, L.G. 1971. *Joint venture survival in multinational corporations.* New York: Praeger.

Galbraith, J.R. 1973. *Designing complex organizations.* Reading, Mass.: Addison-Wesley.

Glaser, B., and Strauss, A. 1967. *Discovery of grounded theory: Strategies for qualitative research..* Chicago: Aldine.

Harrigan, K.R. 1985. *Strategies for joint ventures.* Lexington, Mass.: Lexington Books.

Hedberg, B. 1981. "How organizations learn and unlearn?" In P.C. Nystrom and W.H. Starbuck (eds.), *Handbook of organizational design:* 8–27. London: Oxford University Press.

Hladik, K.J. 1985. *International joint ventures: An economic analysis of U.S.-foreign business partnerships.* Lexington, Mass.: Lexington Books.

Hout, T., Porter, M.E., and Rudden, E. 1982. How global companies win out. *Harvard Business Review,* 60: 98–108.

Jemison, D.B. 1986. *Strategic capability transfer in acquisition integration.* Working Paper. Stanford University, Stanford, Calif.

Killing, J.P. 1982. "How to make a global joint venture work." *Harvard Business Review,* 60 (3): 120–27.

Lawrence, P.R., and Dyer, D. 1983. *Renewing American industry.* New York: Free Press.

Lenz, R.T. 1980. "Strategic capability: A concept and framework for analysis." *Academy of Management Review*, 5 (2): 225–34.

Lyles, M.A. 1986. *Parental desire for control of joint ventures: A case study of an international joint venture.* BEBR Working Paper 1273. College of Commerce, University of Illinois, Urbana.

Lyles, M.A., and Mitroff, I.I. 1980. "Organizational problem formulation: An empirical study." *Administrative Science Quarterly*, 25: 102–19.

Lyles, M.A., and Reger, R.K. 1987. *Upward influence in joint ventures.* Working Paper. University of Illinois-Champaign.

Martin, J. 1982. "Stories and scripts in organizational settings." In A. Hastorf and A. Isen (eds.), *Cognitive social psychology:* 225–305. New York: Elsevier-North Holland.

Meyer, A. 1982. "Adapting to environmental jolts." *Administrative Science Quarterly*, 27: 515–37.

Miles, R.H. 1982. *Coffin nails and corporate strategies.* Englewood Cliffs, N.J.: Prentice-Hall.

Miller, D., and Friesen, P.H. 1980. "Momentum and revolution in organizational adaptation." *Academy of Management Journal*, 23 (4): 591–614.

Pennings, J.M. 1981. "Strategically interdependent organizations." In P.C. Nystrom and W.H. Starbuck (eds.), *Handbook of organizational design*, vol. 1: 433–55.

Pfeffer, J., and Nowak, P. 1976. "Joint ventures and interorganizational interdependence." *Administrative Science Quarterly*, 21: 398–418.

Pfeffer, J., and Salancik, G.R. 1978. *External control of organizations: Resource dependence perspective.* New York: Harper & Row.

Prahalad, C.K., and Doz, Y.L. 1981. "An approach to strategic control in MNCs." *Sloan Management Review* (Summer): 5–13.

Starbuck, W.H. 1983. "Organizations as action generators." *American Sociological Review*, 48: 91–102.

Stopford, J.M., and Wells, L.T. 1972. *Managing the multinational enterprise.* New York: Basic Books.

Thorelli, H.B. 1986. "Networks: Between markets and hierarchies." *Strategic Management Journal*, 7: 37–51.

Wright, R.W. 1979. "Joint venture problems in Japan." *Columbia Journal of World Business*, 14 (1): 25–31.

18

Technology Partnerships between Larger and Smaller Firms: Some Critical Issues

Yves L. Doz

Partnerships between larger and smaller firms have multiplied over the past few years. To large firms, partnerships usually offer a channel to tap into the innovative and entrepreneurial potential of smaller companies, and to overcome some of their own rigidities. In most of the observed partnerships, smaller firms perform research and development for the larger firms and/or transfer innovations to them. These larger firms offer their smaller partners the ability to reach world markets quickly, without having to build their own infrastructure or to negotiate complex agreements with multiple agents. Larger firms also often offer the experience of volume manufacturing. The complementarity is obvious.

Partnerships are also more frequent because of the growing awareness of the drawbacks of the alternatives. Acquisitions of smaller firms have seldom been a success, as the anticipated synergies most often did not materialize. In the microelectronics industry, nearly all acquisitions of smaller entrepreneurial firms by larger, well-established ones have failed (for example, Honeywell–Synertek, GE–Intersil, Schlumberger–Fairchild, Thorn–EMI–Inmos, and Thomson–Mostek). Large firms have become increasingly reluctant to acquire smaller firms, particularly as these usually command a high price. Large pharmaceutical firms have faced similar difficulties with innovative, entrepreneurial firms, mostly in biotechnology. Investments through venture capital funds usually result in conflict of interests between the large investors interested in acquiring the venture's technologies, and the other investors and the entrepreneurs interested in capital gains, two often contradictory objectives (Hardyman, de Nino, and Salter, 1983). Venture fund managers usually shield the ventures, and the larger firms get little technological advantage from their investment (Roberts, 1980).

Managers in large firms have thus put much hope into an intermediate formula which usually involved a direct equity participation by the larger firm in the smaller one (often a minority position but bolstered by various clauses such as preferred stock with higher voting rights, super majority clauses, and other setups allowing the larger firm an influence more than commensurate with its equity participation).

The equity investment itself is usually complemented by various agreements, such as research contracts from the larger firm to the smaller one, exclusive licensing agreements to the larger firm, and loan and other financial arrangements provided by the larger firm to the smaller one. This chapter deals with such partnerships (not with full acquisitions or with the setting of joint ventures as a third independent entity, between partners.

Yet, even a cursory observation of such partnerships suggests that many are a disappointment to partners. They do not actually yield the results expected by either or both partners, and even when a measure of success is achieved the tensions in making partnerships work sometimes dwarf their success in the eyes of the participants.

Critical Issues in Partnerships

Exploratory research on a few selected partnerships suggests that the issues are multiple and complex, while the pitfalls are many. In the partnerships I have analyzed in detail, three sets of issues are critical to success:

Convergence of purpose. While the complementarity of strengths and assets brought to the partnerships is generally obvious at the start of and even prior to negotiations—since this is what usually brings the partners together in the first place—the convergence of purpose is still difficult to achieve. First, a partnership is almost always partly competitive, with the larger firm often attempting to capture the technology of the smaller one, to transfer it to its own operations, and, ultimately, to appropriate it. Some managers in larger firms may also view minority equity investments as a transitional step toward majority or full ownership, a threat to their smaller partner.

Conversely, the smaller firm almost always tries to retain control over its technology or over its replenishment, no matter what the intent of the larger firm is. Technology is, after all, the only bargaining strength of the smaller firm. Within the partnership, this genuine competition over what is contributed over time by each partner translates itself into hidden agendas. It may result in strategic conflict and strategic misrepresentation. Convergence of purpose may also be hampered by an incomplete or insufficient strategic overlap; current technological complementarity may hide future strategic divergence, particularly in a situation where inherent technological and market uncertainties often make joint assessments difficult, but leave room for very different interpretations of the same facts. Finally, cultural distance—not only in its most obvious national and geographic forms, but also between organizations whose ways of operating differ deeply—compounds the problem of convergence of purpose.

Consistency of Position within the Large Firm. Large firms are often characterized by the interplay of parochial subunit goals as well as by the interplay of corporate and personal interests in top management decision and implementation processes. Partnerships are seldom neutral vis-à-vis that interplay: while some stand to gain from the partnership within the big firm, others may stand to lose. Positions toward a partnership may thus be taken on the basis of individual perceptions of gains and losses that are only reconciled through coalitions. The composition and power of such coalitions may vary over time, and the partnership may fall prey to the internal politics of the larger partner.

Interface. In larger firms, in particular, partnerships are usually decided upon by top management, but implemented by middle managers and by technical specialists. While the intrinsic ambiguity of partly collaborative, partly competitive relations can be easily understood and tolerated by top management, operating managers who bear the brunt of the actual interface may find this ambiguity difficult to integrate in their working relationships. Further, cultural differences come into play again; the larger firm may be internally fragmented and bureaucratic ("segmentalist"), while the smaller firm usually functions as a tightly knit clan. Members of either organization may face difficulty in understanding that an organization such as their partner's can not only exist, but can also have some merits. In such situations, misunderstandings and frustrations are bound to erupt and quite often kill the partnership.

Further, since these clusters of issues evolve over time during the life of a partnership, evolutions in markets, technologies, and competitive economic conditions may ruin partnerships. They may change the relative criticality of the two firms' contributions as well as the value of the joint output to one or both of them in ways that cannot be foreseen at the outset. A partnership thus cannot usually be reduced to a one-time legal, technical, and financial agreement. Adjustment and flexibility have to be part of most partnerships. This puts further stress on the operating interface and on the relationship between strategic and operational aspects in managing the partnership over time. A partnership is a dynamic relationship, not a one-time agreement.

This chapter analyzes and discusses these three clusters of issues in turn and points to some approaches that can circumvent, if not eliminate, the pitfalls inherent in partnerships between large and small firms.

The Convergence of Purpose

A minimum common set of operational goals, as well as a high degree of mutual understanding, are needed for partnerships to succeed. This assumes that relatively early in the process of cooperation, the purposes of the two partners—at least in the restricted area of the partnership—are made to converge. Even vis-à-vis the partnership, their respective purposes need not be the same, but they need at least to be sufficiently compatible on specific terms to allow for common operational goals. The required convergence of purpose faces three obstacles in the partnerships I observed:

1. It must overcome the genuine difficulties that managers of two very different firms may have to communicate. Some common language, as a basis for mutual understanding, must be developed. Cultural distance makes this difficult.

2. Convergence of purpose must survive imperfect information and uncertain situations and assessments. Observers of trade in technology have noted that, no matter what the specific arrangements, trade is hampered by the public good nature of technology (Teece, 1986). Full disclosure to allow the buying party to assess the value of what it buys would consume the transaction; the party would gain full access to the technology without having paid for it.

3. Less than full disclosure makes valuation difficult and encourages firms to pursue hidden agendas, to engage in misrepresentations, and to be tempted by opportunist behavior (Williamson, 1975).

Cultural Distance

National cultural differences and their reflections in managers' assumptions about organizational processes and managerial behaviors are an obvious first component of cultural distance (Laurent 1986). Yet, in the partnerships I observed, these differences seem to be dwarfed by interorganizational differences, at least among western companies. While differences between smaller entrepreneurial firms and larger bureaucratic organizations are well known and have been much written about, they are particularly critical when such firms become partners (Burns and Stalker, 1968 and Kanter, 1983). Decision-making processes and organizational structures interact to compound the problems.

Typically, the larger firms are slow, ponderous, and consensual in their decision making, both in entering a partnership and subsequently with respect to the specific decisions to be made over the life of the partnership. When they are not, this usually reflects hasty top management commitments which are open to questioning, change, or mere foot dragging, if not outright sabotage, by operating levels. In the larger firm, decisions typically span multiple levels, with intermediate levels playing a key role. Top management not being knowledgeable of the specifics of all businesses, commitments at intermediate levels in the hierarchy are necessary. Smaller firms are more agile, fast-footed, and nimble in their moves, with strong informal horizontal and vertical communications. They are also driven more tightly from the top. Furthermore, the formality and clarity of hierarchies and the perceived social distance between levels are greater in the established firms than in the entrepreneurial ones.

Differences in decision-making processes may also reflect differences in control over the company's environment. Larger firms may dominate the markets in which they participate and be able to influence the evolution of their environment. Their approach to planning and control reflect this. Smaller firms may exercise little influence over their environment, be in emerging industries whose evolution is difficult to predict, and, thus, have to emphasize flexibility and speed of response over planning and strategizing. While the larger firms develop long-term strategies and implement them with great continuity, the smaller firms keep their options open, remain flexible, and are much more opportunist in their development. While these differences may be rather obvious, they create a gap between the two firms and make it difficult for them to manage strategic convergence. The logic of strategy is too different between the partners.

Both kinds of firms may have difficulties in dealing with members of the partner organization. Members of large firms are used to hierarchical relationships within their firm and to distant relationships outside of it. Members from the partner organization fit neither relational mode. They are not to be personnel from a subsidiary—although the temptation to treat them as such is almost irresistible in the large firm—nor are they to be strangers to the organization. This difficulty in positioning members of a partner firm is particularly true of Japanese firms where the distinction between "insiders" and "outsiders" is sharply drawn, resulting in technology partnerships involving coordinated and shared work, but seldom joint common activities (Sakakibara, 1983).

Conversely, members from the entrepreneurial smaller firm may hold strong views about the deficiencies of large firms. (In fact, in both the electronics and biomedical industries, they are often disgruntled creative and entrepreneurial individuals who have left big firms.) Thus, they may not accept easily the processes of large organizations, and, even though past personal experience may allow them to understand these processes, managers and scientists from the smaller firm may challenge them or at least not feel constrained to abide by them.

The first hurdle, thus, is to overcome cultural distance in the negotiation process, to understand and recognize how different the two organizations are, and to clearly distinguish a partnership from an acquisition, even when the first tangible action in the partnership is the large firm's acquisition of equity in the smaller one.

Uncertainty and Misunderstandings

It is difficult for the large firm to understand clearly what the smaller firm's technology can provide, often because the technologies are unclear and not developed far enough yet, and occasionally because the analysis of complementary and competitive aspects of the partnership is not carried far enough. For instance, when Ciba Geigy (one of the big-three Swiss pharmaceutical companies) entered a partnership with Alza (a small, entrepreneurial, California-based firm specializing in developing advanced drug-delivery systems), both issues were in evidence. One of Alza's technologies was a new controlled-rate drug-release technology using a membrane in a pill (called "OROS"). When the partnership started, the amount of substance-specific application engineering needed to adopt the technology to the delivery of individual drugs was much underestimated by both companies. Alza's scientists and engineers were naturally optimistic about their new technology, while Ciba Geigy's scientists—although working on their own somewhat similar slow-release technology—were not able to estimate accurately the amount of work that remained to be done.

At the broader level, the strategic fit was far from perfect. Alza was developing a broad range of advanced drug-delivery systems (transdermal patches, pill membranes, slow-release implantable polymers, minipumps, and so on) whose potential applications far exceeded the range of Ciba Geigy drugs or the generic drugs which suffered serious drawbacks when administered by conventional means (such as nitroglycerine for angina pectoris). The strategic logic of Alza's delivery systems called for multiple specific partnerships with different pharmaceutical companies—to maximize the number of useful applications—rather than for an exclusive across-the-board alliance with Ciba Geigy. Yet, short-term expediency was the order of the day—Alza was in dire financial straits after having tried to produce and market two relatively unsuccessful product applications of its systems on its own. Thus, an exclusive partnership was quickly established. This was going to be a constant bone of contention between the two companies (Alza's third-party contracts had to be vetted by Ciba Geigy) and much contributed to mar their relationship. Conversely Genentech articulated early in its development a clear concept of what types of partnerships it would enter, why and for what products it would do so, and what kind of products it would manufacture and market itself—the choice being mainly driven by the need for marketing and manufacturing means to reach customers, develop the market, and scale up manufacturing processes (Horwich and Sakakibara, 1984).

This provided Genentech with a strategic framework, selectivity in the use of its own limited resources, and the ability to choose either partners, or internal development, production, and sales for specific products.

The capabilities of the larger firm may also be overrated. For instance, a major pharmaceutical company may not be well equipped to distribute diagnostic products or medical supplies. Some of the finer differences in the distribution system may not be fully appreciated, or the uncertainty surrounding how the new technology will ultimately be used may be such that a precise assessment of its manufacturing and distribution requirements cannot yet be made.

Technical relatedness also often obfuscates strategic divergence. Many of the agreements in the information technology industry that have brought together companies in the components industry, in the telecommunication industry, and in the office equipment industry had to overcome different implicit strategic logics that were inappropriately transferred to the partnership from the industries of origin of the partners and then created confusion. Each partner had to learn about the logic of a different industry and understand where the other partner was coming from.

The evolution of uncertainty over time and the way uncertainties are perceived by each partner also add to the difficulties. When dealing with basic technology development (usually early in a partnership, much before a competitive stage), parity is maintained between the partners through balance in contribution, and the potential output is so distant, still, that precise valuation is not an issue. When dealing with well-developed technologies, a precise valuation of the outcome can be made. We are almost at the stage of OEM (original equipment manufacturer) supply contracts, with precise product or system specifications, costs, and prices plus some volume forecasts. Yet, a "danger zone" often separates these stages in the evolution of a partnership: the transition from precompetitive stages to competitive ones. During that transition, one partner, but not the other, may shift from a valuation of the partnership based on contribution to one based on expected results, and show impatience with a divergence from the position of the other partner. This is most likely when development schedules slip between the two firms or when unanticipated difficulties delay product development and introduction (as in the case of the OROS technologies developed by Alza for Ciba Geigy's applications). The uncertainty of the situation is still such that an analytical agreement is not usually possible, and the divergence is likely to endure until market success or failure may possibly allow one to assess the relative criticality of the partners' contributions.

Hidden Agendas

Genuine uncertainty and the potential for honest misunderstandings also obviously leave ample room for not so honest misunderstandings that derive from hidden agendas and lead to misrepresentation. Partners are often caught in a catch-22 situation where, if they contribute too little to the partnership, it will fail (not meet their expectations), while if they contribute too much too openly, their partner will gain the upper hand in the implicit or explicit bargaining power balance in the partnership. This obviously leads to less than full cooperation, but seldom to a mutual recognition and joint discussion of the competitive dimension within the partnership itself.

This is compounded, in all partnerships I observed, by an almost visceral fear, on the part of managers and owners of the smaller firm, of the bigger firm taking detrimental action that the small firm cannot resist and that could put its future in jeopardy. This may range from an abrupt termination of the partnership to a full acquisition by the bigger firm. The smaller firm is thus likely to keep its technology proprietary and to avoid transferring it to the larger firm; it is also likely to try to keep options to the current partnership(s) open (one more reason for third-party contracts to have been a bone of contention between Alza and Ciba Geigy). Obviously, also, any individual partnership is seldom of critical strategic importance to a larger firm, with multiple businesses and a spider web of partnerships for different technologies and products, while a single partnership may be a matter of life and death for the smaller company. Such differences in strategic criticality add to the difficulties being faced.

Differences in time horizon, often stemming from the partners having products at different stages of their life cycle, also make genuine agreement difficult, and may lead to opportunist behavior. One of the partners may give very high priority to speedy development of a product (for example, the smaller firm who sees a big opportunity) while the other may see no need to hurry (for example, the larger firm which has entered the partnership to gain access to a new-generation product, but sees no need to replace its own mature, older-generation, but highly profitable product). The larger firm may see the partnership as insurance, but not be keen to see it succeed quickly.

Worse, some partnerships are not meant to succeed at all. A partnership may be a blocking position, meant to prevent the partner from entering an alliance with another firm, at least temporarily. In other words, partnerships may be a way to temporarily immobilize or at least constrain the moves of other players in an industry. The value of the partnership lies not so much in its success as in its slowing down competitive actions.

Finally, the relative values of the respective contributions of the partners vary over time and may be very asymmetrical at almost any given point in time. There is a need, then, to keep in perspective the contributions over the life (potential) of the partnership and not to be swayed by what currently looks like a serious imbalance.

Working Out Concepts of Partnership

The preceding three issues—cultural distance, the uncertainty and risk of misunderstandings inherent in new technologies, and the potential for hidden agendas—are inherent in partnerships between large established firms and smaller entrepreneurial ones. Yet, to some extent, their possible negative impact can be minimized. First, and most obviously, concepts of partnerships ought to be carefully worked out with a precise approach. Too many firms have rushed into new types of partnerships with little thought given to their specificity, or with cooperative logics inherited from joint ventures in developing countries which probably do not provide a valid set of assumptions for technology partnerships where the small firm (not the large one) is the technology leader, but where the large firm offers worldwide distribution. Concepts of partnerships must be worked out at several complementary levels:

Technological Complementarity. This is most obviously needed to establish the basis for the partnership, but should probably go beyond the initial assessment to also analyze—as far as possible—the complementarity of skills brought to the further development of the technologies. Part of the difficulties between Ciba Geigy and Alza stemmed from the poor initial understanding of OROS technologies and, thus, of the amount of development work still needed.

Technologies may also be valued differently, according to the partner, with the innovative firm overly committed and the other firm more skeptical. As much joint assessment as possible should be done before the partnership is established or at its start.

Joint Business System Complementarity and Viability. Beyond technological complementarity, the viability of the partnership requires that business system complementarity and viability be achieved. In other words, the partnership needs to be competitively successful and to allow for continued complementarity in the partners' inputs. A complete early assessment may not be possible, but an awareness of this need for complementarity of inputs into the partnership and for competitive viability of the output is critical.

Value of Outcome versus Cost to Partners. Partnerships are going to be viable only insofar as the value of the joint results to both partners is superior to the opportunity cost they incur—in particular, the cost of the loss of control and autonomy that follows the partnership. Over time, the value of the Ciba Geigy partnership became less to Alza than the opportunity cost of missed third-party contracts. First, Ciba Geigy was vetting the third-party contracts of Alza, and, although most were approved, approval was often given only after substantial delay. Further, the mere fact that Alza was associated with Ciba Geigy probably deterred potential contracts—third parties feared that their own technology would leak to Ciba Geigy through Alza or their future product plans would be known by Ciba Geigy. While a large enough mutual benefit could overcome concerns about such opportunity costs, the benefits are future and uncertain (typically royalty streams from products not yet launched), while the opportunity costs are more immediate and often tangible (unsuccessful negotiations with third parties for research contracts, for example).

Focus and Boundaries. Hidden agendas and uncertainties can be best contained if the partnership has a clear focus and visible boundaries in both scope and duration. This may help alleviate the fears of both partners—in particular, the fear of the smaller firm about being taken over and/or destroyed in the relationship. Risks are limited for both parties by a framework providing guidance for their future moves. This allows less room for opportunist behavior by circumscribing where it may apply and providing for future adjustment as a function of the behavior of the partners. To some extent, it allows the phasing-in of commitments as the reputation of the partner gets established over time and its trustworthiness is assessed.

Strategic Continuity. Partnerships may fall prey to strategic gyrations on the part of one or both partners, or to mere hesitancy on their part. Doubts about the strategic commitment of the partner may be enough to scuttle the partnership. Yet, unfortunately, partnerships not only face the intrinsic uncertainty of their technological content, they are also entered by larger firms on the basis of tentative commitments, as a second best alternative to self-development. This does not necessarily provide for strategic continuity. Concerned with the commitment of their larger partners, the smaller firms keep their options open.

Precision of Agreement. Partnerships involve contracts, and contracts have to be precise. Thus, agreements are precisely spelled out. Yet, this has several drawbacks, and the partnerships most likely to succeed are not the most precisely defined. Partnerships are joint-learning exercises, and too much precision may hamper learning. Definition of the partnership must be precise enough to allow commitments, but not so precise as to leave no room for learning and interpretation. This allows operating managers to reinterpret goals in ways that can respond to unforeseen events. While the initial numbers may be important to value outcomes and costs (as previously discussed), they can be revised over time. Further, operating managers should be involved early, not only to develop their own commitment, but also because they—better than top management or technical and financial experts—can give insight about how to get the best out of the partnership and, thus, develop a strong commitment to the substantive success of the partnership over time rather than to its numbers. They can also more credibly allow the evolution of expectations and goals over time than could specialists and early negotiators.

While none of these approaches, alone or in combination, can totally overcome the difficulties faced by partnerships, they can at least minimize them. Yet, even successfully conceived partnerships may fall prey to political decision-making processes within the large firm or to interface difficulties between the two firms.

Consistency of Position within the Large Firm

In the examples I observed, large firms find it difficult to establish and maintain a consistent position vis-à-vis their smaller partners. First, vested interests make a consistent position difficult at any point in time. Uncertainties and lack of detailed knowledge only amplify the interplay of vested interests. Second, the politics of resource commitment and program support threaten the consistency of position over time.

Vested Interests

No partnership offers the same opportunity to various managers or organizational units within the big firm. It may offer solutions and opportunities to some, while it presents problems and threats to others. We can briefly review what the Alza partnership offered to various sides within Ciba Geigy:

> To the newly appointed head of the pharmaceutical division, it offered an opportunity to shake up a somewhat passive research organization by showing that viable alternatives to internal research did exist. It was also a show of quick action in a business where the impact of any action is usually very slow to be seen. Finally, Alza offered, hopefully, a different role model from the structured hierarchical R&D establishment traditionally found in large pharmaceutical companies.

To the traditional galenical and pharmacokinetics specialists in the R&D lab, Alza was a threat and a challenge to their competences and importance.

To a few researchers who had an interest in advanced drug-delivery systems but had been too few to gain a strong voice, Alza was both an ally and a competitor—an ally in mustering support for their concepts and their research, but a competitor for results.

To the U.S. subsidiary of Ciba Geigy, Alza was an opportunity to bolster the importance of the United States for R&D and to increase its independence from headquarters in Switzerland.

I could extend this list further to other players within the Ciba Geigy organization. As in any large company, the list can be quite long and the importance and nature of the stakes to the various players quite varied.

The general point is not the specific list of players and stakes, but the fact that their number and diversity render a consistent position impossible for the big firm because not all players can agree.

The lack of a consistent position is usually reinforced by the behavior of the smaller firm. Purposefully or by mere happenstance, it plays on the rifts that exist between units of the large firm to maintain its freedom of action and to gain a suitable mix of partial commitments from these various units. As the CEO of a small firm confided, "I found myself unwillingly in the position to arbitrate between units of my partner. I had more information than any of their units had, they did not talk among themselves, but each talked to me!" The smaller firm will promote consistency where it needs it and encourage divergence where it suits it. Managers from smaller entrepreneurial firms may also find ambiguity quite acceptable and not strive for consistency.

Vested interests in the large firm are important mainly in that they make reaching an honest assessment of the partnership difficult—all analysis is partisan analysis. Top management—at divisional or corporate level—may have a strong influence (for example, by deciding on the composition of a partnership negotiation team)—but not the ability to create or impose a single unitary view. Furthermore, the intrinsic technological and market uncertainties of many partnerships encourage vested interest. Positions are often more a matter of judgment and belief than a matter of well-defined analysis.

Later on, over the duration of the partnership, the variety of agreements reached between the two partners is often found to fuel vested interests, were it only because the larger firm quite often inflicts upon itself conflicts of interest that are difficult to solve on an ongoing basis.

The most basic conflict of interest within the larger partner is usually that between shareholder and business partner. While, in the agreements I observed, the larger firm is a minority shareholder of the smaller one, it is also its privileged business partner, with the obvious resulting conflicts. The large firm, as any investor, wants returns, but it also wants other benefits, such as technology transfers. This is bound to create tensions concerning transfer prices, royalty payments, focus of R&D activity (the focus more profitable for the small firm or that more profitable for the larger partner?), relationships with third parties, and the extent of strategic control to be exercised by the larger firm over the smaller one (versus the degree of entrepreneurial autonomy left to the smaller firm).

Various units of the larger company are likely to become identified with shareholders' or partner's interest. Conflicts of interest cut between functions (for example, R&D sees the partnership as critical, while finance sees the investment as paramount) and often between the parent company and some subunit. In the cases of European investments in U.S.-based entrepreneurial companies, the investment was often made by the U.S. subsidiary (for fiscal reasons), while the partnership was managed from the home country where R&D centers are located. Such an arrangement, while making sense both operationally and financially, is bound to create tensions.

Partnerships may also affect not only subsidiaries and head offices, but also multiple divisions within the larger firm. For practical reasons, it may be useful to delegate the negotiating responsibility for various aspects of the partnership to the relevant divisions. Yet, this may not only fragment the bargaining strength of the large company, it may also lead to each operating unit trying to get the best deal from the partner and lead to a loss of sight of the total value of the partnership.

Further, tentative observations suggest that slack is important. If the performance pressures on operations are very strong, the learning and joint optimization required for a partnership to succeed cannot take place. Each partner will not be willing to give away anything in the short term, and the relationship between the partners may degenerate into constant bargaining which wears down the willingness to cooperate. While learning needs some pressure, it also needs resources. Joint optimization also requires an ability to make trade-offs in ways that are not immediately favorable.

Vested interests in the larger firm are, thus, likely not only to be important at the outset of a partnership, but also to exist throughout its duration. The politics of resource commitments within large firms are also likely to create more tensions and to maintain vested interests active throughout the partnership.

Politics of Resource Commitments

The intrinsic technological uncertainty makes difficult any clear analysis of either resource commitments to the partnerships or expectations from the partnerships, particularly early on. Yet, since partnerships normally imply equity ownership and contractual agreements, they represent a significant one-time commitment of resources as well as legal obligations. This gives them more visibility to top management than internal resource commitments of a comparable magnitude. Internal resources can be allocated on an annual basis through the regular resource-allocation process, whereas partnerships almost always extend commitments over a number of years, with ad hoc revisions made more difficult by contractual conditions.

The combination of vested interests and uncertainty within the large firm led, in the cases I observed, to an overemphasis of the merits of the agreement early on. While the risks were acknowledged, the internal commitment process put forward the reasons for starting the partnership, but not the intrinsic risks of committing resources to uncertain technologies.

Even when such risks were stressed by the technical and operating managers closest to the issues, top management developed expectations of success rather than a balanced view of risks and advantages. While part of these expectations were geared to putting pressure on lower-level operating executives to do their best to make the partnership succeed, in many cases senior managers became committed to results themselves. Consequently, they were likely to be disappointed when the partnership encountered difficulties and did not fulfill expectations.

Following an early phase of overoptimism—usually triggered by the commitment process within the large firm—there came in the observed partnerships a phase of overpessimism. Such pessimism resulted from disappointment with the early results and from the difficulties faced in the interface between the two partners.

Partnerships have unpredictable ways to succeed. Beyond the technological uncertainty, the strategic issues discussed earlier came to play in the partnerships I observed. Early strategic analyses on the part of the partners were often lacking. First, partnerships were taking place in emerging industries whose structure is hard to analyze and forecast. Usual strategy concepts may be misleading, and the uncertainty constantly leads to reassessment of strategic opportunities and threats. Further, these emerging industries are often strongly impacted by regulatory or deregulatory moves, particularly in such areas as health care, communications, and electronics, adding to the uncertainty in the direction and extent of their development. Last, the partners are often not well placed to forecast and assess their own opportunities. Missionary zeal and lack of resources for environment scanning and planning may not facilitate self-assessment on the part of the small entrepreneurial firm. The large company, particularly when it is a conservative company entering both a new geographic area and a new emerging business, may lack the familiarity with the products, markets, and technologies needed to make reasonable forecasts and assessments.

As a result, expectations could fluctuate widely, with little capability on the part of the partners to establish stable, mutually understood expectations. The swing from overoptimism to overpessimism was also accentuated by the process of cooperation. While early on, the negotiators and sponsors of the partnership tended to emphasize its positive aspects, later on the managers at the interface between the two companies, who had the relatively thankless task of working out the day-to-day problems, tended to blow the difficulties they faced out of proportion. More dangerously, since they constituted the primary informal source of information about the partner in their own company, they often propagated a negative image of the partner and created doubts—among managers and scientists not directly involved in the partnerships—about the value of the partnership. Intrinsic uncertainties, gyrating expectations, and negative perceptions of the quality of the partnership (focusing on short-term operational issues rather than long-term strategic worth) compounded to make the partnerships I observed face increasing difficulties. The shift from early overoptimism to overpessimism as problems grew in the partnership took about two years to develop.

The consequences of this shift were worsened by the "half-empty versus half-full" assessment. To the entrepreneurial innovative firm, considerable progress had usually been accomplished, and resources committed and spent wisely. The entrepreneurial company remained optimistic on the technology and its applications, and its managers were usually quite willing to tolerate further ambiguity and uncertainty. They viewed the partnership as at least half-successful. Managers in the larger firm were often frustrated at what they saw as slow progress—if not foot dragging—on the part of their smaller partner. They also evinced less tolerance for unexpected shifts and changes in outcomes, and often were less adaptive and opportunistic in exploiting unexpected outcomes. They harked back to the earlier plans and early contractual obligations and showed concerns that increasing resources were being ploughed into the partnership with very little to show for them.

At that stage, the situation may deteriorate even further as the partners develop different approaches for evaluating the partnership as it enters the "danger zone" outlined in the first section of this chapter. The smaller entrepreneurial firm remains willing to take the results on faith and to continue to evaluate the partnership on the basis of current contributions and future expectations. This leads the small firm's management to a position to invest even more, and faster, in an increasing commitment to the partnership. Managers in the large firm, on the other hand, may be led to a position of bringing "discipline" to the partnership, of restricting spending, and of focusing the effort toward a few short-term tangible results. (Such results are needed to continue to justify the partnership to top management in the larger firm.) While both positions—that of the small firm and that of the large one—are internally consistent, they may be increasingly incompatible. Not only are the resource commitments different, but so is the content of the work. Priorities for downstream product development and application engineering may clash with priorities for more research on the part of the smaller firm. Competitive motives also come into play. The smaller firm is often concerned with its ability to continue to replenish its stock of technology by doing upstream research. Yet it has to cooperate with the larger firm by devoting more resources to the engineering needed to put products on the market.

These difficulties—although to some extent quite predictable—test again the capabilities of the larger partner to maintain a consistent position over time in how it approaches and manages the partnership. Some within the larger firm will use any argument to denigrate the partnership, while others will support it. Consistency of position is not just a one-time requirement at the outset of the partnership, but one evolving over time.

Beyond the objective aspects, partnerships with smaller entrepreneurial firms do not leave managers in the larger firms indifferent. Some are seduced by the operating modes, entrepreneurial cultures, or personalities of managers in the smaller firms. Others see their beliefs and operating assumptions challenged and tend to retreat from the involvement with the entrepreneurial partners. Parochialism in goals and specialization in practices also play a role, with some professional groups coming closer to the partner and others drifting away.

The initial clinical research suggests little in the way of prescription for the larger companies to develop and maintain a consistent position over time. One rather obvious suggestion is to not rely on the existing hierarchy to provide consistency, but to create horizontal groups and task forces to interface with the smaller partner. Information can be shared and positions made explicit in these groups. Another suggestion, which goes right back to the discussion of strategic convergence, is to strive to develop an explicit understanding of the strategic issues in the partnership as they evolve and to maintain a shared perspective on these issues between the two companies. Regular, relatively frequent top management meetings may, for instance, be a vehicle to share understanding and frame a joint perspective.

Also important, as will become clearer in the next section, is to maintain a clear distinction between corporate- and business-unit–level issues in the partnership. Consistency of position within the bigger firm is also made more difficult by multiple levels of management dealing with the smaller partner, each with different information—at least in level of detail—as well as different priorities, degrees of familiarity with the issues, and involvements with the partnership. Poor vertical communication—a problem that often plagues large established firms with a strong sense of hierarchy—only makes the problems more acute. Vertical as well as horizontal communication within the large firm is thus a key to the successful management of the partnership. Communication between the two firms and the way in which the day-to-day interface allows for communication over time are two other important determinants of success or causes of difficulties.

Interface and Boundary Spanning

The central issue to managing the interface between the two firms is the extent of integration between them, from a complete arm's-length relationship (akin to a portfolio investment) to a close cooperation (akin to the integration of an acquired company). Partnerships obviously differ much on this axis. Several issues, beyond the extent of equity ownership of the large firm into the small one, are important in setting up the interface.

Entrepreneurship versus Technology Transfer

First, a close cooperation without careful preparation can be quite destructive, mainly because of cultural distance. Unless they have already had the experience of similar partnerships, operating managers in both firms are likely to lack a clear understanding of their partner. The two organizations are quite different, have no common language, no way to comprehend each other's operating mode, and no understanding of managers' roles and positions in the other organization. Given these differences in starting points, an unprepared interface might lead to disastrous results. One approach here is to organize joint sessions (orientation, briefings, training, discussion, and so on) between members of both firms so they can start to develop a mutual understanding before they actually have to work together.

Close cooperation may have drawbacks though, even when the preconditions for its success are established. Large companies' intervention into small entrepreneurial firms may lead to their innovative spirit being lost, with some of the key talent leaving—as has often been the case in the electronic industry—and with managers being demotivated. Ciba Geigy made the early choice in its relationship with Alza, for instance, not to mingle with Alza's internal management nor to send Ciba Geigy's research or managerial staff to Alza for any long-term visit or permanent assignment. The head of Ciba Geigy's pharmaceuticals division was concerned with maintaining the free entrepreneurial spirit of Alza and not exposing Alza to too many visitors and persons seconded from Ciba Geigy. He was concerned that some key managers and scientists would leave and others adopt the conservative attitude often found in recently acquired companies.

Yet, an arm's-length relationship obviously makes the transfer of technology more difficult. The interface is poorer and more formal, with only modest knowledge in the large company of the potential of its partners' technologies and with little understanding by the smaller partner of the production, marketing, and application engineering issues that its technologies may face. This may compromise the overall success of the partnership and certainly makes it more difficult. Successful transfer of technology was very much an issue between Alza and Ciba Geigy, particularly for the OROS products. An arm's-length relationship has the most severe drawbacks when the nature of the technology or the desire of the small firm to preserve its autonomy keeps the knowledge about the technology largely tacit. Explicit technology transfer cannot take place in the absence of relatively detailed knowledge, on the part of the larger firm, of the operating modes of its smaller technology partner. Yet, as discussed earlier, these operating modes are themselves tacit and hard to understand.

In the absence of close collaboration, smooth transfers of partly tacit technology seem to hinge on the development of good personal relationships among a handful of individuals at the boundary between the two organizations. In the Alza–Ciba Geigy relationship, the success of the transdermal (TTS) technologies hinged indeed on personal friendships between a few scientists at Alza and their counterpart "product sponsors" at Ciba Geigy. For other technologies and products, Ciba Geigy's sponsors were less available or less dedicated, while the technologies demanded a closer coupling between research, application engineering, and marketing, and progress was slower and more difficult. OROS, for example, did not benefit from such close relationships, yet demanded even more interactions than TTS to succeed.

To a large extent, thus, the trade-off is not merely between arm's-length relationships and close integration. Both have significant risks and drawbacks. Rather, the issue is to be more selective in integrating what is needed for the partnership to succeed, but yet leave sufficient freedom to the entrepreneurial firm.

Studies of the processes used to achieve both differentiation from existing businesses and interdependence with these businesses in the context of a single diversified company suggest that selective differentiation and interdependence can be achieved (Doz, Angelmar, and Prahalad, 1985). In the context of a single large, diverse corporation, the evidence points toward the need for a richly structured organizational context in which many management tools are available to balance forces for autonomy, independence, and differentiation of the innovative activity and forces for control, interdependence, and similarity of the innovative activity, with respect to existing businesses and operations.

Obviously, many of the management tools available to top management in a single firm cannot apply in the context of a partnership. (Examples include management of human resources, common information systems, planning and resource-allocation procedures, and control methods.) Simultaneously preserving the required entrepreneurial autonomy of the small firm and yet establishing the level of interdependence needed for the larger partner to successfully exploit its innovations is thus difficult and costly. It also requires a tolerance for ambiguity in power and control relationships that managers in the larger firm (who are used to hierarchical relationships and assumed full control) may find difficult to tolerate. The lack of hierarchical control may create even more difficulties as the reporting position of the smaller firm into the larger one is unclear.

Locus of Management Linkage

In several of the partnerships observed, discrepancies and vagueness in deciding where the small firm hooked into the big one were major sources of difficulties.

In the negotiating phase, the CEO of the smaller firm typically had a division manager, group vice president, or even the CEO of the larger firm as an interlocutor. Yet, the continuation of relationships at that level proved dysfunctional, at least to the larger firm. In several instances, differences and conflicts at lower levels would be escalated very quickly by the CEO of the small firm to the top management of the larger firm. While top management could have just politely listened, registered the disagreement, and asked for information internally, on more than one occasion, top management (poorly informed—or not informed at all from within) would give agreement to something the small firm wanted. This was immediately taken back by the smaller firm to middle managers in the larger one, or worse, it came back through the hierarchy of the large firm as a disavowal of middle management's actions. Not only did that often lead the larger firm to acquiesce to unwise decisions, it also demoralized the middle managers who were constantly put at a disadvantage in dealing with their smaller partner.

The difference in vertical communication between the two companies allowed this asymmetry to develop. In the cases observed, in the smaller entrepreneurial firm, there were at most two levels of management between the CEO and anybody involved in the interface with the larger partner. Further, vertical communication was frequent and informal, often with daily contacts if needed. In the larger firms, though, about five layers of management might separate the CEO from the managers and specialists directly involved in any partnership with a small firm. Vertical communication was slower, less frequent, open to distortion, and necessarily not so well informed. Top management could not know the context of partnerships precisely, nor devote the time needed to become familiar with the particular issues in conflict. Yet, top management did not always show the discipline to ask for internal analysis and staff work before rushing to a decision, nor would they politely turn the CEO of the smaller company to managers several levels below the top, where the issue truly belonged.

As suggested in the previous section, these difficulties call for a clear definition of the locus of interface within the large firm. First and most obvious, corporate and divisional partnerships need to be distinguished. So, in a global business, local partnerships that can be handled by an individual national subsidiary need to be distinguished from global ones where headquarters need to be involved. Within a product division or a subsidiary, though, partnerships still imply multiple levels of issues, from key policy choices for new research programs or product-development choices to the day-to-day communication of documents, shipments of test samples, and the like. Interface points within the large firms cannot be the same for all these issues; some need top management attention, others are for day-to-day administration. Each needs to be structured and adhered to with a high degree of discipline. Most of the problems I observed with the larger partners derived from confusion of roles and responsibilities between organizational levels (and, in some cases, geographic entities) and poor vertical communication within the larger firm.

Similarly, it seemed useful in the observed partnerships not to limit the interfaces to one function. In one case, top management from the two partners deliberately made the marketing groups from both partners work jointly to develop product policies and specifications first, then putting joint product functionality specifications to their R&D groups, thus forcing them to work toward a fully common set of objectives and to accept common technical parameters. This circumvented the initial reluctance of each partner's R&D team to work toward common objectives. To overcome the "not invented here" syndrome in technology partnerships, it may be useful to extend the interface beyond the technology function to areas where agreement on joint objectives and parameters may be easier.

Single-interface points, although sought by the several large companies I observed, do not work in practice. First, interface managers need to be closely connected with the various parts of their own corporation. This is usually not possible. Operating managers want to deal directly with the partners, rather than go through a contact point. Further, the technological content of the partnership is usually such that contact points cannot fully grasp it or keep abreast of it, and thus they lose personal credibility with their scientists and operating managers. Second, the span of issues defies any single interface point. Placed too high, the interface point may lose touch with the needed substantive details; placed too low, it runs the risk of sinking into a mere "letter-box" role, with little practical usefulness.

Interface managers are useful in that as they can be the intersection of several committees, be the focal point for their action, and (insofar as they can) be entrepreneurial and work on the partner to get things done. Multiple committees, in each of which interface managers participate, can give them a fuller vision of the partnership than that available to any other managers, thus allowing them to be integrators in their own firms vis-à-vis the partnership.

Interface managers also need to be entrepreneurs. In several of the larger companies observed, interface managers had been chosen because of their diplomatic skills. While these are important, the most successful interface managers I observed were also strong entrepreneurs, devoted to the success of the partnership, and able to lobby effectively with both sides.

Boundary-spanning Roles and Individuals

In the partnerships studied, not only the successful interface managers, but also most of the individuals successfully involved in making the partnerships work, had entrepreneurial characteristics that set them apart from their colleagues. First, as has been observed of "intrapreneurs" within large firms, their risk profiles were somewhat unusual. Most of them had little to lose, in career terms, either because they were already marginal in their own company or, on the contrary, because their position was so secure as to be unassailable. In both cases, this allowed them to accept unusual levels of personal risks and to deviate from corporate norms in making the partnership work. The most successful "product sponsors" of Ciba Geigy (who were in charge of shepherding Alza's product toward registration through the Ciba Geigy development organization) were unusual characters who took great risk—and caught much flak—in circumventing or bypassing some of the bottlenecks in product development.

These "boundary-spanning" individuals had the ability to accept and assimilate some of the attitudes and ways of doing things from the partner without losing their capability to deal successfully with their own organization. Some of them were relatively recent recruits of the larger firm and had not adopted their cultures yet.

In several cases, though, the boundary-spanning individuals were ultimately adopted by the other organization, whose values and attitudes they espoused. In many instances, struggling with the fragmentation of their own company, they became such strong advocates of the smaller partner's positions as to lose their personal credibility in their own company. In at least one case, a manager from the larger partner ended as managing director of the smaller partner *after* the partnership had been terminated in a crisis and the larger firm had sold its stake in the smaller one.

Such individuals are critical, though, to assure a measure of flexibility in differentiation and interdependence between the two partners. Their very "deviance" from the big partner's standards mitigates against the smaller partner being overwhelmed and losing its original identity. Yet, their origin with the larger partner allows, at least for a while, a relatively smooth flow of information and exchange of technology between the two partners.

Besides specific boundary-spanning individuals, some partners paid great attention to the reciprocal acculturation of members of the two companies. To be able to do this without overloading the small firm with "visiting" members of the larger company, and without too much emphasis on immediate issues, several large firms invited managers from their smaller partner to participate in their internal management-development programs. When the smaller partner was large enough to have its own internal workshops and seminars, reciprocal arrangements were reached.

Selective mobility of a few key individuals between the partners is also feasible, particularly in the technical management area. Exchanges of personnel from a few weeks to a few years in duration are possible and useful. They are obviously limited by the small size of the entrepreneurial partner and by the usual obstacles of compensation levels, salary scales, incentives, and the like. But these latter obstacles can be overcome relatively easily.

Governance Bodies

The complexity of dealing with the strategic and organizational issues discussed earlier in this chapter calls for explicitly structured governance bodies for the partnership. The larger partner usually appoints some of its top managers following the acquisition of equity in the smaller companies. Board-level relationships, however, are usually not enough. They are complemented by joint "steering committees" and "research boards" which allow the partner companies to coordinate their activities at a more operational level and which usually meet more often than the board of the smaller company.

Unfortunately, not only do the coordinating bodies tend to proliferate, they also often become increasingly disjointed from each other. In several of the cases analyzed, the coordination committees added to the problems of vertical communication within the larger partner: each management layer set its own committee to interact with the partner, but since these committees did not comprise managers from multiple levels, they hampered vertical communication rather than facilitated it.

In order to try to overcome these difficulties, the larger partners had to set up their own internal teams and committees. Following its experience with Ciba Geigy, Alza has now made it standard practice to request its partners—even for a mere product-development subcontract—to set up their own internal coordination committee comprising all the required interfaces with Alza.

In cases where the interdependences between the two partners are simultaneous and reciprocal rather than sequential (such as the joint development of a computer line rather than the transfer of a new drug-delivery–system application for testing), the management processes of both partners may have to be adjusted to provide for explicit meeting points (for instance, joint design reviews and "milestone" assessments). This usually calls for the product-strategy and product-planning processes to be made compatible in schedule and for joint participation of the partners in at least some phases of these processes.

Conclusion

The obstacles that face strategic partnerships between large established bureaucratic companies and smaller, entrepreneurial fledgling firms are formidable indeed. The odds are against such partnerships, and most fail to meet the objectives of both partners. Yet, more and more of these partnerships are undertaken. Although the research reported here is clinical rather than statistical, it very strongly suggests that partnerships are likely to fail because of managerial rather than technical reasons. The analysis leads one to be concerned with three critical areas that may doom partnerships:

1. The initial analysis and the initial agreements emphasize strategic complementarity as a source of value for the partnership, but take subsequent strategic convergence as given. Cultural distance, uncertainties, and misunderstandings, as well as hidden agendas make such convergence difficult unless it is truly desired by the top management of both partners and unless it is actively managed.

2. Managers in the larger partner do not develop a joint coordinated approach to the partner. On the contrary, they use the partnership as a tool to further their own interest in the bureaucratic and political games that take place within large organizations, and they see the partnership from the standpoint of their own parochial interest. While this is unavoidable, awareness of these problems by the top management of the larger partner can help limit the risk of internal politics and enhance its ability to manage a partnership with a small entrepreneurial company.

3. The operating interfaces between the two partners cannot be left to chance and to ad hoc adjustment. They must be designed as a whole, recognizing the various issues and the corresponding levels in the hierarchy of the bigger firm as well as the nature of the interdependences between the partners.

Even more so than with acquisitions or with joint ventures, top-management attention to the requirements of the interaction between the two companies is critical.

Bibliography

Burns, Tom, and G.M. Stalker. 1968. *The Management of Innovation*. London: Tavistock.

Doz, Yves, Reinhard Angelmar, and C.K. Prahalad. 1985. "Technological Innovation and Interdependence: A Challenge for the Large, Complex Firm," *Technology in Society*, vol. 7, nos. 2–3: 105–25.

Hardyman, G., M. de Nino, and M.S. Salter. 1983. "When Corporate Venture Capital Does Not Work," *Harvard Business Review*, May–June: 114–20.

Horwitch, Mel, and Kiyonori Sakakibara. 1984. "The Changing Strategy–Technology Relationship in Technology-Related Industries: A Comparison of the United States and Japan." Sloan School of Management Working Paper no. 1533–84. Massachusetts Institute of Technology, Cambridge, Mass.

Kanter, Rosabeth Moss. 1983. The Change Masters. New York: Simon and Schuster.

Laurent, André. 1986. "The Cross-Cultural Puzzle of International Management," *Human Resource Management*, vol. 25, no. 1: 91–102.

———. (1979). "Cultural Dimensions of Managerial Ideologies: National versus Multinational Cultures." Paper presented at the Fifth Annual Meeting of the European International Business Association, London Business School, December 1979.

Roberts, Edward. 1980. "New Ventures for Corporate Growth," *Harvard Business Review*, July–August.

Sakakibara, Kiyonori. 1983. "From Imitation to Innovation: The Very Large Scale Integrated (VLSI) Semiconductor Project in Japan." Sloan School of Management Working Paper no. 1490–83. Massachusetts Institute of Technology, Cambridge, Mass.

Teece, David. 1986. "Capturing Value From Technological Innovation: Integration, Strategic Partnering and Licensing Decisions." Working Paper. Berkeley Business School, University of California at Berkeley. March 1986.

Williamson, Oliver. 1975. *Markets and Hierarchies*. New York: Free Press.

19

Domestic and Foreign Learning Curves in Managing International Cooperative Strategies

D. Eleanor Westney

I n its 1985 annual report, Nippon Steel, the largest steel company in the world, redefined its industry as "basic industrial materials," including new organic and inorganic materials as well as steel. The same year, General Motors announced that its goal was "to be the leader in all technologies applicable to its core business," which crossed industry lines to include information processing and robotics as well as automobile manufacture (*Business Week*, 1985). Over the past few years, a number of firms that occupy leading positions in copiers, computers, or telecommunication have redefined their industries as "office automation" or "information." Increasingly, long-established, large-scale firms are deliberately changing their definition of their core industry. And even more firms have been finding that the long-standing boundaries of their industry are expanding more rapidly than their ability to find the appropriate labels for their broadening fields of activity.

For some firms, such as Nippon Steel, the change in the way they define their industry is a response to shifts in the comparative advantage of their home society that put them at a competitive disadvantage in their original industry. In other cases, the change is a reaction to the increasingly close interactions between the technologies of the firm's core industry and other technologies that have heretofore been evolving separately. But whether the firm actively seeks to redefine its industry or whether it is faced with the challenge of responding to shifting industry boundaries, it must master a new range of procedures and knowledge if it is to continue to function successfully. In other words, it must embark on the changes in its structures, processes, and portfolio of knowledge and skills that theorists have called "organizational learning." This response goes beyond the entry into new lines of business, an undertaking conventionally defined as diversification; it involves changes in the existing structure and processes of the firm plus the acquisition and use of an array of knowledge and skills that must interact with and change the existing knowledge base of the firm.

A firm whose activities are beginning to cross industry boundaries must acquire knowledge from its environment or, more precisely, from other organizations in its environment: knowledge about new technologies and markets as well as knowledge about how to manage its own operations in adding value to the technology and in dealing with the markets. In this context, cooperative strategies can become an indispensable mechanism for learning, although not all cooperative strategies involve learning. And, because in many fields no one society today monopolizes this kind of knowledge, the firm will probably have to build cooperative linkages that draw on knowledge being generated outside its home country.

But, another dimension of learning in cooperative strategies concerns learning not as an output, to which the firm then adds value internally in order to enhance its competitive advantage, but learning how to manage the processes of cooperative linkages. And the greater the importance of learning as a goal in cooperative strategies, the more important it is for the firm to learn how to manage cooperative linkages effectively. When the boundaries of its industry are shifting, the firm must adopt a learning strategy in at least some of its relationships with external organizations, both within and beyond the borders of its home country, if it is to make a successful transition.

Cooperative Strategies and Organizational Learning

One can distinguish between two types of cooperative linkage. The first has as its goal the production of a certain output for the firm to use. One example might be the linkage between General Motors and Daewoo to build small cars in Korea for sale by General Motors in other Asian markets and the United States. An example from the Japanese building industry is a joint development project between a heavy machinery firm and a building firm to develop a floor-smoothing robot to use in small spaces.

The second type may also focus on the production of a specific output, but it has the additional goal of helping the firm to learn: to internalize new skills, to refashion its procedures or structures. The GM–Toyota joint venture to produce small cars in California has the additional goal of helping GM learn how to produce small cars efficiently and helping Toyota learn how to manage a manufacturing operation in North America. The joint project to develop the building robot was primarily oriented to getting an effective robot, but it also helped some of the building firm's engineers enhance their capabilities in robotics and to understand how the other firm organized its development processes, providing a reference point for improving one's own. Firms may actually engage in cooperative strategies in which learning is virtually the only goal: for example, building firms in Japan have recently been cooperating with various external organizations to hold international conferences on intelligent building technology. Ideally, therefore, "concrete output" and "learning" are two ends of a continuum rather than a dichotomy.

There are many impediments to organizational learning, as organization theorists have been pointing out for years. Organizational change is never easy. At the individual level, many employees may be unwilling or unable to adjust to the demands for new skills and modes of operation. And, as population ecologists have pointed out, at the organizational level the large-scale, differentiated firm faces particular difficulties in organizational change—size, age of organization, and complexity all increase structural inertia.

But, the firm that is trying to shift its definition of its industry faces difficulties beyond those generic to efforts at organizational change. Arthur Stinchcombe has postulated that there is a powerful industry effect on organizational structure and processes: that is, that the organizational patterns of a firm within an industry are shaped by the social technologies of coordination and control and by the nature of labor markets and educational levels that are available when the industry was founded, regardless of the time of founding of that particular firm (Stinchcombe, 1966, pp. 153–69). When a shift in industry involves (as it usually does) a shift from an older to a newer industry, the implications for the firm's structures of coordination and control and its systems of recruitment, reward, and development of human resources are likely to be more far-reaching than may at first be apparent.

A further source of difficulty may be the need to change the firm's normative models—those firms to which it looks as standards of comparison for its own performance. These "significant others," to borrow the language of social psychology from which the concept was drawn, can provide a powerful impetus to change and a source of models. When the boundaries of one's industry change, the normative models must usually change as well, unless the firm is following moves that are being made by another firm within its own industry that has long been identified as a normative model. If a change in normative models is necessary, however, and there is a lag in adopting these new models, or if competing sets of external referents emerge in the firm, what could be a powerful stimulus of learning can become a source of confusion and conflict.

Finally, another impediment to learning in transitions across industries is suggested by the concept of the organization-set. This paradigm of organizational behavior sees the firm as operating in a set of relationships with other organizations that provide inputs, receive outputs, and regulate activities (Evan, 1966). Among the inputs is, of course, technical and managerial knowledge. The change in the firm's range of activities entailed by a shift in industry means weakening or ending many of these relationships and building new ones. In other words, a firm must reconstruct its external "knowledge network": the array of external organizations with which it is cooperating to develop new knowledge or from which it is drawing for existing knowledge. For example, an automobile firm that has traditionally drawn on university research laboratories in mechanical engineering must now build connections with those in materials science and electrical engineering. And, to build those linkages, it must often compete for time and attention with other firms who have already established relationships with those labs and who likely have more of their own people with the training and experience in those fields to make the relationships run smoothly.

These impediments to organizational change make learning-oriented cooperative strategies both more important to the firm in its efforts to change and potentially more difficult to manage, since managing such strategies will itself require organizational change.

Managing Learning-oriented Linkages

Much of the literature on managing cooperative strategies suggests that the more concrete the goals and the more specific the time horizon, the greater is the likelihood of success. Cooperative linkages that focused on specific outputs rather than on learning are more likely to meet these criteria than learning-oriented linkages. The potential for mistrust and asymmetry between the partners in a learning-oriented cooperative relationship is also greater, especially if one partner views the relationship as output-oriented and the other as learning-oriented.

Another reason why learning-oriented cooperative strategies will be harder to manage is that they involve a denser and more varied set of interorganizational resource flows than cooperative strategies aimed at obtaining a specific output. And the denser those flows, the more demanding is the task of managing the relationship.

One reason for the greater difficulty is that the denser the interactions, the greater the potential for what organizational sociologists have called "isomorphism"; that is, the greater the pull on the organizations involved to move toward similar structures and processes. In other words, as the relationships with an external organization (such as an electronics firm or a university laboratory) become closer, there is greater likelihood that the interactions will occur smoothly if the subunits involved in the relationship have or develop similar structures and processes.

The concept of organizational isomorphism has only recently been explored by organizational theorists, and the level of analysis has been the organization as a whole rather than the subunit within the organization. We cannot assume that theories generated at one level of analysis apply with equal validity to different levels, but developing working hypotheses by taking insights derived at one level (for example, the individual) and applying them across levels (by viewing the organization as a whole as a social actor, for example) is an acceptable working tool. And the fact that current management writings are pointing out that firms managing a range of changing technologies have to cope with increasing levels of internal variation in structure and process (Horwitch, forthcoming; Kanter, 1983) suggests that isomorphic pulls are operating at the subunit level as well as at the organizational level.

In the learning-oriented strategies aimed at the firm's redefinition of its industry boundaries, it is likely that the organizations with which the firm has its most important linkages will be from another industry and that, therefore, their structures and processes will differ significantly from the firm's own. And because the learning-oriented firm is likely to be facing greater uncertainty (attendant on the transition), it is the more likely to try to change in order to make the relationship work.

The difficulty of managing increased internal variation is only one of the problems faced by the firm under these circumstances. Another is that although a subunit that changes to resemble its external partner may thereby become more able to make the relationship function smoothly, its growing differentiation from the patterns of its own firm may make it less able to pass its learning on to the other parts of the firm that must use it once it is acquired. A third problem is that in some of the literature on joint ventures, the creation of parallel structures inside the firm has been portrayed as a result of bad faith, of the firm trying to preempt or exploit the knowledge generated (Harrigan, 1985). Yet the isomorphism approach suggests that if a firm is to learn effectively from such partnerships, the creation of analogous structures within its own boundaries is an important way to make the transfer of learning work. If, however, the perspective that such an approach indicates bad faith is shared by the partner, it could cause serious problems in the relationship.

On all these dimensions (generating and managing subunit change, managing the relationship with the partner, and applying the learning that is produced in a cooperative linkage), we would expect to find that firms become more effective as they gain experience.

Learning Curves in the Management of Cooperative Strategies

It seems intuitively obvious that a firm with extensive experience in cooperative strategies will enjoy a greater chance of managing additional linkages effectively. Part of this advantage may be individual-level learning: in the course of engaging in a cooperative venture, the individuals involved can learn how to make the processes more effective and efficient. If the firm continues to involve those people in managing cooperative ventures, it can continue to benefit from their learning. And to the extent that such people disseminate their individual learning by training others and by producing formal analyses that are disseminated within the firm, and to the extent that their learning becomes institutionalized in the organization's rules and routines, we can speak of organizational learning in managing the processes of cooperation.

One key issue for empirical research is the extent to which such organizational learning can be cumulative across different types of linkages. Does learning in the context of managing linkages with one kind of organization (for example, universities or private laboratories) help in managing linkages with others (such as electronics firms)? Does accumulated experience in managing linkages in one area (for example, industrialized housing in the building industry) translate into effective management of linkages in another (such as intelligent buildings)? Or is learning cumulative only in very specific contexts, such that continued experience in cooperating with certain firms means that additional linkages with those firms will work so much more effectively that the firm would be advised to work with its existing partners wherever possible, even if they are not the holders of the most advanced technical or organizational knowledge? And—most important for the consideration of international cooperative linkages—does experience in managing linkages within the firm's home society provide an advantage in building linkages with foreign organizations?

Learning curves in managing cooperative strategies have two dimensions. One is how to manage the relationship between the partners; the other is how to transfer learning (once it has been generated by the cooperation) effectively within the firm and how to add value to it to produce better products, services, or processes. Of the two, it would seem that the latter is much more likely to be cumulative across contexts, because the organizational structures and processes reside within the firm and have therefore more commonality across specific context. For example, one researcher in a major U.S. chemical firm observed that Japanese firms, with their much longer history of building on externally generated technology, were able to benefit much more from cross-licensing agreements than their U.S. counterparts. The Japanese seemed to be better at working on and improving technology they licensed in, so much so that the U.S. firm was increasingly in the position of licensing back technologies developed from its own work—the Japanese firm had licensed it in, worked on it, effectively made the technology its own, and improved on it. In the U.S. firm, by contrast, all too often technology that was licensed in tended to become an "orphan" in that no group or individual within the research organization took—or was effectively charged with—the responsibility for building on that knowledge. The NIH (Not Invented Here) syndrome is only partly attitudinal: it is also organizational, in that the firm has not developed routinized mechanisms for learning from externally generated information.

The folklore on the U.S.–Japan comparison is also useful for framing the prior question: is learning how to manage cooperative relationships transferrable across borders? Japanese firms are believed to have much greater experience in pursuing cooperative strategies for a number of reasons, including a regulatory climate that favors such strategies, a government that encourages them and even constructs them through government-sponsored projects in a wide range of industries, and the cooperative arrangements in the *keiretsu* (industrial groups). Does this mean that the Japanese firm is likely to be more effective in managing cooperative relationships abroad than U.S. firms?

The Japanese management of cooperative relationships within Japan seems to have been facilitated by the development of three institutions: the practice of *shukko* (sending employees on temporary assignments outside the company), the prevalence of what Yoshino and Lifson had dubbed "parallel hierarchies," and the density of internal communications networks.

Shukko takes two forms in Japanese companies. One is the dispatch of workers to other firms when the parent company no longer can provide them with suitable work. The second, and more important for managing cooperative linkages, is the temporary dispatch of employees as part of their career development. Employees are routinely sent on one- or two-year assignments to government ministries or laboratories, private think tanks, joint research projects, associated Japanese or foreign companies, or foreign universities. Because the practice is so routinized, the mechanisms for keeping the employees in touch with the parent company and for debriefing them on their return are well developed.

The communications across firms within Japan are facilitated, as Yoshino and Lifson have pointed out, by the fact that large-scale organizations have very similar formal structures and career paths (1986, pp. 238–41). Employees are recruited from the universities and move upward through very similar organizational ranks at a very similar pace, whether they are in a government ministry, a large trading firm, a bank, or a large manufacturing firm. These "parallel hierarchies" mean that the networks that develop at the early stages of a career (either as a result of a common educational background or in the course of routine business contacts) are maintained as the employees move upward. Parallel hierarchies also reduce the problems of managing cooperative interfirm relationships. The high degree of similarity across the partners means that the "isomorphic pulls" are much slighter, and the resulting degree of internal variation is lower.

Finally, Japanese firms seem to be better able to disseminate and use acquired knowledge more effectively than their U.S. or European counterparts because of dense internal communications networks. Japanese engineers are much more likely than their American counterparts to get together informally after work to discuss work-related matters. They were also more likely to participate after work hours in study groups involving such activities as the assessment of competitors' patents or quality control. Such groups can be effectively used to digest and develop further the information derived from learning-oriented cooperative strategy.

Of these three institutions, the second is the least likely to translate into an advantage in learning from international linkages. Indeed, it may be a handicap, since the Japanese firms have less need within Japan to develop the capacity to handle internal variation. It may well be the U.S. firm, which has had to develop learning curves to handle greater variation across its domestic partners, whose learning curves are in the long run more transferrable into international cooperative strategies. Moreover, as Japanese firms increasingly attempt to move toward less rigid structures of promotion, the system of parallel hierarchies may weaken, creating difficulties for cooperative linkages between firms that are struggling to maintain the old system and those that are stretching to adopt the new.

The practice of *shukko* and the utilization of dense internal networks both are transferrable across national boundaries, however, and underlie much of the advantage the Japanese are perceived to have to learning-oriented cooperative strategies.

The competitive balance between Japanese and Western firms may well be determined in the long run by which can move more quickly to match the advantages of the other: the Japanese in building learning curves in managing greater levels of internal variation in structure and process, or the Western firms in developing effective internal mechanisms for the dissemination and utilization of externally derived knowledge.

Conclusion

Much of the research on cooperative strategies to date has focused on "making the deal": the motivation for cooperation, the modes, and the frequency. An essential and complementary part of understanding the phenomenon is empirical, process-oriented research on how the deals are managed once they are made. This will mean drawing on a different theoretical base for hypotheses, and such studies will view cooperative strategies as a subtype (or set of subtypes) of a more general process, such as organizational learning. It will also involve a narrower focus, at least initially, on a particular set of firms and activities. But, the eventual benefits from such contextual research, and from blending research on making the deals with research on making the deals work, will be enormous.

Bibliography

DiMaggio, P., and Powell, W.W. 1983. "The Iron Cage Revisited: Institutional Isomorphism and Collective Rationality in Organizational Fields." *American Sociological Review*, 48: 147–61.

Evan, W. 1966. "The Organization-set: Toward a Theory of Interorganizational Relations." In J.D. Thompson (ed.), *Approaches to Organizational Design*. Pittsburgh: University of Pittsburgh Press.

Harrigan, K. 1985. *Strategies for Joint Ventures*. Lexington, Mass.: Lexington Books.

Horwitch, M. Forthcoming. *Postmodern Management: Its Emergence and Lessons*.

Kanter, R.M. 1983. *The Change Masters: Innovation for Productivity in the American Corporation*. New York: Simon and Schuster.

Meyer, J.W., and Rowan, B. 1977. "Institutionalized Organizations: Formal Structure as Myth and Ceremony." *American Journal of Sociology*, 83: 340–63.

Stinchcombe, A.L. 1966. "Social Structure and Organizations." In J.G. March (ed.), *Handbook of Organizations*. Chicago: Rand McNally.

Yoshino, M.Y., and Lifson, T.B. 1986. *The Invisible Link: Japan's Sogo Shosha and the Organization of Trade*. Cambridge, Mass.: MIT Press.

20

Underlying Dilemmas in the Management of International Joint Ventures

Willem T.M. Koot

C orporate business life is steadily being enmeshed in the internationalization process. Not only Big Business lives its day-to-day life on a global basis, but quite a few middle-sized corporations hesitantly are trying the intercontinental scene as well.

It seems that during the past decade, even the biggest corporations could not help but form joint ventures with some of their major global competitors. Yet, entrepreneurs and corporate managers are aware of the many problems that they have attributed to this type of venture. Complications mentioned include performance problems in less-developed countries, reluctance to share profits and to trust a major business partner, and the difficulty in directing joint ventures toward one's goals. In particular for medium-sized ($100 million sales) companies, the joint venture is a difficult but at the same time indispensable vehicle for jumping over to another continent.

Would it not be a useful idea, then, to try to sort out the difficulties for different international joint ventures and to come to grips with some of the factors that seem to obstruct, time and again, the noble paths that managers have planned to follow? This chapter accepts this challenge by highlighting and sorting the many experiences of companies located in the Netherlands, whose management has lived through joint venture cases all over the world. In this qualitative research, 55 Dutch and American experts have been asked to put their experiences with more than 100 ventures into words. In-depth interviews lasting up to 5 hours have been supplemented with documents. Extensive data exist for some 20 cases. Most experts have had at least a year of direct experience with a venture. The case studies provide insights for managers and academicians. The data together cover, as much as is possible, the period of original start-up negotiations, midstream life, as well as some end-of-life situations of ventures.

Data and Joint Ventures Defined

A joint venture is defined as a subsidiary company that is established by a corporation together with a partner company in a foreign country, the normal case being the multinational company from an industrialized economy having a share of some 20 percent or more in the equity of a company outside its home country, with the remainder of the equity being in possession of a company located in the country where the joint venture is to be established. The argument of this chapter also pertains to the case of two parent companies both established outside the country where the venture is set up.

During the past two decades, the joint venture has outgrown its traditional status of project vehicle to implement trade deals or substantial construction orders on an international scale. Extensive documentation indicates that many Fortune 500 corporations participate in joint ventures (Janger, 1980; Killing, 1983) and that both in Europe and in North America, even domestic joint ventures are becoming normal business (Harrigan, 1985). Before elaborating further on international joint ventures, a shorthand typology might make a first useful differentiation of the matter at hand and it will put the present data into perspective.

The first type of joint venture is called the *global core business venture*. For the biggest Fortune 500–type corporations, investments in research and development of their core businesses have become so costly or risky that they have to seek partners. Global competitive advantages are the targets, particularly in maturing industries. Partnerships are being sought to divide continents as domains between the partners. It is no longer regarded as shameful to play with the thought of "can't we do that business on our own?" The AT&T/Philips joint venture in the Netherlands and the many joint ventures in the European and U.S. automotive industries highlight this new type of venture. Domestic ventures exist within the United States and inside of the European Common Market, with comparable effects of delineation of domains and tempering of competition among those big corporations (Perlmutter and Heenan, 1986). Strategy implementation and technology exchange are central problem areas of the global core business ventures. The mode of strategy development can perhaps best be described as planning-adaptive in Mintzberg's terms (Mintzberg, 1973). It is a shared concern of divisional and top management, and these managers are ably assisted by elaborate corporate staff departments.

A second type is the *LDC-joint venture*. Here, small as well as big corporations are committed to their own goals of strategic expansion into a nonindustrialized continent or country (Conference Board, 1975). Relatively inexpensive production factors and the opportunity of augmenting mature home markets are bought with the admission of foreign private and government share capital in the distant venture. Relative inequality of northern and southern partners are a fact of life here. Since 1980, more than half of U.S. investment in less-developed countries took the form of joint ventures and similar developments occur in European corporations. In the LDC venture, strategy development may be partly planned, partly locally adaptive in Mintzberg's terms. It is the diplomacy-fueled business of corporate staff and the joint venture manager, as well as the partner and LDC's national government.

The third type of joint venture may for this moment be called the continental partnership. Big, middle-sized, or even small businesses take an option for a capital partner in another industrialized country, with the aim of "conquering a continent" for their capital or product. Successful corporations that feel challenged by opportunities for expansion or profit beyond the ocean increasingly consider the joint venture as a feasible alternative to both fully owned establishment and temporary licensing agreements with distributors. In addition, less successful but profitable companies on both sides of the Atlantic try the joint venture form because the executive board or the president may consider the overseas adventure to be too much of a risk to run on their own. Their own capital reserves, technological advantage, or familiarity with the new territory will not be sufficient for more than a year or two. Strategy development is to be characterized as a mix of formal planning and entrepreneurial thinking. On one hand, it is an impressively tough job for the president of the smaller company with his outside fiscal, legal, and, eventually, management consultants. On the other hand, a variety of inside specialists and managers as well as the joint venture manager all try to explore the other partner and avoid the hazard of an unhappy journey.

Data on continental partnership ventures account for 90 percent of the data behind this report, and the remaining data almost completely refer to LDC-ventures. It is hypothesized, however, that the outcomes of this analysis may be useful to all three types of ventures and be valid at least for the continental partnership venture.

Generally Perceived Problems with International Joint Ventures

Managers and staff specialists of the examined companies confirm the image of the joint venture as a cumbersome form of organization. Its main problems are threefold: the joint venture is hard to direct to its goals; it requires a formation period with hardship; and it is difficult to manage even when it starts operating. In this chapter, special legal, fiscal, and antitrust aspects of joint venturing are not considered, although they should have the attention of the managers involved.

Measuring Effectiveness and Success. Managers of parent companies perceive the joint venture as a vague and risky business, however few the problems that the partnership actually has. The dependence on a partner does make the disposition and commitment of future financial resources insecure or rather less secure than it seems to be without a partner (*Chemical Week*, 1983). There is a fair chance that short- and long-term objectives of partners are misunderstood so that the combined direction of the venture may not be clearly visible to anyone (Roberts, 1980), except perhaps to the joint venture manager. Objectives of both partners in terms of marketing and technical development efforts may almost unnoticeably change over time, no matter how formalized the proposed policy for the joint venture is (Franko, 1971). The supposed risks of a joint venture go together with a tempered publicity: partners are reticent (Berg and Friedman, 1980), joint ventures often are not registered, and the annual reports may quote their proceeds as "other income."

Costly and Cumbersome Formation Period. The long period between the first steps abroad and the rounding up of negotiations does usually require much attention of top managers and their staff (Berg and Friedman, 1980; Otterbeck, 1981). However, the practical experience of participants in this research is such that they think this really is the suitable period to take a clear stand and to make agreements with regard to areas of potential conflict. The list of such sensitive issues is impressive: it contains management contracts, arranging the technical assistance, determining a broad policy for the joint venture, establishing provisions for ending the venture, plus identifying and managing cultural differences between parent companies.

Difficult to Manage. The composition and functioning of the joint venture's board and management, the informal and formal lines of communication, recruitment and compensation of key staff, and adaptation to political forces at hand all form potential built-in difficulties for the interacting companies (Killing, 1983).

If one seriously considers the joint venture for making a substantial international jump, a focus on the process of strategic decision making for the venture might disclose some of the pitfalls. After a study of the literature and of a few companies, this chapter addresses the following question: what creates recurrent problems for the joint venture? First, let us look for more fundamental dilemmas and elements with which managers will have to cope. So, back to a few basics.

Four Unique Features of the Joint Venture: Does Management Choose All of Them?

On the basis of some one hundred joint venture experiences of interviewees, four characteristics can be inductively condensed. These are important because they lead to the dilemmas that I will mention further on. What makes the international joint venture so particular is the combination of (1) sharing of profit and risk, (2) a long-standing relationship with a partner company, (3) partially equal international partners, and (4) a third entity within a Y-form administration.

Sharing Profit and Risk of Loss on Common Equity. Investing capital and management attention involves risks. Taking risks together with a business partner requires the capability of managers to make consistent, sound decisions.

Company A is a 50 percent establishment of a big corporation with a strong leverage and liquidity position. Interviewee stresses: "However difficult it is to administer joint ventures, even for us there are situations in which our independent expansion of a distribution system for fuel would not be wise. Of course, the profitability norm is different for a joint venture. Ah, when things go bad, one has to invest much longer. And joint ventures are ideal occasions for creating disagreements among partners! So the interests must go parallel or else you take too big a risk. With company A, we were not in a position to independently set up a distributors network as we have done in our division Y. We had the supply problem. That is why we made a deal with corporation Z. In this case, our motive has been defensive in nature, and the joint venture is engaged in a substantial core activity of our corporation which justifies the risks and investments."

Cultural inhibitions concerning "sharing" and "not running things your own way" do play a role and sometimes lead to unnecessary reluctance and mistaken zeal. Operational requirements also may impede the sharing.

Company B in the automotive industry reports that it is looking for a partner for local assembly and distribution in an Asian country in order to share risks and improve market penetration. It is, however, not prepared to share either concerns for the joint venture or the care of profits. Its spokesman says they "have a secret contact with a second local partner-applicant as a necessary reserve." After summing up some real problems in Asia, he states, "We refuse to limit our role to being a licensor of automotive knowledge. To run your international business, you need a hammer to make decisions. The joint ownership mode does not provide that hammer."

Long-standing Affair and Contractual Relationship. A good relationship before the "marriage" is logically a necessary condition for any capital investment risk to be taken. It hardly seems surprising that so many managers confirm the imagery found in much of the literature: the joint venture as a sort of marriage. These data are strongly flavored by the Dutch and American cultures, as both produce strongly individualist managers with traditional views of the family and marriage. Yet, I found strong warnings not to be content with misleading ideas about the venture being like a marriage.

First, the joint venture "marriage" is principally an open marriage. Parent companies are happy to do intimate business with many other candidates and there seems no such thing as an internationally valid conception of decency in ending the relationship. As a result, the joint venture manager is quite often treated as a stepchild.

Second, in the international scene, there are as many differences in conception of faithfulness and moral duty as there are interpretations of profitability. U.S. and Dutch partners often discuss how much should be written down in an agreement and what should be left open. Experiences in underdeveloped countries reveal that foreign partners grant themselves the authority as well as the moral right to alter contractual statements unilaterally without any consultation.

The experience of informants in this chapter reveals that managers do not always perceive in time these built-in infidelities of the joint venture relationship. Things may turn out badly. Alternatively, the parent companies gradually detect the true motives of each other. Almost all interviewees point out that they had not realized that the courtship stage in the negotiations takes months longer than expected, although no one was very clear about initial time estimates. Negotiations do have prolonged periods in which there is no point in discussing the content of the business itself. Some preliminary advice to prospective joint venturers is:

Elaborate your company's own network of contacts around the prospective partner. Meet its banks, customers, and government as well as other partners that it may have had.

Reflect on the costs of a prolonged period of tough negotiations as a possibility.

Make your company's plans for the venture, but revise them as you come to view your partner's interests in a new way.

The elder joint venture specialist of a Fortune 500 corporation concludes:

No two joint ventures are similar enough to work with model contractual agreements. There are four or five different basic contracts depending on the negotiations. In LDCs, just the orientation phase will cost one to two years of hard work on the part of a team with double reporting lines within our corporation. I can imagine that no middle-sized company can afford this type of game and it should restrict itself to market surveys and the appointment of a local agent first, and only then consider an eventual partnership. My personal view is that a joint venture should be designed and planned through for at least ten years.

So far, what is clear is the need to assess the joint venture affair as a long-standing one, one that can very well take the form of a dominant partner in an unequal relationship.

A Partially Equal International Partner. The joint venture can be less than a family relationship and turn out to be a "broken" family, a one-parent family with a distant parent contributing in some material respect. In the case of joint ventures, this may be a very happy and stable situation that partners have agreed upon from the outset. Indeed, "the important feature of dominant-parent joint ventures is that they are managed . . . virtually *as if* they were wholly owned subsidiaries" (Killing, 1983, p. 20, emphasis added). But obviously, they are not wholly owned. And a willingness not to share management is not a lasting willingness; sooner or later, a passive parent may show an interest in becoming a more equal partner.

Again, it seems important for parent companies to realize from the outset whether or not they will accept the uneasiness of an unequal balance. In the case of a LDC venture, the inequality may take the form of an inequality agreement that neither partner trusts completely.

> Company C is a supermarket chain. It is a majority interest of a big trading corporation. Years ago, this corporation had approached a German trading company and proposed to jointly internationalize. "In fact, we split the world and agreed on each other's domains. 'In countries that I like, you join us with money,' and vice versa. The leading, 60 percent share partner has management control. Of course, we both tried to attract a local partner for some 3 percent of the shares in Britain and Brazil. No need to say that now these have lost their effect and have been removed from the scene."

Partners in underdeveloped countries quite often are doomed to become silent or even fake partners who after a few years have no effects on the performance or the management of the venture's business.

In the world of joint ventures, there may be another inequality to live with. Parent companies may vastly differ in either size or international business experience. In fact, the complementary nature of the partnership may be precisely what attracts the partners, and the world of business is full of these "natural" inequalities. Again, it seems important to realize the difficulties of a mismatch in size or internationalism. As one of the experts from very experienced Royal Dutch Shell put it:

> Of course, the internal organization then is a big challenge. We invest up to 50 percent of total buildup time into in-house preparation of the project. And, mind you, this should always involve very organic teamwork. Now, in most cases, a small business makes the mistake of not spending this type of preparation effort and doing it in an organic team form. It takes a terrible time to find out what the real objectives of a partner are. . . . The size mismatch between the partners puts extra weight onto the dilemmas involved in the joint venture process.

If one parent should feel that the difference in terms of international cooperative experience is rather uneasy, my advice would be to ask time and again: a joint venture may be a necessary evil, so do you really expect it to be useful for your company?

Third Entity and Y-form Administrative Structure. The joint venture is attached to two parent companies and a common board representing it legally. This organizational form creates a double set of line/staff reporting networks. This situation explains why checking the balance of power in this triangle is a classical theme.

The venture may become a power in itself, or at least a third entity. In any case, the two parent companies can both do their business independently of each other and the venture. This separation distinguishes the joint venture from mergers and ordinary participations in corporate and subsidiary share capital. On the other hand, the joint venture, being a separate corporation and organizational unit, can be distinguished from less powerful forms of cooperation such as international management contracts and service contracts, licensing, and franchising.

The balance of power in the Y-form structure and the chances for "identity" of the joint venture are the objects of explicit care and design. For the shared-management, 50:50 joint venture, this may be best expressed by an expert in the international chemical industry where this type of venture is popular:

> We construct the triangle in such a way that the board is relatively heavy in its staffing. That is a necessity because precisely the 50:50 joint venture becomes a third party within the corporate parent-to-child relationship as soon as it works all right. Within the joint venture then, both the new interests of this party and the interests of the individual partners are included.

The dreadful fantasy of at least one of the partners is the possibility of the successful joint venture manager who exploits this structure by a perfect game of divide-and-rule. This powerful fantasy obscures the fact that both parent companies can simultaneously profit from the venture, as one successful and determined joint venture manager states:

> Our company has had a very good starting period in which there were soon no initial losses anymore—in fact, a unique situation so I got much freedom to attract my type of personnel and to design my way of managing purchasing and contracting. Of course, I have always had the feeling of being a stepchild, even now. It is me who has to maintain the interests of both parties on a lively level, and I am the person to care that new developments within parent *A* can find their way to parent *B* and vice versa. There is a very frequent informal contact with both parents, plus much telephone and telex traffic. The shared interests do need a periodic renewal. Yet at the same time, a joint venture manager is a little captain who has to find his own course.

Reluctance to start a joint venture may exist precisely in order to avoid a fast-growing independent unit, says the advisor on business development of one parent corporation administering this venture:

> We try to start things internationally by getting or selling a manufacturing license. Sometimes, if we do not have the manufacturing capacity, there is a separate company to be developed. With our type of joint businesses being rather small in scale, we prefer to avoid the extremely complex and independent joint venture mode.

Realizing what features one accepts when forming a foreign joint venture, we may now turn to the inevitable dilemmas connected with these joint venture features.

Four Main Dilemmas Putting Weight on Decision Making

A more profound appreciation of how the joint venture functions and what parent companies should do with them is found in terms of at least four dilemmas extracted from all the accounts and interviews in this research project. The dilemmas are in fact recurrent comparisons or balancing operations that take place in the minds of the participating managers. These tasks continuously require managerial attention. The present data reflect in most cases the various development stages of ventures, not only end games or start-ups. Also, what seemed to be wrong in retrospect often was happening in all of the ventures' history.

The management of parent companies have to, time and again, balance the criteria for decisions they make on the commercial, technological, financial, and human resources of the joint venture. On the basis of my data, it is hypothesized here that those dilemmas can be summarized as follows:

1. Exploit or invest in finance and know-how.
2. Mold operations or let them grow.
3. Fight or produce a teamlike cooperative effort.
4. Select your own venture manager or let a joint venture manager develop his staff.

Even in the period of formation and start-up of the joint venture, it is important to realize and explicitly use the dilemmas for decision and action. Since the international joint venture is such a difficult organizational form, success lies in the ability of management not to think solely in terms of their company's objectives and ratios, but to expand decision making into the realm where one is expected to find difficult balances and even admit faulty decisions. Objectives and policies, however important they are as a planning tool to companies involved, do become rather fluid and seem transient when one engages in a partnership with a business firm in a different continent.

Exploit or Invest

In terms of finance and know-how, parties have to internally balance their own projections of what is to be expected from the venture. Thus, the amount of investment in fixed assets and product development is to be balanced against the profitability objectives and self-financing goals of each parent company. It is hoped that partners can then communicate what they really want within a certain time span; often, they are not quite able to do so, which results in a lot of trouble.

For each of the parent companies, one major objective is to make a certain profit after a period of start-up investments. But how big the return on investments should be and how long a payback period would be realistic, are questions that even the most stringent policy statement cannot solve. First, different objectives (for example, "penetrate the market with a share of 3 percent and try to break even after two years") cannot be that precise. In reality, a relatively risky international adventure with a partner, often involving modified products in a relatively undefined market, cannot be too tight in one's control. One might ask: should it be so?

The business interests may actually diverge drastically among partners in such a way that sooner or later, a shared concern about the venture leads to lack of unity in company policy for the venture, with a heightened chance of failure. An important potential for joint venture failures is clearly formed by a conflict of views between an industrial producer or distributor of consumer goods on the one hand and, on the other hand, the financial investment-oriented silent partner. Among our Dutch and American informants, this divergence of interests repeatedly proved to be a particularly dangerous situation.

> Partners like that do form good business together. But they have to do a good business *both* with management resources and adequate capital. The management resources are as important as the finance; they dedicate partners to the venture where they have so little in common. In a way of speaking, running back to your home country after having given your money is complete nonsense. You have to take care, look after a company that has been established. You cannot really "park your capital" here or there to develop a sound industrial or trading business in another continent.

Differences in scale of operations and in financial leverage of the parent companies play a role in this dilemma. Obviously, it is the lack of balance here that causes continuously insecure relationships. The case of a minimultinational with some $60 million sales having a limited possibility to support an eventual rapid expansion of the joint venture forces the parent to exploit the venture or disinvest while new operations are still in the building stage. The bigger diversified multinational involved as a second partner may put its cards, however reluctantly, on the investment side of the dilemma.

> Apart from their policy differences, the parent companies were not financially comparable. Parent A is small, entrepreneurial, and finances with debt. B is much bigger, has a planning bureaucracy, and finances with equity. The size mismatch is important when things go bad. You risk the prolonged investment that is necessary. In the recession of 1982, A approved money to cover substantially more investment than had been planned. To them, it was a cash drain.

The exploitation-investment dilemma strongly relates to the previously mentioned aspect of sharing. The upper and lower limits of this sharing of profits and financial risks should be explored and made clear by each of the partners in a more continuous manner. Parent companies who are interested in profit maximization and not really willing to bear an equal share of the risks choose an extreme basis for solving the dilemma. I would suggest that they should not use the fragile joint venture form at all. Again, it is not the objectives in themselves, but the mode managers choose to communicate the dilemmas between partners, that counts.

The exploit-invest dilemma also applies to know-how or technological information. As is known from the literature, a joint venture is usually a convenient form of transmitting technological value such as patents and industry knowledge among partners (Killing, 1980). The technology-acquisition theme prevails in the present data, as demonstrated in diversification by one or the other parent. Thus, for instance, a high technology company official reports:

> Of course, it was an explicit intention for each of our joint ventures to contribute to the product development of our corporation. It was absolutely essential. The partner had the products in case *Z* and knowledge of the U.S. market. Now they contribute nothing and we develop the technology for the venture.

Limited knowledge and limited funds as well as a desire to constrain the partners' use of their companies' patent positions put a brake on the investment side of the balance.

> This joint venture should not have started in the first place. The parents wanted to invest here and they wanted to get new technology. But they both just gave the money and sat back; they never followed up with technology or development effort. It turned out that our products were simply not theirs. This continent's market is totally different in its cost base and its development function. So only on the surface do we operate in similar markets and products as the parents do. Secondly, the parents were too competitive in attitude. Corporation *A* did not want to give us any support because they said it would go to *B*. Typical response in the board by *B* was: "You are not fast enough in product *X*." After all these years, I can safely conclude that *we* had all the technology in house all the time. They did not exploit any of the technology that they or we had. During an important period of years, they were simply too busy with staying present in this continent's markets at any effort. Nobody has learned anything or even tried to.

This example illustrates how a serious commitment to remain present in the continent's market may postpone the exploitation of immaterial technological assets which are already at hand for product development.

There are, of course, companies that use this dilemma very successfully to get what they want. Here is what managers of high technology corporations who fight their way into new markets report:

> We have an elaborate management information system to monitor projects, license holders, and joint ventures. [shows documents] It should be instantly clear what each month's contribution of each of the projects and companies is or how much is needed on young promising project companies. Of course, everyone hates it, but we think that failure to reach goals should be clear very soon and nobody gets blamed for it then. This fits into our concept that we want high-risk but highly

profitable, 20 percent return-on-equity companies and we aim for very active technology acquisition. We want to make sure that we are getting enough, and joint ventures are an ideal form to get technology. When after a period, the partner does not contribute anymore or does not like the venture anymore, we usually simply buy them out. We also give further licenses on the basis of acquired technology.

A lack of consent on how knowledge should be acquired or transmitted may indeed cause a conflict between parent companies, particularly in industries such as automobiles or machinemaking. In some instances, corporate reluctance to limit license and research fees to the venture seem to have forced a rigid choice for the exploit-side of the exploit versus invest dilemma. Such a direction of the joint venture makes it very difficult to let the venture grow successfully. A way out of this situation may be the suggestion of an expert on chemical joint ventures:

> Joint ventures in our corporation's experience usually stick to the products and product lines that they started with. New products are a problem anyway because they involve new knowledge in most cases. New products are kept and fostered by the parent companies in their own organization; this is one of the most difficult aspects of the joint venture form. We come to the conclusion that the product mix of the venture should be very well demarcated to both parents.

More than just a few companies try to use their joint venture partner as a means to obtain know-how even by stealing it. The others want to market existing products with some modifications to new continental markets, without too much investment in know-how and without an effort to get new technology via the partner. In most cases, it became clear that parent companies judge, but seldom monitor the results of these learning efforts to acquire technology or industry know-how. A formalized evaluation of both partners' contributions is one of the most valuable improvements of the difficult decision-making process in joint venturing. Careful monitoring and top-management evaluation of qualitative contributions is thus an essential check on strategy.

As with finance, sharing involves immediate stipulation by parent companies of exactly what they want. A style of half-open communication is necessary in most cases. In particular, strong, successful companies may play a sophisticated game of trying to use the venture to get access to new technology leading to a buyout of the partner's share after some years. Again, what matters is not just the objectives of one's company, but the way each party prudently approaches the different underlying possibilities while working on the venture. It is how well they realize their common interests, rather than their individual planning, that determines if the joint venture is to be successful.

The exploit-invest dilemma as a whole is primarily a strategic balancing and, as such, is the realm of both headquarters involved plus a small group at the top of the venture. Data on effects at lower levels are not available.

Mold Operations or Let Them Grow Up

The operations of the parent company can be exported in a ready-made form in such a way that no adaptation in manufacture or sales methods is allowed, keeping product quality and brand name intact. Many of the biggest multinationals, particularly in capital-intensive or high-precision–product industries, try to transmit the exact design of managing the new operations to the newborn stepchild company. If the venture is to keep these standards and procedures and negotiate on any adaptations, the parent can be said to mold the venture. In many LDC ventures with a dominant partner, this seems the case as well.

In the continental partnership venture, however, a more liberal managerial standpoint on molding can be judged beneficial by the other partner. And, of course, all joint venture managers tend to plea for the let-them-grow-up side of the balance. Strongly decentralized international corporations may give them what they want, provided that they adhere to the prescribed accounting procedures and reporting mechanisms via the venture's board. A substantial majority of joint ventures in this research are being administered at arms length.

Even so, parent companies and the venture will get into big trouble concerning operations in running the venture after its take-off whenever the parents differ substantially in their degree of decentralizing and delegating operational tasks. The global venture, which can be seen as a large partial merger, has much more potential than most ventures for differing technical and cultural standards leading to vast areas of conflict. This may not be typical for the continental partnership venture. As for middle management in the venture, the little information available suggests that this autonomy dilemma seems to at most create uncertainty on whose plans to follow. "Should one take this headquarters proposal seriously this time?"

Even in unequal partnerships with managing partners, how to manage operations should be a point of early inspection by the other parent during the first talks as well as long after the formative talks are completed. Needless to say, this advice is essential for the shared-management venture as the following comment shows:

> In our chemical corporation, we are used to running ventures as shared ventures with detailed policy agreements. In the starting phase of the talks, we think the dilemma of your "grip" on operations should already by explored and stated as far as is possible then. Because we do not know at this stage how the new company and the new partner will run things, we just take the easy position of putting lots of demands with respect to the new general manager on the table to explore the partner and this dilemma.

At this point we have arrived at the communication dilemma.

Fight or Produce a Teamlike Cooperative Effort

The preferred style of communication between management and staff of the two parent companies can vary with the seriousness of the situations. Negotiating behavior and an attitude to try to get what you want without discontinuing the relationship is probably a nice intermediate point of balance between fight and teamwork. The data suggest that some parties with rather unclear or unconsciously hidden motives for the venture do have a more tough way of interacting. Occurrences include breaking up ongoing talks, threatening with sanctions and ultimatums, and even blackmailing the partner-investor. These are all harmless and feasible acts in a certain stage of severe, stubborn negotiations, or as an outlet for the stress of managers' work. In some companies, however, such a regular fighting behavior puts a strain on the goodwill of all parties involved. A warlike attitude also capitalizes on the ever-present motives of parent companies to remain in a position of dignified autarky, thus restricting the chances of a successful common venture. An account on a failed joint venture reveals:

> The management of the venture was much too autonomous. We had shared management. After our initial investment, there was surplus capacity in the market and we had foreseen a long period of initial losses. This is why we set up the venture, to share these losses with a partner. Both the other partner and we ourselves thought (without saying, of course) that we would be able to get rid of the venture by selling out in a couple of years. With this type of attitude, we made a management mistake to share this particular business with a partner.

On the other hand, a forthcoming attitude in the preparation of the joint venture even before the interests of the partner are clear enough may frighten the parties and make them skip the courtship altogether. It is generally assumed that it is imprudent to show your know-how and the quality of your company's contacts in an eager manner.

The theme of gluing corporate cultures together, one of the fashionable themes in recent literature, is not prevalent in the data. This is due to the joint venture being a third entity that leaves partners independent.

What is stressed in a substantial number of interviews, however, is the necessity of some personal chemistry among a few of the top managers involved. In addition to an ostensible persistence to go together, this feature creates a sound basis for occasional teamwork. This teamwork of managers in turn is regarded as the necessary communicative "cement" with which the joint venture shall become a more viable, continous business affair.

As to the effects on middle managers in the ventures, the data contain a few cases of highly aggressive internal climates. Middle managers and staff (engineers and economic staff belonging to either parent's culture) there tend to be divided into rival camps and to be badly cooperating within the joint venture in those cases.

Select Your Own Joint Venture Manager or Let a Manager Develop His Staff

This dilemma concerns management development and not the authority to manage the operations. Management development is a strategic responsibility of top management, so an inclination to demand staffing authorities on the venture in itself is not a surprise. At one extreme in this dilemma, one finds the partner who, after having stipulated a majority contribution in financing the venture's equity and loans, demands to select and appoint the management of the joint venture by itself. The other partner may then stipulate to put a controller in the venture; at least, this seems the case in the continental partnership venture. This in itself seems to be a reasonable construction, but it turns out dangerous as soon as a non-managing partner wants to restore control evenly: "They had the two managers then. A controller was then appointed on our behalf, for *one should continuously dig informal channels to get grip on the venture*" (emphasis added). (This particular venture being discussed is low-performing and not promising now.) Thus, given this task of quasi-dominant joint venture management, international ventures should be managed by the most competent partner in the field of management development in the foreign country, even if this is not the majority partner in terms of equity.

Another extreme way to develop your venture's management is the corporate entrepreneur's insistence on letting a manager play the game he wants. Even in a distant continent, one could try to let the partners develop the venture's management potential. Staff selection then is the responsibility of the joint venture manager.

> We had little knowledge to offer to our partner. The president knows a lot himself. We knew he likes our company and our reputation and we had worked with him before. He moved us as an interesting individual and a great businessman. So we said, "OK, then we want part of the ownership and profit, 50 percent." We set up this joint company. We simply gave Mr. V. the ball and let the joint venture manager roll it. Yes, it may turn out to be wrong; it's always risks that are involved.

During the life of a joint venture, this fourth dilemma recurrently comes up and it may be clear now that either position has its risks. Constant surveillance of both partners' interest and one's management philosophy may be the only remaining but wise path to follow.

This fourth dilemma is again more or less restricted to the few key officers at the top of the venture, who may be the objects of direct selection by the owning companies. There is no information on perceptions of lower-level managers on this point.

Existing Themes in the Literature Expressing The Dilemmas—and The Need to Rephrase Them

Five themes repeatedly coming up from the literature on joint ventures give support to the idea that four major dilemmas need to be approached. Writings on the subject can be grouped in five themes: rationales for taking a joint venture strategy; ownership and control; venture autonomy; choice of partner; and legal agreement and protection. Figure 20–1 connects the themes to the dilemmas put forward here.

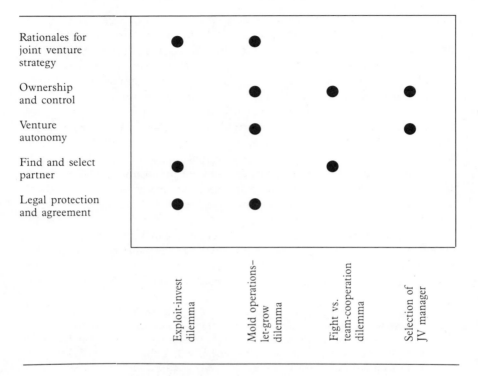

Figure 20–1. Themes in the Management Literature in Connection with the Basic Dilemmas in the Management of Joint Venture Formation

Rationales for Joint Venture Strategy. A major part of literature reflects on the reasons why a joint venture is taken into strategic consideration. Objective industrywide mechanisms, but mostly technological and commercial factors, are suggested to lie behind expansive behavior of corporations (Berg, Duncan, and Friedman, 1982; Bivens and Lovell, 1966; Gullander, 1976; Harrigan, 1985; Killing, 1980; Otterbeck, 1981; Young and Bradford, 1977).

I interviewed many managers whose accounts were also devoted to the "why" of the venture, usually formulated in retrospect. There is a prescriptive tendency expressed like: "We have done it all right. This joint venture is better than doing it alone. It really fits our ideas about the strategy of our parent company." This theme has a strong connection with the previously mentioned "exploit-invest" and "mold operations" dilemmas. While most of the literature formulates pros and cons for a final decision, this connection suggests that strategy is a product of individually and jointly coping with the dilemmas.

Ownership and Control. The question of where a joint venture is unavoidable or when you should be satisfied with what portion of the venture's share capital has been a predominant issue from the moment the joint venture first caught the attention of students of management (Bivens and Lovell, 1966; Conference Board, 1975; Contractor, 1984; Gullander, 1976; Killing, 1983; Otterbeck, 1981). The sharing of profit and risks is usually taken into consideration and sometimes the tone is a prescriptive one: even if you have to share, do try to get the dominant-partner position or at least the management of the venture so as to direct the flows. This theme points at the difficult areas of "molding or not," "fight or cooperate," and whose management development should put its mark on the venture, as reflected in figure 20–1.

Autonomy. The theme of how much autonomy can be given to the joint venture manager recurs in the managerial literature on the subject (*Chemical Week*, 1983; Holton, 1981; Janger, 1980; Killing, 1983). There is a tendency to suggest: "decentralize, but keep control of operations as much as you need." The dilemmas about molding the operations and selecting the management staff of the venture are being reinforced here. Again, there is no question of creating common opinions that solve things once and forever. In practice, management's goals are often replaced by management's dilemmas.

Choice of Partner. How to find partners and how to select one are two difficult tasks (Berg, Duncan, and Friedman, 1982; Young and Bradford, 1977). A number of cases and some practical hints have been suggested in management journals such as *Business Week, Chemical Week,* and *Financial Times.* Some of the informants in this research asked for advice on partner selection. The balance in both the use-invest and fight-cooperate dilemmas is the source of what makes these courtship problems so difficult.

Legal Agreement and Protection. Once the parents have chosen a partner and have formed some opinions about strategy and management control, a lot of attention is needed for written agreements.

Lawyers and tax consultants usually start with this item and this is part of the literature (Herzfeld, 1983; Holton, 1981; Cherin and Combs, 1983). These reports often include protection against abuse of one party's trademarks and patents or statements about an eventual liquidation of the venture still to be established. The wise course is for firms "to go together but not get cheated." The agreements and their meaning as to practical management are also discussed by many of the experts in this research. They point out that basic dilemmas concerning one's investment or one's wishes to mold the foreign operations against the intentions of the partner company remain. (See figure 20–1.)

It seems logical to rephrase these themes, as I have done now, in terms of dilemmas. But generally, one may also redirect the focus of learned writing on joint ventures to issues that deserve a lot of consulting and concern to managers involved. In particular, the issues of ownership and control and partner selection are produced by basic dilemmas about cooperative styles and management development. Should researchers not direct their work to the additional requirements and traits that a joint venture manager needs over a "regular" manager?

In addition, it is suggested that themes such as rational choice for a strategic adventure with a partner, and the formulation of the agreements are a reflection of the three dilemmas. Should not more of our academic writers touch upon the necessity for managers being able to write down a fine business plan and to "fit" the venture convincingly for the other party as well?

Using Dilemmas to Cope with Measuring Ventures' Success

Let us return to one of the problems associated with the joint venture form earlier in this chapter. Effectiveness was said to be difficult to assess. Yet, it is necessary to have a tool for measuring top management's success when forming a partnership company. It seems as if the "joint" feature of the common, distant subsidiary forms a mist around one's ideas of what to expect.

The elusiveness of joint venture success is reflected in the literature. From different sources, one may note a diversity of notions about when parent companies would have been successful in forming a viable venture, and when not (Berg, Duncan, and Friedman, 1982; Berg and Friedman, 1980; Janger, 1980; Harrigan, 1985; Young and Bradford, 1977; Killing, 1980, 1982; Holton, 1981).

Is the joint venture effective when it generates sufficient profit or has a certain continuity? Can it be considered effective with a given market performance or a certain degree of technology development? Or is it all a matter of how well the two partners act together? Most writers elaborate on the instability of the venture and on the management difficulties, or they sum up the factors that facilitate or restrict the use of joint ventures in specific industries. Systematic empirical studies or explicit accounts on joint venture effectiveness, however, are rare (Harrigan, 1985; Young and Bradford, 1977).

Two factors are responsible for this elusive measure of joint venture "success." First, it seems impossible to produce an objective, common ratio of success for the joint venture as a whole. Clearly, the two individual parent companies have different roles and evaluation perspectives. Second, effectiveness cannot without further ado be rationally evaluated. Top managers of the partners do not usually formulate a range of objectives very strictly and, if they do so, such a range is a product of the negotiations rather than an independent planning tool. The rationality of planning the venture is further diminished by practical folklores such as diplomacy in the venture's board and "moves" vis-à-vis governments. Data in this research support this impression of political or emotional performance indices. Thus, effectiveness and top-management success seem to be nothing else than what individual partners want and what they view as feasible in the course of joint venture action.

Of course, particularly when this joint venture is so difficult to be evaluated and easily misread (Roberts, 1980), top management's own consistent direction is of prime importance. So being aware of one's hidden dilemmas may be very useful to the parent companies' management and staff as well as to the joint venture manager. Mapping one's position on the four dilemmas mentioned should produce the ability to assess the direction one is taking at any moment. The dilemmas are the more constant balances that play a role in widely varying circumstances with potentially unwise players.

For example, the content of objectives for the venture may be switched in the view of top management's priorities. One could thus reconsolidate on a position where less profits counterbalance a freshly conquered presence in the distant market, plus, for example, a new peace with the joint venture manager and the partner.

A management's course of action would be clarified if this change in position was to be evaluated as a potentially new position in the exploit-invest dilemma as well. Even if one does not perceive this new position, one might consider enlarging the corporation's concern with molding the venture's operations the year after. The dilemmas, being the underlying factors, can thus be used as the language with which each partner can measure both ambitions and positions of the three entities involved.

Formation Period Shortened by Focus on Dilemmas

The long and cumbersome formation period has been mentioned as a second major practical problem of the international joint venture. Managers of both parent companies must be individually capable of taking long series of decisions on how the joint venture should function in the future. This is not an easy task. In this long process, it is probable that the approach these managers take for coping with the dilemmas will color all decisions that they make for the venture. The formation period is also one of the least predictable and hectic periods. Time and again, the officials involved in the game will be confronted with surprises, ultimata, and even personal problems. Internal corporate parties and government agencies usually demand quick briefings.

The dilemmas can thus be used as personal instruments for risk analysis. An example may reveal what happens:

> Initially, a parent corporation *A* may put an absolute nonnegotiable limit on the total fixed assets to be invested in two years. The other partner then has to be willing to show a similar commitment. But tables might turn when the financial results of the partner corporation in its home

markets drop for several years. Does *A* accept the necessity of supporting the venture on its own disproportionally, and does it reinvest or does it sit back and wait for better times? *A* might reinvest disproportionally; however, then is its management heading for more management control of the venture's operations and is it able to avoid fighting with the troubled partner? Company *A* may realize its basic position has not altered and then decide to let the joint venture board take short-term decisions and make a new marketing plan on which to take appropriate joint actions later.

The decision-making process in the joint venture strategy would be easier and quicker if managers clearly realized which basic positions they should in fact adopt. As a consequence, the process would be faster and conceived by more conscious, autonomous minds. This chapter is devoted to furthering this objective.

Bibliography

Berg, S.V., Duncan, J. and Friedman, P. 1982. *Joint Venture Strategies and Corporate Innovation.* Cambridge, Mass.: Oelgeschlager, Gunn & Hain.

Berg, S.V., and Friedman, P. 1980. "Corporate Courtship and Successful Joint Ventures." *California Management Review*, XXII: 85–91.

Bivens, K.K. and Lovell, E.B. 1966. *Joint Ventures with Foreign Partners.* New York: Conference Board.

Chemical Week. 1983. "Making Joint Ventures Work." August 17.

Cherin, R.E., and Combs, J.J. 1983. "Foreign Joint Ventures: Basic Issues, Drafting, and Negotiation." *The Business Lawyer*, 38 (May): 1033–106.

Conference Board. 1975. *Multinational Corporations and Developing Countries.* Chapter 7. Report 767.

Contractor, F.J. 1984. "Strategies for Structuring Joint Ventures: A Negotiations Planning Paradigm." *Columbia Journal of World Business*, Summer.

Franko, L.G. 1971. *Joint Venture Survival in Multinational Corporations.* New York: Praeger.

Gullander, S. 1976. "Joint Ventures and Corporate Strategy." *Columbia Journal of World Business*, Spring: 104–14.

Harrigan, K.R. 1985. *Strategies for Joint Ventures.* Lexington, Mass.: Lexington Books.

Herzfeld, E. 1983. *Joint Ventures.* Bristol, England: Jordon & Sons.

Holton, R.H. 1981. "Making International Joint Ventures Work." Chapter 11 in L. Otterbeck (ed.), *The Management of Headquarters–Subsidiary Relationships in Multinational Corporations.* Aldershot, England: Gower.

Janger, A. 1980. *Organization of International Joint Ventures.* New York: Conference Board.

Killing, P.J. 1980. "Technology Acquisition: License Agreement or Joint Venture." *Columbia Journal of World Business*: 38–46.

Killing, J.P. 1982. "How to Make a Global Joint Venture Work." *Harvard Business Review*, May: 120–27.

Killing, J.P. 1983. *Strategies for Joint Venture Success.* New York: Praeger.

Mintzberg, H. 1973. "Strategy Making in Three Modes." *California Management Review*, XV: 44–53.

Otterbeck, L. 1981. "The Management of Joint Ventures." Chapter 12 in L. Otterbeck (ed.), *The Management of Headquarters–Subsidiary Relationships in Multinational Corporations*. Aldershot, England: Gower.

Perlmutter, H.V., & Heenan, D.A. 1986. "Cooperate to Compete Globally." *Harvard Business Review* (March-April).

Roberts, E.B. 1980. "New Ventures for Corporate Growth." *Harvard Business Review* (July): 134–42.

G.R. Young, & Bradford, S. 1977. *Joint Ventures: Planning and Action*. Cambridge, Mass.: Arthur D. Little.

21

Formal and Informal Cooperation Strategies in International Industrial Networks

Håkan Håkansson
Jan Johanson

The growing interest in cooperative strategies in international business has mainly focused on formal cooperative arrangements, such as joint ventures, licensing, coproduction agreements, and management contracts. (See chapter 1 in this book.) But cooperation may as well be informal. A supplier and a customer may engage in a lasting, mutually advantageous relationship, where the parties take each other's interests into consideration (Webster, 1979; Levitt, 1983). Similarly, two complementary suppliers may cooperate informally when entering new markets. In a study of cooperations between firms in technical development, more than two-thirds of the cooperative relations were informal (Håkansson, 1986). This chapter argues that both formal and informal cooperation strategies are pursued in international business. Its aim is to analyze some important aspects of their use in international settings.

For that purpose, the first section outlines a model of industrial networks which is the conceptual framework within which different cooperative strategies are discussed. The network is the firm's frame of operation with constraints and possibilities. It constitutes the arena in which the struggle for survival takes place, but it is also an important tool in that struggle.

The network model is based on some assumptions about interaction between firms. In the second section, the role of such interaction in the emergence and development of industrial networks is analyzed. This gives some basic implications for the formation of firms' network strategies. Such strategies concern the development of the role and position of the firm in the industrial network.

The use of cooperation in the network strategies is discussed in the third section. The focus is on the distinction between formal and informal cooperation. The fourth section develops a number of propositions about the use of formal and informal cooperation in international industrial networks.

This chapter is based on research about industrial networks conducted with a number of other Swedish researchers, in particular Lars-Gunnar Mattsson. The authors wish to thank Peter Lorange, Lars Engwall, and Mats Klint for helpful comments.

Characteristics of Industrial Networks

In any field of industrial activity, an observer can identify a network of connected interaction relations between firms engaged in industrial activities—an industrial network.[1] In principle, such industrial networks are unbounded, but the observer (or a specific actor) may, for analytical purposes, set suitable boundaries. Such boundaries may be drawn on the basis of technology, country, a focal organization, and so on. All such boundaries are arbitrary. Different actors will draw different boundaries. They are a result of perspectives, intentions, and interpretations.

An example regarding technical development can illustrate how companies in different industries and countries are bound together into a network (Håkansson, 1987, p. 18f). The start is given by the use of a product—large engines for marine applications. There are few companies (Sulzer, Bursmeister and Wein, Westfalia, and some small producers) specializing in producing large engines and competing worldwide. The users are the shipowners, but the buying company can be a shipyard with quite different interests. The use of the engine is dependent on the kind of fuel used. If cheaper oil (for example, heavy oil) can be used, this decreases the costs. Thus, there is a technical and economic connection to the oil companies. Furthermore, in order to use heavy oil products, special equipment (a separator) is needed. This product is manufactured by a few producers (Alfa-Laval, Mitsubishi, Westfalia, and some small producers) who market their products worldwide. This network of companies is very well structured and the companies have known each other for many years. A special cooperation project where the aim was to develop the use of cheap fuel was initiated by the largest engine producer (Sulzer) approaching Alfa-Laval. The latter responded favorably and, furthermore, asked the Shell oil company to participate. By combining the different resources and knowledge of the three companies, the technical problem could be attacked in a much more efficient way than if any of the companies had attempted it alone. The "effective network" (Epstein, 1969) consisted in this case of companies in three different industries located in different geographic parts of the world.

Industrial networks are not designed by any single actor according to a master plan or a strategic decision. They emerge and develop as a consequence of interaction between semiautonomous, interdependent industrial actors. Every such actor has to establish its own relations in the network and this cannot be done unilaterally. Other actors must be motivated to engage in interaction and this may require adaptations by one, both, or even more actors. On the other hand, any actor can initiate interaction in the network, thus promoting structural change. The actors may be firms, divisions, departments, or even individuals.

Industrial networks are functional entities, in which heterogeneous resources are used in industrial activities to satisfy heterogeneous demands. There is technical, temporal, and social interdependence between the actors. This holds irrespective of how the boundaries are drawn.

In spite of the strong interdependencies, the industrial networks have a plasticity in the sense that single actors, relations, or activities may disappear without jeopardizing the overall functioning of the network. This is largely due to the loose coupling of the networks. Other actors adjust and other relations and activities are adjusted to the new situation, thus keeping the system of activities functionally intact. It is at the same time stable and changing.

In the industrial networks, each actor controls some resources directly and some resources indirectly via dependence relations with other actors. The dependence relations are due to the strength of the bonds between the actors and the relative importance of the actors to each other (Cook and Emerson, 1984). Thus, in every network, there is a power structure where different actors have different powers to act and to influence the action of other actors. This power structure in combination with the interest structure of the network affects the development of the network.

The interest structure is formed by the conflicting and common interests of the actors. Within every relation, subnetwork, or wider network, there is a potential conflict between the actors concerning the distribution of the surplus and the influence on its future development. At the same time, the actors in a relation, subnetwork, or wider network have a common interest in that relation, subnetwork, or wider network as against competing relations, subnetworks, or wider networks. Thus, all over the network, there will be strong incentives to cooperate with and counteract other actors. There will be efforts to form various more or less stable, visible, and overlapping alliances in order to strengthen power in and over the network.

The industrial networks are not transparent. This has to do with the complexity, fluidity, and unequivocality of the interaction. All actors have a rather clear view of their own interaction and bonds with other actors even if the views of interacting actors are not necessarily consistent. Neither does this mean that the views of different individuals in a firm are consistent. To some extent, actors have ideas of the relations of their counterparts, and of those between some other important actors in the network. Generally, however, the ideas are vaguer about more distant relations in the network. The views of distant actors may differ widely. An observer who is not engaged in a network (for instance, a foreign network) cannot but get a very superficial comprehension of it.

The industrial network is a product of its history. The actors—organizational or individual—have memories of their interaction. They have made investments in the relations with other actors, they have developed and invested in their industrial activities on the basis of that interaction, and they have developed knowledge about their parts of the network. In this historical development, there is an inherent tendency to structuring, making the links stronger and more stable, as well as strengthening the power of established actors. On the other hand, other actors, both internal and external, may change and even break up the network. In order to exploit opportunities, they may try to establish new relations inside the network, establish relations with actors outside, change the character of old relations, or even liquidate them, or they may relate different networks to each other. Changes in the network structure, except for breaks of relations, cannot be made unilaterally. But, they can be initiated. Other actors must be influenced to participate in the change. Large changes may require considerable resources, and support by several actors may have to be mobilized. Such mobilization may be based on power relations between the actors or on common interests.

Interaction in Industrial Networks

Industrial networks emerge and develop as a consequence of interaction. Through interaction, firms exchange resources, products, and services. Through interaction, they influence and adapt to each other's ways of performing activities. Through interaction they also develop various kinds of bonds with each other.[2]

Interaction between firms implies that they are active and that their acts are dependent on each other. They base their acts on each other's acts and on anticipation of each other's acts. Interaction takes place over time. Single acts follow or precede each other. Interaction between two parties is a stream of acts. A set of acts in this stream that are close in time and related to each other constitute an episode. Such an episode may concern a negotiation, a delivery, a complaint, a technical problem, and so on.

The stream of interaction may be steady, as when similar episodes follow each other with regular intervals. The stream may also be turbulent, as when episodes of varied character follow each other in irregular or unclear patterns. Sometimes, the stream is some separate streams dealing with issues that are only weakly related to each other. Sometimes a stream parts into two separate streams; sometimes two different streams of acts flow into each other. The character of the streams is partly a matter of objective facts. Partly, however, it is a matter of interpretations and intentions of the parties involved (Weick, 1979; Giddens, 1975).

Firms are engaged in a great number of streams of interaction of different character with different parties. Those streams of interaction are connected with and dependent on each other in various ways. The character of those connections is very much a matter of the industrial activities performed in the firm and the resources needed in those activities. It is also a matter of interpretations and intentions regarding the firm's relations in the industrial network—the strategic identity of the firm. Streams of interaction may also be more directly connected with each other. A firm's interaction with an important supplier may very well be an element in interaction with its customers.

The content of a stream of interaction—or an episode or a single act—is never equivocal. What one actor mainly considers as exchange of products may be viewed by another primarily as communication or by a third as a demonstration of power

(Klint, 1985). Once again, interpretations and intentions are important elements in interaction and they may differ between the actors. Evidently, they may differ between individuals in one company as well as between individuals in different companies. Such differences may be due to differences in professional orientation, management level, or views of the company's position in the network.

Interaction between firms develops over time. It takes time to build functioning relations. The parties have to learn about each other's ways of doing and viewing things and how to interpret each other's acts. Relations are built gradually in a social exchange process through which the parties may come to trust in each other (Blau, 1964). Over time, as a consequence of interaction, bonds of various kinds are formed by the parties. There may be technical bonds which are related to the technologies employed by the firms, knowledge bonds related to the parties' knowledge about their business, social bonds in the form of personal confidence, administrative bonds related to the administrative routines and procedures of the firms, and legal bonds in the form of contracts between the firms. These bonds tend to create lasting relationships between the firms.

Interaction between firms is based on and affects the industrial activities of the firms. In interaction, they exchange resources that are used and produced in the activities. Within a firm, a number of interrelated activities are performed. Single activities are linked to each other in various ways. They constitute parts of more or less repetitive and regular activity cycles, where a number of interdependent activities are performed and adjusted to each other. Through experiential learning of handling more or less heterogeneous resources, single activities and activity cycles are gradually adjusted to and more tightly linked to each other so that, over time, a basic stability of the activities is achieved.

Furthermore, through interaction, the activities of firms are interwoven in a wider system of industrial activities where a number of different firms perform interrelated activities. Through the interaction, the firms modify and develop their activities so that, over time, they develop some kind of balance in relation to the activities of other relevant actors. In this development process, imbalances may and usually do occur.

Throughout our discussion, the importance of intentions and interpretations in the network interaction has been stressed. We mean that the firm has a strategic identity, which refers to the views—both inside and outside the firm—about the firm's role and position in relation to other firms in the industrial network. The strategic identity is formed and developed through the interaction with other firms. The strategic identity in turn governs the development of the industrial activities of the firm and its relations with other firms. The role of interaction in the development of the strategic identity, industrial activities, and interfirm relations is illustrated in figure 21–1.

The role of interaction in industrial networks can also be summarized in two ways. First, interaction is both objective and subjective. It is objective in the sense that the industrial activities and the interfirm relations have an observable effect on

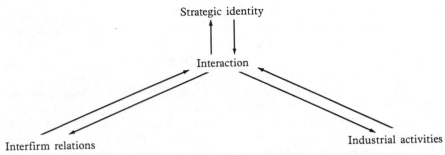

Figure 21-1. The Interplay between Strategic Identity, Industrial Activities, and Interfirm Relations

the interaction and *vice versa*. It is subjective in the sense that the actors make subjective interpretations of its meaning and base their action on this meaning. This aspect of the interaction is related to the strategic identity and cannot be reduced to structural models.

Second, interaction causes both stability and change. It is a way of coordinating the activities of firms in the network and, to that extent, it primarily serves the aim of keeping the system going. At the same time, however, the interaction contains the seeds of change. New opportunities are born in the confrontations between different interpretations of interaction.

Cooperation in Industrial Networks

It has been demonstrated that cooperation is effective in situations where actors have both common and conflicting interests (Axelrod, 1984). Cooperation is also an element in all interfirm interaction and industrial network strategies. For the following discussion, we make distinctions with regard to the formalization and the scope of the cooperation.

The distinction between formal and informal cooperation is interesting for three reasons. First, formal cooperation is more visible both within the cooperating firms and outside to other actors.

Second, informal cooperation is based on trust developed through social exchange. Generally, this cannot be attained but through business exchange. The informal cooperation evolves as a consequence of growing awareness of mutual interests. This takes time and resources. The parties invest in the relationship with each other. Thus, it can be said that informal cooperation implies that business comes first and visibility later—if it comes—whereas, in formal cooperation, visibility comes first and business later—if trust can be developed. This means that formal cooperation does not often lead to real cooperation, and that real cooperation is often not visible.

The third reason is that informal cooperation is developed by those who are directly involved in the business exchange between firms, usually line managers on the middle management level. In contrast, formal cooperation is usually entered into on a higher management level with comparatively high involvement of staff.

Differences in scope may refer to the importance and number of activities included in the cooperation. In some cases, the cooperation concerns some specific and limited activity only (standardization or information, perhaps); in others, more or less the whole strategies of the firms are included.

In the following comments about cooperation, we first focus on the networks as constraints and then on the networks as development potentials. The industrial network is a specific structure which binds together actors, activities, and resources in a certain pattern. The existence of this structure, where each firm has a strategic identity which has been captured over time, is in many ways a serious limitation of the space of action of the firm. Within the network, actors are aware that particular actors' changes also create changes for the others. Therefore, the actors watch each other closely and all acts are judged as to whether they will lead to structural changes or not. The network, in this way, becomes a frame of reference or norm and therefore also a general constraint.

The positions of all actors are continuously questioned and the firm must demonstrate that it still keeps its strategic identity in the network. It must show that it has the strength and capacity that correspond to its position in the network. Both when the firm confirms its image of itself and when it defends its position, cooperation may be instrumental. By demonstrating to others that it cooperates with central network actors, it can prove its own centrality and power. In the same way, the firm can show its loyalty to old friends in various cooperative projects. They may concern technical issues or commercial concerns such as product interchanges and licensing. The formal side of such cooperation is often important as it makes it visible both within the organization and to other network actors. In many cases, this visibility is more important than the stated purpose.

A more specific constraint is formed by all the bonds between the firms. The bonds may be (as has been discussed) technical, knowledge-based, social, administrative, or legal. They refer to the mutual interest between the actors and have to be handled in various ways. If there is a technical dependence, coordinated technical development may be required in response to other current or anticipated network changes. This can be done in technical cooperations. On the other hand, a technical cooperation may have as its main aim to maintain social or knowledge bonds.

In such cases, cooperation is usually an integrated part of the interaction in a current business relation. It is often specific and directed at solving specific problems. It aims at supporting or developing the relation. Formalization is low as a rule. One reason is that formal cooperation is interpreted as antagonistic by non-participating actors.

The network in its specific existing structure is just one of a great number of possible structures. Certain dependencies between certain actors based on certain activity patterns have been manifested, but, in most cases, there is an endless number of latent, not yet exploited relations. For every actor, there are a great number of undeveloped possibilities in terms of potential relations to central actors and to quite different networks. By building new relations, finding new cooperation partners, making new combinations, and copying the present position in other, similar networks, the firm can utilize the network as a development potential. Every such possibility has, of course, its price. Exploiting a possibility requires investments. Every possibility requires that other actors can see it is a possibility. Every possibility competes with other possibilities seen by other actors. The endless number of possibilities is therefore a problem to the firm. It has to choose, to create some internal agreement about how to exploit or develop the network and to influence other actors to see the same development possibilities. Cooperation in all its forms is an element in all development courses, but it implies the same problem as the possibilities. If the cooperations are too many and different, their effect is dividing and weakening rather than integrating and strengthening. From a total development point of view, it is consequently more important how cooperation projects are related to each other than how each of them is designed. Specific projects may have to be combined with general ones, formal projects with informal ones, and so on.

A central element in industrial network strategies is to influence other actors not only directly, but also indirectly via other actors. The network connects actors via various activity chains. Indirect influence can go via one or several actors engaged in the same activity chain as the target actor. As all actors in a network try to influence other actors directly and indirectly, there will emerge a number of partly overlapping alliances of actors promoting different competing interests concerning the future network structure. There is, however, not necessarily a direct confrontation between the alliances as the network, at least partly, can channel the forces out into other networks. Cooperation is used to hold together the alliances, as well as to reconcile differences between them. In the latter case, cooperation is often formalized; in the former cases, it is informal. In the latter case, cooperation is often specific and concentrated to neutral technical issues, such as standardization. The purpose of such cooperation is, however, not always to attain the stated result, but to maintain communication between the alliances.

International Business

The industrial network model has implications for international business analysis. The industrial networks in different countries can be expected to have different characteristics. Such differences may refer to the character of the interaction and relations, the roles of the actors, the transparency, power structure, interest structure, stability of the networks, and interdependencies with networks in other countries. Such characteristics have implications for entry strategies, control of international operations, and management of global interdependencies (Johanson and Mattsson, 1984).

The industrial network model can also cast some light on cooperation between firms in international business. First, it can be assumed that firms cooperate in order either to develop their position in the industrial network where they are already operating or to get involved in the industrial network in which the counterpart is engaged. Many joint ventures, licensing agreements, and management contracts can be interpreted as having that purpose. One party may have relations to networks where critical resources are controlled and the other to local potential customers (Sharma, 1983; Thunman, 1986; Hyder, 1986). Evidently, the same holds for the still much more common cooperations between a firm and its local agents, representatives, or distributors in foreign markets. However, many such cooperations are less formalized and, consequently, less visible.

Generally, we expect formal cooperation to be used when the parties are interested in demonstrating the presence or intended presence in the network of the counterpart. Such messages can be directed at competitors ("this market is nothing for you"), suppliers ("supply us; we are the leaders"), or complementary suppliers ("our systems are worth developing"). Similar messages can be intended for distributors, customers, technical consultants, or public authorities. It can be assumed that the tendency to use formal cooperation is stronger in international business as there are fewer developed channels for informal market communication between countries than within countries.

Informal cooperation will be used when the parties are interested in business with the counterpart's network without visibility. This may, for instance, be the case when the firm considers itself a runner-up and wants to avoid competitive moves by competitors. This is a very plausible strategy in international business with actions in networks that are not transparent to those who are not inside the network.

We can summarize by saying that firms with strong positions in their industrial network will seek formal cooperation with prestigious actors in tightly structured networks that are considered important. Firms with less strong positions will try to develop informal cooperation, thus establishing a position before it is made visible. This tendency will be accentuated in international business because of the comparatively lower transparency there than at home.

Finally, the message of formal cooperation may be intended for internal purposes. The model implies that there is a struggle within the firm about which relations to develop and about in which networks the firm should be involved. In this internal struggle, formal cooperation may be an important tool as it makes it possible for groups who control the formal side of the firm, but not the actual business relations, to commit the firm to new network relations.

Notes

1. For a summary of the network approach to markets, See Hägg and Johanson (eds.), 1982; Hammarkvist et al., 1982; Johanson and Mattsson, 1985; and Håkansson (ed.), 1987.

2. For a summary of the interaction model and its basis in interorganizational and marketing theory, see Håkansson (ed.), 1982; Turnbull and Valla (eds.), 1986; or Ford et al., 1986.

Bibliography

Axelrod, R. 1984. *The Evolution of Cooperation*. New York: Basic.

Blau, P.M. 1964. *Exchange and Power in Social Life*. New York: Wiley.

Cook, K.M., and Emerson, R.M. 1984. "Exchange Networks and the Analysis of Complex Organizations." *Research in the Sociology of Organizations*, vol. 3. New York: JAI Press.

Epstein, E.M. 1969. *The Corporation in American Politics*. Englewood Cliffs, N.J.: Prentice-Hall.

Ford, D., Håkansson, H., and Johanson, J. 1986. "How Do Companies Interact?" *Industrial Marketing & Purchasing*, vol. 1.

Giddens, A. 1975. *New Rules of Sociological Method*. Essex, U.K.: Anchor Press.

Hägg, I., and Johanson, J. (eds.). 1982. *Företag i nätverk* (Firms in Networks). Stockholm: SNS.

Håkansson, H. (ed.). 1982. *International Marketing and Purchasing of Industrial Goods: An Interaction Approach*. Chichester, England: Wiley.

Håkansson, H. (ed.). 1987. *Industrial Technological Development: A Network Approach*. London: Croom Helm.

Håkansson, H. 1986. *Teknisk utveckling genom samarbete mellan företag* (Technical Development through Cooperation between Firms). Working paper. Department of Business Administration, Uppsala University, Sweden.

Hammarkvist, K.O., Håkansson, H., and Mattsson, L.G. 1982. *Marknadsföring för konkurrenskraft* (Marketing for Competitiveness). Malmö, Sweden: Liber.

Hyder, A. 1986. *Swedish–Indian Joint Ventures*. Unpublished manuscript. Department of Business Administration, Uppsala University, Sweden.

Johanson, J., and Mattsson, L.G. 1984. *Internationalization in Industrial Systems—A Network Approach*. Paper prepared for the Prince Bertil Symposium on "Strategies in Global Competition." Stockholm School of Economics.

Johanson, J., and Mattsson, L.G. 1985. "Marketing Investments and Market Investments in Industrial Networks." *International Journal of Research in Marketing*, vol. 2.

Klint, M. 1985. *Mot en konjunkturanpassad kundstrategi—om den social relationens roll vid marknadsföring av massa och papper*. (Toward a Customer Strategy Allied to the Business Cycle: About the Role of the Social Relationship in the Marketing of Pulp and Paper). Ph.D. thesis with an English summary. Department of Business Administration, Uppsala University, Sweden.

Levitt, T. 1983. "After the Sale Is Over." *Harvard Business Review*, September–October.

Sharma, D.D. 1983. "Swedish Firms and Management Contracts." *Acta Universitatis Upsaliensis*, Studia Oeconomiae Negotiorum, 16, Stockholm, Almqvist & Wiksell (diss.).

Thunman, C.G. 1986. *Technology Licensing to Distant Markets: An Interaction Approach.* Unpublished manuscript. Department of Business Administration, Uppsala University, Sweden.

Turnbull, P., and Valla, J.P. (eds.). 1986. *Strategies for International Industrial Marketing.* London: Croom Helm.

Webster, F.E., Jr. 1979. *Industrial Marketing Strategy.* New York: John Wiley & Sons.

Weick, K.E. 1979. *The Social Psychology of Organizing,* 2nd ed. Reading, Mass.: Addison-Wesley.

Part V
A Focus on
Developing Countries

22

Cooperative Strategies in Developing Countries: The New Forms of Investment

Charles P. Oman

N ew forms of international investment—joint equity ventures and contractual interfirm cooperation arrangements—are business operations that lie in a gray area between the traditional international activities of firms (namely, arm's-length exports) and wholly or majority-owned foreign subsidiaries ("traditional" foreign direct investment, or TFDI). The number and importance of new forms of investment (NFI) have grown markedly since the early 1970s in the North–South context and since the early 1980s among industrialized countries. Statistics on international value transfers that occur in conjunction with NFI are often buried in aggregate data on trade, balance of payments, or financial flows: generally, they cannot be isolated or compared with those on TFDI. Data on foreign direct investment thus still mainly reflect TFDI. But, there can be no doubt that NFI have come to occupy a central place in the international strategies of firms around the world.

This chapter focuses on NFI in developing countries. North–South NFI patterns are described in the petroleum, mining, petrochemicals, auto, electronics, textile, and food-processing industries. The chapter also discusses the principal causes of NFI and tries to weigh some of their consequences.

The NFI Concept

The term *new forms of investment* covers a broad, heterogeneous range of international business operations that all have a common denominator: a foreign company supplies goods, either tangible or intangible, which constitute assets for an investment project or enterprise in the host country, but the foreign company does not hold majority ownership of the investment project or enterprise as such. In

The views expressed are those of the author and do not necessarily represent those of the OECD. Many of the points discussed are developed more fully in the author's forthcoming book, *New Forms of Investment in Developing Countries, Volume II: Industry Studies* (Paris: OECD Development Centre).

other words, the foreign company's equity share, if any, does not constitute owner-ship control, as it does in TFDI. But, this does not mean that the foreign company cannot exercise partial or total control over the project by other means.

Among the NFI are joint ventures in which foreign equity does not exceed 50 percent, licensing agreements, management contracts, franchising, turnkey and "product-in-hand" contracts, production-sharing and risk-service contracts, and international subcontracting (when the subcontracting firm is at least 50 percent locally owned). Many of these business forms of course are not particularly new; examples of many of them predate the 1960s. Use of the adjective *new* (it could be replaced with *nontraditional*) is meant to focus attention on the new *importance* of these business forms as a whole, given their significant growth in recent years.

An important question here is whether all these business forms can legitimately be considered investments. From the point of view of the host-country participants, they almost invariably do represent investments. But, from the perspective of the foreign firms supplying technology, equipment, or access to export markets, the answer can vary from one project to the next. Nor does the answer depend on the type of resources the firm supplies; rather, it rests on the nature of the firm's involvement in the project.

This distinction between what a given international business operation represents for the host country and for the foreign supplier of assets—an invest-ment or a sales operation—may seem academic. But, from a managerial standpoint, it is in fact crucial because it sheds light on the logic underlying the types of con-flict of interest, on the one hand, and types of convergences of interest or possibilities for strategic alliances, on the other, that are likely to characterize relations between the two parties.

When a foreign company participtes as an *investor*, it shares with its host-country partner an interest in maximizing the difference between the costs of producing the project's output on the one hand and the value of that output on the other. Often, the two parties also share an interest in generating or defending the market share of the project's output and, if possible, in generating monopoly rents in that market. In short, they share an interest in the project's success as an investment, in its future ability to generate a surplus. Conflicts of interest between the two partners arise primarily over how profits or losses are shared. In some cases, con-flict may also arise over the definition of the geographic boundaries of the market (for example, over whether or not the product is to be exported from the host coun-try, as this could conflict with the foreign company's international marketing strategy).

When, however, an investment project basically represents a sales operation for the foreign company supplying assets to the project, the foreign company's in-terest lies primarily in maximizing the difference between the prenegotiated price to be paid by the host-country partner for the assets supplied (technology, equip-ment, or whatever) and the cost to the foreign company of supplying those resources. The foreign company's concern about the future surplus-generating capacity of the project is secondary at best. The interest of the host-country participant is usually just the opposite: it wants to minimize the price–cost difference for resources supplied by the company; and the host-country party is concerned above all with the success of the project as an investment (with its long-term capacity to generate an economic surplus).

Returning to our definition, then, it is possible to distinguish between a broad and a narrow, more rigorous definition of the "new forms of investment" concept. We have already sketched out the broad definition: NFI projects are ones that are at least 50 percent locally owned, with some assets supplied by one or more foreign companies. For such a project to qualify as NFI in the narrower definition, the project should represent an investment not only for the host-country participant(s), but also for at least one of the participating foreign companies. The foreign company should regard the surplus-generating capacity of the project in the host country as a source—if not *the* source—of income and profit. This implies both that the company has a direct interest in the project's economic viability as an investment and that it has some way to appropriate or control at least part of the surplus generated. The project then represents an investment for the foreign company irrespective of its equity participation. In this definition, the foreign company must perceive its contribution to the project as an asset not only for the project, but for itself.

New Versus Traditional Foreign Direct Investment: The Trends

Is NFI superseding TFDI in the North–South context? In the 1970s, NFI grew more quickly than TFDI, but will this trend be reversed in the coming years? To what extent does NFI substitute for, and to what extend does it complement, TFDI?

Overall, the evidence points to two broad tendencies. During the 1970s, some developing countries promoted NFI over TFDI so as to enhance local control over industry and to circumvent the rent-extracting powers of multinational firms, powers seen as being embodied in TFDI. Today, they may feel as if they had jumped from the frying pan into the fire. When real interest rates were low in the first half of the 1970s, many developing countries no doubt found it easier and cheaper to pursue strategies of debt-financed growth, with greater reliance on NFI for access to nonfinancial assets when necessary. It was frequently easier to borrow than to negotiate with multinational firms over the terms of new flows of TFDI. But by the 1980s, higher interest rates and a feeling that the international banking community and the International Monetary Fund have quasi-monopoly powers in the financial markets—as well as awareness of their continuing, heavy reliance on multinational firms for access to technology and export markets—made many developing countries change their minds. That is why many of these countries, including some of the more ardent promoters of NFI during the 1970s, are now liberalizing their investment policies and trying to attract TFDI.

Even so, there is considerable evidence of a changing division of risks and responsibilities among the three principal groups of participants in North–South investment: multinational firms, international lenders, and host-country elites. It suggests that NFI will continue to gain importance—superseding TFDI in some cases and complementing it in others. In part, this reflects continued interest by some developing countries in acquiring only those components of the TFDI package (technology, management, marketing, and finance) that cannot be obtained locally. Such "unpackaging" and selective overseas acquisition of assets via NFI may be seen by some countries, including some of the more industrialized or heavily indebted developing countries, as a way to minimize the foreign-exchange costs of obtaining only those particular assets required for industrial restructuring or for sustaining local industrial capital formation.

But more importantly, the changing international division of risks and responsibilities reflects a tendency for some multinational companies to modify their views on the advantages and disadvantages of NFI over TFDI as well. Some companies, for example, are finding that they can earn attractive returns from certain tangible or intangible assets that they can supply without necessarily having to own or finance projects. By supplying assets via NFI, they can also, in some cases, benefit from increased leverage on those assets because, for example, local partners or international lenders absorb start-up costs and provide working capital. And, especially important, NFI often means reduced exposure to commercial and political risks that accompany TFDI.

There is also evidence that "newcomer" multinationals and market-share "followers" frequently use NFI to compete with the more established multinational firms. In some cases, they use it *offensively*—to penetrate or increase market shares in industries or countries where the "majors" are reluctant either to share equity (and rents) or to relinquish the decision-making power and information that might dilute their particular competitive advantages (such as state-of-the-art technology or brand names). Newcomers and followers may offer host countries shared ownership or greater access to technology in return for preferred (or exclusive) access to local markets.

In other cases, newcomers and followers are using NFI more *defensively*—in a context of globalized oligopolist rivalry in which their managerial and, especially, financial resources are stretched thin because of increased competitive pressures to take investment positions in numerous markets. By sharing technology, control, and profits with local partners, they can benefit from the latter's knowledge of local markets, access to local finance, and willingness to share or assume important risks. This phenomenon may have received added impetus during the 1970s because of rising capital costs and cash-flow problems that some firms experienced due to depressed demand conditions in their home markets.

Furthermore, whether they resorted to NFI as a competitive tool in developing countries offensively or defensively, newcomers and followers have sometimes brought considerable pressure to bear on the majors to follow suit. Finally, as technologies diffuse and products mature and become increasingly price-competitive, even the majors and market-share leaders sometimes initiate the use of NFI as part of a strategy of *divestment*. For example, if a company perceives that its control over a particular technology is waning, it may decide to obtain additional, marginal returns from that technology by licensing it and using those returns to help finance movement into newer, higher-growth activities—often in its home market or in other industrial countries. Another example is the phenomenon of "industrial restructuring" in Japan, where the government's Ministry of International Trade and Industry (MITI)—either because of changing comparative advantage or for environmental reasons—has joined forces with firms and large trading companies to transfer entire industries or industry segments to developing countries by using the new forms of investment.

Still, industry leaders often resort to NFI only in fairly protected and isolated markets; the new forms generally are considered marketing tools in countries where local production by the joint venture, licensee, or purchaser of a turnkey plant stands little chance of competing internationally with the company's core activities. This may be because the company will not supply its most advanced technology or because of relatively high production costs in the host economy, for example, due to inefficiencies of small-scale production behind tariff barriers. Industry majors that do incorporate production from developing-country affiliates into their global networks, on the other hand, still tend to rely heavily on TFDI for such affiliates.

Thus, the ultimate importance of NFI relative to TFDI in coming years is likely to be determined less by unilateral developing-country government decisions on whether to increase their efforts to attract TFDI or to emphasize selective acquisition of assets through NFI, than it is by the dynamics of interfirm competition—and by the interaction between those dynamics and host-government policies. And even though those dynamics reflect patterns of technological innovation and of supply and demand that are global in scale, they tend to be industry-specific. Hence, it is important to look at investment trends in specific sectors and individual industries, as we shall do in this chapter.

Overall, however, the evidence does point to an emerging international, interactor division of risks and responsibilities whose principal characteristics can be summarized as follows:

Multinational firms will tend to concentrate their efforts in industry segments where barriers to entry and, hence, value-added and profitability ratios are highest, while at the same time seeking to maintain or increase flexibility. They will thus generally focus on such strategic activities as technological innovation, marketing, and certain key aspects of management. These activities could increasingly become their primary bases of control and profits in a world economy characterized by the growing internationalization of production and interfirm competition, coupled with rapid technological change and considerable instability in world product and financial markets. In other words, multinational companies may increasingly become intermediaries for both the input (technology and management) and output (world market) sides of industry in developing countries, while shifting a greater share of the investment risk associated with the investment process onto international lenders and, perhaps even more so, onto their host-country partners.

International lenders—notably multinational banks, but also public national and multilateral financial institutions—may continue to play a leading role in channelling financial capital to developing countries in need of liquidity, at least those with the industrial or primary-products export potential needed to service their debt. Financial institutions may thus continue to assume control or will be delegated control over the financial dimension of the international investment process in developing countries. Within the financial community, however, the division of risks and responsibilities will vary from project to project and period to period, with private banks playing a clearly predominant role in some cases, and national or multilateral financial agencies playing an increasingly important role (via cofinancing, export credits, or mixed credits, for example) in others.

Host-country elites in the private and public sectors may increasingly retain legal ownership of the investment projects in their countries and assume, or be delegated, certain managerial responsibilities. In addition, they may take on important risks and, in some cases, increase their share of returns.

Sectoral Analyses

Risk and Responsibility Sharing in the Extractive Industries

It is in the extractive industries where one finds the strongest empirical evidence to support the argument that TFDI is being superseded by NFI. In *petroleum extraction*, the shift to NFI began to gain momentum in the 1950s and was virtually complete in Third World petroleum-producing countries by the late 1970s. In the major capital-surplus petroleum-exporting countries, service contracts are commonly used, often in conjunction with joint ventures. In contrast, petroleum-producing countries that did not generate large financial surpluses (many of which are major borrowers) often use the production-sharing formula. In the first group of countries, the interactor division of risks and responsibilities is often bilateral, between the host country and the multinational petroleum company. But in the second group, the financial dimension often involves international lending institutions. Mexico's PEMEX and Brazil's PETROBRAS, for example, received huge loans to finance exploration, production, and refining during the 1970s. Less spectacular but also important were loans to state oil companies in Algeria, Indonesia, Nigeria, and

Peru. In both groups of countries, however, there is ample evidence that multinational petroleum companies are concentrating on supplying technology, certain key managerial functions, and international marketing, while the host countries assume ownership of the investment projects along with some important managerial responsibilities.

In *metals mining*, the shift toward NFI became clear in the late 1960s, and the desire for national sovereignty over mineral resources led many developing countries to put ownership of mining operations in the hands of state or private local enterprises. Management contracts in which the managing company's remuneration is based at least in part on profits or production levels are not uncommon in new projects, and they are sometimes combined with minority equity participation by the managing company. Turnkey contracts (which typically call for the contractor to conduct a feasibility study, to provide technology and know-how, and to carry out or supervise the design, engineering, and construction as well as to supply capital equipment) have been widely used in minerals-processing projects. They are less frequent in minerals extraction itself, although they have been used in some mining projects that required major infrastructure investments. The most typical contracts since the late 1960s, however, have been between major developing-country state mining companies and international contractors (for example, a specialized engineering or construction company), in which the latter receive a fixed fee or percentage of total costs and assume little risk associated with or control over the mining project.

In sharp contrast to petroleum, the rapidly rising investment costs in metals mining have been accompanied since the early 1970s by fluctuating and, on average, depressed output prices on the world market. One result is that relatively few new mining projects are being brought to fruition. Another is that, following a period of increased restrictions on TFDI in the late 1960s and early 1970s, a number of mineral-producing countries have switched back to active promotion of TFDI. But the multinational mining companies have shown considerable reluctance to undertake major equity investments in developing countries. Those that are still active increasingly operate as mobilizers of international loan capital from public and private sources, as innovators and suppliers of production and processing technology, as project managers, and, above all, as providers of access to world-market outlets. Engineering companies that often worked as contractors to these multinationals are now contracted directly by state mining companies in developing countries.

Although TFDI has not been as completely displaced by NFI in mining as it has been in petroleum extraction, the evidence nevertheless points to major changes in the international interactor division of risks and responsibilities, with the host countries assuming major risks and costs. And the requirements of finance capital are such that "the attitudes of lenders, be they international agencies, banks, or export credit insurers, are likely to be of critical importance and may well seriously limit the freedom of manoeuvre of the host countries and mining enterprises as they reach for new models of mining agreements for the remainder of this century" (Suratgar, 1984).

The Manufacturing Sector

The evidence on NFI patterns in the manufacturing sector as a whole in developing countries is less clear-cut than for the extractive industries, both as regards the extent to which NFI are superseding TFDI and the extent to which a new interactor division of risks and responsibilities is emerging. The increased importance over the past ten to fifteen years of NFI in manufacturing is clear. But, what stands out most is the great diversity among host countries both in terms of the importance of NFI as a group relative to TFDI, and of their role in gross domestic capital formation in the manufacturing sector.

Differences in host governments' policies on foreign ownership of investments is clearly the single most important explanation for the observed diversity among countries as to the role of NFI in manufacturing. But, this diversity also reflects a complex interaction of other factors whose combined importance, especially in recent years, may well outweigh that of host governments' policies toward foreign investment as such. The factors include potential foreign investors' perceptions of: the size and growth potential of a host country's market; its political stability; the extent of its bureaucracy and the nature of relations between government and the private sector; its long-run development strategy and track record; its macroeconomic and industrial policies; and the availability of local managerial talent and skilled labor.

If one controls for such country-specific factors (and company-specific views of them), a few sectorwide patterns nevertheless seem to emerge. First, NFI are more likely to be found in investment projects whose output is destined for the host country's local or regional market, other things being equal, than in export-oriented manufacturing investments. This is because foreign investors are more likely to be willing to share ownership and some degree of control and profits with local partners in return for access—especially if it is exclusive access—to local markets, than when production is for export. And, in a similar vein, host countries are more likely to accept majority or whole foreign ownership and control in return for access to export markets and the foreign exchange earnings that export-oriented manufacturing investments, it is hoped, will bring.

Second, NFI are more frequent in investment projects using relatively stable or mature technologies than in those using high or rapidly changing technologies. This is because host countries are more likely to accept foreign ownership and control in return for access to high technology and because of their recognition that companies forced to share ownership and control with local partners are less likely to transmit continuing technological improvements that constitute key corporate competitive assets to affiliates they do not fully control. Likewise, foreign investors are more likely to share ownership and control when the technology involved in a given project is widely available and/or does not constitute a key corporate asset at home. And, for analogous reasons, investments to manufacture highly advertising-intensive products, other things being equal, are less likely to be NFI than are those that are not advertising-intensive.

Third, NFI tend to concentrate, like TFDI, in host countries' principal growth industries, or in high value-added segments within industries. This pattern of course reflects the rent-seeking behavior of foreign investment—NFI as well as TFDI. But it also points to an important corollary in terms of the nature of relations—conflicts and convergences of interest—between host-country and foreign partners in different NFI projects: those projects with promising growth and surplus-generating potential more often represent *investments* for the foreign company as well as the host country (that is, they more often correspond to our narrower definition of the NFI concept), even when the foreign company holds no equity; projects whose growth potential appears limited or doubtful more often correspond to *sales* operations for foreign participants—even in cases where they have equity participation.

But the importance of looking at global trends on an industry-by-industry basis cannot be overemphasized, if for no other reason than because of the great diversity among host countries in overall patterns, and because many manufacturing projects use NFI not as a substitute for but in conjunction with TFDI. We thus look briefly at these patterns in the petrochemical, automobile, electronics, textile, and food industries.

Petrochemicals

Until recently, petrochemicals were produced almost exclusively by the industrial (OECD) countries, but today a spectacular change is taking place, to a large extent via NFI in developing countries. Whereas in 1970, only 2–3 percent of world ethylene capacity was found in developing countries, by 1982 that share had surpassed 8 percent. It is expected to reach 20–22 percent by 1990. Similar patterns can be seen in the cases of the five major thermoplastics.

Since the mid-1970s, a large proportion of this expansion in developing countries' production capacity has been on the basis of 50:50 or minority foreign-owned joint ventures, technology licensing agreements, and turnkey contracts. The foreign companies involved in these NFI are some of the world's leading petrochemical producers, including the largest chemical companies as well as the chemical divisions of major petroleum firms.

In Latin America, the transition from a rather limited development of petrochemicals production in the 1950s and 1960s, when foreign investment was primarily via TFDI, to the emergence of large-scale, state-led petrochemical programs during the late 1970s and the 1980s has been accompanied by a marked shift to NFI—primarily joint ventures, but also licensing and turnkey contracts. In Argentina and Brazil, this shift was triggered by the general lack of interest on the part of the petrochemical multinationals in further developing local capacity through TFDI. In Mexico, U.S. companies might have been interested, but the Mexican government's extension of PEMEX's monopoly to basic and secondary petrochemicals in 1960 hindered such a move.

A notable feature of the big petrochemical joint ventures established during the 1970s in Brazil and Mexico (now the major producers in Latin America) and in Asia is the foreign firms' contribution of technology in return for equity shares. In Mexico, despite legislation in 1970 that restricted foreign ownership to 40 percent and despite a sluggish economy since 1982, the local market remains a major attraction to foreign investors—especially to U.S. firms and some large European companies (BASF, Bayer, ICI)—in downstream production. In Brazil, most production is also for the local market, although foreign partners are now being asked to promote exports and to help develop high value-added products as well. Another important feature is the extent to which NFI in Brazil and Mexico have led to major advances not only in substituting local for foreign hardware and detail engineering services, but also in local appropriation of skills and know-how in state-of-the-art process design engineering and in research and development. This trend is reflected, for example, in Brazil's third NFI agreement signed in 1977 with Technip of France and KTI of the Netherlands. These firms agreed to supply all the technical engineering data, including the technology to obtain and update those data, along with technical assistance and training of local technicians. In fact, Brazil has assimilated the technology so well that it now supplies some other developing countries with petrochemical technology and production know-how.

In Asia, several developing countries—India, the Republic of Korea, Taiwan, and the member countries of the Association of Southeast Asian Nations (ASEAN)—have significant petrochemical capacities, and the People's Republic of China is expected to have substantial capacity by the end of the decade. India's production dates back to the 1950s. Its 1963 petrochemical development plan, prepared with the help of the French Petroleum Institute, aimed for a pattern where basic production would be in local hands and downstream production would be in those of joint ventures. But India's experience has been less successful than Mexico's, and there is no clear division of responsibilities between sectors. Some TFDI still exists; some NFI came in, largely during the 1960s (mostly joint ventures with U.S. and European firms); and production is almost exclusively for a not very dynamic domestic market.

In the Republic of Korea, state-led development of the industry by private firms has resulted in considerable use of joint ventures and licensing, mostly involving U.S. and Japanese partners in downstream products, with ethylene now totally in Korean hands. Korea's first complex was completed in 1973, and a world-scale complex came onstream in 1979; the former relied heavily on 50:50 joint ventures, whereas the latter involved fewer joint ventures and more domestic firms with licensing agreements. Downstream production appears to be moving into Korean hands as well: some foreign partners, such as Dow, have been bought out; and technology has been acquired through arm's-length licensing, as happened in 1984 with Union Carbide.

In Taiwan, the pattern is not unlike that of Korea, with the notable difference that all the foreign partners in Taiwan are U.S. majors—perhaps reflecting U.S.

political motivations to help develop the Taiwanese industry. Korea's Lucky Group and Taiwan's Formosa Plastics Corporation have become important suppliers of technology to other developing countries. In 1983, Saudi Basic Industry Corporation (SABIC) chose Lucky to be its joint venture partner in its largest polyvinyl chloride plant, and it chose the Taiwan company as its partner in a urea plant.

In the ASEAN region, Japanese firms are involved in petrochemical joint ventures in most countries but, apart from Singapore, this is largely through turnkey and licensing contracts, with little capital contribution. In Singapore, by contrast, the Japanese have played a leading role since the late 1970s in setting up a world-scale complex in which the Singapore government is a 50 percent shareholder. (Philips and Shell are participants in two downstream facilities.) The project was designed to produce for export to the ASEAN region as well as for the Japanese home market as part of Japan's vertical integration/relocation strategy. Now, however, Japanese commitments to import from Saudi Arabia are highlighting problems of excess supply.

The creation of major petrochemical capacities in the Mideast is undoubtedly the most striking recent development for the industry worldwide and for the OECD countries in particular. Saudi Arabia alone has eleven major production facilities, all of which are 50:50 "first-generation" joint ventures between SABIC and one or more multinational firms (primarily Japanese and U.S. ones, with the latter being mostly petroleum companies). In every instance, SABIC and the foreign partner each put up 15 percent of the project's capital needs as equity, 60 percent is provided by the Saudi Public Investment Fund in the form of long-term low-interest loans, and the remaining 10 percent is raised from commercial banks; a ten-year tax holiday is also provided. Technology has not been capitalized as part of the foreign partner's equity share, but is the object of separate contracts, and usually third-party technology has been chosen. Thus, it is obviously the foreign firms' ability to penetrate OECD petrochemical markets that constitutes their key "immaterial asset"; it also explains both the highly favorable financial and fiscal arrangements provided by the host country and the difference between the foreign firms' 15 percent contribution to financial needs and their 50 percent equity shares.

By and large, the major petroleum and chemical companies' decisions to meet the demands of various Third World countries to help develop their local petrochemical capacities and to use NFI to do so reflect strategies these companies came up with in response to important changes in the industry starting in the early 1970s. One such change was the shift from rapid growth and high profitability during the 1950–70 period to a maturation of the industry in the OECD area, with a slackening of growth potential and profits. Another major change came with the two successive oil-price hikes, which greatly increased the share of naphtha feedstocks in total output costs. The latter has had a crucial impact on profitability as well as on cost structures. In virtually every OECD country except the United States, which has oil and natural gas resources, the petrochemical industry that developed prior to 1973 has been caught between the need to pass on cost increases to safeguard financial viability and the difficulty of doing so because of depressed demand conditions.

The pattern of petrochemical investments in the developing countries points up the fact that newcomers—which in this industry include the Japanese petrochemical firms and U.S. petroleum companies—often use the new form of investment to gain favored access to new markets and to force some of the majors to follow suit. The substitution of NFI for TFDI now appears irreversible. Some of the major developing-country producers are apparently trying to do without foreign investment altogether, except when foreign partners can help penetrate OECD markets. It is also worth noting that South–South collaboration has been growing primarily through NFI. This movement may well be accentuated by China's large demands for technological and industrial NFI in this industry.

The Auto Industry

TFDI still dominates investment in vehicle *production* in developing countries. (Production implies over 50 percent local content, whereas assembly implies over 50 percent of imported parts and components.) But such investment is heavily concentrated in only a few countries: Brazil, Mexico, and Argentina. There were a fair number of joint ventures and licensing agreements during the early years of auto production (notably in the 1960s), but, even then, TFDI accounted for a larger share of production. Since then, most majority locally owned producers based on NFI have folded or have been absorbed by majority or wholly foreign-owned subsidiaries.

The other major auto-producing developing countries today are India and Korea. Foreign investment in India has been limited mostly to licensing, and production has been largely confined to models quite outdated by international standards. Now, however, Japanese investments in minority joint ventures are growing rapidly. In Korea, two firms dominate production. Hyundai was a wholly Korean-owned producer and is now 85 percent Korean-owned. (Mitsubishi has taken a 15 percent equity share in return for its contribution to finance and international marketing.) Hyundai's Pony or "Excel" automobile (developed with the collaboration of various foreign suppliers of design, technology, and finance) is now a competitor in world markets. Daewoo is in a 50:50 joint venture with General Motors (GM); the venture is not yet very active in exports, and Daewoo took over management from GM in 1983.

Car *assembly* presents a very different picture. Minority joint ventures and licensing play an important role in numerous developing countries (including ASEAN members, the Andean countries, Iran, Nigeria, and several North African nations). The investment pattern in assembly operations suggests that: (1) host-government restrictions on foreign ownership are a major factor behind NFI; (2) auto companies that are market-share followers often use NFI offensively to gain favored access to local markets (pressuring the leaders to follow suit in some cases) and/or defensively—to benefit from local partners' sharing risks and contributing to finance and marketing efforts; and (3) the industry leaders tend to use NFI only when local production cannot compete internationally with the core activities of their international integrated production and marketing sytems. NFI, notably joint ventures and licensing, are also somewhat more prevalent in the commercial-vehicle and component segments of the industry than in auto production per se.

The pattern of North–South investment in the auto industry reflects above all the high level of worldwide concentration in this industry, the very significant economies of scale in production (which are greater in passenger cars than in commercial vehicles), and the financial and technological advantages of subsidiaries of the major auto multinationals vis-à-vis majority locally owned firms that rely on NFI. It also reflects the importance that such industry leaders as GM and Ford attach to retaining full control and ownership of their affiliates, which operate within increasingly integrated worldwide production and marketing networks. Meanwhile, the Japanese majors continue to prefer to keep production at home. Korea's experience is thus unique among developing countries; and its success is far from assured, particularly given the relatively limited size of the country's domestic market.

Electronics

The electronics complex may be defined as covering three distinct segments: microelectronic components (semiconductors and integrated circuits), consumer electronics (radios, television, hi-fi equipment, electronic watches, hand calculators, and toys), and computers.

In *microelectronics*, increasing price competition, the relatively labor-intensive nature of the assembly and testing of semiconductors, and the relatively modest fixed-capital requirements led a number of major firms to set up assembly and testing operations in some Asian and Latin American countries in the early 1960s. But those operations, which produce virtually exclusively for OECD markets, involved mostly TFDI. In the late 1960s and especially in the 1970s, however, locally owned subcontracting companies were set up in a number of countries, including Hong Kong, the Philippines, and Taiwan. They were often established on the basis of contracts with smaller OECD-based firms that supplied equipment and technical and marketing assistance. Furthermore, in countries such as Brazil, Korea, and Taiwan, recent efforts to increase semiconductor production capacities have given rise to a number of NFI arrangements. A few examples are the licensing agreements between the Brazilian firms, Itan and Docas, and several European firms; licensing between Korea's Sam Sung and the U.S. firm, Micron Technology; a joint venture between Gold Star in Korea and the U.S. AMI; and licensing between Taiwan's state enterprise, ERSO, and RCA in the United States.

In *consumer electronics*, licensing and joint ventures provided the basis for some developing-country producers, especially in East and Southeast Asia, to develop their production capacities. In the early years, assembly of radios and black-and-white television sets was the principal activity; but this led to greater local production of components, to the production of more sophisticated products, and finally, in countries such as Korea and Taiwan, to the mastery of production techniques and technology by local firms. In the past few years, some of these firms have actually set up production subsidiaries in OECD countries—there are Korean subsidiaries in the United States and Portugal and a Taiwanese color TV producer in the United Kingdom.

In *computers*, foreign investment in developing countries remains limited. This is particularly so in the case of large computers, in which what investment there is tends to be dominated by the TFDI of a few major companies. Efforts to promote the development of national production capacities, notably in Brazil, have given rise to licensing in mini- and microcomputers and in such peripherals as printers, screens, and disks. And it is principally market-share followers—such as Sycor (United States), Logabax (France), Nixdorf (the Federal Republic of Germany), Fujitsu (Japan), and Ferrati (United Kingdom)—that have supplied production technology through NFI. On a much smaller scale, China, Korea, and Mexico have also begun to develop national computer industries, mainly through licensing and joint ventures.

In short, the pattern of NFI in the electronics complex points up the importance of rapid technological change, which explains why the majors are reluctant to share ownership or to license their most up-to-date technologies with developing-country producers. It also highlights the use of NFI by some followers, primarily as an offensive tactic to gain access to potentially important markets in some newly industrializing countries. Such companies may also seek to amortize research and development expenditures through licensing activities in developing countries. Future negotiations in this industry undoubtedly will focus on the issue of access to developing-country markets in exchange for access to rapidly changing production technology, particularly in microelectronics and computers.

Textiles

In the textile industry, international investment has played a less important role in the development of production capacity in developing countries than it has in other manufacturing industries of comparable importance. This is consistent with the observation that both TFDI and NFI tend to concentrate in host countries' major growth industries. The textile industry has not been a major growth industry for the Third World as a whole during the past two decades.

But, in those developing countries where the industry had been a growth leader, foreign investment—especially NFI—usually has been important. Such is clearly the case of the three leading exporters: Korea, Taiwan, and Hong Kong. It is also true in a number of emergent or "second-tier" textile-producing countries, with the notable exception of India.

To understand the patterns of international investment in this industry, it is important to recall that the industry comprises three main segments: fibers (synthetic and natural), textile-mill products (fabrics), and end-use products (notably apparel). Also key is the role played by the international quota system in apparel trade under the Multi-Fibre Arrangement (MFA), which strongly influences the flow of textile production and technology from developed to developing countries and within the Third World.

World production of synthetic fibers is dominated by a handful of OECD-based multinational chemical companies. The top twelve alone accounted for some 60 percent of world output in 1980. One result is that TFDI plays a bigger role than NFI in this segment, especially compared with the other two segments. Large capital costs, economies of scale, and patent protection constitute major barriers to entry; and relatively few developing countries have embarked upon synthetic fiber production. New forms of investment—especially by a few U.S. and European fiber producers (the latter being an integral part of their countries' larger, oligopolist chemical industries)—have been important in some of the larger Latin American countries. Nevertheless, new forms of investment have helped develop fiber-production capacity in some Third World countries. The most active investors have been the Japanese fiber companies, which are part of vertically integrated textile groups; and they have done so primarily through joint ventures, licensing of know-how, and plant exports with technical assistance—particularly in Asia and to some extent in Latin America.

Compared with the fiber industry, the role of international investment in textile-mill products has been limited. This segment has been developed in many Third World countries on the basis of imported, often second-hand machinery. Only Japanese firms have been really active in this segment, and, again, their involvement has been largely through minority joint ventures, licensing, and plant exports with technical assistance. Many of the smaller Japanese firms have used NFI (especially joint ventures) to relocate production capacity, often under the umbrella of the large *sogo shosha* (general trading companies) in conjunction with Japan's restructuring of its textile complex during the 1960s and early 1970s. It is worth noting that about two-thirds of the sales of Japanese textile affiliates in developing countries go to local markets, about a quarter to third-country markets, and less than a tenth to Japan.

But it is in the apparel industry, more than any other segment of the textile complex, that NFI have been of crucial importance—and TFDI has been insignificant—in recent decades. Textile and clothing manufacturers as well as apparel retailers and buying groups in the OECD countries have played a major role in the development of apparel production for export from developing countries. These principals supply designs and raw materials, organize shipping, provide advertising and brand names, and control distribution channels. Most of this is done through international subcontracting with locally owned firms. The contracts are normally short-term (about one year), which allows the principals to shift important risks and costs associated with demand fluctuations onto the subcontractors while retaining virtual control over operations.

Among the first to make extensive use of international subcontracting were Japan's trading companies, which set up agreements with local producers in Hong Kong, Taiwan, and Singapore. Starting in the late 1960s, they worked mostly for export to the U.S. market. Some of this activity has been taken over by U.S. buying groups, and it has been expanded considerably both by these groups and by U.S. textile and apparel manufacturers. Among the European firms, German manufacturers have been the most active in using Asian subcontractors. The main motivations have been labor-cost reductions in a context of slow demand growth and intense price competition (and, in Japan, rapid wage increases).

Whether or not this type of offshore apparel processing continues to grow will depend largely on the nature and speed of technological change in the clothing industry. One of the major transformations that industrial countries may be able to carry off is to reduce labor costs markedly while increasing production flexibility through robotization; apart from high-fashion apparel, they have no comparative advantage today. (If import pressures on textile and clothing manufacturers are creating serious difficulties in some OECD countries, these problems should be attributed less to NFI in developing countries than to domestic restructuring difficulties—for example, in moving up-market or, as in the United States, in modernizing production.) Obviously, continued expansion will also depend on protectionist trends in the OECD region and the distribution of Multi-Fibre Arrangement quotas among developing countries.

It should also be noted that the MFA quotas, along with the high costs of new production technology and other barriers to international marketing, create major obstacles to developing countries aspiring to join the ranks of major textile and apparel exporters. The quota system has had a major influence on the spread of production to second-tier producing countries, a movement in which NFI has played a central role. But the consensus seems to be that most of the emergent producers, with the exception of China, are not likely to join the ranks of the major exporters in the foreseeable future.

Food Processing

Although TFDI predominates foreign investment in food-processing plants, the trend is clearly one of increasing use of NFI. Particularly important are joint ventures in which the foreign partner supplies sophisticated product technology and, often, a brand name and advertising experience, while the local partner provides assured access to raw materials. Other NFI of growing importance in the industry include licensing and franchising, the latter especially in fast foods.

The fact that the majors and market-share leaders in food processing still rely heavily on whole or majority ownership of their processing plants suggests that such firms are reluctant to share equity (and rents) or to relinquish decision-making power that might dilute their competitive advantages, notably in marketing and brand differentiation. But, there is also considerable evidence that some newcomers and followers are using NFI offensively, to penetrate markets in competition with some of the majors. Sharing production technology and control with local partners, such firms benefit from the latter's knowledge of local markets and ability to share risks (as well as to insure supplies of raw materials). They have thus sometimes exerted considerable pressure on competitors, including the majors, to follow suit.

These patterns in turn suggest that the future of NFI will depend largely on the dynamics of interfirm rivalry, especially on whether more newcomers and followers will want to expand through NFI. Although a relatively low level of concentration in the industry works in favor of such a trend, it is important to remember that most international investment is still in the OECD region, where the emphasis is on acquisitions and mergers.

Several observations confirm that the new forms of investment, such as TFDI, tend to be concentrated in the high value-added segments of this industry. The branches in which both the majors and the newcomers have become the most involved are brand-name and differentiated processed foods as well as milk products, fruits, and vegetables. They are not usually in mass-consumption food products, as they tend to concentrate their activities in the higher-income markets. An important exception is, of course, beverages. Some foreign companies have used mass-marketing techniques to create mass-consumption markets for their drinks.

Another phenomenon is the use of new forms of investment (notably contract growing) to shift the risks of primary production onto local growers, while keeping control over the high-value-added segments of the food-chain, namely processing and marketing.

Structural changes in developing countries also account for some increased use of NFI. In many countries, especially in Latin America, the process whereby modern elites have consolidated their power has been accompanied by, and indeed has sometimes depended on, import-substitution industrialization. This has usually created internal terms of trade that are unfavorable to agriculture. Consequently, there has been a massive migration to urban centers with an accompanying rise in urban food demand. It was in this context that the change in foreign-investment patterns in Latin American food production took place: from heavy reliance on TFDI in the production of mostly unprocessed export produce, there was a shift to contract growing by food processors producing primarily for local urban markets.

Implications of New Forms of Investment

From a managerial perspective, few sweeping generalizations should be made about the net advantages to be gained from investing via NFI rather than TFDI in developing countries. Obviously, much depends on the specific competitive strengths and weaknesses of a given firm, as well as on global trends in different industries and conditions in different host countries. But the general observations made earlier are worth reiterating: many companies, including some that first engaged in NFI in developing countries only because host-government regulations left them few alternatives other than complete withdrawal, have come through experience to appreciate the potential advantages of NFI over TFDI in terms of risk shedding and increased leverage, particularly on certain nonfinancial, often intangible assets that they possess. Others, particularly relative latecomers or market-share followers, have found NFI to be an effective means of penetrating new markets and/or increasing market shares in competition with established multinationals. Indeed, these features appear to explain an important number of NFI that have developed in industrialized host countries in the past few years as well. And many companies have found that just as ownership of equity does not necessarily imply effective control, so minority or zero equity does not necessarily imply inadequate control.

Another interesting implication of the continuing proliferation of NFI is that, as familiarity with its use and potential spreads worldwide, it may come to be used as a vehicle by many small- and medium-sized firms to internationalize their operations. Such firms have tended to be excluded from TFDI because of their limited financial and managerial resource bases compared with the major multinationals'. But, in theory at least, smaller firms should be able to exploit via NFI certain types of assets they commonly possess (for example, a unique product technology, or organizational or technical know-how better adapted to small-scale production). And the collective importance of smaller firms in industrialized countries is so great that the stimulus to such firms that would result from their multinationalization via NFI could have a major positive impact on the economies of their home countries. It would also of course greatly increase the potential supply of productive assets to host countries—and, in doing so, could well increase the competitive efficiency of many sectors worldwide—while strengthening the bargaining position of developing countries in their negotiations with potential foreign investors.

But the evidence calls for caution. There has not, as yet, been a massive proliferation of small- and medium-size firms using NFI to internationalize their operations. And of those that have, many are subcontractors or suppliers to a relatively small number of large multinational companies, with the latter generally having retained positions of dominance in international investment in developing countries.

As regards the implications for host developing countries, NFI can offer important advantages compared with TFDI, but greater risks as well. Among the potential risks, perhaps the most important are those associated with the decision of whether to invest and with the choice of the size of capacity to be installed. Under NFI, these decisions are commonly assumed by host-country firms or governments and are thus more likely to be delinked from world market conditions and the supply of technology. Under TFDI, the risks and responsibilities associated with long-term investment decisions, supply of technology, financing, and marketing of output are normally assumed by the multinational firm; its decisions are likely to be based on a careful and knowledgeable assessment of worldwide conditions of supply and demand. The local participant in a NFI venture rarely has an information and planning horizon as international in scope as a multinational, and its ability to keep abreast of technological innovation and changing world-market conditions is likely to be more limited. Decisions may be influenced more by local production potential, investment costs, the country's need for foreign exchange, or even political considerations than by projected global supply and demand.

One result may be continued host-country dependence on foreign firms for access to new technology and world-market outlets, even though those firms may be less committed to the success of the investment project than they would be under TFDI. (They may even take measures to insure that the NFI project cannot compete with their global system.) The danger is that the gains in local control or share of returns obtained by the host country may not be commensurate with the increase in risks assumed and the costs incurred. There have been cases of large NFI projects whose viability depended on exports (as, for example, in mining, steel, petrochemicals, and autos), but whose output could not be sold profitably on world markets. There also have been cases of NFI in highly cost-inefficient, local-market projects to which local elites were more economically and politically committed than they would have been to a TFDI project, but whose survival called for high output prices behind even higher import barriers and large public subsidies. TFDI projects are not immune to such problems, of course, but the potential risks and costs to the host country may be considerably greater under NFI.

Exacerbated long-run disequilibria in global supply and demand trends, with a tendency toward overproduction and overcapacity worldwide in some important industries, are thus also dangers for host countries—and for the global economy. Such dangers undoubtedly explain why some firms approach certain investment projects in developing countries as sales operations rather than as investments. Indeed, certain NFI projects may be a response to short-term problems of host countries and foreign firms alike. But in some cases, these projects risk creating or aggravating disequilibria in host economies and internationally in the longer run. And insofar as NFI not only reflects but also reinforces the tendency of firms to shorten their investment-planning horizon, these disequilibria may be accentuated. It should be emphasized, however, that with the bulk of production capacity in most industries still located in the OECD region, and with the bulk of international investment still occurring (and increasingly so) within this region, such a negative impact of certain NFI projects on the global economy could, at worst, exacerbate problems of overcapacity whose origins lie—and whose solutions must be found—in the industrialized OECD countries.

Among the potential advantages of NFI for host countries, the most important is undoubtedly the possibility for increased local control over the process of capital formation, and for a larger share of returns from investment. There can be little question that NFI have favored such control in some cases: witness the Japanese postwar experience, for example, as well as events in South Korea during the 1960s and 1970s. In other cases, NFI have at least favored a higher host-country share of profits; petroleum extraction is a case in point.

But for a given host country, the crucial question is how to take advantage of what NFI can potentially offer—and whether it might not do better with TFDI (perhaps in conjunction with improved fiscal policies or performance requirements). The evidence suggests that the answer generally depends less on the country's foreign-investment policies as such (although these should be reasonably stable and transparent) than on the coherence and effectiveness of its overall industrial and macroeconomic policies. Much also depends, of course, on the relative bargaining strength of local elites vis-à-vis their international counterparts. This bargaining strength in turn depends on such factors as the size and dynamism of the local market and the level of development of local technological, managerial, and entrepreneurial capacity—and, hence, also on the ability of local elites to take advantage of rivalry among foreign firms.

Insofar as host countries, but also smaller foreign firms and other newcomers to international investment, are able to exploit the potential advantages of NFI, the growing use of NFI could have far-reaching implications. By combining the strengths and interests of host-country elites and the international business and finance communities, certain NFI have already opened the way to the development and capitalization of activities in developing countries that were either new to those countries and to foreign investors (such as petrochemicals) or backward and undeveloped (such as peasant farming). Given the vast development needs and growth potential of the Third World at a time when growth in the OECD region has slowed considerably by postwar standards, it would be reasonable to infer that by opening important new avenues of growth and longer-term business opportunities, NFI may hold important positive-sum-game implications not only for host economies, but also for the global economy. In the extreme, it is conceivable that NFI may in the long run do for accumulation and growth internationally what the advent of the limited liability joint stock corporation did a century ago in the national context of today's industrial economies. Like the corporation, NFI provide a legal and institutional framework in which entrepreneurs, owners of physical assets, and financiers can join forces, separate equity ownership from effective control, and divide risks and responsibilities.

Reference

Suratgar, D. 1980. *International Project Finance and Security for Lenders.* Paper presented to the German Foundation for International Development Conference of International Mineral Resources Development—Emerging Legal and Institutional Arrangements, Berlin.

23

Successes and Failures of Joint Ventures in Developing Countries: Lessons from Experience

William A. Dymsza

A joint venture in a developing country generally involves at least three parties: the transnational corporation (TNC), the national partner (which is often a local firm), and the host government. It can also involve the home country of the TNC (which does not play a major role in many cases); external financial institutions, such as the International Finance Corporation, regional development banks, bank consortia, or individual commercial banks; local investors and financial institutions; and other interests. The negotiations of the basic character and terms of the joint venture arrangement among these parties play a major role in determining its ultimate success or failure, as indicated in figure 23–1.

Criteria of Success or Failure of Joint Ventures

The success or failure of joint ventures is a relative matter, subject to considerable controversy on the part of scholars in the field. Essentially, I here adopt a pragmatic approach based upon field studies of fifteen joint ventures, comprehensive personal interviews of the parties involved in thirty-five others, examination of many writings about these and other ventures, and interviews with government officials in many developing countries, supplemented by mail questionnaires to which over one hundred firms responded. Without going into all the complexities involved, my criteria are that successful joint ventures are those that survive over a reasonable period of time, generally over eight years, and the major parties involved—the TNC, the national partner(s), and the host government—perceive sufficient benefits in relation to costs.

Figure 23–1 shows a model of key factors involved in the success and failure of joint ventures from the standpoint of the TNC, the national partner(s), the host

This chapter is based upon a larger study undertaken for the United Nations Centre on Transnational Corporations. The study involved case studies, personal interviews, and mail questionnaire responses involving a little more than 100 multinational firms, about 80 percent in the United States and the rest in Western Europe. This was supplemented by examination of various other sources of information.

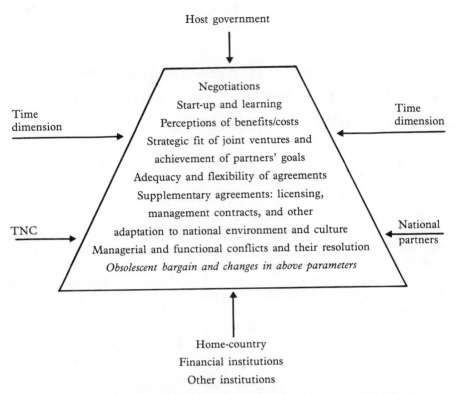

Host government

Time
dimension

Time
dimension

Negotiations
Start-up and learning
Perceptions of benefits/costs
Strategic fit of joint ventures and
achievement of partners' goals
Adequacy and flexibility of agreements
Supplementary agreements: licensing,
management contracts, and other
adaptation to national environment and culture
Managerial and functional conflicts and their resolution
Obsolescent bargain and changes in above parameters

TNC

National
partners

Home-country
Financial institutions
Other institutions

Figure 23-1. Major Factors in Success or Failure of Joint Ventures

government, and other interests involved. This model emphasizes the negotiation process determining the basic aspects of the venture; the start-up and learning period involving the principals in the arrangement; the strategic fit of the venture and its achievement of major goals for the parties; the appropriateness and flexibility of the venture agreement; the character of supplementary agreements; adaptation of the TNC to the country environment and culture; the adjustment of the TNC and national partner(s) to each other's management style and culture; the management and functional conflicts between the principals; and the capability of the TNC, the national partner(s), and host government to resolve conflicts, the obsolescing bargain, and other changes in fundamental conditions. All of these factors have to be considered within a dynamic time frame over the life of the venture. This model essentially shows the complex relationships between the three major parties and others involved—interactions that determine the success and failure of joint ventures in the developing country setting.

In the body of the chapter, I start off with a discussion of broad combinations of factors contributing to successful joint ventures; I then go into specific elements.

To emphasize these factors, I shall show examples from actual joint ventures. Since much of the information I obtained is confidential, I shall disguise the names of the TNCs, the national partners, and occasionally the products involved; in some cases, I shall change the names of the host nations. The same procedure will be followed with respect to the discussion of failures in joint ventures. I have to strongly emphasize that the factors in successful as well as failed joint ventures are often interrelated. Generally, a combination of factors leads to the success or failure of a joint venture.

Key Factors That Lead to Success in Joint Ventures

Achievement of Major Goals

The successful joint venture fosters the achievement of major goals by each party to the joint venture. The major goal of the transnational corporation (TNC) may be to enter into a manufacturing operation in a developing country with a considerable size of market, growing market potential, reasonable risk, and opportunity for a satisfactory rate of return in the medium or longer term. Responding to the foreign investment policies of the host government and taking strategic initiatives to utilize its firm-specific oligopoly advantages, the TNC finds that the joint venture route is the most viable way to attain the goals just stated. On the other hand, the national partners may have the goal of entering into a profitable manufacturing operation with a prestigious TNC, which can provide essential technology, business know-how, and trademarks. The national firm finds that the joint venture is the most feasible way of attaining such goals. Through the joint venture arrangement, the host government aims to attain several possible goals, including contributions to industrialization and economic development, increases in national income and employment, and possibly balance of payments improvement and development of backward areas of the country. It also aims to have nationals to control manufacturing businesses.

> In a pharmaceutical joint venture in South Korea with 51 percent ownership by the U.S. TNC and 49 percent by the national firm, the U.S. company obtained some equity for its contribution of process and product technology and set up a manufacturing plant for production of dosage drugs in the growing Korean market, to which it found export penetration increasingly difficult because of trade barriers and increased competition from foreign licensing. The Korean partner, on the other hand, obtained the manufacturing and product technology, which enabled it to engage in the manufacturing of dosage drugs in a modern plant through the affiliate, develop its production and marketing capabilities, and make a good

return on its investment. The Korean government obtained a drug manufacturing plant (which had a high priority in its economic development) and later some expansion of exports.

Complementary Contributions by Partners

A successful joint venture provides for complementary contribution of resources by the major parties involved—contributions that are valued by the principals. The contribution of the transnational corporation depends upon the industry in which it is involved, its product or product lines, its business orientation, and many other factors. In many manufacturing operations, the major contribution of the TNC comprises manufacturing technology, product know-how, patents (if any), business expertise, technical training, and management development. The significant contributions of marketing-oriented companies may be product differentiation, trademarks, brand names, effective marketing programs, and training. Even though TNCs in joint ventures are not necessarily export-oriented or prefer to export from their home country or wholly owned subsidiaries, some of them do make available their global marketing network to expand exports.

The national partner in a manufacturing joint venture commonly contributes some combination of capital, management, knowledge of the country environment and the market, and contacts with the government, financial institutions, local suppliers, and labor unions.

In a joint venture by a U.S. TNC in packaged foods in Venezuela, initially with majority ownership which was later reduced to 49 percent equity, the U.S. company provided product know-how; trademarks and brand names; and major aspects of promotion, distribution, selling, brand acceptance, and other components of marketing; along with modern design and procurement of equipment for the manufacturing operation. The local partner, a family-run business which had served as import distributor for the TNC in the past, contributed its existing plant and warehouse; local currency financing; on-the-spot supervision of all contractual arrangements and government clearances for modernization of the plant; hiring and training of local workers; its existing sales force as a nucleus for the marketing effort; its knowledge of the local economy, political situation, and culture; and general management.

Synergies of Combining the Contributions of the Partners

A more successful joint venture creates synergies through the partners pooling their resources, capabilities, and strengths. These synergies lead to the establishment of a manufacturing operation in which the total results are greater than the sum of the contributions of the partners. As a result of combining the modern production processes, the product know-how, technical training, management development, and management systems of a transnational company with the national partner's local capital, management, existing plant, marketing expertise, and knowledge of the country environment, the joint venture results in a more efficient and productive enterprise than the participants could achieve on their own. The synergies occur through the partners working closely together, reinforcing each other's strengths, cross-pollinizing with ideas concerning management of the enterprise, responding to competition, and developing the potential of the business in the country environment.

> In a chemical joint venture with 40 percent ownership by a U.S. TNC and 60 percent equity by a Mexican firm and local investors, the synergies occurred by the U.S. company and the Mexican partner assuming joint responsibility in construction of a modern plant suitable to the country; hiring, training, and developing workers, technicians, and managers; establishing appropriate management processes, including strategic and operational planning and control; and developing an effective marketing program, including distribution, selling, pricing, advertising, and customer service, which fitted the conditions of the country. This close cooperation has continued between the partners, even as Mexicans have assumed most of the top and middle management positions.

Entry for Smaller and Medium-size TNCs

The joint ventures can provide a suitable means of entry into a manufacturing operation in a developing company for a smaller or medium-size international company, with limited capital and some management with international experience, but no great breadth in such management. At the same time, it limits the exposure to risk by such an international company. The national partner in such a joint venture provides a combination of local financing, an existing plant and facilities, most of the management, its marketing expertise, and relationships with the government, financial institutions, and other groups. The manufacturing technology, the product know-how, technical training, and business expertise contributed by the TNC lead to a more efficient manufacturing and marketing operation, introduce new products, or improve existing products. The government, in some cases, is more receptive to a joint venture by a smaller or medium-size TNC than to one by a large enterprise. The result is a successful venture.

> Through a joint venture arrangement, a medium-size Dutch firm was able to enter into a manufacturing arrangement in Colombia with 49 percent ownership with a local firm for the manufacture of cotton and synthetic

textiles. The Dutch TNC provided hard currency financing; assisted in procuring additional machinery and its installation; provided know-how to improve the quality of products and expand the product line; and helped to train local personnel. As a result, the Colombian firm, which provided its existing plant, warehouse, and offices, its distribution and marketing expertise, its contacts with local banks, and most of the top and middle management, was able to engage through the joint venture affiliate in a modern and profitable textile operation—one that exported about 15 percent of its output within five years.

Conversion of a Licensing Arrangement into a Successful Joint Venture

A successful joint venture can be established from a licensing arrangement that may have been successful over a number of years, but no longer is suitable to develop the full potentials of a business. The joint venture can induce a TNC to make more significant contributions in a combination of manufacturing and product technology, technical training, management, marketing expertise, and capital for a manufacturing operation in a developing country, since it has much greater potential for profits and return on its investment. When such resources of the TNC are combined with the local capital, the plant and facilities, the management, the marketing organization and expertise, and the knowledge of the country environment of the national firm, the business can be much more successful than the previous licensing arrangement.

A major U.S. electronics TNC and a Philippine manufacturer converted a long-standing licensing agreement into a joint venture to manufacture appliances in the Philippines, after the licensing arrangement was no longer suitable for both firms and the government. The U.S. company negotiated initially for 52 percent of the equity for its contribution of improved manufacturing and product technology, technical assistance, production and financial management, trademarks, and marketing assistance. The Philippine firm contributed local capital, its existing plant and facilities, most of the top and middle management, and its sales organization.

Comprehensive Joint Venture Agreement

The joint venture agreement between the partners should be comprehensive and cover all major aspects of the business. The contract should state the major goals of the partners; their specific contributions of assets, their responsibilities and obligations; the equity contributed by each party and their share of ownership; the means of raising other financing, including working capital; the products; the customers and markets served; the composition and responsibilities of the board of directors; procedures for the selection of top and middle managers; provisions for technical training and management development; the supplementary licensing, technical, and management agreements which are part of the joint venture arrangement; provisions for safeguarding patents, trademarks, and technical secrets; duration of the agreement and ways of modifying it; management processes, including strategic and operational planning and the control and information system; sources of supply for raw materials, intermediates, and components; accounting standards; reporting requirements; the audit and review of financial statements; means of settling disputes, including mediation, arbitration, and use of national courts; and procedures for dissolution of the business and distribution of assets. It would also be advisable for the contract to cover major matters, such as prior agreement on policy concerning declaration and distribution of dividends; reinvestment of earnings; major marketing programs; the capital structure, including debt-equity relationships and future financing; and the rights, if any, of either partner to veto the appointment of top managers or the establishment of key managerial policies. Such comprehensive provisions in the agreement can help to deal with many sources of possible difficulties.

Joint Management Responsibilities

A joint venture generally performs better if the TNC and the national partner assume major managerial responsibilities and share in key decisions. Both parties should participate actively in the meetings of the board of directors and strive for agreement on major policies of the enterprise throughout its life. Based upon its greater managerial experience and competence, the TNC commonly assumes greater managerial responsibilities during the initial phases of the joint venture, but joint management is fostered by using the particular competencies of the national partner, its involvement in major decisions over time, and training and development of local managers to assume top and middle management positions. Involvement of the national partner in more and more managerial decisions develops its capabilities in joint management. The management processes established (such as strategic and operational planning, budgeting, financial and other controls, the information and reporting system, and organizational development) also foster joint management participation, but they have to be adapted to the management styles of the partners and to local customs. Conflicts and disagreements may arise between the TNC and national partner, but they can be resolved through negotiations, compromises, and goodwill, plus thinking of the mutual interest of the parties, the common goals, and the future of the business.

A U.S. TNC and a Thai manufacturer entered into a joint venture with 50:50 ownership to manufacture paper products. The two partners have an equal number of members on the board of directors, have shared responsibility in formulation of major policies, and within four years have engaged in joint decision making on production, marketing, finance, personnel, and other aspects of the operation. The joint venture affiliate adopted a modified type of strategic and operational planning, budgeting, financial controls, an information system, and periodic evaluation of managerial performance and bonuses as part of its joint management. Joint management has become a reality through the learning process and by experience; it has played a major role in the success of the joint venture.

Different Degrees of Allocation of Managerial Responsibilities

A joint venture can succeed with different degrees of sharing of responsibilities in management as long as the partners are content with the allocation. Realistically, complete sharing of management responsibilities is difficult to achieve in many joint ventures, given the differences in the strengths, resources, and experiences of the TNC and the national partner. Further, the determination of managerial responsibilities may vary over time, as the TNC provides managerial training and development and the national partner acquires considerable managerial competence. Many patterns of allocation of managerial responsibilties can exist in successful joint ventures. A number of joint ventures are successful even when the TNC retains critical managerial responsibilities, even with minority ownership. In some cases, the TNC retains authority to appoint key managers or the right to veto crucial managerial decisions. In other circumstances, the national partner shares in the formulation of major policies, but leaves most of the operational decisions to the TNC. On the other hand, the national partners in other joint ventures assume all or most of the top and other executive positions and run the ventures, with some technical and other guidance by the TNC. What is crucial is that the partners accept the allocations of managerial responsibilities, are satisfied with the progress of the venture, and perceive sufficient benefits, including its profitability, growth, and viability.

> In a joint venture by a U.S. chemical TNC with 51 percent equity with a local partner and financial investors in Nigeria for the manufacture of pesticides and other agricultural chemicals, the U.S. company provided the process and product technology, technical assistance, and top and most of the middle management. The U.S. TNC assumed responsibility for production, finance, marketing, organization, planning, control, and the major part of the decision making. The local partner has been represented on the board of directors and has provided information on political, economic, and regulatory conditions; has maintained relationships with the government authorities; and has assisted in improving the marketing effort, particularly sales to farmers.

Control of Key Aspects of Joint Venture Arrangement

Many TNCs with key resources that give them firm, specific advantages enter into joint ventures with local partners if it is required by governments, but they strive to control key aspects of the business. Although many high technology TNCs generally prefer 100 percent ownership, companies that do enter into joint ventures with local partners strive to control the diffusion of their technology. Marketing-oriented companies that emphasize product differentiation, segmentation of markets, trademarks and brand names, and promotion and selling strive to control these activities in joint ventures. Other companies having major strengths in mass production, high productivity, quality control, computerized manufacturing, organization, finance, and other aspects of management make every effort to control these resources in joint ventures. Despite considerable control of key aspects of management and the business by TNCs, the joint venture can prove to be successful from the standpoint of the local partner and the government, as well as the TNC.

Control is a relative matter; even in these types of joint ventures, local partners control other aspects of the business and generally expand their control over time, as they gain technical, production, marketing, financial, organizational, and other competencies. The developing-country governments often impose various requirements with respect to location of plants in less-developed areas of the country, employment and training of nationals, increased local content, placing of nationals in key managerial positions, performance of some research and development in the country, and export expansion. Even though the government performance requirements do not always work and may have some adverse trade-offs, some of these requirements, along with the increased competence of national partners, lead to reduced control by the TNC and a wider diffusion of benefits from a modern manufacturing operation, which probably could not exist without the joint venture arrangement.

A French TNC entered into a 49 percent-owned joint venture with a local firm to manufacture tires in Morocco. Although the French company had major responsibility for setting up the plant and for production, finance, and marketing management at the beginning, the Moroccan firm assumed the key managerial and technical responsibilities and most decision making in the joint venture affiliate within five years.

Licensing Agreements and Management Contracts as Part of Joint Ventures

Successful joint ventures may have supplementary agreements, particularly licensing agreements and management contracts, between the TNC and the affiliate. The TNC partner, which provides significant product and manufacturing technology, patents, trademarks, and secret know-how enters into a licensing agreement, in order to obtain a return for these scarce resources which it has developed over a period of time. The transfer of these resources becomes an essential ingredient for the manufacturing operation to be established and to operate (in many ways similar to a wholly owned foreign manufacturing subsidiary).

The conditions of the licensing agreement, including the payment of royalty, have to be negotiated with the national partner and often have to be approved by the host government. Such licensing agreements as part of joint ventures work out satisfactorily when the TNC provides suitable, modern technology and the royalties are considered reasonable by the national partner and the host government authorities. The royalty should be related to the availability and costs of comparable technology from other sources and its contribution to the successful operation of the venture. Further, the TNC should justify the payment of royalties over the life of the venture on the basis of its continuing contribution of newer process and product technology. In some instances, the TNC may supplement a licensing agreement with a management contract.

In cases where the TNC makes a substantial input of its management and engages in major training of local managers for the affiliate, a joint venture can succeed with a management contract. Some TNCs provide scarce management talent, for example, in manufacturing, finance, marketing, organization, planning, and control; they may also train local managers to assume such responsibilities. Thus, they expect to obtain a return for these vital contributions to the learning process of the joint venture affiliate.

> As part of a 50 percent owned joint venture with a national company in Peru to manufacture chemicals, rayon acetate, and polyester fibers, the U.S. TNC has entered into a licensing agreement with the joint venture affiliate. Under this arrangement, the TNC receives a royalty as a percentage of sales and a percentage of profits earned for its contribution of process and product technology; the TNC makes available its new technology to the affiliate. Under this arrangement, the licensing agreement has been advantageous to the local company and has been approved by the Peruvian government.

> A U.S. TNC with a 51 percent joint venture in Thailand with a family business for production of appliances entered into a management contract for five years, under which it supplied production, technical, and marketing management for a fee. Manufacturing expertise, quality control, product specifications, revamping the marketing effort, training of detailed sales force, and brand management were all of vital importance for the success of the joint venture. These essential aspects of management were furnished by the TNC by means of the management contract; in addition, the TNC trained Thai managers to assume major responsibilities for these functions.

Transfer Pricing and Joint Ventures

While major problems can exist in a joint venture with respect to the purchase of intermediates, components, and other products from a TNC and the issue of transfer prices, the partners involved in a number of these types of businesses have been able to work out satisfactory arrangements. In some cases, the TNC may be the only readily available source of supply for a joint venture operation (at least during the early years of operation) or the TNC may feel that it should supply components and intermediates in order to assure required quality for production of the end product. The national partner, in turn, wants assurance that the prices charged by the TNC are arms-length, competitive, and fair, since so many cases exist of TNCs using transfer pricing as a means of increasing their income or shifting profits from higher-tax to lower-tax countries or using other types of manipulative pricing. Provisions in the joint venture contract that the TNC will base prices upon arms-length pricing, cost plus agreed margins, or competitive international prices can help to deal with this problem, but they do not guarantee a full resolution. Furthermore, similar types of provisions can deal with sales of the end product by the joint venture affiliate to the TNC or its various subsidiaries.

Despite the complexities, a number of TNCs and national partners have worked out satisfactory ways of dealing with these issues. These arrangements can include not only contractual provisions just mentioned, but also agreements that the joint venture affiliate can purchase materials, intermediates, and components from the lowest-cost source available, as long as it meets quality and delivery standards. Further, in many cases, efforts can be made to develop national sources of supply—a matter that the government encourages. The local partner also has an advantage in a joint venture affiliate over a 100 percent-owned subsidiary because it can examine all invoices, evaluate alternative availabilities, and take action to protect the affiliate from abusive transfer pricing. But, in the last analysis, the TNC and the national partner need to have goodwill and sufficient common interests to work out such problems.

In a joint venture between a U.S. TNC and a Mexican firm to manufacture power-generating equipment, the U.S. firm sold essential components to the affiliate at an agreed cost plus a standard margin. Further, the affiliate was permitted to purchase such components from other international or domestic sources if they were available at a lower equivalent price. Over the years, more and more of these components were produced in Mexico and the sales of these components by the U.S. TNC declined appreciably.

Reduction of Ownership by a TNC in a Joint Venture

Over time, as the TNC's contributions become less significant to the operations of the manufacturing joint venture, it may have to reduce its ownership as a result of pressures of its national partner and the government and turn major managerial responsibilities over to its partner. Vernon (1977) has described the "obsolescing bargain," under which the bargaining position of the TNC declines and that of the partner increases, as the partner gains considerable experience and expertise in production, finance, marketing, and other managerial functions and does not need the resources of the TNC as much any more. The TNC makes less significant contributions to the joint venture manufacturing and marketing operation, but continues to obtain an inordinate share of profits and royalties from the business. In some cases, the TNC may strive to make new contributions by making available new process technology and product expertise and by expanding product lines. While the situation varies depending upon the importance of these continuing contributions or resources by the TNC, the role of the TNC in the joint venture operation and its bargaining position may continue to decline. Thus, it may be forced to turn over more ownership and responsibility for management to the national partner as well as to renegotiate the licensing agreement in order to continue to be involved in a successful operation.

> In response to the pressure of its partner (a local manufacturer) and the Philippine government, a U.S. electronics TNC decided to reduce its equity from 52 percent to 40 percent in a joint venture to produce and market appliances in the Philippines. Over the years, the Philippine firm had developed the manufacturing, technical, product, and marketing competencies and taken over most of the managerial responsibilities, except manufacturing and finance. Besides a reduction in its equity to 40 percent, the TNC agreed to a new licensing agreement reducing its royalty from 5 to 2 percent on sales.

Resolution of Disputes in Joint Ventures

Many successful joint ventures provide for ways for resolving disputes between the TNC and the national venture in the operation of joint ventures. Disputes between the partners can take place on many matters, including management appointments, payment of dividends, reinvestment of earnings, joint venture expansion, new financing, salaries and benefits, pricing policies, advertising and promotion, brand management, expansion of product lines, modernization of plant, purchases of raw materials, intermediate and component costs, quality controls, distribution channels for products, and export development. As stated previously, a comprehensive joint venture contract should deal with most of these vital matters, so that a substantial degree of consensus exists between the partners. Close and continuing communications are also essential.

Still, as the operation proceeds, misunderstandings and disputes often occur between the TNC and the national partner on some of these issues. Some of these disputes can be resolved by face-to-face meetings and give-and-take discussion between the parties. An executive committee of the key managers representing both parties can also deal with disputes. Disputes involving major managerial policies can be referred to the board of directors, where both partners are adequately represented. Board of directors may have outside directors agreeable to both partners; these outside directors can play an important role in resolving disputes.

Whenever the TNC and the national partners perceive adequate benefits from the joint venture arrangement, they should be able to make compromises or trade-offs in order to continue a successful operation. In cases of deadlock, the TNC in certain cases has veto power over key matters, such as appointments of top managers and major aspects of manufacturing, marketing, and finance. In some other joint ventures, the local manager has taken over many of the key managerial functions and can exercise control over key areas of contention. Finally, major disputes between a TNC and a national partner can be resolved by arbitration.

A successful 50:50 joint venture in South Korea to manufacture industrial machinery with a U.S. TNC and a Korean firm provides for a board of directors of five members, with two members appointed by the TNC, two members selected by the Korean firm, and an outside member appointed by mutual agreement of the partners. The board of directors meets monthly and deals with all major managerial policy issues. One of their major functions is to resolve any disputes on managerial policies. They have succeeded in doing this, particularly since both parties have vital interest in continuing a successful and growing joint venture manufacturing operation.

Financial Arrangements as Part of Joint Ventures

A number of successful joint ventures have required various types of financing, including local financing by development or commercial banks, TNC debt financing or guarantees, and financing by international commercial banks, Eurodollar banks, and regional and international financial organizations. As the patterns of financing have become more complex, I can hardly go into details about the many intricate ways of arranging financing of establishment or expansion of joint venture industrial operations, but I can show a few examples.

A U.S. TNC involved in a joint venture to manufacture industrial machinery had to restructure the arrangement in 1977 to bring in a new national partner and reduce its equity to 40 percent. As part of the new agreement, it had to guarantee a loan by Mexican banks to the local partner. Two years later, when the joint venture affiliate expanded its manufacturing operation, Eurodollar medium-term loans were obtained through two U.S. banks.

Another U.S. TNC participating in a joint venture to manufacture industrial chemicals in Brazil with a national firm assisted in obtaining a Eurodollar five-year term loan through a commercial bank in New York. At the same time, the Inter-American Bank granted a ten-year loan for the manufacturing operation, guaranteed by the Brazilian government.

A cement-manufacturing joint venture in Sudan involving a Spanish TNC and a local business group has obtained a combination of debt and equity financing from the International Finance Corporation.

Key Factors in Failures of Joint Ventures

Joint ventures have had a high rate of failure, since many of them break up. Although complete data are not available on failures, the 180 U.S. firms studied in the Harvard Multinational Enterprise Project withdrew from a total of 103 joint ventures between 1955 and 1965 and from 831 ventures in the decade from 1966 to 1975. These data include withdrawals by U.S. MNCs from joint ventures in developed nations as well as in developing countries. Still, unquestionably many of these breakups of joint ventures were in developing countries.

Executives of TNCs prefer to discuss successful joint ventures more than those that fail. Further, they prefer to present information about the problems and weaknesses of the joint venture form of business in general terms, rather than grant specific details on projects that failed. Many executives consider this confidential business information which might affect their business standing and future competitive positions. This opinion is understandable, because many TNCs have liquidated their positions in unsuccessful joint ventures with considerable losses. Further, they have undergone difficult and unpleasant experiences. I would have liked to have obtained more complete information from national partners in joint ventures that failed, in order to have a fuller perspective, but this has proved difficult. Nevertheless, I have synthesized considerable information on factors involved in failures of joint ventures and pieced together a number of brief examples from personal interviews, short cases, and other sources of information.

The analysis of factors involved in successful joint ventures presents a good framework for understanding the reason why a number of these ventures fail. The failed joint ventures lack one or a combination of factors which lead to successful arrangements. We turn to a more specific discussion of major elements that have led to failure of joint ventures in developing countries.

Significant Differences in Major Goals of Parties

The TNC and the national partner in a manufacturing joint venture that fails may have significant differences in their goals with respect to the business. Since the partners in a joint venture can have a number of different goals depending upon the size and type of companies involved; their particular business, industry, and products; their international and other experience; and many other factors, I can only mention a few differences in goals. A TNC may desire to enter into a viable and expanding manufacturing operation through a joint venture that will yield a target rate of return on investment in the medium and long term; therefore, it strives to reinvest a substantial portion of earnings in the venture in order to expand the operation and increase its return over this time horizon. The local partner, on the other hand, enters into the joint venture to earn a good immediate rate of return on its investment; therefore, it strives for maximum payout of dividends. The situation, of course, can be the reverse. The TNC may have the goal of a quick payback on its investment of capital, technology, and management—for example, three to five years. The local partner may strive to develop a growing, profitable manufacturing business yielding satisfactory profits over the medium or long terms.

A U.S. TNC involved in a 51 percent-owned joint venture to manufacture industrial machinery in Argentina had a basic goal of expanding the operation in the 1970s by reinvesting most of the profits to take advantage of a growing market; it aimed for a target rate of return of 20 percent on equity over many years. The Argentinian partner, on the other hand, had the goal of obtaining immediate payout of dividends. The partners experienced a stalemate, which interfered with the successful management of the operation. As a result, the U.S. firm sold out its interest in the venture to the Argentinian partner within four years, at a considerable loss.

TNC's Global Integration and Local Partner's National Orientation

A number of joint ventures fail because the TNCs strive for global integration of their business, while local partners emphasize the operations within the country. Many TNCs aim to maximize their profits or earn a target rate of return on their investments globally, rather than maximize their business in a particular country, including those in which they have joint ventures. Accordingly, the TNCs strive to integrate their joint venture affiliates with their system of enterprises around the world in production, finance, marketing, and management. Further, since joint venture affiliates in developing countries are generally a small part of the total international business of most TNCs, they may not grant high priority to them in resource allocation, management, and technological effort. On the other hand, the joint venture manufacturing commonly represents a major business involvement for the local partner. Thus, the national partner commits major capital and management effort to the joint venture affiliate and expects comparable commitment from the TNC in order to have a highly successful business. Serious conflicts can emerge when the local partner finds that the TNC does not grant high priority to the joint venture and does not commit sufficient resources and effort. These conflicts can become deeper and the joint venture may fail.

An Italian TNC, which had a joint venture with a family firm in Turkey to assemble agricultural machinery, strove to integrate production, finance, and management with its European-wide operations and to import and interchange components with its European and African affiliates. The Turkish partner and the government pressed the TNC to increase its investment to produce more components in Turkey, something which the Italian firm resisted. After five years of controversy, the Italian TNC disinvested by selling its interests at a loss to a German company.

Perception of Unequal Benefits and Costs

A perception by the TNC or the national partner that it is not obtaining sufficient benefits from the joint venture in return for its contribution of resources leads to the failure of some ventures. What counts is not only the actual contributions made by each party and the profits and other benefits obtained by each one, but even more what the partners perceive over the life of the operation. In some cases, the TNC perceives that it is not obtaining an adequate return for its contribution of manufacturing and product technology, management, technical training, trademarks, and business expertise. In other instances, the national partner believes that its contribution of existing factories and facilities, management, local capital, sales organization, and contacts with the government are excessive in relation to its share of ownership, the responsibilities it has in the venture, and the profits it earns. These perceptions of benefits obtained in relation to contributions made can change over the years. When one or both partners perceive an unsatisfactory ratio between benefits and costs from the venture, serious conflicts develop, which lead often to the failure of the venture.

A local firm involved in a 51 percent-owned food-processing joint venture with a U.S. TNC in Colombia perceived that the U.S. company was contributing standardized, mature process and product technology and trademarks which had limited value in the country. The Colombian firm believed that its contribution of local capital, a plant and warehouse, general management, distribution system, sales force, and contacts with the government were substantially greater in value than that of the United States TNC. Considerable conflict ensued between the parties when the Venezuelan firm strived to increase its equity and its share of profits and the government restricted remittance of dividends. After the conflicts were not resolved, the U.S. company divested by selling out its interests to the local firm.

Joint Venture Agreements and Failures

When the joint venture contract does not clearly specify the goals of each party, the resources contributed by the partners, their major responsibilities and obligations, their rights, the character of the business, their share of profits and their mode of distribution, ways of resolving disputes, and other key aspects of the venture, disagreements can take place; these can disrupt the venture.

I previously showed major components that should be covered in the agreement. A satisfactory agreement is important but not sufficient, because close and continuous communications between the partners, a learning process, and adaptation to changing conditions are also significant.

Conflicts over Decision Making, Managerial Processes, and Style

The strife between a TNC and a local partner to control major policies and decisions constitutes a major reason for the failure of certain joint ventures. The TNC may strive to control major policies of the venture through appointment of a majority of the board of directors, including outside, allegedly neutral directors, who are favorable to it. The role of the board of directors of joint venture affiliates varies a great deal. Some boards determine major policies of the venture, select the chief and top executives, and monitor the overall management and operations of the enterprise, but many boards primarily grant advice to the chief executive and perform rather perfunctory responsibilities. Other boards assume a legal function to meet the requirements of the law.

TNCs control the management of joint venture affiliates in other ways. They obtain authority to appoint the chief executive and key managers; they establish the managerial and control processes and have the right to veto major decisions. The continuing control by the TNC of combinations of manufacturing, finance, marketing, reinvestments and expansion, sourcing, and other decisions in the venture often leads to major conflicts with the national partners and the host governments. These conflicts can lead to failure of joint ventures.

Major differences with respect to management processes, style of management, and corporate culture between the TNC and national partner can lead to serious conflicts which contribute to the failure of joint ventures. For example, TNCs may strive to impose their processes of strategic and operational planning, an information and control system, budgeting, and accounting on the joint venture affiliate. The local partner may not have any experience with these processes and consider them not suitable. A U.S. TNC may emphasize a more participatory style of management, delegation of responsibility to subordinates, profit centers, and periodic evaluation of performance. The national partner, which is often a family-run business in developing nations, may have a more authoritarian management, with no delegation of responsibility to subordinates and very little formal planning and control. Although such differences in management processes and style can sometimes be harmonized through a learning process in the joint venture, they can often disrupt the venture.

A U.S. TNC involved in a 51 percent-owned joint venture with a national firm in Brazil attained the right in the contract to appoint the president plus top executives in finance, production, and marketing as well as the power to veto key decisions. As the venture proceeded, the Brazilian firm felt that it had highly competent executives in general management and financial and marketing management and was in the process of increasing its competence in manufacturing; it strived to have such managers take over key responsibilities and to eliminate the right of the U.S. company to veto managerial decisions. After the TNC would not yield its managerial prerogatives, a stalemate developed, which led to the dissolution of the venture.

A U.S. TNC involved in a 50 percent joint venture in industrial machinery with a family-run firm in South Korea strived to impose a major part of its strategic and operational planning system, budgeting, reporting and information system, and financial and other controls on the affiliate. The Korean partner resisted the imposition of these management processes on the grounds that they were unsuitable and irrelevant for the management of the affiliate and would interfere with its actual management. As a result of this conflict, along with other disagreements in the management of the joint venture, the operation was terminated within five years.

Differences between the Partners Concerning Marketing

A joint venture between a marketing-oriented TNC and a national firm can fail because of major differences between the parties about marketing policies and procedures. Many highly marketing-oriented TNCs strive to avoid joint ventures, but when they do enter into them because of the requirements of host governments, they strive to adopt their own marketing systems, based upon product differentiation, aggressive promotion and advertising, selling, and emphasis upon trademarks and brand names (Stopford and Wells, 1972). Some TNCs work for standardization of their marketing mixes globally, but they do adapt some aspects of marketing to the national environment and institutional setting. They consider control of the key elements in the marketing mix in a joint venture essential in their type of business. Having a dissimilar experience in their own country, the national partner may strive to adopt different marketing programs and procedures, with less emphasis on product differentiation, promotion, aggressive selling, and trademarks. The TNC and the national partner may also differ on pricing practices, market segmentation, introduction of new products, and marketing expenditures. As a result, the partners may encounter serious conflicts in marketing management which result in stalemates in decision making and, ultimately, a failure in the joint venture.

A highly marketing-oriented European TNC with a 45 percent-owned joint venture with a former distributor in Pakistan to manufacture detergents and personal products encountered major differences in marketing policies and procedures with its partner. The TNC insisted upon controlling product specifications, pricing decisions, promotions, and advertising, and it strived to place emphasis on its trademarks and brand names. The Pakistani firm, on the other hand, wanted to limit promotion, advertising, and brand emphasis; have responsibility for pricing based upon a high markup and low volume; and emphasize its distributions system. The disagreements on marketing paralyzed the operation. With growing dissention, largely unprofitable operations, and problems with the government, the TNC divested its ownership position.

Transfer-pricing Conflicts

Major conflicts can erupt between partners in joint ventures with respect to purchases of materials, intermediates, and components of the affiliate from a TNC and issues of transfer pricing. Some TNCs strive to have the joint venture affiliate purchase intermediate goods or components from it on the grounds that it assures required quality standards and meets delivery requirements and that competitive alternative sources are not readily available. National partners, on the other hand, want to explore alternative sources in order to obtain the materials from lowest-cost suppliers internationally or domestically. They may believe that the TNCs charge excessive prices and aim to earn additional income from selling the intermediates to the affiliate. If the TNC presses aggressively for continued sales of these intermediates to the affiliate, despite the fact that the partner finds other suppliers at competitive or lower prices, serious conflicts arise between the partners to the venture, which can disrupt relationships.

Dow Chemical entered into a 50 percent-owned joint venture with the Korean Pacific Chemical Corporation (KPCC) to produce vinyl chloride monomer (VCM) in South Korea in 1974. Dow Chemical sought to have the joint venture affiliate purchase its chlorine requirements from its wholly owned subsidiary, Dow Chemical Korea, Ltd. Unexpectedly, the Korean partner resisted purchasing the material from the Dow plant, because it felt that it could obtain these intermediates at lower prices from other sources. Sharp conflicts prevailed between Dow and the Korean partner. By 1982, KPCC had decided not to continue to purchase any more chlorine from Dow. Faced with substantial losses from its wholly owned subsidiary and its joint venture affiliate, Dow proposed a merger of both chemical operations in South Korea, with KPCC becoming a minority partner in a restructured joint venture. KPCC rejected the merger proposal. After considerable pressure by Dow and public accusations by Dow against its partner, the Korean government supported its local enterprise rather than give way to a foreign TNC. As a result, Dow sold out its chemical interests in South Korea to a consortium of local firms, taking a loss of $100 million (Levy, 1984; various issues of *I.L.&T. Korea* and *Business Asia*).

Royalties, Management Fees, and Headquarters Charges

Allocation of headquarters administrative costs, royalties on licensing agreements, technical fees, and management fees in supplementary agreements negotiated by TNCs in joint venture arrangements can lead to serious conflicts with the national partners and in some cases with host governments. Even though joint venture contracts may provide for such payments to the TNC in supplementary agreements, the national partner may scrutinize such charges while the joint venture operates, in order to avoid excessive or unreasonable charges to the business. For example, the partner or the government may find royalties on licensing agreements excessive, when the TNC contributes no new technology. Management fees may be considered unjustified, if national managers are not trained to take over managerial positions in the process. Particularly troublesome are allocations of a share of headquarters administrative costs by a TNC to a joint venture affiliate. The national partners in joint ventures may want to revise licensing agreements, management contracts, and other supplementary agreements, when they perceive that the TNCs are not providing the technological, managerial, technical, and training inputs to justify the continued payments of royalties, management and technical fees, and other charges. As a result, serious conflicts between the TNCs and national partners erupt, which can lead to impasses and failures of joint ventures.

> A German TNC involved in a 50 percent-owned joint venture with a local Nigerian partner and investors for the manufacture of industrial and agricultural chemicals had supplementary agreements to charge an allocation of its corporate overhead to the joint venture affiliate and a licensing agreement for ten years under which it obtained a royalty of 5 percent on sales for the technology it provided to the affiliate. After three years of operation, the Nigerian partner initiated negotiations with the TNC to stop payments of the allocation to corporate overhead. The German TNC resisted. A year later, the Nigerian firm started negotiations to reduce the amount of royalty in the licensing agreement. After the German firm refused, the Nigerian government, in support of its local firm, suspended allocations of foreign exchange for corporate overhead payments and authorized limited remission of royalties. Faced with difficult negotiations, dissention, and conflict, the German firm divested.

Decline in Resource Contribution by the TNC

A TNC may not respond to a decline in its bargaining power in a joint venture arrangement resulting from a reduction in the value of its technological, product, managerial, and other contributions to the business. The national partner may have significantly developed the capabilities to take charge of manufacturing, marketing, finance, and other key aspects of the venture and may find that it has far less need for the expertise of the TNC partner. Accordingly, it initiates renegotiation to take over a larger share of the ownership and to assume control over the top management; it may also strive to renegotiate a licensing agreement, particularly to reduce the royalties. Despite the fact that the national partner perceives that it needs the TNC much less than previously, the TNC may resist major reduction in its ownership and managerial responsibilities as well as a renegotiation of the terms of the licensing agreement. As a result, the partners reach a stalemate; the joint venture operation suffers and may break up in time. In other cases, the host government make take the lead in renegotiating for a reduction in equity and control over management by a TNC, which is resisted by the TNC, even though its technological, managerial, and other contributions to the venture have declined over the years. Once again, the result may be failure of the joint venture, as the TNC resists essential changes in its position.

> A U.S. TNC involved in a joint venture with 55 percent equity to manufacture consumer electronics in Mexico resisted pressure of its partner, a Mexican industrial group, to reduce ownership to a minority position. The Mexican company also initiated negotiations to reduce the royalty on the licensing agreement from 4 percent to 2 percent on sales, on the grounds that the process and product technology were not sophisticated. The Mexican government strongly supported the position of the local firm and put major pressure on the U.S. company to comply. After two years of renegotiation, the U.S. TNC sold out its interest in the joint venture affiliate.

Other Factors in Failure of Joint Ventures

Joint ventures in developing countries fail for many other reasons similar to those involved in the lack of success of many wholly owned subsidiaries. For example, host-country regulations, including performance requirements and operational restrictions, can lead to failure of some ventures.

Further, increased political instability and risk, high rates of inflation, frequent and sharp currency devaluations, and exchange control on remittances of dividends and royalties in some developing countries have led to disruptions or failures of joint ventures. Some joint ventures also fail because of severe economic declines in the host country and profitability of the ventures.

Conclusion

Using the experiences of U.S. and Western European transnational corporations, this chapter has analyzed many key factors involved in the success and failure of joint ventures in developing countries. It has considered broad as well as specific factors, but I have to emphasize that many of them are interrelated. Much more research remains to be done on this subject. The information available should be helpful to transnational corporations, potential local partners, and host governments, in view of the increasing importance of joint ventures.

Bibliography

Business Asia. Various issues.

Business Latin America. Various issues.

Davidson, W.H. 1982. *Global Strategic Management.* New York: John Wiley.

Dymsza, W.A. 1984. "Joint Ventures in Developing Countries: Trends and Perspectives." Singapore. *Proceedings of the International Business Conference.*

Franko, L.G. 1971. *Joint Venture Survival in Multinational Corporations.* New York: Praeger.

Friedman, W.G., and Beguin, J.P. 1972. *Joint International Business Ventures in Developing Countries.* New York: Columbia University Press.

I.L.&T. Various issues.

Levy, B. 1984. "The Perils of Partnership: Dow in Korea." In K. Moskowitz (ed.), *From Patron to Partner.* Lexington, Mass.: Lexington Books.

Robinson, R. 1983. *Performance Requirements for Foreign Business.* New York: Praeger.

Stopford, J., and Wells, L.T., Jr. 1972. *Managing the Multinational Enterprise.* New York: Basic Books.

Tomlinson, J.W. 1980. *The Joint Venture Process in International Business.* Cambridge, Mass.: MIT Press.

Vernon, R. 1977. *Storm over Multinationals.* Cambridge, Mass.: Harvard University Press.

24

Countertrade: A Form of Cooperative International Business Arrangement

Donald J. Lecraw

Countertrade—the exchange of goods for goods in international trade—falls within this general rubric of *Cooperative Strategies in International Business.*[1] Countertrade often combines elements of international trade, licensing, foreign direct investment, and international finance. It involves active management cooperation, often over extended time periods, by the exporting firm, the importing firm, other producers and exporters, countertrade intermediaries, and banks.

The next section of the chapter outlines the major forms of countertrade and their distinguishing characteristics. Subsequent sections analyze the economic rationales for and against countertrade; assess the implications of this economic analysis for strategic cooperation between firms; and present some data on the determinants of usage by firms of countertrade and its implications for success in international operations.

Characteristics of Countertrade

Countertrade can be most broadly defined as trade in which a purchase by an importer is made conditional on a reciprocal purchase by the prospective exporter or a third party acting on its behalf. There are four broad groups of characteristics of countertrade: the type of countertrade arrangement, the regulations and requirements governing the countertrade transaction, the institutional mechanisms by which the arrangement is carried out, and the countries involved in the countertrade transaction. These characteristics influence the management of a countertrade arrangement and the cooperative management strategy of each of the parties involved.

Types of Countertrade

There are seven generic types of trade arrangements that fall under the broad definition of countertrade:

Barter: The pure exchange of goods and services.

Counterpurchase: The assumption by an exporter of a transferrable obligation through a separate, but linked, contract to accept as full or partial payment goods and services from the importer or importing country.

Compensation or *buyback:* An agreement by an exporter of plant and equipment to take back part of the output produced by these goods as full or partial payment.

Production sharing: Conceptually similar to buyback, but mostly used for natural resource and energy projects.

Industrial offsets: Requirements placed on the exporter by the importer or importing country to produce part of the product, source parts, or assemble the product in the importing country. Exports from the importing country may also be required.

Switches: The requirement by a country that possesses a trade surplus with a second country that an exporter from a third country accept goods and services from the second country in payment for goods purchased by the first country.

Unblocking funds: Some countries with foreign exchange constraints block the remittance of funds accumulated there. These funds may be used by the firm or transferred to another firm for use there or for export abroad.

Several of these forms of countertrade may also involve taking, as part of the payment, partial equity ownership of the firm supplied by the producer-exporter. In production-sharing and buyback arrangements, although the producer-exporter may receive no formal, legal equity ownership, it receives a claim on a contracted percentage or volume of the operation's output for a number of years or into perpetuity. These forms of countertrade are particularly difficult for firms to manage. Payment for their exports is contingent on the performance of the importing enterprise in the future. Yet, their ability to influence, much less control that performance is limited since, in most cases, they do not have the legal authority based on majority equity ownership. A similar situation arises in some counterpurchase arrangements. The producer-exporter receives payment in the form of goods produced by a third firm that is in turn paid by goods or money from the importing enterprise. The producer-exporter often has no legal authority to insure that the importer pays the third firm, which in turn may be unwilling to ship prior to payment.

Only about one in ten countertrade arrangements is ever finalized and there are numerous examples of countertrade arrangements that have led to losses for one of the participants. Some of these stories seem humorous to those not involved and add spice and an exotic flavor to countertrade operations. For the firms involved,

of new Japanese investments in manufacturing for each three-year period between 1970 and 1984. The growth in the number of these investments is evident.

Within the broader, more obvious trend of increasing numbers of Japanese-owned manufacturing firms in the United States lies another surprising change. There is evidence that Japanese investors are becoming more receptive to partnership arrangements with U.S. companies. This change in Japanese investment practices is important because the "us versus them" distinction is becoming increasingly blurred as more and more collaborative relationships, particularly joint ventures, are established. Joint ventures between Japanese and U.S. companies are hardly a new phenomenon in themselves. What is new is that these joint ventures are being established within the United States. Earlier joint venturing was largely an outgrowth of U.S. companies seeking local partners in overcoming access barriers into the lucrative Japanese market.

The numbers of joint venture investments are also charted in figure 26–1. A joint venture was identified as one in which a Japanese company and a non-Japanese company each had an equity position exceeding 5 percent. Investments with multiple partners were not defined as joint ventures in this analysis if all the partners were Japanese companies or U.S.-based wholly owned subsidiaries of Japanese companies. In the past decade, the number of joint ventures have grown faster than the total number of direct investments. In the 1976–78 period, about 25 percent of the new investments (that is, 12 of 46) involved a joint venture with a U.S. firm. During 1982–84 the number of joint ventures represented 38 of 99, or roughly 40 percent, of the new Japanese investments.

The relative equity position of Japanese versus U.S. partners in these joint ventures showed no evidence that the Japanese demand a controlling position in their joint ventures. There were roughly equal numbers of cases in which the Japanese had a majority position and cases in which they held a minority position. Also, there were a significant number of cases in which U.S. and Japanese partners each held 50 percent of the equity. (See table 26–1.)

In summary, Japanese foreign direct investment has been growing faster than their exports, this investment is being increasingly targeted at industrialized countries

Table 26–1
Equity Structure of U.S.–Japanese Joint Ventures

Equity Owned by Japanese Partner(s)	Number of Cases	Percentage of Cases
80–95%	12	12.4
66–79	10	10.3
51–65	14	14.4
50	26	26.8
35–49	17	17.5
21–34	10	10.3
5–20	8	8.3

including the United States, and joint ventures play an increasingly greater part in the direct investment of Japan in the manufacturing sector of the United States. Taken together, these trends seem to indicate that Japan is moving away from a scenario of confrontation with U.S. companies in the latter's domestic markets to one of creating jobs and adding value in the United States, often in cooperation with a local partner.

And yet, Japan's joint ventures here have been criticized as predatory. The charge levied is that only low-value-added tasks are performed by the joint venture in the United States and the Japanese partner exports from its home base the components and subassemblies with the highest technology content (*Newsweek*, May 28, 1984; Reich, 1984a, 1984b). In these joint ventures, the United States is portrayed as the loser.

In this chapter, I analyze the character of Japanese–U.S. joint ventures in the U.S. manufacturing sector. Why do they occur? Certainly Japanese–U.S. joint ventures in Japan have not been uniformly successful. In the five-year period 1972–76, ninety joint ventures in Japan were dissolved (Killing, 1982). Nor are there any legal barriers to wholly owned foreign investment in the United States. In the remainder of this chapter, I pursue this question of why these joint ventures have been formed. In the next section, a model of joint venture formation is proposed. In the following section, concepts drawn from this model are used to analyze interview data on twenty-one joint ventures.

A Model of Joint Venture Formation

The model discussed in this section has two broad goals. The first is to identify the factors that influence whether or not two potential partners will establish a joint venture. The second is to model the influences on the way a joint venture will be structured. The model is based upon those proposed by Harrigan (1984, 1985) in that it relies on the strategic imperatives facing companies as the primary influence on their willingness to create joint ventures. Second, the relative bargaining power of the partners together with the direness of their strategic need determines the manner in which the joint venture will be configured.

Whether or not a company will enter a joint venture relationship with another will depend upon its *desire to engage in joint ventures*. (See figure 26–2.) This desire may be manifest, in which case the company will actively engage in the search for a partner, or it may be latent in that it is only activated when the management is approached by a potential partner seeking a joint venture relationship. The desire for a joint venture, in turn, is determined by the size of the *strategic gap* facing that firm. The strategic gap is defined as the shortfall between the firm's *strategic goal* and its *realizable goal*, that which it can reach from its *current position* by deploying its *capabilities and resources*, including those it can muster without entering into a cooperative arrangement. Thus, for a firm to have the desire for a joint venture,

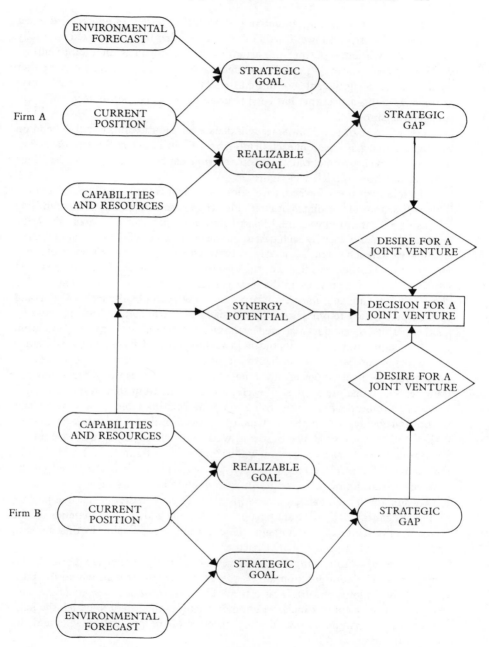

Figure 26–2. The Decision to Create a Joint Venture

it must believe that the cost and/or risk of acquiring resources necessary to meet its strategic objectives is lower if paid for in equity rather than if acquired internally or externally without a partnership arrangement. Analogously, in a joint venture, value is created by bringing together strategic assets of two partners where neither partner incurs a significant loss in its assets by allowing the other to participate in them. It is this aspect that has been referred to as *synergy potential* in joint venture relationships.

Whether or not two companies will decide on a joint venture will depend on both an internal assessment of each firm's strategic gap as well as the external assessment of the synergy potential of the other firm's capabilities and resources. This decision has been modeled in figure 26–2.

If a joint venture is formed, a question of interest is how it will be configured. The *configuration* of the joint venture is reflected in several aspects of each parent's relationship with the joint venture. In particular, two aspects are of interest. First, the *degree of control* exercised by each parent on the venture's operations depends on the extent to which each parent's interests are represented in the venture's board of directors and top management. Second, the *domain of control* depends on the extent to which each partner provides to the joint venture various parts of the value-added chain in producing and marketing its product. For example, the technology could be kept proprietary to one partner, portions of the manufacture kept in-house by another partner, the product marketed by the sales force of one of the parents, and so on.

The degree and domain of control of each parent is determined by its relative *bargaining power*. Since the configuration of the joint venture is a negotiated arrangement, the relative power of the negotiators determines the control they can exercise. The bargaining power of each partner stems from their respective capabilities and resources (what they bring to the negotiating table) as well as the size of the strategic gap (the extent to which they need to find a partner). As we saw earlier, the capabilities and resources as well as the strategic gap played a role in determining whether a joint venture will be formed. (See figure 26–2.) Additionally, the domain of control exercised by each partner will also be determined by the relative capabilities of each partner in each domain and the strategic importance of that domain to each partner's core business. Thus, whether or not one partner will retain control over a certain portion of the value-added chain depends on the strategic importance of this domain, the capability to add value in this domain, and the bargaining power of that partner.

The factors influencing the joint venture's configuration are portrayed in figure 26–3. The configuration affects the extent and manner in which the partners control the joint venture. This control limits the *strategic autonomy* of the joint venture. The concept of strategic autonomy relates to the extent to which the joint venture can determine its own destiny in terms of the products it sells and the markets it serves.

Hladik (1985) considers two issues related to the strategic autonomy of the joint venture, namely whether the joint venture will invest in R&D and whether it

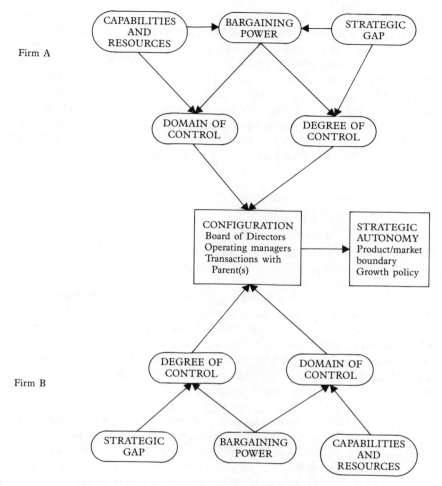

Figure 26-3. Configuration of a Joint Venture

will compete in export markets. Her analysis of joint ventures between a U.S. firm and a partner based outside the U.S. revealed that the joint venture was less likely to engage in R&D if the U.S. parent had a high R&D intensity at home. When the joint venture produced dissimilar or peripheral product lines and, hence, posed less of a potential for conflict in third-country markets, the joint venture was much more likely to export. Similarly, the overwhelming majority of Canadian licensees of foreign firms were not allowed to export when their license agreement included both current and future technology (Killing, 1983, p. 89).

Strategic autonomy is critical to the long-run survival of the joint venture. Franko (1971, p. 73) concludes that the instability of joint ventures is more a result of multinational policies of partners that limit the strategic autonomy or autonomy of the joint venture rather than the mere existence of conflict between the partners. Policies that in particular limit the joint venture's strategic autonomy are centralization, standardization, and specialization. Similarly, higher freedom to manage (as measured by the venture manager's perception of his own autonomy or the number of key decisions this manager could make on his own authority) dramatically increases the likelihood of the joint venture's success (Killing, 1983, p. 84).

The loss of strategic autonomy is of no particular consequence in stable environments. However, when the joint venture must adapt to a rapidly changing environment, the loss of strategic autonomy is a threat to survival.

Characteristics of U.S.–Japanese Manufacturing Joint Ventures

In this section, selective concepts from the model developed in the previous section are used to profile twenty-one joint ventures between a Japanese partner and a U.S. partner. All these joint ventures are in the manufacturing sector and all are located in the United States.

The sample of joint ventures used in this study was drawn from a directory of Japanese investments in the manufacturing sector (MacKnight, 1981; *JEI Report*, 1985). This directory was culled to identify those investments in which there was a U.S. company with an equity position exceeding 5 percent. A total of 97 such investments were identified. The sample was further narrowed using the following criteria: steel and automobile joint ventures were excluded as these were unique in terms of their scale of operations, those manufacturing consumer goods (typically foodstuffs) were excluded as they were very few in number, and those manufacturing commodity bulk goods (for example, newsprint, feedstuffs, or chemicals) were ignored. The general idea was to limit the sample frame to joint ventures making industrial products that were technology-intensive but not capital-intensive or process-intensive. Of the 97 joint ventures originally examined, 37 met these criteria. Of these 37 joint ventures, 25 were randomly selected for survey purposes and each was contacted by telephone at least 5 times to solicit an interview with the most senior manager. Following this procedure, 21 interviews were completed.

Clearly, the nature of the sample restricts the generalizability of the results. The directory did not include joint ventures that had been dissolved. For this reason, the data are probably biased in overrepresenting successful joint ventures. Second, the sample was screened to select only technology-intensive ventures which may well have different character than those in resource-intensive or capital-intensive industries.

Joint Venture Demographics

The twenty-one joint ventures in the sample came from a wide variety of standard industrial classification (SIC) codes. The products represented are communications equipment, auto components, process equipment, electrical equipment, semiconductors, pharmaceuticals, printing machinery, specialty metals and materials, audio devices, and computer peripherals. The joint ventures were young. Seventeen of them had been established in the 1980–85 period and the median age was three years.

It is interesting to note that most of the ventures in the sample do not meet the definition of a joint venture by Harrigan (1985), namely a new entity or child created by two independent parent companies. In eleven of the cases, a Japanese company was buying into an existing business in the United States. However, it was clear from the interviews that though the acquisition of an equity position did not create a new business entity, it wrought significant changes on the business acquired.

Strategic Analysis

The market relationships of the partner firms prior to the formation of the joint venture give insight into the nature of the strategic coalition between the two. Five types of market relationships between the parents were used to characterize each joint venture. These are (1) vertical relationships where the Japanese parent's core business was in a raw material or component which the U.S. partner purchased as an input to its own production process or for value-added resale (Japanese forward integration), (2) vertical relationships reversing the roles of the Japanese and U.S. partners just described (Japanese backward integration), (3) horizontal relationships in which the two partners were direct competitors in the same markets, (4) horizontal relationships where each partner's product line complemented the other's, and (5) no prior relationship. Table 26–2 gives a breakdown by type of relationship for the twenty-one firms studied.

Joint ventures arise predominantly out of two types of relationships between partners, namely where the foreign supplier of raw materials or components is integrating forward into the United States and where the two partners are participants in the same industry but selling noncompeting product lines. An analysis of the

Table 26–2
Prior Relationship of Partners

Type of Relationship	Number of Joint Ventures
Vertical	
Japanese forward integration	7
Japanese backward integration	2
Horizontal	
Direct competition	2
Complementary products	6
Unrelated	3
No data	1

motives of the Japanese partner in forming the joint venture finds that in 14 of the 21 cases, the Japanese objective is to become a first-order participant in the U.S. market so as to establish access to and garner intelligence in this market, establish a base in the United States to gain market experience or further expansion, or hedge against trade barriers. Other motives were to acquire technology (6 cases), to insure a U.S.-based source of supply (2 cases), and to gain access to U.S.-based production facilities (1 case).

In contrast, for U.S. partners, the motive of market access is much less important and, when present, of a very different nature. Only in 5 of the 21 joint ventures were marketing-related factors important in seeking a Japanese partner. Of these 5 cases, in only 2 were the worldwide marketing capabilities of the Japanese partner a specific reason for having formed the joint venture. In 2 of the joint ventures, the reason for seeking a Japanese partner was to be able to access a very specific market segment, namely Japanese-controlled manufacturing facilities in the United States. For example, a supplier to Toyota and a supplier to General Motors formed a joint venture to serve the Toyota–GM joint venture, NUMMI, in California. In one case, the joint venture was with a leading Japanese semiconductor manufacturer and U.S. partner, a supplier to that industry, which wanted to develop new technology in cooperation with a dominant user in the market.

Access to technology was a much more prevalent motive among U.S. partners in these joint ventures. In ten of the cases, the U.S. partner was looking to its Japanese partner for transfer of technology from Japan.

Japanese production skills and supply of raw materials important to the U.S. partner's business were of moderate importance. Access to Japanese manufacturing know-how and/or facilities was important in 8 of the joint ventures. Increased control of supplies critical to the U.S. partner's core business was a factor in 2 of the joint ventures. Additionally, the Japanese partner provided the expansion capital which was being sought by the American partner in 7 of the cases.

The strategic value added by each partner to the joint venture reflects the strategic resources provided by that partner and the strategic gap or need of the other partner. The exchange of value added by the Japanese partner and the U.S. partner is analyzed in table 26–3. The type of value added has been categorized into four broad categories for the purpose of this analysis, namely access to

Table 26–3
Strategic Value Added in Joint Venture Formation

By Japanese Partner	By U.S. Partner			
	Technology	Capital	Production	Marketing
Technology	5	0	1	6
Capital	1	0	2	5
Production	1	0	1	7
Marketing	2	0	2	2

technology, capital, factors of production, and market. Together, these constitute the four major components of the value-added chain in manufacturing industries. The number of entries in table 26–3 exceeds the number of ventures in the study because, in several cases, there were multiple motives for one or both of the partners.

If the cells in table 26–3 with two or fewer entries are ignored, the nature of the strategic value exchanged in the formation of joint ventures is quite specific. These joint ventures give the Japanese strong marketing advantages in exchange for technology, capital, and production advantages. Additionally, when the U.S. partner makes a strong technology contribution to the joint venture, in exchange it gains access to a complementary technology from the Japanese partner.

Configuration of Joint Ventures

Next, the configuration of the joint ventures will be analyzed. Only a few aspects of the configuration will be considered here, namely (1) the representation of each parent in the board of directors and senior management, (2) the role of parents in product engineering, manufacturing, and marketing, and (3) the transactions between the joint venture and one or more of the parents.

In all but one, there was a formal board of directors in place. The size of the board varied from 2 to 9 persons. In 9 cases, there was an even number of members of the board, and in 8 of these 9, the numbers of board members representing Japanese and U.S. partners were equal. Consensus building became particularly important in such arrangements, though in a few cases, the swing vote of the chairperson had the power to break the deadlock. The relationship between equity structure and board structure is given in table 26–4 for 18 of the cases. (In one case, there was no board, while in 2 cases, data on board size and composition were not available.)

Table 26–4
Board Composition and Equity Structure

Board Composition	Japanese Majority	50:50	U.S. Majority
Japanese majority	6	0	0
50:50	0	5	1
U.S. majority	1	1	4
No board		1	
Not data	1	1	
Total	7	8	6

The 15 cases on the diagonal represent the rather conventional situation of board composition mirroring the equity structure. The 3 cases on the off-diagonal are exceptions which warrant further consideration.

The case of the 50:50 equity split with the U.S. partner having board majority is an interesting one. The bylaws of the venture agreement require a 4-to-1 majority for any major decision to carry. This arrangement gives the managing partner a majority on the board, but requires consensus building in that the vote of at least one board member representing the minority is necessary for the majority vote to carry.

The other two cases—one with a 50:50 board but with the U.S. partner holding a majority equity position, and the other with a U.S. majority on the board but majority equity held by the Japanese partner—proved to be unstable joint ventures. Both were in the process of reorganizing at the time of the study.

The president of the joint venture was a U.S. citizen in all but one case. In fifteen cases, the venture was managed by a person who had a previous affiliation with the U.S. partner. In two cases, the venture's manager was on the payroll of the U.S. parent; both these ventures were having problems in that one was virtually inactive and the other was having trouble establishing an identity other than that of a licensee.

In thirteen of the cases, there were Japanese employees transferred from the Japanese parent organization. The positions they occupied were:

Title/Function	Number of Persons
Officers	
Financial officer	1
Vice president	1
Senior managers	
Technical	8
Administrative	2
Marketing and sales	1
Other	5

A little over half the cases had Japanese managers. Those that did have Japanese managers averaged less than two per case. Moreover, in several cases, the Japanese personnel were periodically rotated back to Japan, and the purpose of their presence seemed to be as much a training and development function as it was a contribution to the venture's operations.

The marketing relationships between the joint venture and the parents varied considerably. At the risk of oversimplification, four types of marketing arrangements are typical. (There are no data on two cases.)

1. Both parents' sales forces carry the joint venture's product.   2 cases
2. The U.S. parent's sales force does all the marketing.   8 cases
3. Marketing is handled by an independent sales force of the joint venture.   6 cases
4. The Japanese partner's sales force handles all the marketing.   3 cases

Three issues are of primary concern in defining the parents' marketing roles: first, whether a parent has exclusive rights; second, whether the joint venture can sell outside the United States; and third, what commission will be paid on sales handled by a parent. These are all points for negotiation and are potential areas of conflict.

A significant portion of the manufacturing value added is performed in Japan in the case of nine of the twenty-one ventures. In these cases, either the manufacture is done almost entirely in Japan or a large portion (in excess of 60 percent) of the raw material and component purchases are made from Japan.

The parents were not directly involved in the product engineering at the joint venture. However, there were indirect influences due to transfer of technical know-how, coordination with parent(s) which supplied raw materials and components, and the pressure on the specs of the joint venture's product to meet the requirements of the parent who was the dominant customer of this product.

Transactions between parents and joint venture on an operating basis arise out of various types of transfers:

1. Licensing fees
2. Management fees to operating partner
3. Sales commission to partner assuming the marketing function
4. Purchase of materials, components or, semifinished product from parent
5. Purchase of joint venture's product by the parent

The first three types of flows (licensing royalties, management fees, and sales commissions) are typically on a percentage of sales basis. They are not linked to the physical flow of goods or flow of title. On the other hand, the remaining two types of flows involve a sales transaction between the venture and its parents. The prevalence of these various transactions or flows are given in table 26–5.

Fees when used tend to be small, in the region of 5 percent or less. Moreover, they tend to be equally distributed to both parents. For example, when one parent gets a certain royalty on licenses, the other parent gets a comparable management fee or sales commission.

The financial transaction associated with the transfer of product from/to the joint venture to/from a parent could, in principle, allow one partner to profit more

Table 26-5
Transactions between Parent and Joint Venture

Transactions	U.S. Parent	Japanese Parent
Fees and commissions	3 cases	5 cases
Transfer of product to joint venture from:	4 cases	11 cases
Transfer of product from joint venture to:	8 cases	5 cases

Note: There were only fifteen joint ventures in the sample with a U.S. partner that was a separately operating company.

from the joint venture at the expense of the other. For example, if margins on materials, components, and products purchased by the joint venture from one parent are higher than they would be under an arms-length relationship, or if sales by the joint venture to one of the parents are at lower than market prices, the joint venture is favoring one of the partners. Unlike fees and commissions, these subsidies are hidden. Though this type of conflict was a potential problem in a majority of the ventures, none of the ventures expressed any concern over this situation. The partners seemed to be willing to manage this potential problem on a good-faith basis rather than by specific clauses in the contract.

Product flow is more likely to occur from the Japanese partner into the joint venture (eleven cases). When this type of flow occurs, it can account for a substantial proportion of product cost: 70 percent on the average when the product comes from the Japanese parent and 40 percent on the average when it is from the U.S. parent.

Conversely, the U.S parent is more likely to directly consume the output of the joint venture (eight cases). In such cases, the U.S. parent's purchases accounted for 70 percent of the venture's sales on the average. When the Japanese parent was a customer (four cases), its purchases averaged only 40 percent of the venture's output.

Strategic Autonomy

Only one type of strategic autonomy is considered here—namely, the extent to which the joint venture could enter geographic markets other than the United States. Of the 21 cases in this study, only 5 reported any export sales. Fourteen did not have any exports and 2 were unwilling to discuss their export activities. The major reason that the other joint ventures had not developed export sales was because such sales would conflict with the Japanese parent's activities outside the United States. The joint ventures that did export had one of 3 characteristics: (1) the Japanese parent was in an unrelated business, (2) the export sales were handled entirely by the Japanese parent or a trading company affiliated with it, or (3) a separate marketing agreement was in force whereby the parents were marketing each other's products in certain world regions.

Other areas of potential conflict between partners were not fully investigated in this analysis. However, several joint ventures did express concern that the U.S. partner and Japanese partner had different profit objectives and growth objectives. Typically, the U.S. partner stressed short-term performance, whereas the Japanese had longer horizons. Yet, in the few cases where there was a mismatch of opinion between partners as to how aggressively to invest in growth, it was the U.S. partner that felt that the Japanese were not willing to invest for expansion.

Conclusion

Though the twenty-one joint ventures upon which this chapter's empirical work is based exhibit a large number of individual differences, some generalizations are in order. First, the joint ventures that were the most unstable (those in which the equity relationships, power, and roles of the parents were shifting over time) were those in which one or more of three conditions were not met: (1) the composition of the board in terms of the constituencies represented did not reflect the equity structure, (2) the growth objectives of the parents were not congruent so that one viewed the desirability of investing for growth more aggressively than the other, and (3) the joint venture had evolved out of an arms-length supplier–distributor relationship without any clear idea of why an equity joint venture was a preferred arrangement.

Finally, most of the joint ventures in this analysis are young. The median age is three years. It is too early to address the charge levied by critics of these joint ventures that the partnership does not bode well for U.S. business. Certainly at this early stage, there seems to be exchange of value for both sides. The question is whether the Japanese partner will remain a partner or become a competitor once the joint venture helps it establish a beachhead in a particular product-market sector.

References

Franko, L.G. 1971. *Joint Venture Survival in Multinational Corporations.* New York: Praeger.

Harrigan, K.R. 1984. *"Joint Ventures and Global Strategies." Columbia Journal of World Business* 19(2): 7–17.

Harrigan, K.R. 1985. *Strategies for Joint Ventures.* Lexington, Mass.: Lexington Books.

Hladik, K.J. 1985. *International Joint Ventures.* Lexington, Mass.: Lexington Books.

JEI Report. 1985. "Japan's Expanding U.S. Presence: 1984 Update." Washington, D.C.: Japan Economic Institute. February 15.

Killing, J.P. 1982. "How to Make a Global Joint Venture Work." *Harvard Business Review,* May–June: 120–127.

Killing, J.P. 1983. *Strategies for Joint Venture Success.* New York: Praeger.

MacKnight, S. 1981. *Japan's Expanding Presence in the United States.* Washington, D.C.: Japan Economic Institute.

Newsweek. 1984. "Are Foreign Partners Good for U.S. Companies?" May 28: 58–60.

Reich, R.B. 1984a. "Collusion Course." *New Republic.* February 27: 18–21.
Reich, R.B. 1984b. "Japan Inc., U.S.A." *New Republic.* November 26: 19–23.
Reich, R.B. 1986. "Joint Ventures with Japan Give Away our Future." *Harvard Business Review.* March–April: 78–86.

27

Deference Given the Buyer: Variations across Twelve Cultures

John L. Graham

> In Japan, as in other countries, the "buyer is king," only here he or she is "kinger." Here, the seller, beyond meeting pricing, delivery, special specifications, and other usual conditions, must do as much as possible to meet a buyer's wishes. . . . Many companies doing business in Japan make it a practice to deliver more than called for under the terms of their contracts.
> —Manufactured Imports Organization of Japan, p. 16

There are numerous reasons why American executives have difficulty conducting business in Japan. But perhaps the most important cause of problems for Americans is the basic misunderstanding regarding the structure and process of interpersonal and business relationships. In Japanese society, interpersonal relationships are vertical in nature (Nakane, 1970). That is, in almost all two-person relationships, a difference in status exists. The basis for this status distinction may be any one of several factors: age, sex, education, position in a firm, even which firm. For example, the president of the number one firm in an industry holds a higher status position than the president of the number two firm in the same industry. All Japanese are very much aware of such distinctions and of their position relative to others with whom they interact. And for good reason—knowledge of their status dictates how they will act during interpersonal interactions. Thus, it is easy to understand the importance of exchanging business cards in Japan—such a ritual clearly establishes the status relationships and lets each person know which role to play. The roles of the higher- and lower-status positions are very different, even to the extent that different words are used to express the same idea, depending on which person makes the statement. For example, a buyer would say

The following institutions and people have provided crucial support for this chapter: U.S. Department of Education, Toyota Motor Sales USA, Inc., Solar Turbines, International (a division of Caterpillar Tractors Co.), the Faculty Research and Innovation Fund and the International Business Educational Research (IBEAR) Program at the University of Southern California, and Professors Nancy J. Adler, Nigel Campbell, Richard H. Holton, Alain Jolibert, Dong Ki Kim, C.Y. Lin, Hans-Gunther Meissner, and Theodore Schwarz Gehrke.

otaku (your company), while a seller would say *on sha* (your great company). Status relations dictate not only what can be said, but how it is said.

In the United States, things are, of course, much different. Americans size up one another and act accordingly, but the degree to which it is consciously done is different. And the way in which status distinctions affect how Americans behave is almost the opposite of that in Japan. In Japan, both people feel uncomfortable if status distinctions do not exist and/or are not understood. But in egalitarian American society, people often go out of their way to establish an interpersonal equality. There is little distinction between roles and relatively few rules for adjusting behavior (Graham, 1981, and 1984).

Japan is the United States's second most important trading partner. What about cooperative relationships in Canada, the number one trading partner? Do they work the same way as in the United States? Buyer–seller relationships are the most basic and pervasive form of commercial cooperation. Yet, we have little empirically based knowledge about buyer–seller relationships in foreign countries. Such relationships in twelve cultures are examined here using a negotiation simulation involving more than seven hundred businesspeople in ten countries, all among the United States's most important trading partners. The remainder of the chapter is divided into four sections. First, the theoretical perspectives of the chapter are presented and the hypotheses stated. Next, the methods used are described. Third, results are reported. In the final section of the chapter, the results are interpreted and conclusions are drawn. Implications of the present analysis are discussed in the broader context of cooperative strategies in international business.

Theoretical Perspectives

The basic theoretical perspective underlying all the following hypotheses is drawn from social psychology and exchange theories. Briefly, negotiation outcomes are determined by three clashes of constructs—bargainer characteristics, situational constraints, and the process of bargaining. The focus of this work is on the influence of culture (a bargainer characteristic) on negotiation outcomes (the dependent variables).

Negotiation Outcomes

In practice, outcomes of buyer–seller negotiations are often difficult to measure and compare. Sale versus no sale is one obvious measure of bargaining effectiveness and has been used by Pennington (1968) in a field study of buyer–seller interactions. However, researchers have sought richer measures which make possible comparisons of a variety of effectiveness criteria.

Negotiation outcomes have been operationalized in a number of ways in different studies. In the hundreds of bargaining experiments conducted by social psychologists, an often used measure is profits attained by bargainers in negotiation

Part VI
Cooperating with the Japanese

25

Strategic Partnerships between Technological Entrepreneurs in the United States and Large Corporations in Japan and the United States

Frank Hull
Gene Slowinski
Robert Wharton
Koya Azumi

Problem Background

Small, high tech firms probably have higher rates of invention per dollar of R&D investment than large firms. However, the promising technologies of small firms often fail to reach commercialization because of a lack of resources. Too often, this lack of resources is misdiagnosed as simply financial. Thus, venture capitalists were once seen as the solution to the problems of small, high tech firms. However, money is not enough! Many small firms also need access to markets, manufacturing know-how, and managerial expertise which can best be provided by a cooperative relationship with a large corporation. Thus, a new era is dawning for "strategic partnering."

But how to structure and manage these cooperative relationships with small high tech firms is not well understood. In the past, major corporations simply acquired the small firm and often killed its innovative spirit (Sykes, 1986). Because of this problem, several corporations have recently made minority investments instead of outright acquisitions. Although the influx of cash into the small firm's operations is important, the large firm has much more to offer than money in exchange for access to the small firm's technology. The greater the number of areas of cooperation between small and large partners in high technology, the more

Sponsorship by the Center for Innovation Management Studies at Lehigh University is gratefully acknowledged.

successful the relationship seems to be, especially if the large firm does not dominate (Slowinski, Hull, and Wharton, 1987).

In looking for ways of structuring partnerships so that the small firm retains some autonomy, the Japanese model may offer some insights. Major Japanese firms are highly interdependent with their smaller suppliers and are cooperative in nature. Such experience probably fosters a learned capacity for cooperation (see chapter 17 by Lyles in this book) and could be one reason why major Japanese firms may be offering more attractive deals to U.S. technological entrepreneurs than U.S. corporations. Another is that the supply of technological entrepreneurs is greater in the United States than in Japan. Regardless, we propose to compare the approaches to small-firm–large-firm cooperation in the two nations by evaluating the extent to which cooperative ventures are advantageous between small and large firms in technology-based industries and which factors affect the conditions of mutual advantage. These results may point the way toward criteria that will help management make strategic decisions regarding cooperative ventures in general, especially with regard to interorganizational cooperation in the United States and Japan.

Framework for Comparisons

In comparing high tech cooperative relationships between U.S. and Japanese companies, it is useful to know the strengths and weaknesses participants from each nation bring to the partnership which affect international strategy (Contractor, 1986). For example, the new-product potential of technological entrepreneurs is an important resource, and the United States probably has a greater number of small entrepreneurial firms than Japan. To the extent that this cross-national difference exists in the economics of the two nations, one would expect Japanese corporations to be open to U.S. entrepreneurs, especially to the degree that their intrapreneurial product development strategies are insufficient to meet objectives. (See table 25–1.)

Size as a Competitive Advantage: Small versus Large

Strategic partnering between small and large firms in high tech is usually based on the exchange of the entrepreneur's technology for the corporation's resources. The opportunity for creating synergistic cooperation between these two categories of partners has been noted and resulted in a call for further investigation of what Roberts (1980) terms "new style joint ventures." Yet joint ventures are often resisted by corporations preferring internal development and they frequently fail (Berg and Friedman, 1980). Moreover, controversy remains over the value of resources offered by the entrepreneurial firm. Do small firms actually have more innovative capacity than large ones? The issue is not clear because technology transfers from major corporations and universities to technological entrepreneurs bias the results showing that small firms are more innovative. Thus, further research is needed

Table 25-1

Technology and Organization Characteristics of U.S. and Japanese Industries: Hypothetical Contrasts Pertinent to Cooperative Ventures

	United States	*Japan*
Size and Entrepreneurship		
Small	Many independent entrepreneurs	Few independent entrepreneurs, with many small companies semidependent upon suppliers to larger corporations
Large	Large corporations, including some successful intrapreneurs	Many successful intrapreneurial corporations, especially using technology transferred from suppliers and others
Technology		
Product	Innovatively new, occasionally radical	Many enhancements, few breakthroughs
Process	Medium cost, medium quality	High quality, low cost
Organization		
Type	Mechanistic bureaucracy or organic-professional	Mixed mechanistic/organic
Formalization and control	Contractual, with specific centralized authority concentrated at top of hierarchy	Negotiable, flexible, with centralized authority mitigated by participatory influence of lower-ranking personnel
Interorganizational Relationships		
Number of cooperative relationships	Few	Many, especially suppliers
Type of cooperation	Contractual, short-term contractual exchange (such as competitive bidding)	Informal and implicit as well as contractual exchanges, as with a trusted family member in long-term relationship

at the technological interface between large and small firms to document the flow of technology between them. Although the literature is rather consistent in suggesting that small firms have higher rates of innovation (Gilman and Siczek, 1984; Azumi, Hull, and Hage, 1983), the concept of size needs to be reconceptualized and its effects partialed out in regression analysis to control not only for technology transfer, but also for spurious sources of association such as market maturity as well as the indirect consequences of bureaucratization. Moreover, managerial strategies for creating islands of smallness within the corporation should be examined as many Japanese firms have dramatically succeeded using this approach (Takeuchi and Nonaka, 1986).

Resources for ventures are often discussed in financial terms even though intangible assets and informal exchange may be equally important. Thus, the concept of organizational boundaries needs to be modified to take various kinds of cooperative ventures into account. The distinction between markets and hierarchies might be expanded to include a broader array of exchanges than is implied in this dichotomy (Williamson and Ouchi, 1981). Exchange theories need to be devised to include sociological as well as economic incentives and barriers to cooperation, including such subjective factors as trust (Sullivan and Peterson, 1982). For example, cooperation between small and large firms is essential to the innovative capacity of Japanese industry (Wood, 1984; Imai, Nonaka, and Takeuchi, 1984). Thus, further research must be conducted on interorganizational cooperation not only in the United States, but also in Japan, because it alters the effective size of a partnering firm's operations.

Technology: Product versus Process

Although Japanese industry has now reached parity with U.S. industry in many technology-based markets (Moritani, 1982), historically each nation has brought competing advantages to high technology. The United States has been known for inventions and new products, some of which are radical breakthroughs. By contrast, the Japanese approach has often involved taking Western inventions and perfecting them through many small incremental improvements in product, especially in process. However, Japanese products dominate many markets because they are competitive, in terms of not only low cost, but also high quality.

Organizations

Industrial organizations in the United States have evolved into specialized forms to accommodate different kinds of work. For example, mechanistic bureaucracies (type 2 in figure 25–1) supplanted most traditional crafts (type 1) by the early twentieth century. Because size and concomitant bureaucratization often hamper innovation, organic organizations (type 3) emerged after World War II (Burns and Stalker, 1961). Type 3 organizations are often small and usually staffed by professionally trained employees (Hull and Collins, 1987). The organic-professional organization is highly innovative, but not very productive, which contrasts with the mechanistic-bureaucratic organization. However, as large bureaucracies became more innovative, a mixed-product corporation (type 4) evolved which has moderate competitive advantages in both innovation and productivity (Hage, 1980; Hull and Hage, 1982).

Organic-professional organizations, which are more contemporarily described as "small high tech," usually have the advantage of inventiveness, but lack the resources of the other modern types of organizations. Indeed, many small, high tech companies fail because of resource scarcity and not because their technological

MARKET ENVIRONMENT	WORKLOAD	small-scale	large-scale
Heterogeneous and/or dynamic	High technical complexity	#3 Structure organic-professional *Technology* complex batch *Performance* high innovation low–med. productivity	#4 Structure mixed product *Technology* process, sub batches *Performance* med.–high innovation med.–high productivity
Homogeneous and/or static	Low technical complexity	#1 Structure traditional-craft *Technology* simple batch *Performance* low innovation low productivity	#2 Structure mechanistic bureaucracy *Technology* mass, assembly-line *Performance* low–med. innovation high productivity

WORKLOAD

Small and/or unconcentrated — Large and/or concentrated

MARKET ENVIRONMENT

Figure 25-1. Typology of Organization Design, Workload, and Environment: The Niche of Small High Tech Firms

concept is inadequate. They lack financing, market access, and production capability—not good situations. This lack of resources is a key contributor to the lack of success of many entrepreneurial firms.

The small high tech firm (type 3) is our frame of reference for estimating the opportunity for cooperative ventures. A coalition with the mixed-product corporation (type 4) is the most probable because of type 4's technical capacity and adaptiveness relative to the mechanistic bureaucracies (type 2). The mechanistic type usually is fairly mature and focused in a highly concentrated market niche. Therefore, it lacks flexibility in its production and market capacity (Abernathy and Utterback, 1978). To the extent that size is inversely related to innovativeness, the larger the firm, the greater the benefits of partnering with small high tech firms.

The question then becomes, why should the mixed-product corporation with its extraordinary resources in both technology and scale of operations or the mature-product corporation with its size do anything other than acquire the small high tech firm? One reason is that the innovative potential of the small firm may be stifled by the overpowering bureaucratic structure and influence of the large firm. A second reason is that a considerable amount of data suggest that smaller firms are more innovative relative to large ones in the United States (Gilman and Siczick, 1985) and in Japan (Azumi, Hull, and Hage, 1983; Hull and Azumi, 1985).

Consequently, many major U.S. corporations are increasingly taking minority positions in small high tech firms. The advantage of this strategy is suggested by Exxon Enterprise's striking success with external venture capital investments versus the lackluster performance of internal corporate ventures as well as many other cases where the acquired company's technology became less competitive after acquisition (Sykes, 1986).

How do Japanese industries compare with those of the United States in terms of the preceding typology? First, they are highly stratified by size so that a three-tier system exists: major firms, their suppliers, and the suppliers to the supplier of the majors. Second, they are less differentiated according to the mechanistic versus organic distinction, as well as productive versus innovative performances, in that most firms are distributed along the lower left to upper right quadrants in figure 25–1. Third, Japanese industry is distributed in figure 25–1, so that there are few relatively small high tech firms in the upper-left quadrant. To the extent that large Japanese corporations seek small high tech entrepreneurs, their opportunities are greater in the United States than domestically because small high tech firms in Japan are associated with a family of companies and are not free to cooperate with firms outside the family. In terms of exchange theory, one might expect that major Japanese firms would offer U.S. small high tech firms a better deal than domestic corporations because of their relative scarcity in Japan.

Interorganizational Cooperation

In terms of technology, U.S. entrepreneurs with new products *complement* major Japanese corporations with process advantages. By contrast, major U.S. corporations often have highly inventive R&D labs, which reduces need for technological entrepreneurs.

Organizations in Japan mix mechanistic and organic design characteristics. In some ways, they are easier for organic entrepreneurial firms in the United States to deal with to the extent that Japanese management takes a more evolutionary and less bureaucratic approach than American managers (Kagono, Nonaka, Sakakibara and Okumura, 1985).

In Japan, the large firm often benefits from cooperation with smaller suppliers far more than in the United States. Japanese industry seems to be applying its techniques for managing interorganizational cooperation with its suppliers to cooperative ventures with small high tech firms in the United States. In Japan, our surveys show that the pattern of relationships with suppliers is quite different. For example, Japanese firms obtain only about 5 percent of supplies through competitive bidding, about 40 percent of their supplies come from other sub units of their company (including subsidiaries), and about 55 percent are from "trusted vendors" with whom they cooperate on a long-term basis (Azumi, Hull, and Wharton, 1987). By contrast, U.S. firms are much more reliant upon bidding and open-market purchases, with only 6 percent purchased from trusted vendors.

Japanese industry is beginning to establish a large number of cooperative agreements with small high tech firms in the United States (Levine and Byrne, 1986). Although Japan has relatively few small high tech entrepreneurs, they are applying their experience in cooperating with suppliers to their interface with technological entrepreneurs in the United States. Simplistically stated, some Japanese corporations are telling small high tech firms: "Give us your product inventions. We will reengineer, manufacture, and sell them for you, especially in the Asian market. In exchange, you will receive money and process technology if you want to manufacture for the U.S. market." By contrast, the large U.S. corporation is largely inaccessible to the small firm.

In sum, we propose to identify reasons why some partnerships in high technology between U.S. and Japanese firms are more successful than others. A key factor will be size of the partner firm in each nation because the United States has proportionately more small high tech entrepreneurs than Japan. Thus, we will implicitly compare four types of partnership which vary by size of firm and nation. However, our subsequent analysis focuses only on the partnership between small firms in the United States with large firms in either the United States and Japan because we have no data as yet on small Japanese firms partnerships with large firms. Small Japanese firms in any case only rarely partner with U.S. corporations (Burton and Saelens, 1982). In comparing the success partnership by small U.S. firms partnering with corporations from both nations, our discussion includes three reasons why major Japanese firms may offer the better deal: (1) a domestic scarcity of technological entrepreneurs, (2) an advantage in process technology plus a mixed organization design which is more culturally compatible with the organic style of entrepreneurs, and (3) experience with interorganizational cooperation.

Data. Questionnaires are being administered to large corporations in the United States and Japan having smaller partners in high technology—most commonly

452 • *Cooperative Strategies in International Business*

in electronics and biochemistry. To date, 21 questionnaires from large corporations are available for analysis—15 from the United States, but only 6 from Japan. We therefore present *preliminary* data relevant to our previous theoretical and hypothetical discussion. The reader is cautioned that insufficient data are currently available for statistical analysis, while relationships may change somewhat as more questionnaires are added. However, so far the pattern of responses from the two nations seems to be fairly congruent with a priori expectations.

Results. How do corporations in the United States and Japan rate the success of their partnerships with small firms? Japanese corporations say their partnerships were relatively successful compared to the self-rating given by U.S. corporations, which is consistent with other findings (Sullivan and Peterson, 1982). Table 25–2 shows responses to the question: How would you rate the effectiveness of this strategic partnership in comparison with operating alone?

Our possible reason for the success Japanese corporations report working with small firms in the United States may be their relatively modest amount of control. For example, the more the distribution of influence favors the small firm, the more successful the partnership as rated by both the small and large partner. Thus, Japanese corporations report exercising considerably less influence than U.S. corporations over all types of activity except process technology, which is one of the competitive advantages they bring to the partnership. Table 25–3 shows U.S. and Japanese firms' responses to the question: Of the total amount of influence in making decisions today, what percentage is exerted by the corporate partner?

Despite the fact that U.S. corporations report somewhat less satisfaction with their smaller U.S. partners than with Japanese corporations, they report giving

Table 25–2
Success of the Partnership by Type of Activity Ratings by Large Firms in the United States and Japan

	United States (n = 15)	Japan (n = 6)
Technology		
Product	3.6	4.7
Process	3.6	4.7
Manufacturing	3.3	4.2
Marketing	3.7	4.2
Management	3.7	4.0
Finance	3.5	4.2

Scale: 5 = extremely effective.
    4 =
    3 =
    2 =
    1 = very ineffective.

Table 25–3

Percentage of Total Influence Exerted by the Corporate Partner by Type of Activity: United States versus Japan

	United States (n = 15)	Japan (n = 6)
Technology		
Product	42%	12%
Process	37	60
Manufacturing	35	29
Marketing	63	30
Management	79	14
Finance	45	29

a considerable amount to the partnership—and comparatively more than their Japanese counterparts except in process technology and manufacturing. Table 25–4 shows responses to the question: What percentage of the following resources has your firm given to the strategic partnership: product and process technology, manufacturing, marketing, management, and finance?

Partnering Strategies: Exploring Success Factors

Patience is required for successful partnering in high technology because developments may take considerable time to come to fruition. Because of the risks and uncertainties involved, corporate partners who link with entrepreneurs need to be prepared to be flexible as well as patient.

Giving entrepreneurs considerable autonomy seems to be a key factor in the success of partnerships with large corporations. For corporations to work well with smaller partners, the not-invented-here (NIH) syndrome must be overcome.

Cooperative symbiosis rather than acquisition needs to help shape the thinking of the large corporation. In the United States, this may often require a change

Table 25–4

Resources Given by Large Firm to Small Partner

	United States (n = 15)	Japan (n = 6)
Technology		
Product	22%	16%
Process	20	30
Manufacturing	28	44
Marketing	38	26
Management	38	34
Finance	48	20

in corporate culture to reflect the increasing need for using alliances to accomplish objectives that exceed the grasp of even large, rich corporations going it alone.

Process technology and manufacturing capability need to receive increased appreciation. In the United States, many small firms expressed dissatisfaction with the contribution by their corporate partners, in part because they seem to undervalue the importance of manufacturing processes. But, new product technologies will ultimately require low-cost, high-quality manufacturing to ring the cash register over the course of the product life cycle. If partners focus impatiently on the immediate drama of new-product development, their competitive position downstream may be risked.

The patience Japanese corporations seem to show with their entrepreneurial partners may be in part due to the probability that in the long run, much of the manufacturing process required to succeed will become a kind of in-house trade secret, especially in electronics and to a lesser extent in bioprocess. While many aspects of high tech partnerships lend themselves to specific contractual kinds of negotiation, the know-how technology involved in competitive manufacturing is somewhat subtle and diffuse. Thus, entrepreneurs may tend to underestimate the potential value of the corporate partner's contribution to manufacturing processes over the short term and may be shut out of the relationship over the long term.

Conclusion

Differences between U.S. and Japanese industry in terms of the size distribution of firms, areas of technological expertise, types of organization design, and patterns of interorganizational cooperation present opportunities and challenges for partnerships between the two nations. Interorganizational cooperation practiced by major Japanese corporations with their suppliers may be related to their willingness to allow technological entrepreneurs considerable autonomy and it possibly contributes to their rating partnerships as more highly successful than U.S. corporations. The exchange of new-product technology for process technology seems more complementary for U.S. entrepreneurs with Japanese corporations than with U.S. partners. However, the fruits of the partnership over time are likely to rest largely with the corporation supplying the manufacturing processes to manufacture competitively.

Bibliography

Abernathy, W.J., and Utterback, J.M. 1978. "Patterns of Industrial Innovation." *Technology Review* 80: 40–47.

Azumi, K., Hull, F., and Hage, J. 1983. "Managing High Technology in an International Perspective: A Comparison between Japan and the U.S." In *The Challenge of Japan's Internationalization*. H. Mammari and H. Befu (eds.), Tokyo: Kodansko Int. 111–147.

Azumi, K., Hull, F., and Wharton, R. 1987. *Productivity and Organization Design in Japanese versus American Factories.* Report to the U.S. National Science Foundation.

Berg, S.V., and Friedman P.H. 1980. "Corporate Courtship and Successful Joint Ventures." *California Management Review* XXII: 85–91.

Burns, T., and Stalker, G.M. 1961. *The Management of Innovation.* London: Tavistock.

Burton, F.N., and Saelens, F.H. 1982. "Partner Choice and Linkage Characteristics of International Joint Ventures in Japan: An Exploratory Analysis of the Inorganic Chemical Sector." *Management International Review* 22: 20–29.

Contractor, F. 1986, "International Business: An Alternative View." *International Marketing Review* 3: 74–85.

Gilman, J.J., and Siczek, A.A. 1985. "Optimization of Inventivity." *Research Management* 28 (4): 29–31.

Graham, J.L. 1981. "A Hidden Cause of America's Deficit with Japan." *Columbia Journal of World Business* (Fall): 5–15.

Hage, J. 1980. *Theories of Organizations.* New York: Wiley.

Hambrick, D.C., and McMillan, I.C. 1985. "Efficiency of Product R&D in Business Units: The Role of Strategic Context." *Academy of Management Journal* 28 (3): 527–47.

Hull, F., and Azumi, K. 1985. *Innovative Payoff from R&D in Japanese Industry, 1970s–1980s.* Report JR-1 to the U.S. National Science Foundation.

Hull, F., and Collins, P. 1987. "High-Tech Batch Systems: Woodward's Missing Type." *Academy of Management Journal* (December).

Hull, F., and Hage, J. 1982. "Organizing for Innovation: Beyond Burns and Stalker's Organic Type." *Sociology* 16(4): 564–77.

Hull, F., Hage, J., and Azumi, K. 1984. "Innovation versus Productivity Strategies in Japanese Industry." *Strategic Management of Industrial R&D.* In B. Bozeman (ed.): Lexington, Mass.: Lexington Books, 85–104.

Imai, K., Nonaka, I., and Takeuchi, H. 1984. *Managing the New Product Development Process: How Japanese Companies Learn and Unlearn.* Hitotsubashi University paper no. 118.

Kagono, T., Nonaka, I., Sakakibara, K., and Okumura, A. 1985. *Strategic vs. Evolutionary Management: A U.S.-Japan Comparison of Strategy and Organization.* Amsterdam: North-Holland.

Levine, J.B., and Byrne, J.A. 1986. "Corporate Odd Couples." *Business Week* (July 21): 100–6.

Moritani, M. 1982. *Japanese Technology.* Tokyo: Simul Press.

Nonaka, I., *et al.* 1985. *Managing New Product Introductions.* Hitotshubashi University working paper.

Peterson, R.B., and Shimada, J.Y. 1978. "Sources of Management Problems in Japanese–American Joint Ventures." *Academy of Management Review* 3(4): 796–804.

Roberts, E.B. 1980. "New Ventures for Corporate Growth." *Harvard Business Review* (July): 134–42.

Roberts, E., and Berry, C.A. 1980. "Entering New Business: Selecting Strategies for Success." *Sloan Management Review* (Spring): 3–17.

Slowinski, G., Hull, F., and Wharton, R. 1987. *Strategic Partnerships between Small and Large Firms in High Technology.* Report to the Center for Innovation Management Studies. Bethlehem, Pa.: Lehigh University.

Sullivan, J., and Peterson, R.B. 1982. "Factors Associated with Trust in Japanese–American Joint Ventures." *Management International Review* 22: 30–40.

Sykes, H.B. 1986. "Lessons from a New Venture Program." *Harvard Business Review* (August).

Takeuchi, H., and Nonaka, I. 1986. "The New Product Development Game." *Harvard Business Review* (January–February).

Williamson, O.E., and Ouchi, W.G. 1981. "The Markets-Hierarchies Program of Research: Origin, Implications, Prospects." In W. Joyce and A. Van de Ven (eds.), *Organizational Design.* New York: Wiley.

Wood, R.C. 1984. *Small Business: Foundation of Japan's Leadership.* Report to the U.S. Small Business Administration, preliminary (August).

26

Japan's Joint Ventures in the United States

Tyzoon T. Tyebjee

The 1980s have brought a new dimension to the presence of Japanese business interests in the United States. Though the image of Japan as a competitive threat in the United States market continues to persist, there is evidence that Japanese business in the future may seek more cooperative arrangements within the United States. Joint ventures are already playing a large role in Japanese direct investments in the United States, particularly in the manufacturing sector. This chapter concerns itself with Japan's joint ventures in the United States, why they are established, and how they are structured. To motivate the reader's interest in such joint ventures, the next section addresses the trends in the Japanese direct investment in the United States.

Japanese Investments in the United States

There is no doubt that Japan's exports of goods is an order of magnitude larger than its export of capital as direct investment abroad. For example, in 1984, Japanese exports worldwide amounted to $170 billion as compared to $38 billion in Japanese foreign direct investment in the same year. At the same time, it is clear that in the previous period, 1973–1984, the growth rate of direct investment exceeded the growth in exports by a factor of nearly five. Whereas exports grew only 360 percent in this period, Japan's foreign investment grew over 1500 percent.

Several factors have contributed to this trend. For example, corporate earnings in Japan, which have been extremely strong in the past decade, have provided the corporate chest of funds for foreign investment. Moreover, Japan has often been the target of protectionist sentiment in countries beleaguered with trade deficits, and direct investment abroad both ameliorates the threat of increased protectionism against Japan and hedges against the sensitivity of export-based strategies to quotas and tariffs. Finally, the high value of the yen has made Japanese exports expensive, foreign manufacturing cheaper, and the yen stretch further in the productive assets it can buy abroad.

The record high value of the yen in early 1986 prompted Japan's Economic Planning Agency to survey 1,644 exporting firms to identify their planned response to the exchange rate. A full 1,027 firms replied to the survey in March 1986. The average exchange rate that firms considered to make exports profitable was 207.2 yen to the U.S. dollar. Responses by industry varied: precision machinery, 195; light electronics, 202; textiles, 212; steel, 217; and shipbuilding, 227. In early 1987, the yen is around 150, substantially below the rate at which export-based strategies are profitable. The planned response of the Japanese companies is to increasingly rely on manufacturing outside Japan and, at the same time, invest in cost-reduction programs. A total of 58.4 percent of the firms were already established abroad and 30.5 percent were thinking of moving overseas. One-third of the firms had the goal of overseas production accounting for at least 20 percent of their sales.

Japan's direct investments are also shifting in terms of where they are being invested. Whereas in 1974, approximately an eighth of the direct investments were made in the United States and other industrialized countries, by 1984 this proportion had doubled to 25 percent. In the United States alone, Japan invested $1.7 billion in 1984. This was a sharp increase from the average annual investments of half a billion dollars in the preceding five years. By the end of 1984, Japanese investors had a majority equity position in 342 manufacturing concerns in the United States (*JEI Report*, 1985). Ninety-two of these (over 25 percent) were investments occurring in the three preceding years, 1982–84. Figure 26–1 tracks the number

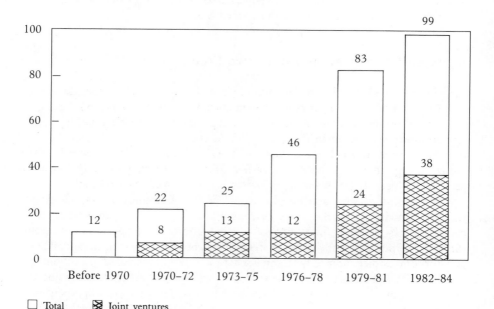

☐ Total   ⬚ Joint ventures

Note: Investments with unknown dates are excluded.

Figure 26–1. Number of Japanese Investments in U.S. Manufacturing

however, countertrade is a serious form of international operations, a form fraught with danger.

Countertrade Regulations

The implications for management and corporate strategy of engaging in countertrade vary from type to type. They also depend on the regulations of the countertrade transaction. These can vary on ten primary dimensions:

Timing: The export may precede or follow the linked import.

Duration: Countertrade arrangements can be discharged over a short time period (as is often the case in barter) or last indefinitely (as when the export is exchanged for a portion of the importer's output or for some share of equity).

Countertrade percentage: The percentage of the value of the export to be offset by countertrade can range from low (5–10 percent) to, in some cases, well over 100 percent. Countertrade can also be undertaken on a "best-efforts" basis.

Mandatory or voluntary: Countertrade can be a mandatory or voluntary part of a trade deal. If voluntary, countertrade may be used by the exporter to sweeten its trade offer.

Penalties for noncompliance: Penalties for noncompliance with the terms of a countertrade arrangement can range from nil, to 100 percent to total disallowance of the export.

Product requirements: Often countertrade obligations can only be discharged by taking back "approved products."

Incremental exports: Often countertraded goods must be incremental to the firm's previous imports from the country or incremental to its home country's previous imports.

Quota limits: When countertraded goods are under quota restraints in importing countries, they may only be used to discharge the countertrade obligation if they are imported outside the quota limits or sold to another country without quota limits.

Country destination: Some countries require that countertraded goods be sold only in the source country of the export or in an approved list of destination countries.

Countertrade mechanism: Some countries require that only the exporter may undertake the countertrade obligation.

Countertrade arrangements are time-consuming and difficult to negotiate since agreements on each of these dimensions must be evaluated, negotiated, and included in the contract in addition to the normal legalities involved in international trade. This task can be a daunting one for the inexperienced exporter and for small firms. Lawyers and those experienced in countertrade may have to be used intensively and at high cost. As well, changing circumstances over the life of the arrangement may lead to problems for one or more of the parties to the arrangement.

Countertrade Institutional Arrangements

Producer-exporters can handle countertrade negotiations and their countertrade obligations through several institutional arrangements: in-house countertraders, external countertrade intermediaries, and bank countertraders.

In-house Countertrade Units. Some firms have developed in-house countertrade expertise, often in a separate countertrade unit. This unit may be in the export department, in a free-standing countertrade unit, or in a countertrade subsidiary. In some firms, this unit becomes a profit center and even begins to market its expertise to unrelated firms facing countertrade situations.

Trader-Countertrader. Most countertrade intermediaries are part of trading firms, although there are an increasing number of countertrade specialists. Countertraders can provide some combination of the following services: negotiating countertrade arrangements; evaluating the price, quality, availability, design, and delivery schedules of prospective countertrade takebacks; marketing these products internationally; giving financial advice and facilitating financing; and arranging legal services. For these services, they charge some combination of a flat fee, fees for services rendered, and commissions. They usually act as pure trade intermediaries, but some will take title to the countertraded goods and pay the exporter a preset amount on a no-recourse basis.

Bank Countertraders. Finance often plays a crucial role in countertrade, especially in the usual case when the timing of the flows of goods does not occur simultaneously. Some banks have expanded out of trade finance to offer countertrade services. This move from export lending to countertrade intermediary has proven to be problematic for many of the banks. The expertise and attitudes that bring success in banking often have not proven to be transferrable to countertrade operations.

A producer-exporter engaged in countertrade then has a range of institutional arrangements through which to organize countertrade deals. Another crucial decision closely linked to the choice of institutional arrangement is to determine what will be done with the products taken back in countertrade. They can be used as inputs within the exporter's own operations; they can be sold through its normal channels of distribution; or they can be sold by a countertrading unit outside the firm's normal channels of distribution.

The characteristics of each type of countertrade and countertrade arrangement form a complex web through which those involved in countertrade must maneuver. This process is often a difficult one and is outside the expertise of many manufacturing firms. In response, experts in the legal, trade, financial, and regulatory aspects of countertrade in general and in particular countries have emerged. An exporter approaching a countertrade arrangement is often besieged with offers of help from these experts. One major problem for the exporter is how to evaluate all the competing offers of assistance. This can be a daunting prospect and has discouraged more than one firm from engaging in countertrade. To know where to start in evaluating a firm's response to countertrade takes considerble expertise. Hence, countertrade per se can be a substantial barrier to trade.

Countries That Countertrade

Of countries that engage in, encourage, or mandate countertrade, one can identify four groupings: the Eastern European nations, low- and middle-income countries, oil-exporting countries, and high-income countries. Each group has different motivations and policies.

Eastern European Nations. Through the early 1970s, most countertrade involved the Eastern European nations on one side of the agreement and a Western exporter on the other (Vernon, 1979). The currencies of the countries of Eastern Europe were nonconvertible; their exchange rates were not allowed to respond to market forces and were usually fixed at nonequilibrium levels. They often suffered chronic balance of trade deficits (which they were unwilling or unable to finance through the requisite international borrowing) and chronically scarce foreign exchange which they rationed according to the priorities of their economic plans. Countertrade was used as a second-best alternative to allowing market forces to operate as a means to circumvent these market distortions. Countertrade also fit well with their centralized, bureaucratic planning systems.

Low- and Middle-Income Countries. During the 1970s, due in part to the rapid rise of oil prices in 1973–74 and 1978, many low- and middle-income countries experienced substantial deterioration in their terms of trade and imbalances in their trade and payments accounts. In response to these imbalances and the need to finance development, they borrowed heavily abroad. The rise of the U.S. dollar and real interest rates in 1978–83, the world recession of 1981–82, and increased trade protection in Western countries increased the magnitude of their debt, the costs of carrying it, and the difficulty of financing it out of export earnings. In a belief that countertrade would increase exports, many of these countries turned to countertrade to access needed imports without increasing the reported amount of foreign indebtedness.

China is something of a special case. Starting in the late 1970s, under its open-door policy, China sought to accelerate the pace of its economic development through increased links to the rest of the world through trade, accessing technology, and foreign direct investment. In order to pay for the large imports of capital goods and technology required by its development plans without accumulating unacceptably large international debt or incurring high levels of foreign equity ownership, China encouraged and/or mandated many forms of countertrade, especially compensation trade and loans backed by exports of output. In joint ventures, the foreign partner often received the return on its equity in the form of the venture's output or, in some cases, in the form of goods from other sources. China also sought to encourge South–South trade, especially with countries on the Asia-Pacific Rim, through countertrade arrangements.

Oil-Exporting Countries. The decline of oil prices in 1981–85 led to large revenue shortfalls for oil exporters. To finance imports by increasing oil exports while not being seen as overtly undercutting OPEC prices and production quotas, some oil-exporting countries engaged in countertrading oil.

High-Income Countries. High-income countries, for political purposes and to foster domestic high tech and military industries, have historically demanded industrial offsets for purchases of military hardware and civilian aircraft. The governments of most high-income countries are philosophically opposed to countertrade, viewing it as a nontariff barrier to trade; they would prefer to see its incidence decrease. This displeasure with countertrade has not led them to prohibit firms in their countries from engaging in countertrade, but rather has been manifested through multilateral institutions under their influence.[2]

Note that in many instances, countries have turned to countertrade as a second-best alternative when market imperfections (such as foreign-exchange constraints, nonequilibrium exchange rates, artificially set international prices, and commodity agreements) have restricted trade, yet increased trade is seen as yielding net benefits.

Rationales for Countertrade

The motivation for a specific countertrade transaction can have important implications for the management of the firms involved. In general, negotiating and executing a countertrade arrangement extends over a long time period, uses scarce management resources intensively, and changes and/or shifts the risks and profits of international operations for the enterprises and countries involved. If the countertrade arrangement is efficiency-enhancing and, hence, there is a net welfare gain, this gain can be used to offset these costs. If it leads to a net welfare reduction for the stakeholders in the countertrade arrangement, it is more difficult for the direct participants to manage so that they benefit from the arrangement. An understanding of the forces motivating countertrade can assist exporters in identifying situations in which a countertrade arrangement would foster trade and increase net welfare.

Firms and countries that encourage, require, and engage in countertrade adduce a wide variety of rationales concerning the benefits of countertrade and their motivations for engaging in it.

> In some situations, countertrade can increase economic efficiency and, hence, lead to welfare gains by reducing or circumventing natural imperfections in international goods, services, and capital markets.

> Countertrade can serve as a second-best alternative to the removal or reduction of government-imposed market imperfections.

> In some cases, the costs of countertrade can be shifted to others such that the direct participants gain even though there is a net welfare loss.

> In some cases, countertrade is motivated by the political or economic expediency of one or more of the stakeholders in the arrangement.

> Countertrade can be used under mistaken perceptions as to its net benefits.

Countertrade and Efficiency Gains

If international goods and financial markets were perfect in an economic sense, countertrade would reduce economic efficiency and the welfare gains of free trade. The international trade and finance system, however, differs from the competitive ideal due to natural market imperfections—transportation costs, incomplete and asymmetric information, incomplete forward and contingent markets for risk bearing—and government-imposed market imperfections—tariffs and nontariff barriers to trade, barriers to capital mobility and access to capital, nonequilibrium exchange rates, and commodity cartels—and firm-level imperfections—proprietary technology, information, and access to markets, and international market power. To the extent that countertrade can be used to arbitrage across these market imperfections, it can increase the efficiency of the world trading system and be a positive-sum game for the participants.[3]

Providing Information. Countertrade can provide information in three ways:

1. A producer-exporter may possess knowledge of the performance characteristics of its product (reliability, speed, durability, efficiency, and so on) that is difficult to convey to the buyer (Caves, 1976). One way to bridge this information gap is for the firm to enter into a buyback or production-sharing arrangement by which the exported machinery is paid for with the output it produces (Akerlof, 1970). This gain of information on the part of the buyer, however,

may be offset by additional information requirements on the part of the producer-exporter concerning the capabilities of the importer to successfully operate not only the equipment, but the enterprise as a whole.[4]

2. Buyback and production-sharing arrangements also can provide the importer with unbiased information of the producer-exporter's projections of future world supply, demand and, price conditions and production costs of the goods produced by the exported equipment (Parsons, 1985a, p. 33). Countertrade can provide the importer with information on both the *technological* and *economic* viability of its investment.

3. Countertrade may also provide information to potential purchasers of the output produced by the imported equipment concerning quality and delivery, if the ongoing involvement of the producer-exporter can serve as a guarantee (Murrell, 1982).

Risk Reduction. Buyback and production-sharing arrangements, by providing information to the importer, may *change* the level of actual or perceived risk of the trade transaction for one or more of the direct participants.

Contingent and Forward Contracts. Forward markets do not exist for most internationally traded products. Buyback, production sharing, and equity joint venture arrangements can represent a form of a one-product forward or contingent contract (Parsons, 1985a). They can be used to shift some of the risk of world price and demand fluctuations as well as technological and quality-control failure back onto the producer-exporter by creating a private forward market when no public one exists. Countertrade can also help a government faced with foreign exchange constraints plan future foreign exchange flows. This acts as a positive externality to the nation, but not to the firms involved in the specific arrangement. If this situation were to exist, government would have to mandate countertrade. This last explanation still leaves open the question of why a government would mandate countertrade to create a forward market rather than simply arrange a long-term contract with a trader abroad.

When countertrade is used to secure access to proprietary, unbiased information, to reduce risk, and to create a forward or contingent market, value is created. There is an incentive for the participants to enter into a countertrade arrangement voluntarily. In most countertrade arrangements, however, one or more of the firms is an unwilling participant. This conclusion implies that either the net gains from countertrade are not shared, or that they accrue to some other stakeholder (for example, the importing country or the producer of the countertrade takebacks).

Countertrade as a Second-Best Alternative

The trade market may fail due to government regulation of international trade flows, the exchange rate, and foreign-exchange availability; it may fail when one party to a trade arrangement has market power. In such circumstances, countertrade may increase trade efficiency by compensating for these deviations from competitive conditions (Goldstein, 1985). The best alternative would be to act to remove the market imperfection directly, but this action may not be possible either for the firms themselves or through government action. In this case, countertrade may be a second-best alternative to some other form of trade or no trade all; that is, countertrade may be the constrained optimum solution.

Failure in the Foreign-Exchange Market. If the foreign-exchange rate is not at its free market, equilibrium level, the opportunity cost of foreign exchange for the economy is not reflected in the cost of national currencies paid by importers or the value in national currencies received by exporters. Countertrade can be used in this situation to increase national welfare by changing relative *domestic* prices of the countertrade takebacks to approach their implicit foreign-exchange values while also raising the implicit costs of their importers.

Market Power of Importers. A government may believe that an importer is making excess profits on the imported products, possibly due to an overvalued exchange rate or its possession of market power in the national market. Countertrade is one way for the government to tax away these profits and use them for other purposes, such as to encourage (subsidize) exports as well as to discourage imports in general.

Market Power of Producer-Exporters. Producer-exporters located in high-income countries may have market power vis-à-vis individual importers. Countertrade requirements might be one way for government to increase the buying power of its importers by placing restrictions on market access at the national level to create a bilateral monopoly situation (Caves, 1976). This is essentially an effort by government to change the terms of trade. In this situation, we would expect that countertrade arrangements would be less profitable for the producer-exporter than simple export operations in the normal course of trade. Yet, the remaining question is why the government in such a situation would not use control over access to the domestic market to extract price concessions rather than to impose countertrade.

Barriers to Entry in Export Marketing. One of the most prevalent rationales for countertrade is put forward by governments of countries trying to increase exports of manufactured products. They believe that their products have the characteristics to be saleable on international markets, yet their producers do not have the expertise, knowledge, or trading ability necessary to overcome barriers to entry arising from lack of information and their low reputation with potential users abroad. They believe that by inducing producer-exporters abroad to take these goods as payment through countertrade, they can force them to use their knowledge of trade and their home markets to market products successfully. Once the intrinsic value of their products is recognized by foreign buyers, they believe their products will be able to be exported and sold abroad based on their merits. This rationale for countertrade is based on several assumptions about international product markets and institutional arrangements. The countries could be trying to build a public good—a national brand image—at an initial cost to the firms involved in the countertrade arrangement, much as Japanese trading companies bore the cost of building a quality image for products made in Japan. As well, using countertrade through a producer-exporter might bring a free ride on its corporate image.

These views of how world trade operates would seem to imply that countertrade would yield net benefits to the country above those attainable through the use of other trading arrangements. Yet there are hundreds of trading firms worldwide to handle new products—for a price. Moreover, many countertrade arrangements involve countertrade intermediaries who could be used directly. There would seem to be no reason why these countertraders or producer-exporters would be more willing to accept countertraded products mandated by government on a more favorable basis than if they were sold in the normal course of trade.

Countertrade as Industrial Policy. Recently, trade theorists (for example, Helpman and Krugman, 1985) have modelled international trade in oligopolist industries with differentiated products and increasing returns to scale. Under certain assumptions of oligopolist response and economies of scale, it is in a country's best interests to follow a policy of subsidizing exporting industries and impeding imports. To the extent that the real world mirrors these assumptions, countertrade could be one means to affect such a trade policy.

Shifting the Costs of Countertrade to Other Stakeholders

Countertrade, whether efficiency-enhancing or efficiency-reducing, may shift the costs and benefits of trade. In some cases, the costs can be shifted so that the direct participants in the arrangement benefit at the expense of other stakeholders.

Cartels and Administered International Prices. Countertrade can be used to disguise price cutting to increase sales and market share at the expense of competitors, while avoiding precipitating an international price war, violating international pricing agreements, or being seen as selling below list prices.

Dumping and Subsidizing Exports. In some instances, countertrade can be used to try to circumvent the antidumping and countervailing duty laws in the destination country. This can be accomplished if a country accepts overpriced imported goods in exchange for its products. This dumping mechanism is hard to identify and act against (Zarin, 1984).

Circumventing Debt Ceilings. Countertrade can also be used to circumvent International Monetary Fund–imposed external debt limits by implicitly borrowing against the foreign-exchange earnings of future exports used as countertraded goods. In this case, countertrade shifts costs onto the holders of a country's external debt. This use of countertrade may have motivated the International Monetary Fund (IMF), World Bank, and General Agreement on Tariffs and Trade (GATT) to act to discourage its use.

Political Rationales

Political considerations can make countertrade attractive. This situation often arises in purchases of military hardware and civilian aircraft. In order to muster support for a purchase from abroad, it may be politically advantageous to be able to an-nounce offset agreements that will create jobs, develop national technological capabilities, or create investment.[5] Such announcements can yield general political advantage; those affected positively by the offsets then have a stake in seeing the countertrade arrangement finalized. This may be a political second-best rationale to promote trade through countertrade.

It is difficult to determine which of these rationales has motivated firms and countries to increase their use of countertrade. Several of the most often articulated rationales—to preserve hard currency, to improve trade balances, and to increase exports—are incorrect in general. Countertrade will not yield these benefits except in special cases.[6] In many situations, however, even though the explicitly ar-ticulated rationale for engaging in countertrade may be incorrect, the actual trade conditions may be such that countertrade will yield net benefits.

The Winners and Losers from Countertrade

The analysis of the winners and losers from countertrade arrangements can be quite complicated. There are often many stakeholders in a countertrade transaction, both direct—the producer-exporter, the importer, producers of the products taken back in countertrade, and countertrade and financial intermediaries (if any)—and indirect—other producers of any of the goods involved in the countertrade transac-tions (both in the countries involved and in the other countries), holders of inter-national debt, and, more generally, all international traders and trading countries. The governments of the countries directly and indirectly affected by a counter-trade arrangement have a stake in it and may become involved in their role as custodi-ans of their national public interests. As well, international organizations such as the GATT, IMF, and the World Bank may try to intervene to protect the interests of their members.

Countertrade can affect both the *net gains* from trade and the *allocations* of gains and losses among all the stakeholders in the arrangement. If there are net gains from a countertrade arrangement and if its costs and benefits are allocated such that each of the stakeholders is better off under the arrangement relative to any other trade arrangement, then there is a basis for an ongoing, stable relationship. As long as one or more of the stakeholders is made worse off relative to some other form of trade relationship or to no trade, then there is always the threat that this stakeholder will intervene or react to counteract, destabilize, or terminate the arrangement.

Often, one or more of the direct participants in a countertrade arrangement does not enter into it willingly or as a first choice. In many, if not most, situations the producer-exporter would prefer a straight trade transaction with payment in cash or a trade supplier's credit. In response, this producer may try to recoup the additional costs plus insurance for the increased risk of entering a countertrade arrangement by increasing the sales price of its product relative to what it would have been in the normal course of trade or by cirumventing the countertrade regulations. The importer-user will try to resist these price increases, particularly when the benefits of countertrade accrue to another firm (such as the exporter of countertrade takebacks) or to the nation as a whole. The producer of the countertraded takebacks may also look unfavorably on the arrangement unless it receives a price in local currency that makes the sale attractive. For these reasons, countertrade can and often does lead to dissatisfaction all around. From this mutual unhappiness, a countertrade arrangement must be negotiated that will withstand the tests of time.

Countertrade arrangements typically take a long time to negotiate and can extend over many years. This time frame may allow any stakeholder to react if it has been damaged. This situation frequently arises during the bidding for large contracts during which countertrade wars can break out, and charges and countercharges of dumping, subsidization, and unfair trade practices are levelled. Over the extended course of a countertrade contract, conditions may change such that it is in the best interests of one of the stakeholders to alter the arrangement or terminate it. This can lead to management problems that are more complex and severe than those faced for normal trade and finance transactions.

There are often high up-front costs in engaging in countertrade negotiations. These costs are magnified since only a small proportion of proposed countertrade arrangements are finalized and discharged. The profits from the one successfully completed countertrade arrangement must then cover the expenses of the unsuccessful attempts. Unless the countertrade arrangement is large or there are prospects of additional ones in the future, it may not be profitable for a firm to proceed. As well, countertraders are often unwilling to participate in small-volume countertrade arrangements since their fixed costs are high. These characteristics of countertrade may discriminate against small firms, infrequent exporters, and firms without extensive experience in international trade.

Countries and producers that are alternative suppliers of countertraded takebacks can also be damaged by countertrade. This problem is particularly severe for producers whose products face inelastic demand worldwide. This is often the case for natural resource products such as petroleum, palm oil, rubber, copper, and petrochemicals. This effect has led, in some instances, to countries imposing countertrade regulations of their own to recoup lost exports, leading to countertrade wars in which everyone loses—except those skilled in countertrade. As one counter-trader remarked, "Just because there's a war doesn't mean that the undertakers shouldn't make money."[7]

Traders may also be damaged by countertrade when countertrading firms out-bid them with their suppliers. As well, requirements on country destination for countertrade takebacks may also disrupt established trading patterns and require liqui-dation of takebacks in home markets.

If a countertrade arrangement enhances the efficiency of world trade or is a second-best alternative when there is market failure, then there is the potential for one or more of the participants to win and the others to not lose relative to the gains from other forms of trade or no trade. Even if countertrade does not yield net gains, some participants can benefit: countertraders, established importers from the country who can liquidate countertrade takebacks, and government officials responsible for countertrade. These participants are in a position to profit from arbitraging across the barriers to trade created by countertrade regulations. They have a vested interest in perpetuating countertrade regulations for their own benefit. There is little incentive for an individual firm or country to move away from counter-trade as long as its competitors do not.[8] Although the OECD, GATT, and IMF have issued negative reports on countertrade, this has not prevented individual firms in high-income countries or the governments of these countries themselves from engaging in countertrade when it is to their advantage. It is difficult to muster a collective agreement to reduce the incidence of trade-distorting countertrade ar-rangements. Even if such a consensus could be reached, it would be difficult in practice to provide guidelines to distinguish between efficiency-enhancing and efficiency-reducing countertrade arrangements. Hence, there is a high risk of pro-liferation of countertrade arrangements that are not efficiency-enchancing and decrease the benefits that can accrue from international trade.

Responses to Countertrade

The strategies of firms toward countertrade can be placed in five categories:

1. Firms may refuse to engage in countertrade and, hence, refuse to pursue trade opportunities with countries in which countertrade may become a factor.

2. Firms may refuse to engage in countertrade, but be willing to pursue trade opportunities until countertrade becomes a factor.

3. Firms may be willing to engage in countertrade arrangements, but only as a last resort when the initiative comes from their trading partner and if they can negotiate satisfactory terms.

4. Firms may actively pursue countertrade opportunities and use their counter-trade capabilities as a proactive marketing device.

5. Firms may offer their countertrade capabilities to others to assist in formulating and implementing countertrade arrangements both internally and for external users.

These five generic strategies toward countertrade are not necessarily mutually exclusive. A firm could follow one or the other depending on the circumstances: the type of countertrade arrangement, its characteristics, the countries involved, and the countertrade mechanism.

In order to analyze the determinants of firms' strategic response to countertrade, data were collected on the countertrade activities of a large sample of firms based in Canada, the United States, and Japan that operated in five countertrade-intensive industries. Based on the analysis in the preceding sections, the following firm-level characteristics might influence a firm's countertrade strategy:

Size. The smaller the firm, the less likely it would be to engage in countertrade. The costs of undertaking a countertrade arrangement are largely fixed, independent of the size of the contract. As well, smaller trade transactions often fall below the threshold set by governments in their countertrade regulations. To the extent that smaller firms engage in smaller transactions, there should be a positive relationship between firm size and countertrade activity.

Export Intensity. The greater the dependence of a firm on exports, the more costly a strategy of avoiding countertrade would be. There should be a positive relationship between export dependence and countertrade activity.

Export Experience. The more experienced a firm is in export markets, the more willing and able it may be to undertake the added complexities of countertrade. There should be a positive relationship between export experience and countertrade activity.

Vertical Integration. The greater the degree of vertical integration of a firm, the higher the probability that it has expertise in selling and/or using products taken back as part of a countertrade arrangement. The greater a firm's vertical integration, the higher should be its countertrade activity.

Output Diversity. The more diversified a firm's output, the greater the probability that it can find countertrade takebacks to sell through its normal channels of distribution. Output diversity should be positively related to countertrade activity.

Input Diversity. The more diversified the inputs a firm purchases, the higher the probability that it can utilize countertraded goods internally and thereby reduce the costs of countertrade arrangements. There should be a positive relationship between a firm's input diversity and its countertrade activity.

Subcontractor or Subsidiary. Often, the prime contractor or a subsidiary's parent organization handles countertrade arrangements, while their subcontractors or subsidiaries are involved only to the extent that ultimately their products are part of a countertrade arrangement. Subcontractors and subsidiaries would then tend to have a less active strategy toward countertrade.

Data from the firms in the sample on these dimensions and their strategic response to countertrade are displayed in table 24–1. On an impressionistic basis, the hypotheses were supported: the larger the firm, the higher its export/sales ratio, the greater its export experience, the greater its degree of vertical integration, the greater its output diversity, the greater its input diversity, the greater the probability that it actively pursued countertrade arrangements. Subcontractors or subsidiaries tended to follow a more passive strategy. Impressions can be misleading, however, since there was obvious multicollinearity between the dependent variables. (For example, small firms tended to be less experienced exporters, have lower export/sales ratios, be subcontractors, be less vertically integrated, require less diverse inputs, and have less diverse outputs.) Ideally, the independent effects of each of the seven variables on a firm's countertrade strategy should be analyzed. The problem in attempting this more thorough analysis is that most of the independent variables and the dependent variable are not measured on an interval scale (hence, multiple

Table 24–1
Firm Characteristics and Countertrade Strategy

Firm Characteristics	Countertrade Strategy					Total
	1	*2*	*3*	*4*	*5*	
Size						
Small	20	23	33	18	6	100
Large	8	11	39	27	15	100
Export intensity						
Low	17	26	35	16	6	100
High	10	10	35	31	14	100
Export experience						
Short	24	25	30	18	3	100
Long	8	9	35	30	18	100
Vertical integration						
Low	16	20	32	23	9	100
High	12	14	32	30	12	100
Output diversity						
Low	17	19	30	24	10	100
High	11	15	38	26	10	100
Input diversity						
Low	18	21	34	18	9	100
High	12	13	32	31	12	100
Subsidiary/subcontractor						
Yes	32	21	20	19	8	100
No	4	8	29	36	23	100

regression is not appropriate), but are divided into more than three categories (hence, multiple discriminant analysis is ruled out as well).

The effect of countertrade arrangements on the volume and profitability of exports for the firms in the sample is reported in table 24–2. Note that the impact of countertrade was not uniform among the firms in the sample. It had a generally negative impact on the firms that had followed an avoidance or passive strategy toward countertrade and a positive impact on the sales and profits of firms that had followed a proactive strategy, although the variance of outcomes was wide.

There is difficulty in interpreting these results, however. They should not be interpreted to mean that firms should take a more proactive stance toward countertrade. The correct (successful) strategy toward countertrade may be a function of a firm's characteristics (such as size and export intensity); hence, a blanket recommendation is inappropriate. Also, the reported success of proactive countertrade strategies may well be contingent on the very fact that many firms and countries avoid countertrade. If this situation were to change in the future, then the determinants of success of any countertrade strategy might change in either of two opposite directions: (1) the increased number of firms active in countertrade might lead to reduced profits for all or (2) the spread of countertrade from country to country might make possession of countertrade expertise a key success factor for any serious producer-exporter.

Countertrade is in a state of growth and change around the world as firms and countries struggle to deal with this complex form of international cooperative arrangement. Countertrade can increase the efficiency of global trade relative to other forms of trading relationships or be a second-best alternative when other, more efficient, arrangements are impeded. Countertrade arrangements can also distort

Table 24–2
The Effects of Countertrade on Sales and Profits
Question: "Has Countertrade Increased (7) or Decreased (1) Sales and Profits?

Countertrade Strategy	Sales	Profits
Active avoidance	1.9 (1.3)	2.8 (1.8)
Refusal to countertrade	2.5 (.9)	3.5 (2.1)
Acquiescence	3.8 (2.1)	4.1 (2.3)
Proactive	4.5 (1.1)	5.0 (2.3)
Countertrade services	5.2 (1.4)	4.3 (2.4)

Note: Numbers in parentheses represent standard deviation of responses world trade patterns and reduce the efficiency of the world trading system even when they bring net benefits to some of the participants. Whatever the motivations and effects of countertrade, however, it is safe to project that countertrade will be a significant factor in world trade into the foreseeable future. Hence, firms and governments will find it necessary to examine their strategic responses to countertrade opportunities and threats, and perhaps take a more active stance toward this form of international business arrangement.

Notes

1. Countertrade can also involve services as well as goods.
2. This reluctance to prohibit firms owned and/or operating within their borders from engaging in countertrade arises from two sources: a commitment to the legal principle of freedom to contract and the fear that a prohibition on their national firms from engaging in countertrade would impose costs on them by reducing their competitiveness on export markets in countries that mandate or encourage countertrade.
3. Evidence of the high profitability of countertrading is the high entry into the industry from 1980 to 1985, the high salaries of countertraders, and the high profits of countertrading firms, as reported in various issues of *Countertrade Outlook*.
4. As described later in this chapter, the risk attached to the export and to total firm operations also is shifted from importer to the exporter in such arrangements.
5. A problem in Indonesia was that:

> As foreign trading partners, both buyers and sellers realized that the "Linkage Unit" [the unit responsible for certifying additionality (incremental exports)] lacked the tools to enforce the countertrade law, and fulfillment of offset obligations became primarily a matter of trading PEBs [certificate of compliance] or to "fulfilling" obligations through "confidential payments." (*Countertrade Outlook*, May 19, 1986, p. 1)

6. See Welt (1984, pp. 12–13) for a good example of such incorrect conclusions on the "reasons for engaging in countertrade" put forward by a countertrade expert.
7. This statement was made during an interview. For particularly insightful comments by a countertrader on the effects of countertrade, see Beckerman (1983).
8. Indonesia is an interesting exception to this trend. In 1986, it de facto rescinded its mandatory countertrade regulations for government import purchases due to its inability to enforce "additionality" requirements.

Bibliography

Akerlof, G. 1970. "The Market for 'Lemons': Qualitative Uncertainty and the Market Mechanism." *Quarterly Journal of Economics*, 74: 488–500.
Banks, G. 1983. "The Economics and Politics of Countertrade." *The World Economy*, 6(2): 1–33.
Beckerman, P.S. 1983. "Statement." *Journal of Comparative Business and Capital Market Law*, 5(4): 37–38.
Caves, R.E. 1976. "The Economics of Reciprocity: Theory and Evidence in Bilateral Trading Arrangements." In W. Sellakaerts (ed.), *Essays in Honor of Jan Timbergen*. London: Croom Helm.

Goldstein, E.A. 1985. *A Theoretical Model of Countertrade.* Research paper. Federal Reserve Bank of New York.

Helpman, E., and Krugman, P. 1985. *Market Structure and Foreign Trade.* Cambridge, Mass.: MIT Press.

Murrell, P. 1982. "Product Quality, Market Signalling, and the Development of East–West Trade." *Economic Inquiry,* 20(4): 589–603.

Parsons, J.E. 1985a. *A Theory of Countertrade Financing of International Business.* Working Paper no. 1632-85. Cambridge, Mass.: Massachusetts Institute of Technology.

Parsons, J.E. 1985b. "Notes on the Optimality of Characteristic Buy Back Contracts." Mimeo. Cambridge, Mass.: Massachusetts Institute of Technology.

U.S. Department of Commerce. 1982. *Analysis of Recent Trends in U.S. Countertrade.* Washington, D.C.: U.S. Government Printing Office.

Vernon, R. 1979. "The Fragile Foundations of East–West Trade." *Foreign Affairs,* 57(4): 1035–52.

Verzariu, P. 1984. *International Countertrade: A Guide for Managers and Executives.* Washington, D.C.: U.S. Department of Commerce.

Verzariu, P. 1985. *Countertrade, Barter, Offsets.* New York: McGraw-Hill.

Welt, L. 1984. *Trade without Money.* New York: Harcourt Brace Jovanovich.

Zarin, D. 1984. "Countertrade and the Law." *George Washington Journal of International Law and Economics,* 20(3): 235–52.

simulations (compare Rubin and Brown, 1975). *Profits* (both individual and joint) in negotiation simulations have been used as dependent measures in marketing studies (for example, Graham, 1984; Dwyer and Walker, 1981; Clopton, 1984). In this chapter, three outcome measures are considered—buyers' profits, joint profits, and the difference between buyers' and sellers' profits. Each of these will be discussed in further detail later.

Culture

A second aspect of the chapter is the search for underlying dimensions of culture. Three sources of information suggest explanations for cultural differences in buyer–seller relationships. Hall (1976) and Cateora (1983) indicate that cultures can be ordered along a high-context/low-context continuum. Hofstede (1984) reports that nine of the twelve cultures considered in this chapter vary along his Power Distance Index. Finally, Schmidt (1979), Copeland and Griggs (1985), Condon (1985), and Harrison (1983) provide a foundation for understanding cultural differences in interpersonal status relations which might be generalized to buyer–seller relationships.

High and Low Context. Hall (1976) describes a crucial dimension of culture to be the importance of the context of communication. He states, "In cultures in which people are deeply involved with each other . . . in which information is widely shared—what we will term high-context cultures—simple messages with deep meaning flow freely" (p. 39). Cateora (1983) interprets Hall's ideas, "Communication in a high-context culture depends heavily on the context or non-verbal aspects of communication, whereas the low-context culture depends more on explicit, verbally expressed communications" (p. 133). A careful reading of both authors suggests that eleven of the twelve cultures considered in this chapter would fall along the continuum presented in table 27–1's "High Context/Low Context" column. Neither Hall nor Cateora explicitly mention Taiwan or Canada. Taiwan was ranked on the "American side" of Mainland China to reflect historical ethnic roots and recent, substantial contact with the United States. Likewise, the Canadian cultures were ranked between the United States and their European counterparts.

As can be seen in table 27–1, Japan is ranked highest on the "context" continuum (see the fourth column in table 27–1). Hall's comments support this view: "I can think of few countries Americans are likely to visit and work in . . . where life is more filled with surprises than Japan" (p. 57). Hall's writings imply that in Japan, the context of interpersonal communication will be a more important determinant of interpersonal interactions than in other countries. Moreover, he specifically states that the importance of context can be generalized to negotiation situations (p. 129). That is, in a high-context country such as Japan, the words used in negotiations are not so important as the status relationships of negotiators determined before bargaining begins. Or, deference will be given Japanese

Table 27-1
Variables and Results for Each Country (Culture) Group

Country (Culture)	Negotiator Characteristics			Independent Variables				Outcome Measures (Means)				Percentage Variation Explained by Role (ANOVA R^2)
	Age	Years Work Experience	Number of Dyads	High Context/ Low Context (Hall, 1976; Cateora, 1983)	Power Distance Index (Hofstede, 1984) Actual	Predicted	Importance of Status	Buyer\$	Seller\$	\$Difference (Buyer\$ − Seller\$)	Joint\$ (Buyer\$ + Seller\$)	
Japan	36.9	12.1	21	10	54	57	1	51.6	44.3	7.3*	95.9	23.2
South Korea	39.1	8.6	24	—	—	—	1	46.8	38.6	8.2*	85.4	14.0
China (Mainland)	35.6	16.0	20	9	—	—	0	45.6	46.7	−1.1	92.3	00.4
China (Taiwan)	37.6	14.2	27	8	58	63	0	44.3	40.1	4.2	84.4	3.9
France	35.4	8.5	24	5	68	42	1	49.0	42.2	6.8	91.2	8.0
United Kingdom	32.5	11.4	22	6	35	45	1	50.0	44.3	5.7*	94.3	11.5
West Germany	31.0	9.4	22	1	35	42	0	42.8	39.0	3.8	81.6	2.3
Canada (Anglophones)	32.1	8.3	37	4	39	36	0	47.9	42.5	5.4*	90.4	7.4
Canada (Francophones)	32.3	8.6	37	3	—	—	0	42.3	44.1	−1.8	86.4	1.0
Mexico	32.4	9.2	34	7	81	70	1	48.6	37.7	10.9*	86.3	17.5
Brazil	36.8	9.6	39	7	69	72	1	47.3	45.5	1.8	92.8	1.0
United States	31.6	9.1	69	2	40	42	0	46.8	43.5	3.3	90.3	2.4
All Groups	33.8	10.0	376					46.8	42.5	4.2	89.2	

*Difference is statistically significant ($p < 0.05$).

buyers because of the context/situation of bargaining—the buyer is "kinger." Based on this reasoning, the following hypotheses are considered:

Hypothesis 1 (a): Buyers will achieve higher profits in high-context cultures than they will in low-context cultures.

Hypothesis 1 (b): The differences between buyers' profits and sellers' profits will be greater in high-context cultures than in low-context cultures.

Power Distance Index. Hofstede (1984) describes one of four basic dimensions of culture to be what he calls the Power Distance Index (PDI). Hofstede's ideas are based on landmark research regarding values of businesspeople working for a multinational firm in thirty-nine different countries. He defines PDI roughly as the deference a "subordinate" gives a "boss." He states "Power Distance is a measure of the interpersonal power or influence between Boss and Subordinate as perceived by the less powerful of the two" (pp. 70–71). Although his work involves internal management relationships, Hofstede states that, "a Power Distance norm spills over from one sphere of life—work organizations—into others; in fact it helps us to find the origin of a Power Distance norm in the early socialization by the family, the school, and the other institutions of society" (p. 72). By implication, culture with a high PDI can also be expected to display a more vertical relationship between buyers and sellers.

Hypothesis 2 (a): Buyers will achieve higher profits in high-PDI cultures than in low-PDI cultures.

Hypothesis 2 (b): The difference between buyers' profits and sellers' profits will be greater in high-PDI cultures than in low-PDI cultures.

Hofstede provides two kinds of PDI scores for the nine cultures. First is PDIA (see table 27–1) based upon *actual* responses of businesspeople to three attitude survey questions. Second is PDIP, *predicted* on the basis of multiple regression on latitude, population size, and wealth of the nine countries.

The Importance of Status. Little information is available regarding business negotiations in most of the twelve cultures considered here. Schmidt (1979) and Copeland and Griggs (1985) do describe business negotiations in several of the twelve cultures, thus providing a unique opportunity for comparisons among them. Based on their descriptions, interpersonal rank and the status of sellers are important in commercial relationships in Japan, South Korea, France, and the United Kingdom. For example, Copeland and Griggs state, "Korean society is highly structured; great respect is paid to age and position" (p. 241). Schmidt concludes, "the French have not traditionally held selling in high esteem" (p. 4). Regarding the other eight cultures, none of their comments imply that status is important. Condon

(1985) devotes an entire chapter to the importance of status in Mexican society: "For Mexicans, such differences are very important. To an extent greater than in the U.S. factors such as age or rank or sex guide a person's actions toward others" (p. 37). Harrison (1983) describes the importance of status in Brazil: "Status defined both by position/rank . . . determines much in business interactions" (p. 75). Thus, status is considered to be a more important influence on business negotiation in the six countries listed previously and in table 27–1. (See "Importance of Status.)

Hypothesis 3 (a): Buyers will achieve higher profits than sellers in Japan, South Korea, France, Britain, Mexico, and Brazil.

Hypothesis 3 (b): Buyers will achieve higher profits in the six "status-important" cultures than buyers in the other six cultures.

Hypothesis 3 (c): The differences between buyers' and sellers' profits will be greater in the six "status-important" cultures than in the other six cultures.

Research Methods

Participants

The participants in the experiment were 42 Japanese, 48 Korean, 94 Chinese (40 Mainland and 54 Taiwanese), 48 French, 44 British, 44 German, 148 Canadian (74 Anglophone and 74 Francophone), 68 Mexican, 78 Brazilian, and 138 American businesspeople. All have been members of executive education programs or graduate business classes and all have at least two years of business experience in their respective countries. The sample was limited to experienced businesspeople because Fouraker and Siegel (1963) reported differences in the bargaining behavior of students and businessmen. The participants were randomly paired and assigned to play the role of either buyer or seller in an intracultural negotiation game. The average age of the 752 participants was 33.8 years and the average work experience was 10.0 years. More detail about each group is provided in table 27–1.

Laboratory Setting

The negotiation simulation, developed by Kelley (1966) and used by Pruitt and Lewis (1975), Lewis and Fry (1977), and Clopton (1984), involves bargaining for the prices of three commodities. Each bargainer is given an instruction sheet, including a price list with associated profits for each price level. The participants are allowed 15 minutes to read the instructions and plan bargaining strategies. As evident in the payoff matrices included in table 27–2, the game has both competitive and cooperative

Table 27-2
Payoff Matrices for Kelley's (1966) Negotiation Game

Prices	Buyer Profits			Seller Profits		
	Product 1	*Product 2*	*Product 3*	*Product 1*	*Product 2*	*Product 3*
A	40	24	16	0	0	0
B	35	21	14	2	3	5
C	30	18	12	4	6	10
D	25	15	10	6	9	15
E	20	12	8	8	12	20
F	15	9	6	10	15	25
G	10	6	4	12	18	30
H	5	3	2	14	21	35
I	0	0	0	16	24	40

Note: Profits are also adjusted (multiples of those listed above) to reflect realistic levels, given the products involved.

characteristics. That is, the combination of *A* product 1, *E* for product 2, and *I* for product 3 allows a higher joint profit (buyer profit + seller profit = 104) than the *EEE* combination (joint profits = 80). The game is simple enough to be learned quickly, but complex enough to provide usually one half-hour of interaction. There was a one-hour time limit and bargainers used face-to-face, free communication. Several other negotiation and bargaining games were reviewed. Kelley's game was selected primarily because it simulates the essential elements of actual business negotiations observed in preliminary field research. All negotiations were conducted in the native languages of the participants.

Measures

Buyers' and sellers' individual profits, ranging from 0 to 80, are a direct result of the simulation. The measures of the independent variables (context, PDI, status) are described in previous sections and in table 27-1.

Results

In tables 27-1 and 27-3 are listed the results of the various hypothesis tests. Hypothesis 1 is partially supported, albeit weakly. Buyers from high-context cultures tended to achieve higher profits than negotiators from low-context cultures. Differences between buyers' and sellers' profits were found to be unrelated to the "context" dimension.

Hypothesis 2 is not supported by the analyses. PDI is not related to any of the negotiation outcome measures.

Hypothesis 3(a) is supported in part. Statistically significant differences ($p < 0.05$) between buyers' profits and sellers' profits were found in five cultures—Japanese, Korean, British, Canadian (Anglophone) and Mexican. (See table 27-1.)

Table 27-3
Results, All Groups Pooled

| Dependent Variables | Independent Variables Pearson Correlation Coefficients | | | Percentage of Variation Explained by STATUS (ANOVA R^2) (n = 376) |
	CONTEXT (n = 352)	PDIA (n = 295)	PDIP (n = 295)	
Buyers$	.113*	.048	.012	2.8*
$Difference	.055	.066	.025	1.2*
Joint$	.145*	−.017	−.014	2.4*

*Difference between groups is statistically significant ($p < 0.05$).

No differences were found between buyers' and sellers' profits for French or Brazilian dyads. Japanese buyers achieved the highest profits and Canadian (Francophone) buyers the lowest. Role of the negotiator explains the highest percentage of variation in profits for the Japanese negotiators (ANOVA $R^2 = .232$). Japanese negotiators also achieved the highest joint profits of all the cultural groups.

Hypotheses 3(b) and 3(c) are consistently supported. Buyers in "status-important" cultures achieved higher profits in the simulation. The differences between buyers' profits and sellers' profits tended to be greater for negotiators from status-important cultures.

Although no hypotheses were stated regarding joint profits, results of an exploratory analysis are also reported in table 27-3. Higher joint profits were found to be associated with both high-context cultures and status-important cultures.

Discussion and Conclusions

Limitations of the Analysis

It is important to be aware of the limitations and shortcomings of the research design. There are several such issues involved in this laboratory experiment.

Perhaps the most important consideration is the validity of the principal outcome measure, individual profits. Kelley's negotiation game (1966) and such measures have been used in other studies, but how well the game represents actual business negotiations is problematic. Any laboratory experiment is open to criticism regarding external validity—this research is no exception.

Interpretation of Findings

The results of this analysis strongly support the idea that in Japan, the buyer is "kingest." Japanese buyers achieved the highest profits (individual and joint) of any of the twelve cultural groups. Role of the negotiator (buyer or seller) explained the highest percentage of variation in profits for the Japanese dyads.

The findings also suggest that greater degrees of deference are given buyers in four other countries—South Korea, the United Kingdom, Canada (by Anglophones), and Mexico. Moreover, these findings dramatically demonstrate the potential problems of regional stereotypes (such as, all Orientals or all Latin Americans behave the same).

This study comprises the only empirical evidence to support Hall's (1976) theories about high/low context being a crucial dimension of culture. The findings of this study are also consistent with the ideas of Schmidt (1979), Copeland and Griggs (1985), Condon (1985), and Harrison (1983) regarding the importance of status/rank in Japan, South Korea, France, the United Kingdom, Mexico, and Brazil.

The results regarding Hofstede's (1984) Power Distance Index are disappointing. Perhaps, the importance of the PDI, measured in the context of boss/subordinate relations, cannot be generalized to buyer–seller relations and commercial dealings between firms. Hofstede's ideas and results, like those of Hall (1976), deserve further empirical scrutiny. Indeed, Hofstede invites such attention, "The concepts of national culture in general . . . should be further underpinned, criticized, and complemented" (p. 279).

Management Implications

The influence of culture on buyer–seller relationships is affirmed here. Managers will need to adjust their bargaining approaches to be effective in different cultures. A greater emphasis in building personal relationships and understanding status relations will be required in Japan and other high-context cultures. Greater deference to buyers' wishes will be expected in those places. Yet in Japan, this deference does not appear to adversely affect sellers' economic rewards. Only in mainland China and Brazil did sellers achieve higher profits than Japanese sellers. Apparently, Japanese buyers "take care of" Japanese sellers as Graham (1981) and others suggest. Graham and Sano (1984) and Levine and Byrne (1986) provide anecdotal evidence that American sellers can also appreciate the benefits of *amae*, the paternalism of Japanese buyers, when relationships are managed with care.

Future Research

All of these issues deserve further attention. This analysis demands replications in similar and different settings. Little work has been undertaken to examine empirically the influence of culture in commercial cooperation across national and organizational boundaries. Because of this lack of evidence, many academics and managers denigrate the importance of "cultural" considerations. But, the lack of evidence is due to the inherent difficulties and associated absence of systematic studies, rather than being due to the triviality of the problem.

Broader Issues

Buyer–seller relationships are the most pervasive form of cooperative strategy in international business. However, other forms are on the increase (compare chapters 6 and 7 in this book)—joint ventures, licensing, franchising, consortia and cartels, ownership, management contracts, and creative combinations of these several options. Despite the legal and financial differences among these several forms of cooperative strategies, they all have two important characteristics in common. First, all these relationships involve exchange. Even in buyer–seller relationships, more than goods and monies are traded. Management and marketing expertise, technology, market access, and market control are other media of exchange in an international business enterprise.

The second key characteristic in common is the problem of developing and managing such agreements not only across corporate cultures, but also across national cultures. The crucial nature of this latter problem is frequently taken for granted in the study of cooperative strategies in international business. Instead, the foci have most frequently been economic and legal issues such as pricing, ownership and profit-sharing percentages, and board of director membership. In this chapter, bridging the cultural difficulties in international cooperative ventures is the primary issue. Indeed, it is argued that culture strongly influences commercial exchange in general and buyer–seller negotiations in particular. Thus, culture is a crucial consideration in understanding all kinds of cross-national commercial relationships.

Exchange Theory. Social exchange theory may be a useful theoretical perspective for investigations of all forms of cooperative strategies in international business. Most of the work accomplished in this burgeoning area of interest has lacked a cohesive theoretical foundation and the dynamism that social exchange theory provides. Heretofore, theoretical perspectives have dictated units of analysis and constrained lists of potential explanatory variables. For example, the transaction costs approaches (as in chapters 1 and 10 in this book) conjure explanations in terms of dollars and cents. Organizational learning theories (as in chapter 17) consider variables such as previous joint venture experience.

Although social exchange theory was developed in the context of interpersonal relationships and social psychology, its application can be broadened to a wider set of phenomena. As mentioned earlier, social exchange theory posits three kinds of explanatory variables—individual characteristics, situational constraints, and process-related factors. In the most narrow sense, this means, for example, that outcomes of negotiations between two people from different countries may be influenced by: (1) their cultural backgrounds, (2) the orders given them by their supervisors before the negotiations, and (3) the strategies and tactics of conversation used during the bargaining sessions. (See table 27–4.)

Table 27-4

Examples of Broader Applications of Social Exchange Theory

	Dependent Variables		
	Individuals' Negotiation Outcomes (profits or satisfaction)	*Profitability of Joint Ventures*	*Total Trade between Two Countries*
Independent Variables			
Individual characteristics	Cultural background	Size, joint venture experience	Technological bases of countries
Situational constraints	Orders of supervisors	Legal restrictions	Worldwide financial conditions
Process-related factors	Conversational tactics used	Kinds and amounts of communication between parents and venture	Customs approval procedures
Units of analysis	Dyads	Firms	Countries

If we apply the same theoretical framework using the firm as the unit of analysis, then a somewhat different set of explanatory factors may come into play. For example, the profitability of a joint venture between firms in two foreign countries may depend upon: (1) the relative size or experience of the firms (see chapter 12 in this book), (2) the legal restrictions in the country of operations, and (3) the kinds and amounts of communications between the venture and the parents (see Pascale, 1978). Or, total trade between two countries might be explained by: (1) technological bases of the countries, (2) worldwide financial conditions, and/or (3) customs approval procedures (see Cateora, 1987).

The addition of the process-related factors is an important contribution of exchange theory. It brings a dynamic aspect into explanatory equations. However, the reader will take note of the difficulties in measuring and monitoring exchange processes. Observation of such processes takes much more time and resources than questionnaire or econometric data–based research designs. Yet, the study of exchange processes will add much to our knowledge regarding cooperative strategies in international business.

Microlevel Explanations for Macrolevel Outcomes. Finally, there is one additional reason for focusing on interpersonal exchanges as part of the effort toward understanding cooperative strategies. That is, microlevel factors may have strong influences on macrolevel outcomes. Consider how the findings reported in this chapter relate to the U.S.–Japanese trade deficit. Given the vertical relationships between Japanese negotiators and the more horizontal relationships typical of American negotiators, what happens in cross-cultural negotiations? It is my belief that a Japanese seller and an American buyer will get along fine, while the American seller and the Japanese buyer will have great problems. Moreover, I believe this consideration to be a key factor in U.S. trade difficulties with Japan. And my observations in the field and the laboratory provide strong evidence for such a proposition.

When Japanese sellers come to the United States to market their products, they naturally assume the lower-status position and act accordingly (with great respect for the American buyer), and a sale is made. Initially, the Japanese sellers are taken advantage of. After all, they expected the American buyer to respect their needs (consistent with *amae*). But in any case, relationships are established between firms. The door is open and the Japanese sellers have the opportunity to learn the "American way," to adjust their behavior, and to establish more viable long-term relationships.

However, if American sellers take their normative set of bargaining behaviors to Japan, then negotiations are apt to end abruptly. The American seller expects to be treated as an equal and acts accordingly. The Japanese buyer is likely to view this rather brash behavior in a lower-status seller as inappropriate and lacking in respect. The Japanese buyer is made to feel uncomfortable and politely shuts the door to trade, without explanation. The American seller never makes the first sale and never gets an opportunity to learn the Japanese system.

Most of the explanations for the U.S. trade deficit with Japan are at the macroeconomic or institutional level; that is, tariffs and quotas, government interference, labor, myopic business leadership, and the like are hypothesized as the causes of U.S. trade problems with Japan. And certainly these causes are important. But how much of the problem results from U.S. ineptitude at the international negotiation table? How much of the trade deficit is caused by thousands of Americans mismanaging face-to-face negotiations with Japanese clients and partners?

References

Cateora, P.R. 1983. *International Marketing*, 5th ed. Homewood, Ill.: Richard D. Irwin.

Cateora, P.R. 1987. *International Marketing*, 6th ed. Homewood, Ill.: Richard D. Irwin.

Clopton, S.W. 1984. "Seller and Buying Firm Factors Affecting Industrial Buyers' Negotiation Behavior and Outcomes." *Journal of Marketing Research*, 21 (February): 39–53.

Condon, J.C. 1985. *Good Neighbors, Communicating with the Mexican*. Intercultural Press.

Copeland, L., and Griggs, L. 1985. *Going International*. New York: Random House.

Dwyer, F.R., and Walker, O.C., Jr. 1981. "Bargaining in an Asymmetrical Power Structure." *Journal of Marketing*, 45 (Winter): 104–15.

Fouraker, L.E., and Siegel, S. 1963. *Bargaining Behavior.* New York: McGraw-Hill.

Graham, J.L. 1981. "A Hidden Cause of America's Trade Deficit with Japan." *Columbia Journal of World Business* (Fall): 5–15.

Graham, J.L. 1984. "A Comparison of Japanese and American Business Negotiations." *International Journal of Research in Marketing* (1): 51–68.

Graham, J.L., and Sano, Y. 1984. *Smart Bargaining, Doing Business with the Japanese.* Cambridge, Mass.: Ballinger.

Hall, E.T. 1976. *Beyond Culture.* Garden City, N.Y.: Anchor Press/Doubleday.

Harrison, P.A. 1983. *Behaving Brazilian.* Rowley, Mass.: Newbury House.

Hofstede, G. 1984. *Culture's Consequences.* Beverly Hills, Calif.: Sage.

Kelley, H.H. 1966. "A Classroom Study of the Dilemmas in Interpersonal Negotiations." In K. Archibald (ed.), *Strategic Interaction and Conflict.* University of California, Berkeley, Institute of International Studies.

Levine, J.B., and Byrne, J.A. 1986. "Corporate Odd Couples." *Business Week,* July 21: 100–5.

Lewis, S.A., and Fry, W.R. 1977. "Effects of Visual Access and Orientation on the Discovery of Integrative Bargaining Alternatives." *Organizational Behavior and Human Performance,* 20: 75–92.

Manufactured Imports Promotion Organization. *Penetrating the Japanese Market.* Tokyo.

Nakane, C. 1970. *Japanese Society.* Berkeley, Calif.: University of California Press.

Pascale, R.T. 1978. "Communication and Decision Making across Cultures: Japanese and American Comparisons." *Administrative Science Quarterly,* 23 (March): 91–110.

Pennington, A.L. 1968. "Customer–Salesman Bargaining Behavior in Retail Transactions." *Journal of Marketing Research* (February): 103–5.

Pruitt, D.G., and Lewis, S.A. 1975. "Development of Integrative Solutions in Bilateral Negotiation." *Journal of Personality and Social Psychology,* 31 (4): 621–33.

Rubin, J.Z., and Brown, B.R. 1975. *The Social Psychology of Bargaining and Negotiation.* New York: Academic Press.

Schmidt, K.D. 1979. *Doing Business in France (et cetera).* Business Intelligence Program (a series of pamphlets on major U.S. trading partners). Menlo Park, Calif.: Stanford Research Institute.

28

Strategic Alliances with the Japanese: Implications for Human Resource Management

Vladimir Pucik

A strategic alliance with a Japanese partner, in most cases through license or distribution agreements or through a joint venture, is still the most common vehicle of entry into the Japanese market for consumer and industrial goods (Ministry of International Trade and Industry, (1980–84). The joint venture form is considered preferable to licensing, because it may provide the Western firm with better control over the exploitation of its know-how, while at the same time, it enables the new company to draw on the resources of the experienced local partner. In fact, the literature discussing foreign investment in Japan often lists joint ventures as the most desirable investment alternative (for example, Wright, 1979; Zimmerman, 1984; Ohmae, 1985). However, as available information points out, the returns from a number of such alliances have so far been negative or, at best, marginal (Sadamoto, 1982).

This chapter reports on research conducted in U.S. and European manufacturing firms that have established joint ventures with partners in Japan and experienced difficulties in managing their partnership. Most were established in order to accomplish one or more of the following strategic objectives: exchange their technological know-how or brand recognition for access to the Japanese market; defend their traditional markets by cooptation of a potential Japanese competitor; or expand segments of worldwide business by combining the competitive advantages of both partners. However, the implementation results were mostly disappointing, in particular from the point of view of Western partners attempting to establish a foothold in Japan.

To examine what causes the problems in the implementation of joint venture strategies, I have interviewed over a period of three years Western and Japanese managers of twenty-three existing or dissolved joint ventures in Japan. Because of the sensitivity of this topic, the sample of firms is not random. To secure access to key sources of information, I used personal contacts gained through academic and consulting activities as well as references from Japanese associates. All firms and individuals participating in the study were assured full confidentiality.

The sample was also limited to ventures between Western and Japanese firms of similar size and/or competitive position. This should reduce the possibility that the analysis will be influenced by an asymmetrical distribution of resources among the partners. The oldest joint venture studied was over twenty years old, the youngest was established two years before the first set of interviews. In all cases, interviews were conducted with both Western and Japanese executives and with key staff in the personnel area. In most firms, interviews were conducted in more than one time period. In addition, I visited a majority of the Western and Japanese parent companies to listen to their perspective of what went right and what went wrong with their joint ventures.

The reason for low performance could often be traced to the poor organizational capability of the Western partner to manage and control the cooperative relationship. This deficiency demonstrated itself in a number of forms ranging from ignorance about or misreading of the strategic intentions of their Japanese partner, to disagreements about the implementation of daily business decisions. In particular, the Western firms observed did not pay sufficient attention to the competitive aspects of the joint venture relationship and were not prepared for a possibility of changes in the relative power of their Japanese partners over time.

Obviously, more than a single problem factor is generally involved, yet many of these factors share a single characteristic: poorly designed and executed human resource management strategies. In turn, the evidence seems to indicate that many of the problems encountered in designing a human resource strategy for the joint venture are embedded in fundamental differences in the way the two partners approach the human resource role in creating and maintaining competitive advantage.

This chapter discusses the most common mistakes made by Western firms with respect to the human resource management of the cooperative ventures. The issues are analyzed on the operational, managerial, and strategic levels (Fombrun, Tichy, and Devanna, 1984), and cover all four key areas of human resource management: recruiting and staffing, training and development, performance appraisal, and the compensation and reward system. A summary of the problem areas is presented in table 28-1. The focus here is limited to human resource strategies in regard to the Japanese staff. It should be pointed out that human resource strategies for expatriate staffing are also of critical importance, as the two sets of strategies are often interrelated.

Recruitment and Staffing

In most joint ventures that were investigated in this study, responsibility for the recruitment of staff for the newly established joint venture was generally assigned to the Japanese parent. In fact, difficulties in recruiting qualified staff were frequently mentioned by the expatriate staff as one of the key reasons why a Western firm would prefer to establish a joint venture partnership, rather than to set up

Table 28-1
Joint Ventures in Japan: Key Human Resource Management Issues

Management Levels	Operational	Managerial	Strategic
Recruitment and Staffing	Low quality of available Japanese staff	Limited access to the pool of qualified recruits	Continuous dependence on the Japanese partner
Training and Development	Lack of independent training infrastructure	Low emphasis on employee socialization	Transfer of know-how is unidirectional
Performance Appraisal	Western appraisal methods not applicable	Limited input from Western managers	Weak link to strategic interests of the Western parent
Reward and Compensation System	Expensive wage structure due to demographics	Multiple system causing internal frictions	Incentives defined in the local context only

an independent wholly owned affiliate. The availability of talented staff is restricted by the dualistic nature of the Japanese labor market with its limited job mobility (Cole, 1979), whereby large employers providing higher wages, superior working conditions, and relative job security enjoy a substantial recruiting advantage (Kono, 1984). Even if, in principle, Western firms could offer an employment package equal or perhaps better than one offered by the best employers in Japan, the limited supply of qualified employees makes the recruiting task difficult.

Under such circumstances, many Western firms entering Japan believed that recruiting through the Japanese parent would eliminate at least some of the disadvantages in accessing the local labor market (American Chamber of Commerce in Japan, 1981). However, the operational reliance on the Japanese partner often backfired. First of all, Japanese firms tend to look at the joint venture as another *kogaisha* (child company) in its corporate family, irrespective of the actual ownership share (Rohlen, 1979). Such firms are expected to have their personnel policies subordinated to the needs of the parent company.

The strategic objectives of the Western partner, far from the scene, become secondary. In practical terms, the joint venture firms may often serve as a reservoir of jobs for surplus or plateaued employees of the Japanese parent firm (Abegglen, 1985). The slowing down of economic growth further accentuates this need, as most large Japanese firms—the most frequent joint venture partners—look carefully on every venue for reducing their core staff without resorting to layoffs (Dore, 1986). As a result, it is not unusual that many of the employees simply do not have the skills necessary for the joint venture to operate in a competitive fashion.

When the joint venture lacks a competent cadre of managers, the deficiencies are often filled with staff temporarily seconded from the Japanese parent. Individually, they may stay five years or longer, but in principle, the management group lacks stability and cohesion. Many of them are unprepared to handle the complexity and ambiguity inherent in cooperative alliances. The learning is on the job, and opportunity costs, while hidden, are high. The frequent changes among Japanese managers also complicate the task of establishing close communication links with the Western partner which, for better or for worse, are often dependent on personal ties.

On the managerial level, too much reliance on the Japanese parent to take care of staffing issues eventually causes serious difficulties. The joint venture continues to be excluded from access to the pool of talented recruits. Especially in the technical fields, direct ties between individual professors and the prospective employers are critical for the identification and recruitment of top-quality engineers and scientists (Pucik, 1984; Sakakibara and Westney, 1985). The lack of linkage to universities leaves the joint venture in the fundamentally weak position of depending on a "fair share" from the Japanese partner's college intake. In fact, most Western executives interviewed had no idea about the quality of the new graduates assigned to the joint venture, relative to those retained by the Japanese parent.

Even if equity in assignment of new graduates is carefully negotiated and established as a policy, talented young employees are often reluctant to transfer to the joint venture on a full-time basis. They see that higher management positions are frequently reserved for short-term transferees and that opportunities for core joint venture employees may be restricted. The perceived lack of opportunities also has negative impact on the motivation of employees already in the joint venture and increases the possibility of frictions and factionalism within the joint venture firm.

Strategically, the reliance on support from the Japanese partner for staffing is seen as a desirable low-cost strategy. In fact, to keep the start-up cost down, a number of business functions are subcontracted back to the Japanese parent or its affiliates, often including critical parts of the total operation, such as manufacturing or distribution. Such strategy not only improves personnel economies of scale, but also minimizes the need to set up an expensive recruitment mechanism, as well as provides a convenient buffer if the Western firm decides to pull out of Japan. In such a case, employees can be transferred back to the Japanese parent, which is far less costly than typical severance payments. What is often overlooked, however, is that, in the long run, lack of control over staffing puts the Western firm into a position of extreme vulnerability.

When the time comes to renegotiate the joint venture agreements, be it in five, ten, or twenty years, it becomes very tempting for the Japanese to walk away from the joint venture and pull the business back into the parent company or into a wholly owned subsidiary. After all, they have already learned all current technology and have not much else to gain by continuing the partnership. The Western firm does not have many options, unless it is ready to start again from scratch. The only alternative is to continue to transfer new technologies as its part of the bargain. If, as has often happened, the Western firm loses its technological advantage (an outcome that the Japanese staffing strategies are designed to foster), the exit from the Japanese market is unavoidable.

Training and Development

Many Western joint ventures in Japan lack the training and development infrastructure that would guarantee continuous improvement of employee skills. As in their home markets, many Western firms often put less emphasis on employee training and development, under an assumption that in the long run, their needs can be more efficiently met through the external job market. In Japan, such an assumption is, however, invalid and dangerous. The external job market is limited and cannot be relied upon as a source of new skills (Koike, 1983). New job requirements have to be anticipated well ahead of time in order to build a corresponding training infrastructure supporting the firm's long-term competitive advantage. Given the expected stability in the bulk of the joint venture labor force, the lack of continuous training can result in a burdensome situation in which the joint venture firms become saddled with an expensive but technically obsolete labor force.

As in the case of staffing strategies, many Western firms have chosen to take advantage of the training infrastructure already put in place by their Japanese partners to keep the operating costs down. New employees enter the joint venture firm in small batches at various levels of the organizational hierarchy and with a different mix of skills and experience. To establish a common training program seems costly, if not methodologically infeasible. In the short term, outside training clearly seems to be a more desirable alternative.

The "subcontracting" of training and development activities may already begin with the introductory training program for the newly hired employees. Many Western firms, however, do not pay much attention to the fact that most of technical and professional training in Japanese firms (introductory training in particular) is traditionally combined with an intensive effort to increase the socialization of employees into the corporate family. This is because employee socialization plays an important control and communication function in the Japanese management process (Rohlen, 1975; Pucik and Hatvany, 1983).

Too much reliance on training conducted outside of the joint venture restricts its ability to socialize the employees into the firm and, thus, weakens its tools of organizational control. In addition, when training is conducted by the Japanese parent, the joint venture employees are in effect socialized into its corporate culture, rather than into the culture of the joint venture. Their sense of identification becomes blurred and commitment to the joint venture firm is replaced with commitment and loyalty to one of the parents only. In the long run, such a condition increases the long-term bargaining position of the Japanese partner. In any crisis, it probably can count on tacit support from the joint venture staff.

Strategically, training of the joint venture personnel is not a high priority for the Japanese parent. To the contrary, from its viewpoint, the transfer of know-how should flow from the joint venture into the parent, not the other way around. The lack of competent personnel in the joint venture gives the Japanese partner leverage in using the long-term need for seconded employees as a tool for management control of the joint venture as well as for transfer of know-how.

The joint venture firm often becomes a training and development center for the Japanese parent firm. Employees with high potential, both managers and technical professionals, are dispatched to the joint venture on a temporary assignment with the task to get acquainted with the latest of the Western partner's skills and know-how. After they return to the parent, they are expected to diffuse the newly acquired knowledge to the rest of the firm. The objective is to close, over a period of time, any "knowledge gap" vis-à-vis the joint venture partner and, thus, improve the long-term bargaining position of the Japanese firm.

Naturally, it is not possible or even desirable to stop the transfer of know-how to the Japanese partner. The issue is what the Western partner gets in return. Paradoxically, because of low attention to its own training and development needs, the Western firm often ends up sharing in the costs of technology transfer and training of its Japanese partner. These costs may be substantial, as they often include a transfer of the trainee to the Western partner's overseas facility. At the same time, the lack of involvement in training activities by joint venture managers limits their ability to use the training process as a method to identify and develop their own core of high-potential employees.

Performance Appraisal

Administration of the appraisal process in a joint venture is seldom a problem at the lower levels of the organizational hierarchy where both appraisors and their subordinates are Japanese. However, when expatriate managers become involved, the superior–subordinate relationship and the appraisal process in particular are influenced by the quality of the cross-cultural interaction. Differences in expectations concerning the purpose and methods of the appraisal may lead to a serious conflict within the joint venture firm.

The Western approach to performance appraisals is often unsystematic but explicit, in contrast to the more implicit but systematic approach favored by the Japanese. Appraisals in the West are less frequent than is customary in Japan. In most cases, performance reviews are conducted annually, as opposed to the Japanese practice of having at least two or three reviews per year (Pucik, 1984). In Japanese firms, the appraisal standards and process are enforced vigorously at all levels of the organization, while in Western firms, individual managers retain considerable freedom of action.

Often, the Western manager's understanding of the performance record achieved by Japanese subordinates is limited by the language barrier. In many cases, what is being evaluated is not job performance, but the ability to speak English or other foreign languages as well as Western-like behavior, such as assertiveness and aggressivity. The language bias in performance appraisal is a frequent source of discontent among the Japanese staff, who naturally expect an intervention from the personnel department of the Japanese parent firm to remedy perceived inequities. When Western managers introduce MBO-type measures, the goal-setting process is critical and those with weak bargaining skills are put in an unfavorable position.

The Japanese are generally uncomfortable with an MBO process linked to individual performance. They fear that such an approach to performance appraisal discourages cooperation within the organization. A group-based MBO process is generally preferred (Hongo, 1980). However, to properly evaluate an individual's contribution to the attainment of a group objective, managers have to be thoroughly familiar with the process of achieving the objective, not just its results. In a joint venture, the complexity of deciphering the process is often increased by the intimacy of the relationship with the Japanese parent, which evolves out of sight of the Western managers, if not behind their backs.

The appraisal feedback process may also cause difficulties. Western managers expect and are ready to give explicit feedback. However, in the Japanese cultural context, it is preferable to avoid one-on-one confrontations where direct criticism may imply a loss of face and claims of credit create a suspicion of unhealthy individualism. Faced with a culturally uncomfortable situation, many Western managers choose to limit their input into the appraisal process to formal approval of ratings prepared by their Japanese assistants. This reluctance to get involved, coupled with the turnover among expatriates, ultimately severely restricts the ability of the Western partner to use the performance appraisal as a meaningful management and control tool.

The lack of leverage is even more pronounced in the case of appraisals given to managers seconded from the Japanese parent. For all practical purposes, they are evaluated by the "invisible" superiors in the parent firm on criteria based on the strategic interest of the Japanese partner. Their loyalty to the joint venture is clearly secondary. Only a few joint ventures established formal procedures that in concrete terms put all seconded employees, Japanese as well as Western, under control of joint venture executives.

However, even managers assigned to the joint venture on a permanent basis found it hard, during the interviews, to define linkage between their performance objective and the global competitive strategies of their Western parent. In contrast, they understood clearly their own role in the context of the competitive strategy of the Japanese parent. Much of their behavior was therefore concentrated on the achievement of short-term goals, making sure that their Western bosses stayed out of their way as much as possible. The objective was to identify the lowest level of satisfactory outcome acceptable to the Western partner and then deliver slightly above that target. Any suggestion of more ambitious targets would be derailed with oblique remarks such as, "You don't understand Japan."

Compensation and Reward System

The wage levels in all joint ventures studied are, as customary in Japan, influenced by the age and seniority of the individual employees. Although the performance record is critical for promotion to most management positions, the difference between an employee's starting salary and the compensation of staff with high seniority can still be anywhere from 200 to 300 percent (McMillan, 1985). One of the significant negative side effects of the heavy reliance on the Japanese joint venture partner in the implementation of human resource management strategies is a wage cost higher than for Japanese firms of similar size, for reasons discussed below.

When the joint venture staff is recruited primarily through transfers from the Japanese parent or from the pool of available midcareer recruits, the age profile of the employee group is heavily skewed toward the older, more expensive employees. This leads to high wage costs without a corresponding increase in productivity. Over the long run, the skewed age structure also imposes higher retirement costs in terms of direct payments of retirement bonuses as well as the cost of replacements. Although a trend toward annuity benefits is on the increase (Fujita, 1984), retirement bonuses are still largely paid on a lump-sum basis and may at times restrict the cash flow position of the joint venture firm.

The wage spiral is further increased by the tendency of most foreign-related firms in Japan to use a superior compensation package as a tool to draw in new employees. Rather than rely on a long-term strategy of building a reliable recruiting network, the trend is to use financial incentives to attract, in particular, capable midcareer employees. Frequently, however, foreign-related firms bid against and raid each other. Or, not knowing their true ability, several joint ventures in the sample ended up hiring expensive Japanese executives pushed out from other foreign firms. As related by an experienced personnel manager: "The best way to get rid of an English-speaking incompetent executive is to pass on his home phone number to a headhunter." The alternative is a very costly termination.

To compensate for the higher staffing costs, not to mention the bias toward short-term profits often exhibited by the Western partner, the joint venture is forced to adopt a premium pricing strategy. Such an approach hinders its penetration of the Japanese market and slows down the growth of the firm. Slowdown of growth relative to that of their Japanese competitors further deepens the labor cost disadvantage as rapidly growing firms can benefit from adding personnel, usually recent school graduates, at costs below the present average wage level. Ultimately, just when the Japanese partner absorbs most of the available know-how, the joint venture is squeezed into a high-price/high-cost situation. With no prospect of improving its competitive position, the Western partner is ready to give up.

Even if the joint venture manages to keep its wage cost in line, the complexity of its compensation system increases potential for friction and conflict within the organization. It is not unusual for three different compensation sytems to be in place within a single firm: one for the core employees of the joint venture, one for employees temporarily transferred from the Japanese parent (which is generally more generous), and one for the Western expatriates (which most Japanese employees consider extravagant, unfair, and wasteful). Expatriate compensation is treated with great secrecy, but as the Japanese partner is involved in some of the decisions, the word gets out. After all, the differences in life-style are too obvious to ignore.

In medium-sized and large-scale joint ventures, the direct "bottom-line" impact of expatriate compensation expenses is limited. More critical is the internal conflict created by frequently encountered perceptions of inequality. While most Japanese employees accept that the firm should cover the inevitable costs of overseas assignments (such as children's education or home leave), the size of the total package is an easy target of resentment. It is quite common that the total cost of maintaining a midlevel expatriate in a joint venture is more than the total compensation of the CEO in the Japanese parent firm. Such staff resentment toward the Western parent can easily result in labor–management friction and/or favoritism toward the interests of the more egalitarian Japanese partner.

Another factor contributing to the shifts in loyalty is the perception of many Japanese employees that, in principle, joint ventures are inherently unstable. Seeing the Western partner muddling in the dark, the dissolution of the joint venture or a buyout by the Japanese partner is often considered only a question of time. Naturally, under such conditions, most employees, including those hired directly by the joint venture, think about their advancement and careers in terms of a fit with the long-term strategic objectives of the Japanese parent. As long as these objectives are complementary or synergistic with the objectives of the Western firm, the joint venture functions relatively smoothly. When the goals begin to differ, the collapse is quick. Without the support of key Japanese managers, chances for the Western partner prevailing are, at best, slim.

Human Resources Practice and Competitive Strategy

The evidence collected during the interviews with the multinational group of managers in Western joint ventures in Japan showed quite clearly that the execution of a successful competitive strategy in the Japanese market was often severely handicapped by deficiencies in the human resource system. The "capability" gap between strategic requirements of the business and the support provided by the human resource management system was evident independently of the products and industries the joint ventures were involved in. This suggests that the neglect of strategic leverage provided by well-designed human resource management systems may be a systemic problem embedded in many Western multinationals operating in Japan.

Over and over, the evidence points in one direction: the Western firms, with few notable exceptions, underestimated the critical role of human resource management strategies for the long-term viabililty of the cooperative venture. This was in contrast to the behavior of the Japanese partner where human resource concerns were often close to the top of managers' agenda. Obviously, a number of other factors may influence the long-term success of the joint venture, ranging from partner selection to compatibility of strategic objectives. On the one hand, if the business strategy underlying the formation of the partnership is misguided to begin with, no amount of organizational wizardry will save the day. On the other hand, even a well-thought-out strategy depends on an adequate organizational capability for its implementation.

The strategic intent of most Japanese partners in the joint ventures studied was often to learn as much as possible about technology contributed to the joint venture by the Western firms. A carefully implemented human resource strategy secured a rapid diffusion and assimilation of the newly available know-how to the Japanese parent, while at the same time, very little of local knowledge filtered back to the Western partner. Without such a reservoir of local knowledge, the Western firm's freedom of action in the Japanese market was greatly reduced.

From the typical Japanese perspective, control over human resource strategies should over time push the joint venture firmly into the orbit of the Japanese parent firm. This was happening irrespectively of the actual distribution of the equity in the joint venture or the initial input or know-how. As confided by the Japanese president of a fifteen-year-old joint venture where the Western partner was the majority owner: "We have constant problems dealing with our guests from overseas. They believe that because they own 65 percent of us, they are entitled to exercise control. But obviously, that can't be the case."

In this particular venture, the main office was in a building next to the headquarters of the Japanese partner. More than half of the top managers were seconded from the Japanese parent; all others, except for a single expatriate without language skills, also came from the Japanese parent firm when the venture was originally formed. New employees were recruited through the personnel office of the parent. Recruiting materials did not even mention the fact that the majority owner of the company is a foreign firm. Training programs at all levels were contracted out to the Japanese partner. The level of bonuses paid to all employees paralleled closely bonuses paid at the parent firm. Under these conditions, the president's statement is rather natural.

Western managers frequently do not think about control over human resources as a means to protect a competitive advantage. Rather, they rely on control tools used in their domestic competitive environment, such as equity ownership or legal agreements limiting what their local partner can or cannot do. As the previous quote shows, there are limits to how much can be gained from a majority control if authority over human resources is fully abdicated to the local partner and the diffusion of the knowledge gained from the joint venture becomes asymmetrical. The experience also shows that legal agreements or alliances do not last very long, once there is a shift in balance between the two partners, which in many cases is the strategic intent of the Japanese firm. Control over human resources is a critical factor, although obviously not the only factor in the total strategic equation.

In principle, despite the generally poor record of Western joint ventures in Japan, partnerships with Japanese firms can work out and be successful. (Fuji–Xerox, Yokogawa–Hewlett Packard, and Smith-Kline–Fujisawa are examples.)

What can a Western firm in Japan do in the human resource management area to improve its chances for success?

To begin with, the Western partner has to build its own local management team which is independent of its Japanese ally. In optimal circumstances, this should take place even before an agreement is reached concerning a specific strategic alliance. In other words, penetration of the Japanese market should start with hiring people to lead the charge; specific organizational forms can be decided on later, with the full participation of the new team. A highly qualified personnel executive should be one of its first members. All this can take more time and resources than to simply jump in and join hands with the most persistent suitor, but the long-term payoff can be substantial.

Once a joint venture is established, the recruitment and deployment of human resources must be constantly monitored. Functions critical to the long-term competitive advantage of the joint venture should be staffed internally even if doing so may increase costs in the short run. The personnel staff should establish direct contacts with leading universities in order to improve access to superior job candidates. (This process, in itself, can take a number of years.) In training programs, the independent identity of the joint venture should be emphasized, in particular during the introductory training.

Clear rules concerning intracompany job transfers and assignments should be established from the outset. Loyalty and commitment can be reinforced if it is understood that once employees are transferred to the joint venture, they will move back to the parent firm only under very special circumstances. The joint venture personnel staff has to have an input in decisions about who will be transferred and under what conditions. Not all of those transferred will be of the highest calibre, but the joint venture should have control over the total quality mix. In this matter, the quality, integrity, and independence of the joint venture's personnel group are essential.

For the joint venture to be successful, the performance appraisal and reward system has to reflect the fundamental strategic interests of both partners, although operationally both systems will probably mirror organizational norms dominant in the Japanese environment. However, sensitivity to local practices should not result in abdication of responsibility. Careful attention should also be given to the cost implications of current staffing decisions as well as to the impact of expatriate compensation practices on the morale within the joint venture enterprise.

All expatriates should be thoroughly trained in the personnel responsibilities expected from executives in similar positions working in Japanese firms. The ultimate objective, although probably unrealistic at short notice, is to develop a cadre of expatriates able to function effectively within the Japanese cultural context. This functioning would include facility with the language. At the same time, the Western partner should use whatever leverage is available to integrate at least some of the promising Japanese employees into its global management infrastructure. In fact, the possibility of worldwide careers can be a powerful motivator for a number of younger Japanese executives.

From a strategic perspective, the role of the human resource function in a joint venture firm is straightforward: at every step, business decisions affecting the critical components of the joint venture and the fundamentals of the strategic alliance have to be backed up by logically designed and carefully implemented human resource management policies. With proper understanding of what drives the human resource strategies of Japanese partners, what is expected from Japanese personnel staff, and what levers are available to control the human resource system, the chances of sustainable success can be substantially improved.

References

Abegglen, J.C. 1985. *Kaisha: The Japanese Corporation.* New York: Basic Books.

American Chamber of Commerce in Japan. 1981. *Successful Entry into the Japanese Market.* Tokyo.

Cole, R.E. 1979. *Work Mobility and Participation.* Berkeley: University of California Press.

Dore, R.P. 1986. *Structural Adjustment in Japan, 1970–82.* Geneva, Switzerland: International Labor Office.

Fombrun, C., Tichy, N., and Devanna, M.A. 1984. *Strategic Human Resource Management.* New York: John Wiley & Sons.

Fujita, Y. 1984. "Employee Benefits and Industrial Relations." *Japanese Industrial Relations Series.* Tokyo: Japan Institute of Labor.

Hongo, T. 1980. *Management by Objectives: A Japanese Experience.* Tokyo: Asian Productivity Organization.

Koike, K. 1983. "Internal Labor Markets: Workers in Large Firms." In T. Shirai (ed.), *Contemporary Industrial Relations in Japan.* Madison, Wis.: University of Wisconsin Press.

Kono, T. 1984. *Strategy and Structure of Japanese Enterprises.* Armonk, N.Y.: M.E. Sharpe.

McMillan, C.J. 1985. *The Japanese Industrial System.* New York: Walter de Gruyter.

Ministry of International Trade and Industry. 1980–84. *Gaishikei Kigyo No Doke.* (Trends in foreign-related enterprises.) Tokyo: Tsusho Sangyo Chosakai.

Ohmae, K. 1985. *Triad Power: The Coming Shape of Global Competition.* New York: Free Press.

Pucik, V. 1984. "White-collar Human Resource Management in Large Japanese Manufacturing Firms." *Human Resource Management,* 23 (3): 257–76.

Pucik, V., and Hatvany, N. 1983. "Management Practices in Japan and Their Impact on Business Strategy." In R. Lamb (ed.), *Advances in Strategic Management.* Greenwich, Conn.: JAI Press.

Rohlen, T. 1975. "The Company Work Group." In E. Vogel (ed.), *Modern Japanese Organization and Decision-making.* Berkeley: University of California Press.

Rohlen, T. 1979. *Technology Import and Organizational Adaptation in Joint Ventures: A Case Study.* Unpublished manuscript. University of California, Santa Cruz.

Sadamoto, K. (ed.) 1982. *Breaking the Barriers.* Tokyo: Survey Japan.

Sakakibara, K., and Westney, D.E. 1985. "Comparative Study of the Training, Careers, and Organization of Engineers in the High-tech Industry in the United States and Japan." *Hitotsubashi Journal of Commerce and Management,* (20): 1–20.

Wright, R.W. 1979. "Joint Venture Problems in Japan." *Columbia Journal of World Business,* 20 (1): 25–31.

Zimmerman, M. 1985. *How to Do Business with the Japanese.* New York: Random House.

Index

Page numbers followed by f indicate figures; page numbers followed by t indicate tabular material.

List of Contributors

Kofi Afriyie, Graduate School of Management, Rutgers University

Koya Azumi, Innovation and Productivity Strategies Group, Rutgers University

Paul W. Beamish, Wilfrid Laurier University, Canada

Sanford V. Berg, College of Business Administration, University of Florida

Peter J. Buckley, Management Center, University of Bradford, United Kingdom

Mark Casson, Department of Economics, University of Reading, United Kingdom

Farok J. Contractor, Graduate School of Management, Rutgers University

Yves Doz, INSEAD, Institut Europeen d'Administration des Affaires, France

William A. Dymsza, Graduate School of Management, Rutgers University

Benjamin Gomes-Casseres, Graduate School of Business Administration, Harvard University

John L. Graham, School of Business, University of Southern California

Håkan Håkansson, Department of Business Administration, Uppsala University

Kathryn Rudie Harrigan, School of Business, Columbia University

Michael Hergert, College of Business Administration, San Diego State University

Karen J. Hladik, McKinsey & Company, Inc., New York

Jacob M. Hoekman, Delta Lloyd Verzeheringsgriep, Amsterdam

Frank Hull, Graduate School of Management, Rutgers University

Jan Johanson, Department of Business Administration, Uppsala University, Sweden

J. Peter Killing, School of Business Administration, University of Western Ontario, Canada

Stephen J. Kobrin, Graduate School of Business Administration, New York University

Bruce Kogut, The Wharton School, University of Pennsylvania

Willem T.M. Koot, Nijenrode, The Netherlands School of Business

Donald J. LeCraw, School of Business Administration, University of Western Ontario, Canada

Peter Lorange, The Wharton School, University of Pennsylvania

Marjorie A. Lyles, College of Business, Ball State University

Deigan Morris, Institut Europeen d'Administration des Affaires (INSEAD), France

Richard W. Moxon, Graduate School of Business Administration, University of Washington

Charles P. Oman, Development Center, Organization for Economic Cooperation and Development, France

Vladimir Pucik, Graduate School of Business, University of Michigan

Thomas W. Roehl, Graduate School of Business Administration, University of Washington

Franklin R. Root, The Wharton School, University of Pennsylvania

Jean-Louis Schaan, Faculty of Administration, University of Ottawa, Canada

Harbir Singh, The Wharton School, University of Pennsylvania

Gene Slowinski, Innovation and Productivity Strategies Group, Rutgers University

J. Frederick Truitt, Graduate School of Business Administration, University of Washington

Tyzoon Tyebjee, School of Business, Santa Clara University

Gordon Walker, The Wharton School, University of Pennsylvania

D. Eleanor Westney, The Sloan School, Massachusetts Institute of Technology

Robert Wharton, Innovation and Productivity Strategies Group, Rutgers University

DATE DUE

GAYLORD			PRINTED IN U.S.A.